Designing Cisco Networks

Diane Teare, Editor

Cisco Press
201 W 103rd Street
Indianapolis, IN 46290

Designing Cisco Networks

Diane Teare, Editor

Copyright© 1999 Cisco Systems, Inc.

Cisco Press logo is a trademark of Cisco Systems, Inc.

Published by:

Cisco Press

201 West 103rd Street

Indianapolis, IN 46290 USA

Printed in the United States of America 1 2 3 4 5 6 7 8 9 0

Library of Congress Cataloging-in-Publication Number: 99-61689

ISBN: 1-57870-105-8

Warning and Disclaimer

This book is designed to provide information about designing Cisco networks. Every effort has been made to make this book as complete and as accurate as possible, but no warranty or fitness is implied.

The information is provided on an "as is" basis. The editor, Cisco Press, and Cisco Systems, Inc. shall have neither liability nor responsibility to any person or entity with respect to any loss or damages arising from the information contained in this book or from the use of the discs or programs that might accompany it.

Trademark Acknowledgments

All terms mentioned in this book that are known to be trademarks or service marks have been appropriately capitalized. Cisco Press or Cisco Systems, Inc. cannot attest to the accuracy of this information. Use of a term in this book should not be regarded as affecting the validity of any trademark or service mark.

Feedback Information

At Cisco Press, our goal is to create in-depth technical books of the highest quality and value. Each book is crafted with care and precision, undergoing rigorous development that involves the unique expertise of members from the professional technical community.

Readers' feedback is a natural continuation of this process. If you have any comments regarding how we could improve the quality of this book or otherwise alter it to better suit your needs, you can contact us through e-mail at ciscopress@mcp.com. Please make sure to include the book title and ISBN in your message.

We greatly appreciate your assistance.

Publisher	John Wait
Executive Editor	John Kane
Cisco Systems Program Manager	Jim LeValley
Managing Editor	Patrick Kanouse
Acquisitions Editor	Brett Bartow
Development Editor	Christopher Cleveland
Project Editor	Jennifer Chisholm
Copy Editor	Clifford Shubs
Technical Editors	Alison Humphries
	Curt Humphries
	Joe Freeman
Team Coordinator	Amy Lewis
Book Designer	Gina Rexrode
Cover Designer	Louisa Klucznik
Production Team	Steve Gifford
Indexer	Tim Wright
Proofreader	Debra Neel

About the Editor

Diane Teare is a Senior Network Architect with GeoTrain Corporation, Cisco's largest worldwide training partner, where she provides training and consulting services to customers in North America and Europe. Diane is a Cisco Certified Systems Instructor with more than 14 years experience in teaching; course design; design, implementation, and troubleshooting of network hardware and software; and project management. She is the Master Instructor for the ICRC, ACRC, and DCN courses at GeoTrain. Diane has a Bachelors of Applied Science in Electrical Engineering and a Masters of Applied Science in Management Science.

About the Technical Reviewers

Joe Freeman is a Technical Analyst with Sprint Paranet, the oldest and largest organization solely devoted to the management and support of distributed computing environments. Joe provides multivendor network design, management, and troubleshooting services to customers spanning the spectrum of business. Currently a CCDA, Joe has more than 18 years experience in IT, ranging from the component level through networking and mainframes.

Curt Humphries is a founder of The Garnett Group, Inc., a Silicon Valley-based company that provides technical course development and delivery services. Curt provides training and consulting services to customers in the Silicon Valley and worldwide. With 25 years in the computer industry, Curt is able to offer significant insights and technical expertise to help bridge the gap between business needs and computer technologies. Curt was instrumental in the development of the Designing Cisco Networks 2.0 CD and instructor-led courses. Curt's areas of expertise include mission-critical systems planning, networking, Internet and intranet technology and implementation, and integrated voice/data systems.

Alison Humphries is a founder of The Garnett Group, Inc., and is responsible for providing technical course development services to computer companies and enterprises throughout the United States. Alison has been consulting with technology companies like Cisco Systems for over 18 years to design and develop educational programs, including the Designing Cisco Networks 2.0 CD and instructor-led courses. Alison's areas of expertise include networking, Internet and intranet technology and implementation, UNIX, and integrated voice/data systems.

Dedications

This book is dedicated to my loving husband, Allan Mertin, who has given me wonderful encouragement and support during the editing of this book and always; and to my great parents Syd and Beryl, who have continually encouraged me in everything I've done. Thank You

Acknowledgments

First, I would like to thank the entire team at Cisco Press for their assistance and guidance during this project. I would especially like to thank Brett Bartow, Acquisitions Editor, for getting me started on this book and coordinating the team, and Chris Cleveland, Development Editor, for his great suggestions and keen eye. Amy Lewis was instrumental in organizing everything required for the production of this book. I'd also like to thank Jennifer Chisholm for her hard work on the production side of this project.

Many thanks are owed to the developers of the original DCN course, and to the technical reviewers of this book, Curt and Alison Humphries, and Joe Freeman, for their thorough review and very valuable input to this book.

I would also like to thank GeoTrain Corporation, especially Richard Gordon, General Manager, and Dan O'Brien, Director of Operations, for their enthusiastic support during the time it took to edit this book. Many thanks also to Eric Dragowski, Network Architect, for answering my obscure questions and for his constant support.

Contents at a Glance

Table of Contents

Foreword

In April 1998, Cisco Systems, Inc., announced a new professional development initiative called the Cisco Career Certifications. These certifications address the growing worldwide demand for more (and better) trained computer networking experts. Building on Cisco's highly successful Cisco Certified Internetwork Expert (CCIE) program—the industry's most respected networking certification vehicle—Cisco Career Certifications enable you to be certified at various technical proficiency levels.

Designing Cisco Networks presents in book format all the topics covered in the CCDA certification preparation course of the same name. Whether you are studying to become CCDA certified or you just need a better understanding of network design methodologies, you will benefit from the insights this book offers.

Cisco and Cisco Press present this material in text-based format to provide another learning vehicle for our customers and the broader user community in general. Although a publication cannot replace the instructor-led environment, we must acknowledge that not everyone responds in the same way to the same delivery mechanism. It is our intent that presenting this material via a Cisco Press publication will enhance the transfer of knowledge to our audience of networking professionals.

This is the fourth in a series of course supplements planned for Cisco Press, following *Introduction to Cisco Router Configuration*, *Advanced Cisco Router Configuration*, and *Cisco Internetwork Troubleshooting*. Cisco will present existing and future courses through these coursebooks to help achieve Cisco Worldwide Training's principal objectives: to educate Cisco's community of networking professionals and to enable that community to build and maintain reliable, scalable networks. The Cisco Career Certifications and classes that define these certifications are directed at meeting these objectives through a disciplined approach to progressive certification. The books Cisco creates in partnership with Cisco Press will meet the same standards for content quality demanded of our courses and certifications. It is our intent that you will find this and subsequent Cisco Press certification and training publications of value as you build your networking knowledge base.

Thomas M. Kelly
Director, Worldwide Training
Cisco Systems, Inc.
June, 1999

Figure Icons Used in This Book

Throughout the book, you will see the following icons used for networking devices:

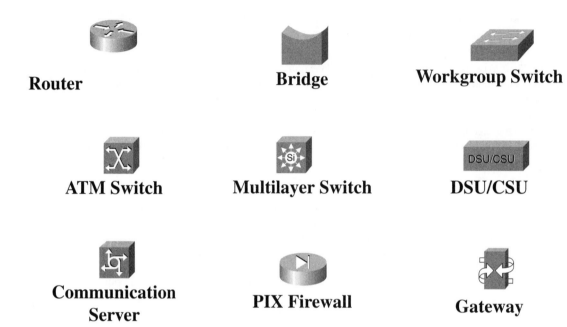

Router   **Bridge**   **Workgroup Switch**

ATM Switch   **Multilayer Switch**   **DSU/CSU**

Communication Server   **PIX Firewall**   **Gateway**

Throughout the book, you will see the following icons used for peripherals and other devices.

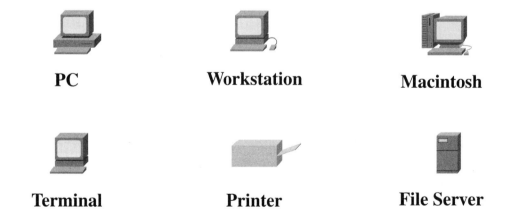

PC   **Workstation**   **Macintosh**

Terminal   **Printer**   **File Server**

IBM Mainframe

Front End Processor

Cluster Controller

Host

Throughout the book, you will see the following icons used for networks.

Line: Ethernet

Token Ring

FDDI

Line: Serial

Line: Switched Serial

Network Cloud

Introduction

To support more protocols and users, internetworks are growing at a fast pace and are becoming more complex. The proper design of these networks is therefore becoming ever more crucial to the efficient and optimal operation and management of the network. Cisco Systems, as the premier designer and provider of internetworking devices, is committed to supporting network designers, implementers, and administrators in the use of its products.

The content, objectives, and organization of this book are based on the current *Designing Cisco Networks* instructor-led and self-paced CD-ROM courses. This book provides a reference and reinforcement of ideas in these courses, as students prepare for their Cisco Certified Design Associate (CCDA) exam.

This book provides the reader with a framework and process to follow when designing internetworks, to ensure that all essential issues necessary to design an optimal network are considered. The process includes steps for defining what the network requirements are, the decisions that need to be made in the design process, and how to document and test the design.

Case studies are used throughout the book to provide you with an opportunity to evaluate your understanding of and to practice applying the concepts presented. The chapters in the book also contain *Tips* and *Notes* to emphasize critical details and other supplementary information to provide useful background and reference information.

Who Should Read this Book

This book contains a broad range of information related to the design of internetworks, including network topologies, LANs, WANs, addressing, protocols, router software features, management strategies, design documents, and prototyping and piloting of a design. It can be used as a general reference for the design of internetworks, as well as a specific reference for designing with Cisco devices. If you are planning to take a Cisco certification exam, particularly the CCDA exam, this book provides you with in-depth study material.

Before reading this book, it is assumed that you have working knowledge of internetworking and Cisco products. If you lack experience with internetworking technologies and Cisco products, it is recommended that you review Cisco's interactive, self-paced *Internetworking Multimedia CD-ROM,* or read the *Internetworking Technologies Handbook* (Cisco-Press) before starting this course. Chapter 1 of this book includes some information from these sources to serve as a reminder and summary of important points on specific topics relevant to this book.

Specifically, it is assumed that you are able to complete the following tasks before beginning the readings and exercises after Chapter 1 in this book:

- Define networking technology terms, such as LAN, WAN, bridging, switching, protocols, and network management.

- Explain the operation and implementation of source-route bridging, transparent bridging, and mixed-media bridging.

- Describe the purpose and operation of routed protocols, including Internet protocols, Novell IPX and SAP, AppleTalk, IBM SNA, DECnet, Open Systems Interconnection, Banyan VINES, and Xerox Network Systems.

- Describe the purpose and operation of routing protocols including RIP, OSPF, IGRP, EIGRP, BGP, IP multicast, RSVP, NLSP, IBM routing, DECnet routing, and OSI routing.

Objectives for this Book

Upon completion of the readings and exercises this book, you will be able to design a network that meets a customer's requirements for performance, security, capacity, and scalability, and assemble Cisco devices into an end-to-end networking solution. The case studies used throughout the book enable you to test your knowledge at each step along the design process.

After you finish this book, you may choose to become certified by completing the CCDA exam through your local Sylvan testing center. The CCDA Sylvan administered examination will verify that you have met the objectives of this book.

Time and Resources Required To Complete This Book

Doing all the readings and case studies suggested in this book will take you about 24 to 40 hours, depending on your networking background and experience.

Access to the Internet is not a requirement to complete this course book because relevant information has been extracted from the Internet (for example from Cisco's Web site) and provided in the book. Access to the Internet would be a benefit though, enabling you to obtain detailed information related to specific topics. All the Web sites referenced in the book are also listed in Appendix C, "Interesting WWW Links and Other Suggested Readings."

NOTE	The Web site references in this coursebook were correct at the time of writing—however, they might change. If you cannot find the document referenced, you might want to try searching for the information using either Cisco's web site search facility or a general search engine.

Case Studies

This book is built around the following four case studies:

- CareTaker Publications, a publishing company

- PH Network Services Corporation, a health care company

- Pretty Paper Limited, a European wall covering company

- Jones, Jones, & Jones, an international law firm

Each case study demonstrates different aspects of network design for small- to medium-sized businesses. The CCDA Sylvan examination will present similar case studies and solutions. For each case study, you will do the following:

- Analyze the existing network

- Determine the customer's requirements

- Answer questions to help you design internetworking solutions

The questions are designed to help you evaluate if you have mastered each section and are ready to move on to the next. After you answer the questions for each case study, you may view the answers provided by our internetworking experts to see how your solution compares. Although there is no single correct answer to internetwork design or to the case studies in this book, our internetworking experts have made recommendations and explained how they made their decision.

TIP	Before starting the exercises in this book, it is suggested that you obtain a binder where you can store information related to each case study. For example, as you progress through the book, you will be asked to draw topology diagrams for each case study; the topology diagrams will be referenced over and over again and expanded upon as you progress through the chapters.

Parts of the Book

This book is organized in seven parts, as described in the following sections.

Part I: Internetworking Technology Review

In Part I, Chapter 1, "Internetworking Technology Review," provides a review of key internetworking technology information. Chapter 1 also includes excerpts from Cisco's interactive, self-paced *Internetworking Multimedia CD-ROM* and the *Internetworking Technologies Handbook* (Cisco Press*)*.

Part II: A Small- to Medium-Sized Business Solutions Framework

In Part II, Chapter 2, "Analyzing Small- to Medium-Sized Business Networks," provides a framework that you can use to easily analyze customer network problems and create Cisco scalable solutions.

Part III: Identifying Customer Needs

Part III provides a process that can be used to determine a customer's requirements for network performance, security, capacity, and scalability.

Chapter 3, "Characterizing the Existing Network," defines the types of data that must be gathered in order to define the existing network and identifies how this data can be obtained. Some of the tools that are available to help in this process are discussed. Many tables and checklists are provided to aid in the collection of the needed data.

Chapter 4, "Determining New Customer Requirements," focuses on determining what a customer wants and needs in their new network. Characterizing the traffic on this network is key to understanding the requirements, and many tables are provided to aid in this process.

Part IV: Designing the Topology

Part IV details the design of a network topology that meets customer requirements for performance, security, capacity, and scalability, given a specified topology and internetworking constraints.

Chapter 5, "Designing the Network Topology," introduces three different topology models available for your internetwork design: Hierarchical Models, Redundant Models, and Secure Models. This chapter discusses the benefits of each model and also references some related Design Guides, which are provided in the Appendixes.

Chapter 6, "Provisioning Hardware and Media for the LAN," delves into the devices and media available in the LAN environment, including routers and switches. The design problems solved by and scalability issues of each device type are identified. Design rules and provisioning of LAN media are also identified. This chapter provides many tables and guidelines that can be followed in your designs.

Chapter 7, "Provisioning Hardware and Media for the WAN," focuses on the WAN portion of your new network. This chapter investigates design considerations, including the type of WANs available and limitations of devices. You will also learn about the available switching modes of routers and router platform selection. In addition, this chapter discusses the provisioning of WANs, including some of the options available for Frame Relay.

Chapter 8, "Designing a Network Layer Addressing and Naming Model," explains how to design Layer 3 addressing and naming for IP and IPX networks. This chapter also introduces Network Address Translation, variable-length subnet masking, and summarization for IP networks.

Chapter 9, "Selecting Routing and Bridging Protocols," identifies topics that should be considered when choosing routing and bridging protocols. This chapter includes a discussion of link-state protocols (for example, OSPF), distance vector protocols (for example, RIP), and hybrid protocols (for example, EIGRP) and compares the different types of protocols. You will also learn to identify scalability issues with bridging protocols, including with transparent bridging, source-route bridging, and Integrated Routing and Bridging (IRB).

Chapter 10, "Provisioning Software Features," explains some of the advanced Cisco IOS features that are available. These features include access lists, encryption, proxy services, compression, traffic shaping, queuing (custom, priority, and weighted fair), resources reservation protocol (RSVP), and tag switching.

Chapter 11, "Selecting a Network Management Strategy," identifies the protocols, SNMP and RMON, and some of the various tools, including CiscoWorks, available to manage today's complex networks. This chapter also discusses a network management process and proactive network management.

Chapter 12, "Writing a Design Document," identifies the role and content of a design document and how to create one.

Part V: Building a Prototype or Pilot for the Network

Part V identifies how to build a prototype or pilot to prove that the network meets the customer's requirements for performance, security, capacity, and scalability.

Chapter 13, "Building a Prototype or Pilot," defines the difference between a prototype and a pilot and identifies the steps to build each. This chapter also identifies products available to help you prove the concepts in your prototype or pilot.

Chapter 14, "Testing the Prototype or Pilot," identifies tools available for the testing, including protocol analyzers and Cisco IOS software commands. This chapter also discusses how to demonstrate your findings to the customer and provides a network health checklist.

Part VI: Sample CCDA Sylvan Exam

In Part VI, Chapter 15 provides a sample CCDA Sylvan examination that you can take to evaluate your understanding of the material in this book.

Part VII: Appendixes

Additional information is provided in the Appendixes and is referenced from within the book when required.

Appendix A, "Case Studies," includes the introductory information on four case studies used throughout the course, for easy reference within the book.

Appendix B, "Answers to Chapter Questions, Case Studies, and Sample CCDA Exam," is self-explanatory.

Appendix C, "Interesting WWW Links and Other Suggested Readings," lists all the Web sites and other external readings referred to in the text, by chapter.

Appendix D contains a PIX Firewall Design Implementation Guide.

Appendix E contains a Router Performance Design and Implementation Guide.

Appendix F contains an ISDN Design and Implementation Guide.

Appendix G contains a Windows NT Design and Implementation Guide.

Appendix H, "Network Address Translation," contains information on Cisco's Network Address Translation feature.

Appendix I contains an OSPF Frequently Asked Questions document.

Appendix J contains an OSPF Design Guide.

Appendix K contains an Enhancements to EIGRP document.

Appendix L, "Workbook," contains job aids, such as procedures, tables, and checklists, which you may use during the case studies and in your real designs later. These items are duplicated here from the chapters within the book so that you can easily find them later.

The Glossary provides definitions for networking concepts and acronyms used throughout the book.

PART I

Internetworking Technology Review

This part of the book provides a review of key internetworking technology information and includes excerpts from Cisco's interactive, self-paced *Internetworking Multimedia CD-ROM,* and the *Internetworking Technologies Handbook* (Cisco Press).

Chapter 1   Internetworking Technology Review

This chapter provides a review of key internetworking technology information.

As noted previously, it is assumed that you have working knowledge of internetworking and Cisco products before reading this book. If you lack experience with internetworking technologies and Cisco products, it is recommended that you review Cisco's interactive, self-paced *Internetworking Multimedia CD-ROM* or read the *Internetworking Technologies Handbook* (Cisco Press) before starting this course. This review chapter includes some information from these sources to serve as a reminder and/or summary of important points on specific topics relevant to this book.

Internetworking Technology Review

An internetwork is a collection of individual networks, connected by intermediate networking devices, which functions as a single large network. *Internetworking* refers to the industry, products, and procedures that meet the challenge of creating and administering internetworks.

The first networks were time-sharing networks that used mainframes and attached terminals. Such environments were implemented by both IBM's System Network Architecture (SNA) and Digital's network architecture.

Local-area networks (LANs) evolved around the PC revolution. LANs enabled multiple users in a relatively small geographical area to exchange files and messages, as well as access shared resources such as file servers.

Wide-area networks (WANs) interconnect LANs across normal telephone lines (and other media), thereby interconnecting geographically dispersed users.

Today, high-speed LANs and switched internetworks are becoming widely used, largely because they operate at high speeds and support high-bandwidth applications such as voice and video conferencing.

Protocols

Computers need to agree on a set of traffic rules to successfully communicate. Such a set of rules is known as a *protocol*. Two computers use the same protocol if they want to communicate. Two computers trying to use different protocols would be like speaking French to a German—it wouldn't work.

There are many different networking protocols in use. In the past, each networking vendor would invent their own protocol; today, standard protocols exist so that devices can communicate with each other. For example, TCP/IP is the most widely used *routed protocol*, but Novell's IPX and Apple Computer's AppleTalk are also used.

The OSI Model

Because sending data, like an e-mail, involves doing so many things, a standards committee—the International Organization for Standardization (ISO)—came up with a list of these functions and divided them into seven categories. These categories are collectively known as the Open Systems Interconnection (OSI) seven-layer model. It represents everything that must happen in order to send data. It doesn't say *how* these things are to be done, just *what* needs to be done. Figure 1-1 illustrates the seven layers of the OSI model.

Figure 1-1   *Each Layer of the Seven-Layer OSI Model Represents a Function that Is Needed When Devices Communicate*

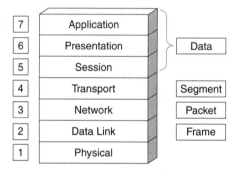

Different vendors will implement the functions at these layers differently. For example, there are different physical layers (wires)—copper and fiber optic are two common ones.

As data is sent through the functions at each of the layers, information is added to allow the data to go through the network. The data is *encapsulated*, or wrapped in, the appropriate information. This encapsulated information includes addressing and error checking.

At Layer 4, the transport layer, the data is encapsulated in a *segment*.

At Layer 3, the network layer, this segment is then encapsulated in a *packet* or *datagram*. At Layer 3, *routed protocols* are used to send data through the network. There are different types of packets for each of the routed protocols at Layer 3; examples include IP and IPX packets.

At Layer 2, the data link layer, this packet is then encapsulated in a *frame*. The data link layer used is determined by the type of LAN or WAN you are connected to. There are different types of frames for each type of LAN or WAN. For example, the frames sent out on Ethernet are different than those sent out on Frame Relay because there are different protocols to be followed.

At Layer 1, the physical layer, the frame is sent out on the wire in bits.

When data is received at the other end of the network, it must have the additional information removed. Thus the data is *decapsulated*, or unwrapped, until the original data sent arrives at its destination

LAN Protocols

A LAN typically has the following characteristics:

* Interconnects devices over a "short" distance (hence the term "local area")
* Is fast
* Belongs to you
* Is there all the time

There are a number of different LAN technologies. Ethernet is the most common. Ethernet runs at 10 millions of bits per second (10 Mbps). New versions, known as Fast Ethernet and Gigabit Ethernet, run at 100 Mbps and 1 Gbps, respectively.

Other LAN technologies include Token Ring and FDDI. Token Ring is an IBM invention and is found mainly at IBM sites. FDDI is based on optical fiber and runs at 100 Mbps.

LAN protocols function at the lowest two layers of the OSI reference model: the physical layer and data link layer.

LAN Physical Network Access

LAN protocols typically use one of two methods to access the physical network medium:

* In the *carrier sense multiple access collision detect (CSMA/CD)* scheme, network devices contend for the use of the physical network. CSMA/CD is sometimes called contention access. Examples of LANs that use the CSMA/CD media access scheme are Ethernet/IEE 802.3 networks.
* In the *token passing media access* scheme, network devices access the physical medium based on possession of a token. Examples of LANs that use the token passing media access scheme are Token Ring/IEEE 802.5 and FDDI.

LAN Data Transmission Types

LAN data transmissions fall into three classifications:

* In a *unicast* transmission, a single packet is sent from the source to a destination on a network. The source node addresses the packet by using the address of the destination node. The packet is then sent to the network, and finally, the network passes the packet to its destination.
* A *multicast* transmission consists of a single data packet that is copied and sent to a specific subset of nodes on the network. The source node addresses the packet by using a multicast address. The packet is then sent to the network, which makes copies of the packet and sends a copy to each node that is part of the multicast address.

- A *broadcast* transmission consists of a single data packet that is copied and sent to all nodes on the network. In these types of transmissions, the source node addresses the packet by using the broadcast address. The packet is then sent to the network, which makes copies of the packet and sends a copy to every node on the network.

WAN Protocols

A wide-area network (WAN) interconnects devices located at different geographical locations. A WAN typically:

- Interconnects devices over a "long" distance (hence "wide-area")
- Is slow (compared to a LAN)
- Belongs to someone else (the "service provider")
- Is there only when you want to send something

WAN protocols function at the lowest two layers of the OSI reference model, the physical layer and data link layer. (X.25 is an exception to this; it functions at layer three also.)

WAN Categories

WANs can be categorized as follows:

- **Point-to-point links**—Provide a single, preestablished WAN communication path from the customer premises through a carrier network, such as the telephone company, to a remote network. A point-to-point link is also known as a leased line because its established path is permanent and fixed for each remote network reached through the carrier facilities.
- **Circuit switching**—A WAN switching method in which a dedicated physical circuit is established, maintained, and terminated through a carrier network for each communication session. Used extensively in telephone company networks, circuit switching operates much like a normal telephone call. Integrated Services Digital Network (ISDN) is an example of a circuit-switched WAN technology.
- **Packet switching**—A WAN switching method in which network devices share a single point-to-point link to transport packets from a source to a destination across a carrier network. Statistical mulitplexing is used to enable devices to share these circuits. Asynchronous Transfer Mode (ATM), Frame Relay, Switched Multimegabit Data Service (SMDS), and X.25 are examples of packet-switched WAN technologies.

WAN Virtual Circuits

Virtual circuits are logical circuits created to ensure reliable communication between two network devices. Two types of virtual circuits exist:

- **Switched virtual circuits (SVCs)**—Virtual circuits that are dynamically established on demand and terminated when transmission is complete. Communication over an SVC consists of three phases: circuit establishment, data transfer, and circuit termination.

- **Permanent virtual circuits (PVCs)**—Permanently established virtual circuits that consist of one mode: data transfer.

WAN Dialup Services

Dialup services offer cost-effective methods for connectivity across WANs. Two popular dialup implementations follow:

- **Dial-on-demand routing (DDR)**—A technique whereby a router can dynamically initiate and close a circuit-switched session as transmitting end stations demand. A router is configured to consider certain traffic interesting (such as traffic from a particular protocol) and other traffic uninteresting. When the router receives interesting traffic destined for a remote network, a circuit is established, and the traffic is transmitted normally. If the router receives uninteresting traffic and a circuit is already established, that traffic also is transmitted normally. The router maintains an idle timer that is reset only when interesting traffic is received. If the router receives no interesting traffic before the idle timer expires, the circuit is terminated. Likewise, if uninteresting traffic is received and no circuit exists, the router drops the traffic.

- **Dial backup**—A service that activates a backup serial line under certain conditions. The secondary serial line can act as a backup link that is used when the primary link fails or as a source of additional bandwidth when the load on the primary link reaches a certain threshold.

WAN Devices

Devices used in WAN environments include:

- **WAN switch**—A multiport internetworking device used in carrier networks. These devices typically switch such traffic as Frame Relay, X.25, and SMDS and operate at the data link layer.

- **Access server**—Acts as a concentration point for dial-in and dial-out connections.

- **Modem**—A device that interprets digital and analog signals, enabling data to be transmitted over voice-grade telephone lines.

- **Channel service unit/digital service unit (CSU/DSU)**—A digital-interface device (or sometimes two separate digital devices) that adapts the physical interface on a data terminal equipment (DTE) device (such as a terminal) to the interface of a data circuit-terminating (DCE) device (such as a switch) in a switched-carrier network. The CSU/DSU also provides signal timing for communication between these devices.

- **ISDN terminal adapter (TA)**—A device used to connect ISDN Basic Rate Interface (BRI) connections to other interfaces, such as EIA/TAI-232. A terminal adapter is essentially an ISDN modem.

Defining the type of WAN and the specifications and options desired is called *provisioning* the network.

Internetwork Addressing

Internetwork addresses identify devices separately or as members of a group. Addressing schemes vary depending on the protocol family and the OSI layer.

MAC Addresses

Media Access Control (MAC) addresses identify network entities in LANs. MAC addresses are unique for each LAN interface on a device. MAC addresses are 48 bits in length and are expressed as 12 hexadecimal digits. The first 6 hexadecimal digits, which are administered by the IEEE, identify the manufacturer or vendor and thus comprise the Organizational Unique Identifier (OUI). The last 6 hexadecimal digits comprise the interface serial number, or another value administered by the specific vendor. MAC addresses sometimes are called burned-in addresses (BIAs) because they are burned into read-only memory (ROM) and are copied into random-access memory (RAM) when the interface card initializes.

Network Layer Addresses

A network layer address identifies an entity at the OSI network layer. Network addresses usually exist within a hierarchical address space and sometimes are called *virtual* or *logical* addresses.

Network layer addresses have two parts: the *network* that the device is on and the *device* (or *host*) number of that device on that network. Devices on the same logical network must have addresses with the same network part; however they will have unique device parts.

This is analogous to the postal "network" addresses: one part indicates the street, city, province/state, and so on, whereas the other part identifies the building number on that street. For example, a building at 27 Main Street is on the same "network" as a building at 35 Main Street. The "network" portion of their addresses, Main Street, is identical, whereas the "device" portions are unique.

Network Devices

The main devices used in networking are as follows:

- Hubs
- Bridges and switches
- Routers

Hubs

A hub is used to connect devices together so that they are on one LAN, as shown in Figure 1-2. The cables normally used for Ethernet have RJ-45 connectors. Because only two devices can be connected with these cables, we need a hub if we want to interconnect more than two devices on one LAN.

Figure 1-2   *A Hub Connects Devices Together So that They Are on One LAN*

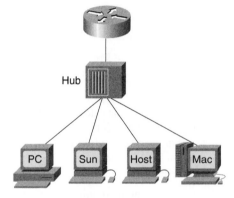

A hub is not a "smart" device. A hub sends all the data from a device on one port to all the other ports. When devices are connected via a hub, the devices all hear everything that the other devices send, whether it was meant for them or not. This is analogous to being in a room with lots of people—if you speak, everyone will hear you. If more than one person speaks at a time, there will just be noise. Rules must be put in place if real conversations are to happen; in networking, these rules are the protocols.

Bridges and Switches

To improve performance, LANs are usually divided into smaller multiple LANs. These LANs are then interconnected by a LAN switch or by a bridge, as shown in Figure 1-3.

Figure 1-3   *LANs Are Split Into Many Smaller LANs, Using Switches or Bridges To Improve Performance*

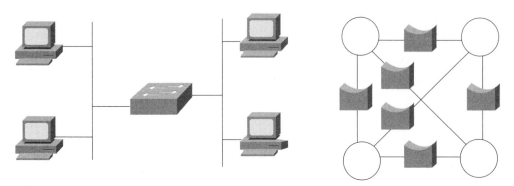

Switches and bridges have some "smarts." When devices are connected via a switch or a bridge, a device will only hear the following:

- Everything that the other devices on its port send
- Any information from devices on other ports that was meant for *everyone* (a *broadcast*)
- Any information from devices on other ports that was meant for devices on its port

A device connected to a switch or bridge will *not* hear any of the information meant just for devices on other ports of the switch.

Upper-layer protocol transparency is a primary advantage of both bridging and switching. Because both device types operate at the data link layer, they are not required to examine upper-layer information. This means that they can rapidly forward traffic representing any network layer protocol. It is not uncommon for a bridge to move AppleTalk, DECnet, TCP/IP, XNS, and other traffic between two or more networks.

By dividing large networks into self-contained units, bridges and switches provide several advantages. Because only a certain percentage of traffic is forwarded, a bridge or switch diminishes the traffic experienced by devices on all connected segments. Bridges and switches extend the effective length of a LAN, permitting the attachment of distant stations that were not previously permitted.

Bridging Protocols

Switches and bridges may communicate with each other by using a bridging protocol. Several types of bridging protocols are supported by Cisco routers (acting as bridges) and switches, including the following:

- **Transparent bridging**—Found primarily in Ethernet environments.
- **Source-route bridging (SRB)**—Found primarily in Token Ring environments.

- **Translational bridging**—Translates from Ethernet bridging to Token Ring bridging.
- **Encapsulating bridging**—Allows packets to cross a bridged backbone network.
- **Source-route transparent (SRT) bridging**—Allows a bridge to function as both a source-routing and transparent bridge.
- **Source-route translational (SR/TLB) bridging**—Allows a bridge to function as both a source-routing and transparent bridge, and to bridge between the two.

NOTE   In source-route bridging terminology, Layer 2 *frames* are also known as *packets*.

Transparent bridges send Bridge Protocol Data Unit (BPDU) frames to each other to build and maintain a spanning tree, as specified in IEEE 802.1d. The Spanning-Tree Algorithm states that there is one and only one active path between two stations. If a physical loop exists in the network (for redundancy reasons), the Spanning-Tree Algorithm handles this loop by disabling bridge ports. This prevents *broadcast storms* in networks with redundancy, which occurs when broadcasts continuously circle the network.

Bridges Versus Switches

Although bridges and switches share most relevant attributes, several distinctions differentiate these technologies. Switches are significantly faster because they switch in hardware, whereas bridges switch in software. Switches can interconnect LANs of unlike bandwidth; a 10-Mbps Ethernet LAN and a 100-Mbps Ethernet LAN, for example, can be connected using a switch. Switches also can support higher port densities than bridges. Some switches support cut-through switching, which reduces latency and delays in the network, whereas bridges support only store-and-forward traffic switching.

Switches also support virtual LANs (VLANs). A VLAN is a *logical,* rather than *physical,* grouping of devices. The devices are grouped using switch management software so that they can communicate as if they were attached to the same wire, when in fact they might be located on a number of different physical LAN segments.

Cisco switches are known as Catalyst switches (because Cisco bought a company called Catalyst). Catalyst switches include the following series:

Catalyst 1900	Catalyst 4000
Catalyst 2820	Catalyst 5000
Catalyst 2900	Catalyst 5500
Catalyst 2900XL	Catalyst 6000
Catalyst 3000	Catalyst 3900
Catalyst 8500 multiservice switch routers	

Generally the bigger the series number, the more LAN ports the switch has.

Routers

A router connects devices on LANs to devices on other LANs, usually via WANs, as shown in Figure 1-4.

Figure 1-4 *A Router Connects Devices on LANs to Devices on Other LANs, Usually Via WANs*

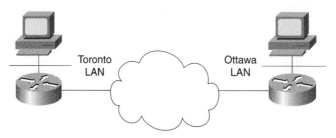

A router has a lot of "smarts." When companies started deploying PCs and connecting them via LANs, they soon wanted to go one step further and interconnect LANs and PCs located at geographically separate locations. The router provides this facility. The router will connect to a local LAN and then connect over a longer distance to another router, which in turn is connected to the remote LAN. Two PCs located hundreds of miles apart can now exchange data.

A router's job is comprised of the following tasks:

- Segment LANs and WANs
- Figure out the best way to send data to its destination
- Talk to other routers to learn from them and tell them what it knows
- Send the data the best way, over a LAN or a WAN

When devices are connected via a router, a device will hear only the following:

- Everything that the other devices on its port send
- Any information from devices on other ports that was meant for devices on its port

A device connected to a router will not hear any of the information meant just for devices on other ports, nor any information from devices on other ports that was meant for *everyone*.

Cisco has a large selection of routers, including the following series:

Cisco 700	Cisco 3600
Cisco 800	Cisco MC3810 multiservice concentrator
Cisco 1000	Cisco 4000
Cisco 1600	Cisco AS5200/AS5300/AS5800 access servers
Cisco 1720	Cisco 7200
Cisco 2500	Cisco 12000
Cisco 2600	
Cisco 7500	

Generally the bigger the series number, the more LAN and WAN ports the router has and the better performance it provides.

Routing

Routing is the act of moving information across an internetwork from a source to a destination. Along the way, at least one intermediate node typically is encountered. Routing occurs at Layer 3, the network layer.

The book *Introduction to Cisco Routers* (Cisco Press) defines *routed protocols* and *routing protocols:*

- A **routed protocol** contains enough network layer addressing information for user traffic to be directed from one network to another network. Routed protocols define the format and use of the fields within a packet. Packets that use a routed protocol are conveyed from end system to end system through an internetwork.
- A **routing protocol** supports a routed protocol by providing mechanisms for sharing routing information. Routing protocol messages move between the routers. A routing protocol allows the routers to communicate with other routers to update and maintain routing tables. Routing protocol messages do not carry end-user traffic from network to network. A routing protocol uses the routed protocol to pass information between routers.

A *metric* is a standard of measurement, such as path length, that is used by routing algorithms to determine the optimal path to a destination. To aid the process of path determination, routing algorithms initialize and maintain *routing tables*, which contain route information. Route information varies depending on the routing algorithm used.

Routing algorithms can be classified by type. Key differentiators include:

- **Static versus dynamic**—Static routing algorithms are hardly algorithms at all, but are table mappings established by the network administrator prior to the beginning of routing. These mappings do not change unless the network administrator alters them.
- **Single-path versus multipath**—Some sophisticated routing protocols support multiple paths to the same destination. .
- **Flat versus hierarchical**—In a flat routing system, the routers are peers of all others. In a hierarchical routing system, some routers form what amounts to a routing backbone. Routing systems often designate logical groups of nodes, called domains, autonomous systems, or areas.
- **Host-intelligent versus router-intelligent**—Some routing algorithms assume that the source end-node will determine the entire route. This is usually referred to as *source routing*. Other algorithms assume that hosts know nothing about routes. In these algorithms, routers determine the path through the internetwork based on their own calculations.
- **Intradomain versus interdomain**—Some routing algorithms work only within domains; others work within and between domains.

- **Link-state versus distance–vector versus hybrid**—Link-state algorithms (also known as *shortest path first* algorithms) flood routing information to all nodes in the internetwork. Each router, however, sends only the portion of the routing table that describes the state of its own links. Distance-vector algorithms (also known as *Bellman-Ford* algorithms) call for each router to send all or some portion of its routing table, but only to its neighbors. In essence, link-state algorithms send small updates everywhere, whereas distance-vector algorithms send larger updates only to neighboring routers. Hybrid, or advanced, routing protocols have attributes associated with both distance-vector and link-state protocols; hybrid protocols send small updates only to neighboring routers.

There are many *suites* of protocols that define protocols corresponding to the functions defined in the OSI seven layers, including routed protocols, a selection of routing protocols, applications, and so forth. They are called protocol *suites* because they have protocols for doing many different things included in their suites. Protocol suites are also known as protocol *stacks*. This section provides a brief overview of some of these protocol suites.

TCP/IP Protocol Suite

TCP/IP is by far the most widely used protocol suite; it is the only one used in the Internet. TCP/IP is short for Transmission Control Protocol/Internet Protocol, after two of the protocols in the suite. It was not invented by any single vendor, but evolved as the Internet grew.

TCP/IP Network Layer

The network layer (Layer 3) includes the following protocols:

- **Internet Protocol (IP)**—Defines a set of rules for communicating across a network. IP contains addressing information and some control information that enables packets to be routed. IP has two primary responsibilities: providing connectionless, best-effort delivery of datagrams through an internetwork, and providing fragmentation and reassembly of datagrams to support data links with different maximum transmission unit (MTU) sizes.

- **Address Resolution Protocol (ARP)**—Allows a host to dynamically discover the MAC-layer address corresponding to a particular IP network layer address. In order for two machines on a given network to communicate, they must know the other machine's physical addresses.

- **Reverse Address Resolution Protocol (RARP)**—Used to map MAC-layer addresses to IP addresses. RARP, which is the logical inverse of ARP, might be used by diskless workstations that do not know their IP addresses when they boot. RARP relies on the presence of a RARP server with table entries of MAC layer-to-IP address mappings.

- **Internet Control Message Protocol (ICMP)**—Used to report errors and other information regarding IP packet processing back to the source.

TCP/IP Transport Layer

At the transport layer (Layer 4), two transport protocols are defined:

- **Transmission Control Protocol (TCP)**—Provides connection-oriented, end-to-end reliable transmission of data in an IP environment. Connection establishment is performed by using a "three-way handshake" mechanism. A three-way handshake synchronizes both ends of a connection by allowing both sides to agree upon initial sequence numbers. This mechanism also guarantees that both sides are ready to transmit data and know that the other side is ready to transmit as well. This is necessary so that packets are not transmitted or retransmitted during session establishment or after session termination.

- **User Datagram Protocol (UDP)**—A connectionless protocol that is basically an interface between IP and upper-layer processes. Unlike the TCP, UDP adds no reliability, flow-control, or error-recovery functions to IP. Because of UDP's simplicity, UDP headers contain fewer bytes and consume less network overhead than TCP.

TCP and UDP use protocol *port numbers* to distinguish multiple applications (described in the next section) running on a single device from one another. The port number is part of the TCP or UDP segment and is used to identify the application to which the data in the segment belongs. There are well-known, or standardized, port numbers assigned to applications, so that different implementations of the TCP/IP protocol suite can interoperate. Examples of these well-known port numbers include the following:

- **File Transfer Protocol (FTP)**—TCP port 20 (data) and port 21 (control)
- **Telnet**—TCP port 23
- **Trivial File Transfer Protocol (TFTP)**—UDP port 69

TCP/IP Application Layer

In the TCP/IP protocol suite, the upper three layers of the OSI model are combined together into one layer, called the application layer. This suite includes many application layer protocols that represent a wide variety of applications, including the following:

- **File Transfer Protocol (FTP) and Trivial File Transfer Protocol (TFTP)**—To move files between devices
- **Simple Network-Management Protocol (SNMP)**—Primarily reports anomalous network conditions and sets network threshold values
- **Telnet**—Serves as a terminal emulation protocol
- **Simple Mail Transfer Protocol (SMTP)**—Provides electronic mail services
- **Domain Name System (DNS)**—Translates the names of network nodes into network addresses

IP Addressing

As mentioned, network layer addresses have two parts: the *network* that the device is on and the *device* (or *host*) number of that device on that network. Devices on the same logical network must have addresses with the same network part; however, they will have unique device parts.

IP addresses are 32 bits, as shown in Figure 1-5. The 32 bits are grouped into four sets of 8 bits (octets), separated by dots, and represented in decimal format; this is known as *dotted decimal* notation. Each bit in the octet has a binary weight (128, 64, 32, 16, 8, 4, 2, 1). The minimum value for an octet is 0, and the maximum decimal value for an octet is 255.

Figure 1-5 *IP Addresses Are 32 Bits, Written in Dotted Decimal Format*

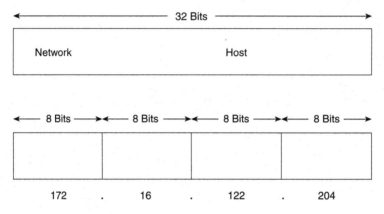

IP Address Classes

IP addressing defines five address classes: A, B, C, D, and E. Only classes A, B, and C are available for addressing devices; class D is used for multicast groups, and class E is reserved for experimental use.

The first octet of an address defines its class, as illustrated in Table 1-1. This table also shows the format of the addresses in each class as defined by the network bits (N) and host bits (H).

Table 1-1 *IP Address Classes A, B, and C Are Available for Addressing Devices*

Class	Format (N= network number, H= host number)	Higher-Order Bit(s)	Address Range
Class A	N.H.H.H	0	1.0.0.0 to 126.0.0.0
Class B	N.N.H.H	10	128.0.0.0 to 191.255.0.0
Class C	N.N.N.H	110	192.0.0.0 to 223.255.255.0

Reference: RFC 1700, available at http://info.internet.isi.edu/in-notes/rfc/files/rfc1700.txt

IP Subnets

IP networks can be divided into smaller networks called *subnetworks* (or *subnets*). Subnetting provides the network administrator with several benefits, including extra flexibility, more efficient use of network addresses, and the capability to contain broadcast traffic (a broadcast will not cross a router).

Subnets are under local administration. As such, the outside world sees an organization as a single network and has no detailed knowledge of the organization's internal structure.

A subnet address is created by "borrowing" bits from the host field and designating them as the subnet field. A *subnet mask* is a 32-bit number that is associated with an IP address; each bit in the subnet mask indicates how to interpret the corresponding bit in the IP address. In binary, a subnet mask bit of *one* indicates that the corresponding bit in the IP address is a network or subnet bit; a subnet mask bit of *zero* indicates that the corresponding bit in the IP address is a host bit. The subnet mask then indicates how many bits have been borrowed from the host field for the subnet field.

The *default subnet mask* for an address depends on its address class. Referring to Table 1-1, class A addresses have one octet, or 8 bits, of network and 3 octets or 24 bits of host; therefore the default subnet mask for a class A address is 255.0.0.0, indicating 8 bits of network (binary ones in the mask) and 24 bits of host (binary zeros in the mask). Similarly, the default subnet mask for a class B address is 255.255.0.0 and for a class C address is 255.255.255.0.

Subnet mask bits come from the high-order (left-most) bits of the host field.

When all the host bits of an address are zero, the address is for the wire (or subnet); when all the host bits of an address are one, the address is the broadcast on that wire.

As an example, a class B network 172.16.0.0 with 8 bits of subnet would have 8 of the available 16 host bits "borrowed" for subnet bits; the subnet mask would be 255.255.255.0. With these 8 subnet bits, there are 2^8 - 2 = 254 subnets; each subnet has 8 host bits, so there are 2^8 - 2 = 254 hosts available on each subnet. (The two hosts and subnets are subtracted in the above calculations because of the network address and broadcast address). The subnets would be 172.16.1.0, 172,16.2.0, 172.16.3.0, and so on. On the first subnet, the available host addresses would be 172.16.1.1, 172.16.1.2, 172.16.1.3, and so on.

Usually within the same "major" network (a class A, B, or C network), the subnet mask used is the same for all subnets of that network. Using *variable length subnet masking* (VLSM) means using a different mask in some parts of the network. Chapter 8, "Designing a Network Layer Addressing and Naming Model," discusses IP addressing and VLSM in more detail.

Tables 1-2 and 1-3 indicate the number of bits of subnetting, associated subnet mask, and resulting number of subnets and hosts available for class B and C networks, respectively.

Table 1-2 *Class B Subnetting*

Number of Subnet Bits	Subnet Mask	Number of Subnets	Number of Hosts
2	255.255.192.0	2	16382
3	255.255.224.0	6	8190
4	255.255.240.0	14	4094
5	255.255.248.0	30	2046
6	255.255.252.0	62	1022
7	255.255.254.0	126	510
8	255.255.255.0	254	254
9	255.255.255.128	510	126
10	255.255.255.192	1022	62
11	255.255.255.224	2046	30
12	255.255.255.240	4094	14
13	255.255.255.248	8190	6
14	255.255.255.252	16382	2

Table 1-3 *Class C Subnetting*

Number of Subnet Bits	Subnet Mask	Number of Subnets	Number of Hosts
2	255.255.255.192	2	62
3	255.255.255.224	6	30
4	255.255.255.240	14	14
5	255.255.255.248	30	6
6	255.255.255.252	62	2

How Subnet Masks Are Used To Determine the Network Number

The router performs a set process to determine the network (or more specifically, the subnetwork) address to which a packet should be forwarded. First, the router extracts the IP destination address from the incoming packet and retrieves the internal subnet mask. It then performs a *logical AND* operation to obtain the network number. This causes the host portion of the IP destination address to be removed, while the destination subnetwork number remains. The router then looks up the destination subnetwork number in its routing table and matches it with an outgoing interface. Finally, it forwards the frame to the destination IP address.

Three basic rules govern logically "ANDing" two binary numbers. First, 1 "ANDed" with 1 yields 1. Second, 1 "ANDed" with 0 yields 0. Finally, 0 "ANDed" with 0 yields 0. The truth table provided in Table 1-4 illustrates the rules for logical AND operations.

Table 1-4   *Rules for Logical AND Operations*

Input	Input	Output
1	1	1
1	0	0
0	1	0
0	0	0

Two simple guidelines exist for remembering logical AND operations: Logically "ANDing" a 1 with any number yields that number, and logically "ANDing" a 0 with any number yields 0.

Table 1-5 illustrates an example of the logical "ANDing" of a destination IP address and the subnet mask. The subnetwork number remains, which the router uses to forward the packet.

Table 1-5   *Example Calculation of Subnet Number*

		Network	Subnet	Host	Host
Destination IP Address	172.16.1.2	10101100	00010000	00000001	00000010
Subnet Mask	255.255.255.0	11111111	11111111	11111111	00000000
Subnet Number	172.16.1.0	10101100	00010000	00000001	00000000

TCP/IP Routing Protocols

The TCP/IP suite defines a selection of routing protocols:

- **Routing Information Protocol (RIP)**—A distance-vector protocol that uses hop count as its metric. RIP is widely used for routing traffic and is an *interior gateway protocol* (IGP), which means it performs routing within a single autonomous system. The latest enhancement to RIP is the RIP 2 specification, which allows more information to be included in RIP packets and provides a simple authentication mechanism.

- The **Interior Gateway Routing Protocol (IGRP)**—A routing protocol that was developed in the mid-1980s by Cisco Systems, Inc. Cisco's principal goal in creating IGRP was to provide a robust protocol for routing within an autonomous system (AS). IGRP is a distance vector interior gateway protocol. IGRP uses a combination (vector) of metrics. *Internetwork delay, bandwidth, reliability,* and *load* are all factored into the routing decision.

- **Enhanced Internet Gateway Routing Protocol (EIGRP)**—Represents an evolution from its predecessor IGRP. Enhanced IGRP is a hybrid routing protocol. It integrates the capabilities of link-state protocols into distance-vector protocols. EIGRP incorporates the *Diffusing-Update Algorithm* (DUAL). Key capabilities that distinguish Enhanced IGRP from other routing protocols include fast convergence, support for VLSM, support for partial updates, and support for multiple network layer protocols (EIGRP supports IPX and AppleTalk, as well as IP).

- **Open Shortest Path First (OSPF)**—A link-state routing protocol that calls for the sending of *link-state advertisements* (LSAs) to all other routers within the same hierarchical area. Information on attached interfaces, metrics used, and other variables is included in OSPF LSAs. As OSPF routers accumulate link-state information, they use the *shortest path first* (SPF) algorithm to calculate the shortest path to each node. Unlike RIP, OSPF can operate within a hierarchy. The largest entity within the hierarchy is the *autonomous system* (AS), which is a collection of networks under a common administration that share a common routing strategy. OSPF is an interior gateway routing protocol, although it is capable of receiving routes from and sending routes to other ASs. An AS can be divided into a number of *areas*, which are groups of contiguous networks and attached hosts.

- **Border Gateway Protocol (BGP)**—An exterior gateway protocol (EGP), which means that it performs routing between multiple autonomous systems or domains and exchanges routing and reachability information with other BGP systems. BGP was developed to replace its predecessor, the now obsolete *Exterior Gateway Protocol* (EGP), as the standard exterior gateway routing protocol used in the global Internet. BGP solves serious problems with EGP and scales to Internet growth more efficiently.

Resource Reservation Protocol

The Resource Reservation Protocol (RSVP) is a network control protocol that enables Internet applications to obtain special qualities of service (QoSs) for their data flows. RSVP is not a routing protocol; instead, it works in conjunction with routing protocols and installs the equivalent of dynamic access lists along the routes that routing protocols calculate. RSVP occupies the place of a transport protocol in the OSI seven layer model.

In RSVP, a data flow is a sequence of messages that have the same source, destination (one or more), and quality of service. QoS requirements are communicated through a network via a *flow specification*, which is a data structure used by internetwork hosts to request special services from the internetwork. A flow specification often guarantees how the internetwork will handle some of its host traffic.

RSVP supports three traffic types: *best-effort*, *rate-sensitive*, and *delay-sensitive*. The type of data flow service used to support these traffic types depends on QoS implemented.

- **Best-effort** traffic is traditional IP traffic. Applications include file transfer, mail transmissions, disk mounts, interactive logins, and transaction traffic. The service supporting best-effort traffic is called *best-effort service.*

- **Rate-sensitive** traffic is willing to give up timeliness for guaranteed rate. Rate-sensitive traffic, for example, might request 100 kbps of bandwidth. If it actually sends 200 kbps for an extended period, a router can delay traffic. An example of such an application is H.323 videoconferencing, which is designed to run on ISDN (H.320) or ATM (H.310) but is found on the Internet. H.323 encoding is a constant, or nearly constant, rate and it requires a constant transport rate. The RSVP service supporting rate-sensitive traffic is called *guaranteed bit-rate service.*

- **Delay-sensitive** traffic is traffic that requires timeliness of delivery and varies its rate accordingly. MPEG-II video, for example, averages about 3 to 7 Mbps, depending on the amount of change in the picture. MPEG-II video sources send key and delta frames. Typically, one or two key frames per second describe the whole picture, and 13 or 28 frames describe the change from the key frame. Delta frames are usually substantially smaller than key frames. As a result, rates vary quite a bit from frame to frame. A single frame, however, requires delivery within a frame time or the CODEC (coder-decoder) is unable to do its job. A specific priority must be negotiated for delta-frame traffic. RSVP services supporting delay-sensitive traffic are referred to as *controlled-delay service* (non-real-time service) and *predictive service* (real-time service).

RSVP data flows are generally characterized by *sessions*, over which data packets flow. A session is a set of data flows with the same unicast or multicast destination, and RSVP treats each session independently.

In the context of RSVP, quality of service is an attribute specified in flow specifications that is used to determine the way in which data interchanges are handled by participating entities (routers, receivers, and senders). RSVP is used to specify the QoS by both hosts and routers. Hosts use RSVP to request a QoS level from the network on behalf of an application data stream. Routers use RSVP to deliver QoS requests to other routers along the path(s) of the data stream. In doing so, RSVP maintains the router and host state to provide the requested service.

To initiate an RSVP multicast session, a receiver first joins the multicast group specified by an IP destination address by using the Internet Group Membership Protocol (IGMP). In the case of a unicast session, unicast routing serves the function that IGMP, coupled with Protocol-Independent Multicast (PIM), serves in the multicast case. After the receiver joins a group, a potential sender starts sending RSVP path messages to the IP destination address. The receiver application receives a path message and starts sending appropriate reservation request messages specifying the desired flow descriptors using RSVP. After the sender application receives a reservation request message, the sender starts sending data packets.

NetWare Protocol Suite

NetWare is a network operating system (NOS) that provides transparent remote file access and numerous other distributed network services, including printer sharing and support for various applications, such as electronic mail transfer and database access. NetWare specifies the upper five layers of the OSI reference model and, as such, runs on virtually any media-access protocol (layer 2). Additionally, NetWare runs on virtually any kind of computer system, from PCs to mainframes. Introduced in the early 1980s, NetWare was developed by Novell, Inc. It was derived from Xerox Network Systems (XNS), which was created by Xerox Corporation in the late 1970s, and is based on a client-server architecture. *Clients* (sometimes called *workstations*) request services, such as file and printer access, from *servers*.

Internetwork Packet Exchange (IPX) is the original NetWare network layer (Layer 3) protocol used to route packets through an internetwork. IPX is a connectionless datagram-based network protocol and, as such, is similar to the Internet Protocol found in TCP/IP networks.

The *Sequenced Packet Exchange* (SPX) protocol is the most common NetWare transport protocol at Layer 4 of the OSI model. SPX resides on top of IPX in the NetWare Protocol Suite. SPX is a reliable, connection-oriented protocol that supplements the datagram service provided by the IPX protocol. SPX was derived from the Xerox Networking Systems (XNS) Sequenced Packet Protocol (SPP).

NetWare supports a wide variety of upper-layer protocols, including the following:

- **NetWare shell**—Runs on clients and intercepts application input/output (I/O) calls to determine whether they require network access for completion. Client applications are unaware of any network access required for completion of application calls.

- **NetWare Remote Procedure Call (NetWare RPC)**—Another more general redirection mechanism similar in concept to the NetWare shell supported by Novell.

- **NetWare Core Protocol (NCP)**—A series of server routines designed to satisfy application requests coming from, for example, the NetWare shell. The services provided by NCP include file access, printer access, name management, accounting, security, and file synchronization.

- **Network Basic Input/Output System (NetBIOS)**—A session layer interface specification from IBM and Microsoft. NetWare's NetBIOS emulation software allows programs written to the industry-standard NetBIOS interface to run within NetWare system.

NetWare application layer services include:

- **NetWare message-handling service (NetWare MHS)**—A message-delivery system that provides electronic mail transport.

- **Btrieve**—Novell's implementation of the binary tree (btree) database-access mechanism.

- **NetWare loadable modules (NLMs)**—Add-on modules that attach into a NetWare system. NLMs currently available from Novell and third parties include alternate protocol stacks, communication services, and database services.

- **IBM Logical Unit (LU) 6.2 network-addressable units (NAUs)**—Support to allow peer-to-peer connectivity and information exchange across IBM networks. NetWare packets are encapsulated within LU 6.2 packets for transit across an IBM network.

IPX Addressing

As with other network addresses, Novell IPX network addresses must be unique. These addresses are represented in hexadecimal format and consist of two parts: a network number and a node number. The IPX network number, which is assigned by the network administrator, is 32 bits long. The node number, which usually is the Media Access Control (MAC) address for one of the system's network interface cards (NICs), is 48 bits long.

NetWare Routing and Service Advertisement Protocols

IPX uses the following protocols for routing and service advertisement:

- **IPX Routing Information Protocol (RIP)**—A distance vector routing protocol that sends routing updates every 60 seconds. To make best-path routing decisions, IPX RIP uses a *tick* as the metric, which in principle is the delay expected when using a particular length. One tick is 1/18th of a second. In the case of two paths with an equal tick count, IPX RIP uses the hop count as a tie breaker.

- **Service Advertisement Protocol (SAP)**—An IPX protocol through which network resources, such as file servers and print servers, advertise their addresses and the services they provide. Advertisements are sent via SAP every 60 seconds. Services are identified by a hexadecimal number, which is called a SAP identifier (for example, 4 = file server and 7 = print server). SAP is pervasive in current networks based on NetWare 3.11 and earlier but is utilized less frequently in NetWare 4.0 networks because workstations can locate services by consulting a NetWare Directory Services (NDS) Server. SAP, however, still is required in NetWare 4.0 networks for workstations when they boot up to locate an NDS server.

- **NetWare Link-Services Protocol (NLSP)**—A link-state routing protocol from Novell designed to overcome some of the limitations associated with the IPX RIP and SAP. As compared to RIP and SAP, NLSP provides improved routing, better efficiency, and scalability. In addition, NLSP-based routers are backward-compatible with RIP-based routers. NLSP-based routers use a reliable delivery protocol, so delivery is guaranteed. NLSP is based on the OSI Intermediate System-to-Intermediate System (IS-IS) protocol and is similar to IS-IS except that a hierarchical topology was not defined until Version 1.1 of NLSP was specified (which is supported in Cisco IOS™ Release 11.1). NLSP now supports hierarchical routing with area, domain, and global internetwork components.

AppleTalk Protocol Suite

AppleTalk, a protocol suite developed by Apple Computer in the early 1980s, was developed in conjunction with the Macintosh computer. AppleTalk's purpose was to allow multiple users to share resources, such as files and printers. The devices that supply these resources are called *servers*, whereas the devices that make use of these resources (such as a user's Macintosh computer) are called *clients*.

AppleTalk was designed with a transparent network interface. That is, the interaction between client computers and network servers requires little interaction from the user. In addition, the actual operations of the AppleTalk protocols are invisible to end users, who see only the result of these operations. Two versions of AppleTalk exist: AppleTalk Phase 1 and AppleTalk Phase 2.

Four main media-access implementations exist in the AppleTalk protocol suite: EtherTalk, LocalTalk, TokenTalk, and FDDITalk. These data link layer implementations perform address translation and other functions that allow proprietary AppleTalk protocols to communicate over industry-standard interfaces, which include IEEE 802.3 (using EtherTalk), Token Ring/IEEE 802.5 (using TokenTalk), and FDDI (using FDDITalk). In addition, AppleTalk implements its own network interface, known as LocalTalk.

AppleTalk Network Components

AppleTalk networks are arranged hierarchically. Four basic components form the basis of an AppleTalk network: sockets, nodes, networks, and zones.

- An AppleTalk **socket** is a unique, addressable location in an AppleTalk node. It is the logical point at which upper-layer AppleTalk software processes and the network layer Datagram-Delivery Protocol (DDP) interact.

- An AppleTalk **node** is a device that is connected to an AppleTalk network. This device might be a Macintosh computer, a printer, an IBM PC, a router, or some other similar device.

- A *nonextended* AppleTalk **network** is a physical-network segment that is assigned only a single network number, which can range between 1 and 1,024. An *extended* AppleTalk network is a physical-network segment that can be assigned multiple network numbers. This configuration is known as a **cable range**.

- An AppleTalk **zone** is a logical group of nodes or networks that is defined when the network administrator configures the network. The nodes or networks need not be physically contiguous to belong to the same AppleTalk zone.

AppleTalk Protocols

There are two protocols at the network layer:

- **AppleTalk Address-Resolution Protocol (AARP)**—Associates AppleTalk network addresses with hardware addresses

- **Datagram Delivery Protocol (DDP)**—Provides a best-effort connectionless datagram service between AppleTalk sockets

Five key implementations exist at the transport layer of the AppleTalk protocol suite:

- **Routing Table Maintenance Protocol (RTMP)**—Responsible for establishing and maintaining routing tables for AppleTalk routers. RTMP is a distance-vector protocol typically used in AppleTalk LANs; it uses hop count as its metric.

- **Name-Binding Protocol (NBP)**—Maps the addresses used at lower layers to AppleTalk names.

- **AppleTalk Update-Based Routing Protocol (AURP)**—Allows two or more AppleTalk internetworks to be interconnected through a TCP/IP network to form an AppleTalk WAN. AURP encapsulates packets in User Datagram Protocol (UDP) headers, allowing them to be transported transparently through a TCP/IP network; this creates a virtual data link between the AppleTalk networks. AURP is also the routing protocol used on this virtual data link; in this capacity, it is similar to distance vector routing protocols but is designed to handle routing update traffic over WAN links more efficiently than RTMP by only sending changed information.

- **AppleTalk Transaction Protocol (ATP)**—Handles transactions between two AppleTalk sockets.

- **AppleTalk Echo Protocol (AEP)**—Generates packets that test the reachability of network nodes.

The session layer protocol implementations supported by AppleTalk include:

- **AppleTalk Data-Stream Protocol (ADSP)**—Establishes and maintains full-duplex communication between two AppleTalk sockets

- **Zone-Information Protocol (ZIP)**—Maintains network number-to-zone name mappings in AppleTalk routers

- **AppleTalk Session Protocol (ASP)**—Establishes and maintains sessions between AppleTalk clients and servers

- **Printer-Access Protocol (PAP)**—Allows client workstations to establish connections with servers, particularly printers

The **AppleTalk Filing Protocol (AFP)** is implemented at the presentation and application layers of the AppleTalk protocol suite. AFP permits AppleTalk workstations to share files across a network.

AppleTalk Addressing

AppleTalk utilizes addresses to identify and locate devices on a network in a manner similar to the process utilized by protocols such as TCP/IP and IPX. These addresses, which are assigned dynamically, are composed of three elements:

- **Network number**—A 16-bit value that identifies a specific AppleTalk network (either a nonextended network or from an extended cable range)

- **Node number**—An 8-bit value that identifies a particular AppleTalk node attached to the specified network

- **Socket number**—An 8-bit number that identifies a specific socket running on a network node

AppleTalk addresses usually are written as decimal values separated by a period. For example, 10.1.50 means network 10, node 1, socket 50. This also might be represented as 10.1, socket 50.

IBM Systems Network Architecture (SNA) Protocols

IBM networking today consists of essentially two separate architectures that branch from a common origin. Before contemporary networks existed, IBM's *Systems Network Architecture* (SNA) ruled the networking landscape, so it is often referred to as traditional or legacy SNA.

With the rise of personal computers, workstations, and client/server computing, the need for a peer-based networking strategy was addressed by IBM with the creation of *Advanced Peer-to-Peer Networking* (APPN) and *Advanced Program-to-Program Computing* (APPC).

Traditional SNA Environments

SNA was developed in the 1970s with an overall structure that parallels the OSI reference model. With SNA, a mainframe running *Advanced Communication Facility/Virtual Telecommunication Access Method* (ACF/VTAM) serves as the hub of an SNA network. ACF/VTAM is responsible for establishing all sessions and for activating and deactivating resources. In this environment, resources are explicitly predefined, thereby eliminating the requirement for broadcast traffic and minimizing header overhead.

IBM SNA model components map closely to the OSI reference model, as shown in Figure 1-6.

Figure 1-6 *The IBM SNA Model Maps Closely to the OSI Model*

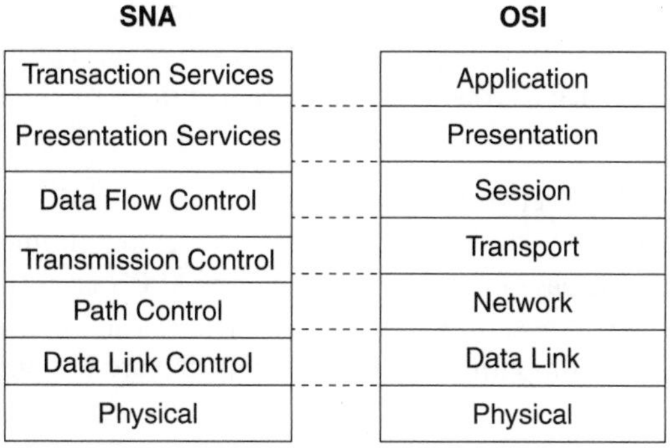

SNA	OSI
Transaction Services	Application
Presentation Services	Presentation
Data Flow Control	Session
Transmission Control	Transport
Path Control	Network
Data Link Control	Data Link
Physical	Physical

The SNA layers are:

- **Data-link control**—Defines several protocols, including the *Synchronous Data Link Control* (SDLC) protocol for hierarchical communication, and the Token Ring Network communication protocol for LAN communication between peers.

- **Path control**—Performs many OSI network-layer functions, including routing and datagram *segmentation and reassembly* (SAR).

- **Transmission control**—Provides a reliable end-to-end connection service, as well as encrypting and decrypting services.

- **Data flow control**—Manages request and response processing, determines whose turn it is to communicate, groups messages together, and interrupts data flow on request.

- **Presentation services**—Specifies data-transformation algorithms that translate data from one format to another, coordinate resource sharing, and synchronize transaction operations.

- **Transaction services**—Provides application services in the form of programs that implement distributed processing or management services.

Traditional SNA physical entities assume one of the following four forms:

- **Hosts**—In SNA, control all or part of a network and typically provide computation, program execution, database access, directory services, and network management. (An example of a host device within a traditional SNA environment is an S/370 mainframe.)

- **Communications controllers**—Manage the physical network and control communication links. In particular, communications controllers (also called *front-end processors* [FEPs]) are relied upon to route data through a traditional SNA network. (An example of a communications controller is a 3745.)

- **Establishment controllers**—Commonly called *cluster controllers*, these devices control input and output operations of attached devices, such as terminals. (An example of an establishment controller is a 3174.)

- **Terminals**—Also referred to as workstations, terminals provide the user interface to the network. (A typical example would be a 3270.)

IBM Peer-Based Networking

Changes in networking and communications requirements caused IBM to evolve (and generally overhaul) many of the basic design characteristics of SNA. The emergence of peer-based networking entities (such as routers) resulted in a number of significant changes in SNA. Internetworking among SNA peers hinges on several IBM-developed networking components.

Advanced Peer-to-Peer Networking (APPN) represents IBM's second-generation SNA. In creating APPN, IBM moved SNA from a hierarchical, mainframe-centric environment to a peer-based networking environment. At the heart of APPN is an IBM architecture that supports peer-based communications, directory services, and routing between two or more Advanced Program-to-Program Computing (APPC) systems that are not directly attached.

Network Management

In general, network management is a service that employs a variety of tools, applications, and devices to assist human network managers in monitoring and maintaining networks.

Most network management architectures use the same basic structure and set of relationships. End stations (*managed devices*), such as computer systems and other network devices, run software that enables them to send alerts when they recognize problems (for example, when one or more user-determined thresholds are exceeded). Upon receiving these alerts, *management entities* are programmed to react by executing one, several, or a group of actions, including operator notification, event logging, system shutdown, and automatic attempts at system repair.

Management entities also can poll end stations to check the values of certain variables. Polling can be automatic or user-initiated, but *agents* in the managed devices respond to all polls. Agents are software modules that first compile information about the managed devices in which they reside, store this information in a *management database*, and finally provide it (proactively or reactively) to management entities within *network management systems* (NMSs) via a *network management protocol*. The Simple Network Management Protocol (SNMP) is a well-known network management protocol. *Management proxies* are entities that provide management information on behalf of other entities.

Simple Network Management Protocol

The Simple Network Management Protocol is an application layer protocol that facilitates the exchange of management information between network devices. It is part of the TCP/IP protocol suite. SNMP enables network administrators to manage network performance, find and solve network problems, and plan for network growth.

Two versions of SNMP exist: SNMP Version 1 (SNMPv1) and SNMP Version 2 (SNMPv2). Both versions have a number of features in common, but SNMPv2 offers enhancements, such as additional protocol operations.

Managed devices are monitored and controlled using four basic SNMP commands:

- The **read** command is used by a network management system (NMS) to monitor managed devices. The NMS examines different variables that are maintained by managed devices.

- The **write** command is used by an NMS to control managed devices. The NMS changes the values of variables stored within managed devices.

- The **trap** command is used by managed devices to asynchronously report events to the NMS. When certain types of events occur, a managed device sends a trap to the NMS.

- **Traversal operations** are used by the NMS to determine which variables a managed device supports and to sequentially gather information in variable tables (such as a routing table).

A Management Information Base (MIB) is a collection of information that is organized hierarchically. MIBs are accessed using a network management protocol such as SNMP. MIBs are composed of managed objects and are identified by object identifiers. A managed object (sometimes called a MIB object, an object, or a MIB) is one of any number of specific characteristics of a managed device. Managed objects are composed of one or more object instances, which are essentially variables. An object identifier (or object ID) uniquely identifies a managed object in the MIB hierarchy.

SNMP is a simple request-response protocol. The NMS issues a request, and managed devices return responses. This behavior is implemented by using one of four protocol operations in SNMPv1:

- The **Get** operation is used by the NMS to retrieve the value of one or more object instances from an agent.

- The **GetNext** operation is used by the NMS to retrieve the value of the next object instance in a table or list within an agent.

- The **Set** operation is used by the NMS to set the values of object instances within an agent.

- The **Trap** operation is used by agents to asynchronously inform the NMS of a significant event.

The Get, GetNext, and Set operations used in SNMPv1 are exactly the same as those used in SNMPv2. SNMPv2, however, adds and enhances some protocols operations. The SNMPv2 Trap operation, for example, serves the same function as that used in SNMPv1; however, it uses a different message format and is designed to replace the SNMPv1 Trap. SNMPv2 also defines two new protocol operations:

- The **GetBulk** operation is used by the NMS to efficiently retrieve large blocks of data, such as multiple rows in a table.

- The **Inform** operation allows one NMS to send trap information to another NMS and receive a response.

Remote Monitoring

Remote Monitoring (RMON) is a standard monitoring specification that enables various network monitors and console systems to exchange network-monitoring data. The RMON specification defines a set of statistics and functions that can be exchanged between RMON-compliant console managers and network probes. As such, RMON provides network administrators with comprehensive network-fault diagnosis, planning, and performance-tuning information. RMON delivers information in nine RMON *groups* of monitoring elements, each providing specific sets of data to meet common network-monitoring requirements. Each group is optional so that vendors do not need to support all the groups within the Management Information Base (MIB).

Summary

Now that you have reviewed key internetworking technology information on specific topics relevant to this book, you are ready to embark on the network design process. The next chapter looks at a framework for understanding how various networking devices can solve your customer's problems, leading into the design process chapters that follow.

PART II

A Small- to Medium-Sized Business Solutions Framework

This part of the book provides a framework that you can use to easily analyze customer network problems and create Cisco scalable solutions.

Upon completion of this chapter, you will be able to describe a framework you can use to analyze customer network problems and create Cisco scalable solutions. It will take you approximately 30 minutes to read this chapter.

CHAPTER 2

Analyzing Small- to Medium-Sized Business Networks

This chapter introduces the role that a Cisco Certified Design Associate (CCDA) will play in designing networks, and presents a framework for you to use in your designs.

Role of the Cisco Certified Design Associate

Your role as a Cisco Certified Design Associate is to be a network design consultant. You will act like an architect, building comprehensive designs that solve your customer's internetworking problems and provide the required functionality, performance, and scalability. In the same way that an architect designs a building or house for a client, you will develop blueprints for an overall internetwork design, as well as component plans for various pieces of the internetwork.

CiscoFusion

Cisco has developed an integrated network architecture, called *CiscoFusion*. With the CiscoFusion architecture, multiple networking technologies operating at different networking layers, can provide the best capabilities to handle different networking issues.

Many of your customers may already be aware of the recent internetworking trend toward an integrated view of networking technologies. As a Cisco Certified Design Associate, you will be uniquely positioned to produce network designs, based on CiscoFusion, that meet the needs of state-of-the-art networks that integrate Layer 2, Layer 3, and Asynchronous Transfer Mode (ATM) services. For example, the intelligent networking services associated with Layer 3 can be combined with the cost-effective, high-capacity services provided by Layer 2 in both local-area networks and wide-area networks.

Evolution of Layer 2 and Layer 3 Services

Layer 2, also known as the data link layer, operates within a specific local-area network (LAN) or wide-area network (WAN) segment. In the last two years, LANs have been revolutionized by the exploding use of switching at Layer 2. Companies are replacing hubs with switches at a quick pace. LAN switches provide performance enhancements for new and existing data networking applications by increasing bandwidth and throughput for workgroups and local servers.

Layer 3, also known as the network layer, operates between and across segments. Protocols such as Internet Protocol (IP), Internetwork Packet Exchange (IPX), and AppleTalk's Datagram Delivery Protocol (DDP) operate at Layer 3. In WANs, Layer 3 networking allows businesses to build global data networks. As an example, the global Internet is based on Layer 3 IP technology.

Layer 3 networking, implemented with routing, interconnects the switched workgroups and provides services such as security, Quality of Service (QoS) options, and traffic management. Routing provides the control needed to build functional, scalable networks.

NOTE   Traditionally, Layer 2 switching has been provided by LAN switches, and Layer 3 networking has been provided by routers. Increasingly, these two networking functions are being integrated into one common platform.

There will still be a wide range of platforms providing different performance and capacity ranges for each networking function, but users will gain fundamental benefits from integration of the layers. Users will be able to reduce the number of networking devices that need to be purchased, installed, supported, and serviced. In addition, users will be able to efficiently apply Layer 3 services, such as security and QoS capabilities, to specific individual users and applications.

Mirroring the integration of Layer 3 networking technology into LAN switching devices, WAN switching equipment likely will increasingly incorporate Layer 3 networking capabilities. As traditional Layer 3 routers gain support for higher capacity and bandwidth, the integration of Layer 2 technologies will enable routers to achieve optimum levels of performance, port density, and cost effectiveness.

Figure 2-1 shows how Layer 2 and Layer 3 switching can be used to facilitate communications between Client X and Server Y, with or without routing.

Figure 2-1   *Layer 2 and Layer 3 Functionality Allows Devices to Communicate*

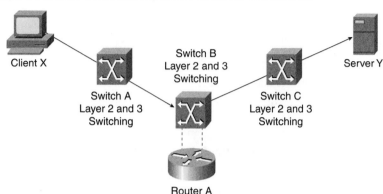

When To Use Layer 2 or Layer 3 Functionality

The decision to use Layer 2 or Layer 3 functionality in a network design depends on which problems you are trying to solve for your customer. These problems can be any of the following:

- Media problems
- Protocol problems
- The need to transport large payloads

Each of these problems is discussed in more detail in the following sections. A solution framework for these problems, using Layer 2 and Layer 3 devices, is then presented.

Media Problems

Media problems occur when too many devices contend for access to a LAN segment, causing an excessive number of collisions on Ethernet networks and long waits for the token on Token Ring or FDDI networks. The level of contention can be estimated by examining network utilization and, in the case of Ethernet, the collision rate. Media contention problems are obvious from complaints from users about slow response time and difficulties accessing services.

Protocol Problems

Problems are caused by protocols that do not scale well. For example, some protocols send too many broadcasts. The number of broadcasts becomes excessive when there are too many clients looking for services, too many servers announcing services, and too many bridge protocol data unit (BPDU) frames. Protocol problems occur when a protocol that was designed for small workgroups is being used for larger networks or for a network that has outgrown the capability of the protocol. The protocol no longer provides the scale required for the business.

Example scenarios of when protocol problems can result include the following:

- Network layer addressing issues, including running out of addresses.
- The requirement to use variable-length subnet masks.
- The need for physically discontiguous subnets.
- The need for a private address space.

Chapter 8, "Designing a Network-Layer Addressing and Naming Model," discusses these issues.

The Need to Transport Large Payloads

The need to transport large payloads, such as multicast video, can require much more bandwidth than is available on a customer's network or backbone. Multicast video will need more bandwidth than standard data. Multicast video may also require support for low and predictable latency.

A Framework for Solving Small- to Medium-Sized Business Network Problems

To help reduce the complexity associated with identifying and analyzing customer problems and designing solutions, Cisco developed a basic framework into which most customer problems fit. The small- to medium-sized business solutions framework is represented as a triangle, as shown in Figure 2-2.

Figure 2-2   *Cisco's Framework for Identifying Small- to Medium-Sized Business Network Solutions*

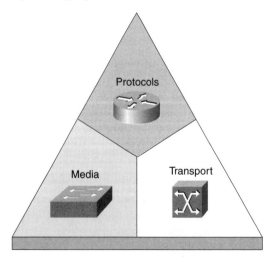

As illustrated in Figure 2-2, use the following simple rules when designing solutions to customer problems:

- If the problems involve media contention, use LAN switching.
- If the problems are protocol related—for example, resulting in an excessive number of broadcasts—use routing.
- If the customer needs to transport payloads that require high bandwidth, use Fast Ethernet switching. In large networks where high bandwidth and predictable low latency are required, consider ATM switching.

Summary

Now that you have an understanding of the problems that customers may encounter on their networks and potential solutions available to you in a network, you are ready to start the network design process.

In the next part of the book, you will learn how to identify customer needs. While reading the chapter content and performing the chapter exercises, keep in mind the small- to medium-sized business solutions framework identified in this chapter to help you understand typical customer problems. At the end of Part III of this book, you will be able to determine whether the needs are related to media, protocols, or bandwidth.

PART III

Identifying Customer Needs

This part of the book provides a process that can be used to determine a customer's requirements for network performance, security, capacity, and scalability.

This chapter covers how to characterize an existing network. It will take you approximately four hours to complete this chapter and its exercises. Upon completion, you will be able to do the following:

- Identify all the data you should gather to characterize the customer's existing network.

- Document the customer's current applications, protocols, topology, and number of users.

- Document the customer's business issues that are relevant to a network design project.

- Assess the health of the customer's existing network and make conclusions about the network's capability to support growth.

CHAPTER 3

Characterizing the Existing Network

This chapter includes some tables and other job aids that you will find useful when completing the case studies at the end of the chapter. References to some World Wide Web (WWW) sites are also included; relevant information has been extracted from these sites and is provided in the chapter. If you have access to the Internet, you may want to access the sites mentioned to obtain detailed information related to specific topics. All of the sites referenced in this chapter are also listed in Appendix C, "Interesting WWW Links and Other Suggested Readings."

Follow these steps to complete this chapter:

1 Study the content in the chapter, including any tables and job aids that appear.

2 Review the case studies at the end of this chapter.

3 Complete the questions in each case study.

4 Review the answers provided by our internetworking experts in Appendix B, "Answers to Chapter Questions, Case Studies, and Sample CCDA Exam."

Tasks for Characterizing a Customer's Network

To characterize a customer's network, you will need to:

- Identify any bottlenecks.
- Determine whether the anticipated growth will cause problems.
- Recognize legacy systems that must be incorporated into the new design.
- Recognize business constraints and inputs to the new design; business constraints are business-related issues (not technical issues) that may place a limitation on your network design.

In order to obtain this knowledge, you will need to gather a lot of data, including administrative and technical data, as discussed in the following sections. Some of the tools available to analyze that data are introduced later in the chapter, followed by a discussion of the steps to follow when characterizing the network. Many tables and other job aids are included in this last discussion for your use when gathering and analyzing the data for your network.

Gathering Administrative Data

Understanding how your customer's company works is an important factor to consider when designing its new network. In order to gain this knowledge, you need to gather administrative data to help you determine the company's business goals, corporate structure, geographical structure, current and future staffing, and policies and politics that might affect your internetwork design. This section identifies the type of administrative data needed and how to gather it.

Determining Company Business Goals

Determine the company's major business goals for the next year and the next five years. This information is important to help you design an internetwork that provides the scalability required. Research your customer's industry and competition. With knowledge of your customer's business, you can position Cisco technologies and products to help strengthen the customer's status in the customer's own industry.

Ask your client if there are any financial constraints that may influence the network design.

Determining Corporate Structure

The final internetwork design usually reflects the corporate structure, so ask your client to help you understand the corporate structure.

For example, a corporation may have Human Resources, Engineering, Accounting, and other departments. The final network design will likely be divided along these same departmental lines, perhaps with a separate network for each department. Other design decisions, such as the placement of servers, may also be influenced by this departmental structure.

Determining Geographical Structure

Locate the client's major user communities. For example, if the client has offices in Europe and Asia, as well as North America, the final network design will likely be divided along these geographical lines. The WAN connections between the offices will also be dependent on this structure; considerations include the type of WANs available in the various locations, the associated costs, and local tariffs and laws.

Determining Current and Future Staffing

Ask the following questions regarding staffing issues:

- How much in-house internetworking expertise is there?
- Does the company plan to expand staff as required to support the new internetwork design?

- Will the company provide you with an Information Technology (IT) or business representative to assist with your design of the internetwork?
- Will the new design cause changes in job functions or possibly eliminate jobs?

Having the necessary staff during the design phase of the new network will help you gather all of the relevant information needed. During implementation, the experience and motivation of the staff could play a key role in the success of the new network.

Determining Policies and Politics

Past successes and failures may help you determine problem areas for your internetwork design. Ask the following questions regarding political and policy issues:

- Has a new design been tried before and failed? Who created and/or owned that design?
- Are there people on the project who do not want to implement changes?

Gathering Technical Data

Technical data will help you understand the customer's current and planned applications, as well as current protocols, internetworking devices, and performance bottlenecks. This section identifies the type of technical data needed and how to gather it.

Identifying Applications

Identify the customer's current applications and plans for future applications.

The applications being used on a network are key to how the network will be used, what protocols will be run, and the amount of traffic that will be on the network. For example, a network used mainly for e-mail will have less traffic than one used for video conferencing between the remote offices of a company. The features required in the internetworking devices are also dependent on the applications being run. For example, some multicasting features may be required for the video conferencing application.

Analyzing Information Flows

Analyze where information flows in the company. Include any data that flows on any network in the company. If the network design involves new applications, the flows for these also need to be analyzed. The type of data, the amount of traffic, and where it is concentrated will all affect how the network performs.

Document any existing data that currently "flows" manually within the company (for example, data copied from one location to another by sending disks) and that will be carried by a network in the new design.

Document any significant changes expected to data as a result of new applications, including the size of files.

If any business process reengineering has been done recently, the information flows may already be documented. If not, it could take considerable time to do the analysis.

Determining Shared Data

Determine where shared data resides (for example, on file and database servers) and which users and applications create and access it.

Determining Network Traffic and Access

Determine how much network traffic flows from one network segment to another. Determine whether data outside the company, such as the Internet, is accessed.

Determining Network Performance Characteristics

Make sure you understand the performance characteristics of the existing network. Document any problems, especially if they will still exist after your new design is implemented.

If time permits, do a baseline analysis of the performance of the existing internetwork. If the internetwork is too large for the baseline analysis to be practical, analyze the backbones and critical network segments.

Tools to Characterize a Network

There are many tools available to help you characterize a customer's network. The World Wide Web contains an abundance of information that you may wish to access if you are unfamiliar with these tools. The following sections document some of the tools available.

NETSYS Tools

The NETSYS Tools (formerly known as NETSYS Enterprise/Solver Performance Tools) analyze interface statistics, routing table sizes, IP/IPX accounting data, and enterprise Remote Monitor (RMON) information to provide an observed performance snapshot of the current network. You can read more about NETSYS tools on Cisco's WWW site; some details from this site are quoted here.

The Network Management section of Cisco's Product and Ordering Information web site at http://www.cisco.com/warp/public/cc/cisco/mkt/enm/index.shtml includes a section titled *Cisco NETSYS Service-Level Management Suite: Providing an integrated end-to-end network management solution*. The following paragraphs cite this information.

NETSYS Service-Level Management Suite (Cisco NSM) provides an integrated end-to-end network management solution combined with service-level management. The NSM consists of four core modules: the enhanced Connectivity Service Manager and Performance Service Manager combined with the new LAN Service Manager and WAN Service Manager.

With Cisco NETSYS Service-Level Management Suite 4.1, Cisco Systems is releasing the industry's first policy-based service-level management solution that enables network managers to define, monitor, and assess network connectivity, security, and performance policies, and to troubleshoot problems quickly when they occur.

The NETSYS Connectivity Service Manager monitors your actual network configuration data and uses built-in intelligence to verify the availability of key network services. It allows you to establish service-level policies for connectivity, reliability, and security services; and it uses the unique VISTA (View, Isolate, Solve, Test, Apply) troubleshooting methodology to automate the diagnosis and repair of problems.

The NETSYS Performance Service Manager complements the capabilities of the Connectivity Service Manager, allowing you to define, monitor, and optimize performance service levels; make the most efficient use of existing network resources; diagnose and solve network performance problems; tune existing networks; and plan network changes. By accurately modeling routing and flow transport over Cisco devices, you can analyze interactions between traffic flows, topologies, routing parameters, router configurations, and Cisco IOS™ software features.

The NETSYS LAN Service Manager complements the Connectivity Service Manager by adding LAN switching topology viewing and diagnostic capabilities. It shows you an integrated view of your router/LAN switching network and traffic paths, and checks the integrity of your LAN switch domain, improving your spanning-tree configuration.

The NETSYS WAN Service Manager adds integrated WAN switching analysis and troubleshooting capabilities to the Service-Level Management Suite. It provides integrated Layer 2/Layer 3 topologies, automated integrity checking, and path tracing via simulation of AutoRoute Layer 2 routing. It incorporates observed Layer 3 traffic to determine how your WAN is really being used, in comparison to the estimated loads it was designed to support. Similar to the Connectivity Service Manager, you can analyze "what-if" scenarios to determine the behavior of your WAN under failure or after configuration changes prior to implementing them on line.

NETSYS is described in the Products Quick Reference Guide on Cisco's WWW site at http://www.cisco.com/univercd/cc/td/doc/cpqrg/index.htm; some details from this site are reproduced here. The following paragraphs describe the purpose of this Reference Guide.

In an effort to provide you with the best product information possible, Cisco is replacing the *Small-Medium Business Solutions Guide*, the *Quick Reference Product Guide*, and the *Reseller Product Catalog* with this new, all-in-one *Cisco Products Quick Reference Guide*. This guide gives you the best of all three previous publications, including product positioning statements, photos, technical specifications, and much more. Cisco is confident that you will find this new guide easy to use, as well as a great resource for quick product information.

New additions include the following:

- A "Cisco Contact Information" page that lists popular Cisco Web sites, fax services, and helpline information.
- "Products at a Glance" and "Port Matrix" pages that briefly highlight features of the products included in that chapter.
- Easy to remember Cisco Web site shortcut URLs for more information on each product.
- Memory and Cisco IOS™ software cross-reference charts for router products.

The Network Management section of Cisco's Product and Ordering Information web site at http://www.cisco.com/warp/public/cc/cisco/mkt/enm/index.shtml, along with the Cisco Network Management section of Cisco's *Products Quick Reference Guide* at http://www.cisco.com/univercd/cc/td/doc/cpqrg/index.htm include information on Cisco's NETSYS Baseliner 4.0 for Windows. The following paragraphs cite this information.

Avoid costly network configuration problems—have your network checked by NETSYS! Fixing network problems is expensive and time-consuming. The combination of costly downtime and time-consuming fault isolation and repair can bring a business to its knees. Geographically dispersed networks amplify the problem because the length and expense of downtime often increase, and fixing the problem can require travel.

Most reported network problems are configuration related. More than 40 percent of technical support calls involve device misconfigurations. As the number of routers grows, configuration problems become harder to detect and avoid. The result is either operational or latent configuration problems.

NETSYS Baseliner 4.0 for Windows NT displays, debugs, and validates your network configuration. With NETSYS, you can do the following:

- Test configurations and changes off line before committing them to the live network. Cisco NETSYS Baseliner 4.0 for Windows NT creates a model of your network and checks for more than 100 common yet difficult-to-isolate configuration problems.
- Graphically view your network as configured, not as planned or discovered. Baseliner gives you the big picture instantly, allowing you to visually navigate your network and gain a complete understanding of how it works.
- Proactively monitor configuration changes. When problems occur, recent configuration changes are often to blame.

NetFlow

Cisco's NetFlow switching traffic management enables full-time monitoring of network traffic and collection of detailed statistics. It also offers advanced accounting and reporting capabilities through the NetFlow Data Export function and applications from Cisco partners. It has advantages over many tools because it does not require an extra protocol, such as RMON. You can read more about Netflow technology on Cisco's WWW site; some details from this site follow.

Cisco's Netflow Technology is discussed at http://www.cisco.com/warp/public/732/netflow/index.html, and a *Netflow White Paper* is available at http://www.cisco.com/warp/public/732/netflow/napps_wp.htm. The following paragraphs cite the information provided in these documents.

Rapid growth in Internet and intranet deployment and usage has created a major shift in both corporate and consumer computing paradigms. This shift has resulted in massive increases in demand for network bandwidth, performance, and predictable quality of service, as well as multimedia and security-oriented network services. Simultaneously, the need has emerged for measurement technology to support this growth by efficiently providing the information required to record network and application resource utilization. Cisco's NetFlow services provide solutions for each of these challenges.

NetFlow also provides the measurement base for Cisco's Internet and Enterprise Quality of Service (QoS) initiatives. NetFlow captures the traffic classification or precedence associated with each flow, enabling differentiated charging based on Quality of Service.

A network flow is defined as a unidirectional sequence of packets between given source and destination endpoints. Network flows are highly granular; flow endpoints are identified both by IP address and transport-layer application port numbers. NetFlow also utilizes the IP Protocol type, Type of Service (ToS), and the input interface identifier to uniquely identify flows.

Non-NetFlow-enabled switching handles incoming packets independently, with separate serial tasks for switching, security, services, and traffic measurements applied to each packet. With NetFlow-enabled switching, security (access lists) processing is applied only to the first packet of a flow. Information from the first packet is used to build an entry in the NetFlow cache. Subsequent packets in the flow are handled via a single streamlined task that handles switching, services, and data collection concurrently.

Thus, NetFlow Services capitalizes on the flow nature of traffic in the network to provide detailed data collection with minimal impact on router performance and efficiently process access lists for packet filtering and security services.

NetFlow enables several key customer applications:

- Accounting/Billing
- Network Planning and Analysis
- Network Monitoring
- Application Monitoring and Profiling
- User Monitoring and Profiling
- NetFlow Data Warehousing and Mining

Cisco provides a set of NetFlow applications to collect NetFlow export data, perform data volume reduction, post-processing, and provide to end-user applications easy access to NetFlow data. Cisco is currently working with a number of partners to provide customers with comprehensive solutions for NetFlow-based billing, planning, and monitoring. NetFlow also provides the measurement base for Cisco's new Internet Quality of Service (QoS) initiatives.

CiscoWorks

CiscoWorks is a set of SNMP-based tools for characterizing a customer's network, monitoring the status of devices, maintaining configurations, and troubleshooting problems.

The Cisco Network Management section of the *Products Quick Reference Guide,* available at http://www.cisco.com/univercd/cc/td/doc/cpqrg/index.htm, provides some details on CiscoWorks. The following paragraphs provide information from this guide.

Current Cisco network management products are a mix of new Web-based products and console-based applications.

CiscoWorks2000 is the new product family designed to carry forward the functionality in CiscoWorks, Cisco Resource Manager, and CiscoWorks for Switched Internetworks (CWSI). Together, the new management products include enhanced tools, significant new functionality, and standards-based third-party integration tools. Specifically, CiscoWorks2000 is comprised of:

- Resource Manager Essentials features tools for managing inventory, availability, change, configuration, Syslog, connectivity, image deployment, and Cisco Management Connection for creating management intranets. This suite of tools is for managing routers, access servers, and switches.

- CWSI Campus is a comprehensive management solution within the CiscoWorks2000 family for managing Cisco Catalyst and LightStream switches. A suite of applications, CWSI Campus offers extensive network discovery and display, configuration, RMON/RMON2 traffic, and LAN/WAN performance management capabilities on a device and network-wide basis.
- CiscoView is a graphical device management tool that provides dynamic status, statistics, and comprehensive configuration information for Cisco Systems' internetworking products (switches, routers, concentrators, and adapters). CiscoView graphically displays a real-time physical view of Cisco devices. Additionally, this SNMP-based network management tool provides monitoring functions and offers basic troubleshooting capabilities.
- Future functional drop-in modules.

Other CiscoWorks products include CiscoWorks Windows and CiscoWorks Blue. CiscoWorks Windows is comprehensive network management software that provides a powerful set of tools to easily manage your small to medium business network or workgroup. Information such as dynamic status, statistics, and comprehensive configuration information is available for Cisco routers, switches, hubs, and access servers. Based on the SNMP industry standard, CiscoWorks Windows provides complete management of Cisco solutions within diverse, heterogeneous networks, using the powerful embedded features of the industry-leading Cisco IOS™ software.

The CiscoWorks Blue suite of applications provides the management tools required to help customers make the transition from legacy networks to multiprotocol networks, including IP. The different tools support different platforms, so whether customers want to manage from the mainframe, from UNIX, or from the Web, there is a CiscoWorks Blue solution for their needs.

Protocol Analyzers

Protocol analyzers such as Network Associate's *Sniffer* network analyzer capture and analyze network traffic, providing both protocol analysis and statistics. Some analyzers, such as the Sniffer network analyzer, include artificial intelligence expert capabilities to simplify and enhance performance management. Network Associates can be reached at http://www.nai.com/.

Network Statistics

The *Scion* software package was developed by Merit Network, Inc. as a freeware, turnkey Internet service provider (ISP) network statistics package. It uses SNMP to collect network management information from network routers, and employs a standards-based client/server architecture to make the information available on the Web. Information about Scion can be found at http://www.merit.edu/~netscarf/.

Steps in Characterizing a Network

This section provides a structured methodology you can use to characterize a customer's network. The procedures, charts, and checklists will help you determine your customer's networking needs so you can design scalable solutions that maximize customer satisfaction.

The next time you plan to investigate the state of a customer's network, you may wish to reproduce the procedures, charts, and so on, from this section to take with you to the customer's site.

Complete the following steps to characterize a customer's network:

Step 1   Characterize the customer's applications.

Step 2   Characterize the network protocols.

Step 3   Document the customer's current network.

Step 4   Identify potential bottlenecks.

Step 5   Identify business constraints and inputs to your network design.

Step 6   Characterize the existing network availability.

Step 7   Characterize the network performance.

Step 8   Characterize the existing network reliability.

Step 9   Characterize network utilization.

Step 10 Characterize the status of the major routers.

Step 11 Characterize the existing network management system and tools.

Step 12 Summarize the health of the existing internetwork.

Step 1: Characterize the Customer's Applications

Use Table 3-1 to characterize the customer's applications, filling in the fields as indicated:

- In the *Name of Application* field, enter the name of each application the customer runs over the network.

- In the *Type of Application* field, enter information that will help you characterize the application—for example, database, multimedia, electronic mail, manufacturing support system, and so on.

- In the *Number of Users* field, enter the number of users who access each application.

- In the *Number of Hosts or Servers* field, enter the number of hosts or servers that provide each application.

- In the *Comments* field, add any comments relevant to the network design. For example, add any scalability concerns you have. Include any information you have about corporate directions, such as plans to migrate from an application.

Table 3-1   *Characterize the Customer's Applications*

Name of Application	Type of Application	Number of Users	Number of Hosts or Servers	Comments

Step 2: Characterize the Network Protocols

Use Table 3-2 to characterize the customer's network protocols, filling in the fields as indicated:

- In the *Name of Protocol* field, enter the name of each protocol on the network.
- In the *Type of Protocol* field, enter some text that will help you identify the protocol: for example, session-layer protocol, client/server, and so on.
- In the *Number of Users* field, enter the number of users who use each protocol.
- In the *Number of Hosts or Servers* field, enter the number of servers that use each protocol.
- In the *Comments* field, enter any comments relevant to the network design. For example, add any scalability concerns you have. Include any information you have about corporate directions, such as plans to migrate from a protocol.

Table 3-2   *Characterize the Network Protocols*

Name of Protocol	Type of Protocol	Number of Users	Number of Hosts or Servers	Comments

Step 3: Document the Customer's Current Network

Documenting the customer's current network is important before any changes are made. Items you should be most attentive to include the following:

- **Network topology**—On a separate piece of paper or in another application, draw a network topology map (or obtain a drawing from the customer). Include the type and speed of each major segment or link. Include the names and addresses of major internetworking devices and servers. See the Tip on drawing a network topology map, following this list.

- **Addressing schemes**—Document addressing schemes used in the current network design. Current addressing might impact your ability to modify the network structure. For example, current IP subnet masking might limit the number of nodes in a LAN or virtual LAN (VLAN).

- **Concerns about the network**—Document any concerns you have about the current topology and any additional information about the architecture of the internetwork that might not be obvious from the topology drawing. Characterize the overall network architecture to help you understand data flow patterns.

TIP   Draw the network topology map in the same, or a compatible, application with which you will be documenting your design. This will save you time later and will ensure that the existing topology is documented before any changes are made.

Step 4: Identify Potential Bottlenecks

Traffic that does not have a source or destination on the local network segment is considered nonlocal and may cause a bottleneck on the network.

Use a Protocol Analyzer to Determine Local Traffic

To identify potential network bottlenecks, obtain a protocol analyzer and determine how much of the network traffic on each major network segment is *not* local.

Specify how much of the traffic travels to different network segments, how much comes from different network segments, and how much just passes through this network segment.

Characterize Traffic That Is *Not Local*

Use Table 3-3 to characterize how much of the traffic on each network segment is *not* local. Source and destination refer to source and destination network-layer addresses. Fill in the fields of Table 3-3 as indicated:

- In the *Network Segment Identification* field, enter an identifier for each segment (for example, number the segments or give them a logical name).

- In the *Both Source and Destination Are Local* field, enter the percentage of traffic on that segment that applies.

- In the *Source Is Local, Destination Is Not Local* field, enter the percentage of traffic on that segment that applies.

- In the *Source Is Not Local, Destination Is Local* field, enter the percentage of traffic on that segment that applies.

- In the *Source Is Not Local, Destination Is Not Local* field, enter the percentage of traffic on that segment that applies.

Table 3-3 *Characterizing Traffic That Is Not Local*

Network Segment Identification	Both Source and Destination Are Local	Source Is Local, Destination Is Not Local	Source Is Not Local, Destination Is Local	Source Is Not Local, Destination Is Not Local
1				
2				
3				
4				

Step 5: Identify Business Constraints and Inputs to Your Network Design

After talking to your customer, check off as many of the following items as possible:

☐ I understand the corporate structure.

☐ I have analyzed the information flow in the corporation.

☐ The customer has identified any mission-critical data or operations.

☐ The customer has explained any policies regarding approved vendors, protocols, or platforms.

☐ The customer has explained any policies regarding open versus proprietary solutions.

☐ The customer has explained any policies regarding distributed authority for network design and implementation: for example, departments that control their own internetworking purchases.

☐ I have a good understanding of the technical expertise of my clients.

☐ I have researched the customer's industry and competition.

☐ I am aware of any politics that might affect the network design proposal.

☐ I am aware of any financial constraints that may influence the network design.

Document any concerns you have about the customer's business constraints.

Step 6: Characterize the Existing Network Availability

Gather statistics on network downtime and the mean time between failure (MTBF) for the internetwork. If some segments are known to be fragile, document the MTBF separately for those segments. Try to get the customer to express the cost of downtime by asking the following questions:

• What is the hourly cost by department for a network outage?

• What is the hourly cost to the company or organization for a network outage?

Use Table 3-4 to help you determine the MTBF for each network segment and the internetwork as a whole, filling in the fields as indicated:

• In the *MTBF* field, enter the mean time between failures for each network segment.

• In the *Date of Last Downtime* field, enter the date on which the last downtime was experienced.

• In the *Duration of Last Downtime* field, enter how long the last downtime lasted.

• In the *Cause of Last Downtime* field, enter the cause (if known) of the last downtime on that segment.

Table 3-4   *Characterize the Existing Network Availability*

Network/ Segment	MTBF	Date of Last Downtime	Duration of Last Downtime	Cause of Last Downtime
Internetwork				
Segment 1				
Segment 2				
Segment 3				

Step 7: Characterize the Network Performance

Use Table 3-5 to document the results of any response time or performance measurements that you completed for each host on the network. This information will help you determine which areas of the network you should concentrate on for performance improvements and which are already satisfactory. This information will also provide you with benchmark measurements with which you can compare your new network.

Table 3-5   *Characterize the Network Performance*

	Host A	Host B	Host C	Host D
Host A				
Host B				
Host C				
Host D				

Step 8: Characterize the Existing Network Reliability

Gather statistics about each major network segment using a monitoring tool, such as a protocol analyzer, network monitor, or network management tool. If possible, monitor each segment for at least a day. At the end of the day, record the following information seen on each segment:

- Total megabytes (MB)
- Total number of frames
- Total number of cyclic redundancy check (CRC) errors
- Total number of MAC layer errors (collisions, Token Ring soft errors, FDDI ring operations)
- Total number of broadcasts/multicast frames

Characterize the current network reliability by completing Table 3-6. To calculate the *average network utilization*, add each hourly average and divide by the number of hourly averages. For the *peak network utilization*, record the highest hourly average. (If you have more granular data than hourly, record any short-term peaks.) For the *average frame size*, divide the total number of MB transferred on the network by the total number of frames.

The rate calculations are more complex. Your concern here is the number of errors or broadcasts compared to the amount of normal traffic. To calculate the *CRC error rate*, divide the total number of CRC errors by the total amount of MB. For the *MAC layer error rate*, divide the total number of MAC layer errors by the total number of frames. For the *broadcasts/multicasts rate*, divide the total number of broadcasts/multicasts by the total number of frames.

For an example of these calculations, assume the following data:

- Hourly average utilization (for 8 hours): 20%, 30%, 30%, 40%, 30%, 40%, 45%, 35%.
- Total Megabytes transferred: 500
- Total number of frames: 500,000
- Total number of CRC errors: 2
- Total MAC layer errors (assuming Ethernet, this would be collisions): 400
- Total number of broadcasts/multicast frames: 35,000

Using the example data, the calculation results would be:

- The average network utilization is: (20% + 30% + 30% + 40% + 30% + 40% + 45% + 35%) /8 = 33.75%
- The peak network utilization is 45%.
- The average frame size is (500 Mbytes/ 500,000) frames = 1000 bytes.
- The CRC error rate is 2 in 500 Mbytes, or (2/500) = .4%.
- The MAC layer error rate is (400/500,000) = .08%.
- The broadcasts/multicast frame rate is (35,000/500,000) = 7%.

Table 3-6   *Characterize the Existing Network Reliability*

Network Segment	Average Network Utilization	Peak Network Utilization	Average Frame Size	CRC Error Rate	MAC layer Error Rate	Broadcasts/ Multicasts Rate
Segment 1						
Segment 2						
Segment 3						
Segment 4						

Step 9: Characterize Network Utilization

Configure the monitoring tool to output an average network utilization statistic once each hour so you can determine when the peak usage hours are. If the network is saturated (that is, it is overutilized), look at network utilization every minute. Especially on Ethernet, peak utilizations of over 40 percent that last for more than one minute cause noticeable performance degradation.

If time permits, characterize how much of the bandwidth on each segment is used by different protocols by completing Table 3-7. Many network monitors let you specify the bandwidth used by protocols as relative or absolute bandwidth. Fill in the fields in Table 3-7 as indicated:

- In the *Relative Network Utilization* field, enter the amount of bandwidth used by each protocol in comparison to the total bandwidth used on this segment.

- In the *Absolute Network Utilization* field, enter the amount of bandwidth used by each protocol in comparison to the total capacity of the segment (for example, in comparison to 10 Mbps on Ethernet).

- In the *Average Frame Size* field, enter the average frame size for each protocol.

- In the *Broadcasts/Multicasts Rate* field, enter the broadcast/multicasts rate for each protocol.

Table 3-7   *Characterize Network Utilization*

Protocol	Relative Network Utilization	Absolute Network Utilization	Average Frame Size	Broadcasts/ Multicasts Rate
IP				
IPX				
AppleTalk				
NetBIOS				
SNA				
Other				

For major protocols, you might want to configure your network monitor to break down the data even further. For example, in an IP environment, it is useful to know how much bandwidth is used by each of the routing protocols, TCP-based applications, and UDP-based applications.

Step 10: Characterize the Status of the Major Routers

Characterize the status of the major routers in the network by completing Table 3-8. Plan to spend about a day studying the routers. The following Cisco IOS™ commands will help you fill out Table 3-8:

show interfaces
show processes
show buffers

Complete Table 3-8 every hour for each interface as follows:

- In the *Router Name* field, enter the name of each major router.

- To complete the remaining fields, add up the appropriate results from the show interfaces, show processes, and show buffers commands. Then divide the total by the number of samples to complete average values for the *5 Minute CPU Utilization, Output Queue Drops per Hour, Input Queue Drops per Hour, Missed Packets per Hour,* and *Ignored Packets per Hour* fields.

- In the *Comments* field, enter any comments that will help you characterize the status of each router.

Table 3-8   *Characterize the Status of the Major Routers*

Router Name	5-Minute CPU Utilization	Output Queue Drops Per Hour	Input Queue Drops Per Hour	Missed Packets Per Hour	Ignored Packets Per Hour	Comments
Router 1						
Router 2						
Router 3						
Router 4						

Step 11: Characterize the Existing Network Management System and Tools

Document the type of platform and network management tools in use. If available, gather recent examples of daily, weekly, and monthly reports.

Step 12: Summarize the Health of the Existing Internetwork

Based on the data you have gathered from the customer's network, check off any of the items that are true in the following *Network Health Checklist*. On a healthy network, you should be able to check off all the items.

Note that these guidelines are just approximations. Exact thresholds depend on the type of traffic, applications, internetworking devices, topology, and criteria for accepting network performance. As every good engineer knows, the answer to most questions about network performance (and most questions in general) is "it depends."

☐ No shared Ethernet segments are saturated (no more than 40 percent network utilization).

☐ No shared Token Ring segments are saturated (no more than 70 percent network utilization).

☐ No WAN links are saturated (no more than 70 percent network utilization).

☐ The response time is generally less than 100 milliseconds (1 millisecond = 1/1000 of a second; 100 milliseconds = 1/10 of a second).

☐ No segments have more than 20 percent broadcasts/multicasts.

☐ No segments have more than one CRC error per million bytes of data.

☐ On the Ethernet segments, less than 0.1 percent of the packets result in collisions.

☐ On the Token Ring segments, less than 0.1 percent of the packets are soft errors not related to ring insertion.

☐ On the FDDI segments, there has been no more than one ring operation per hour not related to ring insertion.

☐ The Cisco routers are not over-utilized (5-minute CPU utilization no more than 75 percent).

☐ The number of output queue drops has not exceeded more than 100 in an hour on any Cisco router.

☐ The number of input queue drops has not exceeded more than 50 in an hour on any Cisco router.

☐ The number of buffer misses has not exceeded more than 25 in an hour on any Cisco router.

☐ The number of ignored packets has not exceeded more than 10 in an hour on any interface on a Cisco router.

Document any concerns you have about the health of the existing network and its capability to support growth.

Summary

In this chapter you learned how to characterize a customer's existing network, including the type of data that you need to gather; how to document the customer's current applications, protocols, topology, number of users, and business issues; and how to assess the overall health of the existing network. Chapter 4, "Determining New Customer Requirements," discusses how to extract the customer's requirements for its new network.

Case Studies

This section introduces four case studies and then asks you to analyze the existing network. These same case studies are used throughout the remainder of the book so that you can continue to evaluate your understanding of the concepts presented. The case study descriptions are provided in Appendix A, "Case Studies."

Read each case study description and complete the questions for each of the case studies. Keep in mind that there are potentially several correct answers to each question.

TIP	As mentioned, in working through the questions to the case studies, you may find it useful to work on some note paper in a separate binder, to accommodate the depth of these exercises.

After you complete each question, you can refer to the solutions provided by our internetworking experts in Appendix B, "Answers to Chapter Questions, Case Studies, and Sample CCDA Exam." Keep in mind that there are potentially several correct answers to each question. These case studies and their solutions will help you prepare for the Sylvan CCDA exam following the course.

The four case studies presented are as follows:

- CareTaker Publications, a publishing company
- PH Network Services Corporation, a health care company
- Pretty Paper Limited, a European wall covering company
- Jones, Jones, & Jones, an international law firm

Case Study: CareTaker Publications

Read the CareTaker Publications case study information in Appendix A, on page 303 and answer the following questions.

CareTaker Case Study Questions

Question 3-1

Has the customer provided you with all of the data that you need to characterize the existing network? What data do you still need to gather from the customer?

Question 3-2

What are the customer's current applications?

Question 3-3

What are the customer's current protocols?

Question 3-4

Draw a high-level topology of the customer's current network.

Question 3-5

Document the customer's business constraints.

Question 3-6

Identify new applications or old applications that will use the new networking structure.

Case Study: PH Network Services Corporation

Read the PH Network Services Corporation case study information in Appendix A on page 306 and answer the following questions.

PH Network Services Corporation Case Study Questions

Question 3-7

What are the customer's current applications?

Question 3-8

Document the customer's business constraints.

Question 3-9

Document any concerns you have about this scenario.

Question 3-10

Identify new applications or old applications that will use the new networking structure.

Case Study: Pretty Paper Limited

Read the Pretty Paper Limited case study information in Appendix A on page 307 and answer the following questions.

Pretty Paper Limited Case Study Questions

Question 3-11

What are the customer's current applications?

Question 3-12

What are the customer's current protocols?

Question 3-13

Draw a high-level topology of the customer's current network.

Question 3-14

Document the customer's business constraints.

Question 3-15

Identify new applications or old applications that will use the new networking structure.

Case Study: Jones, Jones, & Jones

Read the Jones, Jones, & Jones case study information in Appendix A on page 308 and answer the following questions.

Jones, Jones, & Jones Case Study Questions

Question 3-16

What are the customer's current applications?

Question 3-17

Document the customer's business constraints.

Question 3-18

Document any concerns you have about the scenario.

Question 3-19

Identify new applications or old applications that will use the new networking structure.

It will take you approximately four hours to read and complete the exercises in this chapter. Upon completion, you will be able to:

- Determine the customer's requirements for new applications, protocols, number of users, peak usage hours, security, and network management.

- Diagram the flow of information for new applications.

- Isolate the customer's criteria for accepting the performance of a network.

- List some tools that will help you characterize new network traffic.

- Predict the amount of traffic and the type of traffic caused by the applications, given charts that characterize typical network traffic.

CHAPTER 4

Determining New Customer Requirements

The content in this chapter includes some tables and other job aids that you will find useful when completing the case studies at the end of the chapter.

Follow these steps to complete this chapter:

1 Study the content in the chapter, including any tables and job aids that appear in the reading assignment.

2 Review the case studies at the end of this chapter.

3 Complete the questions in each case study.

4 Review the answers provided by our internetworking experts in Appendix B, "Answers to Chapter Questions, Case Studies, and Sample CCDA Exam."

This chapter identifies steps that can be followed to determine the requirements that a network must meet, and then introduces many aspects of network traffic and protocols that must be considered when trying to understand these requirements.

Steps for Determining a Customer's Network Requirements

Determining a customer's requirements for a new network design is one of the most important tasks in internetwork design. This section provides a step-by-step approach to determining these requirements. This approach will ensure the network design specifically meets the needs of the customer. You might want to take a copy of this outline with you to the customer's site and use it as a checklist when requesting information.

Complete the following steps to determine the customer's network requirements:

Step 1 Identify business constraints

Step 2 Identify security requirements

Step 3 Identify manageability requirements

Step 4 Determine application requirements

Step 5 Characterize new network traffic

Step 6 Identify performance requirements

Step 7 Create a customer needs specification document (optional)

Each of these steps is elaborated in the sections that follow.

Step 1: Identify Business Constraints

To identify business constraints, do the following:

- Document the budget and resources available for this project.
- Document the time line for this project.
- Identify staffing requirements, such as hiring or training.

Step 2: Identify Security Requirements

To identify security requirements of the new network, do the following:

- Appraise security risks and determine how much security will be needed and of what type.
- Determine requirements for outsiders to access data.
- Determine the authorization and authentication requirements for corporate branch offices, mobile users, and telecommuters.
- Identify any requirements for authenticating routes received from access routers or other routers.
- Identify any requirements for host security, such as physical security of hosts, user accounts, dated software, access rights on data, and so on.

Step 3: Identify Manageability Requirements

To identify manageability requirements of the new network, do the following:

- Isolate any requirements for fault management.
- Isolate any requirements for accounting management.
- Isolate any requirements for configuration management.
- Isolate any requirements for performance management.
- Isolate any requirements for security management.

Step 4: Determine Application Requirements

To determine application requirements of the new network, do the following:

- Document the names and types of new applications.
- Document the names and types of new protocols.
- Document the number of users who will use new applications and protocols.
- Diagram the flow of information when new applications are introduced.
- Identify peak hours of usage of new applications.

Step 5: Characterize New Network Traffic

To characterize new network traffic, do the following:

- Characterize traffic load
- Characterize traffic behavior including:
  - Broadcast/multicast behavior
  - Frame size(s) supported
  - Windowing and flow control
  - Error recovery mechanisms
- Use tools such as those discussed in Chapter 3 "Characterizing the Existing Network," including:
  - Cisco's NETSYS and NETSYS Baseliner Tools.
  - Cisco's NetFlow switching traffic management.
  - CiscoWorks.
  - Protocol analyzers such as Network Associate's Sniffer network analyzer.
  - The Scion software package, developed by Merit Network, Inc.

Step 6: Identify Performance Requirements

The performance requirements of the new network include the following:

- **Response time**—The amount of time to receive a response to a request for a service from the network system.
- **Accuracy**—The percentage of useful traffic that is correctly transmitted on the system, relative to total traffic, including transmission errors.
- **Availability**—The amount of time that the network is operational, sometimes expressed as Mean Time Between Failure (MTBF).
- **Maximum network utilization**—The maximum percentage of the total capacity (bandwidth) of a network segment that can be used before the network is considered saturated.
- **Throughput**—The quantity of data successfully transferred between nodes per unit of time, usually seconds.
- **Efficiency**—The measurement of how much effort is required to produce a certain amount of data throughput.
- **Latency (or delay)**—The time between a frame being ready for transmission from a node and the completion of successful transmission.

Step 7: Create a Customer Needs Specification Document (Optional)

To create a customer needs specification document, record the customer's requirements and constraints, and the characteristics of the existing network. The goal of this specification is to document, for your customer and for yourself, the current network, the requirements for the new network, and the constraints under which the new network must be constructed. The information identified and gathered in the steps in this chapter and in the steps noted in Chapter 3, are pooled together and organized in one place.

The customer needs document could serve as a basis of agreement between your customer and yourself on the network design requirements. It is also an excellent start for the design document that you will produce upon completion of your network design (see Chapter 12, "Writing a Design Document").

Characterizing Network Traffic

One of the most difficult aspects of determining a customer's requirements is to understand how the customer's protocols behave. Characterizing network traffic and protocols requires you to understand broadcast behavior, frame size, windowing and flow control, and error recovery mechanisms.

NOTE   While reviewing the numbers, guidelines, and tables in this section, remember that the true engineering solution to most questions that characterize network traffic and performance is "it depends." The data provided in this section does not take the place of a thorough analysis of the network in question.

Broadcast Behavior

Broadcasts are used by many protocols as part of their normal operation. If stations are subjected to too many broadcasts, network performance can suffer.

Desktop protocols, such as AppleTalk, NetWare, NetBIOS, and TCP/IP, require broadcast and multicast packets to find services and check for uniqueness of addresses and names. Routing and bridging protocols, which are discussed in Chapter 9, "Selecting Routing and Bridging Protocols," also use broadcasts and multicasts to share information about the internetwork topology. Servers send broadcasts and multicasts to advertise their services.

Layer 2 switches forward broadcasts and multicasts; this becomes a scalability issue as flat, switched networks become larger.

The network interface cards (NICs) in a network station pass broadcasts and relevant multicasts to the Central Processing Unit (CPU) of the station. (Some NICs pass all multicasts to the CPU, even when they are not relevant, because they do not allow you to select broadcasts and multicasts.)

The CPUs in network stations can become overwhelmed when processing broadcasts and multicasts. When investigating the effect of *broadcast radiation* (the way that broadcasts and multicasts radiate from the source to all connected LANs in a flat network), Cisco's technical marketing group discovered that:

- 100 broadcasts/multicasts per second used a noticeable 2 percent of the CPU power on a Pentium 120 MHz CPU with a 3Com Fast Etherlink PCI Ethernet adapter.
- 1300 broadcasts per second used 9 percent of the CPU power.
- 3000 broadcasts per second consumed 25 percent of the CPU power.

CPU performance was measurably affected by as few as 30 broadcasts/multicasts per second on a generic i386 PC. Macintosh CPUs were affected by as few as 15 broadcasts/multicasts per second.

When provisioning hardware for an internetwork design, which is discussed in depth in Chapter 6, "Provisioning Hardware and Media for the LAN," be sure to take into consideration the broadcast behavior of the desktop protocols. Table 4-1 shows recommendations for limiting the number of stations on a single LAN based on the desktop protocol(s) in use. The table also applies to the number of stations in a virtual LAN (VLAN).

Table 4-1   *Scalability Constraints for Flat (Switched and Bridged) Networks*

Protocol	Maximum Number of Workstations
IP	500
IPX	300
AppleTalk	200
NetBIOS	200
Mixed	200

The numbers shown in Table 4-1 are provided as a guide. Actual station limits depend on factors such as broadcast/multicast loads, IP addressing structure constraints, inter-VLAN routing requirements, management and fault isolation constraints, and traffic flow characteristics.

Frame Size

Using a frame size that is the maximum supported for the medium has a significant positive impact on network performance. For file transfer applications in particular, you should use the largest possible maximum transmission unit (MTU). Depending on the protocol stacks in use, the MTU can be configured for some applications.

Avoid increasing the MTU to larger than the maximum supported for the media traversed by the frames in order to avoid fragmentation and reassembly of frames. When devices such as end nodes or routers need to fragment and reassemble frames, performance degrades.

For IP, use a protocol stack that supports *MTU discovery.* With MTU discovery, the software can dynamically discover and use the largest frame size that will traverse the network without requiring fragmentation. If your customers use IP implementations that support MTU discovery, make sure this feature is enabled. Some implementations default to a configuration with MTU discovery disabled.

Table 4-2 demonstrates the importance of using maximum frame sizes.

Table 4-2 *Efficiency Depending on Frame Size*

Data Size in Bytes	Frame Size in Bytes	Overhead	Maximum Efficiency
1492	1518 (maximum)	2.5%	97.5%
974	1000	3.8%	96.2%
474	500	7.4%	92.6%
38 (no PAD)	64 bytes (minimum)	50.0%	50.0%
1 (plus 37 bytes of PAD)	64 bytes (minimum)	98.7%	1.3%

Source: Breyer and Riley, "Switched and Fast Ethernet: How It Works and How to Use It," Ziff-Davis Press, 1995.

Windowing and Flow Control

The next step in characterizing network traffic is to characterize the windowing and flow control.

Some protocols, such as Novell's traditional NetWare Core Protocol (NCP), use a "ping-pong" approach, where each request generates a reply. This approach is an inefficient use of bandwidth, but it can be replaced by the burst mode protocol. With burst mode, a station can send as much data as there is room in the receiver's "receive window."

In the TCP/IP suite, the Transmission Control Protocol (TCP) supports windowing and flow control. Applications that run on top of TCP include the following:

- **File Transfer Protocol (FTP)**—port 20 (data) and port 21 (control)
- **Telnet**—port 23
- **Simple Mail Transfer Protocol (SMTP)**—port 25
- **Hypertext Transfer Protocol (HTTP)**—port 80

NOTE	The port numbers in the preceding list (and in the UDP list later in this section) refer to the "well-known," or standardized, number that the application has been assigned. Recall from Chapter 1, "Internetworking Technology Review," that the port number appears in a TCP or UDP segment to identify the application to which the data in the segment belongs.

The User Datagram Protocol (UDP) does not offer windowing and flow control. (Unlike TCP, UDP is a *connectionless*, *unreliable* protocol—UDP sends data but there are no acknowledgements that the data was received, nor retransmissions of any lost data). Applications that usually run on top of UDP include the following:

- **Simple Network Management Protocol (SNMP)**—port 161
- **Domain Name System (DNS)**—port 53
- **Trivial File Transfer Protocol (TFTP)**—port 69
- **Remote-procedure call (RPC)**—port 111
- **Dynamic Host Configuration Protocol (DHCP) server**—port 67
- **DHCP client**—port 68

Protocols such as Network File System (NFS) and Network Information Services (NIS) use RPC (UDP port 111).

Error Recovery

When characterizing a protocol, you need to understand the error recovery mechanisms used by the protocol. Poorly designed error recovery can use a lot of bandwidth. For example, a protocol that retransmits data quickly without waiting long enough to receive an acknowledgment can cause performance degradation for the rest of the network due to the bandwidth used.

Connectionless protocols usually do not implement error recovery. Most data link layer protocols, such as Ethernet, and network layer protocols, such as IP, IPX, and AppleTalk's DDP, are connectionless. Some transport layer protocols, such as UDP, are connectionless.

A *connection-oriented* protocol establishes a connection between the sender and receiver before any data is sent. Error recovery mechanisms for connection-oriented protocols vary. A good TCP implementation, for example, should implement an adaptive retransmission algorithm, which means that the rate of retransmissions slows when the network is congested. Using a protocol analyzer, you can determine whether your customer's protocols implement effective error recovery. In some cases, you can configure retransmission and timeout timers. Connection-oriented protocols exist at all layers and include SPX, ATM, and Frame Relay.

Characterizing Traffic Loads and Behavior

Use the tables in this section to help characterize traffic load and traffic behavior for new applications that a customer wants to implement.

Again, remember that the true engineering solution to most questions that characterize network traffic and performance is "it depends." The data in the following charts is approximate and does not take the place of a thorough analysis of the network in question.

Size of Objects Transferred Across Networks

Table 4-3 identifies the approximate size of different objects transferred across networks.

Table 4-3   *Approximate Size in MB of "Objects" Transferred Across Networks*

Type of Object	Size in MB
E-mail message	0.01
Spreadsheet	0.1
Computer screen	0.5
Document	1
Still image	10
Multimedia object	100
Database	1000

Source: McDysan and Spohn, "ATM: Theory and Applications," McGraw-Hill, 1995.

Note that the size of a computer screen image depends on the type of screen, the number of pixels, and the number of colors. A "dumb" terminal application transfers much less data than a windowed application. Telnet, for example, sends each character that the user types in one packet. Responses are also very small, depending on what the user is doing.

A 3270 terminal application transfers about 4000 bytes, including characters and "attribute" bytes that define color and style.

Traffic Overhead for Data Link Layer and Network Layer Protocols

Table 4-4 illustrates the amount of traffic overhead associated with various protocols. Understanding the traffic overhead for protocols can be a factor when choosing the best protocol for your network design.

Table 4-4   *Traffic Overhead for Various Protocols*

Protocol	Notes	Total Bytes
Ethernet	Preamble = 8 bytes, Header = 14 bytes, CRC = 4 bytes, Interframe gap (IFG) = 12 bytes	38
802.3 with 802.2	Preamble = 8 bytes, Header = 14 bytes, LLC = 3 or 4 bytes, SNAP (if present) = 5 bytes, CRC = 4 bytes, IFG = 12 bytes for 10 Mbps or 1.2 bytes for 100 Mbps	46
802.5 with 802.2	Starting delimiter = 1 byte, Header = 14 bytes, LLC = 3 or 4 bytes, SNAP (if present) = 5 bytes, CRC = 4 bytes, Ending delimiter = 1 byte, Frame status = 1 byte	29
FDDI with 802.2	Preamble = 8 bytes, Starting delimiter = 1 byte, Header = 13 bytes, LLC = 3 or 4 bytes, SNAP (if present) = 5 bytes, CRC = 4 bytes, Ending delimiter and frame Status = about 2 bytes	36
HDLC	Flags = 2 bytes, Addresses = 2 bytes, Control = 1 or 2 bytes, CRC = 4 bytes	10
IP	With no options	20
TCP	With no options	20
IPX	Does not include NCP	30
DDP	Phase 2 (long "extended" header)	13

Traffic Caused by Workstation Initialization

The tables in this section identify the packets sent and received when different types of workstations initialize. Workstation initialization can cause a load on networks due to the number of packets and, in some cases, the number of broadcast packets.

Novell NetWare Workstation Initialization

Table 4-5 shows the packets that a Novell NetWare client sends when it boots. The approximate packet size is also shown. On top of the packet size, add the data link layer overhead, such as 802.3 with 802.2, 802.5 with 802.2, or FDDI with 802.2, as shown in Table 4-4. Network layer and transport layer overhead are already included in these examples. Depending on the version of NetWare being run, the packets generated might be slightly different than the ones shown here.

Table 4-5   *Packets for NetWare Client Initialization*

Packet	Source	Destination	Packet Size in Bytes	Number of Packets	Total Bytes
GetNearestServer	Client	Broadcast	34	1	34
GetNearestServer response	Server or router	Client	66	Depends on number of servers	66 if 1 server
Find network number	Client	Broadcast	40	1	40
Find network number response	Router	Client	40	1	40
Create connection	Client	Server	37	1	37
Create connection response	Server	Client	38	1	38
Negotiate buffer size	Client	Server	39	1	39
Negotiate buffer size response	Server	Client	40	1	40
Log out old connections	Client	Server	37	1	37
Log out response	Server	Client	38	1	38
Get server's clock	Client	Server	37	1	37
Get server's clock response	Server	Client	38	1	38
Download login.exe requests	Client	Server	50	Hundreds, depending on buffer size	Depends
Download login.exe responses	Server	Client	Depends on buffer size	Hundreds, depending on buffer size	Depends
Login	Client	Server	37	1	37
Login response	Server	Client	38	1	38

AppleTalk Workstation Initialization

Table 4-6 shows the packets that an AppleTalk station sends when it boots. The approximate packet size is also shown. On top of the packet size, add data link layer overhead, as shown in Table 4-4. Depending on the version of Macintosh system software, the packets generated might be slightly different than the ones shown here.

Table 4-6   *Packets for AppleTalk Client Initialization*

Packet	Source	Destination	Packet Size in Bytes	Number of Packets	Total Bytes
AARP for ID	Client	Multicast	28	10	280
ZIPGetNetInfo	Client	Multicast	15	1	15
GetNetInfo response	Router(s)	Client	About 44	All routers respond	44 if one router
NBP broadcast request to check uniqueness of name	Client	Router	About 65	3	195
NBP forward request	Router	Other routers	Same	Same	Same
NBP lookup	Router	Multicast	Same	Same	Same
If Chooser started:					
GetZoneList	Client	Router	12	1	12
GetZoneList reply	Router	Client	Depends on number and names of zones	1	Depends
NBP broadcast request for servers in zone	Client	Router	About 65	Once a second if Chooser still open; decays after 45 seconds	About 3000 if Chooser closed after 45 seconds
NBP forward request	Router	Other routers	About 65	Same	Same
NBP lookup	Router	Multicast	About 65	Same	Same
NBP reply	Server(s)	Client	About 65	Depends on number of servers	Depends
ASP open session and AFP login	Client	Server	Depends	4	About 130
ASP and AFP replies	Server	Client	Depends	2	About 90

An AppleTalk station that has already been on a network remembers its previous network number and node ID and tries 10 times to verify that the *network.node* combination is unique. If the AppleTalk station has never been on a network or has moved, it sends 20 multicasts: 10 multicasts with a provisional network number and 10 multicasts with a network number supplied by a router that responded to the *ZIPGetNetInfo* request.

NetBIOS Workstation Initialization

Table 4-7 shows the packets that a NetBIOS station sends when it boots. The approximate packet size is also shown. On top of the packet size, add data link layer overhead, as shown in Table 4-4. Depending on the version of NetBIOS, the packets might be slightly different than the ones shown here.

Table 4-7   *Packets for NetBIOS Client Initialization*

Packet	Source	Destination	Packet Size in Bytes	Number of Packets	Total Bytes
Check name (make sure own name is unique)	Client	Broadcast	44	6	264
Find name for each server	Client	Broadcast	44	Depends on number of servers	44 if 1 server
Find name response	Server(s)	Client	44	Depends	44 if 1 server
Session initialize for each server	Client	Server	14	Depends	14 if 1 server
Session confirm	Server	Client	14	Depends	14 if 1 server

TCP/IP (without DHCP) Workstation Initialization

Table 4-8 shows the packets that a TCP/IP station not running DHCP sends when it boots. The approximate packet size is also shown. On top of the packet size, add data link layer overhead, as shown in Table 4-4. Depending on the implementation of TCP/IP, the packets might be slightly different than the ones shown here.

Table 4-8   *Packets for Traditional TCP/IP Client Initialization*

Packet	Source	Destination	Packet Size in Bytes	Number of Packets	Total Bytes
ARP to make sure its own address is unique (optional)	Client	Broadcast	28	1	28
ARP for any servers	Client	Broadcast	28	Depends on number of servers	Depends
ARP for router	Client	Broadcast	28	1	28
ARP response	Server(s) or router	Client	28	1	28

TCP/IP (with DHCP) Workstation Initialization

Table 4-9 shows the packets that a TCP/IP station running DHCP sends when it boots. Although a DHCP client sends more packets when initializing, DHCP is still recommended. The benefits of dynamic configuration far outweigh the disadvantages of the extra traffic and extra broadcast packets. (The client and server use broadcast packets until they know each other's IP addresses.)

The approximate packet size is also shown. On top of the packet size, add data link layer overhead, as shown in Table 4-4. Depending on the implementation of DHCP, the packets might be slightly different than the ones shown here.

Table 4-9   *Packets for DHCP Client Initialization*

Packet	Source	Destination	Packet Size in Bytes	Number of Packets	Total Bytes
DHCP discover	Client	Broadcast	576	Once every few seconds until client hears from a DHCP server	Depends
DHCP offer	Server	Broadcast	328	1	328
DHCP request	Client	Broadcast	576	1	576
DHCP ACK	Server	Broadcast	328	1	328
ARP to make sure its own address is unique	Client	Broadcast	28	3	84
ARP for client	Server	Broadcast	28	1	1
ARP response	Client	Server	28	1	28
DHCP request	Client	Server	576	1	576
DHCP ACK	Server	Client	328	1	328

Summary

In this chapter you learned how to determine the customer's requirements for their new network, and how to characterize the traffic on that network. Many tables and other guidelines that you can use when characterizing this traffic were introduced.

This is the conclusion of Part III, "Identifying Customer Needs." Part IV, "Designing the Topology," introduces you to the issues that need to be considered when designing the structure of your network.

Case Studies

In this section, you will complete your analysis of the customer's requirements and business constraints for the four case studies introduced in Chapter 3.

Read each case study description and complete the questions for each of the case studies.

TIP	As mentioned, in working through the questions to the case studies, you may find it useful to work on some note paper in a separate binder, to accommodate the depth of these exercises.

Case Study: CareTaker Publications

You might want to review the CareTaker case study description in Appendix A, on page 303, before proceeding to answer the questions in this section.

CareTaker Case Study Questions

After you complete each question, you can refer to the solutions provided by our internetworking experts in Appendix B. Keep in mind that there are potentially several correct answers to each question. These case studies and their solutions will help you prepare for the Sylvan CCDA exam following the course.

Question 4-1

Diagram the packet flow of information for the new e-mail system. Document any open issues or follow-up questions regarding the e-mail system.

Question 4-2

Diagram the packet flow of information for the TN3270 emulation application. Document any open issues or follow-up questions regarding the TN3270 application.

Question 4-3

Diagram the packet flow of information for the new custom SQL server application. Document any open issues or follow-up questions regarding this application.

Question 4-4

List the customer's performance requirements and constraints.

Question 4-5

What concerns do you have for scalability if the number of users were to double over the next year?

Question 4-6

The manager of Warehouse and Distribution is concerned about PC performance over a leased line. What design constraints and consideration will be taken into account for these concerns?

Case Study: PH Network Services Corporation

You might want to review the PH Network case study description in Appendix A on page 306 before proceeding to answer the questions in this section.

PH Network Services Corporation Case Study Questions

Question 4-7

Diagram the packet flow for the referral approval process.

Question 4-8

Identify the customer's performance requirements.

Question 4-9

Identify the customer's requirements for redundancy.

Question 4-10

What concerns do you have for scalability if the number of doctor offices were to double over the next year?

Case Study: Pretty Paper Limited

You might want to review the Pretty Paper Limited case study description in Appendix A on page 307 before proceeding to answer the questions in this section.

Pretty Paper Limited Case Study Questions

Question 4-11

Diagram the packet flow of client/server traffic for the new business software, as well as traffic for the pattern design documents for film production, based on the requirements as you understand them.

Question 4-12

Identify the customer's performance requirements.

Question 4-13

What concerns do you have for scalability if the number of sales offices were to double over the next two years?

Question 4-14

The manager of Warehouse and Distribution is concerned about PC client performance over the Frame Relay network to the new business software on the HP9000. What design constraints and consideration will be taken into account for these concerns?

Case Study: Jones, Jones, & Jones

You might want to review the Jones, Jones, & Jones case study description in Appendix A on page 308 before proceeding to answer the questions in this section.

Jones, Jones, & Jones Case Study Questions

Question 4-15

Diagram the packet flow of information for the e-mail application.

Question 4-16

Diagram the packet flow of information for the CD-ROM Library Pack application.

Question 4-17

Identify the customer's performance requirements.

PART IV

Designing the Topology

This part of the book details the design of a network structure that meets customer requirements for performance, security, capacity, and scalability, given a specified topology and internetworking constraints.

It will take you approximately four hours to read and complete the exercises in this chapter.

This chapter is the first in Part IV, which aims to enable you to design a network structure that meets the customer's requirements for performance, security, capacity, and scalability, given topology and internetworking design constraints.

Upon completion of this first chapter in Part IV, you will be able to do the following:

- Describe the advantages, disadvantages, scalability issues, and applicability of standard internetwork topologies.

- Draw a topology map that meets the customer's needs and includes a high-level view of internetworking devices and interconnecting media.

CHAPTER 5

Designing the Network Topology

This chapter includes some job aids you will find useful when completing the case studies at the end of the chapter. References to some WWW sites are also included; relevant information has been extracted from these sites and is provided in the chapter. If you have access to the Internet, you might want to access the sites mentioned to obtain detailed information related to specific topics. All the sites referenced in this chapter are also listed in Appendix C, "Interesting WWW Links and Other Suggested Readings."

Follow these steps to complete this chapter:

   A. Study the chapter content, including any job aids that appear.

   B. Answer the multiple-choice questions at the end of this chapter.

   C. Review the case studies at the end of this chapter.

   D. Complete the questions in each case study.

   E. Review the answers provided by our internetworking experts in Appendix B, "Answers to Chapter Questions, Case Studies, and Sample CCDA Exam."

The first part of this chapter includes a discussion of different network topology models available. The second part includes a reference to some network design guides. The design guides are separate documents written by Cisco internetworking experts that detail considerations for different aspects of networking. You can find these design and implementation guides in Appendixes D–G.

Network Topology Models

Three different network topology models are discussed in this section:

   • Hierarchical Models

   • Redundant Models

   • Secure Models

Hierarchical Models

Hierarchical models enable you to design internetworks in layers. To understand the importance of layering, consider the Open System Interconnection (OSI) reference model, which is a layered model for implementing computer communications. Using layers, the

OSI model simplifies the tasks required for two computers to communicate. Hierarchical models for internetwork design also use layers to simplify the tasks required for internetworking. Each layer can be focused on specific functions, allowing you to choose the right systems and features for each layer.

Benefits of Hierarchical Models

The many benefits of using hierarchical models for your network design include the following:

- Cost savings
- Ease of understanding
- Easy network growth
- Improved fault isolation

After adopting hierarchical design models, many organizations report cost savings because they are no longer trying to do it all in one routing/switching platform. The modular nature of the model enables appropriate use of bandwidth within each layer of the hierarchy, reducing wasted capacity.

Keeping each design element simple and small facilitates ease of understanding, which helps control training and staff costs. Management responsibility and network management systems can be distributed to the different layers of modular network architectures, which helps control management costs.

Hierarchical design facilitates changes. In a network design, modularity allows creating design elements that can be replicated as the network grows, facilitating easy network growth. As each element in the network design requires change, the cost and complexity of making the upgrade is contained to a small subset of the overall network. In large, flat, or meshed network architectures, changes tend to impact a large number of systems.

Improved fault isolation is facilitated by structuring the network into small, easy-to-understand elements. Network managers can easily understand the transition points in the network, which helps identify failure points.

Today's fast-converging protocols were designed for hierarchical topologies. To control the impact of routing overhead processing and bandwidth consumption, modular hierarchical topologies must be used with protocols designed with these controls in mind, such as Enhanced IGRP. Chapter 9, "Selecting Routing and Bridging Protocols," further investigates the question of which protocol to use.

Route summarization, which is discussed in Chapter 8, "Designing a Network Layer Addressing and Naming Model," is facilitated by hierarchical network design. Route summarization reduces the routing protocol overhead on links in the network and reduces routing protocol processing within the routers.

Hierarchical Network Design

As Figure 5-1 illustrates, a hierarchical network design has three layers:

- The *core* layer provides optimal transport between sites.
- The *distribution* layer provides policy-based connectivity.
- The *access* layer provides workgroup/user access to the network.

Figure 5-1 *A Hierarchical Network Design Has Three Layers: Core, Distribution, and Access*

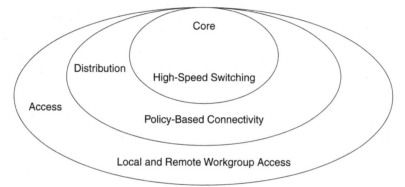

Each layer provides necessary functionality to the network. The layers do not need to be implemented as distinct physical entities. Each layer can be implemented in routers or switches, represented by a physical media, or combined in a single box. A particular layer can be omitted altogether, but for optimum performance, hierarchy should be maintained.

Core Layer

The core layer is the high-speed switching backbone of the network, which is crucial to enable corporate communications. The core layer should have the following characteristics:

- Offer high reliability
- Provide redundancy
- Provide fault tolerance
- Adapt to changes quickly
- Offer low latency and good manageability
- Avoid slow packet manipulation caused by filters or other processes
- Have a limited and consistent diameter

NOTE   When routers are used in a network, the number of router hops from edge to edge is called the *diameter*. As noted, it is considered good practice to design for a consistent diameter within a hierarchical network. This means that from any end station to another end station across the backbone, there should be the same number of hops. The distance from any end station to a server on the backbone should also be consistent.

Limiting the diameter of the internetwork provides predictable performance and ease of troubleshooting. Distribution layer routers and client LANs can be added to the hierarchical model without increasing the diameter because neither will affect how existing end stations communicate.

Distribution Layer

The distribution layer of the network is the demarcation point between the access and core layers of the network. The distribution layer can have many roles, including implementing the following functions:

- Policy (for example, to ensure that traffic sent from a particular network should be forwarded out one interface, while all other traffic should be forwarded out another interface)
- Security
- Address or area aggregation or summarization
- Departmental or workgroup access
- Broadcast/multicast domain definition
- Routing between virtual LANs (VLANs)
- Media translations (for example, between Ethernet and Token Ring)
- Redistribution between routing domains (for example, between two different routing protocols)
- Demarcation between static and dynamic routing protocols

Several Cisco IOS™ software features can be used to implement policy at the distribution layer, including the following:

- Filtering by source or destination address
- Filtering on input or output ports
- Hiding internal network numbers by route filtering
- Static routing
- Quality of service mechanisms (for example, to ensure that all devices along a path can accommodate the requested parameters)

Access Layer

The access layer provides user access to local segments on the network. The access layer is characterized by switched and shared bandwidth LANs in a campus environment. Microsegmentation, using LAN switches, provides high bandwidth to workgroups by dividing collision domains on Ethernet segments and reducing the number of stations capturing the token on Token Ring LANs.

For small office/home office (SOHO) environments, the access layer provides access for remote sites into the corporate network using WAN technologies such as ISDN, Frame Relay, and leased lines. Features such as dial-on-demand routing (DDR) and static routing can be implemented to control costs.

Hierarchical Model Examples

For small- to medium-sized companies, the hierarchical model is often implemented as a hub-and-spoke topology, as shown in Figure 5-2. Corporate headquarters form the hub, and links to the remote offices form the spokes.

Figure 5-2   *The Hierarchical Model Is Often Implemented as a Hub-and-Spoke Topology*

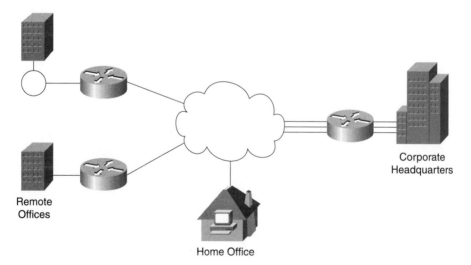

The hierarchical model can be implemented using either routers or switches. Figure 5-3 is an example of a switched hierarchical design, while Figure 5-4 shows examples of routed hierarchical designs.

Figure 5-3 *An Example of a Switched Hierarchical Design*

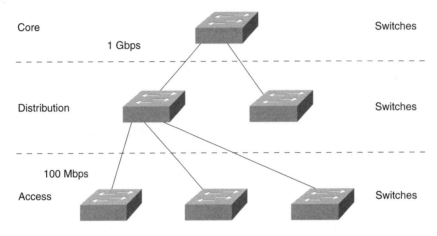

Figure 5-4 *Examples of Routed Hierarchical Designs*

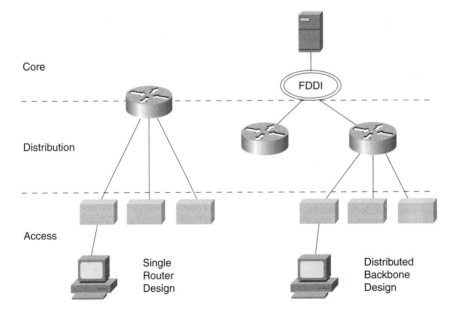

Redundant Models

When designing a network topology for a customer who has critical systems, services, or network paths, you should determine the likelihood that these components will fail and design redundancy where necessary.

Consider incorporating one of the following types of redundancy into your design:

- Workstation-to-router redundancy
- Server redundancy
- Route redundancy
- Media redundancy

Each of these types of redundancy is elaborated in the sections that follow.

Workstation-to-Router Redundancy

When a workstation has traffic to send to a station that is not local, the workstation has many possible ways to discover the address of a router on its network segment, including the following:

- Address Resolution Protocol (ARP)
- Explicit configuration
- Router Discovery Protocol (RDP)
- Routing protocol
- Internetwork Packet Exchange (IPX)
- AppleTalk
- Hot Standby Router Protocol (HSRP)

The sections that follow cover each of these methods.

ARP

Some IP workstations send an ARP frame to find a remote station. A router running proxy ARP can respond with its data link layer address. Cisco routers run proxy ARP by default.

Explicit Configuration

Most IP workstations must be configured with the IP address of a default router. This is sometimes called the *default gateway*.

In an IP environment, the most common method for a workstation to find a server is via explicit configuration (default router). If the workstation's default router becomes unavailable, the workstation must be reconfigured with the address of a different router. Some IP stacks enable you to configure multiple default routers, but many other IP stacks do not support redundant default routers.

RDP

RFC 1256 specifies an extension to the Internet Control Message Protocol (ICMP) that allows an IP workstation and router to run the Router Discovery Protocol (RDP) to facilitate the workstation learning the address of a router.

Routing Protocol

An IP workstation can run the Routing Information Protocol (RIP) to learn about routers. RIP should be used in passive mode rather than active mode. (Active mode means that the station sends RIP frames every 30 seconds.) The Open Shortest Path First (OSPF) protocol also supports a workstation running that routing protocol.

IPX

An IPX workstation broadcasts a *find network number* message to find a route to a server. A router then responds. If the client loses its connection to the server, it automatically sends the message again.

AppleTalk

An AppleTalk workstation remembers the address of the router that sent the last Routing Table Maintenance Protocol (RTMP) packet. As long as there are one or more routers on an AppleTalk workstation's network, it has a route to remote devices.

HSRP

Cisco's Hot Standby Router Protocol (HSRP) provides a way for IP workstations to keep communicating on the internetwork even if their default router becomes unavailable. The HSRP works by creating a *phantom router* that has its own IP and MAC addresses. The workstations use this phantom router as their default router.

HSRP routers on a LAN communicate among themselves to designate two routers as active and standby. The active router sends periodic hello messages. The other HSRP routers listen for the hello messages. If the active router fails and the other HSRP routers stop receiving hello messages, the standby router takes over and becomes the active router. Because the new active router assumes both the IP and MAC addresses of the phantom, end nodes see no change at all.

They continue to send packets to the phantom router's MAC address, and the new active router delivers those packets.

HSRP also works for proxy ARP. When an active HSRP router receives an ARP request for a node that is not on the local LAN, the router replies with the phantom router's MAC address instead of its own. If the router that originally sent the ARP reply later loses its connection, the new active router can still deliver the traffic.

Figure 5-5 shows an example implementation of HSRP.

Figure 5-5   *An Example of HSRP: The* Phantom *Router Represents the Real Routers*

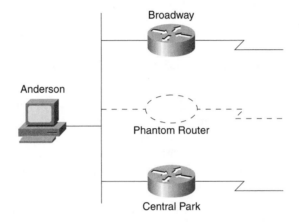

In Figure 5-5, the following sequence occurs:

A. The *Anderson* workstation is configured to use the *Phantom* router as its default router.

B. Upon booting, the routers elect *Broadway* as the HSRP active router. The active router does the work for the HSRP phantom. *Central Park* is the HSRP standby router.

C. When *Anderson* sends an ARP frame to find its default router, *Broadway* responds with the *Phantom* router's MAC address.

D. If *Broadway* goes off line, *Central Park* takes over as the active router, continuing the delivery of *Anderson's* packets. The change is transparent to *Anderson*. If there was a third HSRP router on the LAN, that router would begin to act as the new standby router.

Server Redundancy

In some environments, fully redundant (mirrored) file servers should be recommended. For example, in a brokerage firm where traders must access data in order to buy and sell stocks, the data can be replicated on two or more redundant servers. The servers should be on different networks and power supplies.

If complete server redundancy is not feasible due to cost considerations, mirroring or duplexing of the file server hard drives is a good idea. *Mirroring* means synchronizing two disks, while *duplexing* is the same as mirroring with the additional feature that the two mirrored hard drives are controlled by different disk controllers.

Route Redundancy

Designing redundant routes has two purposes: load balancing and minimizing downtime.

Load Balancing

AppleTalk and IPX routers can remember only one route to a remote network by default, so they do not support load balancing. You can change this for IPX by using the **ipx maximum-paths** command and for AppleTalk by using the **appletalk maximum-paths** command on a Cisco router.

Most IP routing protocols can load balance across up to six parallel links that have equal cost. Use the **maximum-paths** command to change the number of links that the router will load balance over for IP; the default is four, the maximum is six. To support load balancing, keep the bandwidth consistent within a layer of the hierarchical model so that all paths have the same cost. (Cisco's IGRP and Enhanced IGRP are exceptions because they can load balance traffic across multiple routes that have different metrics, using a feature called *variance*.)

A hop-based routing protocol does load balancing over unequal bandwidth paths as long as the hop count is equal. Once the slower link becomes saturated, the higher-capacity link cannot be filled; this is called *pinhole congestion*. Pinhole congestion can be avoided by designing equal bandwidth links within one layer of the hierarchy or by using a routing protocol that takes bandwidth into account.

IP load balancing depends on which switching mode is used on a router. Switching modes are discussed in more detail in Chapter 7, "Provisioning Hardware and Media for the WAN." Process switching load balances on a packet-by-packet basis. Fast, autonomous, silicon, optimum, distributed, and NetFlow switching load balance on a destination-by-destination basis because the processor caches the encapsulation to a specific destination for these types of switching modes.

Minimizing Downtime

In addition to facilitating load balancing, redundant routes minimize network downtime.

As already discussed, you should keep bandwidth consistent within a given layer of a hierarchy to facilitate load balancing. Another reason to keep bandwidth consistent within a layer of a hierarchy is that routing protocols converge much faster if multiple equal-cost paths to a destination network exist.

By using redundant, meshed network designs, you can minimize the effect of link failures. Depending on the convergence time of the routing protocols being used, a single link failure will not have a catastrophic effect. Chapter 9, "Selecting Routing and Bridging Protocols," discusses more about routing convergence.

A network can be designed as a full mesh or a partial mesh. A full mesh network is when every router has a link to every other router, as shown in Figure 5-6. A full mesh network provides complete redundancy and also provides good performance because there is just a single-hop delay between any two sites. The number of links in a full mesh is $n(n-1)/2$, where n is the number of routers. Each router is connected to every other router. (The result is divided by 2 to avoid counting Router X to Router Y and Router Y to Router X as two different links.)

Figure 5-6   *Full Mesh Network: Every Router Has a Link to Every Other Router in the Network*

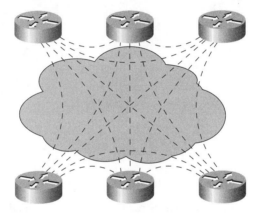

(6*5)/2=15 Circuits

A full mesh network can be expensive to implement due to the required number of links. In addition, there are practical limits to scaling for groups of routers that broadcast routing updates or service advertisements. As the number of router peers increases, the amount of bandwidth and CPU resources devoted to processing broadcasts increases.

A suggested guideline is to keep broadcast traffic at less than 20 percent of the bandwidth of each link; this will limit the number of peer routers that can exchange routing tables or service advertisements. When planning redundancy, follow guidelines for simple, hierarchical design. Figure 5-7 illustrates a classic hierarchical and redundant enterprise design that uses a partial mesh rather than full mesh architecture.

Figure 5-7   *Partial Mesh Design with Redundancy*

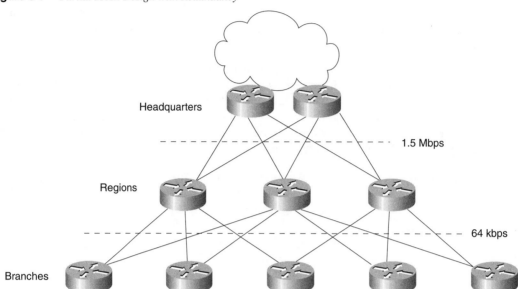

Media Redundancy

In mission-critical applications, it is often necessary to provision redundant media.

In switched networks, switches can have redundant links to each other. This is good because it minimizes downtime, but it may result in broadcasts continuously circling the network, called a *broadcast storm*. Because Cisco switches implement the IEEE 802.1d Spanning-Tree algorithm, this looping can be avoided in the Spanning-Tree Protocol. The Spanning-Tree algorithm guarantees that there is one and only one active path between two network stations. The algorithm permits redundant paths that are automatically activated when the active path experiences problems.

Because WAN links are often critical pieces of the internetwork, redundant media is often deployed in WAN environments. As shown in Figure 5-8, backup links can be provisioned so they become active when a primary link goes down or becomes congested.

Figure 5-8   *Backup Links Can Be Used to Provide Redundancy*

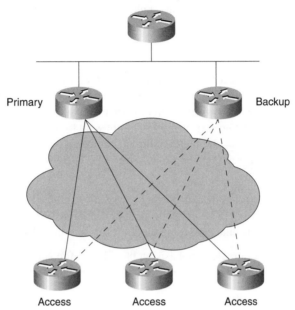

Often, backup links use a different technology. For example, a leased line can be in parallel with a backup dialup line or ISDN circuit. By using what are called *floating static routes*, you can specify that the backup route has a higher administrative distance (used by Cisco routers to select which routing information to use), so it is not normally used unless the primary route goes down. (Administrative distance is discussed further in Chapter 9.)

TIP   When provisioning backup links, learn as much as possible about the actual physical circuit routing. Different carriers sometimes use the same facilities, meaning that your backup path is susceptible to the same failures as your primary path. You should do some investigative work to ensure that your backup really is a backup.

Backup links can be combined with load balancing and channel aggregation. *Channel aggregation* means that a router can bring up multiple channels (for example, Integrated Services Digital Network [ISDN] B channels) as bandwidth requirements increase.

Cisco supports the Multilink Point-to-Point Protocol (MPPP), which is an Internet Engineering Task Force (IETF) standard for ISDN B channel (or asynchronous serial interface) aggregation. MPPP does not specify how a router should accomplish the decision-making process to bring up extra channels. Instead, it seeks to ensure that packets arrive in sequence at the receiving router. Then, the data is encapsulated within PPP and the datagram is given a sequence number.

At the receiving router, PPP uses this sequence number to re-create the original data stream. Multiple channels appear as one logical link to upper-layer protocols.

Secure Models

This section introduces secure topology models. Other aspects of security, such as encryption and access lists, are discussed in Chapter 10, "Provisioning Software Features." The information in this book is not sufficient to learn all the nuances of internetwork security. To learn more about internetwork security, you might want to read the book *Firewalls and Internet Security,* by Bill Cheswick and Steve Bellovin, published by Addison Wesley. Also, by searching on the word "security" on Cisco's Web site (http://www.cisco.com), you can keep up to date on security issues.

Secure topologies are often designed using a *firewall*. A firewall protects one network from another untrusted network. This protection can be accomplished in many ways, but in principle, a firewall is a pair of mechanisms: One blocks traffic and the other permits traffic.

Some firewalls place a greater emphasis on blocking traffic, and others emphasize permitting traffic. Figure 5-9 shows a simple firewall topology using routers.

Figure 5-9   *A Simple Firewall Network, Using Routers*

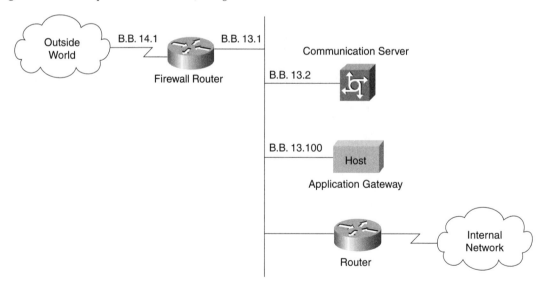

You can design a firewall system using packet-filtering routers and *bastion hosts*. A *bastion host* is a secure host that supports a limited number of applications for use by outsiders. It holds data that outsiders access (for example, web pages) but is strongly protected from outsiders using it for anything other than its limited purposes.

Three-Part Firewall System

The classic firewall system, called the *three-part firewall system*, has the following three specialized layers, as shown in Figure 5-10:

- An *isolation LAN* that is a buffer between the corporate internetwork and the outside world. (The isolation LAN is called the demilitarized zone, or DMZ, in some literature.)

- A router that acts as an *inside packet filter* between the corporate internetwork and the isolation LAN.

- Another router that acts as an *outside packet filter* between the isolation LAN and the outside internetwork.

Figure 5-10 *Structure and Components of a Three-Part Firewall System*

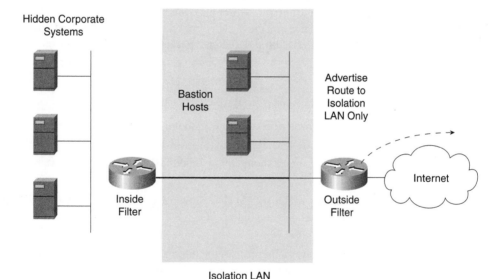

Services available to the outside world are located on bastion hosts in the isolation LAN. Example services in these hosts include:

- Anonymous FTP server
- Web server
- Domain Name Service (DNS)
- Telnet
- Specialized security software such as Terminal Access Controller Access Control System (TACACS)

The isolation LAN has a unique network number that is different than the corporate network number. Only the isolation LAN network is visible to the outside world. On the outside filter you should advertise only the route to the isolation LAN.

If internal users need to get access to Internet services, allow TCP outbound traffic from the internal corporate internetwork. Allow TCP packets back in to the internal network only if they are in response to a previously sent request. All other TCP traffic should be blocked because new inbound TCP sessions could be from hackers trying to establish sessions with internal hosts.

NOTE   In order to determine whether TCP traffic is a response to a previously sent request or a request for a new session, the router examines some bits in the *code* field of the TCP header. If the ACK (acknowledgement field is valid) or RST (reset the connection) bits are set in a TCP segment header, the segment is a response to a previously sent request. The **established** keyword in Cisco IOS™ access lists (filters) is used to indicate packets with ACK or RST bits set.

The following list summarizes some rules for the three-part firewall system.

- The inside packet filter router should allow inbound TCP packets from established sessions.

- The outside packet filter router should allow inbound TCP packets from established TCP sessions.

- The outside packet filter router should also allow packets to specific TCP or UDP ports going to specific bastion hosts (including TCP SYN packets that are used to establish a session).

Block traffic from firewall routers and hosts to the internal network. The firewall routers and hosts themselves are likely to be a jumping-off point for hackers, as shown in Figure 5-11.

Figure 5-11 *Firewall Routers and Hosts May Make Your Network Vulnerable to Hacker Attacks*

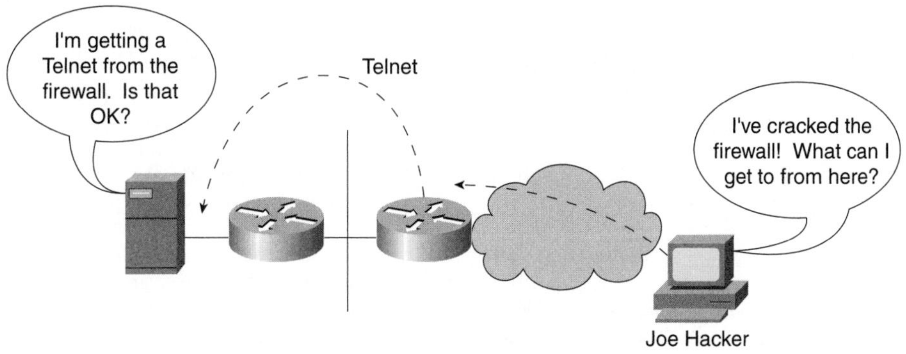

Keep bastion hosts and firewall routers simple. They should run as few programs as possible. The programs should be simple because simple programs have fewer bugs than complex programs. Bugs introduce possible security holes.

Do not enable any unnecessary services or connections on the outside filter router. A list of suggestions for implementing the outside filter router follows:

* Turn off Telnet access (no virtual terminals defined).
* Use static routing only.
* Do not make it a TFTP server.
* Use password encryption.
* Turn off proxy ARP service.
* Turn off *finger* service.
* Turn off IP redirects.
* Turn off IP route caching.
* Do not make it a MacIP server (MacIP provides connectivity for IP over AppleTalk by tunneling IP datagrams inside AppleTalk).

Cisco PIX™ Firewall

To provide stalwart security, hardware firewall devices can be used in addition to or instead of packet-filtering routers. For example, in the three-part firewall system illustrated earlier in Figure 5-10, a hardware firewall device could be installed on the isolation LAN. A hardware firewall device offers the following benefits:

* Less complex and more robust than packet filters
* No downtime required for installation
* No upgrading of hosts or routers is required
* No day-to-day management is necessary

Cisco's PIX Firewall is a hardware device that offers the features in the preceding list, as well as full outbound Internet access from unregistered internal hosts. IP addresses can be assigned from the private ranges, as defined in RFC 1918 (available at http://info.internet.isi.edu/in-notes/rfc/files/rfc1918.txt). The PIX Firewall uses a protection scheme called Network Address Translation (NAT), which allows internal users access to the Internet while protecting internal networks from unauthorized access. Private addresses and NAT are discussed more in Chapter 8.

Further details on the PIX Firewall are available on Cisco's web site at http://www.cisco.com/warp/public/cc/cisco/mkt/security/pix/. The summary from this web site is reproduced here.

Cisco PIX Firewall is the dedicated firewall appliance in Cisco's firewall family. PIX Firewall delivers strong security without impacting network performance. The product line scales to meet a range of customer requirements, with a choice of two hardware platforms, PIX Firewall 510 and PIX Firewall 520, and three capacity license levels. PIX Firewall is the leading product in its segment of the firewall market. The PIX Firewall provides full firewall protection that completely conceals the architecture of an internal network from the outside world. Virtual Private Network (VPN) connections using the IPSec standards can be made with PIX Firewall. PIX Firewall enforces secure access between an internal network and an intranet, extranet links, and the Internet.

PIX Firewall wins the overall performance award in KeyLab's FireBench firewall performance analysis, http://www.keylabs.com/results/firebench/fbenrpt2.pdf, demonstrating nearly 170 megabits per second throughput and over 6,500 connections per second in their network environment.

IDC Research http://www.idcresearch.com/CSS says Cisco PIX Firewall was a strong contender for number one in the overall 1997 firewall marketplace, with a 19% share compared to Check Point Firewall-1 at 23%.

Tests of enterprise-level firewalls by Network Computing http://www.networkcomputing.com/921/921f22.html reconfirm that the "performance of the PIX was by far the best of all the products" and even NAT activation did not slow down performance.

The PIX Firewall provides firewall security without the administrative overhead and risks associated with UNIX-based or router-based firewall systems. The PIX Firewall operates on a secure real-time kernel, not on UNIX. The network administrator is provided with complete auditing of all transactions, including attempted break-ins.

The PIX Firewall supports data encryption with the Cisco PIX Private Link, a card that provides secure communication between multiple PIX systems over the Internet using the data encryption standard (DES).

The PIX Firewall provides TCP and UDP connectivity from internal networks to the outside world using a scheme called *adaptive security.* All inbound traffic is verified for correctness against the following connection state information:

- Source and destination IP addresses
- Source and destination port numbers
- Protocols
- TCP sequence numbers (which are randomized to eliminate the possibility of hackers guessing numbers)

Design Guides

Cisco publishes some design guides that will help you design network topologies for customers. Depending on the solutions you are developing, refer to one or more of the following guides:

- Appendix D, "PIX Firewall Design Implementation Guide"
- Appendix E, "Router Performance Design and Implementation Guide"
- Appendix F, "ISDN Design and Implementation Guide"
- Appendix G, "Windows NT Design and Implementation Guide"

Summary

In this chapter you learned about three network topologies: hierarchical, redundant, and secure. You learned the advantages, disadvantages, scalability issues, and applicability of these topologies and saw some example topology diagrams.

The next chapter discusses the provisioning of the hardware and media for the LAN portion of your network, including routers and switches.

Multiple-Choice Review Questions

Answer the following questions on network design topology by selecting the letter to the left of the correct answer. After you complete each question, you can refer to the solutions provided by our internetworking experts in Appendix B.

Question 5-1

Which of the following characteristics accurately describes the hierarchical model for internetwork design?

- **A.** Alleviates concerns about internetwork diameter.
- **B.** Defines the number of allowed hops in an internetwork.
- **C.** Applies to large internetworks, but not small internetworks.
- **D.** Helps a designer implement scalable internetworks.

Question 5-2

Which one of the following is an issue in large Novell NetWare networks that use a full mesh Frame Relay topology?

A. Split horizon cannot be turned off.

B. SAP broadcasts use a substantial amount of bandwidth.

C. Snapshot routing is not yet supported to reduce bandwidth usage by IPX RIP.

D. Servers do not comply with the CIR.

Question 5-3

When designing load balancing in a WAN network, what is the most important rule?

A. Use equal-cost paths within each layer of the hierarchy.

B. Minimize the number of hops between sites.

C. Use Enhanced IGRP for the most effective load balancing.

D. Use an odd number of routers (rather than an even number).

Question 5-4

Which one of the following conditions would result in recommending routing instead of switching?

A. Many Ethernet collisions.

B. Excessive number of Ethernet runt frames (shorter than 64 bytes).

C. Bandwidth utilization over 40 percent on Ethernet.

D. Many desktop protocols sending packets to find services.

Question 5-5

Which one of the following statements best describes the specialized role that each layer of the hierarchical model plays?

A. The access layer provides policy-based connectivity.

B. The distribution layer provides resource discovery services.

C. The core layer provides optimal transport between sites.

D. The core layer provides workgroups access to the internetwork.

Question 5-6

Cisco's Hot Standby Router Protocol (HSRP) is a useful tool for ensuring which of the following?

A. IPX and AppleTalk sessions do not die when the default router dies.

B. IP sessions do not die when the default router dies.

C. ATM LAN Emulation sessions do not die when the LAN Emulation server dies.

D. Core routing does not die when floating static routes become active.

Question 5-7

In a three-part firewall security system, the outside filter router should support which of the following?

A. Configuration via TFTP

B. Proxy ARP service

C. Static routing only

D. IP route caching

Case Studies

In this section, you will sketch a topology based on the customer requirements for the four case studies introduced in Chapter 3.

Read each case study description and complete the questions for each of the case studies.

TIP	As mentioned, in working through the questions to the case studies, you might find it useful to work on some note paper in a separate binder to accommodate the depth of these exercises.

After you complete each question, you can refer to the solutions provided by our internetworking experts in Appendix B. Keep in mind that there are potentially several correct answers to each question. These case studies and their solutions will help you prepare for the Sylvan CCDA exam following the course.

Case Study: CareTaker Publications

You might want to review the CareTaker case study description in Appendix A, "Case Studies" on page 303 before proceeding to answer the questions in this section.

CareTaker Case Study Questions

In a conversation with Mr. Smith, you point out the load-sharing CSU is not required if you bridge the traffic using the routers. You tell Mr. Smith which Cisco IOS™ software features would be a great value-add to the bridged SNA traffic. Mr. Smith says he has already had this discussion with the parent company. However, the parent company's network administrators require this configuration.

Question 5-8

Draw a topology that will meet CareTaker's requirements. Include only the high-level view of the location of links and internetworking devices. In a few sentences, describe how your topology meets CareTaker's needs.

Question 5-9

After putting your initial topology together, the IS manager has brought up the question of failures. She feels it is important that the warehouse not lose access to the mainframe and its server. In response to your question about the economic trade-offs, she stated that management probably would not accept any kind of fail-safe or redundancy that increases the cost more than 2 to 5 percent. What modification, if any, would you make to your design to accommodate fail-safe operations of the warehouse?

Case Study: PH Network Services Corporation

You might want to review the PH Network Services Corporation case study description in Appendix A on page 306 before proceeding to answer the questions in this section.

PH Network Services Corporation Case Study Questions

Question 5-10

Draw a topology that will meet PH Network's requirements. In a few sentences, describe how your topology meets its needs.

Question 5-11

PH has brought up the question of telecommunication failures. It has had numerous failures in the lines to the hospitals. These are critical communications, and the company would like to know whether anything can be done to reduce communication losses. What modification, if any, would you make to your design to accommodate fail-safe operations to the hospitals?

Case Study: Pretty Paper Limited

You might want to review the Pretty Paper Limited case study in Appendix A on page 307 before proceeding to answer the questions in this section.

Pretty Paper Limited Case Study Questions

Question 5-12

Draw a topology that will meet Pretty Paper's requirements. In a few sentences, describe how your topology meets Pretty Paper's needs.

Question 5-13

The manager of Warehouse and Distribution is concerned about PC client performance over the Frame Relay network to the new business software on the HP9000. What design constraints and considerations will you take into account to answer these concerns?

Question 5-14

How would you respond to the Sales and Marketing organization's questions regarding someone's ability to get to data on the NetWare servers or the HP9000 from the Internet?

Case Study: Jones, Jones, & Jones

You may wish to review the Jones, Jones, & Jones case study in Appendix A on page 308 before proceeding to answer the questions in this section.

Jones, Jones, & Jones Case Study Questions

Question 5-15

Draw a topology that will meet Ms. Jones's requirements. Include only the high-level view of the location of links and internetworking devices. In a few sentences, describe how your topology meets the law firm's needs.

Question 5-16

The managing partner called. She wanted to emphasize that unauthorized workstations should not be allowed access to the Internet. How have you accommodated this request in your design?

It will take you approximately two hours to complete this chapter and its exercises. Upon completion of this second chapter in Part IV you will be able to do the following:

- Recognize scalability constraints and issues for standard LAN technologies.

- Recommend Cisco products and LAN technologies that will meet a customer's requirements for performance, capacity, and scalability in small- to medium-sized networks.

- Update the network topology drawing you created in the previous chapter to include hardware and media.

CHAPTER 6

Provisioning Hardware and Media for the LAN

This chapter includes some tables and other job aids that you will find useful when completing the case studies at the end of the chapter. References to some Web sites are also included; relevant information has been extracted from these sites and is provided in the chapter. If you have access to the Internet, you might want to visit the sites mentioned to obtain detailed information related to specific topics. All the sites referenced in this chapter are also listed in Appendix C, "Interesting WWW Links and Other Suggested Readings."

The *Cisco Product Selection Tool*, available on Cisco's web site, is also referenced in the case studies at the end of this chapter. An introduction to the tool is provided there, and you are encouraged to try the tool if you have access to the Internet.

Follow these steps to complete this chapter:

1 Study the chapter content, including any tables and job aids that appear.

2 Review the case studies at the end of this chapter.

3 Complete the questions in each case study.

4 Review the answers provided by our internetworking experts in Appendix B, "Answers to Chapter Questions, Case Studies, and Sample CCDA Exam."

Provisioning LAN media and hardware involves making many decisions, including which devices to use and what media to use to interconnect these devices. This chapter discusses these issues in the following sections:

- Switching versus Routing in Network Design
- Cisco's Catalyst Switches
- Cisco's Routers
- Selecting Switches, Routers, Access Servers, and Other Cisco Hardware
- Provisioning Network Media

Switching Versus Routing in Network Design

When provisioning internetworking devices for small- to medium-sized networks, you need to decide when LAN switches are appropriate and when routers are appropriate. The sections that follow provide some information on the different types of services offered by routers and switches, and how these devices can be used in your design.

Router Services

If you need internetworking services, routers are needed. Routers offer the following services:

- Broadcast *firewalling* or filtering
- Hierarchical addressing
- Communication between dissimilar LANs
- Fast convergence
- Policy routing
- Quality of Service (QoS) routing
- Security
- Redundancy and load balancing
- Traffic flow management
- Multimedia group membership

Switching Services

Some services are becoming available on switches also. For example, support for multimedia often requires a protocol such as the Internet Group Management Protocol (IGMP), which allows workstations to join a group that receives multimedia multicast packets. Cisco now allows Catalyst switches to participate in this process by using the Cisco Group Management Protocol (CGMP). One router will still be needed, but you will not need a router in every department of a company because with CGMP, switches can communicate with the router to determine whether any users attached to them are part of a multicast group.

Switching and bridging sometimes result in nonoptimal routing of packets because every packet must go through the root bridge of the spanning tree. (Recall that the spanning tree is running in order to prevent *broadcast storms* in a switched network). When routers are used, the routing of packets can be controlled and designed for optimal paths. Cisco supports improved routing and redundancy in switched environments by allowing one instance of the spanning tree per VLAN.

In general, incorporating switches in small-to medium-sized network designs will provide the following advantages:

- High bandwidth
- Low cost
- Easy configuration

Problems Solved with Internetworking Devices

The decision to use an internetworking device depends on which problems you are trying to solve for your client. Recall from Chapter 2, "Analyzing Small- to Medium-Sized Business Networks" that customer problems can be categorized as follows:

- Media problems
- Protocol problems
- Need to transport large payloads

The decision to use routing or switching depends on the problem to be solved. Figure 6-1 illustrates these problems and their solutions, as detailed in the sections that follow.

Figure 6-1   *The Decision to Use Routing or Switching Depends on the Problem to be Solved*

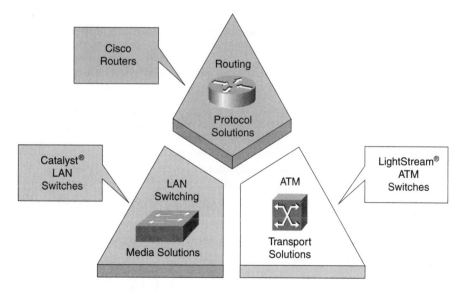

Media Problems

Media problems refer to an excessive number of collisions on Ethernet or long waits for the token in Token Ring or FDDI. Media problems are caused by too many devices on the media, all with a high load for the network segment. Media problems can be solved by dividing a network into separate segments, using one or more switches.

Protocol Problems

Protocol problems are caused by protocols that do not scale well: for example, protocols that send an excessive number of broadcasts. Protocol problems can be solved by dividing a network into separate segments, using one or more routers.

Need to Transport Large Payloads

This category of problems includes the need to offer voice and video network services. These services may require much more bandwidth than is available on a customer's network or backbone. Transport problems can be solved by using high-bandwidth technologies, such as Fast Ethernet or ATM.

Bandwidth Domains and Broadcast Domains

A *bandwidth domain*, known as a collision domain for Ethernet LANs, includes all devices that share the same bandwidth. For example, when using switches or bridges, everything associated with one port is a bandwidth domain.

A *broadcast domain* includes all devices that see each other's broadcasts (and multicasts). For example, all the devices associated with one port on a router are in the same broadcast domain.

Devices in the same bandwidth domain are also in the same broadcast domain; however, devices in the same broadcast domain may be in different bandwidth domains.

All workstations within one bandwidth domain compete for the same LAN bandwidth resource. All traffic from any host in the bandwidth domain is visible to all the other hosts. In the case of an Ethernet collision domain, two stations may transmit at the same time, causing a collision. The stations then have to stop transmitting and try again at a later time, resulting in a delay in transmitting the traffic.

All broadcasts from any host in the same broadcast domain are visible to all other hosts in the same broadcast domain. Desktop protocols, such as AppleTalk, NetBIOS, IPX, and IP, require broadcasts or multicasts for resource discovery and advertisement. Hubs, switches, and bridges forward broadcasts and multicasts to all ports. Routers do not forward these broadcasts or multicasts to any ports. In other words, routers block broadcasts (destined for *all* networks) and multicasts; they only forward *unicast* packets (destined for a specific device) and *directed broadcasts* (destined for all devices on a *specific* network).

Segmenting the Network Using Switches

When analyzing your customer's current network and future needs, as discussed in Part III of this book, determine whether bandwidth domains need to be segmented using switches.

As noted in Chapter 3, "Characterizing the Existing Network," Ethernet networks should be segmented if the network utilization is above approximately 40 percent for long periods of time. Token Ring and FDDI networks should be segmented if network utilization is above approximately 70 percent for long periods of time.

If there are too many hosts on a LAN, broadcast radiation can cause performance degradation. *Broadcast radiation* refers to the way that broadcasts and multicasts radiate from the source to all connected LANs in a flat network, causing all hosts on the LAN to do extra processing. When broadcasts and multicasts are more than approximately 20 percent of the traffic on a LAN, performance degrades.

As seen in Chapter 4, "Determining New Customer Requirements," there are guidelines for an upper limit on the number of workstations on a LAN or VLAN, before broadcast radiation overwhelms the CPUs of the hosts. These limits are shown again in Table 6-1. Actual workstation limits depend on factors such as:

- Broadcast/multicast load
- IP addressing constraints
- Inter-VLAN routing requirements
- Management and fault isolation constraints
- Traffic flow characteristics

Table 6-1   *Scalability Constraints for Flat (Switched/Bridged) Networks*

Protocol	Maximum Number of Workstations
IP	500
IPX	300
AppleTalk	200
NetBIOS	200
Mixed	200

When connecting LANs or VLANs via one or more routers, you need to understand the characteristics of the network traffic. It is also important to understand the performance of the router(s) you plan to use in the network design. You can find out more about router performance and capacity in the next chapter, "Provisioning Hardware and Media for the WAN."

The 80/20 Rule

Campus LANs are easiest to design when the traffic obeys the 80/20 rule, which states that 80 percent of traffic is local to a LAN or VLAN and only 20 percent of the traffic goes to a different LAN or VLAN. This is the case when users primarily access departmental servers and the LANs or VLANs are subdivided by department. However, with the emergence of server farms and corporate web servers, the 80/20 rule does not always apply. In these cases, it is important to provision bandwidth, switches, and routers carefully to avoid congestion and poor performance.

Summary of When to Use Switches Versus Routers

Table 6-2 summarizes the discussion of switching Versus routing.

Table 6-2   *Summary of Considerations for Switches versus Routers*

	Routers	Switches
Problem Solved	Protocol problems	Media (LAN switches), and Transport of large payload (Fast Ethernet and ATM switches) problems
Key Features	Many, including filtering, addressing, connecting dissimilar LANs, security, load balancing, policy and QoS routing, multimedia	High bandwidth, low cost, ease of configuration
Broadcast and Bandwidth Domains	Reduces broadcast domain and bandwidth (collision) domain	Reduces bandwidth (collision) domain

Cisco's Catalyst Switches

Cisco's Catalyst family is a comprehensive line of high-performance switches designed to help users easily migrate from traditional shared LANs to fully switched networks. The Cisco Catalyst family includes many products, such as:

- Catalyst 5000 series switching system
- Catalyst 1900/2820 Ethernet switches

Refer to the *Products Quick Reference Guide*, available at http://www.cisco.com/univercd/cc/td/doc/cpqrg/index.html for information about the complete Cisco Catalyst family for small- and medium-sized businesses. Figure 6-2 shows a sample switched campus network using Catalyst 5000 series switches.

Figure 6-2   *A Sample Switched Network Using Cisco's Catalyst 5000 Series Switches*

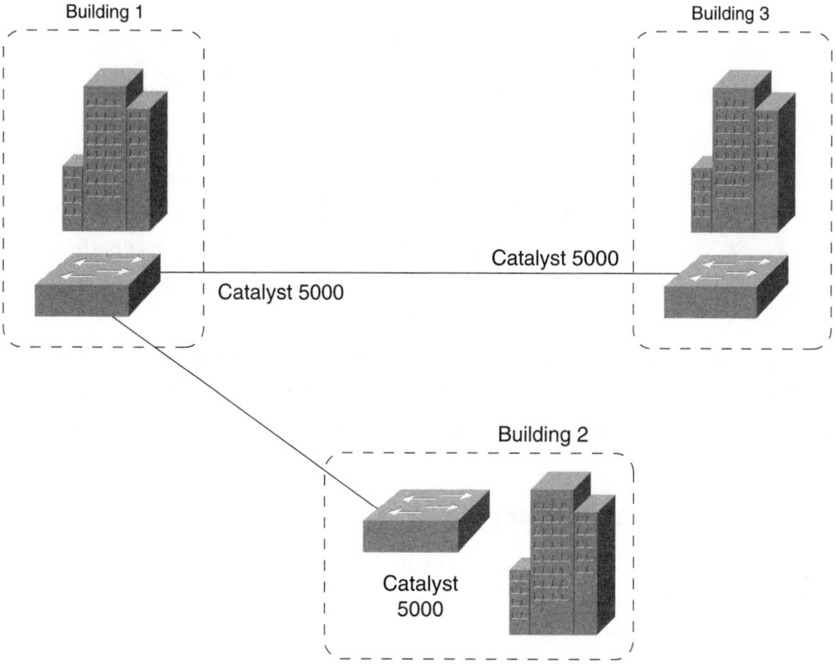

Cisco's Routers

Cisco has a full line of routers for all network needs. The Cisco router family includes many products, such as:

- For the Central Site:
  - Cisco 4500/4700 series access routers
  - Cisco 3600 series access routers
- For the Branch Office:
  - Cisco 2600 series access routers
  - Cisco 2500 series access routers
  - Cisco 1600 series access routers
  - Cisco 1000 series access routers
- For the Small Office/Home Office (SOHO)
  - Cisco 800 series
  - Cisco 700 series

Refer to the *Products Quick Reference Guide*, available at http://www.cisco.com/univercd/cc/td/doc/cpqrg/index.htm for information about the complete line of Cisco routers.

Selecting Switches, Routers, Access Servers, and Other Cisco Hardware

When provisioning Cisco hardware, use the following documents and tools to gather the latest information on ports, interfaces, slots, memory, processors, power supplies, prices, and so on:

- The *Cisco Product Selection Tool*, available at http://www.cisco.com/romeo/select.htm.
- The *Products Quick Reference Guide*, available at http://www.cisco.com/univercd/cc/td/doc/cpqrg/index.htm.
- Cisco Price list (To obtain a copy of the current Cisco price list, log in to the Cisco Reseller's web site. You will require a reseller account in order to do this.)

Each of these items is continuously being updated as Cisco introduces new products and features.

Provisioning Network Media

This section identifies some of the constraints that should be considered when provisioning various LAN media types.

Ethernet Design Rules

Table 6-3 provides scalability information that you can use when provisioning IEEE 802.3 networks:

Table 6-3   *Scalability Constraints for IEEE 802.3*

	10Base5	10Base2	10BaseT	100BaseT
Topology	Bus	Bus	Star	Star
Maximum Segment Length (meters)	500	185	100 from hub to station	100 from hub to station
Maximum Number of Attachments per Segment	100	30	2 (hub and station or hub-hub)	2 (hub and station or hub-hub)
Maximum Collision Domain	2500 meters of 5 segments and 4 repeaters; only 3 segments can be populated	2500 meters of 5 segments and 4 repeaters; only 3 segments can be populated	2500 meters of 5 segments and 4 repeaters; only 3 segments can be populated	See the Details on 100 Mbps Ethernet Design Rules Section that follows

The most significant design rule for Ethernet is that the round-trip propagation delay in one collision domain must not exceed 512 bit times, which is a requirement for collision detection to work correctly. This rule means that the maximum round-trip delay for a 10 Mbps Ethernet network is 51.2 microseconds. The maximum round-trip delay for a 100 Mbps Ethernet network is only 5.12 microseconds because the bit time on a 100 Mbps Ethernet network is 0.01 microseconds as opposed to 0.1 microseconds on a 10 Mbps Ethernet network.

To make 100 Mbps Ethernet work, there are much more severe distance limitations than those required for 10 Mbps Ethernet. The general rule is that a 100 Mbps Ethernet has a maximum diameter of 205 meters when unshielded twisted-pair (UTP) cabling is used, whereas 10 Mbps Ethernet has a maximum diameter of 2500 meters.

10 Mbps Fiber Ethernet Design Rules

Table 6-4 provides some guidelines to help you choose the right media for your network designs. 10BaseF is based on the fiber-optic interrepeater link (FOIRL) specification, which includes 10BaseFP, 10BaseFB, 10BaseFL, and a revised FOIRL standard. The new FOIRL allows data terminal equipment (DTE)—end-node—connections, rather than just repeaters, as allowed with the older FOIRL specification.

Table 6-4   *Scalability Constraints for 10 Mbps Fiber Ethernet*

	10BaseFP	10BaseFB	10BaseFL	Old FOIRL	New FOIRL
Topology	Passive star	Backbone or repeater fiber system	Link	Link	Link or star
Allows DTE (end-node) Connections?	Yes	No	No	No	Yes
Maximum Segment Length (meters)	500	2000	1000 or 2000	1000	1000
Allows Cascaded Repeaters?	No	Yes	No	No	Yes
Maximum Collision Domains in Meters	2500	2500	2500	2500	2500

100 Mbps (Fast Ethernet) Design Rules

100 Mbps Ethernet, or Fast Ethernet, topologies present some distinct constraints on the network design because of their speed. The combined latency due to cable lengths and repeaters must conform to the specifications in order for the network to work properly. This section discusses these issues and provides example calculations.

Understanding Collision Domains

The overriding design rule for 100 Mbps Ethernet networks is that the round-trip collision delay must not exceed 512 bit times. However, the bit time on a 100 Mbps Ethernet network is 0.01 microseconds, as opposed to 0.1 microseconds on a 10 Mbps Ethernet network. Therefore, the maximum round-trip delay for a 100 Mbps Ethernet network is 5.12 microseconds, as opposed to the more lenient 51.2 microseconds in a 10 Mbps Ethernet network.

100BaseT Repeaters

For a 100 Mbps Ethernet to work, you must impose distance limitations, based on the type of repeaters used.

The IEEE 100BaseT specification defines two types of repeaters: Class I and Class II. Class I repeaters have a latency (delay) of 0.7 microseconds or less. Only one repeater hop is allowed. Class II repeaters have a latency (delay) of 0.46 microseconds or less. One or two repeater hops are allowed.

Table 6-5 shows the maximum size of collision domains, depending on the type of repeater.

Table 6-5   *Maximum Size of Collision Domains for 100BaseT*

	Copper	Mixed Copper and Multimode Fiber	Multimode Fiber
DTE-DTE (or Switch-Switch)	100 meters		412 meters (2000 if full duplex)
One Class I Repeater	200 meters	260 meters	272 meters
One Class II Repeater	200 meters	308 meters	320 meters
Two Class II Repeaters	205 meters	216 meters	228 meters

NOTE   The Cisco FastHub 316 is a Class II repeater, as are all of the Cisco FastHub 300 series hubs. These hubs actually exceed the Class II specifications, which means that they have even lower latencies and therefore allow longer cable lengths. For example, with two FastHub 300 repeaters and copper cable, the maximum collision domain is 223 meters.

Example of 100BaseT Topology

Figure 6-3 shows examples of 100BaseT topologies with different media.

Figure 6-3   *Examples of 100BaseT Topologies with Various Media and Repeaters*

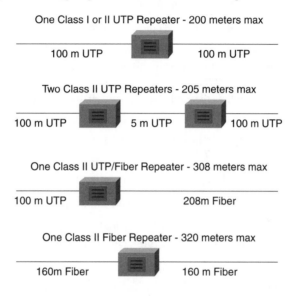

One Class I or II UTP Repeater - 200 meters max

100 m UTP   100 m UTP

Two Class II UTP Repeaters - 205 meters max

100 m UTP   5 m UTP   100 m UTP

One Class II UTP/Fiber Repeater - 308 meters max

100 m UTP   208m Fiber

One Class II Fiber Repeater - 320 meters max

160m Fiber   160 m Fiber

Other topologies are possible as long as the round-trip propagation delay does not exceed 5.12 microseconds (512 bit times). When the delay does exceed 5.12 microseconds, the network experiences illegal (late) collisions and CRC errors.

Checking the Propagation Delay

To determine whether configurations other than the standard ones shown in Figure 6-3 will work, use the following information from the IEEE 802.3u specification.

To check a path to make sure the path delay value (PDV) does not exceed 512 bit times, add up the following delays:

- All link segment delays
- All repeater delays
- DTE delay
- A safety margin (0 to 5 bit times)

Use the following steps to calculate the PDV:

Step 1   Determine the delay for each link segment; this is the link segment delay value (LSDV), including inter-repeater links, using the following formula. (Multiply by two so it is a round-trip delay.)

LSDV = 2 × segment length × cable delay for this segment.

For end-node segments, the segment length is the cable length between the physical interface at the repeater and the physical interface at the DTE. Use your two farthest DTEs for a worst-case calculation. For inter-repeater links, the segment length is the cable length between the repeater physical interfaces.

Cable delay is the delay specified by the manufacturer if available. When actual cable lengths or propagation delays are not known, use the delay in bit times as specified in Table 6-6.

Cable delay must be specified in bit times per meter (BT/m).

Step 2   Add together the LSDVs for all segments in the path.

Step 3   Determine the delay for each repeater in the path. If model-specific data is not available from the manufacturer, determine the class of repeater (I or II).

Step 4   MII cables for 100BaseT should not exceed 0.5 meters each in length. When evaluating system topology, MII cable lengths need not be accounted for separately. Delays attributed to the MII are incorporated into DTE and repeater delays.

Step 5   Use the DTE delay value shown in Table 6-6 unless your equipment manufacturer defines a different value.

Step 6   Decide on an appropriate safety margin from 0 to 5 bit times. Five bit times is a safe value.

Step 7   Insert the values obtained from the preceding calculations into the formula for calculating the PDV:

PDV = link delays + repeater delays + DTE delay + safety margin

Step 8   If the PDV is less than 512, the path is qualified in terms of worst-case delay.

Round-Trip Delay

Table 6-6 shows round-trip delay in bit times for standard cables and maximum round-trip delay in bit times for DTEs, repeaters, and maximum-length cables.

NOTE   Note that the values shown in Table 6-6 have been multiplied by two to provide a round-trip delay. If you use these numbers, you need not multiply by two again in the LSDV formula (LSDV = 2 × segment length × cable delay for this segment).

Table 6-6   *Network Component Delays*

Component	Round-Trip Delay in Bit Times per Meter	Maximum Round-Trip Delay in Bit Times
Two TX/FX DTEs	N/A	100
Two T4 DTEs	N/A	138
One T4 DTE and one TX/FX DTE	N/A	127
Category 3 cable segment	1.14	114 (100 meters)
Category 4 cable segment	1.14	114 (100 meters)
Category 5 cable segment	1.112	111.2 (100 meters)
STP cable segment	1.112	111.2 (100 meters)
Fiber-optic cable segment	1.0	412 (412 meters)
Class I repeater	N/A	140
Class II repeater with all ports TX or FX	N/A	92
Class II repeater with any port T4	N/A	67

Source: IEEE 802.3u—1995, "Media Access Control (MAC) Parameters, Physical Layer, Medium Attachment Units, and Repeater for 100 Mb/s Operation, Type 100BASE-T."

Example Network Cabling Implementation

Refer to Figure 6-4 for this example. Company ABC has all UTP Category 5 cabling. Two Class II repeaters are separated by 20 meters, instead of the standard 5 meters. The network administrators are trying to determine whether this configuration will work.

Figure 6-4 *An Example Network Cabling Implementation for Company ABC (Showing the Two Most Distant DTEs)*

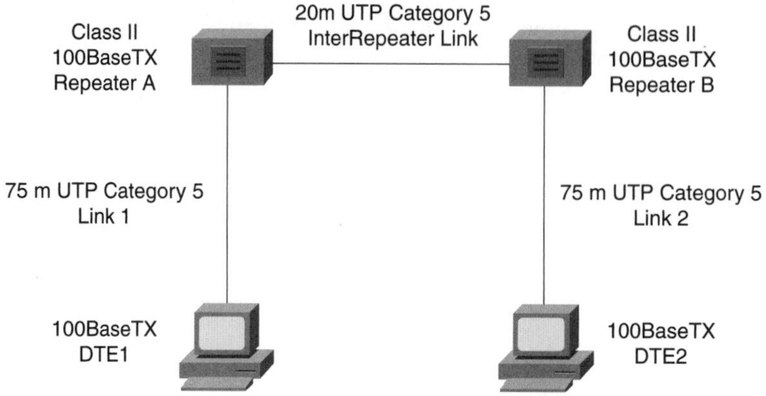

To ensure that the PDV does not exceed 512 bit times, the network administrators must calculate a worst-case scenario using DTE 1 and DTE 2, which are 75 meters from their repeaters.

Assume that DTE 1 starts transmitting a minimum-sized frame of 64 bytes (512 bits). DTE 2 just barely misses hearing DTE 1's transmission and starts transmitting also. The collision happens on the far-right side of the network and must traverse back to DTE 1. These events must occur within 512 bit times. If they take any longer than 512 bit times, then DTE 1 will have stopped sending when it learns about the collision and will not know that its frame was damaged by the collision. To calculate the link delays for the Category 5 cable segments, the repeaters, and DTEs, the administrators use the values from Table 6-6. (Remember that Table 6-6 uses round-trip delay values, so you need not multiply by two.)

To test whether this network will work, the network administrators filled in Table 6-7:

Table 6-7 *Delays of Components in Company ABC's Network*

Delay Cause	Calculation of Network Component Delay	Total (Bit Times)
Link 1	75m × 1.112 Bit Times/m	83.4
Link 2	75m × 1.112 Bit Times/m	83.4
Inter-repeater link	20m × 1.112 Bit Times/m	22.24
Repeater A	92 Bit Times	92
Repeater B	92 Bit Times	92
DTE 1 and 2	100 Bit Times	100
Safety margin	5 Bit Times	5
Grand Total	**Add Individual Totals**	**478.04**

The grand total in Table 6-7 is fewer than 512 bit times, so this network will work.

Calculating Cable Delays

Some cable manufacturers specify propagation delays relative to the speed of light (c) or in nanoseconds per meter (ns/m). To convert these values to bit times per meter (BT/m), use Table 6-8.

Table 6-8   *Conversion to Bit Times per Meter for Cable Delays*

Speed Relative to Speed of Light (c)	Nanoseconds per Meter (ns/m)	Bit Times per Meter (BT/m)
0.4	8.34	0.834
0.5	6.67	0.667
0.51	6.54	0.654
0.52	6.41	0.641
0.53	6.29	0.629
0.54	6.18	0.618
0.55	6.06	0.606
0.56	5.96	0.596
0.57	5.85	0.585
0.58	5.75	0.575
0.5852	5.70	0.570
0.59	5.65	0.565
0.6	5.56	0.556
0.61	5.47	0.547
0.62	5.38	0.538
0.63	5.29	0.529
0.64	5.21	0.521
0.65	5.13	0.513
0.654	5.10	0.510
0.66	5.05	0.505
0.666	5.01	0.501
0.67	4.98	0.498

continues

Table 6-8   *Conversion to Bit Times per Meter for Cable Delays (Continued)*

Speed Relative to Speed of Light (c)	Nanoseconds per Meter (ns/m)	Bit Times per Meter (BT/m)
0.68	4.91	0.491
0.69	4.83	0.483
0.7	4.77	0.477
0.8	4.17	0.417
0.9	3.71	0.371

Source: IEEE 802.3u — 1995, "Media Access Control (MAC) Parameters, Physical Layer, Medium Attachment Units, and Repeater for 100 Mb/s Operation, Type 100BASE-T."

Token Ring Design Rules

Table 6-9 lists some scalability concerns when designing Token Ring segments. Refer to IBM's Token Ring planning guides for more information on the maximum segment sizes and maximum diameter of a network.

Table 6-9   *Scalability Constraints for Token Ring*

	IBM Token Ring	IEEE 802.5
Topology	Star	Not specified
Maximum Segment Length (Meters)	Depends on type of cable, number of MAUs, and so on	Depends on type of cable, number of MAUs, and so on
Maximum Number of Attachments per Segment	260 for STP, 72 for UTP	250
Maximum Network Diameter	Depends on type of cable, number of MAUs, and so on	Depends on type of cable, number of MAUs, and so on

FDDI Design Rules

The FDDI specification does not actually specify the maximum segment length or network diameter. It specifies the amount of allowed power loss, which works out to the approximate distances shown in Table 6-10.

Table 6-10   *Scalability Constraints for FDDI*

	Multimode Fiber	Single-Mode Fiber	UTP
Topology	Dual ring, tree of concentrators, and others	Dual ring, tree of concentrators, and others	Star
Maximum Segment Length	2 km between stations	60 km between stations	100 meters from hub to station
Maximum Number of Attachments per Segment	1000 (500 dual-attached stations)	1000 (500 dual-attached stations)	2 (hub and station or hub-hub)
Maximum Network Diameter	200 km	200 km	200 km

Summary

In this chapter you learned about scalability constraints and issues for switches and routers and for standard LAN technologies. In the case studies that follow you have the opportunity to apply what you have learned to recommend Cisco products and LAN technologies to meet customer requirements.

The next chapter in Part IV discusses the provisioning of the hardware and media for the WAN portion of your network, including routers and switches.

Case Studies

In this section, you are asked to provision media and products for the LANs for the four case studies introduced in Chapter 3. In order to select appropriate products for these case studies, you might want to use some of the many useful tools and documents accessible on Cisco's Web site if you have Internet access. The following section provides some information on two of these items, the *Cisco Product Selection Tool* and the *Products Quick Reference Guide.*

Read each case study description and complete the questions for each.

TIP   As mentioned, in working through the questions to the case studies, you may find it useful to work on some note paper in a separate binder to accommodate the depth of these exercises.

After you complete each question, you can refer to the solutions provided by our internetworking experts in Appendix B. Keep in mind that there are potentially several correct answers to each question. These case studies will help you prepare for the Sylvan CCDA exam following the course.

Product Selection Tool and Products Quick Reference Guide

Cisco's Web site contains many useful tools; they are accessible via http://www.cisco.com/univercd/cc/td/doc/cpqrg/index.html. The *Cisco Product Selection Tool*, available through this link or directly at http://www.cisco.com/romeo/rsmp_home.htm is an easy-to-use tool for aiding you in the product selection task. Alternatively, you can look at the *Products Quick Reference Guide*, also on Cisco's Web site, at http://www.cisco.com/univercd/cc/td/doc/cpqrg/index.htm.

Because the *Product Selection Tool* and *Products Quick Reference Guide* encompass a wealth of information and are constantly being revised, they do not lend themselves to being represented in this book. However, instructions for running the tool are noted here, and excerpts from the results are included in the answers in Appendix B so that you can acquaint yourself with the possibilities available. If you have Internet access you are encouraged to try the tool for yourself.

NOTE   Your results from using the *Cisco Product Selection Tool* may differ from those given in Appendix B, since the tool's output may also change as products change and new products are introduced.

To run the *Product Selection Tool*, go to http://www.cisco.com/romeo/rsmp_home.htm. You will see the initial Cisco Reseller Sales Tools window.

Click on *select a product*. The Product Selection Tool window appears. Click on either *switches*, *access routers/servers*, or *hubs*. The appropriate features selection windows appear. In the left window, click on the product features you want to select in each category, based on your requirements. The right window displays the products that support the currently selected features. As you select more product features, the list of potential products changes in this right-hand window. An example screen is shown in Figure 6-5.

Figure 6-5   *Use the Cisco Product Selection Tool to Determine the Products That Support Your Selected Features*

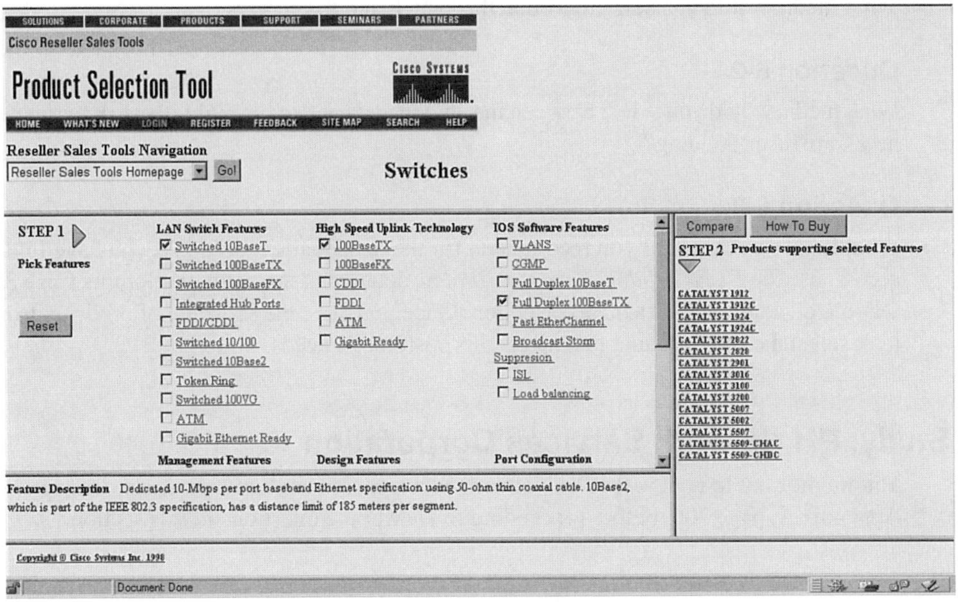

Once you have selected all the required features, you can access more detail on each of the products displayed in the right window by clicking on the product name. This will display an overview of the product; more details can be found by following the links on this overview page.

Case Study: CareTaker Publications

You might want to review the CareTaker case study description in Appendix A, "Case Studies," page 303, before proceeding to answer the questions in this section.

CareTaker Case Study Questions

Refer to the topology drawing you created for CareTaker Publications in Chapter 3 or review the topology drawing solution provided in Appendix B. In this section you will provision LAN hardware and media for CareTaker Publications.

Mr. Smith has indicated that the IS budget has been reduced to provide funding for another project. Mr. Smith wants to complete the project correctly, but needs to lower the costs.

Question 6-1

What media would you select between the switch and the servers?

Question 6-2

What media would you select between the switch and each of the eight network segments in the new CareTaker building?

Question 6-3

What LAN switch would you recommend for the headquarters office? If you have Internet access, use the *Cisco Product Selection Tool* as detailed at the beginning of this Case Studies section, clicking on the *switches* selection. Once you have the short list of products from this tool, select the right product that meets this customer's needs.

Case Study: PH Network Services Corporation

You might want to review the PH Network Services Corporation case study description in Appendix A, page 306, before proceeding to answer the questions in this section.

PH Network Case Study Questions

Refer to the topology drawing you created for Mr. Pero in Chapter 3 or review the topology drawing solution provided in Appendix B. In this section, you will provision LAN hardware and media for PH Network.

Question 6-4

What media would you select between the switch and the servers?

Question 6-5

What media would you select between the switch and each of the network segments in the main office?

Question 6-6

What LAN switch would you select? If you have Internet access, use the *Cisco Product Selection Tool* as detailed at the beginning of this Case Studies section, clicking on the *switches* selection. Once you have the short list of products from this tool, select the right product that meets this customer's needs.

Case Study: Pretty Paper Limited

You may wish to review the Pretty Paper Limited case study in Appendix A, page 307, before proceeding to answer the questions in this section.

Pretty Paper Limited Case Study Questions

Refer to the topology drawing you created for Pretty Paper in Chapter 3 or review the topology drawing solution provided in Appendix B. In this section you will provision LAN hardware and media for Pretty Paper.

Question 6-7

What media would you select between the switch and the servers?

Question 6-8

What media would you select between the switch and each of the network segments in the new Pretty Paper headquarters building?

Question 6-9

What recommendations would you make for media between the switch and central manufacturing in the Pretty Paper design? What about the connection to the warehouse?

Question 6-10

What LAN switch would you select? If you have Internet access, use the *Cisco Product Selection Tool* as detailed at the beginning of this Case Studies section, clicking on the *switches* selection. Once you have the short list of products from this tool, select the right product that meets this customer's needs.

Case Study: Jones, Jones, & Jones

You might want to review the Jones, Jones, & Jones case study in Appendix A, page 308, before proceeding to answer the questions in this section.

Jones, Jones, & Jones Case Study Questions

Refer to the topology drawing you created for Ms. Jones in Chapter 3 or review the topology drawing solution provided in Appendix B. In this section you will provision LAN hardware and media for Jones, Jones, & Jones.

Question 6-11

What media would you select between the switch and the servers?

Question 6-12

What media would you select between the switch and each of the network segments in the law firm's U.S. offices?

Question 6-13

What LAN media would you select for the international offices?

Question 6-14

What LAN switch would you recommend? If you have Internet access, use the *Cisco Product Selection Tool* as detailed at the beginning of this Case Studies section, clicking on the *switches* selection. Once you have the short list of products from this tool, select the product that best meets this customer's needs.

You will need approximately three hours to complete this chapter and its exercises. Upon completion of this third chapter in Part IV, you will be able to do the following:

- Recognize scalability constraints and issues for standard WAN technologies.
- Recognize scalability constraints and performance budgets for major Cisco products.
- Recommend Cisco products and WAN technologies that will meet the customer's requirements for performance, capacity, and scalability in an enterprise network.

CHAPTER 7

Provisioning Hardware and Media for the WAN

This chapter includes some tables and other job aids that you will find useful when completing the case studies at the end of the chapter. References to some Web sites are also included; relevant information has been extracted from these sites and is provided in the chapter. If you have access to the Internet, you might want to access the sites mentioned to obtain detailed information related to specific topics. All the sites referenced in this chapter are also listed in Appendix C, "Interesting WWW Links and Other Suggested Readings."

The *Cisco Product Selection Tool*, available on Cisco's Web site, is also referenced in the case studies at the end of this chapter. An introduction to the tool is provided in Chapter 6, "Provisioning Hardware and Media for the LAN," and you are encouraged to try the tool if you have access to the Internet.

Follow these steps to complete this chapter:

1 Study the chapter content, including any tables and job aids that appear in the reading assignment.

2 Review the case studies at the end of this chapter.

3 Complete the questions in each case study.

4 Review the answers provided by our internetworking experts in Appendix B, "Answers to Chapter Questions, Case Studies, and Sample CCDA Exam."

Provisioning WAN media and hardware involves making many decisions, including which devices to use and what type of WAN to use to interconnect these devices. This chapter discusses these issues in the following sections:

- WAN Design Considerations
- Extending into the WAN
- Selecting Cisco Hardware for Small- to Medium-Sized Networks
- Provisioning Interface Description Blocks on Cisco Routers
- Router Switching Modes
- Choosing a Router Platform
- Provisioning WANs

WAN Design Considerations

WAN designs should provide reliable service, minimize the cost of bandwidth, and optimize bandwidth efficiency. In Figure 7-1, for example, you would want to minimize the cost of bandwidth and optimize bandwidth efficiency between the corporate office and remote offices.

Figure 7-1   *WANs Are Used Between Corporate and Remote Offices*

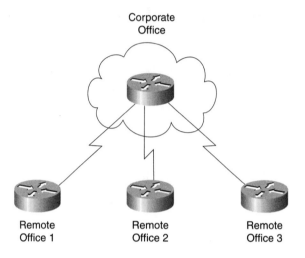

To provide reliable services for end-user applications in a cost-effective and efficient manner, you should select the right type of WAN technology. The following sections review some common WAN technologies and their typical applications.

Analog Modems

Analog modems, which operate over the Public Switched Telephone Network (PSTN), are used in the following applications:

- By telecommuters and mobile users who access the network fewer than two hours per day
- As a backup for another type of link

Figure 7-2 shows analog modems in use over the PSTN.

Figure 7-2   *Analog Modems Are Used Over the Public Switched Telephone Network*

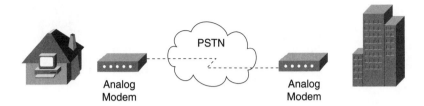

Leased Lines

Leased lines, shown in Figure 7-3, are used in the following applications:

- In point-to-point networks and hub-and-spoke topologies
- As a backup for another type of link

Figure 7-3   *Leased Lines Can Be Used for Point-to-Point Networks*

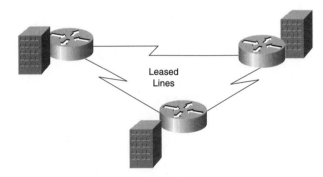

ISDN

ISDN, shown in Figure 7-4, is used in the following applications:

- For cost-effective remote access to corporate networks for telecommuters and remote offices
- As support for voice and video
- As a backup for another type of link

Figure 7-4 *ISDN Is Used by Telecommuters to Access the Corporate Network*

Frame Relay

Frame Relay, shown in Figure 7-5, is used in the following applications:

- For cost-effective, high-speed, low-latency mesh or hub-and-spoke topology between remote sites
- For both private and carrier-provided networks

Figure 7-5 *Frame Relay Provides a Cost-Effective, High-Speed Connection Between Remote Offices*

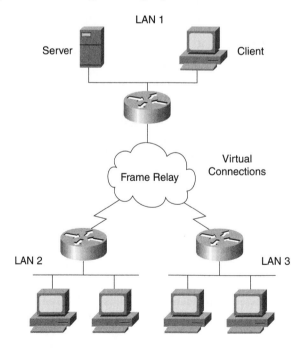

X.25

X.25, shown in Figure 7-6, is used in the following applications:

- As a reliable WAN circuit or backbone
- As support for legacy applications

Figure 7-6   *X.25 Provides a Reliable WAN Backbone*

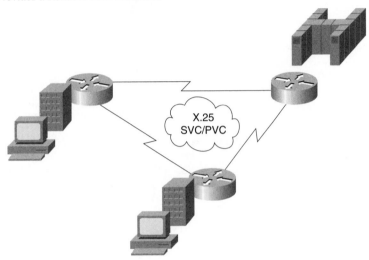

ATM

ATM, shown in Figure 7-7, is used in the following applications:

- As support for accelerating bandwidth requirements
- As support for multiple Quality of Service (QoS) classes for differing application requirements for delay and loss

Figure 7-7 *ATM Provides a High Bandwidth Core Layer*

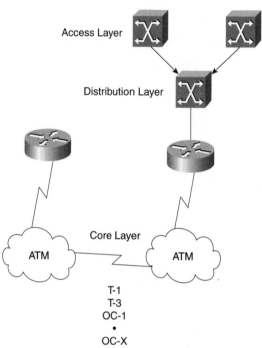

Extending into the WAN

An evolution in networking is occurring in WANs where private businesses and public service providers are deploying a new generation of switching systems. Frame Relay has emerged as the technology of choice for mesh as well as hub-and-spoke topologies. Frame Relay is revolutionizing the data networking infrastructure of corporations and small businesses. The statistical nature of the service means that nationwide networks supporting reasonable speeds can be cost effective.

The area of greatest growth in today's WANs is dialup. With 28.8 kbps (and now 56 kbps) modems and the availability of ISDN, PC users have become mobile. They have remote access to both the Internet and corporate LANs. Some carriers and many Internet service providers are building dialup infrastructures for Internet and telecommuting applications.

Selecting Cisco Hardware for Small- to Medium-Sized Networks

When provisioning Cisco hardware, use the following documents and tools to gather information on ports, interfaces, slots, memory, processors, power supplies, prices, and so on:

- The *Cisco Product Selection Tool*, available at http://www.cisco.com/romeo/select.htm.

- The *Products Quick Reference Guide*, available at http://www.cisco.com/univercd/cc/td/doc/cpqrg/index.htm.

- Cisco Price list (to obtain a copy of the current Cisco price list, log in to the Cisco Reseller's Web site. You will require a reseller account to do this).

Provisioning Interface Description Blocks on Cisco Routers

On Cisco routers, Interface Description Blocks (IDBs) provide a central location in memory for storing information about network interface cards for use by interface driver code.

An IDB must be able to represent all kinds of interfaces, including subinterfaces. Therefore, IDB data structures use a lot of memory. To avoid problems with memory usage, the Cisco IOS™ software limits the number of IDBs. The current IDB limit is 300 per router.

Each physical interface on the router, whether it is configured or not and whether it is active or shut down, uses up one IDB.

Each configured channel on a channelized interface (such as the MultiChannel Interface Processor, MIP) uses one IDB. For example, if an MIP T1 port has 24 configured channels, the interface uses a total of 24 IDBs.

Each configured subinterface also uses one IDB. For example, if a Fast Serial Interface Processor (FSIP) port configured for Frame Relay has 10 configured subinterfaces, the interface uses a total of 11 IDBs (one for the physical interface and one each for the subinterfaces).

Subinterfaces use IDBs, but Frame Relay permanent virtual circuits (PVCs) do not. For example, if a Frame Relay interface has 10 PVCs but does not use any subinterfaces, it uses only a single IDB. If a Frame Relay interface has two subinterfaces, each terminating five PVCs (for a total of 10 PVCs at the interface), it uses three IDBs (one for the physical interface, and one for each of the subinterfaces).

Router Switching Modes

When designing routed networks, take into account the switching (forwarding) mode the router uses to forward packets. Generally, small- to medium-sized networks use either process switching or fast switching. The larger Cisco 7000 series routers also support other advanced switching modes. The following sections explain the different switching modes available:

- Process Switching
- Fast Switching
- Autonomous Switching
- Silicon Switching
- Optimum Switching
- Distributed Switching
- NetFlow Switching

Process Switching

In process switching, the router examines the incoming packet and looks up the Layer 3 address in the routing table located in main memory to associate this address with a destination network or subnet. Process switching is a scheduled process that is performed by the system processor. Process switching is slow compared to other switching modes because it is delayed by the latency caused by scheduling and the latency within the process itself.

An inbound access list (discussed in detail in Chapter 10, "Provisioning Software Features") is an example of something that may be process switched because, normally, each packet must be examined individually and compared to an access list; however, later versions of the Cisco IOS™ now allow access lists to be fast switched. Compression or encryption of packets are also examples of when process switching is used. Anything that requires router processor cycles is process switched. Process switching slows down the network and increases the CPU utilization values.

Fast Switching

With this type of switching, an incoming packet matches an entry in the fast-switching cache (also called the route cache) located in main memory. This cache is populated when the first packet to the destination is process switched. Fast switching is done via asynchronous interrupts, which are handled in real time.

Fast switching results in higher throughput because:

- It uses the cache created by previous packets.
- It runs at the interrupt level.
- The route cache is usually much shorter than a routing table, so the searching takes less time.

Autonomous Switching

With this type of switching, an incoming packet matches an entry in the autonomous-switching cache located on the interface processor. Autonomous switching provides faster packet switching by allowing the ciscoBus controller to switch packets independently without having to interrupt the system processor. It is available only on Cisco 7000 series routers and in AGS+ systems with high-speed network controller cards.

Silicon Switching

With silicon switching, an incoming packet matches an entry in the silicon-switching cache located in the Silicon Switching Engine (SSE) of the Silicon Switch Processor (SSP) module. This module is available only on Cisco 7000 series routers. Silicon switching provides very fast, dedicated packet switching by allowing the SSE to switch packets independently without needing to interrupt the CPU.

Optimum Switching

Optimum switching is available on the Route/Switch Processor (RSP) only, on Cisco 7500 series routers. Optimum switching is similar to fast switching, but is faster. Even though optimum switching does not have a dedicated switching engine such as the SSE, it is nonetheless almost twice as fast as fast switching and almost as fast as silicon switching. This speed is the result of major enhancements in the cache data structure and caching algorithm, the use of certain interface processors to perform packet classification, and the speed and power of the RSP module.

Distributed Switching

On Cisco 7500 series routers with a Route Switch Processor (RSP) and with Versatile Interface Processor (VIP) controllers, the VIP hardware can be configured to switch packets received by the VIP with no per-packet intervention on the part of the RSP. This process is called *distributed switching*. Distributed switching decreases the demand on the RSP.

NetFlow Switching

NetFlow switching identifies traffic flows between internetwork hosts and then, on a connection-oriented basis, switches packets in these flows at the same time that it applies relevant services, such as security, QoS, and traffic accounting. Chapter 3, "Characterizing the Existing Network," has more details on NetFlow switching.

Choosing a Router Platform

Based on the current network and future needs, you should be able to determine which router platform will provide the performance, capacity, and scalability that your customer requires.

In the past, much emphasis was put on the packets-per-second (pps) forwarding rate of routers. Today, less emphasis is placed on pps because routers can process packets so quickly, especially with the newer switching technologies.

To gain an understanding of the significance of pps measurements, the methods for calculating pps capabilities, and the performance of Cisco routers, read the *Router Performance Design and Implementation Guide* in Appendix E, written by Merike Kaeo from the Enterprise Technical Marketing group at Cisco. This clear and concise guide provides accurate and crucial information on router performance and includes pps statistics for some Cisco router platforms.

Provisioning WANs

This section discusses the provisioning of WANs, including the following items:

- **Digital Hierarchy**—Covers the standards for WAN signaling
- **Provisioning Frame Relay networks**—Discusses the steps involved in selecting the router platform for your Frame Relay connection
- **Traffic Shaping over Frame Relay**—Covers the features that provide improved performance on a Frame Relay network

Digital Hierarchy

WAN bandwidth is often provisioned in the United States using the North American Digital Hierarchy, depicted in Table 7-1. Each format is called a digital stream (DS). The lower-numbered digital streams are multiplexed into the higher-numbered digital streams within a certain frequency tolerance. A DS0 is a 64 kbps stream. The term T1 is often used colloquially to refer to a DS1 signal. The term T3 is often used to refer to a DS3 signal. Similar hierarchies have also been developed in Europe and Japan. The term E1 refers to a 2.048 Mbps signal in Europe. The term J1 refers to a 2.048 Mbps signal in Japan.

Table 7-1   *Signaling Standards*

Line Type	Signal Standard	Number of DS0s	Bit Rate
T1[*]	DS1	24	1.544 Mbps
T3[*]	DS3	672	44.736 Mbps
E1[**]	2M	30	2.048 Mbps
E3[**]	M3	480	34.064 Mbps
J1[***]	Y1	30	2.048 Mbps

*The T1/T3 format is used primarily in North America and parts of Asia.

**The E1/E3 format is used in most of the rest of the world.

***The J1 format is used primarily in Japan.

Provisioning Frame Relay Networks

Complete the following steps to provision Frame Relay links:

Step 1   Choose a committed information rate (CIR) based on realistic, anticipated traffic rates

Step 2   Aggregate all CIRs to determine core bandwidth required

Step 3   Determine the link speed and number of interfaces required on the core router

Step 4   Choose a router platform that can handle the job

Each of these steps is expanded in the sections that follow.

Step 1: Choose a Committed Information Rate Based on Realistic, Anticipated Traffic Rates

Step 1 involves the following items:

- Determine how much interactive, file transfer, and broadcast traffic the link must support.

- Use Cisco IOS™ Release 11.2 and later Frame Relay traffic-shaping features for predictability (refer to the section on these features later in this chapter).

- If you opt for an inexpensive zero CIR, try to get a service level agreement from your provider.

Step 2: Aggregate All CIRs to Determine Core Bandwidth Required

Step 2 involves the following items:

- Add up the CIRs used at each access site.
- If an access site has a zero CIR, use half of the link speed as a rough estimate.

Step 3: Determine the Link Speed and Number of Interfaces Required on the Core Router

Step 3 involves the following items:

- Determine the required number of interfaces and the number of data-link connection identifiers (DLCIs) each interface should handle.
- If there are multiple protocols, decrease the number of DLCIs per interface.
- If the applications use many broadcasts, consider static routes and SAP filtering.

Step 4: Choose a Router Platform that Can Handle the Job.

Step 4 involves the following items:

- Consider processing and memory requirements and interface density.
- For example, if you have 10 access sites, each provisioned with a 32 kbps CIR, you will need 320 kbps bandwidth. You can use a router with one T1/E1 port utilizing ten DLCIs.

Traffic Shaping over Frame Relay

The Frame Relay Traffic Shaping feature (in Cisco IOS™ Release 11.2 and later) eliminates bottlenecks in Frame Relay network topologies by providing high-speed connections at the central site and low-speed connections at the branch sites.

The Frame Relay protocol defines the following parameters that are useful for managing network traffic congestion:

- Committed information rate (CIR)
- Forward/Backward Explicit Congestion Notification (FECN/BECN)
- Discard Eligibility (DE) bit

Prior to IOS release 11.2, Cisco provided support for FECN for DECnet and OSI, BECN for SNA traffic using direct LLC2 encapsulation via RFC 1490, and DE bit support.

The Frame Relay Traffic Shaping feature provides the following additional capabilities to improve scalability and performance on a Frame Relay network:

- Rate Enforcement on a per-virtual circuit (VC) basis
- Generalized BECN Support on a per-VC basis
- Priority/Custom Queuing (PQ/CQ) support at the VC level

Cisco IOS™ Release 11.3 has added the Frame Relay Router ForeSight feature.

These traffic shaping capabilities all require the router to buffer packets to control traffic flow and compute data rate tables. Because of this router memory and CPU utilization, these features must be used to regulate critical traffic flows while not degrading overall Frame Relay performance.

The sections that follow provide information on each of these capabilities.

Rate Enforcement on a Per-VC Basis

You can configure a peak rate to limit outbound traffic either to the CIR or to some other defined value, such as the excess information rate (EIR). Use rate enforcement to:

- Limit the rate at which data is sent to the VC at the central site.
- Improve performance in conjunction with the existing DLCI prioritization feature.
- Allow other criteria, such as the CIR, to control the router's transmission speed.
- Preallocate bandwidth to each VC, creating a virtual time-division multiplexing network.

Generalized BECN Support on a Per-VC Basis

The router can monitor BECNs and throttle traffic based on BECN marked packet feedback from the Frame Relay network. The traffic is dynamically throttled based on information contained in BECN-tagged packets received from the network.

With BECN-based throttling, packets are held in the router's buffers to reduce the data flow from the router into the Frame Relay network. The throttling is done on a per-VC basis, and the transmission rate is adjusted based on the number of BECN-tagged packets received.

PQ/CQ Support at the VC Level

The PQ/CQ support at the VC level feature allows for fine granularity in the prioritization and queuing of traffic, providing more control over the traffic flow on an individual VC. These features improve the scalability and performance of a Frame Relay network by increasing the density of virtual circuits and improving response time. The Frame Relay Traffic Shaping feature applies to Frame Relay PVCs and SVCs.

Custom queuing with the per-VC queuing and rate enforcement capabilities enable Frame Relay virtual circuits to be configured to carry multiple traffic types (such as IP, SNA, and IPX), with bandwidth guaranteed for each traffic type.

Frame Relay Router ForeSight

The Cisco IOS 11.3 and later releases include a new feature called ForeSight. Cisco's Web site at http://www.cisco.com/univercd/cc/td/doc/product/software/ios113ed/113ed_cr/wan_c/wcfrelay.htm#xtocid2343228 provides some details on ForeSight:

ForeSight is the network traffic control software used in Cisco StrataCom switches. The Cisco StrataCom Frame Relay switch can extend ForeSight messages over a User-to-Network Interface (UNI), passing the backward congestion notification for virtual circuits.

The Router ForeSight feature allows Cisco Frame Relay routers to process and react to ForeSight messages and adjust virtual circuit level traffic shaping in a timely manner.

Router ForeSight must be configured explicitly on both the Cisco router and the Cisco StrataCom switch. When ForeSight is enabled on the StrataCom switch, the switch will periodically send out a ForeSight message based on the time value configured. The time interval can range from 40 to 5000 milliseconds.

When a Cisco router receives a ForeSight message indicating that certain data-link connection identifiers (DLCIs) are experiencing congestion, the Cisco router reacts by activating its traffic shaping function to slow down the output rate. The router reacts as it would if it were to detect the congestion by receiving a packet with the Backward Explicit Congestion Notification (BECN) bit set.

The difference between the BECN and ForeSight congestion notification methods is that BECN requires a user packet to be sent in the direction of the congested DLCI to convey the signal. The sending of user packets is not predictable and, therefore, not reliable as a notification mechanism. Rather than waiting for user packets to provide the congestion notification, timed ForeSight messages guarantee that the router receives notification before congestion becomes a problem. Traffic can be slowed down in the direction of the congested DLCI.

Summary

In this chapter you learned about provisioning WAN media and devices, including which WANs are suited for various applications, and many details to be considered in your WAN designs. You learned how to provision WANs, including some of the advanced features available to manage your Frame Relay network. In the case studies that follow, you have the opportunity to apply what you have learned by recommending Cisco products and WAN technologies that meet customer's requirements.

In the next chapter in Part IV, you learn how to design a network layer addressing and naming model for your network, for IP and IPX protocols.

Case Studies

In this section, you are asked to provision hardware for the WANs for the four case studies introduced in Chapter 3.

Read each case study description and complete the questions for each.

TIP   As mentioned, in working through the questions to the case studies, you might find it useful to work on some note paper in a separate binder to accommodate the depth of these exercises.

After you complete each question, you can refer to the solutions provided by our internetworking experts in Appendix B. Keep in mind that there are potentially several correct answers to each question. These case studies and their solutions will help you prepare for the Sylvan CCDA exam following the course.

Case Study: CareTaker Publications

You might to review the CareTaker case study description in Appendix A, on page 303, before proceeding to answer the questions in this section.

CareTaker Case Study Questions

Refer to the topology drawing you created for CareTaker Publications in Chapter 3 or review the topology drawing solution provided in Appendix B. In this section you will provision WAN hardware and media for CareTaker Publications.

The parent company HI has advised Mr. Smith that the CareTaker headquarter's router will soon need additional functionality, but it will not make firm recommendations on the media, protocols, or type of interface until next year.

If you have Internet access, use the *Cisco Product Selection Tool* as detailed at the beginning of the Case Studies section in Chapter 6, clicking on the *access routers/servers* selection. Once you have the short list of products from this tool, select the right product to meet this customer's needs.

Question 7-1

Which router would you select for the warehouse?

Question 7-2

Which router would you select for the headquarters office?

Question 7-3

Update your topology diagram from Chapter 3 to reflect your media, LAN, and WAN hardware selections.

Question 7-4

Can you recommend any third-party products for the load-sharing CSU (multiplexer) and the Open Connect gateway products?

Case Study: PH Network Services Corporation

You may wish to review the PH Network Services Corporation case study description in Appendix A, on page 306, before proceeding to answer the questions in this section.

PH Network Services Corporation Case Study Questions

Refer to the topology drawing you created for Mr. Pero in Chapter 3 or review the topology drawing solution provided in Appendix B. In this section, you will provision WAN hardware and media for PH Network.

If you have Internet access, use the *Cisco Product Selection Tool* as detailed at the beginning of the Case Studies section in Chapter 6, clicking on the *access routers/servers* selection. Once you have the short list of products from this tool, select the right product to meet this customer's needs.

Question 7-5

Which router would you select for the main office?

Question 7-6

Which router would you select for the hospitals?

Question 7-7

Which router would you select for the doctors' offices?

Question 7-8

Update your topology diagram from Chapter 3 to reflect your media, LAN, and WAN hardware selections.

Case Study: Pretty Paper Limited

You might want to review the Pretty Paper Limited case study in Appendix A, page 307, before proceeding to answer the questions in this section.

Pretty Paper Limited Case Study Questions

Refer to the topology drawing you created for Pretty Paper in Chapter 3 or review the topology drawing solution provided in Appendix B. In this section, you will provision WAN hardware and media for Pretty Paper.

If you have Internet access, use the *Cisco Product Selection Tool* as detailed at the beginning of the Case Studies section in Chapter 6, clicking on the *access routers/servers* selection. Once you have the short list of products from this tool, select the right product to meet this customer's needs.

Question 7-9

Which router would you select for the main office?

Question 7-10

Which router would you select for the sales offices?

Question 7-11

Which router would you select to provide Internet access?

Question 7-12

The manager of Warehouse and Distribution is concerned about PC clients over the Frame Relay network to the new business software on the HP9000 system. What design constraints and considerations will you take into account to address these concerns?

Question 7-13

Getting products manufactured and delivered to customers is the company's biggest concern. Therefore, it is imperative that the manufacturing/warehouse facilities have uninterrupted access to the HP9000. What modifications, if any, would you make to your design to accommodate fail-safe operations of the warehouses?

Question 7-14

Update your topology diagram from Chapter 3 to reflect your media, LAN, and WAN hardware selections.

Case Study: Jones, Jones, & Jones

You might want to review the Jones, Jones, & Jones case study in Appendix A, page 308, before proceeding to answer the questions in this section.

Jones, Jones, & Jones Case Study Questions

Refer to the topology drawing you created for Ms. Jones in the Chapter 3 or review the topology drawing solution provided in Appendix B. In this section, you will provision WAN hardware and media for Ms. Jones.

If you have Internet access, use the *Cisco Product Selection Tool* as detailed at the beginning of the Case Studies section in Chapter 6, clicking on the *access routers/servers* selection. Once you have the short list of products from this tool, select the right product to meet this customer's needs.

Question 7-15

Which router would you select for the first office?

Question 7-16

Which router would you select for offices 2 and 3?

Question 7-17

Which router would you select for the international offices?

Question 7-18

Update your topology diagram from Chapter 3 to reflect your media, LAN, and WAN hardware selections.

You will need approximately three hours to read this chapter and complete its exercises. Upon completion of this fourth chapter in Part IV, you will be able to do the following:

- Propose an addressing model for the customer's areas, networks, subnetworks, and end stations that meets scalability requirements.
- Propose a plan for configuring addresses.
- Propose a naming scheme for servers, routers, and user stations.

CHAPTER 8

Designing a Network Layer Addressing and Naming Model

This chapter includes some tables and other job aids you will find useful when completing the case studies at the end of the chapter. References to some WWW sites are also included; relevant information has been extracted from these sites and is provided in the chapter. If you have access to the Internet, you might want to access the sites mentioned to obtain detailed information related to specific topics. All the sites referenced in this chapter are also listed in Appendix C, "Interesting WWW Links and Other Suggested Readings."

Follow these steps to complete this chapter:

1 Study the chapter content, including any tables and job aids that appear.

2 Review the case studies at the end of this chapter.

3 Complete the questions in each case study.

4 Review the answers provided by our internetworking experts in Appendix B, "Answers to Chapter Questions, Case Studies, and Sample CCDA Exam."

Designing network layer addressing and naming is one of the most important tasks in internetwork design. It is closely linked with selecting a routing protocol, which is discussed in the next chapter, "Selecting Routing and Bridging Protocols." This chapter discusses some specifics for IP addressing, including variable-length subnet masking, route summarization, private addressing, and address translation, and some specifics for IPX addressing. The steps to follow when designing this aspect of your network are then identified.

IP Addressing

Recall that IP addresses are 32 bits, as shown in Figure 8-1. The 32 bits are grouped into four sets of eight bits (octets), separated by dots, and represented in decimal format; this is known as dotted decimal notation. As in all network layer addresses, part of a device's address represents the network, and part identifies the host number that this device is on that network. IP networks can also be subdivided into subnetworks.

Figure 8-1 *IP Addresses Are 32 Bits, Written in Dotted Decimal Format*

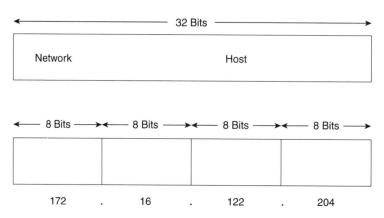

IP addressing defines five address classes: A, B, C, D, and E. Only Classes A, B, and C are available for addressing devices; Class D is used for multicast groups, and Class E is reserved for experimental use.

The first octet of an address defines its class, as illustrated in Table 8-1. The bits that represent network and subnet information in an IP address are known as the *prefix*; the number of such bits is known as the *prefix length*. The *Prefix Length* column in Table 8-1 indicates the default prefix lengths for the three classes of addresses.

Table 8-1 *IP Address Classes A, B, and C Are Available for Addressing Devices*

Class	Format (N= network number, H= host number)	Prefix Length	Higher-Order Bit(s)	Address Range
Class A	N.H.H.H	8 bits	0	1.0.0.0 to 126.0.0.0
Class B	N.N.H.H	16 bits	10	128.0.0.0 to 191.255.0.0
Class C	N.N.N.H	24 bits	110	192.0.0.0 to 223.255.255.0

Reference: RFC 1700, available at http://info.internet.isi.edu/in-notes/rfc/files/rfc1700.txt

A prefix identifies a block of host numbers and is used for routing to that block. According to RFC 1518, *An Architecture for IP Address Allocation with CIDR*, available at http://info.internet.isi.edu/in-notes/rfc/files/rfc1518.txt, a prefix is "an IP address and some indication of the leftmost contiguous significant bits within that address." The indication of the leftmost contiguous bits has traditionally been done with an indication of the address class and a subnet mask. More recently, a length indication has followed a network number and slash. For example, 172.16.168.0/21 indicates that the most significant 21 bits are the prefix; this is equivalent to the address 172.16.168.0 with the subnet mask of 255.255.248.0.

Further information about IP addressing is available in Chapter 1, "Internetworking Technology Review," and in the *Basic IP Addressing and Troubleshooting Guide*, available at http://www.cisco.com/warp/public/779/smbiz/service/troubleshooting/ts_ip.htm.

Classful and Classless Routing Protocols, and Variable-Length Subnet Masking

A *major network* is a Class A, B, or C network; usually, major networks are subnetted to allow the IP addresses to be allocated more efficiently. Traditional *classful routing protocols* (for example, RIP and IGRP) do not transmit any information about the prefix length. When receiving information about routes within the same major network, hosts and routers assume the same prefix length as that on the incoming interface of the route information. Classful routing protocols therefore do not accommodate different prefix lengths being used within a major network.

When receiving information about routes in a different major network, hosts and routers running a classful routing protocol calculate the prefix length by looking at the first few bits of the address to determine the class of the address, as specified in Table 8-1. The prefix length associated with that class of address is then assumed.

Classless routing protocols (for example, OSPF), on the other hand, do include the prefix length with routing updates; routers running classless routing protocols do not have to determine the prefix themselves. Therefore, different prefix lengths within a major network are allowed; this is called variable-length subnet masking (VLSM).

VLSM relies on providing prefix length information explicitly with each use of an address. The length of the prefix is evaluated independently at each place it is used. The capability to have a different prefix length at different points supports more efficient use of the IP address space and reduces routing traffic. Efficient addressing of large subnets (for example, an Ethernet with many hosts) and small subnets (for example, a point-to-point serial line with only two hosts) are allowed. If the small subnets are grouped, routing information can be summarized (aggregated) into fewer routing table entries.

Designing IP Addressing to Facilitate Route Summarization

Whether using VLSM or not, when designing IP addressing it is important to design route summarization, also referred to as *route aggregation* or *supernetting*.

With route summarization, one route in the routing table represents many other routes. Summarizing routes reduces the number of routes in the routing table, the routing update traffic, and overall router overhead.

Reducing routing update traffic can be very important on low-speed lines. If the Internet had not adapted route summarization by standardizing on classless interdomain routing (CIDR), it would not have survived.

NOTE   Classless interdomain routing (CIDR) is a mechanism developed to help alleviate the problem of exhaustion of IP addresses. The idea behind CIDR is that multiple Class C addresses can be combined, or aggregated, to create a larger (that is, more hosts allowed) classless set of IP addresses. CIDR is described in RFC 1519, *Classless Inter-Domain Routing (CIDR): an Address Assignment and Aggregation Strategy*, available at: http://info.internet.isi.edu/in-notes/rfc/files/rfc1519.txt.

The telephone architecture has handled *prefix routing*, or routing based only on the prefix part of the address, for many years. For example, as shown in Figure 8-2, a telephone switch in Detroit, Michigan does not need to know how to reach a specific line in Portland, Oregon. It just needs to recognize that the call is not local. A long-distance carrier needs to recognize that 503 is for Oregon but does not need to know the details of how to reach the specific line in Oregon.

Figure 8-2   *The Telephone Network Uses Prefix Routing; a Switch Does Not Need to Know How to Reach Every Specific Line*

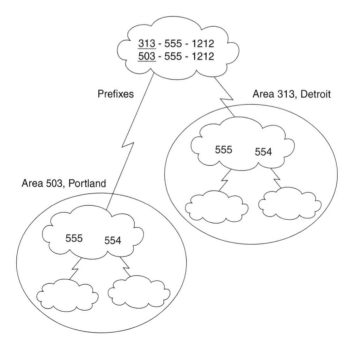

Prefix routing is not new in the IP environment either. A router needs to know only how to reach the next hop. It does not need to know the details of how to reach an end node that is not local. Much as in the telephone example, IP routers make hierarchical decisions. Recall that an IP address is comprised of a prefix part and a host part. Routers use the prefix to determine the path for a destination address that is not local. The host part is used to reach local hosts.

For summarization to work correctly, the following requirements must be met:

- Multiple IP addresses must share the same leftmost bits.
- Routers must base their routing decisions on a 32-bit IP address and a prefix length that can be up to 32 bits.
- Routing protocols must carry the prefix length with the 32-bit IP address.

As an example, assume that a router has the following networks behind it:

192.108.168.0
192.108.169.0
192.108.170.0
192.108.171.0
192.108.172.0
192.108.173.0
192.108.174.0
192.108.175.0

Each of these networks could be advertised separately; however, this would mean advertising eight routes. Instead, this router can summarize the eight routes into one route, and advertise 192.108.168.0/21. By advertising this one route, the router is saying, *"Route packets to me if the destination has the first 21 bits the same as the first 21 bits of 192.108.168.0."*

Figure 8-3 illustrates how this summary route is determined. The addresses all have the first 21 bits in common and include all the combinations of the other 3 bits in the network portion of the address; therefore, only the first 21 bits are needed to determine if the router can route to one of these specific addresses.

Figure 8-3   *To Summarize Routes, Find the Common Bits*

192.108.168.0 =	11000000 01101100 10101	000	00000000
192.108.169.0 =	11000000 01101100 10101	001	00000000
192.108.170.0 =	11000000 01101100 10101	010	00000000
192.108.171.0 =	11000000 01101100 10101	011	00000000
192.108.172.0 =	11000000 01101100 10101	100	00000000
192.108.173.0 =	11000000 01101100 10101	101	00000000
192.108.174.0 =	11000000 01101100 10101	110	00000000
192.108.175.0 =	11000000 01101100 10101	111	00000000

Number of Common Bits = 21
Number of Non-Common Network Bits = 3
Number of Host Bits = 8

Changing IP Addresses

IP addresses used by organizations are likely to undergo changes for a variety of reasons, including the following:

- Enterprise reorganization (for example, people move to different workgroups)
- Physical moving of equipment
- New strategic relationships (for example, merging with another company and merging the networks as well)
- Changing of the Internet service provider (ISP) used to connect to the Internet
- New applications
- The needs of global Internet connectivity (for example, connecting a network to the Internet that was previously standalone)
- Route summarization implementation (for example, redesigning the addressing of your network to facilitate summarization, as elaborated earlier in this chapter)

Therefore, network designers need to devise IP addressing schemes that allow for changes and growth.

Howard Berkowitz, an engineer with a Cisco Training Partner, and Paul Ferguson, a Cisco consulting engineer, have written a document on IP renumbering titled *Network Renumbering Overview: Why would I want it and what is it anyway?* This paper is available at http://info.internet.isi.edu/in-notes/rfc/files/rfc2071.txt.

Howard Berkowitz has also written a helpful draft RFC that outlines the steps for router renumbering titled *Router Renumbering Guide.* It is available at http://info.internet.isi.edu/in-notes/rfc/files/rfc2072.txt.

IP Addressing with Cisco's DNS/DHCP Manager

In IP environments, names of devices are mapped to addresses using the Domain Name Service (DNS) protocol. Addresses can be dynamically assigned using the Dynamic Host Configuration Protocol (DHCP). Cisco has a DNS/DHCP Manager that enables you to synchronize DNS names with addresses dynamically assigned by DHCP. Cisco's product catalog available at http://www.cisco.com/univercd/cc/td/doc/pcat has a section on the DNS/DHCP Manager. Excerpts from this section are reproduced here:

The Cisco DNS/DHCP Manager is a suite of TCP/IP management applications that manage domain names and synchronize IP addresses between a Domain Name System (DNS) server and a Dynamic Host Configuration Protocol (DHCP). The Cisco DNS/DHCP Manager includes the Domain Name Manager—a graphical DNS management tool—and a DHCP server that dynamically updates DNS with IP addresses assigned to DHCP clients. The Cisco DNS/DHCP Manager also includes a DNS server, Trivial File Transfer Protocol (TFTP) server, Network Time Protocol (NTP) server, and a Syslog server.

Managing a large TCP/IP network requires maintaining accurate and up-to-date IP address and domain name information. Today, organizations are forced to manage IP address and domain name information by manually modifying several databases. Organizations maintain IP address and domain name information in DNS servers' text-based configuration files. DHCP servers further complicate the situation by dynamically assigning domain names and IP addressees to nodes on the network. Organizations are therefore forced to manually synchronize the configuration of DNS and DHCP servers. Incorrect IP addresses and domain names can cause problems for people using the World Wide Web, a Network File System (NFS), FTP, and e-mail. The Cisco DNS/DHCP Manager eliminates the need for manually configuring and synchronizing DNS and DHCP servers.

The Cisco DNS/DHCP Manager is designed for the following applications:

- Managing DNS
  - Organizations currently manage DNS by editing configuration files that have a complex syntax. This process is time-consuming and subject to error. The Domain Name Manager browser reduces common configuration errors by checking the syntax of each new entry. The Domain Name Manager is easy to learn, and more people in an organization can use it to manage DNS.
  - The Cisco DHCP server automatically updates the Domain Name Manager with the IP address and domain name of the new nodes on the network. The Domain Name Manager then propagates this information to DNS servers on the network.
  - The Domain Name Manager replaces an organization's existing primary DNS server and becomes the source of DNS information for the entire network.
- DHCP in a switched network
  - The Cisco DHCP server allows organizations to use DHCP in a large switched network. The depletion of IP addresses on the Internet has forced organizations to use classless inter-domain routing (CIDR) blocks or groups of Class C network numbers to build physical networks with more than 256 nodes. This has created a problem for network administrators who want to use DHCP on large switched networks with more than 256 nodes.
  - Organizations building large switched networks with TCP/IP assign multiple logical IP networks on a single physical switched network. At the same time, organizations want to take advantage of DHCP to dynamically configure a large number of PCs on their network. The Cisco DHCP server supports address pools that contain multiple logical networks on the same physical network.
- TCP/IP servers for Windows NT
  - The Cisco DNS/DHCP Manager has a complete range of TCP/IP services used to build and maintain a TCP/IP network. The Cisco DNS/DHCP Manager provides a DNS server for name service, an NTP server for time synchronization, TFTP to load binary images and configuration files to network devices (including Cisco routers and switches), and a syslog server for logging error messages from network devices over the network. All these services are easily configured with a graphical user interface.

Private Addresses and Network Address Translation

Private addresses are reserved IP addresses to be used only internally within a company's network. These private addresses are not to be used on the Internet and therefore must be mapped to a company's external registered address when sending anything on the Internet.

RFC 1918, *Address Allocation for Private Internets*, available at http://info.internet.isi.edu/in-notes/rfc/files/rfc1918.txt, defines the private IP addresses.

The private IP addresses are as follows:

> 10.0.0.0 to 10.255.255.255
> 172.16.0.0 to 172.31.255.255
> 192.168.0.0 to 192.168.255.255

Network Address Translation (NAT) is a feature in the Cisco IOS™ Release 11.2 software that enables you to translate private addresses into registered IP addresses only when needed, thereby reducing the need for registered IP addresses.

When using NAT, the terms *inside* and *outside* networks are used, as shown in the example in Figure 8-4. Table 8-2 defines the terminology for NAT, as used in Figure 8-4.

Figure 8-4   *Network Address Translation Is Used to Translate Addresses Between the* Inside *and* Outside *Networks*

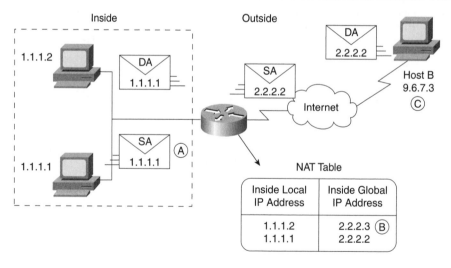

Table 8-2   *NAT Terminology*

Term	Definition
Inside Local IP Address (A)	The IP address assigned to a host on the inside network. The address was globally unique but obsolete, allocated from RFC 1918, *Address Allocation for Private Internet Space*, or randomly picked.
Inside Global IP Address (B)	A legitimate IP address (assigned by the NIC or service provider) that represents one or more inside local IP addresses to the outside world. The address was allocated from globally unique address space, typically provided by the ISP.
Outside Global IP Address (C)	The IP address that was assigned to a host on the outside network by its owner. The address was allocated from a globally routable address space.
Outside Local IP Address (not shown)	The IP address of an outside host as it appears to the inside network. The address was allocated from address space routable on the inside, or possibly allocated from RFC 1918, for example.

Cisco supported NAT features include the following:

- **Static address translation**—Establishes a one-to-one mapping between inside local and global addresses.

- **Dynamic source address translation**—Establishes a dynamic mapping between the inside local and global addresses. This is accomplished by describing the local addresses to be translated, the pool of addresses from which to allocate global addresses, and associating the two. The router will create translations as needed.

- **Address overloading**—Conserves addresses in the inside global address pool by allowing source ports in TCP connections or UDP conversations to be translated. When different inside local addresses map to the same inside global address, each inside host's TCP or UDP port numbers are used to distinguish between them.

- **TCP load distribution**—A dynamic form of destination translation that can be configured for some outside-to-inside traffic. Once a mapping is defined, destination addresses matching an access list are replaced with an address from a rotary pool. Allocation is done on a round-robin basis, and only when a new connection is opened from the outside to the inside. All non-TCP traffic will be passed untranslated (unless other translations are in effect).

For details of NAT operation and configuration see Appendix H, "Network Address Translation."

Dynamic Router IP Addressing

Routers usually are configured with fixed, static IP addresses, while PCs and other hosts may be assigned dynamic addresses. Easy IP is a feature available on selected routers beginning with Cisco IOS™ Release 11.3 that includes dynamic WAN interface IP address negotiation for routers, thereby reducing router configuration tasks and conserving IP addresses.

Details on the Easy IP feature are available on Cisco's web site at http://www.cisco.com/warp/customer/cc/cisco/mkt/ios/nat/tech/ezip1_wp.htm. Excerpts from this web site are reproduced here:

Cisco IOS Easy IP is a combination of the following functionality:

- Port Address Translation (PAT), a subset of Network Address Translation (NAT)
- Dynamic PPP/IPCP WAN interface IP address negotiation
- Cisco IOS DHCP Server

With Cisco IOS Easy IP, router configuration tasks are minimized: simply plug-in the router, configure the dialup number for a central access server, and connect the LAN devices to the router. With Cisco IOS Easy IP, a Cisco router automatically assigns local IP addresses to SOHO hosts via the Dynamic Host Configuration Protocol (DHCP) with the Cisco IOS DHCP Server, automatically negotiates its own registered IP address from a central server via the Point-to-Point Protocol/Internet Control Protocol (PPP/IPCP), and uses Port Address Translation (PAT) functionality to enable all SOHO hosts to access the global Internet using a single registered IP address. Because Cisco IOS Easy IP utilizes existing port-level multiplexed Network Address Translation (NAT) functionality within Cisco IOS software, IP addresses on the remote LAN are invisible to the Internet, making the remote LAN more secure.

IPX Addressing

A Novell Internetwork Packet Exchange (IPX) address has two parts: the network number and the node number. An IPX address is 80 bits long, with 32 bits (4 octets, or 8 hexadecimal digits) for the network number and 48 bits (6 octets, or 12 hexadecimal digits) for the node number. The node number is typically derived from the Media Access Control (MAC) address of an interface. IPX addresses are written in hexadecimal digits.

IPX Address Example

Figure 8-5 illustrates an example of IPX addressing.

Figure 8-5   *A Novell IPX Address Has Two Parts—the Network Number and the Node Number*

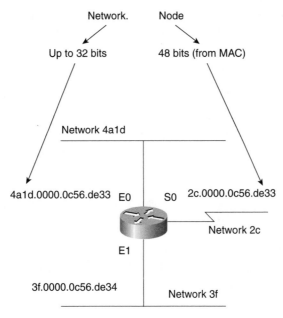

In the IPX example in Figure 8-5, the following is true:

- One IPX network has an address of 4a1d. Other IPX networks shown are 2c and 3f. Note that IPX network numbers are 32 bits long (8 hexadecimal digits), but you do not have to specify leading zeros.

- The IPX node number is 48 bits (12 hexadecimal digits) in length. This number is usually the MAC address obtained from a router interface that has a MAC address.

- The example features the IPX node 0000.0c56.de33. Another node address is 0000.0c56.de34.

- The same node number appears for both the E0 and S0 interfaces of the router. Serial interfaces do not have MAC addresses, so Novell IPX obtained this node number for S0 by using the MAC address from E0.

Each interface retains its own IPX address. The use of the MAC address in the logical address eliminates the need for an Address Resolution Protocol (ARP).

Selecting IPX Addresses

You must use a valid IPX network address when you configure a Cisco router. The IPX network address refers to the *wire*. All devices on the same wire, including routers, must share the same IPX network address.

Because the Novell NetWare networks are probably already established, customers will likely have existing IPX addresses. Determine the IPX address to use for the router using the existing IPX address scheme.

The first and recommended way to find out which network address to use is to ask the NetWare administrator. Make sure that the NetWare administrator specifies the IPX network address for the same network where you want to enable IPX on your Cisco router. The Cisco router must use the same network as the NetWare file server (or other source of the address) specified by the NetWare administrator.

If you cannot obtain an IPX address to use from the NetWare administrator, you can get the neighbor's IPX address directly from a neighbor router. Use any one of the following methods to obtain the IPX address:

- If the neighbor router is another Cisco router, you can use the Cisco Discovery Protocol (CDP) to learn the neighbor's address. Use the **show cdp neighbor detail** command to view this information.

- You can Telnet to the neighbor router, enter the appropriate mode, then display the running configuration on the neighbor.

- If the neighbor router is not a Cisco router (for example, it is a NetWare PC-based router, or a NetWare file server), you may be able to attach or log in and use a NetWare utility *config* to determine the address.

Steps for Designing Network Layer Addressing and Naming

The features of IP and IPX addressing discussed in this chapter are used when designing the network layer addressing and naming of your network. This section identifies eight steps to use in this aspect of your design.

Step 1: Design a Hierarchy for Addressing

Design a hierarchy for addressing as follows:

- Autonomous systems
- Areas
- Networks
- Subnetworks
- End stations

The hierarchy that you use will depend on the network layer protocol and routing protocol that you are using.

Step 2: Design Route Summarization

Summarization, also known as *aggregation,* allows one route to represent many routes, resulting in smaller routing tables. Route summarization is discussed in detail earlier in this chapter.

Step 3: Design a Plan for Distributing Administrative Authority for Addressing and Naming at the Lower Levels of the Hierarchy

Once the high-level plan is made for the network, lower-level addressing and naming may be delegated. For example, if the client has offices in Europe and Asia, as well as North America, the authority to name devices and assign addresses, within established guidelines, could be divided along these geographical lines.

Step 4: Design a Method for Mapping Geographical Locations to Network Numbers

Assigning network numbers by geographical location will also aid in the summarization task. For example, the client who has offices in Europe, Asia, and North America could assign a range of addresses to each continent (with the authority to distribute addresses within the range resting within the appropriate continent office). The summarized address for each continent would then encompass the entire range of addresses assigned to that continent.

Step 5: Develop a Plan for Identifying Special Stations Such as Routers and Servers with Specific Node IDs

To facilitate troubleshooting, devices such as routers and servers should have fixed addresses. For example, all routers could have an IP address with the node part in the range of 1 through 19, while all servers have the node part of their addresses in the range of 20 through 29. Then, if during troubleshooting there is a problem with an address that has a node part of 25, it is immediately obvious that this address belongs to a server.

Step 6: Develop a Plan for Configuring User Station Addresses

For scalability, user station addresses should be assigned dynamically, rather than statically, if possible. Dynamic address assignment allows the automatic assignment of addresses from a pool of addresses as user stations join the network; the addresses are released back into the pool if the device leaves the network. This simplifies the network administrator's task of changing IP addresses on user stations when users move to a new location, for example.

Use the Bootstrap Protocol (BOOTP) or the newer Dynamic Host Configuration Protocol (DHCP) for dynamic IP address assignment. Cisco's DNS/DHCP Manager product, described earlier in this chapter, can be used to aid in this task.

Step 7: If Necessary, Develop a Plan for Using Gateways to Map Private Addresses to External Addresses

As noted earlier, private addresses are reserved IP addresses to be used only within a company's network. These private addresses are not to be used on the Internet and therefore must be mapped to a company's external addresses when sending anything on the Internet. Use the Cisco IOS Network Address Translation (NAT) feature described earlier in this chapter to do this mapping.

Step 8: Design a Scheme for Naming Servers, Routers, and User Stations

Names should be meaningful to facilitate troubleshooting. For example, in the company with offices in Europe, Asia, and North America, the router and server names could all start with an abbreviation of the continent: EUR, ASIA, and NA. This could be suffixed with the last octet of the device's node address—for example, ERU03 for a router. The user's PCs could all have names that start with the abbreviation for the continent, followed by the letters PC, a hyphen, and the user's first initial and last name. An example is EURPC-JSMITH.

To name devices in IP environments, install and configure DNS servers. Use Cisco's DNS/DHCP Manager, described earlier in this chapter, to synchronize DNS names with dynamically assigned IP addresses.

Summary

In this chapter you learned about IP addressing, including address classes, prefix lengths, and summarization. You also learned considerations for IPX addressing and identified steps for designing your network layer addressing and naming model. In the case studies that follow you have the opportunity to apply what you have learned to assign addresses and names for the networks.

The next chapter in Part IV reviews routing and bridging protocols and discusses how to select the right ones for your network.

Case Studies

In this section, you are asked to implement an addressing and naming scheme for the four case studies introduced in Chapter 3, "Characterizing the Existing Network," as well as for a new case study about Virtual University.

Read each case study description and complete the questions for each of the case studies.

TIP   As mentioned, in working through the questions to the case studies, you may find it useful to work on some note paper in a separate binder to accommodate the depth of these exercises.

After you complete each question, you can refer to the solutions provided by our internetworking experts in Appendix B. Keep in mind that there are potentially several correct answers to each question. These case studies and their solutions will help you prepare for the Sylvan CCDA exam following the course.

Case Study: Virtual University

Read the following short case study and answer the questions that follow.

Virtual University has decided to eliminate AppleTalk and use only IP. The university will use the IP network number 172.16.0.0. The university has a North Campus, Central Campus, and South Campus. Each campus has 40 networks and each network has 150 nodes. The network administrators expect to expand to 60 networks and 200 nodes per network within the next five years.

Because of its AppleTalk heritage, Virtual University needs a simple addressing solution with very little end-node configuration. Despite its AppleTalk heritage, Virtual University has some knowledgeable IP gurus who have specified that the addressing scheme must be conducive to route summarization (aggregation).

Virtual University Case Study Questions

Question 8-1

Design and describe a model for dividing up Virtual University's IP address space that will meet the university's current needs and needs for the next five years.

Question 8-2

Explain to the IP gurus at Virtual University how the addressing model that you designed in the previous step will support route summarization. For example, what network number and prefix could a border router at one of the campuses advertise to the other areas or backbone?

Question 8-3

What is special about IP address 172.16.0.0? What will Virtual University require to connect its network to the Internet?

Question 8-4

Propose a plan for naming servers, routers, and end nodes. Describe both the names themselves and the method you will use to configure the names.

Case Study: CareTaker Publications

You might want to review the CareTaker case study description in Appendix A, "Case Studies," page 303, before proceeding to answer the questions in this section.

CareTaker Case Study Questions

Refer to the topology drawing you created for CareTaker Publications in Chapter 3 or review the topology drawing solution provided in Appendix B. In this section you will design an addressing scheme for the network.

The parent corporation, Holdings International (HI), told CareTaker that CareTaker will be protected from Internet "hackers" with a firewall at the corporate facilities. HI has informed CareTaker that it will receive only one Class C address because of the limited number of IP addresses available. CareTaker is to implement *Big Internet* addressing (that is, addressing that will not restrict it from going on the Internet) within the confines of CareTaker.

Question 8-5

Design a model for CareTaker's IP address space that will meet the current needs and needs for the next five years. Describe your model here.

Question 8-6

Propose a plan for naming servers, routers, and end nodes. Describe both the names themselves and the method to be used to configure the names.

Question 8-7

Update your topology diagram to reflect your addressing scheme.

Case Study: PH Network Services Corporation

You may wish to review the PH Network Services Corporation case study description in Appendix A, page 306, before proceeding to answer the questions in this section.

PH Network Services Corporation Case Study Questions

Refer to the topology drawing you created for Mr. Pero in Chapter 3 or review the topology drawing solution provided in Appendix B. In this section, you will design an addressing scheme for the network.

Question 8-8

The hospital system has an existing IP network with its own IP addresses. The hospital will be able to assign two Class C addresses to the PH Network: one for the WAN (202.12.27.0) and one for PH's internal use (202.12.28.0). Describe your IP addressing plans for the implementation of PH's network. You will use a Class C mask of 255.255.255.0 for the PH LAN. What mask will you use for the WAN?

Question 8-9

Update your topology diagram to reflect the new addressing scheme.

Case Study: Pretty Paper Limited

You might want to review the Pretty Paper Limited case study in Appendix A, page 307, before proceeding to answer the questions in this section.

Pretty Paper Limited Case Study Questions

Refer to the topology drawing you created for Pretty Paper in Chapter 3 or review the topology drawing solution provided in Appendix B. In this section you will design an addressing scheme for the network.

Question 8-10

The network administrator has been using the Class B IP address of 199.151.0.0. He does not know where he got it but he is sure that Pretty Paper does not own it. What are your recommendations for an IP address allocation/assignment procedure?

Question 8-11

Propose a plan for naming servers, routers, and end nodes. Describe both the names themselves and the method you will use to configure the names.

Question 8-12

Update your topology diagram to reflect the new IP addressing scheme.

Question 8-13

Recommend an addressing scheme for the IPX network.

Question 8-14

Recommend an addressing scheme for the AppleTalk network.

Case Study: Jones, Jones, & Jones

You may wish to review the Jones, Jones, & Jones case study in Appendix A, page 308, befor proceeding to answer the questions in this section.

Jones, Jones, & Jones Case Study Questions

Refer to the topology drawing you created for Ms. Jones in Chapter 3 or review the topology drawing solution provided in Appendix B. In this section you will design an addressing schem for the network.

Question 8-15

Describe your IP addressing plans for implementation of your proposed system design.

Question 8-16

Propose a plan for naming servers, routers, and end nodes. Describe both the names themselve and the method that will be used to configure the names.

Question 8-17

The managing partner called. She wanted to emphasize that unauthorized workstations shoul not be allowed access to the Internet. How will you plan for this request in your design?

Question 8-18

Update your topology diagram to reflect the new addressing scheme.

It will take you approximately two hours to read this chapter and complete the exercises. Upon completion of this fifth chapter in Part IV, you will be able to do the following:

- Identify scalability constraints and issues for IGRP, Enhanced IGRP, IP RIP, OSPF, IPX RIP/SAP, NLSP, AppleTalk RTMP and AURP, static routing, and bridging protocols.

- Recommend routing and bridging protocols that meet a customer's requirements for performance, security, and capacity.

CHAPTER 9

Selecting Routing and Bridging Protocols

This chapter includes some tables and other job aids that you will find useful when completing the case studies at the end of the chapter. References to some Web sites are also included; relevant information has been extracted from these sites and is provided in the chapter. If you have access to the Internet, you might want to access the sites mentioned to obtain detailed information related to specific topics. All of the sites referenced in this chapter are also listed in Appendix C, "Interesting WWW Links and Other Suggested Readings."

Follow these steps to complete the chapter:

1 Study the chapter content, including any tables and job aids that appear.

2 Answer the multiple-choice questions at the end of this chapter.

3 Review the case studies at the end of this chapter.

4 Complete the questions in each case study.

5 Review the answers provided by our internetworking experts in Appendix B, "Answers to Chapter Questions, Case Studies, and Sample CCDA Exam."

Recall that routers communicate with each other using routing protocols to gather information about available networks and the distance or cost to reach those networks. Bridging protocols define how bridges communicate with each other. This chapter examines various characteristics of different protocols so that you can better select the ones to use in your networks.

You will see later in this chapter that one of the ways to characterize a routing protocol is to determine which of three categories it fits: link-state, distance vector, or hybrid. Recall from Chapter 1, "Internetworking Technology Review," that link-state routing protocols flood routing information to all nodes in the internetwork. Each router, however, sends only the portion of the routing table that describes the state of its own links. Distance vector protocols call for each router to send all or some portion of its routing table, but only to its neighbors. In essence, link-state protocols send small updates everywhere, while distance vector protocols send larger updates only to neighboring routers. Hybrid, or advanced, routing protocols send small updates only to neighboring routers.

The first sections in this chapter examine these three categories of routing protocols. Ways to characterize routing protocols and their scalability constraints are examined next. The chapter concludes with a discussion of bridging protocols and integrated routing and bridging (IRB).

Distance Vector Routing Protocols

Distance vector routers tell neighbors about all known routes. Generally, distance vector protocols are found in small- to medium-sized networks. Distance vector routers usually send the entire routing table, but some versions can be configured to send only updates. The following protocols are distance vector routing protocols:

* Internet Protocol (IP) Routing Information Protocol (RIP) (version 1 and version 2)
* Internetwork Packet Exchange (IPX) RIP
* Interior Gateway Routing Protocol (IGRP)
* AppleTalk Routing Table Maintenance Protocol (RTMP)

With distance vector routing, updates can be easily interpreted with a protocol analyzer that makes debugging easy. Unfortunately, it also makes it easy for a hacker to understand the protocol and compromise it.

NOTE   Because distance vector updates are quite simple, they are easy to understand. One way to prevent hackers from viewing these updates is not to use a routing protocol on networks outside of your control. For example, static routes may be the best way to implement routing to the Internet so that routing information is not sent on the network that connects you to the Internet.

When distance vector routing protocols are used, address consolidation is automatic at subnet and network boundaries. For example, RIP and IGRP always summarize routing information by major network numbers. As was discussed in Chapter 8, "Designing a Network Layer Addressing and Naming Model," these are called *classful routing protocols* because they always consider the IP network class. This has important results:

* Subnets are not advertised across a different major network
* Discontiguous subnets are not visible to each other
* Variable-length subnet masks (VLSMs) are not supported

NOTE   IP RIP version 2 does allow automatic address summarization to be turned off, thereby allowing it to be used with discontiguous subnets and VLSMs. IP RIP version 1 and IGRP do not allow summarization to be turned off.

The following section describes how routers running distance vector routing protocols update their routing tables and discusses some problems and solutions associated with these protocols. Then, each of the distance vector routing protocols is briefly described, including the steps they follow when they detect a network failure so that the network can again be converged. (*Convergence* is how routers arrive at a consistent understanding of the internetwork topology after a change takes place.)

Distance Vector Topology Changes

Distance vector routers discover networks by communicating with neighbor routers and accumulating metrics about networks from these neighbors. When the topology in a distance vector protocol internetwork changes, routing table updates must occur. As with the network discovery process, topology change updates proceed step-by-step from router to router, as shown in Figure 9-1.

Figure 9-1 *Distance Vector Topology Changes Proceed Step-by-Step from Router to Router*

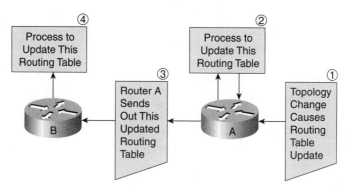

Distance vector algorithms call for each router to send its entire routing table to each of its adjacent neighbors. Distance vector routing tables include information about the total path cost (defined by its metric) and the logical address of the first router on the path to each network it knows about (also called the *next hop router*). For example, recall from Chapter 1 that IP RIP uses hop count as its metric. Example 9-1 displays a routing table from a router running RIP.

Example 9-1   *A Routing Table Shows the Metric and the Next Hop Router for Each Network*

```
Router>show ip route
Codes: C - connected, S - static, I - IGRP, R - RIP, M - mobile, B - BGP
       D - EIGRP, EX - EIGRP external, O - OSPF, IA - OSPF inter area
       E1 - OSPF external type 1, E2 - OSPF external type 2, E - EGP
       i - IS-IS, L1 - IS-IS level-1, L2 - IS-IS level-2, * - candidate default
Gateway of last resort is not set
R     153.50.0.0 [120/1] via 183.8.128.12, 00:00:09, Ethernet0
      183.8.0.0 is subnetted (mask is 255.255.255.128), 4 subnets
R        183.8.0.128 [120/1] via 183.8.128.130, 00:00:17, Serial0
         [120/1] via 183.8.64.130, 00:00:17, Serial1
C        183.8.128.0 is directly connected, Ethernet0
C        183.8.64.128 is directly connected, Serial1
C        183.8.128.128 is directly connected, Serial0
```

In Example 9-1, the networks and subnets that the router is directly connected to are indicated with a "C" in the first column; those learned by RIP are indicated with an "R" in the first column. On the lines displaying networks learned by RIP, numbers in square brackets indicate the administrative distance (or "trustworthiness," as discussed later in this chapter) of the routing protocol, and the metric (hop count). For example, the network 153.50.0.0 is learned by RIP (with an administrative distance of 120) and is one hop away. 183.8.128.12 is the address of the router to which this router will send any information for 153.50.0.0; in other words 183.8.128.12 is the address of the next hop router, the first router in the best path to 153.50.0.0.

When a router receives an update from a neighboring router, it adds the cost of reaching the neighbor router to the path cost reported by the neighbor to establish the new metric. The router compares the update to its own routing table. If the update is a better route (smaller metric) to a network, the router updates its own routing table.

For example, if Router B in Figure 9-1 is one unit of cost from Router A, Router B would add one to all costs reported by Router A when it runs the distance vector processes needed to update its routing table.

Some problems can occur when routers running distance vector algorithms are communicating topology changes. The following sections illustrate two of these problems and discuss three of the solutions that may be implemented in distance vector routing protocols.

NOTE   The solutions shown here are inherent in the operation of the distance vector routing protocols. In some cases, the network administrator may modify router parameters relating to these features, but this should be done with caution to avoid re-creating the problems.

Problem 1: Routing Loops

Routing loops can occur if the internetwork's slow convergence on a new configuration causes inconsistent routing entries. Figure 9-2 illustrates how a routing loop can occur.

Figure 9-2   *Routing Loops Can Occur if the Network Is Slow to Converge, Resulting in Inconsistent Routing Entries*

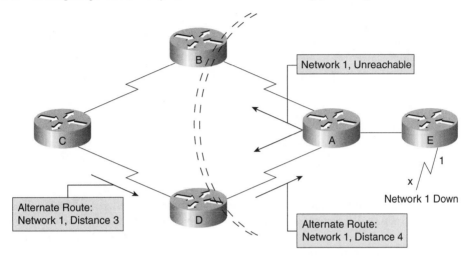

In Figure 9-2, just before the failure of Network 1, all routers have consistent knowledge and correct routing tables. The network is said to have *converged*. Assume for the remainder of this example that Router C's preferred path to Network 1 is by way of Router B, and Router C has a distance of three hops to Network 1 in its routing table.

When Network 1 fails, Router E sends an update to Router A. Router A stops routing packets to Network 1, but Routers B, C, and D continue to do so because they have not yet been informed about the failure. When Router A sends out its update, Routers B and D stop routing to Network 1. However, Router C is still not updated. To Router C, Network 1 is still reachable via Router B.

Router C now sends a periodic update to Router D, indicating a path to Network 1 by way of Router B. Router D therefore changes its routing table to reflect this good, but erroneous, news and propagates the information to Router A. Router A propagates the information to Routers B and E, and so on. Any packet destined for Network 1 will now loop from Router C to B to A to D and back to C.

Problem 2: Counting to Infinity

Continuing the previous example, the invalid updates about Network 1 continue to loop. Until some other process can stop the looping, the routers update each other in an inappropriate way, considering the fact that Network 1 is down. Figure 9-3 illustrates this problem.

Figure 9-3 *Routers Continue to Update Each Other, Despite the Fact that Network 1 Is Down*

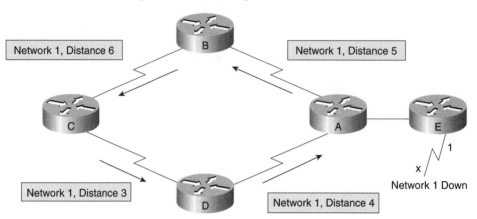

This condition, called *count-to-infinity*, results in the metric (in this case, the hop count) reaching infinity. The routers will continuously loop packets for Network 1 around the network, despite the fundamental fact that the destination Network 1 is down. While the routers are counting to infinity, the invalid information allows a routing loop to exist.

Without countermeasures to stop the process, the distance vector metric of hop count increments each time the routing update passes through another router. The packets for Network 1 loop through the network because of incorrect information in the routing tables.

Solution 1: Defining a Maximum

Distance vector routing algorithms are self-correcting, but the routing loop problem can require a count to infinity first.

To avoid this prolonged problem, distance vector protocols define infinity as some maximum number. This number refers to a routing metric (for example, a simple hop count).

With this approach, the routing protocol permits the routing loop to occur until the metric exceeds its maximum allowed value.

Figure 9-4 shows this defined maximum as 16 hops. For hop count distance vectors, a maximum of 15 hops is commonly used (as it is in IP RIP). In any case, once the metric value exceeds the maximum, Network 1 is considered unreachable.

Figure 9-4   *Defining a Maximum Metric Is One Solution to the Routing Loop Problem*

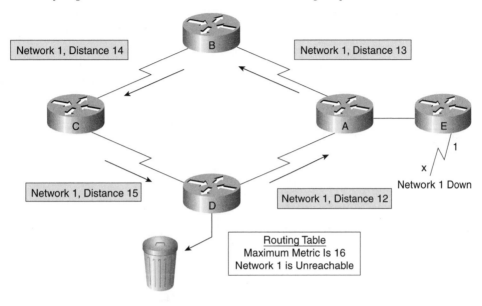

Solution 2: Split-Horizon

The *split-horizon* rule states that a router cannot send routing information about a network out the same interface from which it learned that information. A router knows the interface from which it learned information by looking in its routing table.

NOTE   The split-horizon feature is turned on by default for all distance vector routing protocols in Cisco routers.

A possible source for a routing loop occurs when incorrect information sent back to a router contradicts the correct information it sent. Refer back to Figure 9-2 to see how this problem occurs.

Router A passes an update to Router B and Router D indicating that Network 1 is down. However, Router C transmits an update to Router D indicating that Network 1 is available at a distance of four by way of Router B. This situation does not violate split-horizon rules.

Router D concludes (incorrectly) that Router C still has a valid path to Network 1, although at a much less favorable metric. Router D sends an update to Router A advising A of the "new" route to Network 1.

Router A now determines it can send to Network 1 by way of Router D; Router D determines it can send to Network 1 by way of Router C; and Router C discerns it can send to Network 1 by way of Router B. Any packet introduced into this environment will loop between routers.

Split-horizon attempts to avoid this situation. As shown in Figure 9-5, if a table update about Network 1 arrives from Router A, Router B or D cannot send information about Network 1 back to Router A. Split-horizon thus reduces incorrect routing information and reduces routing overhead.

Figure 9-5 *Split-Horizon Stops One Router from Sending Information to the Same Router from Which It Learned that Information*

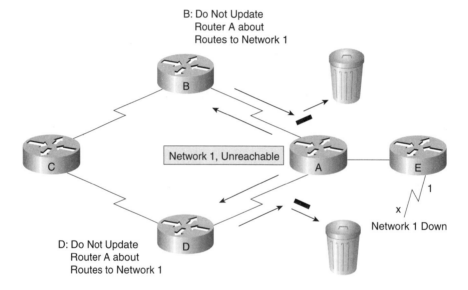

Solution 3: Hold-Down Timers

The count-to-infinity problem can be avoided by using hold-down timers, as detailed in this section and illustrated in Figure 9-6. *Hold-down timers* tell routers to hold any changes that might affect routes for a period of time, so that the entire network has a chance to learn about the change.

NOTE   Hold-down timers are implemented for most distance vector routing protocols in Cisco routers. Their default values may be changed, but as noted earlier, this should be done with caution.

Figure 9-6   *Hold-Down Timers Help Avoid Routing Loops*

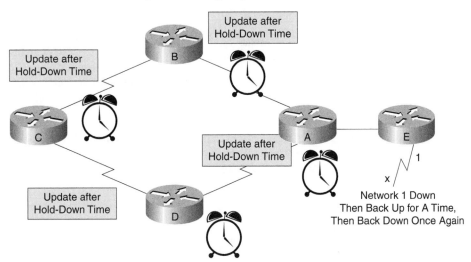

When a router receives an update from a neighbor, indicating that a previously accessible network is now inaccessible, the router marks the route as inaccessible and starts a hold-down timer. If at any time before the hold-down timer expires an update is received from the same neighbor indicating that the network is again accessible with a *better* metric than originally recorded for the network, the router marks the network as accessible and removes the hold-down timer.

If an update arrives from a different neighboring router with a better metric than originally recorded for the network, the router marks the network as accessible and removes the hold-down timer.

If at any time before the hold-down timer expires an update is received from a different neighboring router with a poorer metric, the update is ignored. Ignoring an update with a poorer metric when a hold-down is in effect allows more time for the knowledge of a disruptive change to propagate through the entire network.

IP RIP

IP RIP is a distance vector protocol that uses hop count as its metric. RIP is widely used for routing traffic and is simple to understand and implement. The latest enhancement to RIP is the RIP version 2 specification, which allows more information to be included in RIP packets, and allows VLSM.

The RIP routing protocol follows these steps for convergence:

Step 1   The link failure is detected.

Step 2   The router sends a periodic update (default is every 30 seconds) of its routing table, including the unreachable networks, to all its neighbors.

Step 3   The routers continue to send their routing tables at the normal update interval. The hold-down timer (default is 180 seconds) allows information to stabilize.

Configuring RIP on a Cisco router is relatively simple. Example 9-2 shows a sample configuration, enabling RIP for all interfaces that the router has in network 10.0.0.0. Refer to the technical documentation on Cisco's Web site or to the *Introduction to Cisco Router Configuration* book (Cisco Press) for details on configuring RIP.

Example 9-2   *A Sample Configuration for IP RIP*

```
Router(config)#router rip
Router(config-router)#network 10.0.0.0
```

IPX RIP

Novell's RIP is a distance vector routing protocol that sends routing updates periodically (every 60 seconds by default). To make best-path routing decisions, IPX RIP uses a tick as the metric, which is the delay expected when using a particular link. One *tick* is one eighteenth of a second. In the case of two paths with an equal tick count, IPX RIP uses the hop count as a tie breaker.

The IPX RIP routing protocol follows these steps for convergence:

Step 1   The link failure is detected.

Step 2   The router sends a triggered, or flash, update, indicating unreachable networks. (A *flash* update is the sending of an update sooner than the standard periodic update interval to notify other routers of a metric change.)

   Step 2a   The triggered update is sent immediately to adjacent routers.

   Step 2b   Adjacent routers generate triggered updates in turn.

Step 3   Routers continue to send their routing tables at the normal update interval (default is every 60 seconds)—this action might coincide with the triggered updates. Routes are set to invalid in the routing table if they haven't been heard about within three times the update interval (by default) and are removed from the table if they haven't been refreshed within four times the update interval.

On a Cisco router, IPX RIP is enabled by default on any interface configured with an IPX network number.

IGRP

IGRP is a routing protocol that was developed in the mid-1980s by Cisco. Cisco's principal goal in creating IGRP was to provide a robust protocol for routing within an autonomous system (AS). An *autonomous system* is a collection of networks under a common administration that share a common routing strategy. IGRP is a distance vector interior gateway protocol and uses a combination of metrics; internetwork delay, bandwidth, reliability, and load are all factored into the routing decision.

Cisco's IGRP routing protocol follows these steps for convergence:

Step 1 The link failure is detected.

Step 2 The router sends a triggered, or flash, update, indicating unreachable networks.

   Step 2a The triggered update is sent immediately to adjacent routers.

   Step 2b Adjacent routers generate triggered updates in turn.

Step 3 Routers continue to send their routing tables at the normal update interval (default is every 90 seconds)—this action might coincide with the triggered updates. The hold-down timer (default is 280 seconds) allows information to stabilize.

Configuring IGRP on a Cisco router is relatively simple. Example 9-3 shows a sample configuration, enabling IGRP for all interfaces that the router has in network 10.0.0.0 and using an autonomous system number of 100. The autonomous system number must be configured the same on all routers in that logical group. Refer to the technical documentation on Cisco's Web site or to the *Introduction to Cisco Router Configuration* book (Cisco Press) for details on configuring IGRP.

Example 9-3 *A Sample Configuration for IGRP*

```
Router(config)#router igrp 100
Router(config-router)#network 10.0.0.0
```

AppleTalk Routing Protocols

Recall from Chapter 1 that AppleTalk is a protocol suite developed by Apple Computer in the early 1980s in conjunction with the Macintosh computer. The Routing Table Maintenance Protocol (RTMP) is responsible for establishing and maintaining routing tables, while the Zone Information Protocol (ZIP) maintains network number-to-zone name mappings in AppleTalk routers.

RTMP is a distance vector protocol typically used in AppleTalk LANs. It uses hop count as a metric and is by default enabled on a Cisco router on any interface configured with an AppleTalk cable-range or network number. RTMP has a default update timer of 10 seconds.

The RTMP routing protocol follows these steps for convergence:

Step 1   The link failure is detected.

Step 2   The router sends a periodic update (default is every 10 seconds) of its routing table, including the unreachable networks, to all its neighbors.

Step 3   The routers continue to send their routing tables at the normal update interval. Routes are set to *suspect* in the routing table if they haven't been heard from within the update interval. Routers are set to *bad* in the routing table if they haven't been heard from within 20 seconds (by default) and are removed from the table if they haven't been refreshed within 60 seconds (by default).

RTMP can also be used on WAN interfaces but may result in too much traffic on the WAN. To reduce routing traffic in an AppleTalk environment, you can use the AppleTalk Update Routing Protocol (AURP). AURP is similar to distance vector routing protocols, but it is designed to handle routing update traffic over WAN links more efficiently than RTMP by only sending changed information.

AURP allows two or more AppleTalk internetworks to be connected through a foreign network (such as an IP network), typically over a WAN. This is done by creating a *tunnel*, which functions as a *virtual data link* between the AppleTalk internetworks. Over the tunnel, AURP converts both RTMP routing information and ZIP zone information packets into AURP packets and vice versa. On Cisco routers, AURP also converts Enhanced IGRP (EIGRP) packets. As well as being a routing protocol, AURP is responsible for encapsulating the AppleTalk packets inside the IP packets over the tunnel. In this context, AURP is called the *tunnel mode*. AURP can only be used on tunnel interfaces; it does not replace RTMP in the LAN environment.

AURP has many features, including the following:

- Reduced routing traffic on WAN links because only updates are sent
- Tunneling through IP internetworks or other network systems
- Basic security, including device hiding and network hiding
- Remapping of remote network numbers to resolve numbering conflicts
- Internetwork clustering to minimize routing traffic and storage requirements
- Hop count reduction to allow the creation of larger internetworks

As indicated at the beginning of this section, RTMP is enabled by default on a Cisco router on any interface configured with an AppleTalk cable-range or network number. Configuring AURP involves creating a tunnel and using AURP over the tunnel. Refer to the technical documentation on Cisco's Web site or to the *Advanced Cisco Router Configuration* book (Cisco Press) for details on configuring tunnels.

Link-State Routing Protocols

Routers running link-state protocols tell peers about directly connected links. Generally, larger networks utilize link-state protocols, including the following:

- Open Shortest Path First (OSPF)
- Intermediate System-to-Intermediate System (IS-IS)
- NetWare Link Services Protocol (NLSP)

Link-state protocols were designed to overcome some of the limitations of distance vector protocols so that they can be used in the larger networks. Recall that link-state algorithms send small updates everywhere, whereas distance vector algorithms send larger updates only to neighboring routers. Link-state protocols have many more features available, which can make them more difficult to understand and configure.

With IP link-state routing protocols, the IP address space can be mapped so that discontiguous subnets and VLSMs are supported. The IP address space must be mapped carefully so that subnets are arranged in contiguous blocks, allowing routing advertisements to be summarized at area boundaries, which reduces the number of routes advertised throughout the internetwork. If correctly configured, contiguous blocks of subnets can be consolidated as a single route. Recall that route summarization is discussed in more detail in Chapter 8.

When route summarization is not configured, links going up and down generate many updates, causing a lot of traffic and router CPU overhead as the link-state routers recalculate the topology. The process of links going up and down is often called *link flapping,* which means a link is intermittently nonoperational. Link flapping can be caused by noise, misconfigurations or reconfigurations, or hardware failures.

The following sections briefly describe each of the link-state routing protocols, including the steps they follow for convergence after detecting a network failure.

OSPF

Recall from Chapter 1 that OSPF is a link-state routing protocol that calls for the sending of *link-state advertisements* (LSAs) to all other routers within the same area. Information on attached interfaces, metrics used, and other variables is included in OSPF LSAs. As OSPF routers accumulate link-state information, they use the *Shortest Path First* (SPF) algorithm to calculate the shortest path to each node. Unlike RIP, OSPF can operate within a hierarchy. The largest entity within the hierarchy is the autonomous system. An autonomous system can be divided into a number of *areas*, which are groups of contiguous networks and attached hosts.

The OSPF routing protocol follows these steps for convergence:

Step 1   The link failure is detected.

Step 2   The routers exchange routing information and build a new routing table.

Step 3   A built-in delay (default of 5 seconds)—between when OSPF receives a topology change and when it starts an SPF calculation—prevents rapid changes from causing unstable routing.

Appendix I, "OSPF Frequently Asked Questions," contains a list of frequently asked questions about OSPF. For information about how to design and configure OSPF networks, refer to the OSPF Design Guide in Appendix J. Further information on configuring OSPF can be found in the technical documentation on Cisco's Web site and in *Advanced Cisco Router Configuration* and *OSPF Network Design Solutions*, available from Cisco Press.

IS-IS

IS-IS is an International Organization for Standardization (ISO) dynamic routing specification. Although IS-IS was created to route in ISO Connectionless Network Protocol (CLNP) networks, a version has been created to support both CLNP and IP networks. This version of IS-IS is usually referred to as *Integrated IS-IS*.

In the IS-IS protocol, the term end system (ES) refers to any nonrouting network node, whereas the phrase intermediate system (IS) refers to a router. Thus the ES-IS protocol allows ESs and ISs to discover each other, and the IS-IS protocol provides routing between ISs. A hierarchical topology of areas is supported by IS-IS.

As a link-state protocol, the convergence steps for IS-IS are similar to those for OSPF.

Configuring IS-IS on a Cisco router involves creating an IS-IS routing process and assigning it to specific interfaces (rather than to networks). Refer to the technical documentation on Cisco's Web site for detailed information on configuring IS-IS.

NLSP

Recall from Chapter 1 that NLSP is a link-state routing protocol from Novell designed to overcome some of the limitations associated with the IPX RIP and its companion protocol SAP. As compared to RIP and SAP, NLSP provides improved routing, better efficiency, and scalability because, as a link-state protocol, NLSP only advertises routing and services incrementally. In addition, NLSP-based routers are backward-compatible with RIP-based routers. NLSP-based routers use a reliable delivery protocol, so delivery is guaranteed. NLSP is based on the IS-IS protocol and is similar to IS-IS except that a hierarchical topology was not defined until Version 1.1 of NLSP was specified (which is supported in Cisco IOS™ Release 11.1). NLSP now supports hierarchical routing with area, domain, and global internetwork components.

As a link-state protocol, the convergence steps for NLSP are similar to those for OSPF.

Configuring NLSP on a Cisco router involves defining an internal network number for the router, creating an NLSP routing process, and defining the networks that will be part of the NLSP area. Refer to the technical documentation on Cisco's Web site and to *Advanced Cisco Router Configuration* (Cisco Press) for detailed information on configuring NLSP.

Enhanced IGRP—Hybrid or Advanced Routing Protocol

Enhanced IGRP (EIGRP) is a hybrid protocol that has attributes associated with both distance vector and link-state protocols. Enhanced IGRP can scale to hundreds of routing nodes in an internetwork.

EIGRP has protocol-dependent modules that support routing for IP, IPX, and AppleTalk. The IPX module also supports Novell Service Advertising Protocol (SAP). EIGRP works on the ships-in-the-night (SIN) model, which means that each routed protocol has its own separate hellos, timers, and metrics.

Enhanced IGRP also supports discontiguous subnets and VLSMs. Like the link-state protocols, summarization of address blocks with prefix routing must be manually configured. Although EIGRP automatically summarizes its own networks at the network class boundary like IGRP, this feature can be turned off for EIGRP.

In May 1996, Cisco introduced a new version of EIGRP. It was incorporated into Cisco IOS™ Releases 10.3(11), 11.0(8), 11.1(3), 11.2(1), and later releases and is compatible with older versions. Raja Sundaram of Cisco's Technical Assistance Center (TAC) has written an excellent paper that includes detailed information on the enhancements plus additional detail on EIGRP in general; this paper is in Appendix K, "Enhancements to EIGRP."

EIGRP is an excellent choice when smaller networks connect to larger networks. Running desktop routing protocols such as AppleTalk RTMP or IPX RIP/ SAP on the enterprise network is often not a good idea because of the amount of traffic that these protocols cause. Running EIGRP is especially a good idea on slow serial links.

Cisco routers automatically redistribute IPX EIGRP information into IPX RIP and SAP and vice versa. By default, IPX EIGRP advertises full SAP updates on LAN interfaces and incremental SAP updates only on WAN interfaces.

By default, the Cisco IOS™ software redistributes AppleTalk RTMP routes into AppleTalk EIGRP and vice versa.

EIGRP Convergence

The EIGRP routing protocol follows these steps for convergence:

Step 1 The link failure is detected.

Step 2 The router looks at its own routing table and its neighbors' routing tables (stored locally) for an alternate route.

Step 3 The router switches to an alternate route immediately if found locally.

Step 4 The router sends a query to its neighbors if no alternate route is found locally.

Step 5 The query propagates until a new route is found.

Step 6 Affected routers update their routing tables.

Configuring basic EIGRP on a Cisco router is relatively simple. Example 9-4 shows a sample configuration, enabling EIGRP for IP on all interfaces that the router has in network 10.0.0.0 and using an autonomous system number of 100. The autonomous system number must be configured the same on all routers in that logical group. Note the similarity between this configuration and the configuration for IGRP shown in Example 9-3. Refer to the technical documentation on Cisco's Web site or to *Advanced Cisco Router Configuration* (Cisco Press) for details on configuring the advanced features of EIGRP for IP and EIGRP for IPX and AppleTalk.

Example 9-4 *A Sample Configuration for EIGRP for IP*

```
Router(config)#router eigrp 100
Router(config-router)#network 10.0.0.0
```

Characterizing Routing Protocols

Routing protocols may be characterized in many ways, as presented in this section. The information in this section will help you characterize routing protocols so you can recommend ones that will meet a customer's requirements for performance, security, capacity, and scalability. Some of the methods you can use to characterize a routing protocol include the following:

- **Routed protocols supported**—Which routed protocol does the routing protocol support?

- **Category of routing protocol**—Does the protocol fall under the distance vector, link-state, or hybrid category of routing protocol?

- **Interior or exterior routing protocol**—Is the protocol used by routers within the same autonomous system or is it used by routers between autonomous systems?

- **Bandwidth Used**—What is the overhead involved with using the routing protocol?

- **Administrative Distance**—What is the "trustworthiness" of the source of the routing information?
- **Information Exchanged between Routing Peers**—What type of information does the routing protocol pass between routing peers?

Routed Protocols Supported

A specific routing protocol typically can be used only with one routed protocol. Table 9-1 indicates the routing protocols available for use with the three most popular routed protocols: IP, IPX, and AppleTalk.

Table 9-1   *Routing Protocols Available for Each Routed Protocol*

Routed Protocol	Routing Protocol
IP	IP RIP, IGRP, OSPF, IS-IS, EIGRP
IPX	IPX RIP, NLSP, EIGRP
AppleTalk	RTMP, AURP, EIGRP

Categories of Routing Protocols

As mentioned previously, there are two main categories of routing protocols: distance vector and link-state. A third category, hybrid, includes characteristics from both of the other two categories. Table 9-2 summarizes how the various routing protocols fit in these categories.

Table 9-2   *Categorizing Routing Protocols*

Category	Routing Protocol
Distance Vector	IP RIP, IGRP, IPX RIP, RTMP
Link-State	OSPF, NLSP, IS-IS
Hybrid	EIGRP

NOTE   The AppleTalk Update Routing Protocol (AURP) may also be used in AppleTalk networks. AURP, similar to a distance vector protocol, is discussed earlier in the chapter.

Interior and Exterior Routing Protocols

Routing protocols can also be characterized by where they are used. Recall that an *autonomous system* is a group of routers and networks under one administration—for example, a corporation or a department within a large corporation.

Interior routing protocols, such as RIP, IGRP, and EIGRP, are used by routers *within* the same autonomous system. Exterior routing protocols, such as the Border Gateway Protocol (BGP), are used *between* autonomous systems.

Interior routing protocols exist to find the best path through the network. Although exterior routing protocols also find the best path through the network, they provide additional functionality. For example, BGP, used throughout the Internet by Internet service providers (ISPs), enables a routing system that guarantees a loop-free exchange of routing information between autonomous systems. BGP is a "policy-based" routing protocol, making its routing decisions based on the network policy as defined by the network administrators.

Small- to medium-sized businesses will usually use only interior routing protocols. When connecting to an ISP, a static or default route will probably be sufficient.

Static routes are often used to connect to a *stub network*, which is a part of an internetwork that can be reached only by one path. An example of a stub network is an autonomous system that connects to the Internet. If only one path exists to the autonomous system, routers in the Internet can use static routing to reach the autonomous system, and the autonomous system can use a default route to reach networks in the Internet. By not using a routing protocol on the connection between the autonomous system and the Internet, bandwidth is conserved, and unnecessary routing information is not sent.

Bandwidth Used by Distance Vector Routing Protocols

Distance vector routing protocols, being periodic in nature, use a defined amount of bandwidth for sending their routing updates. Table 9-3 illustrates many characteristics of these routing protocols; you can use this information to determine the bandwidth used by the routing protocol in your network.

NOTE	The last three routing protocols in Table 9-3, DECnet IV, VINES VRTP, and Xerox Network Systems (XNS), have not been discussed in this book but are included here for completeness. These routing protocols are used for the DECnet, VINES, and XNS routed protocols, respectively. More information on these protocols can be found on Cisco's Web site.

Table 9-3   *Calculating Bandwidth Used by Routing Protocols*

Routing Protocol	Default Update Timer (Seconds)	Route Entry Size (Bytes)	Network and Update Overhead (Bytes)	Routes per Packet
IP RIP	30	20	32	25
IP IGRP	90	14	32	104
AppleTalk RTMP	10	6	17	97
IPX SAP	60	64	32	7
IPX RIP	60	8	32	50
DECnet IV	40	4	18	368
VINES VRTP	90	8	30	104
XNS	30	20	40	25

NOTE   For AppleTalk: DDP header = 13 bytes, RTMP header = 4 bytes, each route update = 6 bytes, maximum DDP data = 586. 586 − 4 = 582. 582/6 = 97 routes in a route update packet.

For NetWare: IPX RIP limits the number of routes in an update packet to 50. IPX SAP limits the number of SAPs in an update packet to 7. These limits apply regardless of the maximum transmission unit (MTU).

For IP: RIP is limited to 25 routes per update, regardless of the MTU.

Routing Protocol Administrative Distance

In some network designs, more than one IP routing protocol is configured. If a router learns about more than one route to a destination from different sources, the route with the *lowest administrative distance* is placed in the routing table. Table 9-4 defines the default administrative distances for IP routes learned from different sources.

TIP   Think of the administrative distance as the *trustworthiness* of the source of the routing information. If a router has learned about the same network from more than one source (for example, from a static route and from RIP), it must decide which source is the most *trustworthy.* The lower the administrative distance, the more trustworthy the source.

Table 9-4   *Default Administrative Distances for IP Routes*

IP Route	Administrative Distance
Connected interface	0
Static route using a connected interface	0
Static route using an IP address	1
EIGRP summary route	5
External BGP route	20
Internal EIGRP route	90
IGRP route	100
OSPF route	110
IS-IS route	115
RIP route	120
Exterior Gateway Protocol (EGP) route	140
External EIGRP route	170
Internal BGP route	200
Route of unknown origin	255

Static routes are traditionally implemented so they always take precedence over any dynamically learned routes to the same destination network. Cisco IOS™ software also supports a *floating static route*, which is a static route that has a higher administrative distance than a dynamically learned route, so that it can be overridden by dynamically learned routing information. Thus, a floating static route can be used to create a *path of last resort* that is used only when no dynamic information is available. Floating static routes are available for IP, IPX, and AppleTalk.

One important application of floating static routes is to provide backup routes in topologies where dial-on-demand routing (DDR) is used.

Information Exchanged between Routing Peers

The type of information that is exchanged between routing peers is another characteristic of a routing protocol. For example, protocols may:

- Send periodic updates
- Have a separate hello mechanism
- Exchange information about links
- Exchange information about routes

Routing Protocol Scalability Constraints

The scalability constraints for routing protocols can be characterized by the following items:

- Limits on metrics
- Convergence
- Resource requirements

The sections that follow provide detailed information on each of these scalability constraints for routing protocols.

Limits on Metrics

Some protocols have metric limitations that will not allow them to be used in large networks. For example, no IP RIP-based internetwork can have a diameter greater than 15 hops. AppleTalk's RTMP has the same 15-hop limitation. Recall that this limitation on hop count is to prevent routing loops.

IGRP limits the hop count to 100 by default but allows it to be configured up to 255 hops.

IPX RIP limits the hop count to 15 and will ignore any updates with a hop count greater than this, by default. However the software might learn routes that are farther away than 15 hops if it is using protocols other than RIP. The router can be configured to increase the maximum number of hops that it will accept as reachable, as well as the maximum number of hops that an IPX packet can traverse before it is dropped by the router. The maximum value that can be configured is 254.

Link-state protocols do not have metric limitations.

Routing Protocols Convergence

Convergence is when routers arrive at a consistent understanding of the internetwork topology after a change takes place. Packets might not be reliably routed to all destinations until convergence takes place. The time it takes to reach convergence is a critical design constraint for some applications. For example, the time to convergence is critical when a time-sensitive protocol, such as SNA, is transported in IP packets.

The time to reach convergence depends on the following factors:

- Routing protocol update and other timers
- Network diameter and complexity
- Frequency of routing protocol updates
- Features of the routing protocol

In general, EIGRP and the link-state protocols converge more quickly than distance vector protocols.

The time to reach convergence has two components:

- The time it takes to detect the link failure
- The time it takes to determine a new route

Table 9-5 indicates the time required by an interface to detect a link failure, for common interface types. The "Keepalive Timer" column in Table 9-5 indicates how often keepalive messages are sent on the interface; keepalive messages are used by some data link layer protocols to indicate that the link is still alive. If a device does not hear an expected keepalive message, the link may no longer be alive. Devices typically wait for two or three keepalive intervals before declaring the link dead.

Table 9-5   *Time to Detect Link Failure*

Interface Type	Time to Detect Link Failure	Keepalive Timer
Serial lines	Immediate if Carrier Detect (CD) lead drops. Otherwise, between two and three keepalive times.	Keepalive timer is ten seconds by default.
Token Ring or FDDI	Almost immediate due to beacon protocol.	N/A
Ethernet	Immediate if caused by local or transceiver failure. Otherwise, between two and three keepalive times.	Keepalive timer is ten seconds by default.

Once the link failure has been detected by a router, the router will pass the information on within its routing protocol. Convergence steps of specific protocols are discussed earlier in this chapter.

Routing Protocol Resource Requirements

Routing protocols use resources, including CPU, memory, and bandwidth in the routers and networks they are running on. The resource requirements of a routing protocol depend on many factors, including the following:

- How often routing updates are transmitted. This may be a function of the update timer, or updates might be triggered by events.
- How much data is transmitted, the whole routing table or just changes.
- How widely routing updates are distributed. They may be distributed to neighbors, to a bounded area, or to all routers in the autonomous system.

- How static and default routes are used.
- Whether route summarization is supported and how it is supported.

Bridging Protocols for Cisco Routers and Switches

Several types of bridging protocols are supported by Cisco routers (acting as bridges) and switches, including the following:

- **Transparent bridging (TB)**—Found primarily in Ethernet environments.
- **Source-route bridging (SRB)**—Found primarily in Token Ring environments.
- **Translational bridging**—Attempts to translate from Ethernet bridging to Token Ring bridging.
- **Encapsulating bridging**—Allows packets to cross a bridged backbone network.
- **Source-route transparent bridging (SRT)**—Allows a bridge to function as both a source-routing and transparent bridge.
- **Source-route translational bridging (SR/TLB)**—Allows a bridge to function as both a source-routing and transparent bridge, and to bridge between the two, as shown in Figure 9-7.

Figure 9-7   *SR/TLB Allows Devices in a Source-Route Domain to Communicate with Devices in a Transparent Bridged Domain*

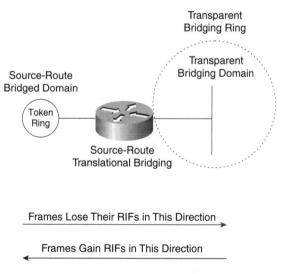

Refer to the technical documentation on Cisco's Web site or to *Advanced Cisco Router Configuration* (Cisco Press) for details on configuring bridging. The sections that follow identify the scalability issues associated with transparent and source-route bridging. The other types of bridging identified above combine both of these types of bridging and therefore inherit scalability issues from both.

Transparent Bridging Scalability Issues

A transparent bridge floods all multicast and broadcast frames, and frames with an unknown destination address out every port except the port on which the frame was received. Multicasts and broadcasts create a scalability issue, as discussed in Chapters 4, "Determining New Customer Requirements," and 6, "Provisioning Hardware and Media for the LAN."

In the case of unknown addresses, a transparent bridge listens to all frames and learns what port to use to reach devices. The bridge learns by looking at the source address in all frames, so an unknown address becomes a known address after a device has sent a frame. Scalability is an issue if the bridge has a limited number of addressees that it can learn about. Cisco devices do not have severe limitations. Refer to product information on Cisco's Web site (at http:// www.cisco.com) for more detailed information on limitations for specific Cisco devices.

Transparent bridges implement the Spanning-Tree algorithm, which is specified in IEEE 802.1d. The Spanning-Tree algorithm states that there is one and only one active path between two stations. If a physical loop exists in the network (for redundancy reasons), the Spanning-Tree algorithm handles this loop by disabling bridge ports.

Transparent bridges send bridge protocol data unit (BPDU) frames to each other to build and maintain a spanning tree. The spanning tree selects one *root bridge,* and a set of active bridge ports is selected by determining the lowest-cost paths to the root bridge. The BPDU frames are sent to a multicast address every two seconds. The amount of traffic caused by BPDU frames can be a scalability issue on very large flat networks with numerous switches or bridges.

Source-Route Bridging Scalability Issues

In Token Ring environments, source nodes as well as bridges and switches must understand bridging. With source-route bridging, a source node finds another node by sending explorer packets. Scalability is affected by the type of explorer packet the source sends. An explorer packet can be either an all-routes explorer or a single-route explorer.

All-Routes Explorer Packets

For an all-routes explorer, the source node specifies that the explorer packet should take all possible paths. The source node usually specifies that the response should take just one path back.

The main scalability issue for source-route bridging is the amount of traffic that can arrive on the destination station's ring when all-routes explorer packets are used. To reduce the amount of traffic on the network, you need to do the following:

- Limit the size of flat, bridged networks
- Introduce routers to segment the network
- If a nonroutable protocol such as NetBIOS is prevalent, investigate implementations that support NetBIOS on top of a network layer protocol, such as IP or IPX

Single-Route Explorer Packets

For a single-route explorer, the source node specifies that the explorer packet should take just one path and that the response should take either all paths or just one path back.

When single-route explorer packets are used, the bridges can use the Spanning-Tree algorithm to determine a single path to the destination. If the Spanning-Tree algorithm is not used, the network administrator must manually choose which bridge should forward single-route explorers when there are multiple redundant bridges connecting two rings.

Integrated Routing and Bridging

For customers who need to merge bridged and routed networks, Cisco IOS™ Release 11.2 has an integrated routing and bridging (IRB) feature that interconnects LANs, VLANs, and bridged domains to routed domains within the same router. IRB provides the capability to route between bridged and routed interfaces, using a software-based interface called the Bridged Virtual Interface (BVI) (see http://www.cisco.com/warp/public/732/Releases/ for details on Cisco IOS releases and features). Prior to the introduction of IRB, routing and bridging of the same protocol between interfaces on the same router was not supported.

Another advantage of IRB is the flexibility to extend a bridge domain across a router's interfaces to provide a temporary solution for moves, adds, and changes, which can be useful during migration from a bridged environment to a routed environment.

IRB supports IP, IPX, and AppleTalk. IRB is supported for transparent bridging, but not for source-route bridging. IRB is supported on all types of interfaces, except X.25 and ISDN bridged interfaces.

Refer to the technical documentation on Cisco's Web site or to *Advanced Cisco Router Configuration* (Cisco Press) for details on configuring IRB.

Summary

Routing protocols have many characteristics. This chapter defined these and identified scalability constraints and issues that affect the choice of routing protocol. Switches and bridges, and routers acting as bridges, implement bridging protocols. These protocols and their constraints and features were reviewed here.

The next chapter in Part IV identifies some of the software features that are available on Cisco routers.

Multiple-Choice Review Questions

Following are 12 statements about scalability constraints for routing protocols. Each statement refers to a specific routing protocol. Answer the questions by selecting the letter to the left of the correct answer. After you complete each question, you can refer to the solutions provided by our internetworking experts in Appendix B.

Question 9-1

This protocol sends routing updates every 10 seconds, which can consume a large percentage of the bandwidth on slow serial links.

A. IP RIP

B. RTMP

C. NLSP

D. IGRP

Question 9-2

This protocol limits the number of networks in a routing table update to 50, which means many packets are required to send the routing table within a large internetwork.

A. OSPF

B. IPX RIP

C. IPX SAP

D. Static Routing

Question 9-3

This protocol does not support discontiguous subnets or variable-length subnet masks.

A. Static Routing

B. OSPF

C. IGRP

D. EIGRP

Question 9-4

This protocol can advertise seven services per packet, which causes many packets on enterprise internetworks with hundreds of services.

A. IPX SAP

B. RTMP

C. IPX RIP

D. IGRP

Question 9-5

This protocol uses 14 bytes to define a route entry, so it can send 104 routes in a 1500-byte packet.

A. AURP

B. OSPF

C. IGRP

D. IPX RIP

Question 9-6

This protocol should be recommended in hub-and-spoke topologies with low bandwidth even though it can be hard to maintain because it is not dynamic.

A. Static Routing

B. OSPF

C. EIGRP

D. RIPv2

Question 9-7

This protocol is similar to OSI's IS-IS protocol except that a hierarchical topology was not defined until Version 1.1 of the routing protocol was specified (which is supported in Cisco IOS™ Release 11.1).

A. NLSP

B. OSPF

C. IGRP

D. EIGRP

Question 9-8

This protocol supports route summarization but it must be configured. It is not automatic. If link flapping occurs when route summarization is not configured, a stream of updates is generated, causing serious traffic and router CPU overhead.

A. AURP

B. RTMP

C. IGRP

D. OSPF

Question 9-9

If a customer is looking for ways to reduce WAN routing traffic and is also considering tunneling AppleTalk in IP, you could recommend this protocol.

A. IPX RIP

B. Static Routing

C. EIGRP

D. AURP

Question 9-10

This protocol can be compromised because the routing updates are easy to read with a protocol analyzer, and an unsophisticated hacker can send invalid routing updates that routers will accept.

A. IP RIP

B. OSPF

C. NLSP

D. EIGRP

Question 9-11

Cisco refined the implementation of this protocol in May 1996 to increase stability in environments with many low-speed links in NBMA WANs, such as Frame Relay, ATM, or X.25 backbones, and in highly redundant dense router-router peering configurations.

A. IPX RIP

B. RTMP

C. EIGRP

D. IGRP

Question 9-12

If a customer wants a protocol with fast convergence that can scale to hundreds of networks and that will fit well with a hierarchical topology, recommend this protocol.

A. IGRP

B. OSPF

C. IP RIP

D. RTMP

Case Studies

In this section, you are asked to select protocols for the four case studies introduced in Chapter 3, "Characterizing the Existing Network."

Read each case study description and complete the questions/exercises for each of the case studies.

TIP   As mentioned, in working through the questions to the case studies, you will find it useful to work on note paper in a separate binder, to accommodate the depth of these exercises.

After you complete each question/exercise, refer to the solutions provided by our internetworking experts in Appendix B. Keep in mind that there are potentially several correct answers to each question. These case studies and their solutions will help you prepare for the Sylvan CCDA exam following the course.

Case Study: CareTaker Publications

You might want to review the CareTaker case study description in Appendix A, page 303, before you begin answering the questions in this section.

CareTaker Case Study Questions

Refer to the topology drawing you created for CareTaker Publications in Chapter 3 or review the topology drawing solution provided in Appendix B. In this section you will select routing protocols for the network.

Question 9-13

The corporate Network Operations people from the parent corporation will be in town, and the IS manager wants to meet you to describe how your IP addressing scheme will work and how it will interface with the corporate network and the Internet. Which routing protocol would you implement on the WAN between CareTaker and the corporate Cisco 7000 series router?

Question 9-14

Are there any protocols between corporate and CareTaker's facilities that cannot be routed?

Question 9-15

What routing protocol is the most efficient between the warehouse and CareTaker's facilities?

Question 9-16

Assuming the routing protocol between CareTaker and HI is IGRP, what additional parameter must you know before the main office router can be configured for IGRP?

Case Study: PH Network Services Corporation

You may wish to review the PH Network Services Corporation case study description in Appendix A, page 306, before you begin answering the questions in this section.

PH Network Services Corporation Case Study Questions

Refer to the topology drawing you created for Mr. Pero in Chapter 3 or review the topology drawing solution provided in Appendix B. In this section, you will select routing and bridging protocols for the network.

Question 9-17

Are there any protocols between PH's facilities that cannot be routed?

Question 9-18

Each hospital will be using existing routers that are not necessarily Cisco routers. Which routing protocol will be the most efficient to implement between the PH Network Services network and the hospitals?

Question 9-19

Which routing protocol would you select to support the doctor offices dialing in via ISDN to the PH Network Services network?

Case Study: Pretty Paper Limited

You might want to review the Pretty Paper Limited case study in Appendix A, page 307, before you begin answering the questions in this section.

Pretty Paper Limited Case Study Questions

Refer to the topology drawing you created for Pretty Paper in Chapter 3 or review the topology drawing solution provided in Appendix B. In this section you will select routing and bridging protocols for the network.

Question 9-20

Are there any protocols between the facilities that cannot be routed?

Question 9-21

Who will you contact to determine which protocol to use for the router providing Internet connectivity?

Question 9-22

Because all the remote sites have Cisco routers attached to the WAN, which routing protocol is the most efficient for implementation?

Case Study: Jones, Jones, & Jones

You may want to review the Jones, Jones, & Jones case study in Appendix A, page 308, before you begin answering the questions in this section.

Jones, Jones, & Jones Case Study Questions

Refer to the topology drawing you created for Ms. Jones in Chapter 3 or review the topology drawing solution provided in Appendix B. In this section you will select routing and bridging protocols for the network.

Question 9-23

Are there any protocols between facilities that cannot be routed?

Question 9-24

Because all the remote sites have Cisco routers attached to the WAN, which routing protocol is the most efficient for implementation?

Question 9-25

Who will you contact to determine which protocol to use for the router providing Internet connectivity?

Question 9-26

Which routing protocol would you select to support the remote PCs dialing in via asynchronous/ISDN to the local office's network?

You will need approximately three hours to complete this chapter and its exercises. Upon completion of this sixth chapter in Part IV you will be able to:

- Recognize scalability issues for various Cisco IOS™ software features, such as access lists, encryption, proxy services, compression, and queuing.

- Recommend Cisco IOS software features that meet a customer's requirements for performance, security, capacity, and scalability.

CHAPTER 10

Provisioning Software Features

This chapter includes some tables and other job aids that you will find useful when completing the case studies at the end of the chapter. References to some WWW sites are also included; relevant information has been extracted from these sites and is provided in the chapter. If you have access to the Internet, you might want to access the sites mentioned to obtain detailed information related to specific topics. All the sites referenced in this chapter are also listed in Appendix C, "Interesting WWW Links and Other Suggested Readings."

Follow these steps to complete this chapter:

1 Study the chapter content, including any tables and job aids that appear.

2 Review the case studies at the end of this chapter.

3 Complete the questions in each case study.

4 Review the answers provided by our internetworking experts in Appendix B, "Answers to Chapter Questions, Case Studies, and Sample CCDA Exam."

Cisco's IOS software provides many features that you can use to enhance the operation of your network. This chapter first identifies some goals that provisioning these software features can meet and then details many of the more interesting features.

Goals for Provisioning Router Software

When designing internetworks that meet your customer's needs for performance and security, you will need to provision router software features. Your goals for provisioning software features might include one or more of the following:

- Optimize bandwidth usage on WAN links to improve performance
- Optimize bandwidth usage on WAN links to save money
- Implement security policies
- Implement policies regarding some traffic having priority over other traffic
- Scale internetworks to a large size and retain good performance

Cisco IOS Software Features

Depending on your customer's requirements for network performance and security, you might need to implement the following Cisco IOS software features:

- Access lists
- Encryption
- Proxy services
- Compression
- Traffic shaping
- Queuing: custom, priority, weighted fair
- Resource Reservation Protocol (RSVP)
- Tag switching

Each of these features is discussed in the following sections. For details on configuring these features in the Cisco IOS software, refer to the Command Reference and Command Configuration documentation for the release of the IOS running on your router. Cisco IOS documentation can be found on Cisco's web site at http://www.cisco.com/univercd/cc/td/doc/product/software/index.htm.

Access Lists

Use access lists to do the following:

- Control whether network traffic is forwarded or blocked at a router's interfaces.
- Provide a basic level of security.
- Control the amount of traffic on networks to improve performance. For example, a NetWare Service Advertising Protocol (SAP) filter can be used to avoid advertising services unnecessarily. Reducing the number of services advertised can have a significant impact on performance because of the reduction in network traffic and reduction in required processing at the routers.

When configuring access lists, you provide a set of criteria that will be applied to each packet that is processed by the router. The router decides whether to forward or block each packet based on whether the packet matches the access list criteria.

There are two types of access lists: standard and extended. *Standard* access lists allow only simple criteria to be specified, such as packet source address. *Extended* access lists allow additional, more complex, criteria to be specified, such as the packet destination address, upper-layer protocol, and application port number. Each protocol has its own specific set of criteria that can be defined.

You define each criterion in separate **access-list** statements. These statements specify whether to block (deny) or forward (permit) packets that match the criteria listed. An access list is the sum of individual statements that all share the same identifying name or number.

Access List Order

The order of **access-list** statements is important. When the router is deciding whether to forward or block a packet, the Cisco IOS software tests the packet against each criteria statement in the order the statements were created. After a match is found, no more criteria statements are checked.

At the end of every access list is an implied "deny all traffic" criteria statement. If a packet does not match any of your criteria statements, the packet will be blocked.

If you create a criteria statement that explicitly permits all traffic, no statements added later will ever be checked. If you need additional statements, you must delete the access list and retype it with the new entries.

Applying Access Lists Inbound or Outbound to Interfaces

With most protocols, you can apply access lists to interfaces as either inbound or outbound (or both). (Earlier releases of the Cisco IOS software allowed only outbound access lists for some protocols. Refer to the Command Reference documentation for the release of the IOS you are running for further details.)

If the access list is applied inbound to an interface, the Cisco IOS software checks the access list's criteria statements for a match when the router receives a packet. If the packet is permitted, the software continues to process the packet. If the packet is denied, the software discards the packet.

If the access list is applied outbound to an interface, the software checks the access list's criteria statements for a match after receiving and routing a packet to the outbound interface. If the packet is permitted, the software transmits the packet. If the packet is denied, the software discards the packet.

The **access-group** command is used to apply an access list to an interface. Parameters in this command indicate whether the list is applied inbound or outbound.

Access Lists Numbering

With the exception of named IP and IPX access lists, configuring an access list requires you to number the list. A range of numbers has been reserved for each type of access list, as identified in Table 10-1.

Table 10-1   *Access List Numbers*

Type of Access List	Range
IP standard	1–99
IP extended	100–199
Bridge type code	200–299
DECnet standard and extended	300–399
XNS standard	400–499
XNS extended	500–599
AppleTalk zone	600–699
Bridge MAC	700–799
IPX standard	800–899
IPX extended	900–999
IPX SAP	1000–1099
Bridge extended	1100–1199
NLSP route aggregation	1200–1299

TIP   In Cisco IOS Release 11.2, a feature was added so that you no longer need to number IP standard or extended access lists; you can now use an alphanumeric name. To use this feature, type **ip access-list** followed by the keyword **standard** or **extended**, followed by a chosen name. Named IP access lists also let you delete individual entries from a specific access list, which enables you to modify access lists without deleting and reconfiguring them. Cisco IOS Release 11.2(4)F added support for named access lists for IPX.

Access List Wildcard Masks

When configuring an **access-list** statement, a *wildcard mask* is used to specify the portion of the source or destination address specified in that **access-list** statement that must exactly match the address in the packet, in order for the statement to apply to the packet. Each bit in the wildcard mask indicates how to interpret the corresponding bit in the address. In binary, a wildcard mask bit of one indicates that the corresponding bit in the address can be ignored; a wildcard mask bit of zero indicates that the corresponding bit in the address must exactly match.

TIP	The concept of a wildcard mask is similar to the wildcard character used in DOS-based computers. For example, to delete all files on your computer that begin with the letter *f*, you would type:

```
delete f*.*
```

The * character is the wildcard; any files that start with *f*, followed by any other characters, then a dot, and then any other characters, will be deleted.

Instead of using wildcard characters, routers use wildcard masks to implement this concept.

Access List Example

Example 10-1 shows the use of a standard access list for IP. In this example, the **ip access-group 1 in** command applies the statements in **access-list 1** *inbound* to interface ethernet 0 of the router. The two **access-list 1** statements permit packets with source addresses that have the first octet equal to 10 or 20. The wildcard mask of 0.255.255.255 indicates that only the first octet of the address, in this case 10 or 20, must exactly match; all other bits in the address can be ignored. All other packets—that is, those whose source address does not start with 10 or 20—are denied entry into interface ethernet 0 because of the implied "deny all traffic" criteria statement at the end of the access list.

Example 10-1   *A Standard Access List for IP*

```
access-list 1 permit 10.0.0.0   0.255.255.255
access-list 1 permit 20.0.0.0   0.255.255.255
interface ethernet 0
  ip access-group 1 in
```

Example Use of an Access List in a Hub-and-Spoke Topology

Consider the example in Figure 10-1 of a hub-and-spoke topology where remote offices attach to corporate headquarters in Connecticut.

Figure 10-1 *An Example Hub-and-Spoke Topology Using Access Lists*

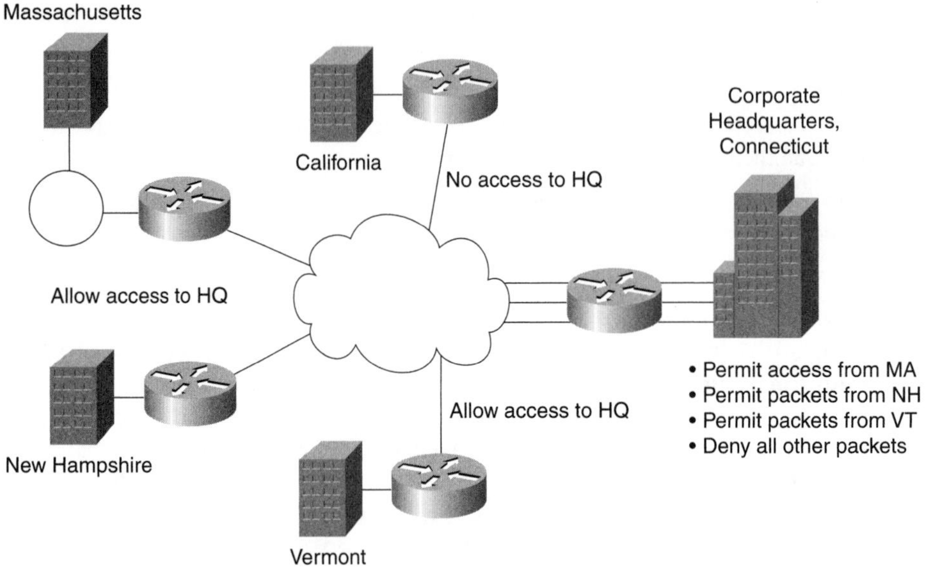

The following are the constraints and requirements for the topology in Figure 10-1:

- Most remote users are in Massachusetts.
- Many remote users are in New Hampshire.
- Some remote users are in Vermont.
- A few remote users are in California, but they are not allowed access to corporate headquarters in Connecticut.
- No outside users are allowed access to corporate headquarters in Connecticut.

To maximize performance, an inbound access list would be implemented on the headquarters router as follows:

- Permit packets from Massachusetts
- Permit packets from New Hampshire
- Permit packets from Vermont
- Implicitly deny all other packets (including packets from California)

Impact of Access Lists on Router Performance

Over the years, Cisco engineering has improved the performance of handling IP access lists on various platforms. Table 10-2 shows the history.

NOTE	When reviewing Table 10-2, recall that Chapter 7, "Provisioning Hardware and Media for the WAN," discusses router switching modes including fast switching, Netflow switching, silicon switching using the Switching Engine (SSE), and distributed switching. Chapter 3, "Characterizing the Existing Network," also has more details on NetFlow switching.

Table 10-2   *Enhancements to Access Lists*

Cisco IOS Software Release	Performance Enhancement
9.21	Inbound and outbound access lists can be fast switched.
10.0	Standard outbound access lists can be SSE switched on Cisco 7000 series routers.
10.3	Extended outbound access lists can be SSE switched on Cisco 7000 series routers.
11.0 (3)	Inbound and outbound, standard and extended lists can be SSE switched on Cisco 7000 series routers.
11.1	Access lists can use NetFlow switching on Cisco 7500 series and Cisco 7000 series routers with an RSP.
11.1 (5)	Access lists can use NetFlow switching on Cisco 7200 series routers.
11.2	IP named access lists supported, except with Distributed Fast Switching.
11.2(3)F	AppleTalk access lists can be fast switched. Inbound AppleTalk access lists supported.
11.2(4)F	IPX named access lists supported.
11.3	IP policy routing can be fast switched.

Enabling an inbound access list on any interface of a Cisco 7000 series router with Cisco IOS Release 11.0 and earlier versions disables SSE switching. Cisco IOS Release 11.0(3) was the first release to support SSE switching of inbound IP access lists.

Cisco IOS software has never supported autonomous switching of inbound access lists. Autonomous switching of outbound access lists is disabled for some interface types. On Cisco 7000 series routers, enable SSE switching to avoid performance problems when access lists are used. (It must be configured; it is not on by default.) On routers with Route/Switch Processors (RSPs), enable NetFlow switching.

NetFlow switching can apply access list filtering very quickly without going through the list for each packet that must be switched. Recall from Chapter 3 that with NetFlow switching, access list processing is applied only to the first packet of a flow. Information from the first packet is used to build an entry in the NetFlow cache, and subsequent packets in the flow are handled via a single streamlined task that handles switching, services, and data collection concurrently.

With most types of switching, however, the Cisco IOS software tests the packet against each criteria statement until a match is found. You should design your access lists with care to provide good performance. Study your traffic flow so that you can design the list so most packets will match the first few conditions. The fewer conditions the router needs to check, the better the performance will be.

Encryption Options

Safeguarding network data has become increasingly important to many organizations as they extend their private internetworks to use public, unprotected networks such as the Internet. To safeguard IP data, Cisco IOS Release 11.2 implements Cisco Encryption Technology (CET). CET provides packet-level encryption that enables you to protect the confidentiality and integrity of network data traveling between cooperating (peer) encrypting routers, as shown in Figure 10-2.

Figure 10-2 *Encryption Enables You to Protect the Confidentiality and Integrity of Network Data*

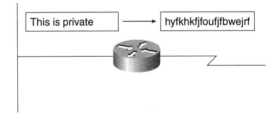

In Cisco IOS Release 11.3(3)T and later, another encryption option, IPSec, is available. IPSec is a framework of open standards developed by the Internet Engineering Task Force (IETF). IPSec services are similar to those provided by CET; however, IPSec provides a more robust security solution and is standards-based.

The following sections provide more information on these encryption options. The Security Configuration Guide for Release 12.0 of the IOS software, available on Cisco's web site at http://www.cisco.com/univercd/cc/td/doc/product/software/ios120/12cgcr/secur_c/index.htm, provides more details on the operation and configuration of these features.

Cisco Encryption Technology

The mechanisms used by CET to authenticate peer routers and exchange encrypted data are described in the following sections.

Authenticate Peer Routers

Authentication of peer routers is done using Digital Signature Standard (DSS) private and public keys.

Peer router authentication occurs during the setup of each encrypted session before encrypted data can be sent. However, before peer routers can authenticate each other, you must generate public and private DSS keys for each peer router, and you must exchange and verify the DSS public keys with each peer router. The exchange and verification of the DSS public keys includes a *manual* process involving yourself and the peer router's administrator, typically done via a telephone call. Generation of the keys, and exchange and verification of the public keys, is only done once for each peer router. DSS private keys are stored in a private portion of the router's NVRAM, which cannot be viewed.

To establish a session, two peer routers exchange connection messages. The connection messages have two purposes: to authenticate each router to the other router and to generate a temporary Data Encryption Standard (DES) key (a *session key*), which will be used to encrypt data during the encrypted session.

Authentication is accomplished by attaching signatures to the connection messages; a *signature* is a character string that is created by each local router, using its own DSS private key, and verified by the remote router, using the local router's DSS public key that was previously exchanged. A signature is always unique to the sending router and cannot be forged by any other device. When a signature is verified, the router that sent the signature is authenticated.

Encrypt the Data

To generate the DES key, Diffie-Hellman (DH) numbers are exchanged in the connection messages. The DH numbers are then used to compute a common DES session key that is shared by both routers.

After both peer routers are authenticated and the DES key has been generated, data can be encrypted and transmitted. A DES encryption algorithm is used with the DES key to encrypt and decrypt IP packets during the encrypted session.

An encrypted communication session will terminate when the session times out. When the session terminates, both the DH numbers and the DES key are discarded. When another encrypted session is required, new DH numbers and DES keys will be generated.

CET Supported Platforms

Cisco's packet-level encryption is supported in the following implementations:

- In Cisco IOS Release 11.2 and later
- In the Versatile Interface Processor, Version 2 (VIP2) software, available on the Cisco 7500 series platform
- In the VIP2 Encryption Port Adapter (EPA) software, available on the Cisco 7500 series platform

The VIP2 EPA greatly improves encryption performance because the encryption is offloaded to the dedicated port adapter hardware. It also has added tamper-proof features for session keys.

In Cisco IOS Release 11.2, packet-level encryption can be used with any Layer 2 encapsulation. IP is the only Layer 3 protocol that is supported. Other Layer 3 protocols, such as IPX and AppleTalk, can be encrypted if they are encapsulated in IP.

IPSec

CET was introduced in Cisco IOS Software Release 11.2. In Cisco IOS Release 11.3(3)T and later, IPSec services are also available. The solution offered by the two services is similar, but IPSec is standards-based and provides a more robust security solution. IPSec provides data authentication services (including authenticating the origin of the data) and antireplay services (so that the receiver can reject old or duplicate packets) in addition to the data confidentiality services that CET provides. Because it is standards-based, IPSec allows Cisco devices to interoperate with other non-Cisco IPSec-compliant networking devices, including PCs and servers.

IPSec also allows the use of digital certificates, using the Internet Key Exchange (IKE) protocol and Certification Authorities (CAs). A *digital certificate* contains information to identify a user or device, such as the name, serial number, company, or IP address. It also contains a copy of the device's public key. The certificate is itself signed by a CA, a third party that is explicitly trusted by the receiver to validate identities and to create digital certificates. When using digital certificates, each device is enrolled with a CA. When two devices want to communicate, they exchange certificates and digitally sign data to authenticate each other. Manual exchange and verification of keys is not required.

When a new device is added to the network, it simply needs to be enrolled with a CA; none of the other devices need modification. When the new device attempts an IPSec connection, certificates are automatically exchanged, and the device can be authenticated.

Proxy Services

Cisco offers numerous *proxy services* you can recommend at customer sites where there are performance or connectivity concerns due to the topology and behavior of network applications. This section identifies some examples of proxy services that the Cisco IOS software provides.

Resource Discovery on Serverless LANs

To aid in resource discovery on serverless LANs, as shown in Figure 10-3, the router provides the following services:

- A router can respond to an IPX GetNearestServer request from a NetWare client if there is no local NetWare server.

- A router can respond when a VINES client boots and sends a broadcast request asking a server to provide it with a network layer address if there is no local VINES server.

- A router can respond to an Address Resolution Protocol (ARP) request when a local IP station looks for a remote station. This is called *proxy ARP*.

- By configuring a helper address you can cause a router to forward certain types of broadcast frames so that a client can reach a service on the other side of the router.

Figure 10-3 *A Router Can Aid Resource Discovery on Serverless LANs*

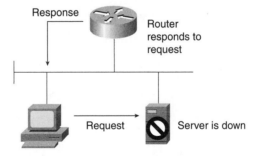

Traffic Reduction on Bridged Networks and WANs

On bridged networks and WANs, the router provides the following services:

- A source-route bridging (SRB) router can convert an all-routes explorer frame into a single-route frame, thus reducing the number of frames in a network that has many redundant paths.

- NetBIOS name caching allows a router to convert NetBIOS name-lookup frames from explorers to single-route frames.

- NetWare servers running the NetWare Core Protocol (NCP) send a keepalive message to all connected clients every five minutes. If clients are connected by DDR circuits, the keepalive keeps the DDR link open indefinitely. To avoid this situation, use watchdog spoofing on the router at the server end. The router then answers session keepalives locally, and the DDR link is allowed to drop.

- Novell Sequenced Packet Exchange (SPX) spoofing does the same thing as watchdog spoofing except that it is for applications that use SPX instead of NCP.

Improved Performance for Time-Sensitive Applications

As shown in Figure 10-4, the Logical Link Control (LLC) Local acknowledgement (ACK) feature allows a router to respond to LLC frames so that SNA and other time-sensitive applications do not time out when used on large routed networks.

Figure 10-4   *The LLC Local ACK Feature Allows a Router to Respond to LLC Frames*

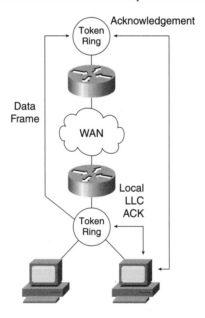

Compression Services

The basic function of data compression is to reduce the size of a frame of data to be transmitted over a network link. Data compression algorithms use two types of encoding techniques: statistical and dictionary.

Statistical Compression

Statistical compression, which uses a fixed, usually nonadaptive encoding method, is best applied to a single application where the data is relatively consistent and predictable. Because the traffic on internetworks is neither consistent nor predictable, statistical algorithms are usually not suitable for data compression implementations on routers.

Dictionary Compression

An example of *dictionary* compression is the Lempel-Ziv algorithm. This algorithm is based on a dynamically encoded dictionary that replaces a continuous stream of characters with codes. The symbols represented by the codes are stored in memory in a dictionary-style list. This approach is more responsive to variations in data than statistical compression.

Data Compression Algorithms

Cisco internetworking devices use the Stacker (abbreviated as STAC) and Predictor data compression algorithms. STAC, developed by STAC Electronics, is based on the Lempel-Ziv algorithm. The Cisco IOS software uses an optimized version of STAC that provides good compression ratios but requires many CPU cycles to perform compression.

The Predictor compression algorithm tries to predict the next sequence of characters in the data stream by using an index to look up a sequence in the compression dictionary. It then examines the next sequence in the data stream to see if it matches. If so, that sequence replaces the looked-up sequence in the dictionary. If not, the algorithm locates the next character sequence in the index and the process begins again. The index updates itself by hashing a few of the most recent character sequences from the input stream.

The Predictor data compression algorithm was obtained from the public domain and optimized by Cisco engineers. When compared with STAC, it makes more efficient use of CPU cycles but requires more memory.

Data Compression Solutions

The Cisco IOS software provides the following data compression solutions:

- Van Jacobson header compression for TCP/IP conforms to RFC 1144.
- Link compression has one set of dictionaries per hardware link (interface).
- Payload compression has one set of dictionaries per virtual circuit.
- The SA-Comp/1 and SA-Comp/2 data compression service adapters provide hardware-based data compression capabilities on Cisco 7200 series routers, the VIP2 in Cisco 7500 series routers, and Cisco 7000 series routers that have an RSP7000 or RSP7000CI.

RTP Header and Frame Relay Compression (Cisco IOS Release 11.3 Features)

The Release Notes for Cisco IOS Release 11.3 include information about RTP Header Compression and Frame Relay enhancements. These notes are available at http://www.cisco.com/univercd/cc/td/doc/product/software/ios113ed/rn113m/rn113mft.htm. The RTP section of these release notes is summarized as follows:

Real-time Transport Protocol (RTP) is a protocol used for carrying packetized audio and video traffic over an IP network. RTP is not intended for data traffic, which uses Transmission Control Protocol (TCP) or User Datagram Protocol (UDP). RTP provides end-to-end network transport functions intended for applications transmitting real-time requirements, such as audio, video, or simulation data over multicast or unicast network services.

The minimal 12 bytes of the RTP header, combined with 20 bytes of IP header and 8 bytes of UDP header, create a 40-byte IP/UDP/RTP header. The RTP packet has a payload of approximately 20 to 150 bytes for audio applications that use compressed payloads. It is inefficient to transmit the IP/UDP/RTP header without compressing it.

The RTP header compression feature compresses the IP/UDP/RTP header in an RTP data packet from 40 bytes to approximately 2 to 5 bytes. It is a hop-by-hop compression scheme similar to RFC 1144 for TCP header compression.

RTP header compression is supported on serial lines using Frame Relay, HDLC, or PPP encapsulation. It is also supported over ISDN interfaces.

Enabling compression on both ends of a low-bandwidth serial link can greatly reduce the network overhead if there is a lot of RTP traffic on that slow link. This compression is beneficial, especially when the RTP payload size is small (for example, compressed audio payloads of 20–50 bytes).

The Frame Relay enhancements section of these release notes is summarized as follows:

The Frame Relay Enhancements introduced with this feature include:

*   Standard-based FRF.9 Frame Relay compression for Cisco routers
*   Hardware compression support for FRF.9 with the Compression Service Adapter (CSA)
*   Support for VIP Software Distributed Compression on the VIP2 model VIP2-40

Frame Relay compression can now occur on the VIP board, on the CSA, or on the main CPU of the router. FRF.9 is standard-based and therefore provides multivendor compatibility. FRF.9 compression uses higher compression ratios, allowing more data to be compressed for faster transmission.

The CSA hardware has been in use on the Cisco 7200 series and Cisco 7500 series platforms, but it has had no support for Frame Relay compression. FRF.9 compression provides the capability to maintain multiple decompression/compression histories on a per-DLCI basis.

Impact of Compression and Encryption on Router Performance

When compression or encryption is performed in software instead of hardware, system performance can be affected. To determine whether these services are stressing a router's CPU:

*   Use the **show processes** Cisco IOS software command to get a baseline reading before enabling encryption or compression.
*   Enable the service and use the **show processes** command again to assess the difference.

Cisco recommends that you disable compression or encryption if the router CPU load exceeds 40 percent. Cisco also recommends that you disable compression if encryption is enabled. Also, if the files being sent across the network are already compressed, do not enable compression on your routers.

Traffic Shaping

Cisco IOS Release 11.2 supports both generic traffic shaping and Frame Relay traffic shaping, as detailed in the sections that follow.

Generic Traffic Shaping

Generic traffic shaping helps reduce the flow of outbound traffic from a router interface into a backbone transport network when congestion is detected in the downstream portions of the backbone transport network or in a downstream router. Generic traffic shaping works on a variety of layer 2 data link technologies including Frame Relay, Switched Multimegabit Data Service (SMDS), and Ethernet.

Topologies that have high-speed links (such as at a central site) feeding into lower-speed links (such as at remote or branch sites) often experience bottlenecks at the remote end because of the speed mismatch. Generic traffic shaping helps eliminate the bottleneck situation by throttling back traffic volume at the source end.

Routers can be configured to transmit at a lower bit rate than the interface bit rate. Service providers or large enterprises can, for example, use the feature to partition T1 or T3 links into smaller channels to match service ordered by customers. Figure 10-5 illustrates this example. Packet loss in the service provider's network can be limited by throttling the traffic back at the source, thus improving service predictability.

Figure 10-5 *Generic Traffic Shaping Helps Eliminate Bottleneck Situations*

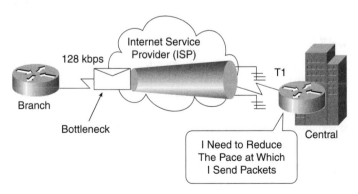

Frame Relay Traffic Shaping

As detailed in Chapter 7 and shown in Figure 10-6, the Frame Relay traffic shaping feature introduced in Cisco IOS Release 11.2 offers the following capabilities:

- **Rate enforcement on a per-virtual circuit (VC) basis**—A peak rate can be configured to limit outbound traffic to either the Committed Information Rate (CIR) or some other defined value.

- **Generalized backward explicit congestion notification (BECN) support on a per-VC basis**—The router can monitor BECNs and throttle traffic based on BECN marked packet feedback.

- **Priority/custom queuing support at the VC level**—This allows for finer granularity in the queuing of traffic, based on an individual VC.

Figure 10-6 *Frame Relay Shaping Allows the Router to Take Advantage of the Frame Relay Congestion Detection Parameters*

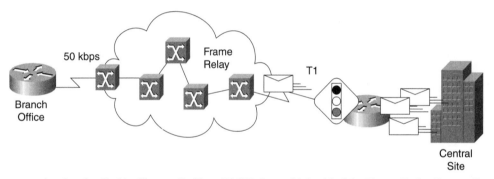

As also detailed in Chapter 7, Cisco IOS Release 11.3 added the Frame Relay Router ForeSight feature that allows Cisco Frame Relay routers to process and react to StrataCom switch ForeSight messages and adjust virtual circuit level traffic shaping in a timely manner.

Queuing Services

Queuing services enable a network administrator to manage the varying demands that applications put on networks and routers. Since Cisco started supporting weighted fair queuing in Cisco IOS Release 11.0, there has been less need for more drastic types of queuing, such as priority and custom queuing. However, in some cases, mission-critical applications running on congested serial links might still require priority or custom queuing.

Custom queuing is a less drastic solution for mission-critical applications than priority queuing. Custom queuing guarantees some level of service to all traffic, whereas priority queuing makes sure that one type of traffic will get through at the expense of all other types of traffic.

Priority Queuing

Priority queuing is particularly useful for time-sensitive, mission-critical protocols such as SNA. It is appropriate for cases where WAN links are congested from time to time. If the WAN links are constantly congested, the customer needs more bandwidth or should use compression. If the WAN links are never congested, priority queuing is unnecessary. Because priority queuing requires extra processing, do not recommend it unless it is necessary.

Priority queuing has four queues: high, medium, normal, and low. As shown in Figure 10-7, the high-priority queue is always emptied before the lower-priority queues are serviced. Traffic can be assigned to the various queues based on protocol, port number, or other criteria.

Figure 10-7 *Priority Queuing Has Four Queues; the High-Priority Queue Is Always Emptied First*

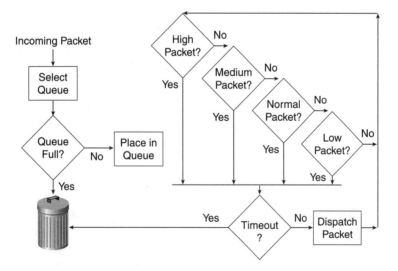

Custom Queuing

Custom queuing is a different approach for prioritizing traffic. Like priority queuing, traffic can be assigned to various queues based on protocol, port number, or other criteria. However, custom queuing handles the queues in a round-robin fashion.

Custom queuing works by establishing interface output queues. (Originally only 10 queues were available; however, there are now 16). The transmission window size of each queue is specified in bytes. When the transmission window size has been reached by transmitting the appropriate number of frames from a queue, the next queue is checked. Figure 10-8 illustrates this process.

Figure 10-8 *Custom Queuing Services Each Queue in a Round-Robin Fashion*

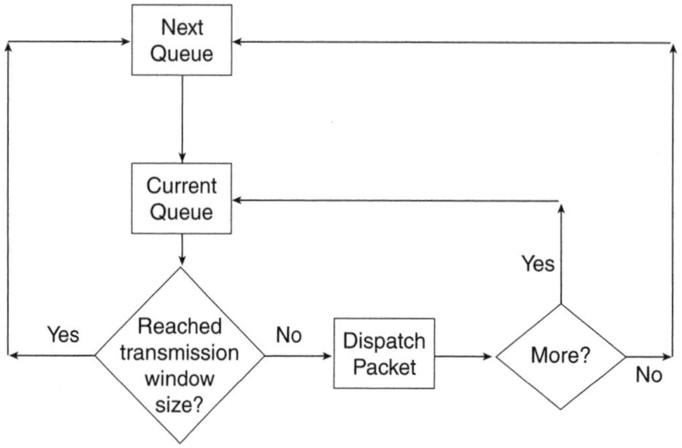

Custom queuing is more "fair" than priority queuing, although priority queuing is more powerful for prioritizing a mission-critical protocol. For example, a particular protocol can be prioritized by assigning it more queue space, but it will never monopolize the bandwidth.

TIP	Like priority queuing, custom queuing causes the router to do extra processing. Do not recommend custom queuing unless you have determined that one or more protocols need special processing.

Weighted Fair Queuing

Weighted fair queuing was first implemented in Cisco IOS Release 11.0. It is enabled by default on most low-bandwidth interfaces; no configuration is required to use weighted fair queuing. Weighted fair queuing is more "fair" than either priority or custom queuing because it handles the problems inherent in queuing schemes that are essentially first-come, first-serve.

The main problem with first-come, first-serve algorithms is that sessions using large packets can impede sessions using small packets. For example, FTP can negatively affect the performance of Telnet. The weighted fair queuing implementation looks at sizes of messages and ensures that high-volume senders do not crowd out low-volume senders.

Weighted fair queuing queues packets based on the arrival time of the last bit rather than the first bit, which ensures that applications that use large packets cannot unfairly monopolize the bandwidth.

RSVP

RSVP is another service that supports varying requirements for bandwidth and delay. RSVP is an outgrowth of the Internet Engineering Task Force's (IETF's) work on integrated services, which enable networks to support special qualities of service for applications that need them while preserving current internetworking methods. Cisco supports RSVP in Cisco IOS Release 11.2.

Traditional network functions, such as file transfers, are not sensitive to delay. Although network users may prefer that a file transfer occur quickly, the transfer will take place regardless of the amount of time it takes. Traffic generated by these applications is called *elastic* because it can stretch to work under any delay conditions.

However, new multimedia network applications, such as voice and video, require that certain minimum numbers of bits be transferred within a specific time frame. The *inelastic* traffic generated by these applications requires the network to allocate specific resources for it.

The mission of RSVP is to allow routers to communicate among themselves and with end systems so that they can reserve end-to-end network resources for inelastic applications.

RSVP is a receiver-based protocol. Applications that receive inelastic traffic inform networks of their needs, while applications that send inelastic traffic inform these receivers about traffic characteristics. The router that is connected to the receiver of a particular data flow (for example, the transmission of a video file) is responsible for initiating and maintaining the resources used for that data flow.

Tag Switching

Cisco IOS Release 11.1CT introduced tag switching on the Cisco's 7200, Cisco 7500, Cisco 7000 with RSP7000 series routers, as well as Cisco's BPX 8620 wide-area switch and BPX 8650 IP+ATM switch.

Tag switching is a new technology that combines the performance and traffic management capabilities of Layer 2 (data link layer) switching with the proven scalability of Layer 3 (network layer) routing. Tag switching assigns tags to multiprotocol frames for transport across packet or cell-based networks. It is based on the concept of label swapping, in which units of data carry a short, fixed-length label that tells switching nodes how to process the data.

Information about tag switching is available on Cisco's Web site at http://www.cisco.com/warp/public/732/tag/index.html. The following are excerpts from this site:

Although Internet traffic and the number of users are growing rapidly, IT budgets are increasing only by modest proportions. Internet service providers and enterprises are challenged to scale the performance of their existing network infrastructures with minimal budgets. Cisco IOS^{TM} software delivers scalability to enhance network capacity and performance while protecting your network investments.

Tag Switching: Evolving Your Network

Cisco IOS Tag Switching, a new technology from Cisco Systems, is an ideal solution to meet these challenges. Tag Switching fuses the intelligence of routing with the performance of switching to scale existing networks to meet future growth demands. With this technology, networks can handle more traffic, users, media-rich data, or bandwidth-intensive applications. This approach also means that ISPs and large-enterprise networks can enjoy more benefits from the performance of Asynchronous Transfer Mode (ATM) switches, like the Cisco StrataCom®, BPX®, and the LightStream® 1010, to provide Internet and ATM/frame relay services on the same platform.

A Tag Switching Internetwork

By "tagging" the first in a flow of data, subsequent packets of related data are expedited to the final destination. Request times and router processing are both minimized. Tag Switching uses a form of label swapping across packet- or cell-based networks that involves three solution elements:

- **Tag edge routers**—Located at the boundaries of a network, edge routers perform network layer services and apply tags to packets. Traffic from multiple sources going to the same destination can share tags, avoiding the label explosion problem of current IP switching implementations.
- **Tag switches**—The ATM switches or routers within the network can switch tagged packets based on the tags. These network elements can also support full Layer 3 routing or Layer 2 switching in addition to Tag Switching.
- **Tag Distribution Protocol (TDP)**—Coexisting with standard network layer protocols including routing protocols, TDP distributes tag information between devices in a Tag Switching network. Because TDP decouples tag distribution from the data flows, Tag Switching can be used over a wide variety of media, including ATM links, Packet-over-SONET (POS) links, Ethernet, Gigabit Ethernet, and others.

Leading the Industry

The worldwide leader in networking for the Internet, Cisco Systems introduces Tag Switching based on proven industry experience. To maximize the effectiveness of Tag Switching, Cisco is committed to the standardization of the architecture. Tag Switching specifications have already been submitted to the IETF for standardization.

Summary

Cisco's IOS software provides many features that you can use to enhance the operation of your network. In this chapter you learned about and discovered the scalability issues for various Cisco IOS software features, including access lists, encryption, proxy services, compression, traffic shaping, and queuing.

The next chapter in Part IV identifies how to select a network management strategy.

Case Studies

In this section, you are asked to provision Cisco IOS software features for the devices in the customer's networks in the four case studies introduced in Chapter 3, as well as for a new case study on Market Mavericks, a money management firm.

Read each case study description and complete the questions for each of the case studies.

TIP   In working through the questions to the case studies, you will find it useful to work on note paper in a separate binder to accommodate the depth of these exercises.

After you complete each question, you can refer to the solutions provided by our internetworking experts in Appendix B, "Answers to Chapter Questions, Case Studies, and Sample CCDA Exam." Keep in mind that there are potentially several correct answers to each question. These case studies and their solutions will help you prepare for the Sylvan CCDA exam following the course.

Case Study: Market Mavericks

Ms. Martin is the MIS manager at Market Mavericks, a money market management firm in New York City. Ms. Martin has the task of planning a new state-of-the-art network for the brokers that work at Market Mavericks. The 80 brokers will be on floors 74 through 77 in a skyscraper.

Ms. Martin has the task of designing a WAN that will connect the 60 branch offices at Market Mavericks. She has chosen Frame Relay and a hub-and-spoke topology. At her site (corporate headquarters), she will have a 1.5 Mbps T1/E1 serial link to the Frame Relay cloud. She plans to route IP using IGRP. She also plans to route AppleTalk using RTMP and Novell NetWare using IPX RIP. (She will upgrade to Enhanced IGRP for IP, AppleTalk, and NetWare.)

At headquarters, five NetWare print servers and five NetWare file servers are installed. Each remote site has one NetWare print server and one NetWare file server.

The corporate router is a Cisco 4000 series running Cisco IOS Release 10.3. The branch offices have Cisco 2500 routers also running Cisco IOS Release 10.3.

Market Mavericks Case Study Questions

Question 10-1

Users at corporate headquarters need to access all the Novell file servers. Users at the branch offices need to access only their own servers and the corporate file servers (though not the corporate print servers). Ms. Martin is tentatively planning to apply an outbound SAP filter on the serial link of the Cisco 4000 router to deny all branch-office servers from being advertised. She will also deny all corporate print servers. What scalability constraints should you discuss with Ms. Martin as she considers using the scheme to filter SAPs?

Question 10-2

Ms. Martin has been asked to implement a security scheme that requires the use of IP access lists. At the corporate site, she has been asked to filter any IP packets coming from the California branch office. This branch office will be shut down soon. Executives at corporate headquarters are concerned that people who will soon end their employment with the company could get proprietary information before they leave the company.

How will an inbound IP access list at the corporate router affect IP performance for all the other branch offices? Remember that Ms. Martin has a Cisco 4000 router running Cisco IOS Release 10.3 at headquarters.

Question 10-3

The financial data that the brokers at the branch offices send over TCP/IP is highly confidential. Ms. Martin is considering using encryption features on the branch routers and the corporate router. How might these features affect performance?

Question 10-4

Ms. Martin wants to know if you recommend priority queuing for the TCP/IP brokerage applications. The data that the brokers generate is considered mission-critical, but the marketing and administrative data on the AppleTalk and Novell networks is not as critical. What would you tell Ms. Martin regarding priority queuing? What are the advantages and disadvantages? Would custom queuing work better for her?

Case Study: CareTaker Publications

You might want to review the CareTaker case study description in Appendix A, "Case Studies," page 303, before you begin answering the question in this section.

CareTaker Case Study Question

Refer to the topology drawing you created for CareTaker Publications in Chapter 3 or review the topology drawing solution provided in Appendix B. In this section you will recommend software features for the network.

Question 10-5

The manager of Warehouse and Distribution is concerned about PC performance over a leased line. What recommendations could you make to increase performance using Cisco IOS software?

Case Study: PH Network Services Corporation

You may wish to review the PH Network Services Corporation case study description in Appendix A, page 306, before you begin answering the question in this section.

PH Network Services Corporation Case Study Question

Refer to the topology drawing you created for Mr. Pero in Chapter 3, "Characterizing the Existing Network," or review the topology drawing solution provided in Appendix B. In this section you will recommend software features for the network.

Question 10-6

The general manager of PH called again to ask about the possibility of patients' medical information being exposed within the system you will present. How will you accommodate for this concern in your design?

Case Study: Pretty Paper Limited

You might want to review the Pretty Paper Limited case study in Appendix A, page 307, before you begin answering the question in this section.

Pretty Paper Limited Case Study Question

Refer to the topology drawing you created for Pretty Paper in Chapter 3, or review the topology drawing solution provided in Appendix B. In this section you will recommend software features for the network.

Question 10-7

The Sales and Marketing managers are concerned about the possibility of someone stealing new designs as they are being transmitted over the network and when they are stored on the servers. What are the performance trade-offs they should be aware of when considering encryption of all data transmissions on the Frame Relay network?

Case Study: Jones, Jones, & Jones

You might wish to review the Jones, Jones, & Jones case study in Appendix A, page 308, before you begin answering the question in this section.

Jones, Jones, & Jones Case Study Question

Refer to the topology drawing you created for Ms. Jones in Chapter 3, or review the topology drawing solution provided in Appendix B. In this section you will recommend software features for the network.

Question 10-8

Ms. Jones has been reading about hackers accessing confidential data by hacking into the network from the Internet. How have you addressed her concerns with your design?

You will need approximately one and a half hours to complete this chapter and its exercises. Upon completion of this seventh chapter in Part IV, you will be able to:

- Recommend protocols and products that meet a customer's requirements for network management.

- Describe the steps a customer should take to develop a proactive network management strategy.

CHAPTER 11

Selecting a Network Management Strategy

This chapter includes some tables and other job aids you will find useful when completing the case studies at the end of the chapter. References to some WWW sites are included; relevant information has been extracted from these sites and is provided in the chapter. If you have access to the Internet, you might want to access the sites mentioned to obtain detailed information related to specific topics. All of the sites referenced in this chapter are also listed in Appendix C, "Interesting WWW Links and Other Suggested Readings."

Follow these steps to complete this chapter:

1 Study the chapter content, including any tables and job aids that appear.

2 Review the case studies at the end of this chapter.

3 Complete the questions in each case study.

4 Review the answers provided by our internetworking experts in Appendix B, "Answers to Chapter Questions, Case Studies, and Sample CCDA Exam."

As internetworks grow in scope and complexity, robust network management capabilities become increasingly important. Many companies require a broad range of network management functions to help them maximize the availability of critical applications and minimize the overall cost of ownership. This chapter examines the goals of network management and addresses how to meet those goals, including Cisco's multiplatform, standards-based solutions.

Network Management Goals

In general, most companies have the following goals for their network management products and strategies:

- Connectivity
- Security
- Cost optimization
- Manageable growth

Cisco's goal for its network management products is to provide customers with complete, up-to-date knowledge of the configuration and behavior of their networks. This goal is achieved through coupling network management products with access to on line diagnostic information and help provided by Cisco's support staff or Cisco partners.

Network Management Processes

Though the goals for network management can be stated simply, understanding all the tasks required to meet the goals is difficult. According to Cisco Enterprise Network Management marketing material, network management tasks can be divided into three main areas:

- Design and optimize
- Implement and change
- Monitor and diagnose

These tasks, detailed in Table 11-1, are carried out by network planners, administrators, engineers, operators, technicians, and help desk personnel. An understanding of the tasks your customer is working on will help you recommend appropriate network management products.

Table 11-1 *The Network Management Process*

Design and Optimize	Implement and Change	Monitor and Diagnose
Data collection definition	Installation	Defining thresholds
Baseline creation	Configuration	Monitoring exceptions
Trend analysis	Address management	Isolating problems
Response time analysis	Adds, moves, and changes	Validating problems
Capacity planning	Security management	Troubleshooting problems
Procurement	Accounting and billing	Bypassing and resolving problems
Topology design	Assets and inventory management	
	User management	
	Data management	

Most network management is reactive, though the industry is moving toward a proactive approach to network management. Vendors have been encouraging proactive network management for years, but due to reduction in staff and training at many companies, networking professionals have been required to spend most of their time implementing changes and troubleshooting problems. However, as companies recognize the strategic importance of their internetworks, more emphasis is being put on proactive network management.

Proactive Network Management

Proactive network management means monitoring the network even when it is not having problems. The following tasks comprise proactive network management:

- Collecting statistics and watching trends.

- Conducting routine tests, such as response time measurements.

- Allocating time at least once a month to compile statistics and write a baseline report that describes the current status of the network.

- Defining service goals for the network: for example, acceptable downtime, response time, throughput, ease of use, and scalability.

- Writing reports on the quality of service that has been delivered in the last month.

Many companies have network operation centers (NOCs) that include equipment, software, and staff that are dedicated to monitoring the health of the network. This staff may include help desk personnel and technicians who work on problems, as well as engineers and planners who develop long-term strategies to keep the network functioning.

Developing Proactive Network Management Strategies

When selling Cisco network management applications, help your customers develop proactive network management strategies by assisting them with the following steps for proactive network management:

- Determine network service goals

- Define metrics for measuring whether goals have been met

- Define processes for data collection and reporting

- Implement network management systems

- Collect performance data and record trends

- Analyze results and write reports

- Locate network irregularities and bottlenecks

- Plan and implement improvements to the network

- Review and adjust metrics and processes if necessary

- Document changes

Multiplatform, Standards-Based Solutions

Cisco network management applications run on standard hardware and operating system platforms, such as UNIX, Microsoft Windows, Hewlett Packard's OpenView for Windows, and other industry standards. SNMP Version 2 (SNMPv2) is supported on all platforms and devices that have Cisco IOS™ software. The following RFCs provide details about the mechanics and features of SNMP:

- RFC 1155, available at http://info.internet.isi.edu/in-notes/rfc/files/rfc1155.txt, defines the mechanisms used for describing and naming objects for the purpose of management. The mechanisms are called the structure of managed information, or SMI.

- RFC 1212, available at http://info.internet.isi.edu/in-notes/rfc/files/rfc1212.txt, defines a more concise description mechanism, which is consistent with the SMI.

- RFC 1157, available at http://info.internet.isi.edu/in-notes/rfc/files/rfc1157.txt, defines the SNMP, the protocol used for network access to managed objects.

- RFC 1213, available at http://info.internet.isi.edu/in-notes/rfc/files/rfc1213.txt, defines the Management Information Base II (MIB II), the core set of managed objects for the Internet suite of protocols.

The following draft standards define SNMPv2:

- RFC 1902, available at http://info.internet.isi.edu/in-notes/rfc/files/rfc1902.txt, defines the SMI for SNMPv2.

- RFC 1905, available at http://info.internet.isi.edu/in-notes/rfc/files/rfc1905.txt defines protocol operations for SNMPv2.

Cisco Network Management Applications

The following sections briefly describe a few of Cisco's network management applications. Other tools, including those noted in Chapter 3, "Characterizing the Existing Network," to help you characterize your network, are also useful for network management. To get more information on these products and Cisco's network management products in general, refer to Chapter 3 of this book and to the Network Management section of the *Cisco Products Quick Reference Guide,* available at http://www.cisco.com/univercd/cc/td/doc/cpqrg/index.htm. Some excerpts from this Guide are provided in this section.

CiscoWorks Applications

CiscoWorks is a series of SNMP-based internetwork management software applications that allow device status monitoring, configuration maintenance, and troubleshooting, as shown in Figure 11-1.

Figure 11-1 *CiscoWorks Allows Device Status Monitoring, Configuration Maintenance, and Troubleshooting*

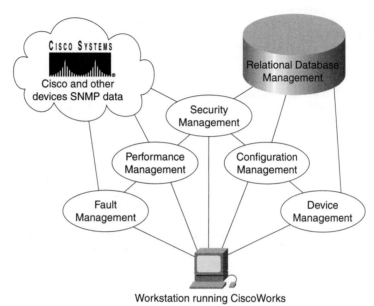

Workstation running CiscoWorks

CiscoWorks2000

Chapter 3 provides an introduction to the CiscoWorks2000 product family, announced in September 1998. Recall from that discussion that CiscoWorks2000 is comprised of Resource Manager Essentials, CiscoWorks for Switched Internetworks (CWSI) Campus, and CiscoView tools.

Details about the components of CiscoWorks2000 can be found at http://www.cisco.com/univercd/cc/td/doc/product/rtrmgmt/cw2000/index.htm; summaries of the CWSI Campus (including CiscoView) and Resource Manager Essentials sections are provided here.

CWSI Campus

CWSI Campus is a suite of network management applications that enable you to configure, monitor, and manage a switched internetwork. The CWSI Campus applications provide you with a graphical user interface (GUI) of your network topology, configuration, and management.

Table 11-2 describes the CWSI Campus applications.

Table 11-2 *CWSI Campus Applications*

CWSI Campus Application	What It Does
CWSI Campus map	CWSI Campus map provides a map of the physical devices and links in your discovered network. It enables you to locate a specific device or link in the network, and view and understand how the devices are linked together. CWSI Campus map also enables you to view the virtual topology of your virtual LAN (VLAN) configuration in relation to the physical topology.
VlanDirector	VlanDirector is a VLAN configuration and management tool that enables you to display, configure, modify, and manage VLANs. It also enables you to display reports on VLAN status and membership.
UserTracking	UserTracking simplifies moves within VLANs and tracks end user information. If an end station is moved and plugged into another port, UserTracking provides configuration information from the Media Access Control (MAC)—VLAN mapping that allows the device to remain on the original VLAN without manual reconfiguration. You can also verify and look up end-station changes in the UserTracking database.
CiscoView	CiscoView displays a graphical representation of a device and enables you to configure and monitor device chassis, port, and interface information. It also provides color-coded indicators to monitor port status.
TrafficDirector	TrafficDirector provides Remote Monitoring (RMON), protocol analysis, application usage monitoring, traffic analysis, and troubleshooting of network performance problems.
AtmDirector	AtmDirector discovers Asynchronous Transfer Mode (ATM) switches, physical links, and permanent and switched virtual circuits. It provides performance monitoring of ATM switches and links within the ATM network, and traffic analysis of RMON-enabled ATM links. AtmDirector also enables you to display and monitor ATM-VLANs and Private Network-to-Network Interface (PNNI) components and their status in the network.

Resource Manager Essentials

The Resource Manager Essentials (Essentials) package provides an enterprise solution to network management. This suite of web-based network management tools enables administrators to collect the monitoring, fault, and availability information needed to track devices that are critical to the network. Essentials also provides the administration tools needed to rapidly and reliably deploy and upgrade Cisco devices.

Essentials is based on a client/network architecture that connects multiple web-based clients to a server residing on the network. As the number of devices on the network increases, additional servers or collection points can be added to manage network growth with little impact on the client browser application.

By taking advantage of the scalability inherent in the intranet architecture, Essentials supports multiple users anywhere on the network. The web-based infrastructure gives network operators, administrators, technicians, Help Desk staff, IS managers, and end users access to network management tools, applications, and services.

Essentials provides the functions in Table 11-3.

Table 11-3   *Resource Manager Essentials*

Function	Details
Availability	Monitor the reachability and response time of user-selected devices on the network.
	Collect fault and performance information for routers and switches.
Change Audit	View and search a central repository of all network changes (for example, Inventory, Software Management, and so on), set up periods of time to monitor network changes, and maintain the repository.
Device Configuration	Maintain an active archive of switch and router configuration files.
	Search the archive for configuration files based on user-specified criteria.
	Create custom reports for repetitive tasks.
Inventory	Import devices from databases or files.
	Add, delete, change, and list devices in your network inventory.
	Schedule polling and collection to update your network inventory.
	Display reports and graphs of your hardware and software inventory.
Software Management	Schedule, download, and monitor software image upgrades for Cisco devices on your network.
	Validate images with devices before initiating downloads and define and monitor the progress of scheduled jobs.
Syslog Analysis	Troubleshoot and track device problems.
	View summaries of real-time reports on events that are being logged to syslog on behalf of a router.
	Process these messages to generate reports and statistical summaries.
	Configure automatic actions that occur when certain message types are received.
System Administration	Create, modify, and browse device views (groups of devices).
	Review your package options before installing or uninstalling task sets.
	Check log file status.
	Back up, move, and restore data.
	Manage user accounts.
	Start, stop, and check the status of processes running on the back-end server.

continues

Table 11-3 *Resource Manager Essentials (Continued)*

Function	Details
Tools	CCO tools, including technical tips, troubleshooting, a bug toolkit, open forum, and connections to the TAC and CCO software.
	Case Management links you to Cisco's Customer Service department for opening and querying cases.
	Connectivity tools to check device connections to the Essentials server.
	Contract Connection verifies which of your Cisco devices are covered by a service contract.
	Device Navigator connects to the HTTP server running on a Cisco router or a Cisco access server.
Management Connection	Create and install connection files that link Essentials to external applications.
Troubleshooting	Collect server and self-test information.
	View process failures.
	Find error message log files.

Previous Versions of CiscoWorks

The CiscoWorks network management application suite, the precursor to CiscoWorks2000, provides an automatic data collection and e-mail link to Cisco or partner support in order to automate the otherwise lengthy and error-prone process of gathering diagnostic information before troubleshooting begins. Some of the applications bundled in previous versions of CiscoWorks include:

- **AutoInstall Manager**—Enables you to remotely install a new router using a neighboring router.

- **CiscoConnect**—Enables you to provide Cisco and Cisco partners with debugging information, configurations, and topology information to speed resolution of network problems. The CiscoConnect application captures information about a customer's routers, including interfaces, controllers, processes, buffer utilization, configuration, protocols, firmware levels, and system software versions. This profile is registered with the Cisco Connection Online (CCO) service to provide a quick reference for technical support staff when solving problems. CiscoConnect can also notify customers via customized news bulletins of new features and bug fixes relevant to their networks.

- **CiscoView**—Provides a graphical device view along with dynamic status, statistics, troubleshooting, and comprehensive configuration information for switches, routers, access servers, concentrators, and adapters. CiscoView is bundled with CiscoWorks and is also available as a standalone product.

- **Configuration File Management**—Provides an audit trail for who made changes and when. It can also detect unauthorized configuration.

- **Contacts**—Provides information about the contact person for a specific device, including the name, phone number, e-mail address, title, location, and address.

- **Device Management**—Creates and maintains a database that holds an inventory of your network, including hardware, software, release levels, individuals responsible for maintaining devices, and location of devices.

- **Global Command Facility**—Creates configuration "snap-ins" that can be applied automatically to groups of routers that share configuration parameters.

- **Health Monitor**—Enables you to view information about the status of a device, including buffers, CPU load, memory available, and protocols and interfaces being used.

- **Offline Network Analysis**—Collects historical network data for offline analysis of performance trends and traffic patterns in a SQL relational database.

- **Path Tool**—Enables you to view and analyze the path between two devices to collect utilization and error data.

- **Security Manager**—Sets up authority checking procedures to protect selected CiscoWorks applications and network devices from unauthorized individuals.

- **Software Manager**—Provides management and central distribution of router software versions.

CiscoWorks Blue

The CiscoWorks Blue suite of applications provides the management tools required to help customers make the transition from legacy (SNA) networks to multiprotocol networks, including IP. The applications available are as follows:

- CiscoWorks Blue Native Service Point
- CiscoWorks Blue Internetwork Status Monitor
- CiscoWorks Blue Internetwork Performance Monitor
- CiscoWorks Blue Maps
- CiscoWorks Blue SNA View

More information about these products can be found in the *Cisco Products Quick Reference Guide* and at the CiscoWorks Blue Web site at http://www.cisco.com/warp/public/cc/cisco/mkt/enm/cworks/cwblue/index.shtml.

CiscoWorks Blue Maps

CiscoWorks Blue Maps enable you to view logical maps of Cisco routers that are running Cisco IOS Release 11.0 or later and are configured with remote source-route bridging (RSRB), data-link switching (DLSw), or Advanced Peer-to-Peer Networking (APPN), as shown in Figure 11-2.

Each application (RSRB, DLSw, or APPN) presents the network administrator with a dynamic, color-coded network map of routers that are enabled with a specific SNA-related protocol. CiscoWorks Blue Maps requires the related Management Information Bases (MIBs) (RSRB, DLSw, and APPN) that are installed on the routers.

Figure 11-2 *CiscoWorks Blue Maps Enable You to View Logical Maps of Cisco Routers Running SNA-Related Protocols*

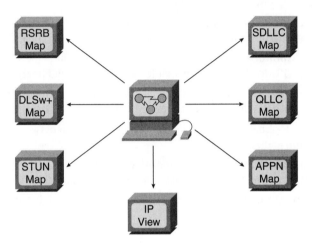

You can manage an entire network from a single workstation by using both CiscoWorks and CiscoWorks Blue Maps. For example, using the DLSw Map application, you can accomplish the following tasks:

- Discover your network of DLSw-enabled routers.

- View a map of DLSw-enabled routers.

- Obtain details about any single router, or statistics about any router, as known by a neighbor.

- Display a list of circuits maintained by any router and details about each circuit.

Remote Monitoring

The SNMP Remote Monitoring (RMON) standard allows for monitoring packet and traffic patterns on LAN segments. RMON tracks the following items:

- Number of packets

- Packet sizes

- Broadcasts

- Network utilization

- Errors and conditions, such as Ethernet collisions
- Statistics for hosts, including errors generated by hosts, the busiest hosts, and which hosts talk to which hosts

RMON features include historical views of RMON statistics based on user-defined sample intervals, alarms based on user-defined thresholds, and packet capture based on user-defined filters.

RMON is defined as a portion of the MIB II database. RFC 1757 available at http://info.internet.isi.edu/in-notes/rfc/files/rfc1757.txt, defines the objects for managing remote network monitoring devices. RFC 1513, available at http://info.internet.isi.edu/in-notes/rfc/files/rfc1513.txt, defines extensions to the RMON MIB for managing 802.5 Token Ring networks.

RMON Specification

The RMON specification comprises nine groups of managed objects. RMON agents can implement some or all of the following groups:

- Statistics
- History
- Alarms
- Hosts
- Hosts Top N (used to prepare reports that describe the hosts that top a list ordered by one of their statistics)
- Traffic Matrix (stores statistics for conversations between sets of two addresses)
- Filters
- Packet Capture
- Events

The Token Ring MIB adds enhancements for gathering data on specific Token Ring information, such as source-route bridging statistics, ring configuration, and ring station order.

Router RMON Support

When used as an agent on routers, RMON enables customers to view traffic events and alarms for the network segments that the router is on. By using a network management console, network managers can detect problems and gather information for developing a baseline understanding of the health of the network. RMON support is available as an option with Cisco IOS software.

Switch RMON Support

Cisco's optional embedded RMON agent in switches provides RMON capabilities for both 10BaseT and 100BaseT. Depending on the revision level of the switch software, RMON support is available for other switches also. Refer to Cisco's Web site at http://www.cisco.com for the latest information on RMON support in switches.

TrafficDirector RMON Console Application

TrafficDirector™ is an RMON console application that analyzes traffic and enables proactive management of internetworks. TrafficDirector provides a graphical user interface for analyzing RMON data. Network traffic information is collected from the following:

- RMON agents in Cisco's Catalyst switches
- Cisco IOS software embedded RMON agents in routers
- Cisco SwitchProbe standalone network monitoring probes
- Any RMON standard-compliant agent

TrafficDirector packet filters enable users to monitor all seven layers of network traffic, including data link, network, transport, and application layers. Performance and fault management are supported using TrafficDirector's multilayer traffic analysis, proactive alarms, and remote packet capture features. TrafficDirector's protocol analysis tool provides centralized troubleshooting for most protocol-related network problems. TrafficDirector supports full seven-layer decodes for the AppleTalk, DECnet, IP, ISO, Novell, SNA, Sun NFS, Banyan VINES, and XNS protocol suites.

TrafficDirector is part of both the CWSI Campus and CWSI application suites.

Summary of Cisco's Internetwork Management Applications

Table 11-4 displays a brief summary of Cisco's internetwork management applications.

Table 11-4 *Cisco's Network Management Applications*

Network Management Application	Devices Supported or Managed by the Application	Product Platform(s)
CiscoWorks	Various Cisco devices	SunNet Manager
		HP OpenView on SunOS/Solaris
		HP OpenView HP-UX
		IBM NetView for AIX
Network Management Application	**Devices Supported or Managed by the Application**	**Product Platform(s)**
CiscoWorks Blue Maps	SNA-enabled Cisco routers	NetView for AIX on RS/6000
		HP OpenView on HP-UX on HP
		HP OpenView or SunNet Manager on Solaris on Sun
CiscoWorks Blue SNA View	SNA-enabled Cisco routers and SNA devices managed by mainframe	Requires CiscoWorks Blue Maps
CiscoWorks Blue Native Service Point	Cisco routers	IBM NetView
		Sterling NetMaster
Cisco Hub/Ring Manager for Windows	Cisco 2517, 2518, 2519 routers	PC with Microsoft Windows 3.1 or higher and HP OpenView Windows
CiscoWorks Windows	Cisco routers, switches, access servers, concentrators, adapters, and ATM switches	PC with Microsoft Windows NT 3.51 or 4.0 or Windows 95 running CastleRock SNMPc (bundled with CiscoWorks Windows) or HP OpenView Windows (optional)
CiscoView	Cisco routers, switches, access servers, concentrators, adapters, and ATM switches (LightStream 100 and LightStream 2020)	Standalone on UNIX workstations Also bundled with CiscoWorks, CiscoWorks Windows, and CWSI
NETSYS Tools	Cisco routers	SunOS, Solaris, HP-UX, and AIX
NETSYS Baseliner for NT	Cisco routers	PC with Microsoft Windows NT 4.0

continues

Table 11-4 *Cisco's Network Management Applications (Continued)*

ControlStream StreamView VirtualStream	LightStream 2020	Sun SPARCstation with SunOS, and optionally HP OpenView
TrafficDirector	RMON console management	SunNet Manager HP OpenView IBM NetView for AIX PC with Windows 95 or NT Standalone on UNIX workstations Version 5.2 is only available as part of CWSI (on Solaris and NT)
Network Management Application	**Devices Supported or Managed by the Application**	**Product Platform(s)**
Total Control Manager/ SNMP	Modem and T1 cards in Cisco 5100 access server	PC with Microsoft Windows 3.1
CWSI (includes VlanDirector, TrafficDirector, CiscoView and others)	Comprehensive support for Cisco Catalyst switches	SunNet Manager on Solaris HP OpenView on Solaris PC with Windows NT
Resource Manager Essentials	Various Cisco devices	Solaris Microsoft Windows NT 4.0 AIX HP UNIX
CWSI Campus (includes VlanDirector, TrafficDirector, CiscoView, and others)	Comprehensive support for Cisco Catalyst switches	Solaris Microsoft Windows NT 4.0 AIX HP UNIX Resource Manager Essentials

Summary

Network management is becoming increasingly important as networks become more complex. In this chapter you learned about protocols used for network management and were introduced to many of Cisco's multiplatform, standards-based solutions.

In the next, final chapter in Part IV, you will learn how to put all of your design considerations, including your network management selections, into a design document for your customer.

Case Studies

In this section, you are asked to select Cisco network management tools to be used in the customer's network for the four case studies introduced in Chapter 3.

Read each case study description and complete the questions for each.

TIP   As mentioned previously, when working through the questions to the case studies, you will find it useful to work on note paper in a separate binder to accommodate the depth of these exercises.

After you complete each question, you can refer to the solutions provided by our internetworking experts in Appendix B. Keep in mind that there are potentially several correct answers to each question. These case studies and their solutions will help you prepare for the Sylvan CCDA exam following the course.

Case Study: CareTaker Publications

You might wish to review the CareTaker case study description in Appendix A, "Case Studies," page 303, before proceeding to answer the questions in this section.

CareTaker Case Study Questions

Refer to the topology drawing you created for CareTaker Publications in the Chapter 3, or review the topology drawing solution provided in Appendix B. In this section, you will select network management products and protocols for the network.

Mr. Smith has the following words to say regarding his network management requirements, "My network administrators are very junior. When new routers come on board, we want to minimize the configuration. In addition, we would like to keep track of the status of the routers here at headquarters and be able to access the router configurations remotely."

You say to Mr. Smith, "Everything you have asked for is feasible. Do you have any requirements for troubleshooting tools, protocol analysis, or performance monitoring?"

Mr. Smith says, "I'm glad you mentioned that. We want to access information on network utilization, errors, broadcasts, which stations talk to which stations, which stations talk the most…that sort of thing. We would like the application to support alarms and to have some protocol analysis when there are problems."

Now that you know Mr. Smith's requirements for network management products and protocols at CareTaker Publications, answer the following questions.

Question 11-1

The IS manager is not sure that she has the personnel it will take to manage the new network. Her administrators are junior and have never worked with routers before. She understands the need for training and has planned for it, but she is still concerned. Recommend specific network management protocols and products that will meet CareTaker's needs.

Question 11-2

In addition to training, recommend steps that CareTaker should take to develop a proactive network management strategy that will not tax the junior staff.

Case Study: PH Network Services Corporation

You may wish to review the PH Network Services Corporation case study description in Appendix A, page 306, before proceeding to answer the question in this section.

PH Network Services Corporation Case Study Question

Refer to the topology drawing you created for Mr. Pero in Chapter 3, or review the topology drawing solution provided in Appendix B. In this section, you will select network management products and protocols for the network.

Question 11-3

The general manager is not sure that he has the personnel it will take to manage the new network. His administrator is very junior and has never worked with routers before. He understands the need for training and has planned for it but is still concerned. Recommend specific network management protocols and products that will meet the needs.

Case Study: Pretty Paper Limited

You might want to review the Pretty Paper Limited case study in Appendix A, page 307, before proceeding to answer the questions in this section.

Pretty Paper Limited Case Study Questions

Refer to the topology drawing you created for Pretty Paper in Chapter 3, or review the topology drawing solution provided in Appendix B. In this section, you will select network management products and protocols for the network.

Question 11-4

The network administrator at Pretty Paper has been managing an X.25 network for a long time and knows something about Frame Relay, mostly from reading. Recommend specific network management protocols and products that will meet the company's needs and allow the administrator to be immediately productive.

Question 11-5

What recommendations would you make to Pretty Paper about proactively monitoring the network and data collection?

Case Study: Jones, Jones, & Jones

You may want to review the Jones, Jones, & Jones case study in Appendix A, page 308, before proceeding to answer the questions in this section.

Jones, Jones, & Jones Case Study Questions

Refer to the topology drawing you created for Ms. Jones in Chapter 3, or review the topology drawing solution provided in Appendix B. In this section, you will select network management products and protocols for the network.

Question 11-6

The managing partner believes that she has a pretty savvy individual ready to hire as the administrator of the new network. She had to commit to him that good network management tools would be in place when the network is completed. Recommend specific network management protocols and products that will meet the needs of this demanding person.

Question 11-7

Recommend steps that should be taken to develop a proactive network management strategy.

You will need approximately one hour to complete this chapter and its exercises. Upon completion of this last chapter in Part IV you will be able to:

- Develop a response to a customer's request for proposal (RFP).
- Create a design document for a customer.

CHAPTER 12

Writing a Design Document

This chapter includes some job aids you will find useful when completing the case studies at the end of the chapter. References to some WWW sites are included; relevant information has been extracted from these sites and is provided in this chapter. If you have access to the Internet, you might want to access the sites mentioned to obtain detailed information related to specific topics. All the sites referenced in this chapter are listed in Appendix C, "Interesting WWW Links and Other Suggested Readings."

Follow these steps to complete this chapter:

1 Study the chapter content, including any job aids that appear.

2 Review the case study at the end of this chapter.

3 Complete the questions in the case study.

4 Review the answer provided by our internetworking experts in Appendix B, "Answers to Chapter Questions, Case Studies, and Sample CCDA Exam."

This chapter first identifies what a design document is used for and leads you through the content of a design document.

Role of the Design Document

After you have identified your customer's needs and designed a solution, the next step is to communicate your solution to the customer and explain how it meets the needs. A design document is an excellent tool to help you communicate your solution, whether you are responding to a request for proposal (RFP) or submitting an unsolicited proposal.

If the customer provided you with an RFP, your design document should follow the format specified in the request. Some RFPs are strict, and your proposal will be rejected if it does not follow the specified format exactly.

If you did not receive an RFP and are submitting an unsolicited proposal, organize your design document to ensure that Cisco's most important selling points and the most important selling points offered by your company are clearly and concisely presented.

Content of the Design Document

Your design document should include the following sections, at a minimum, although you may choose to include additional sections:

- Executive Summary
- Design Requirements
- Design Solution
- Summary
- Appendixes
- The cost of the proposed design may be provided separately.

Section 1: Executive Summary

The Executive Summary is directed at the key decision makers for the project. This part of the design document should be no more than two pages and should include only high-level points that clearly articulate your strategy for the project. Be sure to focus on benefits that you and Cisco can offer, based on the customer's needs. You may include the following items:

- **Purpose of the project**—Including one or two paragraphs that state the purpose of this document as it relates to the company's strategic objectives.

- **Strategic recommendations**—Including one or two paragraphs that outline your internetworking design strategy. Be sure to relate your recommendations to the company's strategic objectives.

- **Implementation considerations**—Including one paragraph that lists implementation considerations for the project, such as integration issues, training, support, and transition issues.

- **Benefits of the solution**—Summarizing the overall benefits of your solution. Make sure the benefits relate to the company's strategic objectives.

Section 2: Design Requirements

The Design Requirements summarizes your conclusions as a result of identifying the customer's needs (as explained in Part III, "Identifying Customer Needs"). You may include characterization of the existing network and customer requirements.

Characterization of The Existing Network

Characterization of the existing network includes the following items:

- A description of the existing network, including a topology map if available
- Current applications, protocols, topology, and number of users
- Business issues relevant to the network design project
- Health of the customer's existing network

Customer Requirements

Customer requirements include the following items:

- Requirements for performance, security, capacity, and scalability to support new applications
- Flow of information for new applications

Section 3: Design Solution

Describe your recommended solution, along with the features and benefits it provides. Organize the content in this section according to the client's needs, listed in order of the client's priorities. Be sure to include the following components:

- **Proposed network topology**—Including a topology map and the advantages offered by the network topology you designed.
- **Hardware and media recommended for the LAN**—Including features and benefits of each component you selected, related to the customer's needs for performance, security, capacity, and scalability. Use the *Products Quick Reference Guide,* available at http://www.cisco.com/univercd/cc/td/doc/cpqrg/index.htm, to help articulate the features and benefits of each component.
- **Hardware and media recommended for the WAN**—Including features and benefits of each component you selected, related to the customer's needs for performance, security, capacity, and scalability. Use the *Products Quick Reference Guide* to help articulate the features and benefits of each component.
- **Network-layer addressing and naming model**—Including an addressing model and naming model for all components on the network, related to the customer's needs for performance, security, capacity, and scalability.
- **Routing and bridging protocols recommended for the network**—Including recommended routing and bridging protocols related to the customer's needs for performance, security, and capacity.

- **Software features recommended for the network**—Including Cisco IOS™ software features, such as access lists, proxy services, encryption, compression, and queuing. Relate your selection of software features to the customer's needs for performance, security, capacity, and scalability.

- **Network management strategy**—Including recommended products and protocols related to the customer's needs. Include a description of a proactive network management strategy.

Section 4: Summary

This section of your design document includes a summary of your solution and articulates how it solves the customer's needs. Use bulleted lists to summarize Cisco's key differentiators, as well as those of your company.

Section 5: Appendixes

Include as many appendixes as required to provide necessary detailed information. Be sure to consider how much content your customer will be able to read and comprehend. That is, keep in mind your customer's threshold for accepting large amounts of information. Appendixes may include the following content:

- A list of contacts at Cisco, your company, and the customer's site

- A project implementation time line or schedule

- Additional information on Cisco products

- Details of addressing and naming schemes that you developed for the customer

- Details of strategies for managing the network that you developed for the customer

- Results of prototype tests (as described in Part V of this book, "Building a Prototype or Pilot for the Network.")

- Test results of any performance measurements you performed on the customer's current network

Section 6: Cost

The cost of your design should be presented in enough detail so that the customer can understand how the total cost was determined. For example, you might want to itemize equipment costs and installation costs.

If appropriate, ongoing network operation costs should also be specified. Even if the customer has not requested these operation costs, you might wish to calculate them while doing your design and keep them for future reference.

The customer may request that the cost of the design be provided separately from other sections, especially if the proposal is large and will be reviewed by many people. This would allow a technical review of your design to be done separately from a cost review.

Summary

A design document is a key tool in communicating your solution to the customer and explaining how that solution meets the customer's needs. This chapter covered the key sections required in a design document and concludes Part IV of this book, "Designing the Topology."

The next chapter is the first in Part V.

Case Study

In this section, you will create a design document for the case study Jones, Jones, & Jones. Although this section requires that you create only one proposal for Jones, Jones, & Jones, you might want to select one of the other case studies and practice creating design documents that address specific customer needs.

TIP

In working through the exercise for the Jones, Jones, & Jones case study, you will find it useful to work on note paper in a separate binder to accommodate the depth of the exercise.

After you complete the exercise for this case study, you can refer to the solution provided by our internetworking experts in Appendix B. Keep in mind that there are potentially several correct answers to this question. The case studies in this book and their solutions will help you prepare for the Sylvan CCDA exam following the course.

Case Study: Jones, Jones, & Jones

You might want to review the Jones, Jones, & Jones case study in Appendix A, "Case Studies," page 308, before proceeding to answer the question in this section.

Jones, Jones, & Jones Case Study Question

Refer to the topology drawing you created for Ms. Jones in Chapter 3, "Characterizing the Existing Network," or review the topology drawing solution provided in Appendix B. In this section, you will create a design document for the network.

Question 12-1

Create a design document using the outline provided in this module. Be sure to emphasize the customer's needs, listed in priority. The format of unsolicited design documents should emphasize key Cisco differentiators and key reseller differentiators as they relate to the client's requirements.

PART V

Building a Prototype or Pilot for the Network

This part of the book identifies how to build and test a prototype or pilot to prove that the network structure meets the customer's requirements for performance, security, capacity, and scalability.

Chapter 13   Building a Prototype or Pilot

Chapter 14   Testing the Prototype or Pilot

You will need approximately one hour to complete this chapter and its exercises. Upon completion of this first chapter in Part V you will be able to do the following:

- Determine how much of the network structure must be built to prove that the network design meets the customer's needs.

- List the tasks required to build a prototype or pilot that demonstrates the functionality of the network design.

CHAPTER 13

Building a Prototype or Pilot

This chapter includes some job aids you will find useful when completing the case studies at the end of the chapter. References to some WWW sites are included; relevant information has been extracted from these sites and is provided in this chapter. If you have access to the Internet, you might want to access the sites mentioned to obtain detailed information related to specific topics. All the sites referenced in this chapter are also listed in Appendix C, "Interesting WWW Links and Other Suggested Readings."

Follow these steps to complete this chapter:

1 Study the chapter content, including any job aids that appear.

2 Review the case studies at the end of this chapter.

3 Complete the questions in each case study.

4 Review the answers provided by our internetworking experts in Appendix B, "Answers to Chapter Questions, Case Studies, and Sample CCDA Exam."

After your design is complete, you must validate it for yourself and your customer. This section discusses both prototypes and pilots.

A *prototype* of a network is an implementation of a portion of the network to prove that the design meets the requirements. A *pilot* is simply a scaled-down prototype used to demonstrate basic functionality.

Steps to follow to build a prototype are presented first, followed by steps needed to build a pilot.

Validating Your Design with a Prototype Versus Pilot

In order to prove that your design works, you can build either a prototype or build a pilot, depending on your customer's requirements. The decision of which to build will probably be made by your customer based on cost versus need.

For larger configurations, a prototype is generally more feasible. For smaller configurations, a pilot might be more practical. The decision will probably be made on relative costs; the costs for prototyping a portion of the network will be relatively small for a larger network. However, if the network itself is small, then prototyping it could involve costs that are relatively large compared to the total costs of the project, so demonstrating basic functionality with a pilot might be more feasible.

Steps to Build a Prototype

You can follow these steps to build a prototype network structure to prove to a customer that your design works:

Step 1   Review the customer requirements.

Step 2   Determine how big the prototype needs to be.

Step 3   Understand what your competition plans to propose.

Step 4   Develop a test plan.

Step 5   Purchase and configure the equipment.

Step 6   Practice.

Step 7   Conduct final tests and demonstrations.

Step 1: Review the Customer Requirements

Review the work you did in Chapter 4, "Determining New Customer Requirements":

- Synthesize the customer's requirements for performance, security, capacity, and scalability into a short list of the customer's major goals.

- List ideas for demonstrations you can conduct that will please the customer.

- List any pitfalls or outcomes to avoid because they could cause a negative reaction.

Step 2: Determine How Big the Prototype Needs to Be

Determine how much of the network structure must be built to prove that the design meets the customer's major goals.

Investigate services and tools you can use to simplify the task of purchasing, installing, and configuring equipment for a prototype. For example, investigate testing services and network simulation tools.

Step 3: Understand What Your Competition Plans to Propose

Gain an understanding of what your competition plans to propose. If possible, work with your account manager to find out the exact design and products that your competitors plan to propose. If it is not possible to get details, make assumptions based on the types of products that will meet the customer's requirements.

Step 4: Develop a Test Plan

Draw a topology map of the test environment. Include major configuration parameters in the map.

List simulation tools, Cisco hardware and software, and non-Cisco hardware and software you will need for the prototype. Include cables, modems, null modems, WAN connections, Internet access, workstations, servers, design simulation tools, telephone-equipment simulators, and so on.

List and plan for any other resources you will need, including scheduling time in a lab either at Cisco or the customer's site, and any help you will need from co-workers or customer staff.

Develop a list of the tests and demonstrations you will run. In this list, explain the following:

- How each test will prove that the design meets the customer's needs
- How each test will showcase Cisco's strengths
- How each test will cause a competitor's product or design to fail (if possible)

Write a script for each test or demonstration, including a list of the steps to prove the design and a description of how to avoid pitfalls during the test.

Step 5: Purchase and Configure Equipment

Purchase (if necessary) and configure the following equipment:

- Network simulation tools
- Cisco hardware and software
- Non-Cisco hardware and software

Step 6: Practice

Make sure to practice demonstrations before you execute them in front of the customer.

Step 7: Conduct Final Tests and Demonstrations

Refer to Chapter 14, "Testing the Prototype or Pilot," for more information on conducting the tests and demonstrations.

Steps to Build a Pilot

For small businesses, a pilot might be more practical. The case studies in this section provide some practical examples of how to design and build a pilot based on customer requirements.

If applicable, the following are some minimum recommendations for a pilot of your design:

Step 1   Test the design.

Make sure you test the design, including meeting the customer's stated response-time requirement. For example, a requirement could state that users should see their screens within one-tenth of a second.

Step 2   Investigate the competition.

Investigate what your competitors will be proposing.

Step 3   Script a demonstration of the test results.

Write a script for a demonstration of the test results. In your script, do the following things:

— Make sure the tests will prove that the design meets the customer's needs.

— Make sure the tests will showcase Cisco's strengths.

— If possible, make sure the tests will showcase competitors' weaknesses.

Step 4   Practice.

Practice demonstrations before you execute them in front of the customer.

Step 5   Schedule and present the demonstration.

Schedule time with the customer and present the demonstration.

Products and Services to Prove the Concept

The following products and services can help you prove the concept to the customer without installing and configuring the whole internetwork. Chapter 14 has more details on testing your prototype or pilot.

Industry Tests

Sometimes it is not necessary to build a test yourself. Instead, you can take advantage of tests already done in the industry or by Cisco personnel. For example, if you are proposing Catalyst 5000 switches and the competition is proposing Cabletron MMAC-Plus switches, download the results of the Strategic Networks Consulting, Inc. (SNCI) switch tests from the SNCI's Web site at http://www.snci.com/ and use these results in your presentation.

Tools

Chapter 3, "Characterizing the Existing Network," discusses some tools that you can use to characterize your network. These tools can also be useful in your network demonstrations.

For example, you can use Network General Corporation's Sniffer network analyzer to generate traffic and simulate new network designs. It is not a true network simulator, but if you are knowledgeable about the amount of network traffic caused by new applications you plan to install on a network, you can use the Sniffer to gain an understanding of the effect new applications will have on your network. For more detail, see Network Associate's Web pages at http://www.nai.com.

Summary

In order to prove that your design works, you can either build a prototype or a pilot. In this chapter, you learned the steps needed to build each of these.

The next chapter in Part V discusses how to test the prototype or pilot.

Case Studies

In this section, you are asked to describe how a prototype or a pilot of the network would be built for the four case studies introduced in Chapter 3.

Read each case study description and complete the questions for each of the case studies.

TIP   As mentioned, when working through the questions to the case studies, you will find it useful to work on note paper in a separate binder to accommodate the depth of these exercises.

After you complete each question, you can refer to the solutions provided by our internetworking experts in Appendix B. Keep in mind that there are potentially several correct answers to each question. These case studies and their solutions will help you prepare for the Sylvan CCDA exam following the course.

Case Study: CareTaker Publications

You might want to review the CareTaker case study description in Appendix A, "Case Studies," page 303, before proceeding to answer the questions in this section.

CareTaker Case Study Questions

Refer to the topology drawing you created for CareTaker Publications in Chapter 3, or review the topology drawing solution provided in Appendix B. In this section you will describe how to create a pilot for the network.

Question 13-1

Mr. Smith of CareTaker Publications has accepted your recommendations but has made it clear that both the parent corporation's and CareTaker's management have repeatedly expressed the requirement that everything work before the move takes place.

Describe how you will "pilot" the system prior to the move. You need not worry about the mainframe and the SNA traffic; that will be the parent corporation's Network Operations personnel's responsibility.

Question 13-2

What additional recommendations for a pilot would you make?

Case Study: PH Network Services Corporation

You might wish to review the PH Network Services Corporation case study description in Appendix A, page 306, before proceeding to answer the question in this section.

PH Network Services Corporation Case Study Question

Refer to the topology drawing you created for Mr. Pero in Chapter 3, or review the topology drawing solution provided in Appendix B. In this section you will describe how to build a prototype or a pilot for the network.

Question 13-3

The general manager of PH wants to make sure that the system can be installed in a manner that will allow all offices to "come on line" in a phased-in approach. Describe your method of installing the system.

Case Study: Pretty Paper Limited

You may wish to review the Pretty Paper Limited case study in Appendix A, on page 307, before proceeding to answer the question in this section.

Pretty Paper Limited Case Study Question

Refer to the topology drawing you created for Pretty Paper in Chapter 3, or review the topology drawing solution provided in Appendix B. In this section you will recommend a pilot for the network.

Question 13-4

Before spending all the effort and money needed to do this conversion, Pretty Paper management would like an assurance that this solution will work. However, it does not have the time or money to do a prototype or proof-of-concept. How would you propose to pilot the system so that most of the effort for the pilot is moving toward the final system while demonstrating the functionality of the final system?

Case Study: Jones, Jones, & Jones

You may wish to review the Jones, Jones, & Jones case study in Appendix A, page 308, before proceeding to answer the question in this section.

Jones, Jones, & Jones Case Study Question

Refer to the topology drawing you created for Ms. Jones in Chapter 3, or review the topology drawing solution provided in Appendix B. In this section you will recommend a pilot for the network.

Question 13-5

The firm has decided to implement one U.S. office and the Europe office as a pilot network. Describe a project plan (at a high level) that will pilot the system to prove the concept for a full implementation.

You will need approximately one hour to complete this chapter and its exercises. Upon its completion, you will be able to do the following:

- List the Cisco IOS™ software commands you need to use to determine whether a network structure meets the customer's performance and scalability goals.

- Describe how to demonstrate the prototype or pilot to the customer so that the customer understands that the proposed design meets requirements for performance, security, capacity, and scalability, and that the costs and risks are acceptable.

CHAPTER 14

Testing the Prototype or Pilot

This chapter includes some job aids that you will find useful when completing the case studies at the end of the chapter. References to some WWW sites are included; relevant information has been extracted from these sites and is provided in the chapter. If you have access to the Internet, you might want to access the sites mentioned to obtain detailed information related to specific topics. All of the sites referenced in this chapter are also listed in Appendix C, "Interesting WWW Links and Other Suggested Readings."

Follow these steps to complete this chapter:

1 Study the chapter content, including any job aids that appear.

2 Review the case studies at the end of the chapter.

3 Complete the questions in each case study.

4 Review the answers provided by our internetworking experts in Appendix B, "Answers to Chapter Questions, Case Studies, and Sample CCDA Exam."

Testing of your prototype or pilot is key in getting the customer's acceptance of your design. This chapter addresses some ways to do the testing and discusses how to demonstrate the test results to your customer. A Network Health checklist is provided to use when checking a prototype for proper network functionality and scalability.

Testing the Prototype or Pilot

After you have installed and configured a pilot or a subset of the network structure, the next step is to test it. This can be done using:

- Cisco IOS software commands
- A protocol analyzer, if the network is more sophisticated
- Simulation tools

Cisco IOS software commands and protocol analyzers are discussed in this section. Specific product documentation provides details on how to test with the simulation tools.

Information on the various products discussed in this book can be found at the WWW sites noted in those discussions. Some other useful product documentation links are as follows:

- Cisco Connection Documentation is available at http://www.cisco.com/univercd/home/home.htm.

- The NETSYS Connectivity Tools User Guide is available at http://www.cisco.com/univercd/cc/td/doc/product/rtrmgmt/netsys/netsysug/index.htm.

- The NETSYS Connectivity Tools Reference Manual is available at http://www.cisco.com/univercd/cc/td/doc/product/rtrmgmt/netsys/netsysrg/index.htm.

Using Cisco IOS Software to Test a Prototype or Pilot

You can use Cisco IOS software commands to make sure your network design will work. The following commands are helpful when testing a network structure:

- The **show interface** command identifies Layer 2 errors, router errors such as dropped or ignored packets, and broadcast rates.

- The **show processes** command identifies router CPU usage, including CPU time used by processes.

- The **show buffers** command checks buffer usage and buffer misses.

- The **ping** and **trace** commands help troubleshoot connectivity and performance problems.

- The **show** *protocol* **route** command displays the protocol routing table to help troubleshoot routing problems.

- The **show access-lists** command displays the contents of access lists to help troubleshoot security problems.

- Various **debug** commands can be used for troubleshooting and verifying packets sent and received.

TIP   Many of the Cisco IOS software **show** commands result in a lot of information being displayed, some of which may be difficult to interpret (due to the large volume of information, and because parts of it are intended only for Cisco engineering support personnel). Some very useful documents for interpreting this information are the Command Reference Manuals, available on the Cisco Documentation CD-ROM, and on line at http://www.cisco.com/univercd/home/home.htm. The CD-ROM version of the documentation includes a search capability; simply search for the command of interest in the appropriate command reference manual to find the details of the displayed information.

Using Protocol Analyzers to Test a Prototype or Pilot

Protocol analyzers can be very useful tools when testing your network. The following sections identify some generic topics to consider when using a protocol analyzer.

Configuring for Correct Media

Make sure you have a protocol analyzer that can attach to the media you are testing, whether it is a WAN link, 10-Mbps or 100-Mbps Ethernet, Token Ring, ATM, or so on. If necessary, configure the analyzer for the media. For example, you might need to tell it whether a Token Ring network is 4 Mbps or 16 Mbps. For WAN analyzers, you often need to specify the data link layer, whether it is HDLC, Frame Relay, a proprietary format, and so on.

Capturing Data

Assuming that the prototype network is installed and users are running the appropriate applications, use the protocol analyzer to perform the following tasks:

- Capture data for at least a day
- Identify errors and irregularities
- Check the network utilization
- Determine what percentage of the traffic is broadcasts or multicasts

To verify that there are no problems, use the Network Health Checklist provided later in this chapter.

Testing

You can also use a protocol analyzer to generate traffic when testing a prototype or pilot. If it is impractical to purchase, install, and configure all the devices required to do a true simulation, you can purchase a subset of them and generate traffic to cause the load that would be present if all the devices were installed. This simulation will give you an approximation of the performance, though not an exact view of the actual performance you should expect.

Demonstrating Security

If the customer has security concerns and your prototype or pilot implements access lists, use a protocol analyzer to demonstrate that traffic filtering is working correctly. For example, if Network A should not be able to reach Network B, run some network applications on hosts in Network A while a protocol analyzer is attached to Network B. Prove to yourself and your customer that no traffic from Network A reaches Network B.

Demonstrating Your Findings to the Customer

After you have run some tests and proved to yourself that the network design works, you must prove this to the customer. Using the results of your tests, you should demonstrate that the design meets the customer's requirements for performance, security, capacity, and scalability, and that the design is within the customer's thresholds for costs and risks. You can demonstrate your findings in many ways, including the following:

- Publish your findings in a concise but comprehensive report.
- Add the results of your tests to the network design document or response to an RFP, discussed in Chapter 12, "Writing a Design Document."
- Create slides that graphically demonstrate the correlation between your test results and the customer's requirements, and present these to the customer.
- Meet with the customer and present your findings.
- Meet with the customer and reproduce the test results as the customer watches.

Network Health Checklist

Use the following checklist when checking a prototype or pilot for proper network functionality and scalability. This checklist provides guidelines, not rules. As mentioned in Chapter 3, "Characterizing the Existing Network," the correct answer to questions regarding thresholds for network health is usually, "It depends." Thresholds depend on topologies, router configurations, network applications, user requirements, how measurement tools calculate thresholds, and many other factors.

NOTE   This is a duplicate of the checklist in Chapter 3, reproduced here for your convenience.

☐ No shared Ethernet segments are saturated (no more than 40% network utilization).

☐ No shared Token Ring segments are saturated (no more than 70% network utilization).

☐ No WAN links are saturated (no more than 70% network utilization).

☐ The response time is generally less than 100 milliseconds (1 millisecond = 1/1000 of a second; 100 milliseconds = 1/10 of a second).

☐ No segments have more than 20% broadcasts/multicasts.

☐ No segments have more than one CRC error per million bytes of data.

☐ On the Ethernet segments, less than 0.1 percent of the packets result in collisions.

☐ On the Token Ring segments, less than 0.1 percent of the packets are soft errors not related to ring insertion.

- [ ] On the FDDI segments, there has been no more than one ring operation per hour not related to ring insertion.

- [ ] The Cisco routers are not over-utilized (five minute CPU utilization no more than 75%).

- [ ] The number of output queue drops has not exceeded more than 100 in an hour on any Cisco router.

- [ ] The number of input queue drops has not exceeded more than 50 in an hour on any Cisco router.

- [ ] The number of buffer misses has not exceeded more than 25 in an hour on any Cisco router.

- [ ] The number of ignored packets has not exceeded more than 10 in an hour on any interface on a Cisco router.

Document any concerns you have about the health of the existing network and its capability to support growth.

Summary

In this chapter you learned methods to test your prototype or pilot and to demonstrate the test results to your customer. Testing and demonstrating are key final steps in the network design process. This concludes Part V of this book, "Building a Prototype or Pilot for the Network."

The next part of this book provides a sample CCDA Sylvan Exam so that you can test your understanding of the concepts presented in this book.

Case Studies

In this section, you are asked to determine how to validate the prototypes or pilots designed in the last chapter, for the four case studies introduced in Chapter 3.

Read each case study description and complete the questions/exercises for each of the case studies.

TIP   As mentioned, when working through the questions to the case studies, you may find it useful to work on note paper in a separate binder to accommodate the depth of these exercises.

After you complete each question/exercise, you can refer to the solutions provided by our internetworking experts in Appendix B. Keep in mind that there are potentially several correct answers to each question. These case studies and their solutions will help you prepare for the Sylvan CCDA exam following the course.

Case Study: CareTaker Publications

You might want to review the CareTaker case study description in Appendix A, page 303, before proceeding to answer the questions in this section.

CareTaker Case Study Questions

Refer to the topology drawing you created for CareTaker Publications in the Chapter 3, or review the topology drawing solution provided in Appendix B. In this section, you will validate the pilot for the network.

Recall the solution developed in the last chapter:

- Because the network will be installed in a new building, we proposed that the new communication lines be installed between the three locations in parallel with the existing lines.

- One of the new servers would be used as a test server. The server would be placed on a 100-Mbps port of the switch.

- A minimum of one PC would be attached to each LAN segment in the new building. This attachment should be done in the computer room at the Catalyst 5000 switch to eliminate cable issues that are not the responsibility of the internetwork design. A single PC at the warehouse would be connected to the Cisco 2524 router. All circuits and paths would then be tested.

Question 14-1

What criteria will you use to validate that the pilot is a success?

Question 14-2

Provide a list of the Cisco IOS commands you will use to test your pilot network structure.

Case Study: PH Network Services Corporation

You may want to review the PH Network Services Corporation case study description in Appendix A, page 306, before proceeding to answer the questions in this section.

PH Network Services Corporation Case Study Questions

Refer to the topology drawing you created for Mr. Pero in Chapter 3, or review the topology drawing solution provided in Appendix B. In this section, you will validate the pilot for the network.

Recall the solution developed in the last chapter:

- The critical path on the implementation of the PH Network system will be obtaining circuits from the local provider.

- The Frame Relay circuits should be ordered as soon as possible.

- A structured plan should be established for doctor offices to place orders for ISDN lines as a coordinated order for the entire network.

- One hospital, one doctor office with an existing LAN, and one single-PC doctor office should be selected as a Phase I Group. The communication lines for these offices and the PH Network office should be installed first.

- The Catalyst 1900 switch and Cisco 3620 router should be installed in the PH Network office. Access to the Windows NT server by local PCs should be verified.

- The pilot network of one hospital, one LAN-based doctor office, and one standalone-based office should then be connected and completely tested by ping tests and user logins.

- The new SQL Server could then be added and the connection tested for the pilot network. Once these tests have proven the operational status of the network, the other hospitals should be added, followed by doctor offices, with an orderly, planned methodology.

Question 14-3

What criteria will you use to validate that the pilot is a success?

Question 14-4

Provide a list of the Cisco IOS commands you will use to test your pilot network structure.

Case Study: Pretty Paper Limited

You might want to review the Pretty Paper Limited case study in Appendix A, page 307, before proceeding to answer the question in this section.

Pretty Paper Limited Case Study Question

Refer to the topology drawing you created for Pretty Paper in the Chapter 3 or review the topology drawing solution provided in Appendix B. In this section you will validate the pilot for the network.

Recall the solution developed in the last chapter:

- The software vendor probably has been asked to provide this kind of proof in the past. Ask whether this vendor has a lab or test-bed facility that could be used to simulate the environment if the routers and switch were provided. The lab or test-bed facility would provide the most controllable environment.

- If a test-bed is not available, all packet flow and performance requirements can be evaluated by implementing a subset of the new network consisting of a group of users in the main office and a remote manufacturing facility.

- The pilot would consist of the installation of the Catalyst 5000 switch, Cisco 2503 routers at headquarters and at a selected manufacturing facility, the HP9000, two Frame Relay circuits, and the necessary subset of cabling.

- Demonstrate that the solution enhances and does not degrade the flow of packets from the warehouse to the main office. This demonstration would be accomplished most definitively through the use of network monitoring devices for both the Frame Relay and the existing X.25 networks. At the application level, this is not a direct comparison. At the packet transport level, it will be a comparison of the new network's capability to deliver what it was asked to deliver.

Question 14-5

What criteria will you use to validate that the pilot is a success?

Case Study: Jones, Jones, & Jones

You may want to review the Jones, Jones, & Jones case study in Appendix A, page 308, before proceeding to answer the question in this section.

Jones, Jones, & Jones Case Study Question

Refer to the topology drawing you created for Ms. Jones in Chapter 3, or review the topology drawing solution provided in Appendix B. In this section, you will validate the pilot for the network.

Recall that the firm decided to implement one U.S. office and the Europe office as a pilot network. The main pilot office was located in the United States. Both offices were fully cabled for the final design and the facilities in both appropriately prepared.

Question 14-6

What criteria will you use to validate that the pilot is a success?

PART VI

Sample CCDA Sylvan Exam

The single chapter in this part of the book provides a sample CCDA Sylvan examination that you can take to evaluate your understanding of the material in this book.

The following test is an example of the type of Sylvan exam you can take to obtain CCDA status after completing this coursebook.

For more information on Cisco certifications in general and the CCDA exam specifically, refer to Cisco's career certification web site at http://www.cisco.com/warp/public/10/wwtraining/certprog/index.html or call Cisco's career certifications number, 1-800-829-NETS.

This sample test exam contains 32 questions. Use a blank sheet of paper to write your answers. You can refer to Appendix B, "Answers to Chapter Questions, Case Studies, and Sample CCDA Exam," for the correct answers, supplied by our internetworking experts.

Some questions relate to case studies you have covered in this book. You can review these case studies in Appendix A, "Case Studies." Read over the case studies and answer the questions with the best answer. The CCDA exam at a Sylvan testing center uses new case studies that are not covered in this book.

Each question is designed to test a specific objective of the course. We recommend that you review the sections that you answered incorrectly in this sample test before going to the Sylvan testing center. Appendix B indicates the chapter in this book where the material relating to each question is covered.

CHAPTER 15

Sample CCDA Sylvan Exam

Question 15-1

To help reduce the complexity associated with identifying and analyzing customer problems and designing solutions, Cisco has developed a basic framework into which most customer problems fit. The framework is a triangle that contains the following three components:

A. Protocols, Transport, and Media

B. Transport, Media, and Network Management

C. Media, Protocols, and Network Management

D. Protocols, Transport, and Network Management

Question 15-2

To list the network protocols and the number of users and hosts, you can use a table similar to the one shown in Table 15-1. To which category in Table 15-1 would "X.25" belong?

Table 15-1 *Network Protocols*

Name of Protocol	Type of Protocol	Number of Users	Number of Hosts or Servers	Comments

A. Name of protocol

B. Number of users

C. Type of protocol

D. Number of hosts or servers

Question 15-3

The goal of internetwork design is to design a cost-effective, scalable, working network. What is the *first* step to take when designing a small- to medium-size internetwork?

A. Identify the customer's needs.

B. Analyze the network load requirements.

C. Characterize data flows over the network.

D. Evaluate traffic-intensive applications and protocols.

Question 15-4

Which one of the following tasks would you complete to identify a customer's organizational objectives that will affect your network design?

A. Identify and document the customer's internal data-flow patterns.

B. Identify and document the customer's existing technology investment.

C. Identify and document the technical competencies of the support staff.

D. Identify and document the business objectives, schedule requirements, and political issues.

Question 15-5

Before making network design recommendations, you will need to characterize the existing network's availability and performance. As a general guideline, WAN links are saturated when network utilization exceeds _____.

A. 20 percent

B. 30 percent

C. 40 percent

D. 70 percent

Question 15-6

The failure rate of a network segment is a good indicator to measure that the network lacks _____.

A. accuracy

B. availability

C. throughput

D. response time

Question 15-7

Figure 15-1 is taken from the Jones, Jones, & Jones Case Study (see Appendix A for details). It represents:

A. A high-level topology of the customer's network

B. E-mail packet flow

C. TN3270 packet flow

D. Office productivity application packet flow

Figure 15-1   *Jones, Jones, & Jones Case Study Diagram for Question 15-7*

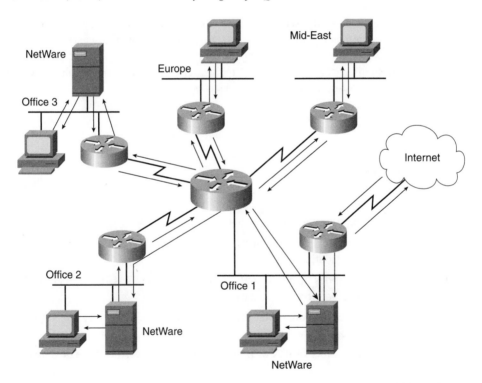

Question 15-8

Isolating requirements for fault management, accounting management, configuration management, and performance management would fall under which one of the following customer requirements?

A. Identifying business issues

B. Identifying security requirements

C. Identifying performance requirements

D. Identifying manageability requirements

Question 15-9

In the CareTaker Case Study (see Appendix A for details), the IS manager is not sure that she has the personnel to manage a new network. The system administrators are junior and have never worked with routers. The IS manager understands the need for training and has planned for it, but she still is concerned. Of the following network management tools, which would be the best and most cost-effective for this case study?

A. Cisco Fast Step

B. CiscoWorks Windows

C. NETSYS

D. CiscoWorks ConfigMaker

Question 15-10

When designing a flat switched network you can:

A. Have more IP nodes than you could have IPX nodes on the same segment without any performance degradation

B. Have more IPX nodes than you could have IP nodes on the same segment without any performance degradation

C. Have more AppleTalk nodes than you could have IP nodes on the same segment without any performance degradation

D. Have the same number of IPX or IP nodes without any performance degradation

Question 15-11

In Figure 15-2, the Cisco Catalyst 5002 switch represents the _____ of the network design.

A. Core layer

B. Access layer

C. Workgroup layer

D. Distribution layer

Figure 15-2 *Network Design Diagram for Question 15-11*

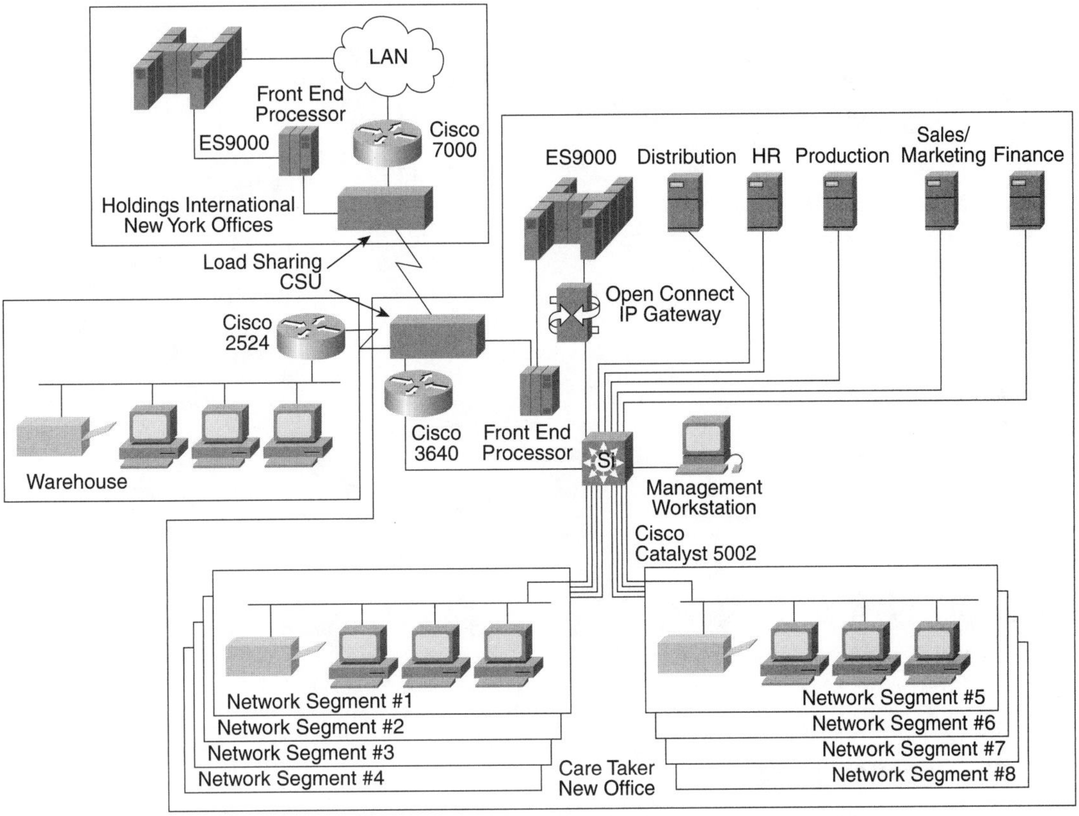

Question 15-12

Figure 15-3 is taken from the Jones, Jones, & Jones Case Study (see Appendix A for details). It represents which of the following?

A. A high-level topology map of the customer's current network

B. A high-level topology map that meets the customer's future needs

C. A high-level topology map of the customer's proposed e-mail packet flow

D. A high-level topology map of the customer's proposed intranet security system

Figure 15-3 *Jones, Jones, & Jones diagram for Question 15-12*

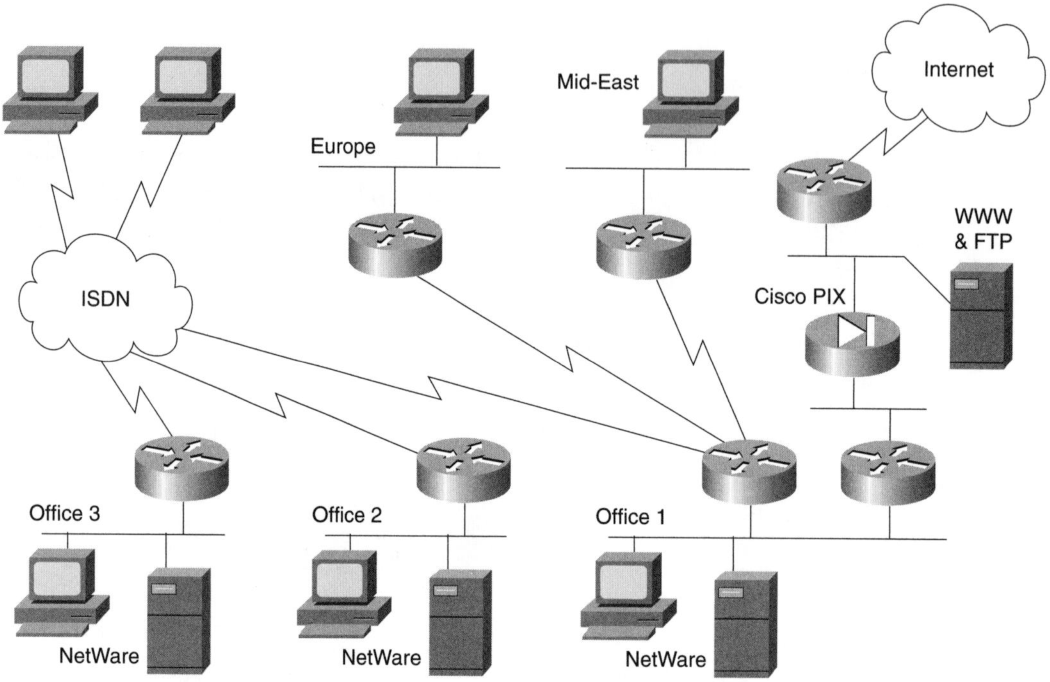

Question 15-13

If the number of users is expected to double over the next year in the CareTaker Case Study (see Appendix A for details), which of the following is the *least* acceptable solution today to allow for future scalability?

A. Use large file servers to segment file and print sharing traffic on the network.

B. Allow for proper segmentation in the design so there is no problem with growth.

C. Assume that TN3270 traffic is not significant and should not require segmentation.

D. Assume that the use of e-mail will be heavy and allow for significant e-mail traffic in the design.

Question 15-14

Which application and positioning statement best describes the Catalyst 1900 series switch?

A. Workgroup stackable with WAN option

B. Standalone, low-cost switch for 10BaseT

C. Multilayer, multiple LAN, backbone switch

D. Stackable, high-performance workgroup switch

Question 15-15

Figure 15-4 represents which of the following?

A. A high-level topology map that meets a customer's needs

B. A high-level topology map of a customer's TN3270 traffic flow

C. A high-level topology map of a customer's current e-mail packet flow

D. A high-level topology map of a customer's proposed e-mail packet flow

Figure 15-4 *Diagram for Question 15-15*

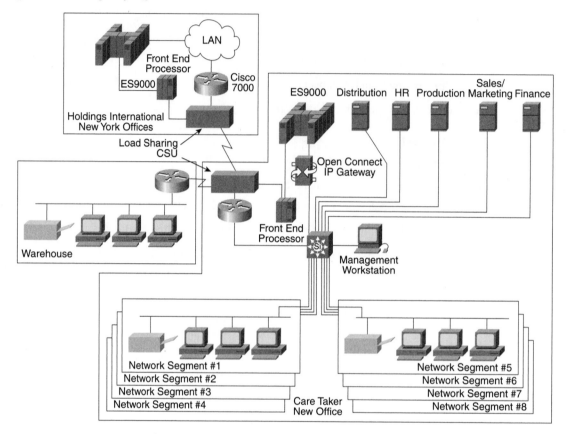

Question 15-16

Which one of the following network designs is commonly used to support remote offices accessing the central headquarters of a company?

A. The central site has a fractional T1 connection and each remote site has a full T1 connection to the central site.

B. The central site uses a hub-and-spoke topology, including an Ethernet concentrator that has multiple WAN interfaces.

C. Each remote site has a router with one ISDN BRI and the central site has a router with ISDN PRI.

D. The central site has a multiservice WAN ATM switch that offers Personal Communication Services to the remote sites.

Question 15-17

When comparing the advantages and disadvantages of a full mesh versus a partial mesh Frame Relay design, which statement is most accurate?

A. A full mesh is more expensive due to more routers.

B. Split horizon limits connectivity in a full mesh.

C. A partial mesh is less expensive due to fewer virtual circuits.

D. Broadcast copying overhead is higher in a partial mesh.

Question 15-18

In the CareTaker Case Study (see Appendix A for details), the company plans to add leased lines but has not made a determination on the protocol, interface, and media. This decision will not be made for another six months or so. Of the following products, which one would be the best solution for this scenario? (Remember to use the *Cisco Product Selection Tool* and the *Cisco Products Quick Reference Guide* to answer this question.)

A. Cisco 770

B. Cisco 2503

C. Cisco 2514

D. Cisco 3640

Question 15-19

Which one of the following is the first step in designing network layer addressing and naming for a network?

A. Design route summarization (aggregation).

B. Design a method for mapping geographical locations to network numbers.

C. Design a hierarchy for addressing autonomous systems, areas, networks, subnetworks, and end stations.

D. Design a plan for distributing administrative authority for addressing and naming at the lower levels of the hierarchy.

Question 15-20

You have a customer with a Class B network number of 172.16.0.0 and divided the network into the following four areas:

172.16.0.0 was assigned to the Backbone.
172.16.64.0 was assigned to the North Campus.
172.16.128.0 was assigned to the Central Campus.
172.16.192.0 was assigned to the South Campus.

The _____ of the third octet can be used to identify the area portion of the networking addressing scheme.

A. First bit

B. First 2 bits

C. First 3 bits

D. Last 6 bits

Question 15-21

Which one of the following tools will synchronize names with dynamically assigned IP addresses?

A. DNS/DHCP Manager

B. CiscoWorks Windows

C. Cisco Fast Step

D. NETSYS

Question 15-22

Which of the following is true of the IP Routing Information Protocol (RIP)?

A. Handles the process of updating the Time To Live field in an IP header.

B. Specifies no more than 15 hops between end stations.

C. Is the same as the IPX RIP implementation.

D. Sends network numbers, subnet masks, and hop count in its routing updates.

Question 15-23

Both distance vector and link-state routing protocols converge more quickly if which of the following items is implemented?

A. Redundancy in the network topology

B. Route redistribution between protocols

C. Consistent use of the Network Time Protocol (NTP)

D. Consistent use of the Time To Live field in the IP header

Question 15-24

Access lists enable you to do which of the following?

A. Reduce the size of a frame of data to be transmitted over a network link.

B. Control whether network traffic is forwarded or blocked at a router's interfaces.

C. Let a network administrator manage the varying demands applications put on networks and routers.

D. Assign different amounts of queue space to different protocols and handle the queues in round-robin fashion.

Question 15-25

Which statement is true about network security policies?

A. Security policies should be based on an understanding of which company assets are most valuable.

B. Security systems should be designed to maximize the number of secrets—for example, passwords and encryption keys.

C. End users do not need training on network security.

D. A company that has an inflexible security policy that is hard to change is less vulnerable than a company with a flexible policy.

Question 15-26

You are developing a network management strategy that includes tools used to troubleshoot physical layer errors. Which one of the following tools should you recommend?

A. A cable tester

B. Remote Monitoring (RMON)

C. Network management software

D. Network modeling and simulation software

Question 15-27

As companies recognize the strategic importance of their internetworks and intranets, more emphasis is being placed on _____ network management.

A. Reactive

B. Security

C. Proactive

D. PC-based

Question 15-28

When writing a Request for Proposal (RFP), which of the following sections should you direct at the key decision makers in a company to clearly articulate your strategy for the project?

A. Summary

B. Design Solution

C. Executive Summary

D. Design Requirements

Question 15-29

Which of the following tasks should you perform when planning your network design prototype?

A. All of the following.

B. Develop a list of the tests and demonstrations you will run.

C. Gain an understanding of what your competition plans to propose.

D. Determine how much of the network structure must be built to prove that the design meets the customer's major goals.

Question 15-30

Which one of the following tasks is the *first step* in building a prototype network structure to prove to a customer that your design works?

A. Develop a detailed test plan.

B. Gain an understanding of what your competition plans to propose.

C. Review the extracted new customer requirements to determine those that affect your design.

D. Determine how much of the network structure must be built to prove the design concept.

Question 15-31

To identify Layer 2 errors, router errors such as dropped or ignored packets, and broadcast rates, which Cisco IOS™software command would you use?

A. ping

B. show buffers

C. show interface

D. show processes

Question 15-32

In the CareTaker Case Study (see Appendix A for details), both the parent corporation's and CareTaker's management have repeatedly expressed the requirement that everything work before the move takes place. Read the following solution and select the best answer.

Because the network will be installed in a new building, your proposal is that the new communication lines be installed between the three locations in parallel with the existing lines. One of the new servers would be used as a test server. A minimum of one PC would be attached to each LAN segment in the new building. This attachment should be done in the computer room at the Catalyst 5002 switch to eliminate cable issues, which are not the responsibility of the internetwork design. The server would be placed on a 100-Mbps port of the switch. A single PC at the warehouse would be connected to the Cisco 2524 router. All circuits and paths would then be tested.

Will error-free pinging and tracing of packets on the various segments and the WAN links test the network design enough to validate that the pilot is successful?

- **A.** Yes. For a network this size, error-free pinging and tracing of packets on the various segments and the WAN segments will be adequate.

- **B.** No. Additional and more thorough testing should be done using various Cisco IOS software commands and possibly a protocol analyzer.

Appendixes and Glossary

The Appendixes and Glossary provide additional information on Cisco network designs and concepts that is referenced from within the book when required.

This appendix presents the four core case studies that are used throughout Chapters 3–15. The four case studies presented are as follows:

- CareTaker Publications, a publishing company
- PH Network Services Corporation, a health care company
- Pretty Paper Limited, a European wall covering company
- Jones, Jones, & Jones, an international law firm

Case Studies

This appendix introduces four case studies that are used throughout the book so you can evaluate your understanding of the concepts presented.

Read each case study and complete the questions in Chapters 3–15. After you complete each question, refer to the solutions provided by our internetworking experts in Appendix B, "Answers to Chapter Questions, Case Studies, and Sample CCDA Exam." These case studies and solutions will help you prepare for the Sylvan exam that you might want to take after reading this course book.

Case Study: CareTaker Publications

This first case study involves CareTaker Publications, a publishing company.

The Client

Mr. Smith of CareTaker publications is responsible for updating the network to use new technologies. Though he has a broad understanding of the options available to him, he needs your help to plan a good network design.

Company Background

CareTaker is a venerable publisher of citation reference material. Though it operates as an independent business, CareTaker is owned by Holdings International (HI). It has two locations across town from each other: a main office facility and a warehouse/distribution facility. The decision has been made to build a new CareTaker headquarters office several miles away from the current main office facility.

Applications

Administration, production, and support of the company's products and services are accomplished with LAN-based applications. Publication media consist of both books and CD-ROM products. CareTaker's publication data is collected and maintained on an IBM ES9000 system. The IBM system, TN3270 terminals, and PCs are connected to a single Token Ring network.

CareTaker has standardized on Microsoft Office applications and Microsoft Exchange for internal e-mail and, therefore, will use the SMTP Connector for SMTP mail to HI and the Internet. Quark Express will be used for publishing functions. A custom SQL Server application has been developed in-house for both order processing, and shipping and receiving functions.

Departmental Servers

Each of five departments (Sales and Marketing, Production, Finance, Distribution, and Human Resources) will have its own Windows NT file and print server, which means adding three servers because Sales and Marketing, and Distribution share one server and the remaining departments share a second server. The IS staff is divided over where to locate the servers and wants a recommendation on the physical location of the servers.

Clients and Terminals

The company now wants to convert the 73 TN3270 terminals to PCs or network computers (NCs). In all, 113 PCs will be on the network over three floors. Ninty-seven PCs will access the ES9000 via Open Connect TN3270 emulation. Of the 97 PCs to have mainframe access, the 73 replacement terminals will generate the most traffic. The warehouse has 10 terminals that will be replaced with PCs or NCs.

Existing Network

The company has a leased-line connection between the main offices and the warehouse. A T1/E1 point-to-point circuit is maintained between CareTaker and HI in New York. This circuit is a part of a much larger WAN owned and maintained by HI. SNA is the only traffic on this line.

The new PCs and NCs will create a great deal of terminal emulation traffic over the LAN. The Token Ring environment will be completely replaced with Ethernet. Logistics issues require that the mainframe remain up until such time as the entire staff is moved and is operational.

In conjunction with the network and system changes, HI will provide parent-corporation–wide e-mail, as well as Internet e-mail and access services. Only 40 employees, based on name and position, will be allowed to have browsing access to the Internet; all others will be restricted.

HI also will be responsible for the host-to-host communications between CareTaker's ES9000 and HI's IBM mainframe. All these services will be provided to CareTaker by HI over the T1 line.

The new routed traffic will be shared with the SNA traffic using a load-sharing CSU (CSU with built-in multiplexer) so SNA traffic is not routed and is maintained separate from the routed traffic. Only IP will be allowed to be routed over the WAN. HI's Network Operations personnel will be responsible for all WAN functions from CareTaker's FEP and router outward.

Goals for the New Network

The IS manager has asked for an internetwork design to connect all the systems within the new facility, the warehouse, and HI's Cisco 7000 series router located in another city. HI's Network Operations personnel will be responsible for the configuration and connection to HI's router, but CareTaker will be responsible for the router purchase on its end. The Network Operations group has specified IGRP as the routing protocol used by the corporate router.

Cabling Intermediate Distribution Facilities are located in the center of each floor with a Main Distribution Facility located in the computer room. The computer room is located on the first floor and takes up half of that floor. The IS department is located in the remaining half of that floor.

Mr. Smith hands you some data gathered from his network, as shown in Table A-1:

Table A-1   *CareTaker's Monthly Report*

Monthly Report	Site: Medford
	Date: September 30, 1997
	Administrator: Jane Stevens
Downtime	September 2nd
Duration of downtime	1/2 hour
Cause of downtime	Loose lobe cable
Average network utilization	5%
Peak network utilization	30%
Average frame size	Unknown
CRC error rate	Unknown
Soft errors	Very few except during problem with loose cable and first thing in the morning when stations boot
Broadcasts	About 10% of the traffic
Comments	We did not have time to gather all the required data this month.

Case Study: PH Network Services Corporation

This case study involves PH Network Services Corporation, a health care company.

The Client

Mr. Pero of PH Network is responsible for updating the network to use new technologies.

Company Background

PH Network is a joint venture between the New Life hospital system and 750 physicians in the community served by New Life. The company was formed to improve patient services by the hospital and physicians, and to provide leverage when negotiating with managed care health plan companies.

One problem area and cost for the doctors is the specialist referral authorization system. The doctors must get authorized referrals for specialist services for their patients before the managed care health plans will cover the cost for the patient. PH Network has negotiated with a number of health plans to take on the risk of these referrals in exchange for more of the premium. PH has determined that this scenario will make economic sense if it can implement an automated referral authorization system. Mr. Pero has indicated that referrals are nearly always made during normal office hours of 8 a.m. to 12 p.m. and 1 p.m. to 5 p.m.

Current Network

The company maintains a 56-kbps leased-line connection to the hospital facilities and dial-up terminal connections to some of the larger doctor offices for access to the hospital's patient records. Both direct terminal access and Telnet access are available on the hospital hosts. There are a total of 120 doctor offices and 4 hospitals. The actual PH Network staff consists of 50 employees in a single office location. Because the number of these referral transactions will average 20 per day, PH Network plans to use ISDN to network to all the doctor offices, and a Frame Relay network between the PH office and the four hospitals. The connection between doctor offices and the PH referral system will be a "dial as needed" design. Each doctor's office will have a PC for this purpose.

Some of the larger offices already have small Ethernet LANs. However, PH is concerned that the doctors will simply stop using the system if it is not available when needed, which would mean failure for the venture.

Goals for the New Network

PH also knows doctors do not like to spend nonmedical money. Therefore, it wants a network with the best estimate of sufficient ISDN connections to start and the capability to add new connections rapidly. The software is being developed for a Windows NT/SQL Server system with a Microsoft Access front end using an ODBC interface to the SQL Server. The hospital connection is critical, so PH would like to look at possible redundancy or backup for this connection.

Case Study: Pretty Paper Limited

This case study involves Pretty Paper Limited, a European wall covering company.

The Client

Mr. Mick of Pretty Paper Limited, is responsible for updating the network to use new technologies.

Company Background

Pretty Paper is a family-owned company that has grown over the last 50 years to be a major supplier of wall coverings throughout Europe. Until now, it has been able to manage its business with a Prime computer system located in its Paris headquarters offices, and an X.25 switched network between two manufacturing plants and five sales offices in three time zones. However, the Prime system can no longer keep up with the demands of the business.

Pretty Paper will be converting to client/server technology using Oracle-based software. The capital for this conversion has been budgeted, and the time line has been established as a three-month project, after which the new business system will operate in parallel with the Prime until all applications are fully converted and verified. Management has stipulated that the new system must reduce the current processing time by half.

Client Systems and Applications

There are 31 existing PCs, 21 Apple Macintosh computers, and 120 Prime terminals at headquarters. The PCs, Macintosh computers, and a single Novell NetWare file server are on an Ethernet network in the headquarters administrative facilities. The headquarters campus consists of the administrative office building, the main warehouse building (300 meters from the main building), and the central production plant (200 meters from the main building).

In the sales offices, three to five Prime terminals will be replaced with PCs. The two manufacturing plants have four Macintosh computers each. Pretty Paper has standardized on Lotus SmartSuite for productivity applications.

Pattern designs for wall covering products will be accomplished on the Macintosh computers, published with Quark Express, and given to the production department to generate printing film.

Server Systems and Applications

The business software is Oracle-based and will run on an HP9000 server. A NetWare file server will be added and all 120 Prime terminals will be replaced with PCs.

Goals for the New Network

In the new environment, Frame Relay is planned as a replacement for the X.25 network. Management wants pattern designs to be available over the WAN for evaluation and sales presentations. It also wants final pattern designs to be transmitted over the LAN directly to film equipment that would then create film for printing. These files are approximately 100 KB in size; 20 to 25 patterns will be sent for processing each evening in the last three hours of the day, 3 p.m. to 6 p.m. Also, 5 to 10 patterns will be transmitted to sales offices each day.

Pretty Paper would like a proposal for a turnkey LAN/WAN solution that will be brought online in parallel with the Prime system until all conversions have been made.

Case Study: Jones, Jones, & Jones

This case study involves Jones, Jones, & Jones, an international law firm.

The Client

Ms. Jones, senior partner of Jones, Jones, & Jones, is responsible for updating the network to use new technologies.

Company Background

The firm is a regional law firm with three offices in the United States and two international offices. Each U.S. office has approximately 50 computer users; the international offices have 10 users each. The firm is feeling the pinch of competition with larger firms that have all the latest technology available. The partners know "protocol" as something used at international negotiations and they do not want to know any more about it. They need their people to be able to share documents and work together as if they were in the same office. Even though their competition has more advanced technology, they cannot keep buying new hardware.

Need for Information

The firm also needs to reduce the cost of its reference library. It would like to have CD-ROM libraries for research and reference publications. The partners envision as many as four or five researchers using the CD-ROM library at any given time. They also want a fax server for each office. Most faxes received by the international offices are from the U.S., and the managing partner wants to know if there is any way to receive those faxes in the U.S. and make them available to the Europe and Middle East offices over the network. The partner believes there would be about 30 faxes a day.

Jones, Jones, & Jones has built an international reputation in its specialty of international oil and gas law. Throughout recent years, the firm has discovered a significant interest in information on this area of law. Therefore, the partners have decided to sell this research in the form of research papers to be offered on an Internet web site. This commercial site will use credit card transactions and FTP downloads of the research papers.

Desktop Applications

The partners have been long-time WordPerfect users and intend to stay standardized on the WordPerfect suite. Each office has an Ethernet LAN, but the offices are not interconnected. The partners want the lawyers to be able to work from home and on the road just as efficiently as if they were in the office. The attorneys work at all times of the day, but the system is in heavy word processing use from 7 a.m. until 6 p.m.

Goals for the Network

The managing partner is looking for a proposal for a network design that can support the business as well as the firm's selection of Novell's GroupWise product for document management and e-mail. Internet access will be required for e-mail and research. The managing partner knows this upgrade will be expensive, but she is looking for three-year cost savings. She also wants the lowest three-year cost for the WAN solution. She does not care if the solution is leased lines or interim connections, as long as the lawyers never know the difference—that is, as long as information is always available within a couple of minutes. However, she is convinced that point-to-point leased lines will be necessary for the international connections.

The managing partner stated that she has an administrative assistant who enjoys computers and who is excited about learning new technology anytime he gets a chance.

Answers to Chapter Questions, Case Studies, and Sample CCDA Exam

This chapter provides solutions from our internetworking experts to the multiple-choice and case study questions in each chapter, by chapter number. The sample CCDA exam answers are provided in the Chapter 15 section. Keep in mind that there are potentially several correct answers to each question.

NOTE   Some of the questions require the use of the *Cisco Product Selection Tool*, available at http://www.cisco.com/romeo/select.htm. Your results from using this tool might differ from those given here, because as products change and new products are introduced, the tool's output may also change.

Chapter 3

CareTaker Case Study Questions

Question 3-1

Has the customer provided you with all of the data that you need to characterize the existing network? What data do you still need to gather from the customer?

Mr. Smith has provided you with a lot of data that will help you characterize the current internetwork at CareTaker Publications. The monthly report from the site is not very helpful because you need to design an Ethernet LAN to replace the Token Ring when the move is made to the new building. More information on MTBF and downtime might prove to be helpful. Although no redundancy has been requested, MTBF and downtime information might help you justify some redundancy in your design.

If possible, try to gather more information about the corporate network. For example, collecting some performance information about the Cisco 7000 series router might help in the event there are problems when the new T1/E1 connection is activated. Because the Cisco 7000 series router is not connected to the CareTaker T1/E1 connection, no bandwidth or error reports will be available for the Cisco 7000 series router. The only traffic currently on the T1/E1 is nonrouted SNA. You will need information about what portion of the T1/E1 the SNA traffic is utilizing. Also, understand that you will not be responsible for or involved with any SNA on this project.

Question 3-2

What are the customer's current applications?

- Open Connect TN3270 terminal emulation
- Microsoft Office productivity applications
- Microsoft Exchange e-mail application
- Quark Express desktop publishing
- Custom order processing based on SQL Server
- Custom shipping and receiving based on SQL Server

Question 3-3

What are the customer's current applications?

- TCP/IP
- SNA
- NetBIOS

Question 3-4

Draw a high-level topology of the customer's current network.

Figure B-1 provides a high-level topology of CareTaker's current network.

Figure B-1   *CareTaker's Current Network*

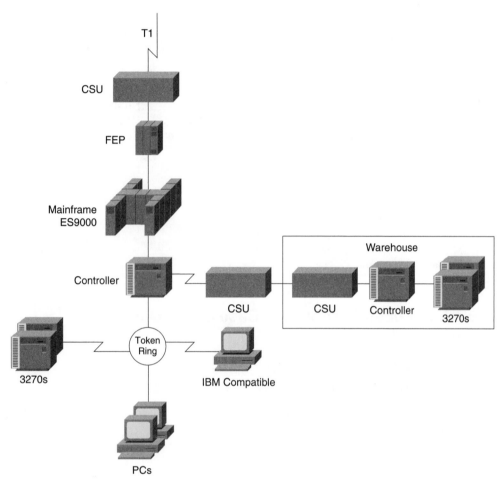

Question 3-5

Document the customer's business constraints.

- New facilities are being built.
- The two existing facilities are across town from each other.
- The parent company is responsible for the WAN and SNA.
- TN3270 is used (there will be no SNA traffic on the LAN or warehouse link).
- There is limited Internet access, probably filtered at the router.
- The Windows NT file servers will require NetBIOS.

Question 3-6

Identify new applications or old applications that will use the new networking structure.

Table B-1 identifies the applications that will use the new networking structure.

Table B-1 *Applications Used in the CareTaker Case Study*

Name and Type of Application	Protocols	Number of Users	Number of Hosts or Servers	Peak Usage Hours
Open Connect TN3270 emulation	TCP/IP TN3270	97	1	Unknown
Microsoft Exchange e-mail	TCP/IP	113	1	Unknown
Internet access	TCP/IP	40	1	Unknown
Department file servers (including Microsoft Office, Quark Express, custom SQL applications)	TCP/IP	113	5	Business hours

PH Network Services Corporation Case Study Questions

Question 3-7

What are the customer's current applications?

SQL/Microsoft Access is used for automated referral system and to store hospital patient records.

Question 3-8

Document the customer's business constraints.

- An average of 20 referrals per day for each of 120 offices, or 2400 referral transactions per day.
- The project must be done at minimum cost. If PH Network Services cannot complete the project within budget, the project will be cancelled.
- High level of availability is a concern.

Question 3-9

Document any concerns you have about this scenario.

PH's capability to manage this network is a concern because it has no real control over the hospitals or the doctor offices.

The capability of a service provider to supply ISDN might be a problem.

Question 3-10

Identify new applications or old applications that will use the new networking structure.

Table B-2 identifies the applications that will use the networking structure.

Table B-2   *Applications Used in the PH Network Case Study*

Name and Type of Application	Protocols	Number of Users	Number of Hosts or Servers	Peak Usage Hours
Automated referral system	TCP/IP	120	1	8-12 a.m., 1-5 p.m.
Hospital patient records (current)	Async	Unknown	~4	8-12 a.m., 1-5 p.m.
Hospital patient records (replaces the current terminal access)	Telnet	Unknown	~4	8-12 a.m., 1-5 p.m.

Pretty Paper Limited Case Study Questions

Question 3-11

What are the customer's current applications?

- Prime business applications operate via asynchronous terminals.
- Quark Express runs on Macintosh computers.
- We assume other office and personal productivity software.

Question 3-12

What are the customer's current protocols?

- X.25
- Ethertalk
- IPX

Question 3-13

Draw a high-level topology of the customer's current network.

Figure B-2 provides a high-level topology of Pretty Paper's current network.

Figure B-2 *Pretty Paper's current network*

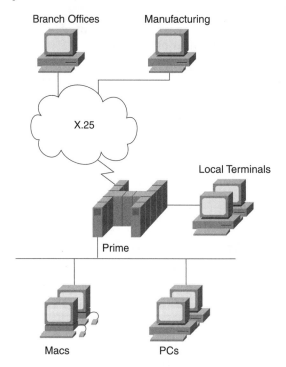

Question 3-14

Document the customer's business constraints.

- The entire upgrade must occur within three months.
- Funds are budgeted.
- New client/server software is to be purchased and installed.
- Pattern designs are to be delivered over LAN and WAN.
- There are parallel operations with the legacy system.

Question 3-15

Identify new applications or old applications that will use the new networking structure.

Table B-3 identifies the applications that will use the networking structure.

Table B-3 *Applications Used in the Pretty Paper Case Study*

Name and Type of Application	Protocols	Number of Users	Number of Hosts or Servers	Peak Usage Hours
Quark Express	AppleTalk	29 (21 local and 8 at warehouses)	3 servers	3 to 6 p.m.
Oracle	TCP/IP	~121-171	1 server	6 a.m. to 6 p.m.
Lotus SmartSuite	IPX	171	3 servers	6 a.m. to 6 p.m.

Jones, Jones, & Jones Case Study Questions

Question 3-16

What are the customer's current applications?

Primarily word processing.

Question 3-17

Document the customer's business constraints.

- Budget is limited.
- They want to get the most out of the new technology.
- Computer literacy is low.
- Document sharing and timely communications are critical.

Question 3-18

Document any concerns you have about the scenario.

The expectation of collaboration and dial-in system use may be unrealistic. They do not seem to have a grasp of what it will take to implement and stay on top of the network. Their willingness and ability to hire the necessary personnel is probably the greatest concern.

Question 3-19

Identify new applications or old applications that will use the new networking structure.

Table B-4 identifies the applications that will use the new networking structure.

Table B-4 *Applications Used in the Jones, Jones, & Jones Case Study*

Name and Type of Application	Protocols	Number of Users	Number of Hosts or Servers	Peak Usage Hours
WordPerfect word processing	IPX	170	1	7 a.m. to 6 p.m.
CD-ROM server	IPX	15	3	7 a.m. to 6 p.m.
Fax server	IPX	30 faxes/day	3	7 a.m. to 6 p.m.
Novell Groupwise (e-mail and document management)	IP	170	1	7 a.m. to 6 p.m.

Chapter 4

CareTaker Case Study Questions

Question 4-1

Diagram the packet flow of information for the new e-mail system. Document any open issues or follow-up questions regarding the e-mail system.

Figure B-3 diagrams the packet flow of CareTaker's e-mail system.

Figure B-3   *CareTaker's E-mail System Packet Flow*

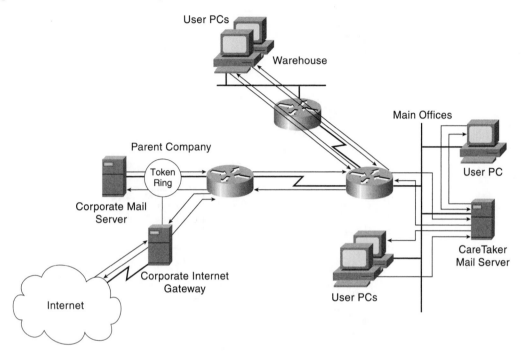

Some open questions about the e-mail system are as follows:

- When the users retrieve their mail, do they send mail also?
- When they send mail, does the mail go to the local server first?
- How are new users added to the system? Do new users create traffic on the WAN?
- When the servers update each other, do they send one query to get new mail and one query to send new mail?

If you are an expert on electronic mail systems, you might think of additional questions.

Question 4-2

Diagram the packet flow of information for the TN3270 emulation application. Document any open issues or follow-up questions regarding the TN3270 application.

Figure B-4 diagrams the packet flow of CareTaker's TN3270 application.

Figure B-4 *CareTaker's TN3270 Application Packet Flow*

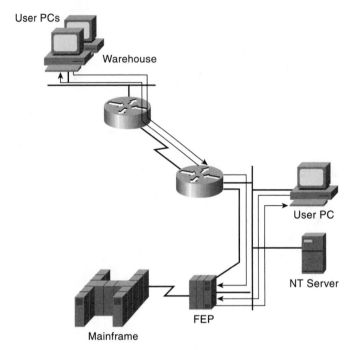

Question 4-3

Diagram the packet flow of information for the new custom SQL server application. Document any open issues or follow-up questions regarding this application.

Figure B-5 diagrams the packet flow of CareTaker's custom SQL server application.

Figure B-5   *CareTaker's Custom SQL Server Application Packet Flow*

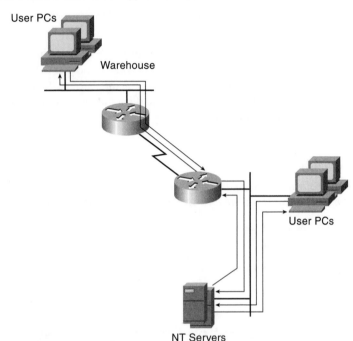

Question 4-4

List the customer's performance requirements and constraints.

- The network in the new building must be fully installed and tested before the move.

- The new corporate link must be tested before the move of the ES9000 to test the IP routing for e-mail and Internet access.

- The servers should be centrally located in the computer rooms for administration and security.

- Because the company's publication data is collected and maintained on an IBM ES9000 system, we can assume that the TN3270 traffic is critical. Verify that TN3270 traffic is critical.

- It does not appear that there are any unusual or demanding performance requirements other than the load of 113 office application and e-mail users.

Question 4-5

What concerns do you have for scalability if the number of users were to double over the next year?

With proper segmentation in the design, there should be no problem with growth. The implementation of five servers will allow traffic to be segmented for file and print sharing. The TN3270 traffic is significant but should be segmentable because 97 of the users are primarily terminal users and light file and print users. We do not know how heavy their use of e-mail will be, so we must assume that it might be heavy.

Question 4-6

The manager of Warehouse and Distribution is concerned about PC performance over a leased line. What design constraints and consideration will be taken into account for these concerns?

- Speed of the leased line
- Location of servers
- Selection of network computer (diskless workstations) technology for the warehouse systems

PH Network Services Corporation Case Study Questions

Question 4-7

Diagram the packet flow for the referral approval process.

Figure B-6 diagrams the packet flow of PH Network's referral approval process.

Figure B-6   *PH Network's Referral Approval Process Packet Flow*

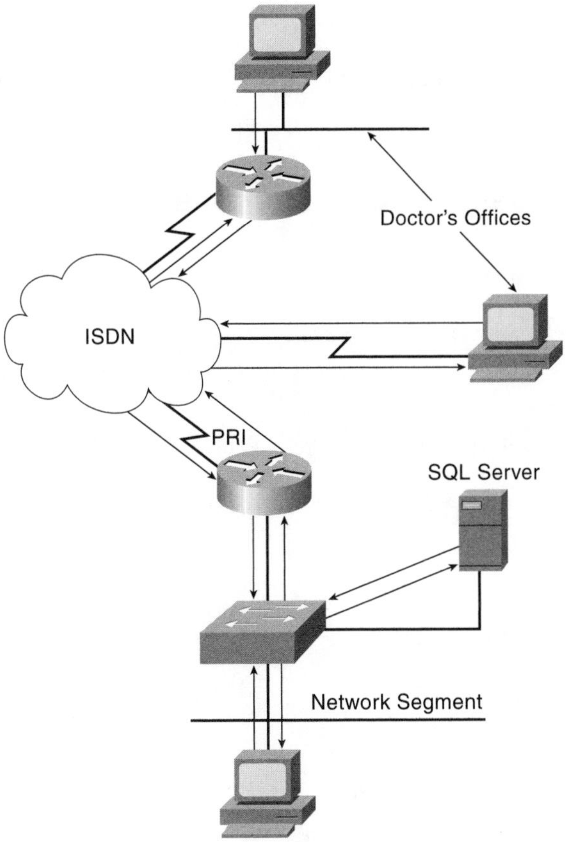

Question 4-8

Identify the customer's performance requirements.

Assuming 2000 characters per transaction and 100 characters per packet (worst case), only 48,000 data packets will be routed per day.

Question 4-9

Identify the customer's requirements for redundancy.

High availability is a requirement. The hospital connection is critical.

Question 4-10

What concerns do you have for scalability if the number of doctor offices were to double over the next year?

Even at twice the number of offices, the traffic would still be fewer than 100,000 data packets per day.

Pretty Paper Limited Case Study Questions

Question 4-11

Diagram the packet flow of client/server traffic for the new business software, as well as traffic for the pattern design documents for film production, based on the requirements as you understand them.

Figure B-7 diagrams the packet flow of Pretty Paper's new business software client/server traffic.

Figure B-7   *Pretty Paper's New Business Software Client/Server Packet Flow*

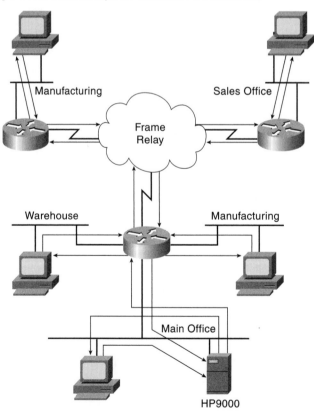

Figure B-8 diagrams the packet flow of Pretty Paper's pattern design documents.

Figure B-8   *Pretty Paper's Pattern Design Documents Packet Flow*

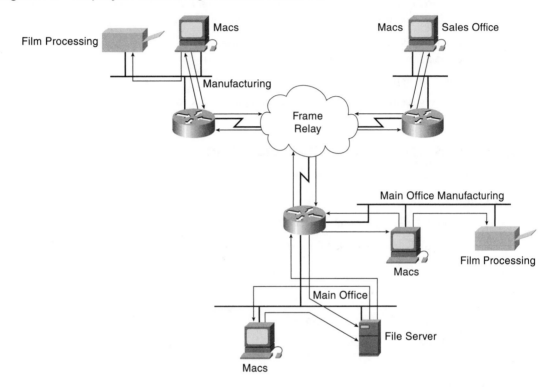

Question 4-12

Identify the customer's performance requirements.

Transaction processing time must be cut in half. This is a requirement primarily on the new business software and the HP9000 system.

Question 4-13

What concerns do you have for scalability if the number of sales offices were to double over the next two years?

Scalability should raise no real concerns, but might affect the router selection.

Question 4-14

The manager of Warehouse and Distribution is concerned about PC client performance over the Frame Relay network to the new business software on the HP9000. What design constraints and consideration will be taken into account for these concerns?

- Obtain traffic characteristics of the application software from the vendor or measure the characteristics with a protocol analyzer
- Select an appropriate Frame Relay CIR
- Possibly recommend use of network computers or X terminals

Jones, Jones, & Jones Case Study Questions

Question 4-15

Diagram the packet flow of information for the e-mail application.

Figure B-9 diagrams the packet flow of the Jones, Jones, & Jones e-mail application.

Figure B-9 *Jones, Jones, & Jones E-mail Application Packet Flow*

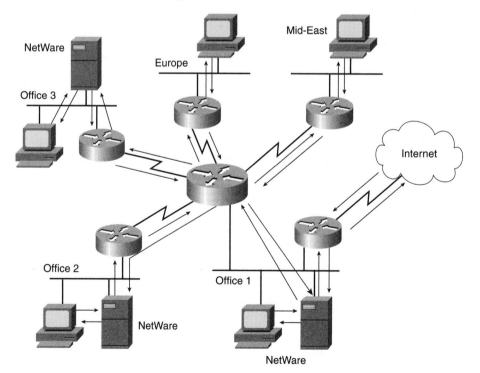

Question 4-16

Diagram the packet flow of information for the CD-ROM Library Pack application.

Figure B-10 diagrams the packet flow of the Jones, Jones, & Jones CD-ROM Library Pack application.

Figure B-10 *Jones, Jones, & Jones CD-ROM Library Pack Packet Flow*

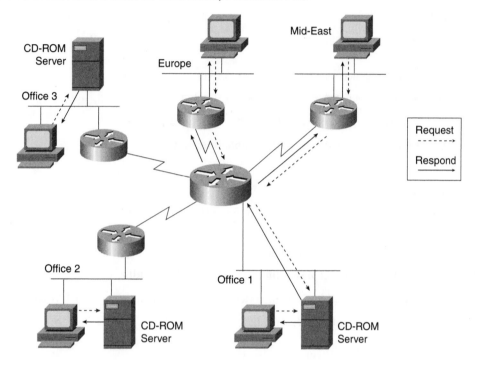

Question 4-17

Identify the customer's performance requirements.

- At home and on the road, users should be able to work as effectively as if they were in the office.

- Attorneys should be able to share documents effectively, regardless of location.

Chapter 5

Multiple-Choice Review Questions

Question 5-1

Which of the following characteristics accurately describes the hierarchical model for internetwork design?

    A. Alleviates concerns about internetwork diameter.

    B. Defines the number of allowed hops in an internetwork.

    C. Applies to large internetworks, but not small internetworks.

    D. **Helps a designer implement scalable internetworks.**

Question 5-2

Which one of the following is an issue in large Novell NetWare networks that use a full mesh Frame Relay topology?

    A. Split horizon cannot be turned off.

    B. **SAP broadcasts use a substantial amount of bandwidth.**

    C. Snapshot routing is not yet supported to reduce bandwidth usage by IPX RIP.

    D. Servers do not comply with the CIR.

Question 5-3

When designing load balancing in a WAN network, what is the most important rule?

    A. **Use equal-cost paths within each layer of the hierarchy.**

    B. Minimize the number of hops between sites.

    C. Use Enhanced IGRP for the most effective load balancing.

    D. Use an odd number of routers (rather than an even number).

Question 5-4

Which one of the following conditions would result in recommending routing instead of switching?

A. Many Ethernet collisions.

B. Excessive number of Ethernet runt frames (shorter than 64 bytes).

C. Bandwidth utilization over 40 percent on Ethernet.

D. Many desktop protocols sending packets to find services.

Question 5-5

Which one of the following statements best describes the specialized role that each layer of the hierarchical model plays?

A. The access layer provides policy-based connectivity.

B. The distribution layer provides resource discovery services.

C. The core layer provides optimal transport between sites.

D. The core layer provides workgroups access to the internetwork.

Question 5-6

Cisco's Hot Standby Router Protocol (HSRP) is a useful tool for ensuring which of the following?

A. IPX and AppleTalk sessions do not die when the default router dies.

B. IP sessions do not die when the default router dies.

C. ATM LAN Emulation sessions do not die when the LAN Emulation server dies.

D. Core routing does not die when floating static routes become active.

Question 5-7

In a three-part firewall security system, the outside filter router should support which of the following?

A. Configuration via TFTP

B. Proxy ARP service

C. Static routing only

D. IP route caching

CareTaker Case Study Questions

Question 5-8

Draw a topology that will meet CareTaker's requirements. Include only the high-level view of the location of links and internetworking devices. In a few sentences, describe how your topology meets CareTaker's needs.

Figure B-11 diagrams the topology of CareTaker's network.

Figure B-11 *CareTaker Topology*

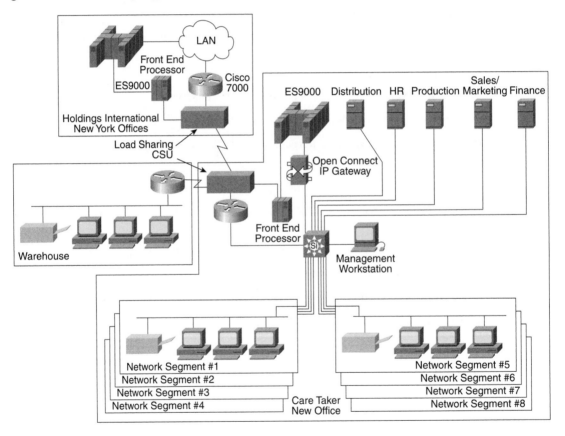

Within the new facilities, the entire internetwork can be configured and tested without interruption to the existing operations. The router link to HI will be configured and tested prior to any move. HI's network operations personnel will be able to simulate SNA traffic while TCP/IP traffic is shared on the link (pings, traces, and e-mail could be used for this purpose).

Question 5-9

After putting your initial topology together, the IS manager has brought up the question of failures. She feels it is important that the warehouse not lose access to the mainframe and its server. In response to your question about the economic trade-offs, she stated that management probably would not accept any kind of fail-safe or redundancy that increases the cost more than 2 to 5 percent. What modification, if any, would you make to your design to accommodate fail-safe operations of the warehouse?

- Consider locating the distribution server at the warehouse
- Consider an additional lower-speed leased line connection between the parent company's router and the warehouse
- Consider either a redundant leased line supplied by a different provider with a different central office or a standby ISDN connection between the warehouse and the Cisco router

PH Network Services Corporation Case Study Questions

Question 5-10

Draw a topology that will meet PH Network's requirements. In a few sentences, describe how your topology meets its needs.

Figure B-12 diagrams the PH Network topology.

Figure B-12 *PH Network's Topology*

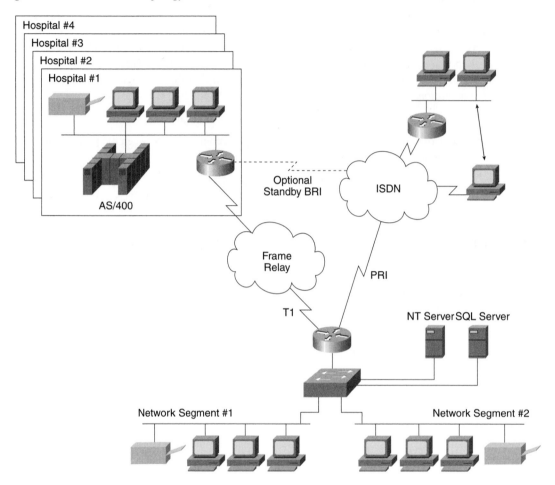

The capability to provide Frame Relay and ISDN support in the Cisco router is important. PH Network's primary concern appears to be availability. The Cisco router will provide the capability to add an ISDN PRI if needed. The use of ISDN also provides a redundant path to the hospitals.

The customer specified 56 kbps Frame Relay and ISDN, which will be adequate for terminal access to patients' records. Using a Cisco switch will allow the NetWare and SQL Server to be placed on Fast Ethernet ports. The Cisco switch will provide good throughput to the SQL Server.

Question 5-11

PH has brought up the question of telecommunication failures. It has had numerous failures in the lines to the hospitals. These are critical communications, and the company would like to know whether anything can be done to reduce communication losses. What modification, if any, would you make to your design to accommodate fail-safe operations to the hospitals?

A backup ISDN connection could be added to the hospitals. This backup will provide a redundant route if the Frame Relay link fails.

Pretty Paper Limited Case Study Questions

Question 5-12

Draw a topology that will meet Pretty Paper's requirements. In a few sentences, describe how your topology meets Pretty Paper's needs.

Figure B-13 diagrams the topology of Pretty Paper's network.

Figure B-13 *Pretty Paper's Topology*

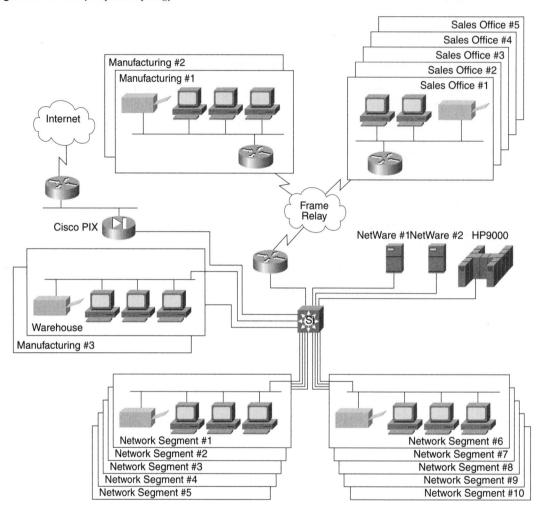

Improvement in overall system performance seems to be Pretty Paper's main concern. On the main office local level, an ethernet switch will provide high bandwidth for the transmission of the graphic files, as well as the heavy client/server traffic for the new Oracle application. The servers, including the HP9000, should each be on dedicated 100 Mbps ports to significantly increase access speeds.

The distance from the main facilities to the local warehouse and manufacturing facilities dictates the use of fiber-optic cable to link between a hub in these facilities and the Catalyst 5000 switch in the main facility.

The 56 kbps Frame Relay links are the limiting factor on the WAN. With the use of client/server technology, this bandwidth should be sufficient.

The Internet connection will be secured through the firewall to address Pretty Paper's security needs.

Question 5-13

The manager of Warehouse and Distribution is concerned about PC client performance over the Frame Relay network to the new business software on the HP9000. What design constraints and considerations will you take into account to answer these concerns?

Obtain traffic characteristics of the application software from the vendor or measure the characteristics with a protocol analyzer.

Question 5-14

How would you respond to the Sales and Marketing organization's questions regarding someone's ability to get to data on the NetWare servers or the HP9000 from the Internet?

Cite the enterprise-level firewalls tests by Network Computing (see http://www.networkcomputing.com/921/921f22.html). Provide printed copies of the test for the customer to review.

Jones, Jones, & Jones Case Study Questions

Question 5-15

Draw a topology that will meet Ms. Jones's requirements. Include only the high-level view of the location of links and internetworking devices. In a few sentences, describe how your topology meets the law firm's needs.

Figure B-14 diagrams the topology of the Jones, Jones, & Jones network.

Figure B-14 *Jones, Jones, & Jones Network Topology*

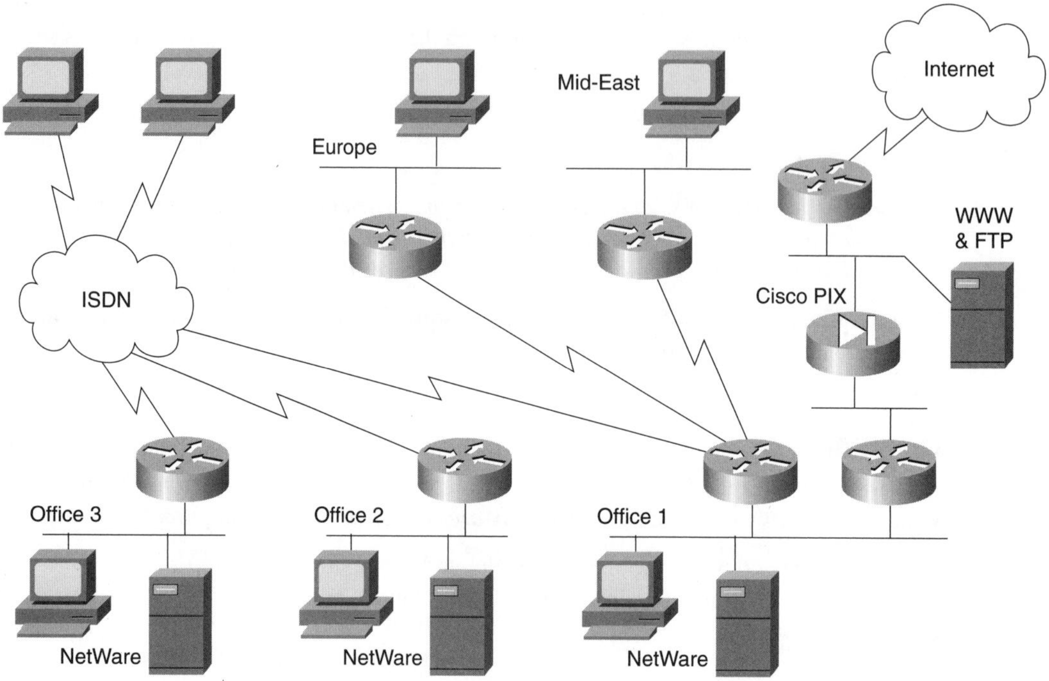

Jones's need to improve competitiveness with technology is met with the deployment of the Cisco routers. These products will provide the company with the connectivity and functionality to operate on a global basis with the capability to collaborate on its work as if it were a single office with very affordable products that will not become obsolete. The private network and firewall to the Internet will provide adequate security. The use of the Ethernet switch in the larger offices will provide significant performance advantages. The use of ISDN and asynchronous dial-in through the main Cisco router provides a very economical, high-performance, and ubiquitous dial-in solution.

For foolproof network security, a three-part firewall system locates Jones's Web/FTP server behind the first tier. To access this tier, users come through a router that provides initial security. Beyond this first tier is Cisco's PIX Firewall series, which represents the second-tier security perimeter. In case there is a breach of security on the exposed segment, the PIX Firewall series acts as a strong security barrier to prevent outside users from gaining access to Jones's private network. Coupling Cisco's PIX Firewall series with Cisco routers running Cisco IOS™ software will provide Jones with a powerful security solution that will allow it to sell its research papers without fear of exposure of internal documents and files. It forces hackers to penetrate multiple lines of defense.

Question 5-16

The managing partner called. She wanted to emphasize that unauthorized workstations should not be allowed access to the Internet. How have you accommodated this request in your design?

Static IP addresses should be assigned to specific users at the DHCP server. All other addresses will then be filtered by the Internet router.

Chapter 6

CareTaker Case Study Questions

Question 6-1

What media would you select between the switch and the servers?

Because switched 100 Mbps Ethernet is a relatively inexpensive solution, use Category 5 cabling throughout the network with 100 Mbps network interface cards in the servers.

Question 6-2

What media would you select between the switch and each of the eight network segments in the new CareTaker building?

Use Category 5 cabling, which saves some expense and allows more flexibility with cable type and length.

Question 6-3

What LAN switch would you recommend for the headquarters office? If you have Internet access, use the Cisco Product Selection Tool *as detailed at the beginning of the Chapter 6 Case Studies section, clicking on the switches selection. Once you have the short list of products from this tool, select the right product that meets this customer's needs.*

Using the *Cisco Product Selection Tool*, the following products were selected:

Catalyst 1912	Catalyst 2926T	Catalyst 1912C
Catalyst 2926F	Catalyst 1924	Catalyst 3016
Catalyst 1924C	Catalyst 3100	Catalyst 2822
Catalyst 3200	Catalyst 2828	Catalyst 5007
Catalyst 2901	Catalyst 5002	Catalyst 2902
Catalyst 5507	Catalyst 5509 CHAC, CHDC	

Recommend the Catalyst 5002 switch with a switched 10/100 Mbps module because it best fits the needs for server performance and cost. The network segments can be connected at 10 Mbps, and the servers can be connected at 100 Mbps.

By clicking on the product name in the right-hand window of the product selection tool, you can display an overview of the product. Part of this overview for the Catalyst 5002 is reproduced here:

The Catalyst 5002 Switching system provides high-performance, flexible switching for the wiring closet and workgroups. The Catalyst® 5002 switch delivers award-winning Catalyst 5000 Family performance in a compact chassis. The Catalyst 5002 is a fully modular, two-slot Catalyst 5000 switch that uses the same architecture and software as the Catalyst 5000. The switch can deliver more than one million packets-per-second (PPS) throughput across a 1.2-Gbps media-independent backplane that supports Ethernet, Fast Ethernet, Token Ring, Fiber Distributed Data Interface (FDDI), and Asynchronous Transfer Mode (ATM).

The Catalyst 5002 can be configured with any of the current or future Catalyst 5000 Family modules. Slot one is reserved for the Supervisor Engine, which provides Layer 2 switching and network management. The Supervisor Engine includes two full-duplex Fast Ethernet uplinks for redundant connections to switches, routers, and servers. Users can choose dual 100BaseTX, dual-multimode 100BaseFX, or dual single-mode 100BaseFX uplinks. Further, with Cisco Fast EtherChannel® technology, the two ports can be configured as a single 400-Mbps fault-tolerant connection.

The second slot accepts any Catalyst 5000 line card, enabling flexible solutions for a variety of applications. High-density switched Fast Ethernet, Ethernet, and group-switched Ethernet modules meet today's wiring closet requirements. Gigabit Ethernet and Fast EtherChannel solutions for can be deployed in distribution layer and server connectivity applications for intermediate-sized networks. With an ATM LAN Emulation (LANE) module, the Catalyst 5002 functions as a compact, high-performance LANE server.

The Catalyst 5002 chassis fits into a standard 19-inch rack, and all system components are accessible from the same side of the chassis. The chassis includes dual load-sharing, redundant power supplies. A single supply can support any configuration, making the system highly reliable. The Catalyst 5002 complements the Catalyst 5000 Family, letting users benefit from common hardware, software, and spares from the data center to network periphery.

PH Network Services Corporation Case Study Questions

Question 6-4

What media would you select between the switch and the servers?

100-Mbps Ethernet is the best solution for the servers.

Question 6-5

What media would you select between the switch and each of the network segments in the main office?

The 10 Mbps switched ports will allow for adequate performance and scalability for the main office.

Question 6-6

What LAN switch would you select? If you have Internet access, use the Cisco Product Selection Tool *as detailed at the beginning of the Chapter 6 Case Studies section, clicking on the switches selection. Once you have the short list of products from this tool, select the right product that meets this customer's needs.*

Using the *Cisco Product Selection Tool*, the following products were selected:

Catalyst 1912	Catalyst 3016
Catalyst 1912C	Catalyst 3100
Catalyst 1924	Catalyst 3200
Catalyst 1924C	Catalyst 5007
Catalyst 2822	Catalyst 5002
Catalyst 2828	Catalyst 5507
Catalyst 2901	Catalyst 5509 CHAC, CHDC

Recommend the Catalyst 1924 switch to allow the NetWare and SQL Server machines to be placed on 100-Mbps Ethernet ports. The Catlyst 1924 Switch will provide for good throughput to the SQL Server machine.

You can display an overview of the product by clicking on the product name in the right-hand window of the product selection tool. Part of this overview for the Catalyst 1900 and 2820 switches, which includes the 1924, is reproduced here:

Cisco Catalyst 1900 and 2820 series Ethernet switches are the ideal desktop complements to the complete line of high-performance switching and routing products from Cisco Systems, the leader in networking. The payoff: better network performance and manageability at an exceptionally affordable price.

Available in Standard and Enterprise editions, Catalyst 1900 and 2820 switches are distinguished by their ease of use, flexible configuration, and upgradability. Standard Edition switches are designed to work directly out of the box and connect desktops to high-speed servers or the network backbone. Enterprise Edition software adds unmatched scalability, as well as flexible network configuration options, including virtual LAN (VLAN) support, bandwidth optimization, enhanced security, and comprehensive management capabilities. You can acquire the rich performance and management features of the Enterprise Edition now or later; the software comes preinstalled on the Catalyst 1900 and 2820 Enterprise Edition switches or is available as an upgrade for Standard Edition switches.

Enterprise Edition

Cisco Catalyst 1900 and 2820 Enterprise Edition switches provide high-capacity links and stackability through Fast EtherChannel port aggregation. Fast EtherChannel can deliver up to 400 Mbps of bandwidth per link in full duplex mode, providing optimal uplinks to high-speed backbones and high-performance servers. The switches also deliver simplified administration, enhanced security, and broadcast control through ISL VLAN trunking. The Catalyst 1900 and 2820 Enterprise Edition series switches provide enhanced security by enabling centralized access control through TACACS+. Multilevel console passwords enable implementation of a secure, flexible access control policy for the switch console. For ease of deployment in a large network, Enterprise Edition switches support autoconfiguration of multiple switches through a boot server and can be managed via the widely used Cisco IOS™ command line interface (CLI). Used in conjunction with Cisco routers, chassis switches, and access servers, Enterprise Edition switches provide unmatched network performance, management control, and ease of use in a Cisco end-to-end network.

In addition to industry-leading software functionality, the Catalyst 1900 and 2800 families of switches are available with a broad range of configurations to meet specific network requirements. The Catalyst 1900 family is available with either 12 or 24 10BaseT ports, with two high-speed Fast Ethernet uplinks configurations, including two 100BaseTX ports, two 100BaseFX fiber ports, or one of each. The Catalyst 2820 family offers 24 10BaseT ports, with several plug-in modules, including Fast Ethernet 100BaseTX, 100baseFX ports, ATM 155-Mbps ports, and FDDI fiber or UTP ports.

Pretty Paper Limited Case Study Questions

Question 6-7

What media would you select between the switch and the servers?

The servers, including the HP9000, will each be on dedicated 100-Mbps ports to significantly increase access speeds.

Question 6-8

What media would you select between the switch and each of the network segments in the new Pretty Paper headquarters building?

All the other Ethernet links will be shared 10 Mbps 10BaseT.

Question 6-9

What recommendations would you make for media between the switch and central manufacturing in the Pretty Paper design? What about the connection to the warehouse?

The distance from the main facilities to the local warehouse and manufacturing facilities dictates the use of fiber-optic cable to link a hub in these facilities with a Catalyst 5000 switch in the main facility.

Question 6-10

What LAN switch would you select? If you have Internet access, use the Cisco Product Selection Tool, *clicking on the switches selection. Once you have the short list of products from this tool, select the right product that meets this customer's needs.*

Using the *Cisco Product Selection Tool*, the following products were selected:

- Catalyst 3200
- Catalyst 5007
- Catalyst 5002
- Catalyst 5507
- Catalyst 5509 CHAC, CHDC

Given the number of interfaces required, recommend a Catalyst 5000 switch with 100-Mbps ports to support the NetWare servers and the HP9000 system and fiber for the connection to the warehouse and production facilities.

Part of the overview for the Catalyst 5000 series switches is reproduced here:

Cisco Systems' flagship Catalyst 5000 series switches are the industry's most powerful switching solutions in the wiring closet, data center, or backbone.

The series features a Gigabit Ethernet and ATM-ready platform offering users high-speed trunking technologies including Fast EtherChannel® and OC-12 ATM. The Catalyst 5000 series also features a redundant architecture, dynamic VLANs, complete intranet services support, and media-rate performance with a broad variety of interface modules.

Modules for the Catalyst 5000 family models—the Catalyst 5500, 5000, and 5002—are designed for complete interoperability and investment protection. New functionalities in the Catalyst 5000 series support multiprotocol NetFlow Switching for scalable convergence of Layer 2 and Layer 3 switching, adding the benefits of multiprotocol, multilayer switching and other Cisco IOS™ network services.

The range of media support in the Catalyst 5000 series enables network managers to deliver high-performance backbone access to accommodate Web browser-based traffic across the intranet. A growing number of interface modules operate in any Catalyst 5000 series switch to deliver dedicated bandwidth to users through high-density group switched and switched 10BaseT or 100BaseT Ethernet; flexible 10/100BaseT Ethernet, fiber-based Fast Ethernet, and Fast EtherChannel; Token Ring; CDDI/FDDI; ATM LAN Emulation (LANE); the Route/Switch module (based on the Route/Switch Processor for the Cisco 7500 router series); and future Gigabit Ethernet. Unique to the Catalyst 5500 platform are the ATM Switch Processor and ATM switch interface modules and port adapters.

Jones, Jones, & Jones Case Study Questions

Question 6-11

What media would you select between the switch and the servers?

Use 100 Mbps Ethernet for the NetWare and CD-ROM servers, which will provide adequate access bandwidth for the document management and research functions.

Question 6-12

What media would you select between the switch and each of the network segments in the law firm's U.S. offices?

Connect the desktop PCs over shared 10 Mbps 10BaseT cable.

Question 6-13

What LAN media would you select for the international offices?

The desktop PCs will be connected over shared 10 Mbps 10BaseT cable.

Question 6-14

What LAN switch would you recommend? If you have Internet access, use the Cisco Product Selection Tool *as detailed at the beginning of the Chapter 6 Case Studies section, clicking on the switches selection. Once you have the short list of products from this tool, select the product that best meets this customer's needs.*

Using the *Cisco Product Selection Tool*, the same products as selected for Question 6-3 were selected.

Recommend the Catalyst 5002 switch to provide two 100 Mbps ports for the NetWare and CD-ROM servers. This solution provides adequate access bandwidth for the document management and research functions. Connect the desktop PCs over shared 10 Mbps 10BaseT cable.

Part of the overview of the 5002 switch is provided with the answer to Question 6-3.

Chapter 7

CareTaker Case Study Questions

Question 7-1

Which router would you select for the warehouse?

Using the *Cisco Product Selection Tool*, the following products were selected:

- Cisco 1602
- Cisco 1605-R
- Cisco 1720
- Cisco 2524
- Cisco 2610
- Cisco 2611
- Cisco 2612

Recommend the Cisco 2524; it offers modular WAN connectivity including a module with a built-in DSU.

By clicking on the product name in the right-hand window of the product selection tool you can display an overview of the product. Part of this overview for the Cisco 2524 (and 2525) is reproduced here:

The Cisco 2524 and Cisco 2525 routers provide LAN and WAN access in a low-cost modular router platform that can grow with your internetworking needs. The Cisco 2524 offers an Ethernet (attachment unit interface (AUI) or 10BaseT) LAN connection, and the Cisco 2525 offers a Token Ring (shielded twisted-pair [STP] or unshielded twisted-pair [UTP]) LAN connection. Both routers can accommodate up to three WAN modules—two synchronous serial and one Integrated Services Digital Network (ISDN).

The choice of synchronous serial WAN modules is as follows:

- Two-wire switched 56-kbps data service unit/channel service unit (DSU/CSU)
- Four-wire 56/64-kbps DSU/CSU
- Fractional T1/E1 DSU/CSU
- Five-in-one synchronous serial

The choice of ISDN WAN modules is as follows:

- ISDN Basic Rate Interface (BRI)
- ISDN with integrated network termination 1 (NT1) device

The ISDN WAN modules are designed so that you cannot insert them into the synchronous serial WAN slots. A blank slot cover is installed over unused slots.

Question 7-2

Which router would you select for the headquarters office?

Using the *Cisco Product Selection Tool*, the following products were selected:

Cisco MC3810	Cisco AS5200	Cisco 2612
Cisco AS5300	Cisco 3620	Cisco 7202
Cisco 3640	Cisco 7204	Cisco 4500
Cisco 7206	Cisco 4700	

Recommend the Cisco 3640; it can accommodate two high-speed (T1/E1) ports and provides future expandability. Cisco IOS™ software will address any new protocol requirements, and the plug-in network modules provide a high-performance RISC processor.

You can display an overview of the product by clicking on the product name in the right-hand window of the product selection tool. Part of this overview for the Cisco 3600 is reproduced here:

The Cisco 3600 is the industry's first true multifunction platform with the versatility to support branch/enterprise dial access applications, LAN-to-LAN or routing applications, and multiservice applications in a single server. It provides unprecedented modularity options with a broad range of available network modules, enormous flexibility with a variety of configurable options for customer-specific application scenarios, and, above all, high performance to support any of these applications.

The Cisco 3640 server is equipped with four network module slots, the Cisco 3620 with two. Dial connectivity is supported with a series of network modules offering Integrated Services Digital Network (ISDN) Primary Rate Interface (PRI), ISDN Basic Rate Interface (BRI), integrated digital modems, very high-density asynchronous interfaces, and asynchronous/synchronous serial interfaces. LAN and WAN connectivity are provided by a series of mixed-media cards supporting Ethernet, Token Ring, and a variety of WAN technologies. Routing applications are supported with high-density Ethernet and a single-port, autosensing, Fast Ethernet network module. Finally, multiservice applications are supported by integrated voice network modules.

Question 7-3

Update your topology diagram from Chapter 3 to reflect your media, LAN, and WAN hardware selections.

Figure B-15 diagrams the updated topology of the CareTaker network.

Figure B-15 *CareTaker's Updated Network Topology*

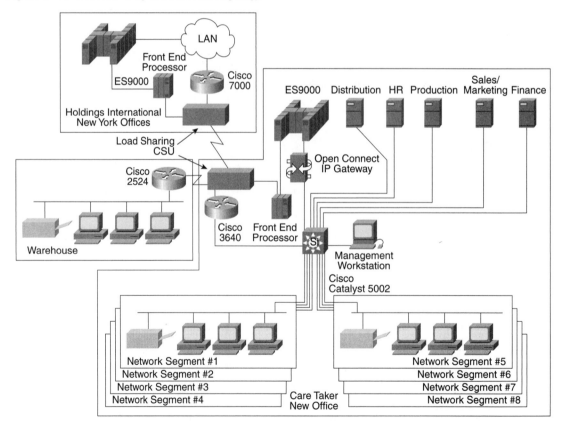

Through the employment of Cisco's Ethernet switching technology, peak performance will be achieved for all user nodes on the network. This performance is accomplished by combining minimal user nodes on segmented dedicated 100-Mbps paths to servers. On average, each user should see virtually the full 10-Mbps path between the user and a given server.

The TN3270 users are also given a dedicated port to the ES9000.

The network design is simple and easy to manage for CareTaker's inexperienced administrators. It is a single-protocol, logically flat network. The naming and addressing is simple and easy to understand and track. The central location of all shared networking devices, servers, routers, switches, and so on makes for easy administration and maintenance.

Question 7-4

Can you recommend any third-party products for the load-sharing CSU (multiplexer) and the Open Connect gateway products?

Load-sharing CSUs are available from Adtran, Inc. (see http://www.adtran.com) and ADC Kentrox (see http://www.kentrox.com). The Open Connect gateway could be the Open Connect Server OC/3030 from Open Connect Systems (see http://www.oc.com).

PH Network Services Coporation Case Study Questions

Question 7-5

Which router would you select for the main office?

Using the *Cisco Product Selection Tool*, the following products were selected:

- Cisco 3620
- Cisco 3640
- Cisco 4500
- Cisco 4700
- Cisco AS5300
- Cisco 7202
- Cisco 7204
- Cisco 7206

Recommend the Cisco 3620 router to provide Frame Relay and ISDN support, including built-in NT1. A 56-kbps Frame Relay for each of the four hospitals terminating into a T1/E1 at the main office and ISDN will be adequate for terminal access to patients' records.

You can display an overview of the product by clicking on the product name in the right-hand window of the product selection tool. Part of this overview for the Cisco 3600 is reproduced in the answer to question 7.2.

PH Network's primary concern appears to be availability. The Cisco 3620 router will provide the capability to add an ISDN PRI if needed. The use of ISDN also provides a redundant path to the hospitals.

Question 7-6

Which router would you select for the hospitals?

Using the *Cisco Product Selection Tool*, the following products were selected:

Cisco 1601	Cisco 1720	Cisco 1602
Cisco 2524	Cisco 1603	Cisco 2610
Cisco 1604	Cisco 2611	Cisco 1605-R
Cisco 2612		

Recommend the Cisco 2524 router; this will provide both ISDN and Frame Relay support for the hospitals.

By clicking on the product name in the right-hand window of the product selection tool you can display an overview of the product. Part of this overview for the Cisco 2524 (and 2525) is reproduced in the answer to Question 7-1.

Question 7-7

Which router would you select for the doctors' offices?

Using the *Cisco Product Selection Tool*, the following products were selected:

Cisco 762	Cisco 1004	Cisco 766
Cisco 1601	Cisco 772	Cisco 1602
Cisco 776	Cisco 1603	Cisco 802
Cisco 1604	Cisco 804	Cisco 1720

Recommend the Cisco 1004 router; the economics and features make this a good choice for the doctor offices.

By clicking on the product name in the right-hand window of the product selection tool you can display an overview of the product. Part of this overview for the Cisco 1004 is reproduced here:

Cisco is introducing a new Integrated Services Digital Network (ISDN) router in the Cisco 1000 series of inexpensive, easy-to-install and manage, multiprotocol access products. The new Cisco 1004 ISDN router has an ISDN Basic Rate Interface (BRI) port with an integrated Network Termination 1 (NT1) device, thus reducing the number of devices required to connect to ISDN in North America. The Cisco 1004 connects small, remote sites with Ethernet LANs to wide-area networks using ISDN at speeds up to 128 kbps; with 4:1 data compression, raw throughput speeds of 512 kbps are possible. The Cisco 1004 has a built-in ISDN BRI port with an integrated NT1, a 10BaseT Ethernet port, a console port, and an external Personal Computer Memory Card International Association (PCMCIA) slot for an optional Flash ROM card. This "plug-and-play" product is designed to be installed easily by nontechnical personnel at remote sites. The Cisco 1004 ISDN router extends Cisco's range of ISDN scalable solutions.

The Cisco 1004 router decreases the total cost of ownership in several ways:

- Deployment costs are reduced because Cisco 1004 routers are easily installed at the remote sites by nontechnical personnel, eliminating the need to send technical personnel to these sites.

- Support costs are reduced, because configuration and management can be performed at a central site, where technical expertise typically resides. Initial configuration files can be stored on optional Flash ROM cards and sent to remote sites. Software upgrades and configuration modifications can be downloaded over the WAN.

- WAN costs are reduced because the Cisco 1004 supports Cisco's bandwidth optimization features, such as DDR, BOD, PPP compression, snapshot routing, IPX spoofing, and access control lists. Priority and custom queuing ensure that delay-sensitive data gets the priority it deserves.

- Equipment costs are reduced because the Cisco 1004 router has an integrated BRI port with NT1 and supports inexpensive unshielded twisted-pair (UTP) wiring for Ethernet.

Question 7-8

Update your topology diagram from Chapter 3 to reflect your media, LAN, and WAN hardware selections.

Figure B-16 diagrams the updated PH Network topology.

Figure B-16 *PH Network's Updated Topology*

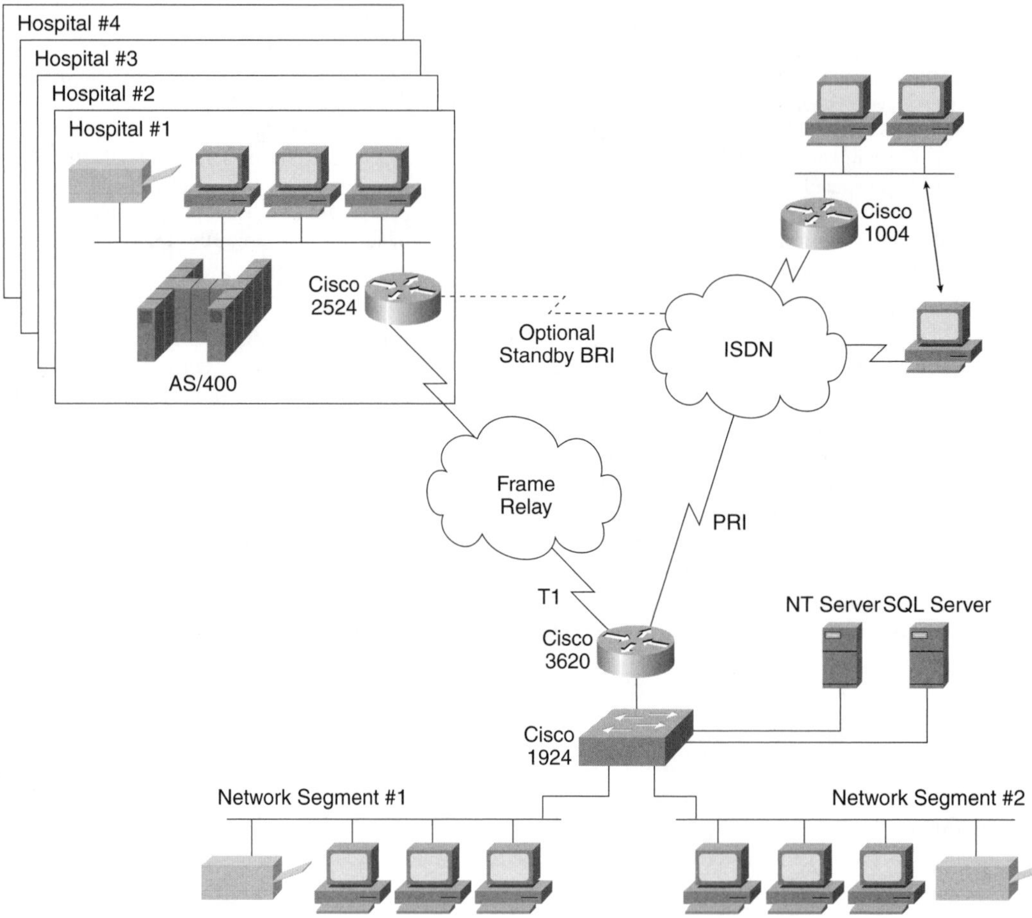

Pretty Paper Limited Case Study Questions

Question 7-9

Which router would you select for the main office?

Using the *Cisco Product Selection Tool*, the same products selected for Question 7-2 were selected.

Recommend the Cisco 3620 to provide a cost-effective main office solution.

You can display an overview of the product by clicking on the product name in the right-hand window of the product selection tool. Part of this overview for the Cisco 3600 is reproduced in the answer to Question 7-2.

Question 7-10

Which router would you select for the sales offices?

Using the *Cisco Product Selection Tool*, the following products were selected:

Cisco 1005	Cisco 2509 and 2590RJ
Cisco 1601	Cisco 2511 and 2511RJ
Cisco 1602	Cisco 2513
Cisco 1603	Cisco 2514
Cisco 1604	Cisco 2516
Cisco 1605-R	Cisco 2520
Cisco 1720	Cisco 2522
Cisco 2501	Cisco 2524
Cisco 2503	Cisco 2610
Cisco 2505	Cisco 2611
Cisco 2507	Cisco 2612

Recommend the Cisco 2503 at the sales offices to provide a logistics and support advantage. The Cisco 2503 router has one ethernet interface, two serial interfaces, and one ISDN interface.

Part of the overview for the Cisco 2500 series routers, which includes the Cisco 2503, is reproduced here:

The Cisco 2500 series of routers, the world's most popular brand of branch office router, provides a variety of models. These routers are typically fixed configuration with at least two of the following interfaces: Ethernet Token Ring, synchronous serial, asynchronous serial, ISDN BRI, and hub. Two modular models are also available.

Key Features include:

- Proven technology with a full suite of Cisco IOS™ software
- Setup with Cisco ConfigMaker, a free tool for configuring a network of routers
- With CiscoWorks Windows, allows remote management and maintenance from a central location

Question 7-11

Which router would you select to provide Internet access?

Using the *Cisco Product Selection Tool*, the same products selected for the sales offices in Question 7-10 were selected.

Recommend the Cisco 2503 for Internet access to provide a logistics and support advantage. Part of the overview of the Cisco 2500 series routers is provided in the answer to Question 7-10.

Question 7-12

The manager of Warehouse and Distribution is concerned about PC client over the Frame Relay network to the new business software on the HP9000 system. What design constraints and considerations will you take into account to address these concerns?

The 56-kbps Frame Relay links are the limiting factor on the WAN. With the use of client/server technology, this bandwidth should be sufficient.

You should obtain traffic characteristics of the application software from the vendor or measure the characteristics with a protocol analyzer. Understanding traffic characteristics will help in the selection of an appropriate Frame Relay CIR.

You might also recommend network computers or X terminals.

Question 7-13

Getting products manufactured and delivered to customers is the company's biggest concern. Therefore, it is imperative that the manufacturing/warehouse facilities have uninterrupted access to the HP9000. What modifications, if any, would you make to your design to accommodate fail-safe operations of the warehouses?

Include a redundant, alternate path fiber run to the local warehouse to be manually switched.

Include either a redundant, second-vendor Frame Relay circuit or a backup, auto-dial telephony path.

Router redundancy would not appear to be economically feasible for this situation.

Question 7-14

Update your topology diagram from Chapter 3 to reflect your media, LAN, and WAN hardware selections.

Figure B-17 diagrams the updated Pretty Paper topology.

Figure B-17 *Pretty Paper's Updated Topology*

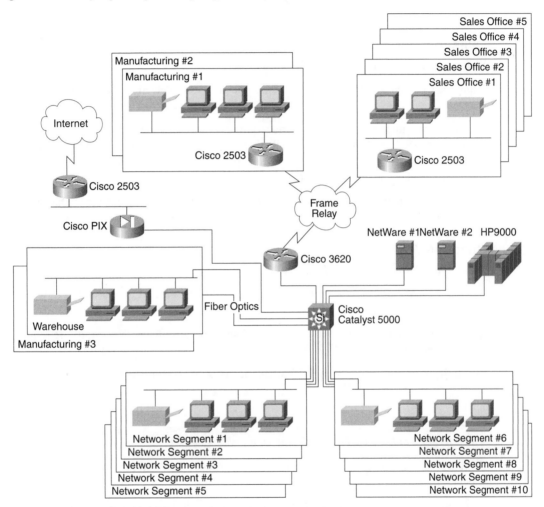

The distance from the main facilities to the local warehouse and manufacturing facilities dictates the use of fiber-optic cable to link between a hub in these facilities and the Catalyst 5000 switch in the main facility.

The Internet connection will be secured through the Cisco PIX. The Cisco PIX Firewall will address Pretty Paper's security needs without the overhead and performance limitations of a proxy server. Its high performance and low cost of ownership make it ideal for Pretty Paper.

Jones, Jones, & Jones Case Study Questions

Question 7-15

Which router would you select for the first office?

Using the *Cisco Product Selection Tool*, the same products selected for Question 7-2 were selected.

Because of the number and types of ports required for this location and its expandability, recommend the Cisco 3640 router with plug-in interfaces. Cisco IOS software will already address any new protocol requirements, but the plug-in network modules with a high-performance RISC processor make this the right choice.

Part of the overview of the Cisco 3600 series routers is provided in the answer to Question 7-2.

Question 7-16

Which router would you select for offices 2 and 3?

Using the *Cisco Product Selection Tool*, the same products selected for Question 7-2 were selected.

Recommend the Cisco 3620 router for offices 2 and 3 because fewer WAN ports are required at these locations.

Part of the overview of the Cisco 3600 series routers is provided in the answer to Question 7-2.

Question 7-17

Which router would you select for the international offices?

Using the *Cisco Product Selection Tool*, the same products selected for Question 7-10 were selected.

Recommend either the Cisco 2503 or the Cisco 1603 router. Based on the cost concerns of the customer, we would recommend the Cisco 1603.

Part of the overview for the Cisco 1600 series routers, including the Cisco 1603, is reproduced here:

The demand for remote access at small offices has grown rapidly as companies discover the benefits of connecting to the Internet and corporate intranets. However, typical products targeted at small offices lack important features, security, and flexibility required for the small office.

The Cisco 1600 Series routers connect small offices with Ethernet LANs to wide-area networks (WANs) through Integrated Services Digital Network (ISDN), asynchronous serial, and synchronous serial connections. The five models in the Cisco 1600 product family offer the following ports:

- **Cisco 1601**—One Ethernet, one serial, one WAN interface card slot.
- **Cisco 1602**—One Ethernet, one serial with integrated 56-kbps DSU/CSU, one WAN interface card slot.
- **Cisco 1603**—One Ethernet, one ISDN Basic Rate Interface (BRI) (S/T interface), one WAN interface card slot.
- **Cisco 1604**—One Ethernet, one ISDN BRI with integrated NT1 (U interface), one S-bus port for ISDN phones, one WAN interface card slot.
- **Cisco 1605-R**—Two Ethernets, one WAN interface card slot.

The WAN interface card slot enables customers to change or add WAN interface cards as their WAN requirements grow or change. With this feature, the Cisco 1600 series routers offer more flexibility and investment protection than any other product in its class.

The Cisco 1600 series routers are designed to be plug-and-play devices: preconfigured software can be loaded into Flash memory PC cards (also known as PCMCIA cards) at a central site and then sent to remote sites, where users can simply insert the Flash cards and plug in WAN, LAN, and power cables. Software upgrades and configuration modifications can be downloaded over the WAN from a central site.

Question 7-18

Update your topology diagram from Chapter 3 to reflect your media, LAN, and WAN hardware selections.

Figure B-18 provides the updated Jones, Jones, & Jones topology.

Figure B-18 *Jones, Jones, & Jones Updated Topology*

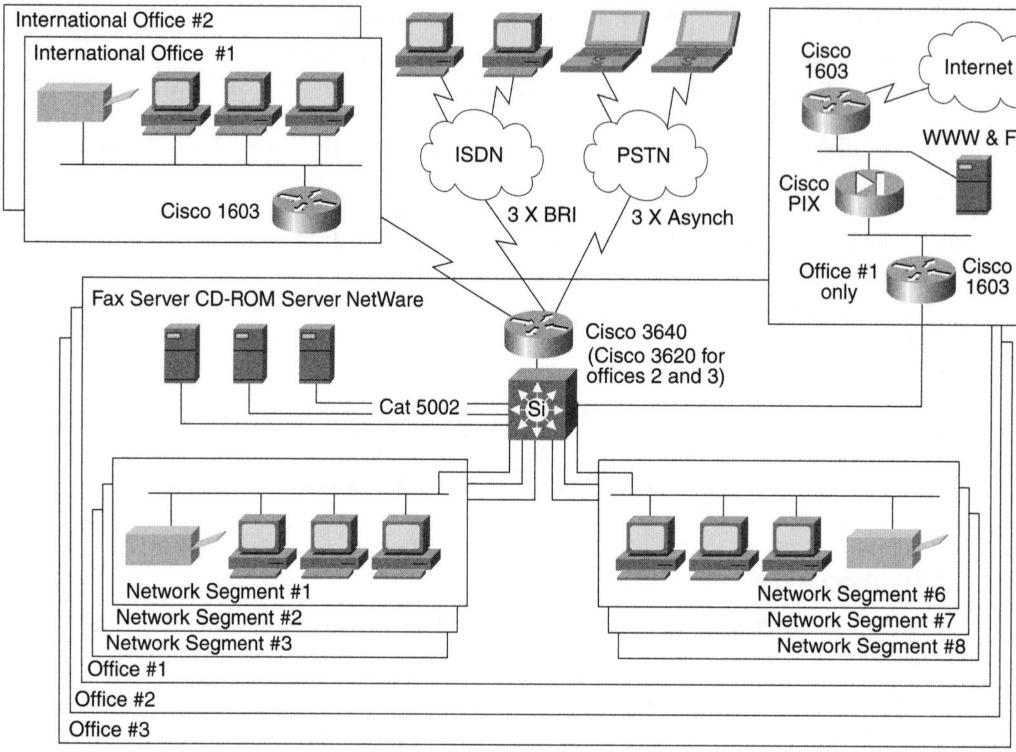

Chapter 8

Virtual University Case Study Questions

Question 8-1

Design and describe a model for dividing up Virtual University's IP address space that will meet the university's current needs and needs for the next five years.

Virtual University's Class B network number 172.16.0.0 can be divided into four, as follows:

- 172.16.0.0 for the backbone area
- 172.16.64.0 for the North Campus
- 172.16.128.0 for the Central Campus
- 172.16.192.0 for the South Campus

This division uses the first two bits of the third octet. The remaining six bits of the third octet will allow 62 subnets in each of the campuses. The fourth octet can be used for the node addresses in each campus.

Question 8-2

Explain to the IP gurus at Virtual University how the addressing model that you designed in the previous step will support route summarization. For example, what network number and prefix could a border router at one of the campuses advertise to the other areas or backbone?

The first two bits of the third octet will be used to identify the area that supports route summarization. For example, a border router at the North Campus can advertise all 40 network numbers with one route, 172.16.64.0/18 (18 bits are relevant; in other words, a subnet mask of 255.255.192.0).

The next six bits of the third octet will be used to identify the 40 networks and will work even when there are 60 networks five years from now.

The last octet will be used to identify the 150 nodes on each network and will work even when there are 200 nodes per network. This solution means that the internal campus routers and end-user nodes support a simple 172.16.x.0/24 configuration—in other words, a 255.255.255.0 subnet mask. This is an attractive solution for Virtual University, which requires simplicity because of its AppleTalk heritage.

Because of Virtual University's history, you should recommend dynamic addressing for the end nodes. The network administrators should install DHCP servers on each of the internal campus networks.

Question 8-3

What is special about IP address 172.16.0.0? What will Virtual University require to connect its network to the Internet?

Virtual University is using a private IP network number, 172.16.0.0. In order to reach the Internet, the network administrators should install a gateway, such as Cisco's PIX Firewall product, which will give Virtual University security features in addition to the capability to use a private network number.

Question 8-4

Propose a plan for naming servers, routers, and end nodes. Describe both the names themselves and the method you will use to configure the names.

To name the routers, servers, and end nodes at Virtual University, DNS servers should be installed and configured. To name the routers and servers, use a naming scheme that requires the name to start with North, South, Central, or Back (for Backbone) to facilitate troubleshooting. The router names could also have a number suffix that identifies the network number. The servers should have a nonnumeric suffix that is meaningful to users.

The users should be encouraged to name their stations with names that will facilitate troubleshooting; for example, last name-first name. However, because the users are students and professors, creative solutions should be tolerated also! Use Cisco's DNS/DHCP Manager to synchronize DNS names with dynamically assigned IP addresses.

CareTaker Case Study Questions

Question 8-5

Design a model for CareTaker's IP address space that will meet the current needs and needs for the next five years. Describe your model here.

Use the contiguous Class C private addresses defined in RFC 1918 Section 3 (192.168.0.0 to 192.168.255.255) within the bounds of CareTaker. (Using this addressing will not restrict CareTaker from going on the Internet because they will be able to use Network Address Translation to translate from these private addresses to registered addresses.) A separate network will be defined for the WAN connection to the parent's router. This network address will be obtained from the parent company's Network Operations. To keep things simple, a separate Class C address will be used for each LAN and WAN, so subnetting will not be required.

For expansion, you might create address groups for the LAN and WAN, such as with the following examples:

- 192.168.10.x through 192.168.19.x for the LANs
- 192.168.20.x through 192.168.29.x for the WANs

With this grouping, we would then make the following assignments:

- 192.168.10.x for the main facility
- 192.168.11.x for the warehouse facility
- 192.168.20.x for the main-to-warehouse WAN

The last octet can be used to identify the network nodes on each network, which will provide 254 nodes for each of the facilities (main and warehouse). With this solution, the internal routers and PC/server nodes will support a simple 255.255.255.0 subnet mask. This is an attractive solution because it provides simplicity for an administrative staff that is not experienced with routers. Use of a 255.255.255.0 mask on the WANs could be seen as a waste, but there are so many addresses available that the mask is not important.

The nodes should then be grouped for ease of identification, as in the following examples:

- 192.168.x.1 through 192.168.x.39 for the communications equipment
- 192.168.x.40 through 192.168.x.59 for the servers (file, print, mail, and so on) and hosts
- 192.168.x.60 through 192.168.x.254 for the user nodes

The Windows NT DHCP should be installed on at least two of the Windows NT servers (depending on their location). Use these servers to dynamically assign IP addresses to the user computers.

Question 8-6

Propose a plan for naming servers, routers, and end nodes. Describe both the names themselves and the method to be used to configure the names.

It would probably be best to name the servers with their department names suffixed with the last octet of the node address, which will aid in troubleshooting. The user nodes should have names that aid troubleshooting, such as the letters "PC," followed by a hyphen and the user's first initial and last name, such as PC-BSMITH.

Because CareTaker is a Windows NT only shop, the Windows NT DNS should be installed as a local DNS, which will allow, at a minimum, addressing the ES9000 with something like es9000.caretaker.com. You should use Cisco's DNS/DHCP Manager to synchronize DNS names with dynamically assigned IP addresses from DHCP.

Question 8-7

Update your topology diagram to reflect your addressing scheme.

Figure B-19 diagrams the updated CareTaker topology.

Figure B-19 *CareTaker's Updated Topology Diagram Reflecting the Addressing Scheme*

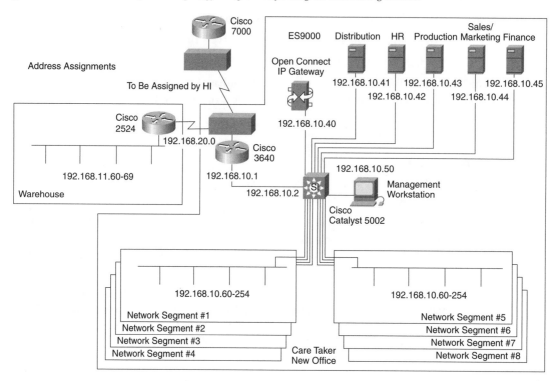

PH Network Services Corporation Case Study Questions

Question 8-8

The hospital system has an existing IP network with its own IP addresses. The hospital will be able to assign two Class C addresses to the PH Network: one for the WAN (202.12.27.0) and one for PH's internal use (202.12.28.0). Describe your IP addressing plans for the implementation of PH's network. You will use a Class C mask of 255.255.255.0 for the PH LAN. What mask will you use for the WAN?

A ratio of 10 percent could normally be used for remote users to access dial-up connections. Because the network must have high availability to the doctor offices, it would be better to raise this number to approximately 20 percent (20 percent of 120 is 24 simultaneous ISDN connections). A single PRI will provide 23 ISDN channels. Within the design, a second PRI could be added if PH finds that the network is not always available as required. A second PRI would bring the total to 46 simultaneous connections if needed.

PH Networks is attached to two WANs (the Frame Relay and the ISDN), and therefore needs two subnets on the WAN side. The address 202.12.27.0 could be divided into two subnets: 202.12.27.64/26 and 202.12.27.128/26; each would have 62 hosts. The mask used would be 255.255.255.192.

One subnet would be for the ISDN connections. Because a maximum of 46 calls could be made at once on the ISDN (assuming two PRIs), at any one time there would be a maximum of 46 (Doctor's offices) + 1 (PH Network) + 1 (optional hospital link) = 48 addresses required on the ISDN at any one time. The Doctor's offices addresses should be dynamically assigned by the router at PH Network because there are more than 60 Doctor's offices, so we would otherwise run out of addresses. The PH Network and hospital link addresses should be permanently assigned.

NOTE   In order for the IP addresses at the Doctor's offices to be dynamically assigned, the routers would require that the Cisco IOS™ Easy IP feature, as described in Chapter 8. With the Easy IP feature, a router at a Doctor's office could automatically negotiate its own IP address from the Central PH Network router via the Point-to-Point Protocol/Internet Control Protocol (PPP/IPCP). The router could also automatically assign local IP addresses to that office's PCs via the Dynamic Host Configuration Protocol (DHCP).

The second subnet would be for the Frame Relay connections. This subnet has only five hosts: four hospitals plus the PH Network. Using one subnet assumes that the Frame Relay is fully meshed. If a partial mesh network is used, then subinterfaces on different subnets may be used.

The PH Network LAN is relatively simple, but it would still be advisable to organize address assignments for troubleshooting. Assign addresses 1 to 10 as communication equipment and servers, and the PH office PCs as 11 to 254. The subnet mask would be a simple 255.255.255.0 mask.

Within the Doctor's offices that have LANs, private addresses and network address translation (NAT) could be used.

Question 8-9

Update your topology diagram to reflect the new addressing scheme.

Figure B-20 diagrams the updated PH Network topology.

Figure B-20 *PH Network Updated Topology Diagram Reflecting the Addressing Scheme*

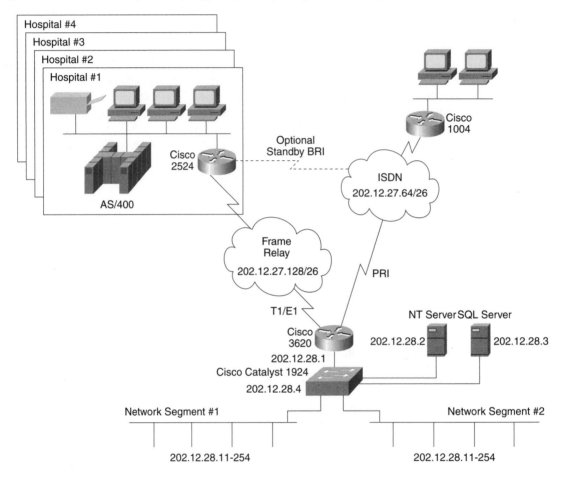

Pretty Paper Limited Case Study Questions

Question 8-10

The network administrator has been using the Class B IP address of 199.151.0.0. He does not know where he got it but he is sure that Pretty Paper does not own it. What are your recommendations for an IP address allocation/assignment procedure?

Because this is a closed network with the Cisco PIX in use for the Internet connection, private Internet addressing should be implemented. Use one of the Class B private addresses defined in RFC 1918 Section 3 (172.16.0.0 to 172.31.255.255), say 172.16.0.0/24. In other words, use

172.16.0.0 with a simple 255.255.255.0 mask; the network would then be divided with one subnetwork per site, perhaps as follows:

- 172.16.0.0 for the headquarters
- 172.16.1.0 for the WAN
- 172.16.10.0 through 172.16.99.0 for the sales offices
- 172.16.100.0 through 172.16.199.0 for the manufacturing/warehouses

NOTE   If you use 172.16.0.0 subnet, all eight of the subnet bits will be zero. By default, Cisco routers will not allow this to be configured. If you want to use this zero subnet, you must configure the **ip subnet-zero** command first before assigning any addresses in this subnet.

Using one subnet for the WAN assumes that the Frame Relay is fully meshed. If a partial mesh network is used, then subinterfaces on different subnets may be used.

Within each network, the last octet can be used to identify the network nodes, which will provide 254 nodes for each of the facilities. With this solution the internal routers and PC/server nodes will support a simple 255.255.255.0 subnet mask. This solution is attractive because it provides simplicity for an administrative staff that is not experienced with routers. Use of a 255.255.255.0 mask on the WAN could be seen as a waste as there are only eight nodes connected, but there are so many addresses available that the mask is not important.

The nodes should then be grouped for ease of identification. This solution would involve something similar to the following:

- For communication equipment, use nodes 1 through 9
- For servers and hosts, use nodes 10 through 59
- For user nodes, use nodes 60 through 254

Cisco's DNS/DHCP Manager should be installed on the HP9000 used to dynamically assign IP addresses to the user computers.

Question 8-11

Propose a plan for naming servers, routers, and end nodes. Describe both the names themselves and the method you will use to configure the names.

It would probably be best to name the servers by location and type, which will allow for the possibility of servers being at locations other than headquarters. For example, the servers could be headquarters NW1, headquarters NW2, and headquarters BS1. These names might be suffixed with the last octet of the node address to aid in troubleshooting. The user nodes should be named with names that aid troubleshooting, such as the letters "PC," followed by a hyphen and the user's first initial and last name, such as PC-BSMITH.

A naming scheme for routers should be devised that will aid in troubleshooting, such as by location and function. For example, the router attached to the Frame Relay at headquarters might be PARIS-FR and the Internet router might be PARIS-IN.

To name the various devices, a single DNS with a single domain could be installed on the HP9000.

Question 8-12

Update your topology diagram to reflect the new IP addressing scheme.

Figure B-21 diagrams the updated Pretty Paper topology.

Figure B-21 *Pretty Paper Updated Topology Diagram Reflecting the Addressing Scheme*

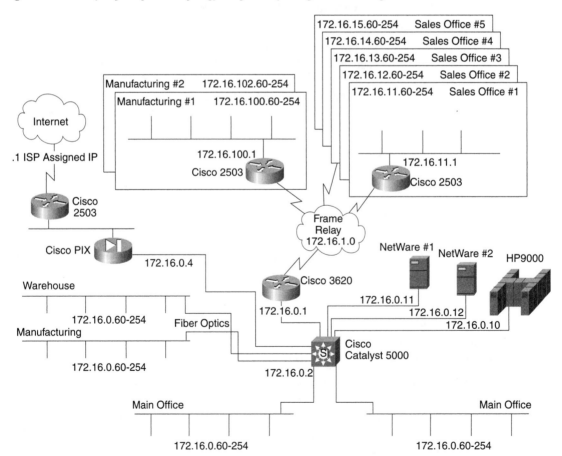

Question 8-13

Recommend an addressing scheme for the IPX network.

IPX network numbers also need to be assigned. Because headquarters is on an Ethernet switch, it is logically "flat," and, therefore, a single IPX number will be assigned for the headquarters facilities, including the warehouse and manufacturing facilities. Each of the other facilities and the WAN link will have a unique IPX network number assigned.

As always it will help in troubleshooting if there is some logic to the assignment of these numbers. For example, you might use two-digit network numbers for locations and three-digit numbers for the WAN link and give meaning to the positions. For locations, the first digit might represent the type of network and the second the location identifier.

Table B-5 provides an example IPX addressing scheme.

Table B-5   *IPX Addressing Scheme*

Network	IPX Network Number
Headquarters	AA
Sales Office #1	BA
Sales Office #2	BB
Sales Office #3	BC
Sales Office #4	BD
Sales Office #5	BE
Manufacturing #1	CA
Manufacturing #2	CB
WAN Link	DAA

Question 8-14

Recommend an addressing scheme for the AppleTalk network.

Likewise, AppleTalk zones need to be defined. The number of Macintosh nodes would suggest a single zone per location and one for the WAN link. The zones should be given meaningful names for troubleshooting purposes. Names by location and names by link would be appropriate.

Table B-6 provides an example AppleTalk addressing scheme.

Table B-6 *AppleTalk Addressing Scheme*

Zone	Assigned Name
All of the headquarters facilities	Headquarters
Sales Office 1-5	SO1–SO5
Manufacturing 1-2	MFG1–MFG2
WAN Link	FR

Jones, Jones, & Jones Case Study Questions

Question 8-15

Describe your IP addressing plans for implementation of your proposed system design.

You should use the contiguous Class C private addresses defined in RFC 1918 Section 3 (192.168.0.0 to 192.168.255.255) within the bounds of Jones, Jones, & Jones. Of course, separate networks will be defined for the WAN connections. To keep things simple, the third octet will be used as a network number. For expansion, you might group these for LAN and WAN, as in the following examples:

- 192.168.1.x through 192.168.99.x for the WANs
- 192.168.100.x through 192.168.199.x for the U.S. LANs
- 192.168.200.x through 192.168.254.x for the international LANs

Plenty of addresses are available, which makes it easy to immediately recognize networks. With this grouping, we would then make the following assignments:

- 192.168.101.x for Office 1
- 192.168.102.x for Office 2
- 192.168.103.x for Office 3
- 192.168.201.x for the Europe Office
- 192.168.202.x for the MidEast Office

The last octet can be used to identify the network nodes on each network, which will provide 254 nodes for each office. With this solution, the routers and PC/server nodes will support a simple 255.255.255.0 subnet mask. This is an attractive solution because it provides simplicity for an administrative staff that is not experienced with routers. Use of a 255.255.255.0 mask on the WANs could be seen as a waste, but there are so many addresses available that it is not important.

The nodes should then be grouped for ease of identification. This solution would involve something similar to the following:

- 192.168.x.1 through 192.168.x.59 for the communications equipment.
- 192.168.x.60 through 192.168.x.99 for the servers (file, print, mail, and so on). Consider that there are many printers in a law firm.
- 192.168.x.100 through 192.168.x.254 for the user nodes.

The NetWare DHCP should be installed on the servers and used to dynamically assign IP addresses to the user computers.

Question 8-16

Propose a plan for naming servers, routers, and end nodes. Describe both the names themselves and the method that will be used to configure the names.

It would probably be best to name the servers with their office location names suffixed with the last octet of the server node address, such as DENVER001, which will aid in troubleshooting. The user nodes should be named with names that aid troubleshooting. For example, a prefix of "PC" for desktop PCs and "NB" for notebook computers, followed by a hyphen and the user's first initial and last name, such as PC-BSMITH or NB-BSMITH.

Question 8-17

The managing partner called. She wanted to emphasize that unauthorized workstations should not be allowed access to the Internet. How will you plan for this request in your design?

Static IP addresses should be assigned to specific users at the DHCP server. All but these addresses will then be filtered at the Internet router.

Question 8-18

Update your topology diagram to reflect the new addressing scheme.

Figure B-22 diagrams the updated Jones, Jones, & Jones topology.

Figure B-22 *Jones, Jones, & Jones Updated Topology Diagram Reflecting the Addressing Scheme*

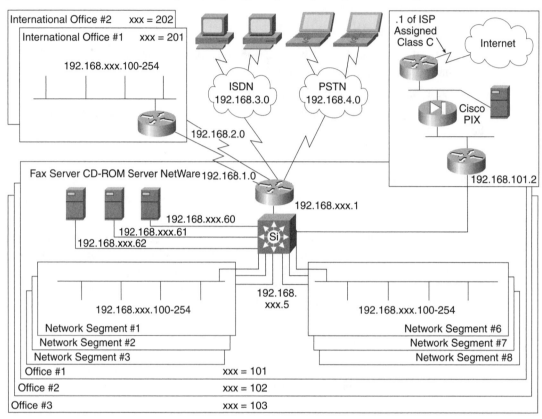

Chapter 9

Multiple-Choice Review Questions

Question 9-1

This protocol sends routing updates every 10 seconds, which can consume a large percentage of the bandwidth on slow serial links.

A. IP RIP

B. RTMP

C. NLSP

D. IGRP

Question 9-2

This protocol limits the number of networks in a routing table update to 50, which means many packets are required to send the routing table within a large internetwork.

A. OSPF

B. IPX RIP

C. IPX SAP

D. Static Routing

Question 9-3

This protocol does not support discontiguous subnets or variable-length subnet masks.

A. Static Routing

B. OSPF

C. IGRP

D. EIGRP

Question 9-4

This protocol can advertise seven services per packet, which causes many packets on enterprise internetworks with hundreds of services.

A. IPX SAP

B. RTMP

C. IPX RIP

D. IGRP

Question 9-5

This protocol uses 14 bytes to define a route entry, so it can send 104 routes in a 1500-byte packet.

A. AURP

B. OSPF

C. IGRP

D. IPX RIP

Question 9-6

This protocol should be recommended in hub-and-spoke topologies with low bandwidth even though it can be hard to maintain because it is not dynamic.

A. Static Routing

B. OSPF

C. EIGRP

D. RIPv2

Question 9-7

This protocol is similar to OSI's IS-IS protocol except that a hierarchical topology was not defined until Version 1.1 of the routing protocol was specified (which is supported in Cisco IOS™ Release 11.1).

A. NLSP

B. OSPF

C. IGRP

D. EIGRP

Question 9-8

This protocol supports route summarization but it must be configured. It is not automatic. If link flapping occurs when route summarization is not configured, a stream of updates is generated, causing serious traffic and router CPU overhead.

A. AURP

B. RTMP

C. IGRP

D. OSPF

Question 9-9

If a customer is looking for ways to reduce WAN routing traffic and is also considering tunneling AppleTalk in IP, you could recommend this protocol.

A. IPX RIP

B. Static Routing

C. EIGRP

D. AURP

Question 9-10

This protocol can be compromised because the routing updates are easy to read with a protocol analyzer, and an unsophisticated hacker can send invalid routing updates that routers will accept.

A. IP RIP

B. OSPF

C. NLSP

D. EIGRP

Question 9-11

Cisco refined the implementation of this protocol in May 1996 to increase stability in environments with many low-speed links in NBMA WANs, such as Frame Relay, ATM, or X.25 backbones, and in highly redundant dense router-router peering configurations.

A. IPX RIP

B. RTMP

C. EIGRP

D. IGRP

Question 9-12

If a customer wants a protocol with fast convergence that can scale to hundreds of networks and that will fit well with a hierarchical topology, recommend this protocol.

A. IGRP

B. OSPF

C. IP RIP

D. RTMP

CareTaker Case Study Questions

Question 9-13

The corporate Network Operations people from the parent corporation will be in town, and the IS manager wants to meet you to describe how your IP addressing scheme will work and how it will interface with the corporate network and the Internet. Which routing protocol would you implement on the WAN between CareTaker and the corporate Cisco 7000 series router?

You will need to determine the routing protocol by talking to corporate Network Operations. More likely than not, it will be IGRP.

Question 9-14

Are there any protocols between corporate and CareTaker's facilities that cannot be routed?

No. Even though it is a Windows NT environment, the NetBIOS names will be encapsulated within IP.

Question 9-15

What routing protocol is the most efficient between the warehouse and CareTaker's facilities?

Because both routers are Cisco, EIGRP will be the most efficient.

Question 9-16

Assuming the routing protocol between CareTaker and HI is IGRP, what additional parameter must you know before the main office router can be configured for IGRP?

The autonomous system number.

PH Network Services Corporation Case Study Questions

Question 9-17

Are there any protocols between PH's facilities that cannot be routed?

No. The common application between the doctor offices, the hospitals, and the PH office is IP based. Windows NT names are not required over the WAN. Therefore, NetBIOS support will not be required over the WAN links.

Question 9-18

Each hospital will be using existing routers that are not necessarily Cisco routers. Which routing protocol will be the most efficient to implement between the PH Network Services network and the hospitals?

Because the routers might not all be the same, OSPF would represent the routing protocol of choice.

Question 9-19

Which routing protocol would you select to support the doctor offices dialing in via ISDN to the PH Network Services network?

In the case of a remote network connecting to the PH Network Services network, you might not be able to control which router is used by the doctor offices, so OSPF would make the most sense, if a routing protocol is needed. Otherwise, if a routing protocol is not needed, static routes would be a good choice to allow the Doctor's offices to connect to the PH Network Services network.

Pretty Paper Limited Case Study Questions

Question 9-20

Are there any protocols between the facilities that cannot be routed?

No. Pretty Paper uses IP, IPX and AppleTalk; these are all routed protocols.

Question 9-21

Who will you contact to determine which protocol to use for the router providing Internet connectivity?

Contact the ISP to coordinate the configuration.

Question 9-22

Because all the remote sites have Cisco routers attached to the WAN, which routing protocol is the most efficient for implementation?

There are three protocols (IP, IPX, and AppleTalk) at Pretty Paper, and all routers are from Cisco. Because Enhanced IGRP has protocol-dependent modules that support IP, IPX, and AppleTalk, a single routing protocol can be used for all three protocols.

Jones, Jones, & Jones Case Study Questions

Question 9-23

Are there any protocols between facilities that cannot be routed?

No. Jones, Jones, & Jones uses two protocols: IP and IPX. These are both routed protocols.

Question 9-24

Because all the remote sites have Cisco routers attached to the WAN, which routing protocol is the most efficient for implementation?

Jones, Jones, & Jones uses two protocols: IP and IPX. Because EIGRP has protocol-dependent modules that support IP and IPX, a single routing protocol can be used for both protocols.

Question 9-25

Who will you contact to determine which protocol to use for the router providing Internet connectivity?

Contact the ISP to coordinate the configuration.

Question 9-26

Which routing protocol would you select to support the remote PCs dialing in via asynchronous/ISDN to the local office's network?

Use static routes for the remote nodes dialing in to the network.

Chapter 10

Market Mavericks Case Study Question

Question 10-1

Users at corporate headquarters need to access all the Novell file servers. Users at the branch offices need to access only their own servers and the corporate file servers (though not the corporate print servers). Ms. Martin is tentatively planning to apply an outbound SAP filter on the serial link of the Cisco 4000 router to deny all branch-office servers from being advertised. She will also deny all corporate print servers. What scalability constraints should you discuss with Ms. Martin as she considers using the scheme to filter SAPs?

The problem with this scheme is that it requires Ms. Martin to write 121 **deny** statements, as follows:

- One **deny** statement for each branch network with file servers (60)
- One **deny** statement for each branch network with print servers (60)
- One **deny** statement for the print servers on the corporate network

A list of this length is hard to maintain and keep current. This scheme does not scale very well.

The other problem is that processing this list every 60 seconds will require a significant percentage of the CPU power available on the Cisco 4700 router at corporate headquarters.

Luckily, the solution is simple. Instead of writing **deny** statements, Ms. Martin should write **permit** statements for each of the corporate file servers. Because there are only five corporate file servers, this is a much more scalable solution. When you use a **permit** statement, the router assumes an implicit **deny** statement for everything that does not match the **permit** statement. All the branch office file servers can be denied without requiring the router to process 121 deny statements.

Question 10-2

Ms. Martin has been asked to implement a security scheme that requires the use of IP access lists. At the corporate site, she has been asked to filter any IP packets coming from the California branch office. This branch office will be shut down soon. Executives at corporate headquarters are concerned that people who will not be employees soon could get proprietary information before they leave the company.

How will an inbound IP access list at the corporate router affect IP performance for all the other branch offices? Remember that Ms. Martin has a Cisco 4000 router running Cisco IOS Release 10.3 at headquarters.

Because Ms. Martin is running Cisco IOS™ Release 10.3 at headquarters, the access list will not seriously affect the IP performance for all the other branch offices. Cisco has been able to fast-switch packets even when there are inbound access lists for a long time.

However, Ms. Martin should investigate purchasing a faster router platform. Her Cisco 4000 router can fast-switch packets at approximately 14,000 packets per second. If she upgraded to a Cisco 4700 router, fast switching would be approximately 50,000 packets per second.

If Ms. Martin had a Cisco 7500 series router, she could use NetFlow switching. NetFlow switching determines which sessions require special processing and quickly applies the special processing while switching packets, which means that inbound access lists do not have a significant impact on performance. The list doesn't need to be processed with each packet that needs switching.

Ms. Martin should be careful when designing the access list. If she makes sure that most packets match the first few conditions, she can maximize performance. She should study traffic flows before designing the access list. The first condition should match the most packets, the second condition the next most packets, and so on. The goal should be to minimize the number of statements the router must process.

Question 10-3

The financial data that the brokers at the branch offices send over TCP/IP is highly confidential. Ms. Martin is considering using encryption features on the branch routers and the corporate router. How might these features affect performance?

When running services such as encryption and compression on the Cisco 4000 series and Cisco 2500 series routers, you run the risk of overwhelming the router CPU. To determine whether the router is overwhelmed, use the **show processes** Cisco IOS software command to get a baseline reading before enabling encryption or compression. Then enable the service and use the **show processes** command again to assess the difference. Cisco recommends that you disable compression or encryption if the router CPU load exceeds 40 percent.

Question 10-4

Ms. Martin wants to know if you recommend priority queuing for the TCP/IP brokerage applications. The data that the brokers generate is considered mission-critical, but the marketing and administrative data on the AppleTalk and Novell networks is not as critical. What would you tell Ms. Martin regarding priority queuing? What are the advantages and disadvantages? Would custom queuing work better for her?

Priority queuing is probably not necessary. Priority queuing is a drastic solution that should be recommended for slow serial links that are experiencing congestion. You should do some testing to determine whether the links at each of the sites is congested. You should also determine whether the TCP/IP applications are experiencing poor performance. If you determine that the performance for the TCP/IP applications should be improved and that the links are congested, then you could run a trial of priority queuing.

Priority queuing could improve performance of the TCP/IP applications because it specifies that packets identified as "high" priority are always sent before other packets. The caveat is that the performance of the AppleTalk and Novell applications could suffer drastically. These applications are not mission-critical, but they are probably important to the company. Custom queuing could be a less drastic solution.

CareTaker Case Study Question

Question 10-5

The manager of Warehouse and Distribution is concerned about PC performance over a leased line. What recommendations could you make to increase performance using Cisco IOS software?

Check router performance. If CPU utilization is less than 40 percent, try compression.

PH Network Services Corporation Case Study Question

Question 10-6

The general manager of PH called again to ask about the possibility of patients' medical information being exposed within the system you will present. How will you accommodate for this concern in your design?

Access to hospital records is always over the Frame Relay network. Cisco's Network Encryption Services could be implemented on the Cisco 3620 and Cisco 2524 routers. This solution, however, does not protect the information on the ISDN to the doctor offices. Adding encryption over these links could be very expensive. Either Cisco routers would be needed at each doctor's office (with the appropriate software feature pack) or application-layer encryption will need to be implemented. If security is of paramount importance to PH, the best solution would be to combine the two by implementing Network Encryption Services over the Frame Relay and application-layer security between the servers and PCs.

Pretty Paper Limited Case Study Question

Question 10-7

The Sales and Marketing managers are concerned about the possibility of someone stealing new designs as they are being transmitted over the network and when they are stored on the servers. What are the performance trade-offs he should be aware of when considering encryption of all data transmissions on the Frame Relay network?

A network-level encryption process will consume router processor cycles. The question suggests that the company really wants the images encrypted on its server. With a Frame Relay PVC, most organizations would not worry about network encryption and would rather have performance. However, Cisco's Network Encryption Services could be implemented throughout the network, including secure transmissions over the Internet through the PIX.

Jones, Jones, & Jones Case Study Question

Question 10-8

Ms. Jones has been reading about hackers accessing confidential data by hacking into the network from the Internet. How have you addressed her concerns with your design?

For foolproof network security, a three-part firewall system locates Jones's Web/FTP server behind the first tier. To access this tier, users come through a router that provides initial security. Beyond this first tier is Cisco's PIX Firewall, which represents the second-tier security perimeter. In case there is a breach of security on the exposed segment, the PIX Firewall series acts as a strong security barrier to prevent outside users from gaining access to Jones's private network. The use of Cisco's PIX Firewall series with Cisco routers running Cisco IOS™ software will provide the firm with a powerful security solution that will allow it to sell its research papers without fear of exposure of internal documents and files. It forces hackers to penetrate multiple lines of defense.

Chapter 11

CareTaker Case Study Questions

Question 11-1

The IS manager is not sure that she has the personnel it will take to manage the new network. Her administrators are junior and have never worked with routers before. She understands the need for training and has planned for it, but she is still concerned. Recommend specific network management protocols and products that will meet CareTaker's needs.

Recommend that CareTaker purchase CiscoWorks Windows.

Question 11-2

In addition to training, recommend steps that CareTaker should take to develop a proactive network management strategy that will not tax the junior staff.

In addition to recommending the CiscoWorks network management product, you should give CareTaker some basic training on how to use Cisco Connection Online. This tool will enable CareTaker to work closely with Cisco to keep the network functioning at maximum performance.

CareTaker should define the service goals for the network. For example, what is the goal for downtime? Is it that the network should never be down or is there a more realistic goal that the network should be up 98 percent of the time? Once the goals have been defined, metrics for measuring the accomplishment of the goals can be defined. This process of defining service goals will also lead to the hardware and software maintenance policies such as next day, 7x24, and so on.

CareTaker may already have a network management console installed in a central computer room or NOC. If not, you should recommend that it install a central console.

If possible, engineers and planners should be assigned to proactively monitor the network even when it is not having a problem. In addition to checking for irregularities and bottlenecks, the staff should make sure that the data collection processes and reporting are working correctly and adjust them if necessary. Assuming sufficient resources are available, the engineers or planners should compile baseline statistics approximately once a month and write a report that characterizes the current health of the network and the service level achieved in the last month.

PH Network Services Corporation Case Study Question

Question 11-3

The general manager is not sure that he has the personnel it will take to manage the new network. His administrator is very junior and has never worked with routers before. He understands the need for training and has planned for it but is still concerned. Recommend specific network management protocols and products that will meet the needs.

The actual need for network management will depend on the number of Cisco 1004 routers deployed into doctor offices. If this number is small, say 5 to 10, it will probably not be economically justifiable to implement formal onsite network management. You might suggest that you provide network management services for PH remotely.

If a formal network management tool is justified, implement CiscoWorks Windows.

Pretty Paper Limited Case Study Questions

Question 11-4

The network administrator at Pretty Paper has been managing an X.25 network for a long time and knows something about Frame Relay, mostly from reading. Recommend specific network management protocols and products that will meet the company's needs and allow the administrator to be immediately productive.

Recommend CiscoWorks for Windows. The configuration file management, device management, software management, and other features of the CiscoWorks software will help manage the central and remote sites at Pretty Paper.

The network administrators can use AutoInstall to enter the initial configuration.

In addition to recommending the CiscoWorks network management product, you should give Pretty Paper some basic training on how to use Cisco Connection Online. This tool will let Pretty Paper work closely with Cisco to keep the network functioning at maximum performance.

Pretty Paper should define what the service goals for the network will be. For example, what is the goal for downtime? Is it that the network should never be down or is there a more realistic goal that the network should be up 98 percent of the time? Once the goals have been defined, metrics for measuring the accomplishment of the goals can be defined. This process of defining service goals will also lead to the hardware and software maintenance policies such as next day, 7x24, and so on.

Question 11-5

What recommendations would you make to Pretty Paper about proactively monitoring the network and data collection?

If possible, engineers and planners should be assigned to proactively monitor the network even when it is not having a problem. In addition to checking for irregularities and bottlenecks, the staff should make sure that the data collection processes and reporting are working correctly and adjust them if necessary.

Assuming sufficient resources are available, the engineers or planners should compile baseline statistics approximately once a month and write a report that characterizes the current health of the network and the service level achieved in the last month.

Jones, Jones, & Jones Case Study Questions

Question 11-6

The managing partner believes that she has a pretty savvy individual ready to hire as the administrator of the new network. She had to commit to him that good network management tools would be in place when the network is completed. Recommend specific network management protocols and products that will meet the needs of this demanding person.

CiscoWorks for Windows should be used as the network management tool set. Once installed, the network will be very static and should not require much in the way of reconfiguration. The tool will be primarily needed to monitor the health of the devices and links. CiscoWorks provides RMON and Health Monitor to monitor all the routers closely and reconfigure them if necessary.

Question 11-7

Recommend steps that should be taken to develop a proactive network management strategy.

In addition to recommending the CiscoWorks network management product, you should give Jones, Jones, & Jones some basic training on how to use Cisco Connection Online. This tool will let Jones, Jones, & Jones work closely with Cisco to keep the network functioning at maximum performance.

Chapter 12

Jones, Jones, & Jones Case Study Question

Question 12-1

Create a design document using the outline provided in this module. Be sure to emphasize the customer's needs, listed in priority. The format of unsolicited design documents should emphasize key Cisco differentiators and key reseller differentiators as they relate to the client's requirements.

The following document is an example design document for the Jones, Jones, & Jones case study.

Note that this design document does not include a cost section; that would be provided separately.

ABC Networks Design Center Network Design

Prepared For:

Ms. L. Jones

Managing Partner

Jones, Jones, & Jones, P.C.

777 Somestreet

Somecity, CA 99999

Submitted By:

John Doe

Networking Engineer

ABC Networks Design Center

200 Creekside Drive

Ourcity, CA 95134

Date Submitted:

January 28, 1999

Section 1: Executive Summary

Purpose of the Project

Jones, Jones, & Jones has requested that ABC Networks provide a proposal for the design and implementation of an international network to connect the firm's three U.S. offices and two international offices. The three U.S. offices have approximately 50 computer users each, and each international office has 10 users. Jones' objective for the new network is to provide the technology to do the following:

- Enable its people to be able to share documents and work together as if they were in the same office.

- Reduce the cost and increase the effectiveness of its reference library through the availability of CD-ROM libraries for research and reference publications.

- Improve client and internal communication through the use of fax servers.

- Provide additional revenue opportunities through the sale of research papers to be offered on a Web site on the Internet.

Strategic Recommendations

In today's fast-paced business environment, immediate access to critical data is key for small- to medium-sized businesses to be successful. Bandwidth-intensive applications, more powerful PCs and servers, and large files downloaded from the Internet, however, are all contributing to an increase in LAN traffic. These factors, along with the additional demands placed by multiple offices and mobile users accessing main LAN services, are challenging the performance of 10BaseT networks, slowing response times and productivity.

Implementation Considerations

ABC Networks will manage the project for its life cycle, providing product installation, training, and support. After the network is installed and functioning correctly, ABC Networks will provide some basic training on how to use Cisco Connection Online. This tool will let Jones, Jones, & Jones work closely with Cisco to keep the network functioning at maximum performance.

Benefits of the Solution

The high-performance solutions provided by ABC Networks will minimize network congestion and substantially improve performance to the desktop, server, and backbone. The new network will:

- Enable Jones, Jones, & Jones employees to share documents and work together as if they were in the same office.

- Reduce the cost and increase the effectiveness of the CD-ROM reference library by making it available to everyone.
- Improve client and internal communication through the use of fax servers on the network.
- Provide additional revenue opportunities by enabling customers to purchase research papers through a Web site on the Internet.

Section 2: Design Requirements

Existing Network

The primary network application is word processing.

Business constraints include:

- Budget is limited
- Maximize the use of new technology
- Provide a solution that requires minimal computer knowledge
- Provide a solution that offers document sharing and timely communications

Table B2-1 shows the applications that will use the new network.

Table B2-1   *Applications That Will Use the New Network*

Name and Type of Application	Protocols	Number of Users	Number of Hosts or Servers	Peak Usage Hours
WordPerfect word processing	IPX	170	1	7 a.m. to 6 p.m.
CD-ROM server	IPX	15	3	7 a.m. to 6 p.m.
Fax server	IPX	30 faxes/day	3	7 a.m. to 6 p.m.
Novell Groupwise (e-mail and document management)	IP	170	1	7 a.m. to 6 p.m.

Network Requirements

At home and on the road, users should be able to work as effectively as if they were in the office.

Attorneys should be able to share documents effectively, regardless of location.

The network should support the flow of information for the e-mail application shown in Figure B2-1.

Figure B2-1 *Jones, Jones, & Jones E-mail Application Flow of Information*

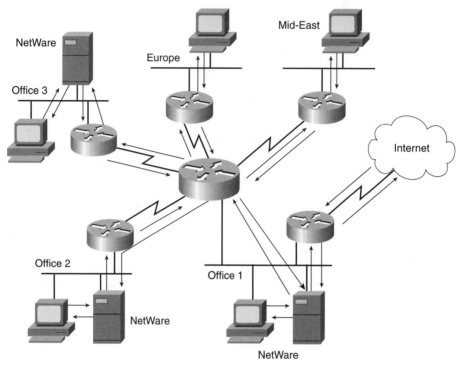

The network should also support the packet flow of information for the CD-ROM Library Pack application shown in Figure B2-2.

Figure B2-2 *Jones, Jones, & Jones CD-ROM Library Pack Application Flow of Information*

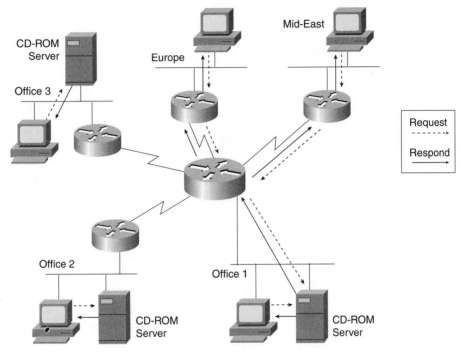

Section 3: Design Solutions

Proposed Network Topology

Figure B3-1 shows the proposed network topology for Jones, Jones, & Jones.

Figure B3-1 *Jones, Jones, & Jones Proposed Network Topology*

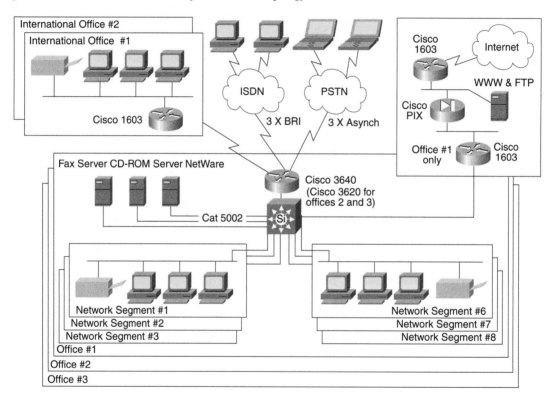

Hardware and Media Recommended for the LAN

The Catalyst 5002 switch provides two 100 Mbps ports that will be used for the NetWare and CD-ROM servers. This solution will provide adequate access bandwidth for these servers for the document management and research functions. The desktop PCs will be connected over shared 10 Mbps 10BaseT cable to provide excellent, affordable performance.

Hardware and Media Recommended for the WAN

The company's need to improve competitiveness with technology is met with the deployment of the Cisco 1600 and 3600 series routers. These products will provide Jones, Jones, & Jones with the connectivity and functionality to operate on a global basis with the ability to collaborate its work as if it were a single office. This ability is provided with affordable Cisco products that will not become obsolete.

Cisco's Private Internet Exchange (PIX) Firewall provides full firewall protection by completely concealing the internal network from the outside world.

This firewall, which offers a variety of LAN connectivity options, resides between the corporate network and the Internet access router. The PIX Firewall offers strong connection-oriented security using a protection scheme based on the adaptive security algorithm (ASA) to ensure the utmost in security. Its cut-through proxy feature dramatically improves performance over traditional proxy servers, and simple installation and minimal maintenance lower the cost of ownership. With the PIX Firewall, you can start with a base of 128 simultaneous connections and scale up to over 65,536 as your business grows.

Network Layer Addressing and Naming Model

Figure B3-2 shows the network layer addressing and naming model for Jones, Jones, & Jones.

Figure B3-2 *Jones, Jones, & Jones Network Layer Addressing and Naming Model*

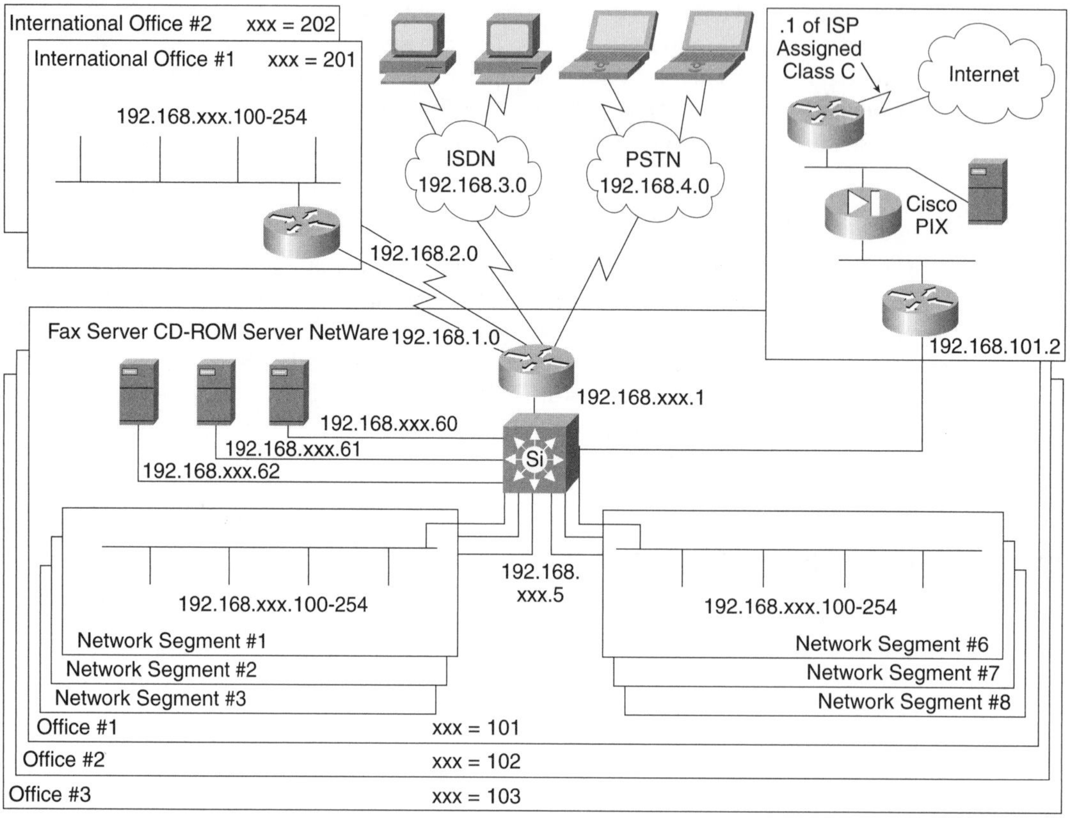

Routing and Bridging Protocols Recommended for the Network

Jones, Jones, & Jones uses two protocols: IP and IPX. Because Enhanced IGRP has protocol-dependent modules that support IP and IPX, a single routing protocol can be used for both protocols.

To support the remote PCs dialing in via ISDN/asynchronous to the local office's network, we recommend using static routes for the remote nodes dialing in to the network.

Software Features Provisioned for the Network

For foolproof network security, the three-part firewall system locates the company's Web/FTP server behind the first tier. To access this tier, users come through a router that provides initial security. Beyond this first tier is Cisco's PIX Firewall series, which represents the second-tier security perimeter. In case there is a breach of security on the exposed segment, the PIX Firewall series acts as a strong security barrier to prevent outside users from gaining access to Jones, Jones, & Jones' private network. Coupling Cisco's PIX Firewall series with Cisco routers running Cisco IOS software will provide Jones, Jones, & Jones with a powerful security solution that will allow it to sell its research papers without fear of exposure of internal documents and files. It forces hackers to penetrate multiple lines of defense.

Network Management Strategy

All Catalyst switches and Cisco routers are manageable by CiscoWorks Windows, a comprehensive, Windows-based network management system. CiscoWorks Windows features are based on the SNMP industry standard and provide a powerful set of management tools for easily managing Cisco products.

CiscoWorks for Windows is recommended as the network management tool set. Once installed, the network will be very static and should not require reconfiguration. This tool will be primarily needed to monitor the health of the devices and links. CiscoWorks provides RMON and Health Monitor to monitor all the routers closely and reconfigure them if necessary.

Section 4: Summary

Benefits of Working with Cisco Systems

Cisco Systems, Inc. is the worldwide leader in networking for the Internet. Cisco routers are the basis for over 80 percent of the Internet infrastructure, and Cisco supplies 60 percent of the access solutions used by companies to provide connectivity for remote users and connectivity to the Internet. Additionally, Cisco, the inventor of switched Ethernet and Fast Ethernet—today's most popular high-performance LAN technologies—leads the way in providing affordable, high-performance LAN solutions.

Cisco's solutions designed for small- to medium-sized businesses help you maximize your business potential and cost-effectively meet your expanding networking requirements. These solutions leverage Cisco's vast networking experience, innovative technologies, outstanding service, and high-quality products, and they help organizations make the transition from today's shared 10BaseT networks to high-performance networks required by organizations such as Jones, Jones, & Jones that extend beyond the main office to multiple offices, mobile users, and telecommuters, and to the Internet. These solutions give network managers the tools they need to build networks that are scalable, flexible, and powerful enough to handle the challenges of today's business environment.

Cisco products include a wide range of high-performance LAN products, such as 100BaseT hubs and Ethernet switches, routers, dial access servers, and network management software solutions. All of these products are based on the Cisco IOS technologies—an integrated suite of network services that provides the native intelligence for more than 1 million installed Cisco units and comprises an integral part of the products of many global partners. All Cisco products provide quality, reliability, network security, and interoperability based on industry standards.

Headquartered in San Jose, California, Cisco employs more than 12,000 people in over 125 worldwide locations. The company's stock is traded over the counter on the Nasdaq National Market under the symbol *CSCO*.

Benefits of Working with ABC Networks

ABC Networks specializes in managing complex network integration projects encompassing varied vendors, suppliers, cabling firms, software developers, architects, and so on. A properly implemented network reduces overall operating costs while greatly enhancing productivity. Identifying ABC Networks as responsible for network installation and integration will ensure continuity in the process. As the integrator, ABC Networks will accept responsibility for the big picture, providing a single point of contact and coordination.

Success in the network industry demands imagination, sound management, dependability, and most of all, the ability to integrate diverse technologies into a single resource, provided by ABC Networks.

The past decade has seen an unprecedented proliferation of computing equipment in the workplace. In most businesses, the objective of a successful network is to enable computers in different physical locations to exchange programs, business data, information, and messages in the most economical fashion while satisfying certain performance, reliability, availability, and expandability requirements—and thus the need for workgroup and network computing was introduced. Although workgroup computing began with the integration of desktop computers into a network, network computing involves the integration of LAN and WAN technologies to provide enterprise-wide connectivity.

Conclusion

We at ABC Networks believe we have provided a design and product selection that meets all of Jones, Jones, & Jones' requirements, is cost effective, and is manageable and maintainable. The system also meets Jones, Jones, & Jones' performance and security needs.

The Cisco products selected will provide Jones, Jones, & Jones with the highest-performance, quality products available. Cisco is the worldwide leader in networking. Cisco routers are the basis for over 80 percent of the Internet infrastructure, and Cisco supplies 60 percent of the access solutions used by companies to provide connectivity for remote users and connectivity to the Internet. Additionally, Cisco, the inventor of switched Ethernet and Fast Ethernet—today's most popular high-performance LAN technologies—leads the way in providing affordable, high-performance LAN solutions. These technologies, when implemented, will provide the stable investment Jones, Jones, & Jones needs to be able to provide the needed improvements in employee and partner performance without the threat of an immediate upgrade or replacement.

Appendix A: Cisco Product Information

Catalyst 5002 Switch

The Catalyst 5000 series switches are the industry's most powerful switching solutions in the wiring closet, data center, or backbone. The series features an ATM-ready platform offering users high-speed trunking technologies and media-rate performance with a broad variety of interface modules.

The Catalyst 5000 series offers a clear migration path to Gigabit Ethernet through modular uplinks to meet scalability needs in the future. These features can be added while retaining all existing card investments.

Cisco 1603 Router

The Cisco 1600 series of Internet/intranet access routers combines all the benefits of multiprotocol routing and transparent bridging with unmatched performance, configuration flexibility, affordability, and integrated security and management. Providing cost-effective LAN-to-WAN connectivity, the Cisco 1600 series extends the reach of network services to local and remote sites and provides access to business resources on the Web.

The Cisco 1603 series router features a built-in single Ethernet port (10BaseT/AUI) and an ISDN BRI S/T port and includes an extra WAN slot for handling growth and WAN technologies of the future. Available optional WAN cards include serial synchronous/asynchronous, ISDN BRI S/T, and ISDN BRI U (with NT1).

Cisco 3620 Router

The Cisco 3620 modular access router offers unmatched price/performance for connecting remote office LANs to centralized network resources at medium-sized companies. Fully supported by Cisco IOS software, the router offers dialup connectivity, LAN-to-LAN routing, data and access security, and access to emerging technologies and multimedia features. Configurable to precise needs, the Cisco 3620 router features two network module slots that accept your choice of mixed-media (Ethernet and Token Ring) network modules and WAN interface cards supporting asynchronous/synchronous serial and ISDN primary rate and basic rate connections, for true, integrated LAN and WAN connectivity within a single platform.

Cisco 3640 Router

The Cisco 3640 modular access router offers unmatched price/performance for connecting remote office LANs to centralized network resources at medium-sized companies. Fully supported by Cisco IOS software, the router offers dialup connectivity, LAN-to-LAN routing, data and access security, and access to emerging technologies and multimedia features. Configurable to your precise needs, the Cisco 3640 router features four network module slots that accept your choice of mixed-media (Ethernet and Token Ring) network modules and WAN interface cards supporting asynchronous/synchronous serial and ISDN primary rate and basic rate connections, for true, integrated LAN and WAN connectivity within a single platform.

PIX Firewall

The Cisco PIX Firewall series delivers strong security in an easy-to-install, integrated hardware/software appliance that offers outstanding performance. The series allows you to rigorously protect your internal network from the outside world—providing full firewall security protection. Unlike typical CPU-intensive proxy servers that perform extensive processing on each data packet at the application level, Cisco PIX firewalls use a non-UNIX, secure, real-time, embedded system. The firewalls deliver superior performance of more than 65,536 simultaneous connections, over 6,500 connections per second, and nearly 170 megabits per second (Mbps) throughput. This level of performance is dramatically greater than that delivered by other appliance-like firewalls or those based on general-purpose operating systems.

Firewalls have traditionally provided perimeter security by maintaining stateful control of all connections between connected network segments. Today, more and more customers are looking to the firewall for virtual private network (VPN) services in addition to access control. For IP-layer VPNs, the Internet Engineering Task Force (IETF) IP Security working group has drafted a collection of standards referred to as IPSec. These emerging IETF IPSec standards are designed to provide secure private communications over the Internet or any IP network. IPSec ensures confidentiality, integrity, and authenticity. With a Ravlin IPSec encryption card installed, a PIX Firewall supports secure VPNs between multiple endpoints, including remote or mobile Windows PCs with Ravlin Remote Access client software, Cisco IOS routers, other PIX Firewalls, or Red Creek Communications Ravlin 4 and Ravlin 10 encryption devices.

To provide the platform extensibility you need without sacrificing the benefits of an embedded system, the PIX Firewall series includes two hardware platforms, the PIX Firewall 510 and 520, which now support a broad range of network interface cards (NICs).

The heart of the Cisco PIX Firewall series high performance is a protection scheme based on the adaptive security algorithm (ASA), which effectively protects access to the internal host network by comparing inbound and outbound packets to entries in a table. Access is permitted only if an appropriate connection exists to validate passage. Another performance feature is cut-through proxy, which enhances authentication. Cut-through proxy challenges a user initially at the application layer, but once the user is authenticated and policy is checked, the PIX Firewall shifts session flow to a lower layer for dramatically faster performance. The Cisco PIX Firewall 520 supports up to 65,536 simultaneous sessions, accommodating thousands of users without affecting end-user performance. Fully loaded, the PIX Firewall 520 operates at higher speeds and supports more simultaneous connections than competitors.

Appendix B: Internet Access Recommendations

Internet Access

Innovative companies have turned to World Wide Web servers as an alternative channel to reach new customers and a vehicle for online customer service, as well as for transacting everyday business. The more successful companies are now seeking ways to continue providing excellent and timely service to a customer and prospect base that is increasing exponentially.

In providing this Internet connectivity, a company faces the challenge of keeping pace with the demands and costs of integrating multiple systems and tools from different vendors. This complexity is increasing continuously with the rapid growth in new technology and products, prompting small- to medium-sized businesses to seek highly integrated, end-to-end solutions.

At the same time, these solutions must also ensure that the security of the company's data and applications is not compromised. The chosen product or products must allow the business to control who accesses its information resources as well as the network path over which it flows.

Cisco Solutions for Internet Access

According to the Yankee Group market research firm, approximately 80 percent of the Internet backbone is run on Cisco routers. Cisco now brings this leadership to bear on solutions for small- to medium-sized businesses to meet their Internet access needs. All of Cisco's access routers incorporate the industry-leading Cisco IOS software. Cisco IOS software offers a rich variety of security features, such as access lists to keep out unwanted traffic, and the comprehensive authentication and authorization Password Authentication Protocol (PAP) and Challenge Handshake Authentication Protocol (CHAP) that allow only authorized users into the network. Event logging and audit trails, data encryption, virtual private networking functions, and network address translation (NAT) provide additional network security. NAT allows a privately addressed network to access public registered networks such as the Internet without requiring a registered subnet address. This feature eliminates the need for host renumbering and allows the same IP address range to be used in multiple intranets. NAT features conserve address space by requiring only a single IP address.

All of Cisco's routers can be used for connectivity to the Internet. Two series of access routers that feature a dual LAN architecture for additional firewall capabilities are highlighted here, as well as a cost-effective access router for multiple offices.

The Cisco 1600 series represents an inexpensive, easy-to-use, multiprotocol router ideal for Internet access. This series of access routers offers a flexible choice of built-in LAN and WAN ports and supports an extra WAN card to accommodate multiple WAN connections.

In addition to the comprehensive list of security features mentioned, the Cisco IOS software supports robust multiprotocol routing, as well as features to reduce WAN connection costs and provide enhanced support for multimedia. Data compression and multiple traffic prioritization techniques ensure that critical data is accommodated, whereas features such as protocol spoofing, snapshot routing, NLSP route aggregation, dial-on-demand routing (DDR), and bandwidth-on-demand (BOD) ensure that dialup costs are minimized. Support for a variety of protocols such as Internet Group Management Protocol (IGMP) and Resource Reservation Protocol (RSVP), to name two, makes the Cisco routers ideally suited to meet the demanding needs of exciting new audio and video services.

Appendix C: Recommendations for the Future

Interoffice Connectivity

Communication becomes challenging for small- to medium-sized companies with multiple offices, warehouses, or business partners located in various geographical areas. They frequently need to share customer information, check inventory, look up sales data, transfer files, process invoices, and exchange e-mail. Yet a dispersed organization cannot communicate effectively and efficiently without the right technology.

To increase productivity and stay competitive, companies require cost-effective interoffice connectivity solutions that combine applications availability with fast and timely access to business information, low cost of ownership to control wide-area connection and ongoing management costs, and scalability to protect investments and allow for expansion.

Cisco Solutions for the Central Site

Cisco offers a range of central site products ideal for connecting to your multiple offices. The Cisco 3600 series routers offer network administrators modular, flexible solutions that will meet changing needs as the company grows while preserving investment. In addition, these routers support extensive features to increase WAN security and reduce WAN costs.

The Cisco 3600 series routers also offer a modular solution for dialup connectivity over asynchronous, synchronous, and ISDN lines at an industry-leading price-for-performance value. The Cisco 3620 and 3640 routers allow small- to medium-sized businesses to increase dialup density and take advantage of current and emerging wide-area services and internetworking technologies. The Cisco 3640 router has four network module slots, whereas the Cisco 3620 router is equipped with two—each slot accepts a variety of mixed-media and WAN network modules. The Cisco 3600 series is also a member of the NetBeyond System. NetBeyond is an extended network system of modular, stackable LAN and WAN products that increase network performance, connect mobile users and multiple offices, and deliver secure access to the Internet. NetBeyond is an ideal networking foundation for small- to medium-sized businesses and multiple offices of larger enterprises.

All the Cisco router products incorporate the industry-leading Cisco IOS software. Cisco IOS supports robust multiprotocol routing, as well as features to ensure WAN security, reduce WAN connection costs, and provide enhanced support for multimedia. Comprehensive authentication and authorization, such as PAP and CHAP, allow only approved traffic into the network. Event logging and audit trails, encryption, virtual private networking functions, and NAT provide additional network security. Data compression and multiple traffic prioritization techniques ensure that critical data is accommodated, whereas features such as protocol spoofing, snapshot routing, NSLP route aggregation, DDR, and BOD ensure that dialup costs are minimized. Support for a variety of protocols such as Internet Group Management Protocol (IGMP) and

Resource Reservation Protocol (RSVP), to name two, makes the Cisco routers ideally suited to meet the demanding needs of exciting new audio and video services.

Cisco Solutions for Multiple Offices

Cisco also offers a wide range of router products perfect for the branch office. These branch office routers support the same comprehensive set of Cisco IOS features that are available with the central site routers.

For branch offices, the Cisco 1600 series represents an inexpensive, easy-to-use, multiprotocol router. This series of routers offer a flexible choice of built-in LAN and WAN ports and supports an extra WAN card to accommodate multiple WAN connections.

Mobile Computing

To be successful, small- to medium-sized businesses require more flexible remote-access solutions. These businesses must find new strategies for increasing the amount of time their mobile sales representatives can spend with customers. They must provide remote access to e-mail and other network resources to key employees who travel or telecommute. They must ensure that representatives can access the most up-to-date pricing, product, and inventory information in order to dramatically improve customer service. They must also quickly collect time-sensitive data from field personnel to more efficiently manage their resources and services.

This changing world of network access requires a new class of remote-access equipment. Products must be powerful enough to handle today's needs and flexible enough to grow and adapt to tomorrow's requirements—while protecting a company's investment in equipment and training. They must integrate dialup connectivity with traditional, remote LAN-to-LAN access. Solutions must also ensure security, data privacy, and availability as users connect from any location, including multiple offices, home offices, and hotel rooms. And they must support the higher levels of performance required for new applications, such as Internet commerce, intranet communications, and multimedia.

Cisco Solutions for Telecommuting and Mobile Users

The CiscoRemote product is a scalable and comprehensive solution for remote-access client software. CiscoRemote Lite extends the benefits of the Cisco IOS software to the mobile user's desktop and together with Cisco access servers provide a complete, remote-access solution.

CiscoRemote Lite provides basic remote-node connectivity to the corporate network. It includes an installer, dialer, modem discovery, TCP/IP stack, ping, telnet, and and Point-to-Point Protocol (PPP)/Serial Line Internet Protocol (SLIP) over IP or IPX for use with Windows PCs. Registered Cisco Connection Online (CCO) users may download CiscoRemote Lite.

Chapter 13

CareTaker Case Study Questions

Question 13-1

Mr. Smith of CareTaker Publications has accepted your recommendations but has made it clear that both the parent corporation's and CareTaker's management have repeatedly expressed the requirement that everything work before the move takes place.

Describe how you will "pilot" the system prior to the move. You need not worry about the mainframe and the SNA traffic; that will be the parent corporation's Network Operations personnel's responsibility.

Because the network will be installed in a new building, we would propose that the new communication lines be installed between the three locations in parallel with the existing lines.

One of the new servers would be used as a test server. The server would be placed on a 100 Mbps port of the switch.

A minimum of one PC would be attached to each LAN segment in the new building. This attachment should be done in the computer room at the Catalyst 5000 switch to eliminate cable issues that are not the responsibility of the internetwork design. A single PC at the warehouse would be connected to the Cisco 2524 router. All circuits and paths would then be tested.

Question 13-2

What additional recommendations for a pilot would you make?

- Test the design. Make sure you can meet Mr. Smith's response-time requirement (for example, users should see their screens within one-tenth of a second).

- Investigate what competitors will be proposing.

- Write a demonstration script of the test results. Make sure the tests will prove that the design meets Mr. Smith's needs and will emphasize Cisco's strengths.

- Practice the demonstration.

- Schedule some time with Mr. Smith and show him the demonstration.

PH Network Services Corporation Case Study Question

Question 13-3

The general manager of PH wants to make sure that the system can be installed in a manner that will allow all offices to "come on line" in a phased-in approach. Describe your method of installing the system.

- The critical path on the implementation of the PH Network system will be obtaining circuits from the local provider.

- The Frame Relay circuits should be ordered as soon as possible.

- A structured plan should be established for doctor offices to place orders for ISDN lines as a coordinated order for the entire network.

- One hospital, one doctor office with an existing LAN, and one single-PC doctor office should be selected as a Phase I Group. The communication lines for these offices and the PH Network office should be installed first.

- The Catalyst 1900 switch and Cisco 3620 router should be installed in the PH Network office. Access to the Windows NT server by local PCs should be verified.

- The pilot network of one hospital, one LAN-based doctor office, and one standalone-based office should then be connected and completely tested by ping tests and user logins.

- The new SQL Server could then be added, and the connection tested for the pilot network. After these tests have proven the operational status of the network, the other hospitals should be added, followed by doctor offices, with an orderly, planned methodology.

Pretty Paper Limited Case Study Question

Question 13-4

Before spending all the effort and money needed to do this conversion, Pretty Paper management would like an assurance that this solution will work. However, it does not have the time or money to do a prototype or proof-of-concept. How would you propose to pilot the system so that most of the effort for the pilot is moving toward the final system while demonstrating the functionality of the final system?

The software vendor probably has been asked to provide this kind of proof in the past. Ask whether this vendor has a lab or test-bed facility that could be used to simulate the environment if the routers and switch were provided. The previous lab or test-bed facility would provide the most controllable environment.

If a test-bed is not available, all packet flow and performance requirements can be evaluated by implementing a subset of the new network consisting of a group of users in the main office and a remote manufacturing facility.

The pilot would consist of the installation of the Catalyst 5000 switch, Cisco 2503 routers at headquarters and at a selected manufacturing facility, the HP9000, two Frame Relay circuits, and the necessary subset of cabling.

Demonstrate that the solution enhances and does not degrade the flow of packets from the warehouse to the main office. This demonstration would be accomplished most definitively through the use of a network monitoring device for both the Frame Relay and the existing X.25 networks. At the application level, this is not a direct comparison. At the packet transport level, it will be a comparison of the new network's capability to deliver what it was asked to deliver.

Jones, Jones, & Jones Case Study Question

Question 13-5

The firm has decided to implement one U.S. office and the Europe office as a pilot network. Describe a project plan (at a high level) that will pilot the system to prove the concept for a full implementation.

The main office should be the U.S. office used in the pilot. At a minimum, it will be necessary to purchase the following for the pilot:

- Cisco 3640 router
- Cisco Catalyst 5002 switch
- Cisco 1603 router
- File server
- CD-ROM server
- Fax server
- Necessary modems and services for at least one each of ISDN and asynchronous dial-in

Both offices should be fully cabled for the final design and the facilities in both appropriately prepared.

A detailed project plan should be developed and the systems installed and tested with the same attention to detail required for a full implementation.

Chapter 14

CareTaker Case Study Questions

Question 14-1

What criteria will you use to validate that the pilot is a success?

The criteria that you will use to validate that the pilot is a success for a network this simple should be error-free pinging and tracing of packets on the various segments and the WAN links.

Question 14-2

Provide a list of the Cisco IOS commands you will use to test your pilot network structure.

Use the following Cisco IOS software commands to determine whether the design meets performance, scalability, and stability goals:

- Check for errors with **show interface** commands.
- Check broadcast rates per interface with **show interface** commands.
- Check for dropped packets with **show interface** commands.
- Check router CPU usage with the **show processes** command.
- Check router buffer usage with the **show buffers** command.
- Check response times with the **ping** command.
- Check for correct routing with the **trace** and **show** *protocol* **route** commands.

PH Network Services Corporation Case Study Questions

Question 14-3

What criteria will you use to validate that the pilot is a success?

The pilot network of one hospital, one LAN-based doctor office, and one standalone-based office, should be connected and completely tested by ping tests and user logins. The new SQL Server could then be added and the connection tested for the pilot network.

After these tests have proven the operational status of the network, the other hospitals should be added, followed by doctor offices, with an orderly, planned methodology.

Question 14-4

Provide a list of the Cisco IOS commands you will use to test your pilot network structure.

Use the following Cisco IOS software commands to determine whether the design meets performance, scalability, and stability goals:

- Check for errors with **show interface** commands.
- Check broadcast rates per interface with **show interface** commands.
- Check for dropped packets with **show interface** commands.
- Check router CPU usage with the **show processes** command.
- Check router buffer usage with the **show buffers** command.
- Check response times with the **ping** command.
- Check for correct routing with the **trace** and **show** *protocol* **route** commands.

Pretty Paper Limited Case Study Question

Question 14-5

What criteria will you use to validate that the pilot is a success?

First you should demonstrate that the new system enhances and does not degrade the flow of packets from the warehouse to the main office. This demonstration would be accomplished most definitively through the use of a network monitoring device for both the Frame Relay and the existing X.25 networks.

At the application level, this is not a direct comparison. At the packet transport level, it will be a comparison of the new network's capability to deliver what it is asked to deliver.

Jones, Jones, & Jones Case Study Question

Question 14-6

What criteria will you use to validate that the pilot is a success?

To validate that the pilot is successful, you should concentrate the validation and acceptability testing on the dial-in users and the CD-ROM library.

If it is possible to test the prototype network structure, attach a WAN protocol analyzer to the serial link at corporate headquarters. Capture data for about a day. Also attach a WAN analyzer at one or more of the branch offices and capture data for about a day.

Chapter 15

Table B-7 provides the answers to the sample CCDA exam and gives a reference to the chapter where the relevant information for each question was discussed.

Table B-7   *Sample CCDA Exam Answers*

Question	Answer	Reference Chapter
1	A	Chapter 2
2	A	Chapter 3
3	A	Chapter 3
4	D	Chapter 3
5	D	Chapter 3
6	B	Chapter 3
7	B	Chapter 4
8	D	Chapter 4
9	B	Chapter 4
10	A	Chapter 4
11	A	Chapter 5
12	B	Chapter 5
13	C	Chapter 6
14	B	Chapter 6
15	A	Chapter 6
16	C	Chapter 7
17	C	Chapter 7
18	D	Chapter 7
19	C	Chapter 8
20	B	Chapter 8
21	A	Chapter 8
22	B	Chapter 9
23	A	Chapter 9
24	B	Chapter 10
25	A	Chapter 10
26	A	Chapter 11

continues

Table B-7   *Sample CCDA Exam Answers (Continued)*

Question	Answer	Reference Chapter
27	C	Chapter 11
28	C	Chapter 12
29	A	Chapter 13
30	C	Chapter 13
31	C	Chapter 14
32	A	Chapter 14

Interesting WWW Links and Other Suggested Readings

Table C-1 provides location/reference information for WWW links and other suggested readings in each chapter.

NOTE The WWW references were correct at the time of writing; however, they may change. If you cannot find the document referenced, you may wish to try searching for the information using either Cisco's web site search facility or a general search engine.

Table C-1 *Location/Reference Information for WWW Links and Other Suggested Readings in Each Chapter*

Chapter	Item	Location/Reference Information
Overview	Internetworking information	Cisco's interactive, self-paced *Internetworking Multimedia CD-ROM*
	Internetworking information	*Internetworking Technologies Handbook* (Cisco Press)
Chapter 1	RFC 1700, *Assigned Numbers*	http://www.cis.ohio-state.edu/htbin/rfc/rfc1700.html
Chapter 3	Network Management section of Cisco's Product and Ordering information web site	http://www.cisco.com/warp/public/cc/cisco/mkt/enm/index.shtml
	Cisco Products Quick Reference Guide	http://www.cisco.com/univercd/cc/td/doc/cpqrg/index.htm
	Cisco Network Management Products section of the *Products Quick Reference Guide*	http://www.cisco.com/univercd/cc/td/doc/cpqrg/index.htm
	Netflow information	http://www.cisco.com/warp/public/732/netflow/index.html

Table C-1   *Location/Reference Information for WWW Links and Other Suggested Readings in Each Chapter*

Chapter	Item	Location/Reference Information
	Netflow white paper	http://www.cisco.com/warp/public/732/netflow/napps_wp.htm
	Network Associates (producer of the Sniffer network analyzer) web site	http://www.nai.com/
	Scion product information on Merit Network Inc.'s web site	http://www.merit.edu/~netscarf/
Chapter 5	Internetwork security information	*Firewalls and Internet Security* by Bill Cheswick and Steve Bellovin, published by Addison Wesley.
	Cisco's web site	http://www.cisco.com
	RFC 1918, *Address Allocation for Private Internets*	http://info.internet.isi.edu/in-notes/rfc/files/rfc1918.txt
	PIX Firewall information	http://www.cisco.com/warp/public/cc/cisco/mkt/security/pix/
	KeyLab's FireBench firewall performance analysis	http://www.keylabs.com/results/firebench/fbenrpt2.pdf
	IDC Research firewall market information	http://www.idcresearch.com/CSS
	Tests of enterprise-level firewalls by Network Computing	http://www.networkcomputing.com/921/921f22.html
Chapter 6	*Cisco Products Quick Reference Guide*	http://www.cisco.com/univercd/cc/td/doc/cpqrg/index.htm
	Cisco Product Selection Tool	http://www.cisco.com/romeo/select.htm
	Sales Tools Central, on Cisco's web site	http://www.cisco.com/warp/public/779/smbiz/service/
Chapter 7	*Cisco Product Selection Tool*	http://www.cisco.com/romeo/select.htm
	Cisco Products Quick Reference Guide	http://www.cisco.com/univercd/cc/td/doc/cpqrg/index.htm

Table C-1   *Location/Reference Information for WWW Links and Other Suggested Readings in Each Chapter*

Chapter	Item	Location/Reference Information
	Configure Frame Relay Traffic Shaping section of the *Wide-Area Networking Configuration Guide* for IOS™ 11.3	http://www.cisco.com/univercd/cc/td/doc/product/ software/ios113ed/113ed_cr/wan_c/ wcfrelay.htm#xtocid2343228
Chapter 8	RFC 1700, *Assigned Numbers*	http://www.cis.ohio-state.edu/htbin/rfc/rfc1700.html
	RFC 1518, *An Architecture for IP Address Allocation with CIDR*	http://info.internet.isi.edu/in-notes/rfc/files/rfc1518.txt
	Basic IP Addressing and Troubleshooting Guide	http://www.cisco.com/warp/public/779/smbiz/service/ troubleshooting/ts_ip.htm
	RFC 1519, *Classless Inter-Domain Routing (CIDR): An Address Assignment and Aggregation Strategy*	http://info.internet.isi.edu/in-notes/rfc/files/rfc1519.txt
	RFC 2071, *Network Renumbering Overview: Why would I want it and what is it anyway?*, by Howard Berkowitz and Paul Ferguson	http://info.internet.isi.edu/in-notes/rfc/files/rfc2071.txt
	RFC 2072, *Router Renumbering Guide*, by Howard Berkowitz	http://info.internet.isi.edu/in-notes/rfc/files/rfc2072.txt
	DNS/DHCP Manager section of the *Cisco Product Catalog*	http://www.cisco.com/univercd/cc/td/doc/pcat/
	RFC 1918, *Address Allocation for Private Internets*	http://info.internet.isi.edu/in-notes/rfc/files/rfc1918.txt
	Cisco Easy IP feature information	http://www.cisco.com/warp/customer/cc/cisco/mkt/ios/ nat/tech/ezip1_wp.htm

Table C-1 *Location/Reference Information for WWW Links and Other Suggested Readings in Each Chapter*

Chapter	Item	Location/Reference Information
Chapter 9	Router Configuration Information	*Introduction to Cisco Router Configuration* (Cisco Press)
		Advanced Cisco Router Configuration (Cisco Press)
		OSPF Network Design Solutions (Cisco Press)
	Cisco's web site	http://www.cisco.com
	Details on Cisco IOS™ releases and features	http://www.cisco.com/warp/public/732/Releases/
Chapter 10	Cisco IOS documentation	http://www.cisco.com/univercd/cc/td/doc/product/ software/index.htm
	Security Configuration Guide	http://www.cisco.com/univercd/cc/td/doc/product/ software/ios120/12cgcr/secur_c/index.htm
	Release Notes for Cisco IOS™ Release 11.3	http://www.cisco.com/univercd/cc/td/doc/product/ software/ios113ed/rn113m/rn113mft.htm
	Tag Switching information	http://www.cisco.com/warp/public/732/tag/index.html
Chapter 11	RFC 1155, Structure and Identification of Management Information for TCP/IP-based Internets	http://info.internet.isi.edu/in-notes/rfc/files/rfc1155.txt
	RFC 1212, *Concise MIB Definitions*	http://info.internet.isi.edu/in-notes/rfc/files/rfc1212.txt
	RFC 1157, *A Simple Network Management Protocol (SNMP)*	http://info.internet.isi.edu/in-notes/rfc/files/rfc1157.txt
	RFC 1213, *Management Information Base for Network Management of TCP/IP-based Internets: MIB-II*	http://info.internet.isi.edu/in-notes/rfc/files/rfc1213.txt
	RFC 1902, *Structure of Management Information for Version 2 of the Simple Network Management Protocol (SNMPv2)*	http://info.internet.isi.edu/in-notes/rfc/files/rfc1902.txt

Table C-1   *Location/Reference Information for WWW Links and Other Suggested Readings in Each Chapter*

Chapter	Item	Location/Reference Information
	RFC 1905, *Protocol Operations for Version 2 of the Simple Network Management Protocol (SNMPv2)*	http://info.internet.isi.edu/in-notes/rfc/files/rfc1905.txt
	Cisco Network Management Products section of the *Products Quick Reference Guide*	http://www.cisco.com/univercd/cc/td/doc/cpqrg/index.htm
	CiscoWorks2000 product documentation	http://www.cisco.com/univercd/cc/td/doc/product/rtrmgmt/cw2000/index.htm
	CiscoWorks Blue web site	http://www.cisco.com/warp/public/cc/cisco/mkt/enm/cworks/cwblue/index.shtml
	RFC 1757, *Remote Network Monitoring Management Information Base*	http://info.internet.isi.edu/in-notes/rfc/files/rfc1757.txt
	RFC 1513, *Token Ring Extensions to the Remote Network Monitoring MIB*	http://info.internet.isi.edu/in-notes/rfc/files/rfc1513.txt
	Cisco's web site	http://www.cisco.com
Chapter 12	*Cisco Products Quick Reference Guide*	http://www.cisco.com/univercd/cc/td/doc/cpqrg/index.htm
Chapter 13	Strategic Networks Consulting, Inc.'s (SNCI) web site	http://www.snci.com/
	Network Associates (producer of the Sniffer network analyzer) web site	http://www.nai.com/
Chapter 14	Cisco Connection Documentation	http://www.cisco.com/univercd/home/home.htm
	NETSYS Connectivity Tools User Guide	http://www.cisco.com/univercd/cc/td/doc/product/rtrmgmt/netsys/netsysug/index.htm
	NETSYS Connectivity Tools Reference Manual	http://www.cisco.com/univercd/cc/td/doc/product/rtrmgmt/netsys/netsysrg/index.htm

Table C-1   *Location/Reference Information for WWW Links and Other Suggested Readings in Each Chapter*

Chapter	Item	Location/Reference Information
Chapter 15	Cisco's career certification web site	http://www.cisco.com/warp/public/10/wwtraining/certprog/index.html
Appendix B	Tests of enterprise-level firewalls by Network Computing	http://www.networkcomputing.com/921/921f22.html
	Adtran, Inc.'s web site	http://www.adtran.com
	ADC Kentrox's web site	http://www.kentrox.com
	Open Connect Systems web site	http://www.oc.com
	Cisco Product Selction Tool	http://www.cisco.com/romeo/select.htm
Appendix D	Where NTMAIL is available from	http://www.net-shopper.co.uk/software/ntmail/
Appendix E	Product Bulletin #284 for the Cisco 4000 series routers	http://www.cisco.com/warp/customer/417/49.html
	Product Bulletin #290 for the Cisco 2500 series routers	http://www.cisco.com/warp/partner/synchronicd/cc/cisco/mkt/access/2500/290_pb.htm
Appendix F	For information on DHCP	http://web.syr.edu/~jmwobus/comfaqs/dhcp.faq.html
Appendix H	CiscoNAT Packaging Update	http://www.cisco.com/warp/public/cc/cisco/mkt/ios/nat/prodlit/792_pp.htm
Appendix J	OSPF Design Guide	http://www.cisco.com/warp/public/104/1.html
Appendix L	RFC 1700, *Assigned Numbers*	http://www.cis.ohio-state.edu/htbin/rfc/rfc1700.html
	RFC 1918, *Address Allocation for Private Internets*	http://info.internet.isi.edu/in-notes/rfc/files/rfc1918.txt

This guide contains detailed configuration examples for the PIX Firewall. It assumes the reader is familiar with the configuration commands and syntax for the PIX product, as well as for DNS servers. You might want to refer to both the PIX documentation and DNS server documentation while reviewing this guide. This guide was originally written by Cisco and has been edited here for formatting.

PIX Firewall Design Implementation Guide

Cisco Systems' Private Internet Exchange Firewall (PIX™ Firewall) provides full firewall protection that completely conceals the architecture of an internal network from the outside world. PIX Firewall allows secure access to the Internet from within existing private networks and the capability to expand and reconfigure TCP/IP networks without being concerned about a shortage of IP addresses.

With PIX Firewall, users can take advantage of larger address classes than they might have been assigned by using the Network Address Translation (NAT) algorithm. NAT makes it possible to use either existing IP addresses or the addresses set aside in the Internet Assigned Numbers Authority's (IANA's) reserve pool (RFC 1597).

NOTE RFC1597 was made obsolete in Feb 1996 by RFC1918.

PIX Firewall provides "bulletproof" firewall security without the administrative overhead and risks associated with UNIX-based firewall systems. The network administrator is provided with a complete accounting and logging of all transactions, including attempted break-ins.

PIX Firewall offers controlled access to all the services of the Internet. Its streamlined software is scalable and simple to install; typical configuration takes five minutes or less. It offers an inexpensive, low-maintenance firewall solution that enables users to take advantage of the Internet's potential. Encryption is available with PIX Private Link to provide secure communication between multiple PIX Firewall systems over the Internet.

This document shows real-life examples of firewall configurations using PIX Firewall to completely conceal the architecture of an internal network from the outside world.

NOTE This document contains data adapted from real-life installations. The names and IP addresses of the original installations have been changed to protect their confidentiality. Some configurations make security and performance trade-offs because of the limited availability of hosts for public access server—such security shortcomings are noted in the text.

Example of a Dual DNS/Double Spooling Configuration—twotier.com

twotier.com is probably the most desirable example of a two-tier PIX Firewall configuration. Internal and external Domain Name Services (DNSs) are handled by separate servers, so there is no exposure of internal host names to the Internet. In addition to acting as the gateway server, gate.twotier.com serves as the File Transfer Protocol (FTP) server and mail relay. Since sendmail potentially allows security breaches, placing the mail relay host on the demilitarized zone (DMZ) eliminates the risk of exposing passwords and aliases on the outside DMZ network. The web server is set up to minimize the risk of damage to the host containing real data (db.twotier.com) in the event that the web server is compromised. Figure D-1 illustrates this configuration.

Figure D-1 *twotier.com Firewall Setup (Dual Host Dual DNS)*

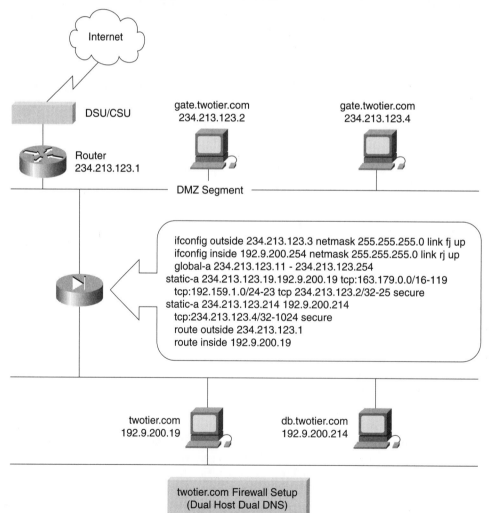

Routing

The Internet router has a gateway of last resort at the provider's end of the WAN link and broadcasts a default route to the DMZ segment. Both gate and WWW point their default gateway to the Internet router. No "rip outside" configuration is necessary on the PIX Firewall because the global address pool (234.213.123.11 through 254) borrows from the DMZ. The PIX Firewall will proxy ARP for the global pool of addresses when required.

The PIX Firewall is configured to broadcast a default route to the inside. UNIX systems running in.routed (or the equivalent) need not be reconfigured to specifically point to the PIX Firewall as a default gateway. PC and Macintosh hosts must be configured to point to the PIX Firewall for a default route (unless a router is set up on the inside, in which case they should point to the internal router for a default gateway).

whois and DNS

According to the whois database, twotier.com has the following domain servers in the order listed:

- **gate.twotier.com**—234.213.123.2
- **ns1.noc.provider.net**—204.31.1.1
- **ns2.noc.provider.net**—204.31.1.2

An MX query of twotier.com shows the following:

>twotier.com	preference = 90, mail exchanger = mail.provider.com
>twotier.com	preference = 20, mail exchanger = gate.twotier.com
>mail.provider.com internet address = 192.100.81.99	
>gate.twotier.com internet address = 234.213.123.2	

The backup MX record (mail.provider.com) facilitates inbound mail spooling from the Internet in the event that the WAN link to the provider breaks.

Bastion Host gate.twotier.com

The following are nameserver entries for the outside DNS server in the named.zone file on gate.twotier.com:

gate.twotier.com.	IN	A	234.213.123.2
msmail.twotier.com.	IN	MX 20	gate.twotier.com.
msmail.twotier.com.	IN	MX 100	mail3.provider.com.
twotier.com.	IN	MX 20	gate.twotier.com.
twotier.com.	IN	MX 90	mail3.provider.com.
twotier.com.	IN	A	234.213.123.19
twotier-g.twotier.com.	IN	CNAME	twotier.com.
mail.twotier.com.	IN	CNAME	twotier.com.
ftp	IN	CNAME	gate.twotier.com.
loghost	IN	CNAME	gate.twotier.com.
www	IN	A	234.213.123.4
nntpserver	IN	CNAME	gate.twotier.com.
newshost	IN	CNAME	gate.twotier.com.
localhost.	IN	A	127.0.0.1
c2500.twotier.com.	IN	A	234.213.123.1
;global ip addresses below			
twotier3.twotier.com	IN	A	234.213.123.3
twotier5.twotier.com	IN	A	234.213.123.5
twotier6.twotier.com	IN	A	234.213.123.6
twotier7.twotier.com	IN	A	234.213.123.7
…..all the way to…			
twotier251.twotier.com.	IN	A	234.213.123.251
twotier252.twotier.com	IN	A	234.213.123.252
twotier253.twotier.com	IN	A	234.213.123.253
twotier254.twotier.com.	IN	A	234.213.123.254

DNS Entries for the Global Cloud

The last section of the zone file contains host-name-to-IP mapping of host names corresponding to the global cloud of addresses. This setup allows access to those sites on the Internet (for example, ftp.uu.net) that require host name verification. Be sure to set up the reverse DNS file for 123.213.234.IN-ADDR.ARPA. Refer to textbooks on DNS for further detail on the need for reverse name servers.

Revealing Internal Names for cc:mail and msmail

msmail.twotier.com is revealed as an MX record. Some Internet mailers attempt to reply to the envelope instead of the "from:" address. Envelopes of messages originating from these PC mail gateways contain the host name of the gateway and are not replyable if the mailer replies to the envelope.

Consider mail originating from the internal msmail gateway that is addressed to a user on the Internet and copied to an internal user. The recipient on the Internet gets a message addressed to lisa@apple.com and copied to joe@msmail.twotier.com. Lisa's reply message will also be directed to joe@msmail.twotier.com. If msmail.twotier.com does not exist as an MX record, the reply message will bounce.

Sendmail

Sendmail on the outside is configured to smart-forward to an inside host.

In the example shown in Figure D-2, gate.twotier.com uses Berkeley sendmail 8.X.

Figure D-2 *gate.twotier.com Uses Berkeley sendmail 8.X.*

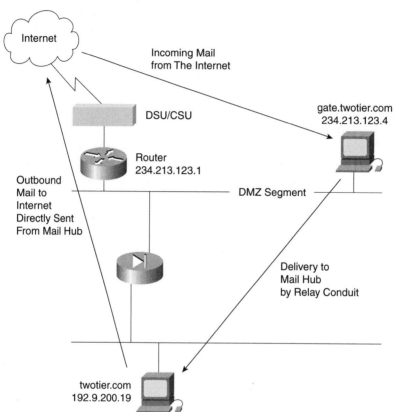

Example D-1 is a cutout of a section of the sendmail.cf on gate.

Example D-1 *Cutout of sendmail.cf on gate*

```
# "Smart" relay host (may be null)
DSsmtp:twotier.com
```

For details, see ftp.translation.com:/pub/sendmail/forwarding.cf.

An nslookup of twotier.com reveals an outside address, as demonstrated in Example D-2.

Example D-2 *nslookup of twotier.com*

```
Name:    twotier.com
Address:  234.213.123.19
```

NOTE	The *A* record of twotier.com is *not* an inside IP address, but a global-to-private mapping. The PIX Firewall is configured with a secure conduit for mail to be delivered only from gate.twotier.com to the internal host twotier.com.

See the MX records on gate.twotier.com. Gate smart-forwards mail addressed to either user@twotier.com or user@msmail.twotier.com to twotier.com, the inside mail host.

Zmailer

Example D-3 shows what the /etc/zmailer.conf for Zmailer (*not* zmail) should look like.

Example D-3 */etc/zmailer.conf for Zmailer*

```
ZCONFIG=/etc/zmailer.conf
HOSTENV=SunOS4.1
SHELL=/bin/sh
MAILBIN=/usr/local/lib/mail
MAILSHARE=/usr/local/share/mail
MAILVAR=/usr/local/share/mail
MAILBOX=/var/spool/mail
POSTOFFICE=/var/spool/postoffice
LOGDIR=/var/log
#LOGLEVEL="file: recipient:"
MANDIR=/usr/local/man
#CC=gcc # gcc -Wall -pedantic
CC=cc
#COPTS="-traditional -g"
COPTS=-g
#RANLIB=true # : ar does the work of ranlib under System V
RANLIB=ranlib # : ar does the work of ranlib under System V
INSTALL="/usr/bin/install -o root -g bin"
NOBODY=65534
#NROUTERS=10
#MAILSERVER=yonge.cs.toronto.edu
SMTPOPTIONS="-l /var/log/smtpserver"
PUNTHOST=twotier.com
SMARTHOST=mail3.provider.com
```

/usr/local/share/mail/db/routers should look like the following:

.twotier.com	smtp!twotier.com

The first field represents the domain name; the second field represents the host to which mail should be "punted" for that domain.

Internal Host twotier.com

This section shows the DNS and Sendmail information for the internal host twotier.com.

DNS

The inside mail host is twotier.com, running DNS for the inside networks.

The following is twotier.com's zone file:

twotier.com.	IN	A	192.9.200.19
msmail	IN	A	192.9.200.57
exchange	IN	A	192.9.200.179
twotier_east	IN	A	192.9.202.2
www	IN	A	234.213.123.4
gate	IN	A	234.213.123.2
news	IN	CNAME	gate.twotier.com.
twotier.com.	IN	MX 20	twotier.com.

NOTE   In the preceding DNS entry, twotier.com's MX record points to itself, so all mail is kept in /var/spool/mail unless otherwise redirected in /etc/aliases.

Sendmail

twotier.com has a rather generic sendmail configuration, except for the rule that stamps the domain name twotier.com for outbound mail. See Example D-4 for excerpts from a Berkeley sendmail v8 cf file. You can find the complete file in ftp.translation.com:/pub/sendmail/sendmail.cf.

Example D-4 *Excerpts from Berkeley sendmail v8 cf file for twotier.com*

```
DDtwotier.com
Dmtwotier.com
```

...CONTINUED...

S31		
R$+	$: $>51 $1	sender/recipient
common		
R$* :; <@>	$@ $1 :;	list:; special case

# do special header rewriting		
R$* <@> $*	$@ $1 <@> $2	pass null host through
R< @ $*> $*	$@ < @ $1> $2	pass route-addr through
R$=E < @ $=w .>	$@ $1 < @ $2>	exposed user as is
R$* < @ $* $m.>	$@ $1 < @ $m>	NTI addition
R$* < @ $=w .>	$: $1 < @ $2 @ $M>	masquerade as domain
R$* < @ $+ @>	$@ $1 < @ $2>	in case $M undefined
R$* < @ $+ @ $+>	$@ $1 < @ $3>	$M is defined --
Use it		
R$*	$@ $>61 $1	qualify unqual'ed names

twotier.com PIX Firewall Configuration

The configuration displayed in Example D-5 allows mail into the global map of twotier.com from gate.

Note that the outside host (www.twotier.com) can access 192.9.200.214 (the database server) via port 1024 (see the static assignments).

Example D-5 *Configuration for Allowing Mail into the Global Map of twotier.com from Gate*

```
ifconfig outside 234.213.123.3 netmask 255.255.255.0 link rj up
ifconfig inside 192.9.200.254 netmask 255.255.255.0 link rj up
global -a 234.213.123.11-234.213.123.254
static -a 234.213.123.19 192.9.200.19 tcp:234.213.123.2/32-25 secure
static -a 234.213.123.214 192.9.200.214 tcp:234.213.123.4/32-1024 secure
route outside 234.213.123.1
route inside 192.9.200.19
timeout xlate 24:00:00 conn 12:00:00
rip inside default passive
rip outside passive
loghost 192.9.200.19
telnet 192.9.200.19
telnet 192.9.200.2
arp -t 600
```

Dual DNS Using Windows NT Gateway Hosts

junction.com uses a Windows NT server as the gateway host and another NT server as the internal mail host (see Figure D-3). This configuration is similar to the two-tier.com example. Bastion.dmz.junction.com serves as the external DNS server, mail relay, FTP server, and web server. Ijserver.junction.com serves as the mail host and internal DNS server.

For simplicity of network stacks management, Windows clients within junction.com do not run an IP stack. Instead, they use the Cisco Internet Junction™ IPX-to-IP protocol conversion software whose server part resides on ijserver.junction.com. With the Internet Junction software, all sessions from PC clients going out to the Internet appear as if they come from a single IP address on ijserver-g.junction.com. UNIX clients take any address assigned dynamically by the PIX Firewall.

Figure D-3 *junction.com Firewall Setup (Dual NT Server Dual DNS)*

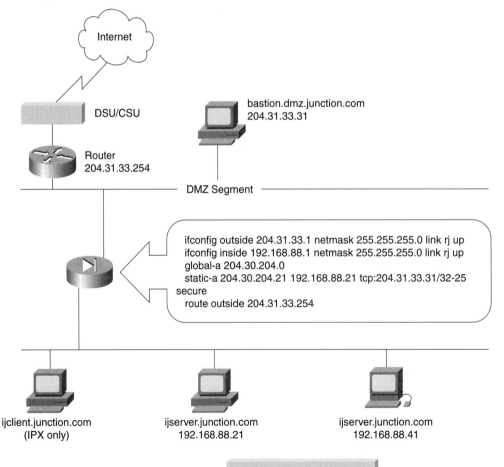

Whois and DNS

According to the whois database, junction.com has the following domain servers in the order listed:

- **bastion.dmz.junction.com**—204.31.33.31
- **ns.translation.com**—204.31.33.2
- **ns2.translation.com**—204.31.33.3

An MX query of junction.com shows the following:

| junction.com | preference = 10, mail exchanger = bastion.junction.com |
| junction.com | preference = 15, mail exchanger = gate.translation.com |

Bastion Host bastion.dmz.junction.com

bastion.dmz.junction.com is a Windows NT 3.51 server configured as follows.

Windows NT Resource Kit 3.51 provides:

- Graphical user interface (GUI)-based FTP server configuration
- A beta copy of EMWAC's http server
- Perl 5.0.X
- Microsoft's DNS server
- Software.com's Post.Office sendmail package for mail relay
- NNS beta 2.06 for Usenet News services

Some alternative sources for Internet services on Windows NT include the following:

- DNS
  - FLBI's DNS is available from ftp.winsite.com/pub/pc/winnt/netutils.
  - Software.com has a port of BIND 4.9.3.
- Mail
  - Windows NT 3.51 Resource Kit has a point of presence (POP) server, mailsrv, with limited features.
  - Krypton Communications has a full-featured mail daemon/POP server package available from ftp.winsite.com/pub/pc/winnt/netutils.
  - Another package, NTMAIL, is available from http://www.net-shopper.co.uk/software/ntmail/.

- HTTPD
  - Commercial web servers for NT are available from Netscape and O'Reilly and Associates.
- TELNETD
  - telnetd is *not* recommended for security reasons.

DNS

Refer to the Microsoft Windows 3.51 Resource Kit for installation instructions.

The following is a listing of the boot file in c:\winnt35\system32\drivers\etc:

cache	.	cache
primary	127.in-addr.arpa.	arpa-127.rev
primary	junction.com	junction.com
primary	33.31.204.in-addr.arpa.	named.rev
primary	204.30.204.in-addr.arpa.	global.rev

The following is the junction.com file (note that $INCLUDE is not used here):

@ IN SOA bastion.junction.com.			
postmaster.bastion.junction.com. (			
			1996031403; serial number
			2400; refresh [3h]
			3000; retry [1h]
			604800; expire [7d]
			86400; minimum [1d]
;;$WINS 192.5.29.2 192.5.29.3			
@	in	ns	bastion.junction.com.
@	in	ns	ns1.translation.com.
@	in	ns	ns2.translation.com.
bastion	in	a	204.31.33.31
localhost	in	a	127.0.0.1
;@	in	mx	5 ijserver.junction.com.
@	in	mx	10 bastion.junction.com.

continues

continued

mail-g	in	a	204.30.204.22
WINSsrv1	in	cname	bastion.junction.com.
ftp	in	cname	bastion.junction.com.
www	in	cname	bastion.junction.com.
ijserver-g	in	cname	ijserver-g.junction.com.
;			
dmz	in	cname	bastion.junction.com.
bastion.dmz	in	cname	bastion.junction.com.
host1.junction.com.	in	a	204.30.204.1
....			
Host254.junction.com.	in	a	204.30.204.254

NOTE   With Krypton's XKIMS mail server, you must configure the mail relay host bastion.dmz.junction.com to be a member of a subdomain, such as dmz.junction.com, to enable mail redirection to the inside host without needing to use aliases. This configuration is not necessary, however, if you are using Post.Office.

Sendmail

The Internet Junction architecture achieves double spooling through the use of the bastion.dmz.junction.com mail relay. Bastion does not contain any user passwords or aliases.

Most commercial NT-based sendmail implementations (such as Post.Office) support mail redirection configuration via a GUI or a Web client.

If you are using Post.Office, the directive to enable mail forwarding to the internal mail host is configurable on the screen (Internet) message channel configuration using the following syntax as shown in Example D-6.

Example D-6   *Enabling Mail Forwarding to the Internal Mail Host*

```
*.junction.com:ijserver-g.junction.com
```

Internal Host ijserver.junction.com

The Internal host ijserver.junction.com runs the same DNS server as the external host but also contains information for the 192.168.88 network and 204.31.33.31.

DNS

The following is a listing of the boot file in c:\winnt35\system32\drivers\etc:

cache	.	cache
primary	127.in-addr.arpa.	arpa-127.rev
primary	Junction.com.	junction.com
primary	88.168.192.in-addr.arpa.	named.rev

The following is a listing of junction.com (note that $INCLUDE is not used here):

@ IN SOA ijserver.junction.com.			
postmaster.ijserver.junction.com. (			
			1996031403; serial number
			2400; refresh [3h]
			3000; retry [1h]
			604800; expire [7d]
			86400; minimum [1d]
;;$WINS 192.5.29.2 192.5.29.3			
@	in	ns	ijserver.junction.com.
bastion	in	a	204.31.33.31
ijserver	in	a	192.168.88.21
localhost	in	a	127.0.0.1
@	in	mx	5 ijserver.junction.com.
ftp	in	cname	bastion.junction.com.
www	in	cname	bastion.junction.com.
dmz	in	cname	bastion.junction.com.
bastion.dmz	in	cname	bastion.junction.com.
unixserver	in	a	192.168.88.41

Sendmail

Internal sendmail uses a generic configuration, but all outbound mail must be stamped as if from [user]@junction.com. Because most mail packages for NT now support MX record lookup, there is no need for the external mail host to act as an outbound mail relay.

junction.com PIX Firewall Configuration

Example D-7 shows the junction.com PIX Firewall configuration.

Example D-7 *junction.com PIX Firewall Configuration*

```
ifconfig outside 204.31.33.1 netmask 255.255.255.0 link rj up
ifconfig inside 192.168.88.1 netmask 255.255.255.0 link rj up
global -a 204.30.204.0
static -a 204.30.204.21 192.168.88.21 tcp:204.31.33.31/32-25 secure
route outside 204.31.33.254
```

Managing the NT Bastion Using NetBIOS

For security reasons, Cisco does not recommend allowing NetBIOS over TCP/IP services to pass from bastion to ijserver. However, if such communication is required, add the following command to the PIX Firewall:

```
conduit 204.30.204.21 udp:204.31.33.31/32-137
```

This command enables the ijserver internal host to map to a shared resource on bastion.

The following command enables the external host to map a file system local to ijserver (referred to as ijserver-g in its DNS). You must preload ijserver's IP address of 204.30.204.21 in c:\winnt35\system32\drivers\etc\LMHOSTS. This setup also allows a user on bastion to log in to the internal NT domain of JUNCTION.

```
conduit 204.30.204.21 tcp:204.31.33.31/32-139
```

NOTE Cisco strongly discourages this configuration for security reasons.

Single DNS and Mail Host Hidden Behind a PIX Firewall

basic.ca.us has a suboptimal security configuration because the web server/mail relay/FTP/ DNS server is located inside the secure network with "holes" to which the outside world has access (see Figure D-4). There is a risk of the internal network being compromised if services like sendmail are compromised. Furthermore, the old server (nafta) contains the real "production"/etc/passwd file. If FTP is not secured in a chrooted fashion, the password file might be compromised.

basic.ca.us has adopted this configuration because nafta is both the authoritative DNS server for basic.ca.us and the internal file server. No other UNIX host is available to serve as a bastion, and basic.ca.us does not want to reregister the authoritative name server to another IP address. In the future, services such as Web, FTP, and mail relay will be migrated to a bastion host on the DMZ network, leaving only DNS open to direct Internet access.

Figure D-4 *Basic Firewall Setup (Single Host Single DNS No Bastion)*

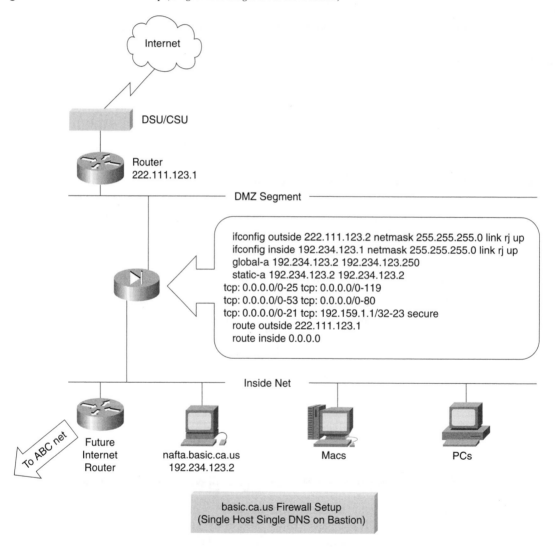

Routing

The Internet router is controlled by the Internet service provider and does not broadcast a default route via Routing Information Protocol (RIP). The PIX Firewall is configured to point to the Internet router for an outside route. basic.ca.us uses a range of 192.234.123.2 to 250 as the global cloud; this is different from the DMZ segment (222.111.123.X).

In order to make the 192.234.123.X net visible from the Internet, a static route is configured on the Cisco 2500 Internet router to the outside interface of the PIX Firewall, as follows:

```
ip route 192.234.123.0 255.255.255.0 222.111.123.2
```

Technical Support Note

Ensure that the second IP address is routed to the customer's Internet router before performing any further debugging. You can accomplish this using **traceroute** from the Internet to verify that both addresses (222.111.123 and 192.234.123) are routed to 222.111.123.1 (or at least to the serial interface IP of the Internet router).

Route inside 0.0.0.0 denotes no routers installed on the network inside.

Route inside can be changed to IP of internal router once it is set up.

DNS

Host nafta.basic.ca.us serves DNS to the outside and inside. The /var/named/named.boot file at Basic serves only the inside addresses (which also fully make up the global pool).

directory /usr/local/named		
primary	basic.ca.us	db.basic
primary	123.234.192.in-addr.arpa	db.192.234.123
primary	123.111.222.in-addr.arpa	db.222.111.123
primary	0.0.127.in-addr.arpa	db.127.0.0
cache	.	named.ca

The named.zone file has some real hosts and some names for global IP addresses, as follows:

basic.ca.us	IN	MX 10 nafta.basic.ca.us.	
basic.ca.us.	IN	MX 100 mail3.provider.com.	
nafta.basic.ca.us.	IN	MX 10 nafta.basic.ca.us.	
luna	IN	A	192.234.123.3
moe	IN	A	192.234.123.27
TiredMac	IN	A	192.234.123.249
MediaPPC	IN	A	192.234.123.250
NSC	IN	A	192.234.123.150
nafta.basic.ca.us.	IN	A	192.234.123.2
www	IN	CNAME	nafta.basic.ca.us.
news	IN	CNAME	nafta.basic.ca.us.
ftp	IN	CNAME	nafta.basic.ca.us.
ns	IN	CNAME	nafta.basic.ca.us.
host5.basic.ca.us.	IN	A	192.234.123.5
host6.basic.ca.us.	IN	A	192.234.123.6
...all the way to...			
host252.basic.ca.us.	IN	A	192.234.123.252
host253.basic.ca.us.	IN	A	192.234.123.253
host254.basic.ca.us.	IN	A	192.234.123.254

Sendmail

The sendmail configuration on nafta is generic (it is similar to twotier.com). Nafta is the most preferred MX host for the basic.ca.us domain.

basic.ca.us's PIX Firewall Configuration

Example D-8 shows the PIX Firewall configuration for basic.ca.us.

Example D-8   *basic.ca.us PIX Firewall Configuration*

```
ifconfig outside 222.111.123.2 netmask 255.255.255.0 link rj up
ifconfig inside 192.234.123.1 netmask 255.255.255.0 link rj up
global -a 192.234.123.2-192.234.123.250
static -a 192.234.123.2 192.234.123.2 tcp:0.0.0.0/0-25 tcp:0.0.0.0/0-119
tcp:0.0.0.0/0-53 tcp:0.0.0.0/0-80 tcp:204.30.204.0/24-23 tcp:0.0.0.0/0-21
tcp:192.159.1.1/32-23 secure
route outside 222.111.123.1
route inside 0.0.0.0
rip inside default passive
rip outside passive
loghost 192.234.123.2
telnet 192.234.123.4
telnet 192.234.123.2
```

NOTE   The static here reveals the IP of nafta, which is the DNS, news, mail, Web, and FTP server. In this configuration, the inside addresses and global addresses are the same. Inside addresses are not actually revealed in this case, because outgoing connections will use IP addresses starting from 192.234.123.254 backwards and resolve back to names like host254.basic.ca.us.

DIGICORP (Another Example of a Single DNS and Mail Host Hidden Behind a PIX Firewall)

Digicorp uses the PIX Firewall to grow its network without needing to acquire new addresses from its Internet service provider (ISP). Digicorp has its own authoritative name server and legitimate IP addresses. As part of a project to implement Internet security, Digicorp has configured a firewall similar to that of Basic. Digicorp will move web servers to the DMZ and will add a mail relay host to further enhance Internet security.

Whois and DNS

A "whois" query of digicorp.com reveals the following:

SUN.DIGICORP.COM	204.31.17.2
PROVIDERSV.PROVIDER.COM	192.100.81.101

digicorp.com's PIX Firewall Configuration

The PIX Firewall will assign all hosts inside digicorp.com an IP address of 206.222.111.X when they go outside. There is only one exception; 204.31.17.2 goes to the outside with its internal IP address. Digicorp thus hides all internal hosts, with the exception of the DNS server. Example D-9 shows the PIX Firewall configuration for digicorp.com.

Example D-9 *digicorp.com PIX Firewall Configuration*

```
ifconfig outside 206.222.111.2 netmask 255.255.255.0 link bnc up
ifconfig inside 204.31.17.1 netmask 255.255.255.0 link bnc up
global -a 206.222.111.11-206.222.111.254
global -a 204.31.17.2-204.31.17.3
static -a 204.31.17.2 204.31.17.2 tcp:204.31.1.0/24-119
tcp:163.179.0.0/16-53 tcp:0.0.0.0/0-25 secure
route outside 206.222.111.1
route inside 204.31.17.254
```

Special Case 1: DNS Server Using Private IP Addresses

If the internal network of Digicorp uses a private or unregistered IP, and internal.digicorp.com uses 192.168.1.2, then a static should be configured as illustrated in Example D-10.

Example D-10 *digicorp.com PIX Firewall Configuration When Using Private IP Addresses*

```
static -a 204.31.17.2 192.168.1.2 tcp:204.31.1.0/24-119
tcp:163.179.0.0/16-53 tcp:0.0.0.0/0-25 secure
```

Also, DNS must be set up as follows:

@ IN		SOA	gate-g.digidemise.com. postmaster.digicorp.com. (		
			96011788	; serial	
			7200	; refresh	
			1800	; retry	
			2592000	; expire	
			345600)	; Minimum	
			IN	NS	gate-g.digicorp.com.
gate.digidemise.com.		IN	A	192.168.88.2	
gate-g		IN	A	204.31.17.2	
digidemise.com.		IN	MX 10	gate.digicorp.com.	
digidemise.com.		IN	MX 15	gate-g.digicorp.com.	

Special Case 2: Same IP Used on DMZ and Internal Network

When there is only one class C available from the ISP, it is still possible to use the same IP address on the outside segment/global cloud and inside network without changing the IP addresses of the internal network. A major drawback with this configuration, however, is that the outside Internet router is unmanageable from the inside LAN. In addition, hosts on the DMZ zone cannot be reached from the inside network.

If Digicorp were to use the same 204.31.17.X network, the PIX Firewall configuration would look like Example D-11.

Example D-11 *digicorp.com PIX Firewall Configuration When Same IP Used on DMZ and Internal Network*

```
ifconfig outside 204.31.17.254 netmask 255.255.255.0 link bnc up
ifconfig inside 204.31.17.1 netmask 255.255.255.0 link bnc up
global -a 204.31.17.2-204.31.17.253
static -a 204.31.17.2 204.31.17.2 tcp:0.0.0.0/0-119 tcp:0.0.0.0/0-53
tcp:0.0.0.0/0-25 secure
route outside 204.31.17.1
route inside 204.31.17.254
```

NOTE   As can be seen in the **static** command, only mail, DNS zone transfer, and news are open to the Internet. This configuration is suboptimal because the Sun host, which contains passwords and aliases, is subject to direct Internet Simple Mail Transfer Protocol (SMTP) connections. The Sun host is also subject to security compromises caused by sendmail bugs.

Single Outside DNS Server Serving Outside and Inside Addresses

Bigcorp, San Jose, has a Class B subnet of the Korean Bigcorp headquarters' network configured internally. To minimize load on the T1 serving IP/IPX traffic, the router in Korea filters out access to the Internet from the San Jose network. A default route (pointing to the PIX Firewall) is configured on the Cisco 7000 to enable San Jose clients to access the Internet seamlessly.

Bigcorp must also protect the msmail SMTP gateway (which cannot handle multiple inbound connections). Unauthorized users could stall the SMTP gate by Telnetting to port 25 of msmail.bigcorp.com if it were to be exposed. Figure D-5 shows the firewall setup for Bigcorp.

Figure D-5 *bigcorp.com Firewall Setup (Single Host Single DNS)*

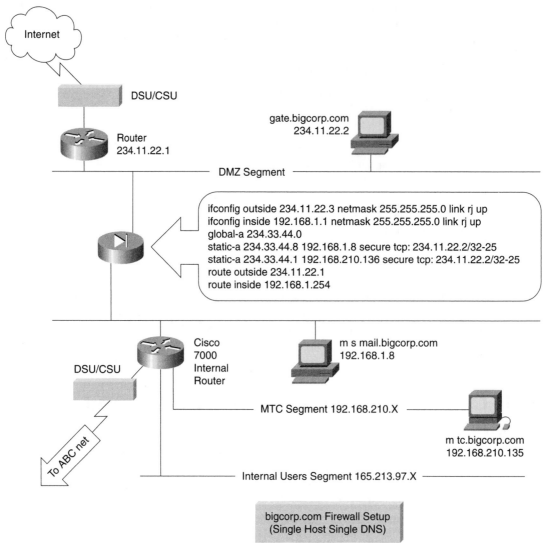

```
ifconfig outside 234.11.22.3 netmask 255.255.255.0 link rj up
ifconfig inside 192.168.1.1 netmask 255.255.255.0 link rj up
global-a 234.33.44.0
static-a 234.33.44.8 192.168.1.8 secure tcp: 234.11.22.2/32-25
static-a 234.33.44.1 192.168.210.136 secure tcp: 234.11.22.2/32-25
route outside 234.11.22.1
route inside 192.168.1.254
```

bigcorp.com Firewall Setup
(Single Host Single DNS)

Routing

The outside DMZ zone (234.11.22.0) has a different IP address than the global cloud
(234.33.44.0). A static route on the Internet router routes 234.33.44.X to 234.11.22.3. The
Internal Cisco 7000 has a default gateway set to 192.168.1.1.

Whois and DNS

Whois on bigcorp.com shows authoritative name servers as follows:

NS1.NOC.PROVIDER.NET	204.31.1.1
NS2.NOC.PROVIDER.NET	204.31.1.2

However, nslookup shows that the SOA belongs to the host gate.bigcorp.com as illustrated in Example D-12.

Example D-12   *Using nslookup to Reveal that SOA Belongs to Host gate.bigcorp.com*

```
jma.com% nslookup
Default Server:  jma.com
Address:  192.159.1.1

>set q=soa
>bigcorp.com
Server:  jma.com
Address:  192.159.1.1
```

bigcorp.com		
	origin = gate.bigcorp.com	
	mail addr = postmaster.bigcorp.com	
	serial = 96020102	
	refresh = 1800 (30 mins)	
	retry = 900 (15 mins)	
	expire = 2592000 (30 days)	
	minimum ttl = 345600 (4 days)	
bigcorp.com	nameserver = gate.bigcorp.com	
bigcorp.com	nameserver = ns1.noc.provider.net	
bigcorp.com	nameserver = ns2.noc.provider.net	
gate.bigcorp.com		internet address = 234.11.22.2
ns1.noc.provider.net		internet address = 204.31.1.1
ns2.noc.provider.net		internet address = 204.31.1.2

Gate.bigcorp.com is the actual primary DNS server, with ns1.noc.provider.net and ns2.noc.provider.net serving as secondary servers, periodically transferring zone files from gate.bigcorp.com.

Gate.bigcorp.com's zone file looks like the following:

gate.bigcorp.com.	IN	A	234.11.22.2
bigcorp.com.	IN	MX 20	gate.bigcorp.com.
bigcorp.com.	IN	MX 60	mail2.provider.com.
ftp	IN	CNAME	gate.bigcorp.com.
loghost	IN	CNAME	gate.bigcorp.com.
www	IN	A	203.241.132.36
nntpserver	IN	CNAME	gate.bigcorp.com.
newshost	IN	CNAME	gate.bigcorp.com.
localhost.	IN	A	127.0.0.1
irx	IN	A	234.11.22.1
msmail	IN	A	234.33.44.8
msmail.bigcorp.com.	IN	MX 10	msmail.bigcorp.com.
msmail.bigcorp.com.	IN	MX 90	gate.bigcorp.com.
abcipo.msmail.bigcorp.com.	IN	MX 20	msmail.bigcorp.com.
abcipo.msmail.bigcorp.com.	IN	MX 30	gate.bigcorp.com.
ssi.bigcorp.com.	IN	MX 20	msmail.bigcorp.com.
ssi.bigcorp.com.	IN	MX 30	gate.bigcorp.com.
hub	IN	A	192.168.1.3
master.bigcorp.com.	IN	A	192.168.210.136

Sendmail for msmail.bigcorp.com and Related Post Offices

In this configuration, mail "trickles" through to the msmail smtpgate from the Internet, as follows:

First, mail from outside will attempt to connect to:

abcipo.msmail.bigcorp.com.	IN	MX 20	msmail.bigcorp.com.

and fail; then it resorts to:

abcipo.msmail.bigcorp.com.	IN	MX 30	gate.bigcorp.com.

This trickling occurs for all other msmail post offices configured as subdomains, as well as the subdomain mtc.bigcorp.com., which we will discuss later on.

A Note About this Mail Configuration

Gate.bigcorp.com's sendmail is not modified to do any special rewriting because msmail.bigcorp.com relies on gate to pass outbound messages. If gate is configured to smart-forward mail to msmail as in the two-tier example, a mail loop results.

If we place a UNIX host that can be used as a mail relay inside or on the DMZ, we can eliminate this awkward mail setup. The resulting configuration would use gate as the MX host for all *.bigcorp.com domains, smart-forward mail to the UNIX host inside Bigcorp's network, and fan out mail to the different mail servers internally.

As an alternative, we could install Zmailer on gate.bigcorp.com. Zmailer will intelligently route mail addressed to user@msmail.bigcorp.com, user@abcipo.msmail.bigcorp.com, and any subdomains on msmail to the msmail SMTP gateway. Zmailer will intelligently route outbound Internet messages for msmail without looping (see Figure D-6).

Figure D-6 *gate.bigcorp.com Mail Routing*

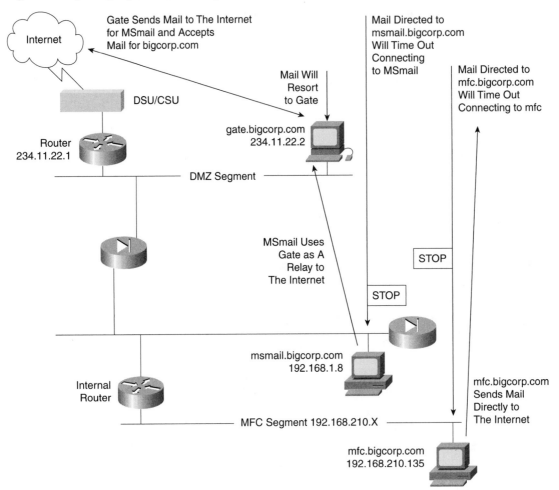

gate.bigcorp.com's named.boot serves all legitimate, private, and bogus addresses, as follows:

directory	/var/named
xfrnets	204.31.1.0
cache	. named.ca
primary bigcorp.com	named.zone
primary ssi.bigcorp.com	ssi.bigcorp.com
primary 226.30.204.in-addr.arpa	named.rev
primary 61.33.204.in-addr.arpa	global.rev
primary 1.168.192.in-addr.arpa	inside.rev
primary 210.168.192.in-addr.arpa	mtc.rev
primary 97.213.165.in-addr.arpa	165.rev
primary 97.213.174.in-addr.arpa	174.rev
primary 0.0.127.in-addr.arpa	local.rev

The following entries in the inside.zone file cover the private addresses inside:

inside1.bigcorp.com.	IN	A	192.168.1.1
inside2.bigcorp.com.	IN	A	192.168.1.2
inside3.bigcorp.com.	IN	A	192.168.1.3
inside4.bigcorp.com.	IN	A	192.168.1.4
inside5.bigcorp.com.	IN	A	192.168.1.5
inside6.bigcorp.com.	IN	A	192.168.1.6

Sendmail for Subdomain Mail Hosts

The configuration in Example D-13 applies to subdomains inside the Bigcorp firewall (such as mtc.bigcorp.com) that have their own UNIX mail host:

Example D-13   *Sendmail for Subdomain Mail Hosts*

```
>set q=MX
>mtc.bigcorp.com
Server: gate.bigcorp.com
Address: 234.11.22.2
```

mtc.bigcorp.com preference = 10, mail exchanger = master.bigcorp.com	
mtc.bigcorp.com preference = 20, mail exchanger = abc-g.bigcorp.com	
mtc.bigcorp.com preference = 30, mail exchanger = gate.bigcorp.com	
master.bigcorp.com	internet address = 192.168.210.136
abc-g.bigcorp.com	internet address = 234.33.44.136
gate.bigcorp.com	internet address = 234.11.22.2

NOTE   Abc-g.bigcorp.com is a static map of 192.168.210.136 and has a conduit for mail delivery only from gate.bigcorp.com because the sendmail daemon of master.bigcorp.com is not security enhanced.

Normally, only the following entries are required in DNS:

mtc.bigcorp.com preference = 20, mail exchanger = abc-g.bigcorp.com	
mtc.bigcorp.com preference = 30, mail exchanger = gate.bigcorp.com	
abc-g.bigcorp.com	Internet address = 234.33.44.136
gate.bigcorp.com	Internet address = 234.11.22.2

However, master.bigcorp.com runs Sun sendmail.mx, which blindly follows MX records. If the entry

```
mtc.bigcorp.com preference = 10, mail exchanger = master.bigcorp.com
```

is omitted, mail reaching master.bigcorp.com will loop to its global address (the most preferred MX host), which it can never reach (because a machine cannot ping its global address from the inside). The mail subsequently loops back to gate.bigcorp.com, based on the MX records on gate.bigcorp.com:

```
mtc.bigcorp.com preference = 20, mail exchanger = abc-g.bigcorp.com
mtc.bigcorp.com preference = 30, mail exchanger = gate.bigcorp.com
```

NOTE   You can avoid this awkward sendmail problem by using ZMAILER (not zmail) on gate.bigcorp.com or Berkeley sendmail on all inside hosts.

Bigcorp.com's PIX Firewall Configuration

Example D-14 illustrates the PIX Firewall Configuration for bigcorp.com.

Example D-14 *bigcorp.com PIX Firewall Configuration*

```
ifconfig outside 234.11.22.254 netmask 255.255.255.0 link rj up
ifconfig inside 192.168.1.1 netmask 255.255.255.0 link rj up
global -a 234.33.44.1-234.33.44.254
static -a 234.33.44.8 192.168.1.8 tcp:234.11.22.2/32-25 secure
static -a 234.33.44.136 192.168.210.136 tcp:234.11.22.2/32-25 secure
static -a 234.33.44.145 192.168.1.145 tcp:234.11.22.2/32-25 secure
route outside 234.11.22.1
route inside 192.168.1.3
timeout xlate 1:00:00 conn 12:00:00
rip inside default passive
rip outside nonpassive
loghost 0.0.0.0
telnet 192.168.210.136
telnet 234.11.22.2
telnet 192.168.202.253
telnet 192.168.1.253

arp -t 600
: version 2.7.1
```

PIX Private Link Example

twoface.com has multiple sites connected via PIX Private Link. Like Digicorp and basic.ca.us, twoface has public access servers both on the DMZ and behind the PIX Firewall. These public access servers are accessed from the Internet via static conduits. (See Figure D-7.)

Figure D-7 *twoface.com Private Link Setup*

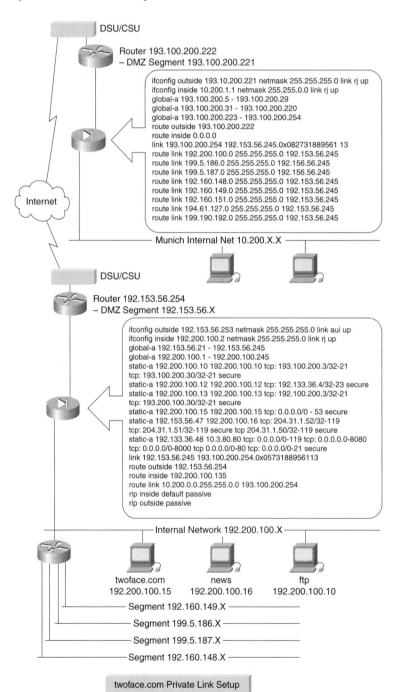

DSU/CSU

Router 193.100.200.222
– DMZ Segment 193.100.200.221

ifconfig outside 193.10.200.221 netmask 255.255.255.0 link rj up
ifconfig inside 10.200.1.1 netmask 255.255.0.0 link rj up
global-a 193.100.200.5 - 193.100.200.29
global-a 193.100.200.31 - 193.100.200.220
global-a 193.100.200.223 - 193.100.200.254
route outside 193.100.200.222
route inside 0.0.0.0
link 193.100.200.254 192.153.56.245.0x082731889561 13
route link 192.200.100.0 255.255.255.0 192.153.56.245
route link 199.5.186.0 255.255.255.0 192.156.56.245
route link 199.5.187.0 255.255.255.0 192.156.56.245
route link 192.160.148.0 255.255.255.0 192.153.56.245
route link 192.160.149.0 255.255.255.0 192.153.56.245
route link 192.160.151.0 255.255.255.0 192.153.56.245
route link 194.61.127.0 255.255.255.0 192.153.56.245
route link 199.190.192.0 255.255.255.0 192.153.56.245

Internet

Munich Internal Net 10.200.X.X

DSU/CSU

Router 192.153.56.254
– DMZ Segment 192.153.56.X

ifconfig outside 192.153.56.253 netmask 255.255.255.0 link aui up
ifconfig inside 192.200.100.2 netmask 255.255.255.0 link rj up
global-a 192.153.56.21 - 192.153.56.245
global-a 192.200.100.1 - 192.200.100.245
static-a 192.200.100.10 192.200.100.10 tcp: 193.100.200.3/32-21
tcp: 193.100.200.30/32-21 secure
static-a 192.200.100.12 192.200.100.12 tcp: 192.133.36.4/32-23 secure
static-a 192.200.100.13 192.200.100.13 tcp: 192.100.200.3/32-21
tcp: 193.200.100.30/32-21 secure
static-a 192.200.100.15 192.200.100.15 tcp: 0.0.0.0/0 - 53 secure
static-a 192.153.56.47 192.200.100.16 tcp: 204.31.1.52/32-119
tcp: 204.31.1.51/32-119 secure tcp 204.31.1.50/32-119 secure
static-a 192.133.36.48 10.3.80.80 tcp: 0.0.0.0/0-119 tcp: 0.0.0.0-8080
tcp: 0.0.0.0/0-8000 tcp 0.0.0.0/0-80 tcp: 0.0.0.0/0-21 secure
link 192.153.56.245 193.100.200.254.0x0573188956113
route outside 192.153.56.254
route inside 192.200.100.135
route link 10.200.0.0.255.255.0.0 193.100.200.254
rip inside default passive
rip outside passive

Internal Network 192.200.100.X

twoface.com   news   ftp
192.200.100.15   192.200.100.16   192.200.100.10

———— Segment 192.160.149.X ————
———— Segment 199.5.186.X ————
———— Segment 199.5.187.X ————
———— Segment 192.160.148.X ————

twoface.com Private Link Setup

DNS

twoface.com	NS	twoface.com
twoface.com	NS	NS1.NOC.PROVIDER.NET
twoface.com	NS	NS2.NOC.PROVIDER.NET
twoface.com	A	192.200.100.15

NOTE   Before Twoface configured the firewall, twoface.com had a valid IP address. The firewall configuration approximately follows that of basic.com and digicorp.com.

Twoface Sunnyvale Site PIX Firewall Configuration

Example D-15 illustrates the PIX Firewall Configuration for the Twoface Sunnyvale site.

Example D-15   *Twoface Sunnyvale Site PIX Firewall Configuration*

```
ifconfig outside 192.200.101.253 netmask 255.255.255.0 link aui up
ifconfig inside 192.200.100.2 netmask 255.255.255.0 link rj up
global -a 192.200.101.21-192.200.101.245
global -a 192.200.100.1-192.200.100.254
static -a 192.200.100.10 192.200.100.10 tcp:193.100.200.3/32-21
  tcp:193.100.200.30/32-21 secure
static -a 192.200.100.12 192.200.100.12 tcp:192.200.101.4/32-25 secure
static -a 192.200.100.13 192.200.100.13 tcp:193.100.200.3/32-21
  tcp:193.100.200.30/32-21 secure
static -a 192.200.100.15 192.200.100.15 tcp:0.0.0.0/0-53 secure
static -a 192.200.101.47 192.200.100.16 tcp:204.31.1.52/32-119 tcp:204.31.1.51/
  32-119
tcp:204.31.1.50/32-119 secure
static -a 192.200.101.48 10.3.80.80 tcp:0.0.0.0/0-119 tcp:0.0.0.0/0-8080
  tcp:0.0.0.0/0-8000
tcp:0.0.0.0/0-80 tcp:0.0.0.0/0-21 secure
link 192.200.101.245 193.100.200.254 0x08273188956113
route outside 192.200.101.254
route inside 192.200.100.136
route link 10.200.0.0 255.255.0.0 193.100.200.254
timeout xlate 5:00:00 conn 1:00:00
rip inside default passive
rip outside passive
```

Twoface Zurich Site PIX Firewall Configuration

This site has one flat network, as illustrated in Example D-16.

Example D-16 *Twoface Zurich Site PIX Firewall Configuration*

```
ifconfig outside 193.100.200.221 netmask 255.255.255.0 link rj up
ifconfig inside 10.200.1.1 netmask 255.255.0.0 link rj up
global -a 193.100.200.5-193.100.200.29
global -a 193.100.200.31-193.100.200.220
global -a 193.100.200.223-193.100.200.254
route outside 193.100.200.222
route inside 0.0.0.0
link 193.100.200.254 192.200.101.245 0x08273188956113
route link 192.200.100.0 255.255.255.0 192.200.101.245
route link 199.5.186.0 255.255.255.0 192.200.101.245
route link 199.5.187.0 255.255.255.0 192.200.101.245
route link 192.160.148.0 255.255.255.0 192.200.101.245
route link 192.160.149.0 255.255.255.0 192.200.101.245
route link 192.160.151.0 255.255.255.0 192.200.101.245
route link 194.61.127.0 255.255.255.0 192.200.101.245
route link 199.190.192.0 255.255.255.0 192.200.101.245
```

NOTE   There are multiple **route link** commands setting up routes from the Zurich network to almost all internal networks at the Sunnyvale site.

Syslog

This section provides examples of syslog files generated on a Sun SPARCstation running SunOS 4.1.4.

The following is a cutout of /etc/syslog.conf (be sure to use tabs instead of spaces in this file):

local4.crit	/var/log/pix/security
local5.err	/var/log/pix/resource
local6.notice	/var/log/pix/system
local7.info	/var/log/pix/acct

The following is a directory listing of /var/log/pix:

inside.sinai-balt.com% ls -la	
total 53484	
drwxr-sr-x 2 root	512 Jun 14 1995 .
drwxr-sr-x 4 root	512 Feb 10 04:05 ..
-rw-r--r-- 1 root	54359851 Feb 15 20:00 acct
-rw-r--r-- 1 root	306741 Feb 15 19:58 resource
-rw-r--r-- 1 root	40450 Feb 14 08:11 security
-rw-r--r-- 1 root	1878 Jan 3 16:41 system

Annotated Examples of PIX Firewall Logs

acct

Example D-17 records the start of an SMTP (25) connection from 204.33.212.2 to 21.84.5.1 via a the global address 204.33.212.4:

Example D-17   *Start of PIX Firewall Log for SMTP Connection*

```
Feb 15 19:56:44 pixin  conn start faddr 204.33.212.2 fport 2485  gaddr
   204.33.212.4 laddr 21.84.5.1 lport 25
```

Example D-18 records the end of the same connection with information on byte count transferred:

Example D-18   *End of PIX Firewall Log for SMTP Connection*

```
Feb 15 19:56:50 pixin  conn end faddr 204.33.212.2 fport 2485 gaddr
204.33.212.4 laddr 21.84.5.1 lport 25 duration 0:00:06 bytes 3672
```

Example D-19 logs the start an outbound mail sent from 21.84.5.1:

Example D-19   *Start of PIX Firewall Log for Outbound Mail*

```
Feb 15 20:00:28 pixin  conn start faddr 198.69.28.2 fport 25  gaddr 204.33.212.4
   laddr 21.84.5.1 lport 1721
```

Example D-20 logs the end of another outbound mail connection:

Example D-20   *End of PIX Firewall Log for Outbound Mail*

```
Feb 15 20:00:35 pixin  conn end faddr 198.69.28.2 fport 25 gaddr 204.33.212.4 laddr
   21.84.5.1 lport 1700 duration 0:02:09 bytes 0
```

Example D-21 logs the start of a connection to a Web server on the Internet from 21.84.5.1:

Example D-21 *Start of PIX Firewall Log for Connection to Web Server*

```
Feb 15 20:06:00 pixin  conn start faddr 17.254.3.61 fport 80  gaddr 204.33.212.4
   laddr 21.84.5.1 lport 1787
```

acct.txt Generated from WIN95 Syslog32

An example of the acct.txt file generated by pixlog32 follows. The other files—security.txt, resource.txt, and system.txt—are the same as their UNIX syslog counterparts. Note that host names are resolved based on IP addresses and displayed in the log files.

Mar 7 11:6:47	192.168.88.252	Accounting (23)	Informational (6)	conn end faddr
204.31.17.3 fport 21 gaddr 204.30.204.252 laddr 192.168.88.141 lport 1274 duration 0:20:01 bytes 1438				
Mar 7 11:7:22	192.168.88.252	Accounting (23)	Informational (6)	conn end faddr
204.31.17.3 (ns.snoopy.com) fport 23 (telnet) gaddr 204.30.204.252 laddr 192.168.88.141 (johnson-pc.translation.com) lport 1272 (Unknown Service) duration 0:21:36 bytes 1864				
Mar 7 11:7:23	192.168.88.252	Accounting (23)	Informational (6)	conn start faddr
204.31.17.3 (ns.snoopy.com) fport 23 (telnet) gaddr 204.30.204.252 laddr 192.168.88.141 (johnson-pc.translation.com) lport 1284 (Unknown Service)				
Mar 7 11:7:58	192.168.88.252	Accounting (23)	Informational (6)	conn end faddr
204.31.17.3 (ns.snoopy.com) fport 23 (telnet) gaddr 204.30.204.252 laddr 192.168.88.141 (johnson-pc.translation.com) lport 1284 (Unknown Service) duration 0:00:34 bytes 319				
Mar 7 11:11:22	192.168.88.252	Accounting (23)	Informational (6)	conn start faddr
204.30.228.2 (gate.usdla.org) fport 3641 (Unknown Service) gaddr 204.30.204.21 laddr 192.168.88.21 (ntilocal.translation.com) lport 119 (nntp)				
Mar 7 11:13:5	192.168.88.252	Accounting (23)	Informational (6)	conn start faddr
204.31.33.1 (gate.translation.com) fport 2718 (Unknown Service) gaddr 204.30.204.3 laddr 192.168.88.3 (pao.translation.com) lport 25 (smtp)				
Mar 7 11:13:21	192.168.88.252	Accounting (23)	Informational (6)	conn end faddr
204.31.33.1 (gate.translation.com) fport 2718 (Unknown Service) gaddr 204.30.204.3 laddr 192.168.88.3 (pao.translation.com) lport 25 (smtp) duration 0:00:16 bytes 3742				

Security

Sendmail uses port 113 for IDENT purposes. Because the PIX Firewall is blocking IDENT, we see in Example D-22 apparent violations to port 113 on host 192.234.123.252. You can safely ignore these apparent violations.

Example D-22 *PIX Firewall Log of Apparent Violations to Port 113*

```
Feb 1 13:43:12 pix-in  deny tcp out 202.255.181.6 4739 in 192.234.123.252
113 flags SYN
Feb 1 13:43:24 pix-in  deny tcp out 202.247.130.38 1446 in 192.234.123.252
113 flags SYN
```

Example D-23 is a log of an attempt to Telnet to port 23 of 192.234.123.2 from 204.30.228.2:

Example D-23 *PIX Firewall Log of Attempt to Telnet*

```
Feb 15 18:09:52 pix-in deny tcp out 204.30.228.2 4042 in 192.234.123.2 23 flags SYN
```

Resource

The resource file reports at 15-minute intervals on issues such as license usage (see Example D-24).

Example D-24 *PIX Firewall Log of Resource File Report*

```
Feb  1 13:11:15 pix-in  conns 256 conns_used 2 xlate 249 xlate_used 16
Feb  1 13:24:11 pix-in  conns 256 conns_used 2 xlate 249 xlate_used 16
Feb  1 13:37:02 pix-in  conns 256 conns_used 4 xlate 249 xlate_used 16
```

NOTE   The first four fields (Feb 1 13:37:02 pix-in) are not part of the PIX Firewall output. These fields are prepended by the syslog daemon on the UNIX log host.

Some UNIX systems append an "ERR" string after the time field, which sometimes misleads users to believe that the PIX Firewall has an error.

The PIX Firewall sends warning messages to syslog upon reaching 80 percent or higher usage of the connection license (see Example D-25).

Example D-25 *PIX Firewall Log of Reaching High Usage of Connection License*

```
Feb 12 09:36:24 twoface-gw  PIX out of connections! 24/256
```

System

The system file in Example D-26 logs Telnet access.

Example D-26   *PIX Firewall Log of Logging Telnet Access*

```
Feb 1 13:56:14 pix-in PIX logged out at 192.234.123.2
Feb 1 14:00:28 pix-in PIX logged in from 192.234.123.2
Feb 1 14:00:55 pix-in PIX logged out at 192.234.123.2
```

NOTE   In this example, Telnet to the PIX Firewall is allowed only from 192.234.123.2.

Special Application: Connecting Networks with the Same IP Addresses

twonet.com has two networks with the same 192.9.200.X addresses. Normally, it would be impossible to connect the two networks without changing the address of one network. However, using two PIX Firewalls and two DNS servers, we can allow hosts to talk to servers on the other side of the network (see Figure D-8).

Figure D-8   *Connecting Two Networks with the Same IP Addresses*

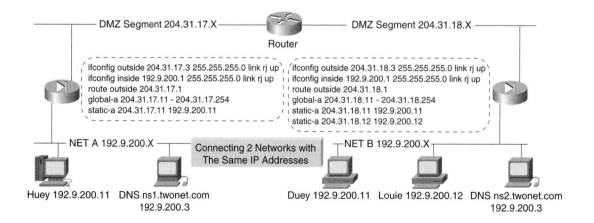

DNS for Network A Name Server

NS1 is the name server for network A. The named.boot file looks like the following:

directory	/var/named
cache	named.ca
primary twonet.com	named.zone
primary 192.9.200.in-addr.arpa	named.rev
primary 17.31.204.in-addr.arpa	global.rev

named.zone contains entries for:

ns1	IN	A	192.9.200.3
huey	IN	A	192.9.200.11
duey	IN	A	204.31.18.11
louie	IN	A	204.31.18.12

named.rev contains entries for:

3	IN	PTR	ns1.twonet.com.
11	IN	PTR	huey.twonet.com.

global.rev contains:

11	IN	PTR	huey.twonet.com.

as well as entries for dynamic mappings:

12	IN	PTR	a12.twonet.com.
......			
254	IN	PTR	a254.twonet.com.

DNS for Network B Name Server

NS2 is the name server for network B. The named.boot file looks like the following:

directory	/var/named
cache	. named.ca
primary twonet.com	named.zone
primary 192.9.200.in-addr.arpa	named.rev
primary 18.31.204.in-addr.arpa	global.rev

named.zone contains entries for:

ns2	IN	A	192.9.200.3
huey	IN	A	204.31.17.11
duey	IN	A	192.9.200.11
louie	IN	A	192.9.200.12

named.rev contains entries for:

3	IN	PTR	ns1.twonet.com.
11	IN	PTR	duey.twonet.com.
12	IN	PTR	louie.twonet.com.

global.rev contains:

11	IN	PTR	duey.twonet.com.
12	IN	PTR	louie.twonet.com.

as well as entries for dynamic mappings:

13	IN	PTR	b13.twonet.com.
......all the way thru			
254	IN	PTR	a254.twonet.com.

NOTE   The file named.ca in named.boot is the official cache file containing entries of the root name servers provided by ftp.internic.net. Therefore, access to the Internet will still be seamless.

PIX Firewall Configuration for Network A

Example D-27 shows the PIX Firewall configuration for Network A.

Example D-27   *Network A PIX Firewall Configuration*

```
ifconfig outside 204.31.17.3 255.255.255.0 link rj up
ifconfig inside 192.9.200.1 255.255.255.0 link rj up
route outside 204.31.17.1
global -a 204.31.17.11-204.31.17.254
static -a 204.31.17.11 192.9.200.11
```

PIX Firewall Configuration for Network B

Example D-28 shows the PIX Firewall configuration for Network B.

Example D-28   *Network B PIX Firewall Configuration*

```
ifconfig outside 204.31.18.3 255.255.255.0 link rj up
ifconfig inside 192.9.200.1 255.255.255.0 link rj up
route outside 204.31.18.1
global -a 204.31.18.11-204.31.18.254
static -a 204.31.18.11 192.9.200.11
static -a 204.31.18.12 192.9.200.12
```

NOTE   Statics are not required except for servers to which clients on the other network require access.

Issues with Simple Network Management Protocol— Configuring SNMP/Extended Remote Monitoring Across the PIX Firewall

The PIX Firewall itself does not support Simple Network Management Protocol (SNMP) as a manageable device.

The following cases describe how devices can be managed across the PIX Firewall.

SNMP Case 1

In Figure D-9, an SNMP monitoring station inside manages a Web server on the outside. A conduit is required for 222.111.222.2 to pass the SNMP traps to 192.9.200.2.

Figure D-9   *Setting Up SNMP across the PIX Firewall (Case 1)*

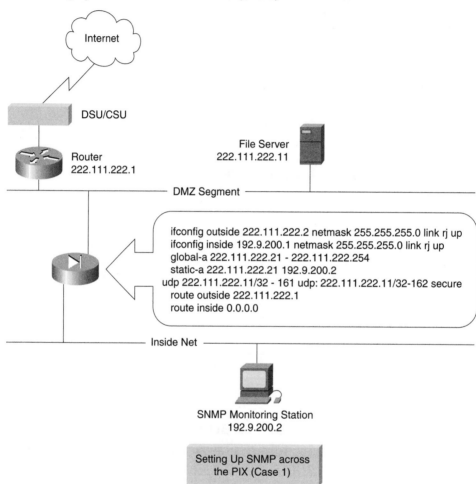

SNMP Case 2

In Figure D-10, the outside SNMP monitoring station manages the file server on the Internal network. The inside network must have a legitimate IP address so that the static translation for the file server is the same as the IP address of the server itself. The source IP address of the SNMP packet sent by the file server will be consistent with the IP address described in the SNMP data.

Figure D-10 *Setting Up SNMP across the PIX Firewall (Case 2)*

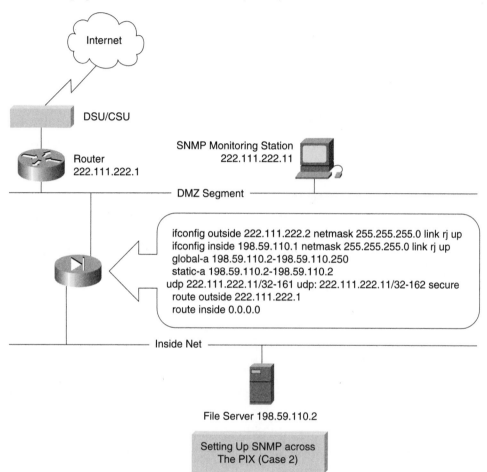

SNMP Case 3

In Figure D-11, the SNMP monitoring station will see an SNMP packet from 222.111.222.21 rather than from 192.9.200.2. This address is inconsistent with the address in the SNMP-protocol data unit (PDU) header of a trap PDU and with the address in a varbind in the varbindlist.

Figure D-11 *SNMP Will Not Work (Case 3)*

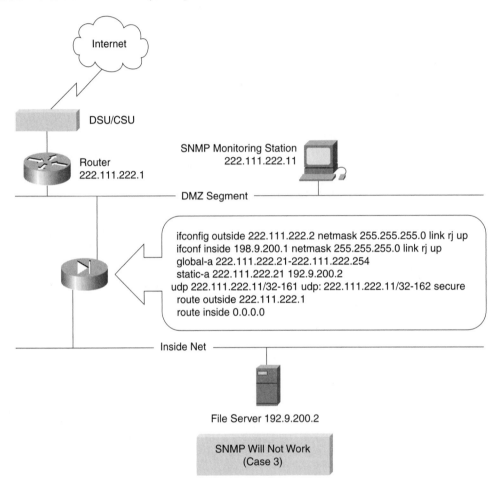

SNMP Case 4

In contrast with Case 3, if a PIX Private Link is used between the management station and the server, the network 192.9.200.X will be recognized as an immediate neighbor with no access restrictions. SNMP will work because the IP source of the packet from 192.9.200.2 will be received with no address modification. Additionally, the monitoring workstation can manage the PIX Firewall used at the customer site.

In Case 4, shown in Figure D-12, you must configure a reverse DNS entry for 200.9.192.IN-
ADDR.ARPA for the file server on the monitoring station to ensure that the name resolved from
192.9.200.2 is fs.foo.com and not the real owner of 192.9.200.X out on the Internet.

Figure D-12 *Establishing a Private Link to Manage the Customer's Network and PIX Firewall (Case 4)*

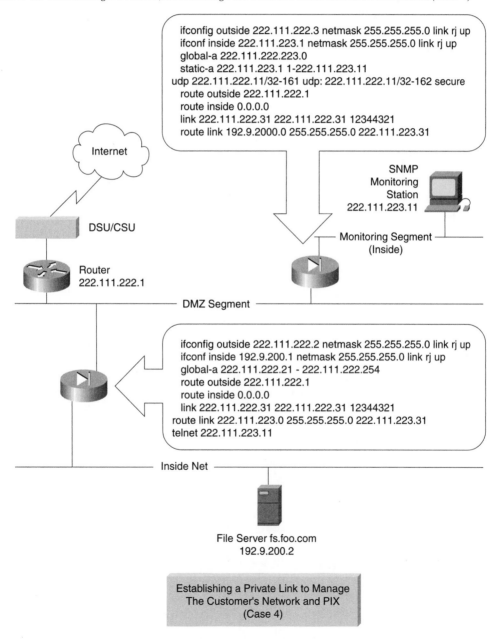

ifconfig outside 222.111.222.3 netmask 255.255.255.0 link rj up
ifconf inside 222.111.223.1 netmask 255.255.255.0 link rj up
global-a 222.111.222.223.0
static-a 222.111.223.1 1-222.111.223.11
udp 222.111.222.11/32-161 udp: 222.111.222.11/32-162 secure
route outside 222.111.222.1
route inside 0.0.0.0
link 222.111.222.31 222.111.222.31 12344321
route link 192.9.2000.0 255.255.255.0 222.111.223.31

Internet

SNMP
Monitoring
Station
222.111.223.11

DSU/CSU

Monitoring Segment
(Inside)

Router
222.111.222.1

DMZ Segment

ifconfig outside 222.111.222.2 netmask 255.255.255.0 link rj up
ifconf inside 192.9.200.1 netmask 255.255.255.0 link rj up
global-a 222.111.222.21 - 222.111.222.254
route outside 222.111.222.1
route inside 0.0.0.0
link 222.111.222.31 222.111.222.31 12344321
route link 222.111.223.0 255.255.255.0 222.111.223.31
telnet 222.111.223.11

Inside Net

File Server fs.foo.com
192.9.200.2

Establishing a Private Link to Manage
The Customer's Network and PIX
(Case 4)

This Router Performance Design and Implementation Guide was originally written by Merike Kaeo from the Enterprise Technical Marketing group at Cisco. It has been edited here for formatting.

Router Performance Design and Implementation Guide

With the proliferation of Cisco router products in the past few years and the ever-increasing features and functionality available, understanding some of the intricate interworkings of these devices is necessary to design optimal performance networks. In the early days of routers, raw packet-per-second performance was a valid concern, but with the increased improvements in processor power and memory management, the increasing performance numbers are reaching a point where perception and reality are becoming blurred. This paper focuses primarily on the realities of real network performance considerations and how the varying router platforms that Cisco provides can meet the appropriate criteria for any given network.

The network performance considerations will not address issues regarding latency of routers because, in a network system as a whole, latency per switch or router has been found to be negligible when compared to normal workstation or PC disk access speeds and lower-speed media bandwidth considerations.

It is important to note that raw performance numbers in packets per second should never be the sole criterion for choosing any product because criteria based on support responsiveness, company financials, feature enhancements, software reliability, troubleshooting capability, and a variety of other criteria factor heavily into a final product decision. Performance of the varying platforms should be understood to determine what meets the user's requirement, allowing for future growth and expansion of a user's network.

A description of how to determine what a user's performance requirements may be follows, including some sample calculations that can then be used as a guideline and extrapolated to fit into specific network designs. The traffic patterns and network applications may not be well understood in new network designs, but it is important for some investigation to be done to determine approximate traffic patterns and worst-case scenarios (not to be misconstrued as theoretical worst-case scenarios). Next, the switching paths of varying Cisco router platforms are listed and platform aggregate numbers are specified to help determine the most optimal platform in a given network design scenario. The last section of the paper lists some common features that may affect switching paths and gives general guidelines for optimum network designs.

Realities of Network Performance Criteria

The bottom line of any given network is that it becomes a medium whereby users (the people relying on the network to do their work) accomplish their jobs without incurring any noticeable delays. Performance criteria are met when every user is satisfied in terms of network responsiveness. To ensure user satisfaction, every aspect of the network must be examined, from the media to the applications to the individual devices creating the network as a whole. This task is complex.

Differentiating Performance Tests Versus Real Network Performance

Three areas require classification:

- What comprises a performance test?
- How does one interpret results?
- How does one compare the results to any realistic performance requirements?

The more common performance tests include blasting traffic from an input port to an output port of a device. For a given device, injecting traffic through multiple input ports to multiple output ports on the same device gives aggregate performance numbers. Usually, these tests are performed on Ethernet because Ethernet-based testers were the first available. Aggregate performance numbers are media-independent, but the type of media used plays an important role in defining what the theoretical packet-per-second limitation is. Table E-1 shows characteristics of some of the more common media in use today.

Table E-1   *Media Characteristics*

	Interframe Gap	Minimum Valid Frame	Maximum Valid Frame	Bandwidth
Ethernet	96 bits	64 bytes	1518 bytes	10 Mbps
Token Ring	4 bits	32 bytes	16K bytes	16 Mbps
Fiber Distributed Data Interface (FDDI)	0	34 bytes	4500 bytes	100 Mbps
Asynchronous Transfer Mode (ATM)	0	30 bytes (AAL5)	16K bytes (AAL5)	155 Mbps
Basic Rate Interface (BRI)	0	24 bytes (PPP)	1500 bytes (PPP)	128 kbps
Primary Rate Interface (PRI)	0	24 bytes (PPP)	1500 bytes (PPP)	1.472 Mbps
T1	0	14 bytes (HDLC)	None (Theoretical) 4500 (Real)	1.5 Mbps
Fast Ethernet	96 bits	64 bytes	1518 bytes	100 Mbps

Calculating the theoretical maximum packets per second involves all the variables listed in Table E-1: interframe gap, bandwidth, and frame size. The formula to compute this number is:

Bandwidth/Packet Size = Theoretical Maximum Packets per Second (where packet size may incorporate interframe gap in bits)

Table E-2 lists the theoretical packet-per-second limitations for three common media—10 Mbps Ethernet, 16 Mbps Token Ring, and FDDI—each for eight different Ethernet frame sizes. These eight frame sizes, widely used in the industry, are derived from the performance testing methodology as outlined in the Internet standard for device benchmarking in RFC 1944. The numbers are derived by using the above formula.

NOTE	RFC 1944 has recently been made obsolete by RFC 2544.

Table E-2   *Packet-per-Second Limitation*

Ethernet Size (bytes)	10-Mbps Ethernet (pps)	16-Mbps Token Ring (pps)	FDDI (pps)
64	14,880	24,691	152,439
128	8,445	13,793	85,616
256	4,528	7,326	45,620
512	2,349	3,780	23,585
768	1,586	2,547	15,903
1024	1,197	1,921	11,996
1280	961	1,542	9,630
1518	812	1,302	8,138

More specific detail in how the numbers in Table E-2 were derived for the three media (10 Mbps Ethernet, 16 Mbps Token Ring, and FDDI) follow.

10 Mbps Ethernet

The frame size needs to incorporate the data and header bytes as well as the bits used for the preamble and interframe gap, as shown in Figure E-1.

Figure E-1 *10 Mbps Ethernet Frames*

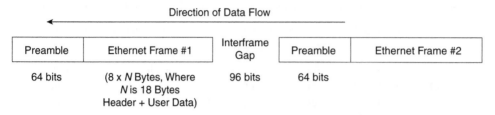

In Figure E-1 the fields have the following lengths:

- **Preamble**—64 bits
- **Frame**—(8×N) bits (where N is Ethernet packet size in bytes, this includes 18 bytes of header)
- **Gap**—96 bits

16 Mbps Token Ring

Neither token nor idles between packets are accounted for because the theoretical minima are hard to pin down, but by using only the frame format itself the maximum theoretical packets per second can be estimated, as shown in Figure E-2. Because we are basing our initial frame on an Ethernet frame, note that we need to subtract the Ethernet header bits for the correct calculation of the data portion. So, for a 64-byte Ethernet frame, we get $64 - 18 = 46$ bytes of data for the Data portion of the Token Ring frame shown in Figure E-2.

Figure E-2 *16-Mbps Token Ring Frames*

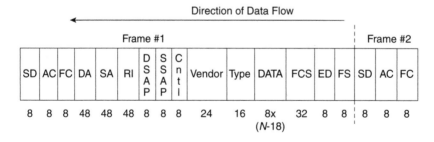

In Figure E-2 the fields have the following lengths:

- **SD**—8 bits
- **AC**—8 bits
- **FC**—8 bits
- **DA**—48 bits
- **SA**—48 bits
- **RI**—48 bits

- **DSAP**—8 bits
- **SSAP**—8 bits
- **Control**—8 bits
- **Vendor**—24 bits
- **Type**—16 bits
- **Data**—8×(N–18) bits (where N is original Ethernet frame size)
- **FCS**—32 bits
- **ED**—8 bits
- **FS**—8 bits

FDDI

Neither token nor idles between packets are accounted for because the theoretical minima are hard to pin down, but by using only the frame format itself the maximum theoretical packets per second can be estimated, as shown in Figure E-3. Note that, because we are basing our initial frame on an Ethernet frame, we need to subtract the Ethernet header bits for the correct calculation of the data portion. So, for a 64 byte Ethernet frame, we get 64 – 18 = 46 bytes of data for the Data portion of the FDDI frame shown in Figure E-3.

Figure E-3   *FDDI Frames*

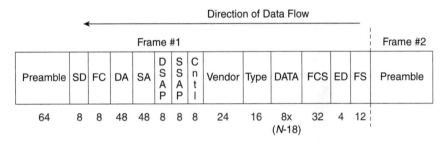

In Figure E-3 the fields have the following lengths:

- **Preamble**—64 bits
- **SD**—8 bits
- **FC**—8 bits
- **DA**—48 bits
- **SA**—48 bits
- **DSAP**—8 bits
- **SSAP**—8 bits
- **Control**—8 bits

- **Vendor**—24 bits
- **Type**—16 bits
- **Data**—8×(N–18) bits (where N is original Ethernet frame size)
- **FCS**—32 bits
- **ED**—4 bits
- **FS**—12 bits

Frame and Packet Size

The packet size is a major factor in determining the maximum packets per second, and, in the theoretical test world, one packet size at a time is tested. Eight standard packet sizes are tested: 64-, 128-, 256-, 512-, 768-, 1024-, 1280-, and 1518-byte packets. Figure E-4 shows a graph of the theoretical maximum packets per second for 10 Mbps Ethernet.

It is important to note that as the frame size increases, the maximum theoretical packets per second decrease.

Figure E-4 *10 Mbps Ethernet Theoretical Performance*

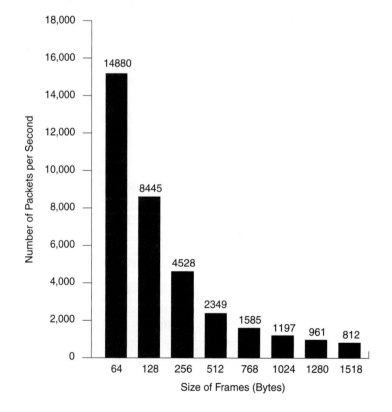

Having seen how maximum theoretical performance is determined, we now see how that data fits in with the performance requirements of real user networks. Each medium has a specific fixed-size bandwidth pipe associated with it, and each one may or may not define a minimum and maximum valid frame size. The minimum and maximum frame sizes are important because most good applications written for workstations or PCs make efficient use of bandwidth available and use maximum-sized frames. The smaller the frame size, the higher the percentage of overhead relative to user data; in other words, smaller frame sizes mean less effective bandwidth utilization as illustrated in Figure E-5.

Figure E-5   *Bandwidth Efficiency for Small Versus Large Frames*

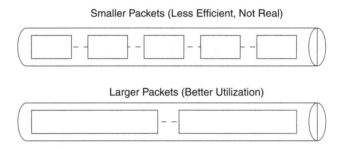

Bandwidth + Packet Size = Theoretical Performance

Smaller Packets (Less Efficient, Not Real)

Larger Packets (Better Utilization)

An understanding of real traffic patterns is important when designing networks. At least some typical applications should be known so that the average packet sizes on the network can be determined. Sniffer traces to look at typical packet sizes for varying applications are helpful; some of the more common ones include:

- **Hypertext Transfer Protocol (HTTP) (World Wide Web)**—400 to 1518 bytes
- **Network File System (NFS)**—64 to 1518 bytes
- **Telnet**—64 to 1518 bytes
- **NetWare**—500 to 1518 bytes
- **Multimedia**—400 to 700 bytes

For optimal network designs, an understanding of the kinds of applications that will be used is necessary to determine the typical packet sizes that will be traversing your network. The following example, taken from a real network, shows how to optimize your network design.

Example

Consider a very simple network, depicted in Figure E-6.

Figure E-6   *Sample Network*

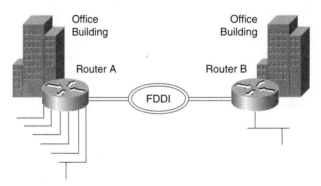

The network consists of six Ethernet networks that are interconnected via an FDDI backbone. Router A interconnects the Ethernet networks to the FDDI backbone. For simplicity, we assume that all the Ethernets have traffic characteristics similar to those shown in Figure E-7.

Figure E-7   *Graph of Typical Ethernet Network*

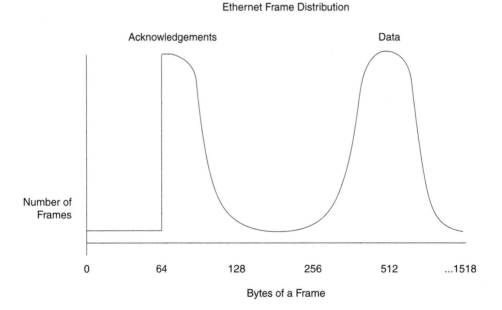

Most of the traffic falls between 256-byte and 1280-byte packets, with numerous 64-byte packets that are typically acknowledgment packets. Our calculations assume that the Ethernet network is fairly busy with average utilization at 40 percent; in other words, 4 Mbps of Ethernet bandwidth is utilized. For average traffic rates, 40 percent utilization of Ethernet bandwidth is a rather heavily utilized network because collisions are very probable and most of the traffic on the network is retransmission traffic. However, the example is intended to show a worst-case, real-world performance scenario.

For simplicity, we assume that the following traffic is on the Ethernet:

- 768-byte packets, 35%
- 1280-byte packets, 20%
- 512-byte packets, 15%
- 64-byte packets, 30%

To calculate the total packets per second that would be on the Ethernet, we need to apply the following formula for each of the different packet sizes: (Bandwidth × Percent Media Used)/ (Packet Size × bits/byte) = Packets per Second.

Using this formula yields:

- (4 Mbps × 35%)/(768 bytes × 8 bits/byte) = 228 pps
- (4 Mbps × 20%)/(1280 bytes × 8 bits/byte) = 79 pps
- (4 Mbps × 15%)/(512 bytes × 8 bits/byte) = 147 pps
- (4 Mbps × 30%)/(64 bytes × 8 bits/byte) = 2344 pps

The total, 2798 pps, is *not* the pps rate that goes through the router. If it is, the network design is not optimal and should be changed. Rather, the 80/20 rule applies to most nonswitched networks, where 80 percent of the traffic stays on the local network and 20 percent goes to a different destination. Then we have 2798 × 20% = 560 pps that the router must deal with from that single Ethernet network. If we take six Ethernets with similar characteristics, we get an aggregate of 3360 pps that the router must support.

Now consider a scenario with central servers and assume that the 80/20 rule does not apply; only 10 percent of the traffic stays local and 90 percent goes through the router to the servers that are off the backbone. In this scenario, the router must support 6 × (2798 × 90%) = 15,110 pps for our example of six Ethernets. The appropriate router platform must be chosen that will meet the traffic requirements.

This example shows how the packets-per-second requirement for varying networks is computed. As will be shown in subsequent sections, all Cisco router platforms meet and greatly exceed the pure packets-per-second requirements of real networks.

Router Platform Switching Paths

This section will list the switching paths that the various router platforms support.

Low-End/Midrange Routers

This category of routers includes the Cisco 2500, 4000, 4500, and 4700 series routers. The switching paths supported for these routers are process switching and fast switching. Fast switching is on by default for all protocols.

The aggregate performance numbers in packets per second are listed in Table E-3.

Table E-3 *Aggregate Maximum Performance for Low-End/Midrange Routers (in Packets-per-Second)*

Switching Paths	2500 Series	4000	4500	4700
Process Switching	1,000	1,800	10,000	11,000
Fast Switching	6,000	14,000	45,000	50,000

Features Affecting Performance

Understanding how a given feature will affect the router's switching paths is critical when designing networks. Many new features are initially incorporated into the process switching path and, in subsequent releases, incorporated into faster switching paths. The most current enhancements are listed in Cisco Connection Online (CCO) under Technical Assistance/Tech Tips: Hot Tips/IOS Information. There you will find new features for Cisco Internetwork Operating System (Cisco IOS™) releases and any performance enhancements to previously implemented features.

Low-End and Midrange Router Memory Considerations

Most performance concerns arise from the need for sufficient memory to run in certain environments and the necessity to prevent overstrain on the CPU. The memory considerations are primarily issues for the low-end and midrange platforms. Product Bulletins #284 and #290 address these issues for the Cisco 4000 and 2500 series routers, respectively. They can be accessed via the Web as follows:

- **PB # 284**—http://www.cisco.com/warp/customer/417/49.html
- **PB # 290**—http://www.cisco.com/warp/partner/synchronicd/
  cc/cisco/mkt/access/2500/290_pb.htm

NOTE   Only registered users can access these product bulletins on Cisco's Web site. Contact your Cisco representative for details on obtaining an account if you do not already have one.

Other Considerations

Additional features that affect CPU utilization are link-state routing protocols, such as Open Shortest Path First (OSPF) and NetWare Link Services Protocol (NLSP), tunneling, access lists, accounting, Layer 2 Forwarding (L2F), multichassis multilink Point-to-Point Protocol (MP), queuing, compression, and encryption.

No boilerplate mechanism that gives hard-and-fast platform limitations exists. What needs to be considered is that for any given platform, the number of interfaces you can support depends greatly on the encapsulations and features used. The aggregate maximum packets per second is a useful number for approximating the maximum number of interfaces to put into a given platform, as long as some real-world analysis of the traffic flow is done. If designs follow a more theoretical maximum packets-per-second approach, the Cisco routers will be greatly underutilized.

Some common rules to follow include:

- Because access lists are checked sequentially, always optimize your access lists so that most traffic meets the criteria of the first entries of the list. If a customer has extensive access lists and this problem is the major performance bottleneck, it may be time to look at a higher performance router.

- Custom, priority, and weighted-fair-queuing activate only when the serial line is congested. As of Release 11.1 they are fast-switched; as long as the serial line is not congested, the fastest switching path that the interface supports and is configured for will be used.

- For low-end and midrange router platforms, compression should be performed for serial lines running at 128 kbps or lower. At higher line rates, compression may tax the CPU.

- Encryption is very CPU- and memory-intensive, so careful consideration of appropriate platforms is necessary.

Network Design Guidelines

Some common network designs are suboptimal in terms of performance; most of these are based on media mismatch as illustrated in Figure E-8.

Figure E-8 *Media Mismatch*

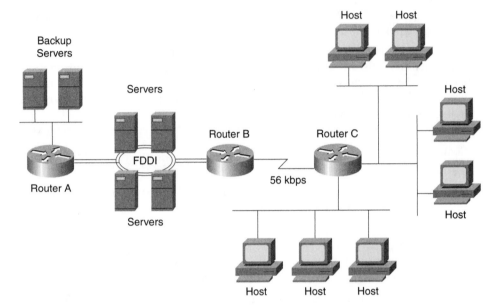

This scenario shows two separate cases of common media mismatch problems. The first problem is between Router B and Router C where multiple clients are trying to access a centralized server farm. What may not be obvious at first glance is that the 56-kbps line is the primary connection between the clients and the servers, and it will quickly become oversubscribed with traffic. At the very least, enough bandwidth to support the maximum expected peak traffic between the clients and servers should be in place. Or, if certain Ethernet segments make extensive use of a particular server, distributing servers to local Ethernet segments will greatly improve network performance.

The second performance problem is through Router A, where the server farm gets backed up to a network of backup servers. The media mismatch from 100 Mbps FDDI to 10 Mbps Ethernet is the bottleneck. To gain optimal performance for high-speed backups going through the router, the media speeds should be maximized.

Conclusion

Choosing the appropriate router interface media and router platform is important to designing optimized performance networks. Choose the appropriate media by understanding what the average and peak traffic flows are for different points of the network. At the very least, an approximate calculation can be performed for worst-case traffic scenarios. Next, the appropriate protocol feature set needs to be determined to ensure that sufficient memory and CPU requirements are met. Armed with the knowledge of media interfaces, memory, and CPU requirements, the appropriate router platform for a given scenario should be clear.

This ISDN Design and Implementation Guide was originally produced by Cisco and has been edited here for formatting.

This guide contains some information on older products and software. The Cisco 750 series of routers has now been replaced by the 760 and 770 series, and some of the configuration commands for these routers have changed. Versions of the IOS™ software released since the 11.0(3) version mentioned herein have additional features than those included in this guide. However, this guide does provide useful information regarding the design and implementation of ISDN networks. Refer to the Cisco 760 and 770 series documentation and the latest version of the IOS documentation for further information.

ISDN Design and Implementation Guide

Like many of today's technologies, Integrated Services Digital Network (ISDN) is rapidly growing and changing. As a result of these changes, Cisco is constantly refining both its product offerings and its software features.

Most notable is the acquisition of Combinet, Inc., which helps to expand Cisco's low-end ISDN product offerings. The first wave of new products comprise the 750 series, a new line of low-end ISDN solutions for homes and small offices.

Cisco has also released a set of new software features as part of Release 11.0 (3) of the Cisco IOS™ software. These features are designed to make more efficient and effective use of ISDN services with Cisco products.

This addendum is intended to address the new additions to the Cisco product line as well as provide in-depth coverage of the latest ISDN-related Cisco IOS features.

The Combinet Acquisition

Cisco's acquisition of Combinet, Inc. extends Cisco's ISDN offerings to small offices, home offices, and individual users.

The Combinet products give Cisco an instant presence in the fast-growing telecommuting market. In particular, the Combinet 2000 series brings to Cisco a family of low-cost, entry-level ISDN products that support IP and IPX routing, bridging, Simple Network Management Protocol (SNMP) management, and multilevel security. Combinet has a 27 percent share of the U.S. telecommuting market, and its products are available in over 20 countries.

In addition to the 2000 series, the Combinet product line includes a family of ISA bus PC adapter cards, an ISDN Primary Rate Interface (PRI) product for central site applications, and Connection Manager, a Windows-based call management, device configuration, and accounting application.

Versions of the Combinet 2000 series products were introduced into the Cisco and CiscoPro™ product lines beginning in November 1995. Enterprise products will be known as the Cisco 750 series, and products intended for the two-tier channel will be known as the CiscoPro 750 series.

Product Positioning: Cisco 750 and Cisco 1000

The Cisco 750 series provides an ISDN access solution that is complementary to the Cisco 1000 family. Although the Cisco 1000 series is ideal for branch office connectivity, the Cisco 750 series is targeted toward telecommuters, professional offices, and home offices that need IP and IPX routing functionality over ISDN.

The Cisco 750 series represents the lowest-cost entry point into the Cisco family of access routers, and provides an optional analog plain old telephone service (POTS) interface (Cisco 753) to reduce the overall cost of the telecommuting solution. The ConnectPro software provides a Windows-based graphical user interface that simplifies the process of installing, configuring, and managing Cisco 750 series products.

The standard version of the Cisco 750 series supports up to four devices on the directly attached LAN. A software upgrade option is available for users who require support for more than four devices on the local LAN.

The Cisco 1000 series is targeted at remote offices and branch offices. It features IP, IPX, and AppleTalk routing, as well as advanced routing protocols, such as Enhanced IGRP and snapshot routing. The Cisco 1000 series also supports priority queuing and custom queuing to optimize WAN bandwidth utilization.

Table F-1 provides a feature comparison of the Cisco 750 and Cisco 1000 products.

Table F-1   *Cisco 750 and Cisco 1000 Feature Comparison*

Cisco 750	Cisco 1000
Telecommuter, home office professional office	Branch office, remote office
IP and IPX routing	IP, IPX, and AppleTalk routing
Low cost	Enhanced IGRP
ConnectPro and personal network profiles	Optional Flash ROM
Optional POTS integration	PCMCIA card
Up to four LAN devices (standard version)	No restriction on LAN devices

Combinet Product Line

Although not all Combinet products have been integrated into the Cisco product line, Table F-2 is a brief overview of ConnectPro Combinet's complete product offerings.

Table F-2   *ConnectPro Combinet Product Offerings*

Product	Description	Target Market
PF-1000	PC ISA card BRI	Telecommuting, single-user Internet access
CB-2000	Ethernet/BRI IP/IPX router	Telecommuting, professional office, Internet
CB-900	Ethernet/PRI IP/IPX router	Telecommuting, regional office
Connection Manager	Windows-based remote access management application	
ConnectPro	Windows-based GUI configuration tool	

The CB-2000 products are available in four versions as detailed in Table F-3.

Table F-3   *CB-2000 Versions*

Product	Description
CB-2050B	ISDN router—four network devices
CB-2050D	ISDN router—unrestricted devices
CB-2060A	ISDN router with NT1—four network devices
CB-2060D	ISDN router with NT1—unrestricted devices

The Combinet 2050B was introduced in the Cisco enterprise product line as the Cisco 751, and the 2060A will become the Cisco 752. Features and functionality of the Cisco and CiscoPro versions will be differentiated over time.

The Cisco 753 is a newer product that includes a basic telephone service interface and a built-in Network Termination 1 (NT1). The telephone service interface allows a standard analog telephone, fax machine, or modem to share the ISDN BRI line with data traffic.

<table>
<tr>
<td>**NOTE**</td>
<td>The following section, "Cisco 750 Series Configuration," details the concepts and terminology used in the configuration of the 750 series routers. This family of routers does not run the IOS software, and therefore has a different user interface and uses different commands than other Cisco routers. Example configurations for 750 series routers are provided in this section, along with configuration examples for a Cisco 4500 series router that would communicate with the 750 series routers. The Cisco 4500 series routers do run the IOS software, and this paper assumes that the reader is familiar with the user interface and commands for IOS routers. The Cisco 1000 series routers, mentioned previously, also run the IOS software and would therefore have a configuration similar to the Cisco 4500 series routers.

For further information on the IOS user interface and commands, refer to the Cisco IOS documentation on Cisco's web site.</td>
</tr>
</table>

Cisco 750 Series Configuration

This section discusses the operation of the 750 series routers and provides configuration examples for various functions available within these routers. Topics addressed include:

- Use of profiles
- Profile parameters
- System parameters
- Basic setup
- Sample configurations
- Advanced configurations

Use of Profiles

The 750 Series products provide for varying profiles, which are a set of configurations customized for and associated with a specific remote device. Once defined by the user, profiles are stored and saved in NVRAM.

The profile types supported are as follows:

- **Permanent**—Can be modified but not deleted.
  - **LAN**—Determines how data is passed from a router to the LAN.
  - **Standard**—Used for incoming ISDN connections that do not have profiles; does not support routing. It should be used to provide the appropriate configuration and security measures for unknown callers.
  - **Internal**—Determines how data is passed between the bridge engine and the IP/IPX router.

- **User**—Set up for each individual user/remote site; up to 17 profiles can be configured in 750 series units. Note: Due to memory limitations and depending on the complexity of the profiles, 17 profiles may be unattainable. Remember, however, that these products are intended for the house and small office so 17 profiles are probably not needed.

Profile Parameters

Profile parameters can be configured on a per-profile basis and apply solely to the specific profile. Any configuration changes to profile parameters while in profile mode apply only to that profile. The following are all profile parameters:

- Auto Calling
- Bridge Type Filters
- Bridging
- Callback
- Callback ID Security
- Callback Receive Numbers
- Called Number
- CHAP Host Secret
- Compression
- Demand Parameters
- Encapsulation
- IP Parameters
- IPX Parameters
- Learning
- Line Speed
- Loopback
- PAP Host Password
- Passwords
- PPP Authentication Outgoing
- Protocol
- Ringback Number

System Parameters

System parameters are independent of profiles and affect the router as a system. System parameters can be changed only at the system-level prompt. If modified while in profile mode, they will apply to all profiles. The following are all system parameters:

- Caller ID Parameters
- Date and Time
- Delay Times
- Directory Number
- Forwarding Mode
- Multidestination
- Numbering Plan
- Passthru
- Patterns
- PPP Parameters
- PS 1 Detect
- Screen Echo
- Screen Length
- SNMP Parameters
- System Passwords

Changing any profile parameters at the system level changes the values for the profile template.

To simplify configuring a multitude of profiles, a profile template can be configured at the system level to configure the same profile parameters throughout all profiles. Any profile that has a specific profile parameter redefined within the profile is not affected by a change to the profile template configuration.

Basic Setup

After a Cisco 750 series unit is cabled and powered on, ensure that the Line and NT1 LEDs are illuminated. Use the LED status to verify that the ISDN line and built-in NT1 are functioning. Then use the **show config** command to verify current ISDN-specific settings.

Enter the commands detailed in Table F-4 at the system level to configure ISDN parameters to adhere to a site's specific ISDN setup:

Table F-4   *Commands to Configure ISDN Parameters for an ISDN Site-Specific Setup*

Command	Function
set switch [type]	(default is 5ess) Refer to documentation for ISDN switch support
set directory [*number*]	Directory number assigned by local telephone company
set [*spid id*] **SPID** [*SPID number*]	Number identifying service to which you have subscribed

To test the ISDN connection, change to profile mode (**cd test**) and place a call from one B channel to a second one with the following command:

```
call [channel] [number]
```

The channel is either B1 or B2, and the *number* is the phone number associated with the BRI interface. Once the connection is working, you can be assured that the local site has its ISDN line ready for configurations to the remote site.

Sample Configurations

The following section shows sample configurations for the network depicted in Figure F-1. The Cisco 4500 BRI router is acting as a branch office router connecting multiple incoming telecommuters from around the area who are using Cisco 750 Series routers.

Figure F-1 *Cisco 750/Cisco IOS Network Design Scenarios*

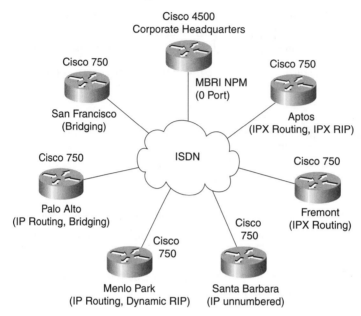

A Brief Note about the Cisco 750 Series User Interface

For UNIX and DOS users, the Cisco 750 Series user interface will be familiar ground. The Cisco 750 Series interface is command-line driven and uses the concept of a root directory and subdirectories to configure parameters. The root directory or system level is represented using the ">" symbol. If the **set system name** command is used to assign a name to the device, the root prompt will change to reflect the new system name. For example, **set system name jackstraw** will change the root prompt to "jackstraw>."

The subdirectories come into play when configuring profiles. To configure the LAN profile or a user profile, you must navigate to the respective subdirectory. Navigating subdirectories is done by using the **cd** command, just like UNIX or DOS. Typing **cd lan** will move you to the LAN profile. The prompt will change to ":LAN>" to reflect this move. For user profiles, the **set user <user profile name>** command will automatically move you into the newly created user profile subdirectory. For example **jackstraw set user stellablue** will automatically put you in the ":stellablue>" subdirectory. The command **cd** will return you to the system level.

It is also important to note that commands need not be input in full in order for them to be accepted. For example, to enter a system name the **set system name <system name>** command can be abbreviated as follows: **SE SY <system name>**. The best place to go to familiarize yourself with the Cisco 750 Series abbreviated commands is the Cisco 750 Series manual.

The manual is extremely useful from this standpoint as well as for learning more about the units and all of the different command options.

The section that follows provides a variety of different configurations for connecting Cisco 750 Series units to Cisco IOS-based units. The Cisco 750 Series syntax provided is intended to illustrate the requisite commands. The configurations, however, do not show the prompt and therefore do not reflect directory changes.

Configuring Bridging Profiles

Use the configuration in Table F-5 for the Cisco 750 Series router in San Francisco, which only needs to bridge.

Table F-5   *Configuring Bridging Profiles for the San Francisco Cisco 750 Series Router in Figure F-1*

Command	Function
set system sanfrancisco	System name cannot exceed 16 characters
set wan mode any	Enable bridging unknown packets to the WAN
set user sanjose	Creates profile named San Jose—profiles can be up to 20 characters long
set encapsulation ppp	
set number 5551212	Remote router's ISDN number
cd	Return to root prompt
reboot	Enables modifications

Table F-6 shows the configuration of the Cisco 4500 using bri0 to communicate with the router in San Francisco.

Table F-6   *Configuring Bridging on the Cisco 4500 Series Router in Figure F-1*

Command	Function
hostname sanjose	
!	
username sanfrancisco	
no ip routing	Disables IP routing
isdn switch-type basic-5ess	
!	

continues

Table F-6   *Configuring Bridging on the Cisco 4500 Series Router in Figure F-1 (Continued)*

Interface Ethernet0	
no ip address	
no mop enabled	
bridge-group 1	Enables bridging for interface
no shutdown	
!	
Interface BRI0	
no ip address	
Encapsulation ppp	
dialer map bridge name sanfrancisco 5551414	Dialer map to call the Cisco 750's BRI interface
no ip route-cache	
dialer-group 1	Assigns the dialer list 1 to interface BRI 0
bridge-group 1	Enables bridging for interface
bridge-group 1 spanning-disabled	Disables BPDU transmissions
no shutdown	
!	
!	
dialer-list 1 protocol bridge permit	Permits bridge traffic over the ISDN link
bridge 1 multicast-source	Permits the forwarding of multicast frames
bridge 1 protocol ieee	Enables IEEE bridging

Configuring IP Routing Profiles

IP Static Routing

The configuration detailed in Table F-7 is used for the Cisco 750 Series router in Palo Alto, which needs to route IP. A default static route is used to get to the branch office and beyond.

Table F-7 *Configuring Static IP Routing for the Palo Alto Cisco 750 Series Router in Figure F-1*

Command	Function
set system paloalto	
cd lan	
set ip address 150.150.150.1	IP address for local Ethernet
set ip netmask 255.255.255.0	
set ip routing on	
set ip rip update periodic	Enables periodic RIP updates (every 30 sec.)
cd	
set user sanjose	
set ip address 150.150.151.2	IP address for local BRI interface
set ip netmask 255.255.255.0	
set ip routing on	Enables IP routing
set ip framing none	Enables IPCP
set ip rip update off	Disables RIP on this profile
set encapsulation ppp	
set ip route destination 200.200.200.0/24 gateway 150.150.151.1 pr=on	Static route entry; "pr=on" propagates the static route
set number 5551212	
set timeout=30	Idle timeout value
set bridging=off	
cd reboot	

Table F-8 shows the configuration of the Cisco 4500 using bri0 to communicate with the router in Palo Alto. A static route is used to get to the 750's Ethernet.

Table F-8   *Configuring a Static Route on the Cisco 4500 Series Router in Figure F-1*

Command	Function
hostname sanjose	
!	
username paloalto	
ip routing	
isdn switch-type basic-5ess	
!	
interface Ethernet0	
ip address 200.200.200.1 255.255.255.0	
no shutdown	
!	
interface BRI0	
ip address 150.150.151.1 255.255.255.0	
encapsulation ppp	
dialer map ip 150.150.151.2 name paloalto 5551414	Dialer map pointing to the Cisco 750's BRI interface
no ip route-cache	
dialer-group 1	
no shutdown	
!	
router rip	
redistribute static	
passive interface b 0	Disables RIP updates on the int b 0
network 200.200.200.0	
redistribute connected	
ip route 150.150.150.0 255.255.255.0 150.150.151.2	Static route to the Cisco 750's Ethernet
dialer-list 1 protocol ip permit	Permits IP packets over the ISDN link

IP Dynamic Routing

Use the configuration detailed in Table F-9 for the Cisco 750 Series router in Menlo Park, which needs to route IP. RIP is used as the dynamic IP routing protocol. Bridging is disabled in this example.

Table F-9   *Configuring Dynamic IP Routing for the Menlo Park Cisco 750 Series Router in Figure F-1*

Command	Function
set system menlopark	
cd lan	
set ip address 150.150.150.1	
set ip netmask 255.255.255.0	
set ip routing on	
set ip rip update periodic	
cd	
set user sanjose	
set ip address 150.150.151.2	
set ip netmask 255.255.255.0	
set ip routing on	
set ip rip update periodic	Enables RIP on this profile
set encapsulation ppp	
set ip framing none	
set number 5551212	
set bridging=off	Disables bridging on this profile
cd	
reboot	

Table F-10 details the configuration of the Cisco 4500 using bri0 to communicate with the router in Melno Park. RIP is configured as the routing protocol.

Table F-10   *Configuring RIP on the Cisco 4500 Series Router in Figure F-1*

Command	Function
hostname sanjose	
!	
username menlopark	
isdn switch-type basic-5ess	
!	
interface Ethernet0	
ip address 200.200.200.1 255.255.255.0	
no mop enabled	
no shutdown	
!	
interface BRI0	
ip address 150.150.151.1 255.255.255.0	
encapsulation ppp	
dialer map ip 150.150.151.2 name menlopark 5551414	
dialer-group 1	
no shutdown	
!	
router rip	Enters RIP configuration mode
network 200.200.200.0	Enables RIP for network 200.200.200.0
network 150.150.0.0	Enables RIP for network 150.150.0.0
!	
!	
Dialer-list 1 protocol ip permit	

IP Unnumbered

An IP connection may be unnumbered only if *all* of the following criteria are met:

- The connection is a WAN connection (not the internal or LAN connection) to a router or single node.
- PPP IPCP encapsulation is being used (framing is set to NONE).
- Static routes, *not* periodic or demand RIP, are being used to establish routes to the connection.

An IP connection can be made unnumbered by setting its IP address to 0.0.0.0. Static routes should be created for unnumbered connections by issuing a **set ip route** field in the connection's profile. The gateway field in the **set ip route** command should be set to 0.0.0.0. Example F-1 shows an example configuration of creating an unnumbered IP connection on a Cisco 750 series router.

Example F-1   *An Unnumbered IP Connection Configuration on a Cisco 750 Series Router*

```
set ip framing none
set ip address 0.0.0.0
set ip rip update off
set ip rip receive off
set ip route dest 144.172.17.0/24 gateway 0.0.0.0
set ip routing on
```

Table F-11 details how you would configure a Cisco 750 Series router in Santa Barbara using IP unnumbered.

Table F-11   *Configuring IP Unnumbered for the Santa Barbara Cisco 750 Series Router in Figure F-1*

Command	Function
set system santabarbara	
cd lan	
set ip address 150.150.150.1	
set ip netmask 255.255.255.0	
set ip routing on	
set ip rip update periodic	
cd	
set user sanjose	
set ip routing on	Enables IPCP on this profile
set ip framing none	
set ip rip update off	Disables RIP updates
set encapsulation ppp	
set ip route destination 0.0.0.0 ga 0.0.0.0	
set number 5551212	
set timeout=30	
set bridging=off	Disables bridging on this profile
cd	
reboot	

Table F-12 details the configuration of the Cisco 4500 using unnumbered bri0 to communicate with the router in Santa Barbara.

Table F-12   *Configuring IP Unnumbered on the Cisco 4500 Series Router in Figure F-1*

Command	Function
hostname sanjose	
!	
username santabarbara	
isdn switch-type basic-5ess	
!	
interface Ethernet0	
ip address 200.200.200.1 255.255.255.0	
no mop enabled	
no shutdown	
!	
interface BRI0	
ip unnumbered Ethernet0	Enables IP on BRI 0; BRI 0 uses the ethernet 0 IP address (200.200.200.1)
encapsulation ppp	
dialer map ip 150.150.150.1 name santabarbara 5551414	
dialer-group 1	
no shutdown	
!	
router rip	
redistribute static	
passive interface b 0	RIP updates are not sent on interface BRI 0
network 200.200.200.0	
!	
ip route 150.150.150.0 255.255.255.0 BRI0	
!	
access-list 101 permit ip any any	
!	
dialer-list 1 list 101	

Configuring IPX Routing Profiles

The Cisco 750 series routers support IPX static routing and dynamic routing; examples are provided in the following sections. Combinet does not support the IPX/SPX default gateway, however.

IPX Static Routing

The configuration in Table F-13 is for a Cisco 750 Series router in Fremont that routes IPX. A static route is used back to corporate headquarters. The Cisco 750 Series router supports up to 15 static IPX routes.

Table F-13   *Configuring Static IPX Routing for the Fremont Cisco 750 Series Router in Figure F-1*

Command	Function
set system fremont	
set user sanjose	
cd sanjose	
set ipx network 100	
set ipx routing on	
set ipx rip update off	
set encapsulation ppp	
set ipx framing none	Enables IPXCP framing
set number 5551212	
set timeout=30	
set ipx route destination=200 gateway=100:0000c6067f5a	Static route to Cisco 4500's Ethernet
set ipx route destination=3039e670 gateway=100:0000c6067f5a	Static route to NetWare server's internal network
set ipx server name corp_fs1 ty 4 address 3039e670:01:0451	Static IPX SAP entry
set bridging=off	
cd	
cd lan	
set ipx network 150	
set ipx framing 802.2	
set ipx routing on	
set ipx rip update periodic	
cd	
Reboot	

Table F-14 details the configuration of the Cisco 4500 using bri0 to communicate with the router in Fremont. IPX static routes are configured.

Table F-14   *Configuring IPX Static Routes on the Cisco 4500 Series Router in Figure F-1*

Command	Function
hostname sanjose	
!	
username fremont	
!	
no ip routing	
ipx routing 0000.0c3b.c743	Enables IPX routing
isdn switch-type basic-5ess	
!	
interface Ethernet0	
ipx network 200	Configures IPX address on interface ethernet 0 (this also automatically enables IPX RIP on the interface)
ipx encapsulation sap	Configures IPX frame type
no mop enabled	
no shutdown	
!	
interface BRI0	
encapsulation ppp	
ipx network 100	Configures IPX address on interface BRI 0 (this also automatically enables IPX RIP on the interface)
dialer map ipx 100.0040.f902.c7b4 name fremont 5551414	Dialer map pointing to Fremont's BRI interface
no shutdown	
!	
ipx route 150 100.0040.f902.c7b4	Static route to Fremont's Ethernet
!	
ipx router rip	

continues

Table F-14   *Configuring IPX Static Routes on the Cisco 4500 Series Router in Figure F-1 (Continued)*

Command	Function
no network 100	Disables IPX RIP on interface BRI 0
!	
dialer-list 1 protocol ipx permit	Permits IPX packets over the ISDN link

IPX Dynamic Routing

Table F-15 shows the configuration for a Cisco 750 Series router in Aptos that routes IPX and wants to use periodic RIP updates:

Table F-15   *Configuring IPX with Periodic RIP Updates for the Aptos Cisco 750 Series Router in Figure F-1*

Command	Function
set system aptos	
set user sanjose	
cd sanjose	
set ipx network 100	
set ipx routing on	
set ipx rip update periodic	Enables periodic IPX RIP on this profile
set ipx framing none	
set encapsulation ppp	
set number 5551212	
set timeout=30	
set br=off	Disables bridging on this profile
cd	
cd lan	
set ipx network 150	
set ipx fr 802.2	
set ipx routing on	
set ipx rip update periodic	Enables periodic IPX RIP on this interface
cd	
reboot	

Table F-16 shows the configuration of the Cisco 4500 using bri0 to communicate with the router in Aptos. IPX RIP routing is configured.

Table F-16 *Configuring IPX RIP Routing on the Cisco 4500 Series Router in Figure F-1*

Command	Function
hostname sanjose	
!	
username aptos	
!	
no ip routing	
ipx routing 0000.0c3b.c743	
isdn switch-type basic-5ess	
!	
interface Ethernet0	
ipx network 200	Configures IPX address on interface ethernet 0 (this also automatically enables IPX RIP on the interface)
ipx encapsulation sap	
no mop enabled	
no shutdown	
!	
interface BRI0	
encapsulation ppp	
ipx network 100	Configures IPX address on interface BRI 0 (this also automatically enables IPX RIP on the interface)
dialer map ipx 100.0040.f902.c7b4 name aptos 5551414	
dialer-group 1	
no shutdown	
!	
!	
dialer-list 1 protocol ipx permit	

Advanced Configurations

The Cisco 750 Series routers also support the following advanced features:

- PAP/CHAP
- Filtering
- Caller ID
- Callback
- Point-to-Point Protocol (PPP) Multilink
- Debugging

PAP/CHAP

The Cisco 750 Series supports both PPP CHAP and PAP authentication. The Cisco 750 Series uses the keyword **password** for PAP authentication and the keyword **secret** for CHAP authentication. The CHAP/PAP **secret/password** is limited to 16 characters. PPP will always send the system name as the user identification. Although either CHAP or PAP can be used for authentication between a Cisco 750 Series and a Cisco IOS-based unit, CHAP is recommended because of its greater security. Table F-17 shows what must be configured in order for CHAP to work.

Table F-17   *Required Configuration for CHAP Operation on a Cisco 750 Series Router*

Required Configuration	Explanation
750 system name = Cisco username	The Cisco 750 Series system name must be entered as a username on the Cisco IOS device.
750 profile name = Cisco hostname	A profile must be created on the Cisco 750 Series that has the same name as the Cisco IOS host name.
750 Chap Host secret = Cisco Username Secret	The Cisco 750 Series secret must be the same as the Cisco IOS username password.
750 Chap Client secret = Cisco Username Secret	The Cisco 750 Series secret must be the same as the Cisco IOS username password.

The 750 Series uses four commands to address PPP authentication:

- **Host Password**—The host password is used during PAP authentication when the unit is the authenticator. The remote device sends its client password to this unit. (If the client's password matches the authenticator's host password, the call is allowed.) *The host password is a profile-based command.*

- **Client Password**—The client password is used during PAP authentication when this unit is the device authenticated. This unit sends its client password to the authenticator. If the client password matches the authenticator's host password, the call is allowed. *The client password is a system-level parameter.*

- **Host Secret**—The host secret is used during CHAP authentication when this unit is the authenticator. This unit sends a challenge to the remote device in the form of a random number. The remote device uses its client secret to perform a calculation on the number. This unit uses its host secret to perform a calculation on the same number. If the answers to both calculations match, the call is allowed. *The host secret is a profile-based command.*

- **Client Secret**—A client secret is used during CHAP authentication when this unit is the device being authenticated. The authenticator sends this unit a challenge in the form of a random number. This unit uses its client secret to perform a calculation on the number. The authenticator uses its host secret to perform a calculation on the same number. If the answers to both calculations match, the call is allowed. *The client secret is a system-level parameter.*

A 750 Series unit can have one host **password/secret** per profile and one client **password/secret** per unit.

Table F-18 shows the configuration for a Cisco 750 Series router with PAP authentication:

Table F-18   *Configuring a Cisco 750 Series Router with PAP Authentication*

Command	Function
set system 2060	
cd lan	
set ip address 150.150.150.1	
set ip netmask 255.255.255.0	
set ip routing on	
set ip rip update period	
cd	
set user 2503	
set ip address 100.100.100.2	
set ip netmask 255.255.255.0	

continues

Table F-18   *Configuring a Cisco 750 Series Router with PAP Authentication (Continued)*

Command	Function
set ip routing on	
set ip framing none	
set encapsulation ppp	
set ip route destination 200.200.200.0/24 ga 100.100.100.1 pr=on	
set number 5551212	
set bridging=off	
set timeout=30	
cd	
set ppp authentication in pap	Sets ppp authentication for incoming packets
set ppp authentication out pap	Sets ppp authentication for outgoing packets
set ppp password client	Sets ppp password
cisco	Password must be input twice for verification
cisco	Password must be input twice for verification
cd 2503	
set ppp password host	Configures host ppp password
cisco	Password must be input twice for verification
cisco	Password must be input twice for verification
reboot	

Table F-19 shows the configuration of the Cisco 4500 using bri0 to communicate with the Cisco 750 series router. PPP with PAP authentication is configured.

Table F-19   *Configuring PPP with PAP Authentication on a Cisco 4500 Series Router*

Command	Function
hostname 2503	
!	
username 2060 password cisco	Password will be displayed in encrypted form
username 2503 password cisco	
isdn switch-type basic-5ess	

continues

Table F-19 *Configuring PPP with PAP Authentication on a Cisco 4500 Series Router (Continued)*

Command	Function
!	
interface Ethernet0	
ip address 200.200.200.1 255.255.255.0	
no mop enabled	
no shutdown	
!	
interface BRI0	
ip address 100.100.100.1 255.255.255.0	
encapsulation ppp	Enable PPP encapsulation
ppp authentication pap	Enable PAP authentication
dialer map ip 100.100.100.2 name 2060 5551414	
dialer-group 1	
no shutdown	
!	
router rip	
redistribute static	
network 200.200.200.0	
redistribute connected	
!	
ip route 150.150.150.0 255.255.255.0 100.100.100.2	
!	
dialer-list 1 protocol ip permit	

Table F-20 shows the configuration for a Cisco 750 Series router with CHAP authentication.

Table F-20   *Configuring a Cisco 750 Series Router with CHAP Authentication*

Command	Function
set system 2060	
cd lan	
set ip address 150.150.150.1	
set ip netmask 255.255.255.0	

Command	Function
set ip routing on	
set ip rip update periodic	
cd	
set user 2503	
set ip address 100.100.100.2	
set ip netmask 255.255.255.0	
set ip routing on	
set ip framing none	
set encapsulation ppp	
set ip route destination 200.200.200.0/24 ga 100.100.100.1 pr=on	
set number 5551212	
set bridging=off	
set timeout=30	
cd	
set ppp authentication in chap	Sets ppp authentication for incoming packets
set ppp authentication out chap	Sets ppp authentication for outgoing packets
set ppp secret client	Sets ppp password
cisco	Password must be input twice for verification
cisco	Password must be input twice for verification
cd 2503	
set ppp secret host	Configures host ppp password
cisco	Password must be input twice for verification
cisco	Password must be input twice for verification
set bridging=off	
reboot	

Table F-21 shows the configuration of the Cisco 4500 using bri0 to communicate with the Cisco 750 series router. PPP with CHAP authentication is configured.

Table F-21 *Configuring PPP with CHAP Authentication on a Cisco 4500 Series Router*

Command	Function
hostname 2503	
!	
username 2060 password cisco	
isdn switch-type basic-5ess	
!	
interface Ethernet0	
ip address 200.200.200.1 255.255.255.0	
no mop enabled	
no shutdown	
!	
interface BRI0	
ip address 100.100.100.1 255.255.255.0	
encapsulation ppp	Enables PPP encapsulation
ppp authentication chap	Enables CHAP authentication
dialer map ip 100.100.100.2 name 2060 5551414	
dialer-group 1	
no shutdown	
!	
router rip	
redistribute static	
network 200.200.200.0	
redistribute connected	
!	
ip route 150.150.150.0 255.255.255.0 100.100.100.2	
!	
dialer-list 1 protocol ip permit	

Filtering

The filtering capabilities documented in the sections that follow are available with the Cisco 750 Series routers.

IP Filters

The Cisco 750 series routers support the following features for filtering IP traffic:

- TCP, UDP, ICMP filtering
- Filtering of various TCP and UDP ports
- Filtering of all addresses, nets of addresses, and single addresses
- Blocking or accepting traffic
- Implicit deny-all

IPX Filters

The user will need to know the hex values of the protocol if filtering is to be done. (No filtering for IPX except for serialization packets.)

Filtering Example

Table F-22 shows an example of IP filtering on a Cisco 750 Series Router.

Table F-22   *Configuring IP Filtering on a Cisco 750 Series Router*

Command	Function
set system 2060	
cd lan	
set ip address 150.150.150.1	
set ip netmask 255.255.255.0	
set ip routing on	
set ip rip update periodic	
cd	
set user 2503	
set ip address 100.100.100.2	
set ip netmask 255.255.255.0	
set ip routing on	

continues

Table F-22 *Configuring IP Filtering on a Cisco 750 Series Router (Continued)*

Command	Function
set ip framing none	
set encapsulation ppp	
set ip route destination 200.200.200.0/24	
ga 100.100.100.1 pr=on	
set number 5551414	
set bridging=off	
set timeout 30	
cd	
cd 2503	
set ip filter tcp in destination=0.0.0.0:23 block	Creates an IP filter to block incoming tcp port 23 (telnet)
set ip filter tcp in destination=0.0.0.0:513 block	Creates an IP filter to block incoming tcp port 513 (rlogin)
set ip filter tcp in destination=0.0.0.0:514 block	Creates an IP filter to block incoming tcp port 514 (rsh)
set ip filter tcp in destination=0.0.0.0:21 block	Creates an IP filter to block incoming tcp port 21 (ftp)
set ip filter tcp out destination=0.0.0.0:21 block	Creates an IP filter to block outgoing tcp port 21 (ftp)
set ip filter udp in destination=0.0.0.0:69 block	Creates an IP filter to block incoming udp port 69 (tftp)
set ip filter udp out destination=0.0.0.0:69 block	Creates an IP filter to block outgoing udp port 69 (tftp)
cd	
set bridging=off	
reboot	

Caller ID

Use the Caller ID feature to filter dial-in access based on an incoming ISDN phone number as shown in the configuration in Table F-23.

Table F-23 *Configuring Caller ID on a Cisco 750 Series Router*

Command	Function
set system menlopark	
cd lan	
set ip address 150.150.150.1	
set ip netmask 255.255.255.0	
set ip routing on	
set ip rip update periodic	
cd	
set user sanjose	
set ip address 100.100.100.2	
set ip netmask 255.255.255.0	
set ip routing on	
set ip rip update periodic	
set encapsulation ppp	
set ip framing none	
set number 5551212	
set bridging=off	
cd	
set callerid on	Enables callerID
set callid 5551212	Maps callerID to incoming ISDN number
reboot	

Table F-24 shows the configuration of a Cisco 4500 using bri0 and caller ID to communicate with the Cisco 750 series router.

Table F-24 *Configuring Caller ID on a Cisco 4500 Series Router*

Command	Function
hostname sanjose	
!	
username menlopark	
isdn switch-type basic-5ess	
!	
interface Ethernet0	
ip address 200.200.200.1 255.255.255.0	
no mop enabled	
no shutdown	
!	
interface BRI0	
ip address 100.100.100.2 255.0.0.0	
encapsulation ppp	
dialer map ip 150.150.150.1 name menlopark 5551414	
dialer-group 1	
isdn caller 5551414	Maps callerID to ISDN number
no shutdown	
!	
router rip	
network 200.200.200.0	
network 100.0.0.0	
!	
!	
dialer-list 1 protocol ip permit	

PPP Callback

Use PPP Callback to enable callback to sites attempting to dial in as illustrated in the configuration in Table F-25.

Table F-25   *Configuring PPP Callback on a Cisco 750 Series Router*

Command	Function
set system menlopark	
cd lan	
set ip address 150.150.150.1	
set ip netmask 255.255.255.0	
set ip routing on	
set ip rip update periodic	
cd	
set user sanjose	
set ip address 100.100.100.2	
set ip netmask 255.255.255.0	
set ip routing on	
set ip framing none	
set ip rip update periodic	
set encapsulation ppp	
set ppp callback request always	Establishes a callback request. The **always** keyword forces the calling unit to disconnect after negotiation.
set number 5551212	
set bridging=off	
cd	
reboot	

Table F-26 shows the configuration of a Cisco 4500 using bri0 and PPP Callback to communicate with the Cisco 750 series router.

Table F-26 *Configuring PPP Callback on a Cisco 4500 Series Router*

Command	Function
hostname sanjose	
!	
username menlopark	
isdn switch-type basic-5ess	
!	
map-class dialer bri0	Configures a dialer map class for PPP callback
dialer callback-server username	Specifies whether the dialstring to call is to be identified by looking up the authenticated hostname or is determined during callback negotiation
!	
!	
!	
interface Ethernet0	
ip address 200.200.200.1 255.255.255.0	
no mop enabled	
no shutdown	
!	
interface BRI0	
ip address 100.100.100.2 255.0.0.0	
encapsulation ppp	
ppp callback accept	Configures the interface to accept PPP callback
dialer map ip 150.150.150.1 name menlopark class bri0 5551414	Uses **class** command to map to a defined map-class
dialer-group 1	
ppp authentication chap	
dialer hold-queue 10 timeout 15	Allows queuing of packets while link comes up
dialer enable-timeout 1	Allows the interface to be re-enabled after only 1 second
no shutdown	
!	
router rip	

continues

Table F-26 *Configuring PPP Callback on a Cisco 4500 Series Router (Continued)*

Command	Function
network 200.200.200.0	
network 100.0.0.0	
!	
!	
dialer-list 1 protocol ip permit	

Multilink PPP

Multilink PPP is enabled by default on the Cisco 750 series and disabled by default on Cisco IOS platforms. Table F-27 shows the multilink PPP configurations for Cisco 750 platform.

Table F-27 *Multilink PPP Configuration for a Cisco 750 Series Router*

Command	Function
set system menlopark	
cd lan	
set ip address 150.150.150.1	
set ip netmask 255.255.255.0	
set ip routing on	
set ip rip update periodic	
cd	
set user sanjose	
set ip address 100.100.100.2	
set ip netmask 255.255.255.0	
set ip routing on	
set ip framing none	Multilink PPP is enabled by default, no additional configuration required.
set ip rip update periodic	
set encapsulation ppp	
set number 5551212	
set bridging=off	
cd	
reboot	

Table F-28 shows the configuration of a Cisco 4500 using bri0 and multilink PPP to communicate with the Cisco 750 series router.

Table F-28   *Configuring Multilink PPP on a Cisco 4500 Series Router*

Command	Function
hostname sanjose	
!	
username menlopark	
isdn switch-type basic-5ess	
!	
interface Ethernet0	
ip address 200.200.200.1 255.255.255.0	
no mop enabled	
no shutdown	
!	
interface BRI0	
ip address 100.100.100.2 255.0.0.0	
encapsulation ppp	
dialer map ip 150.150.150.1 name menlopark 5551414	
ppp multilink	Enables Multilink PPP
dialer load-threshold 50 either	Enables B-channel aggregation regardless of traffic direction
dialer-group 1	
no shutdown	
!	
router rip	
network 200.200.200.0	
network 100.0.0.0	
!	
!	
dialer-list 1 protocol ip permit	

Debugging

The **log *n* traffic verbose** command can be used on Cisco 750 Series routers to perform debugging, where *n* is the connection number (only required when you want to specify a connection corresponding to other than the current profile).

You can add the optional keywords **incoming** or **outgoing** to log packets in the specified direction only.

The **log packets** command gives traffic statistics for the specified connection once per second. There is no verbose option for **log packets**.

For more information on the **log** command, refer to the Cisco 750 Series documentation.

Interoperability Issues

Bridging right now does *not* operate if the Cisco 75x Combinet product calls the Cisco router; it only operates when the Cisco router calls the Combinet product.

The default ISDN packet encapsulation protocol is Combinet Packet Protocol (CPP). If you are connecting to a Cisco IOS router, you must change the encapsulation to PPP with the **set encapsulation ppp** command.

The Cisco 750 Series implements Multilink PPP (RFC 1717). Multilink PPP is available in Cisco IOS Releases 11.0(3) and later. If you are connecting a Cisco 750 Series to a Cisco IOS router running a Cisco IOS release prior to 11.0(3), you must disable Multilink PPP with the **set ppp multilink off** command.

When configuring the Cisco 750 Series for IP and/or IPX routing to a Cisco IOS router, the Cisco 750 must be configured for Internet Protocol Control Protocol (IPCP) and/or Internetwork Packet eXchange Control Protocol (IPXCP). In the Cisco 750 remote profile, use the **set ip framing none** and/or **set ipx framing none** commands. Do not use these values in the LAN profile.

The Cisco 750 series implements RIP version 2 (RFC 1723) and Demand RIP (RFC 1582). These proposed standards are not implemented in the Cisco IOS software. If you are connecting to a Cisco IOS router and want to use a dynamic routing protocol, you must configure the Cisco 750 for RIP version 1 using the **set IP RIP version 1** command and disable demand RIP with the **set ip rip update periodic** command.

The Cisco 750 series implements compression only over the CPP protocol. This is not compatible with the Cisco IOS software as mentioned above.

Cisco IOS routers can only bridge to a single remote site at a time over ISDN. IP and IPX routing do not have this restriction.

For more information on the Cisco 750 series, refer to the Cisco 750 series documentation.

Cisco IOS 11.0(3) Features

In addition to the Cisco 750 series, the Cisco IOS software has also gained increased ISDN functionality. Below is a discussion of the principal ISDN features available in Cisco IOS Release 11.0(3) and later.

Multilink PPP for ISDN Interfaces

Refer to the "Cisco 750 Configuration" section for an example of Multilink PPP for ISDN on Cisco IOS platforms. The sections that follow provide a definition for, benefits of, and considerations for using Multilink PPP (MP) for ISDN Interfaces.

Description

MP is a method of B-channel aggregation that is defined in Internet Engineering Task Force (IETF) RFC 1717 (which you can find at http://info.internet.isi.edu/in-notes/rfc/files/rfc1717.txt). This RFC defines a means by which packets can be sequenced and transmitted over multiple physical interfaces. To reduce potential latency issues, Multilink PPP also defines a method of fragmenting and reassembling large packets.

Multilink PPP is supported and can be used with any Cisco ISDN BRI or PRI interface. Multilink PPP can be used in conjunction with other ISDN features including PPP Compression (CCP), PPP Authentication, PPP Callback, and IP Address Negotiation.

It is important to note that Multilink PPP does *not* define how or why B-channel links should be initiated or torn down. The design of this mechanism has been left to the vendors. Cisco's implementation enables the user to define a loading factor (the percentage of bandwidth being used on a B channel), at which point a second or subsequent B channel call should be initiated. This loading factor can be defined for only incoming, only outgoing, or either incoming or outgoing loads. This allows Multilink PPP to be used effectively in many different environments, such as collecting information from the Internet/WWW (mostly incoming traffic) or sending files to colleagues (mostly outgoing traffic).

Figure F-2 illustrates a basic Multilink PPP session. Here a second B channel is already in use and Multilink PPP is in operation. Incoming packets A and B are both fragmented into smaller packets. These are then given sequence numbers by Multilink PPP and shared over the two B channels. Note that all packets greater than 30 bytes are subject to fragmentation. When the fragments of packet A and B arrive at the receiving router, Multilink PPP reassembles the original packets and sequences them correctly in the datastream.

Figure F-2   *Multilink PPP Operation*

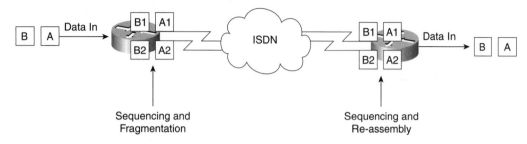

Sequencing and
Fragmentation

Sequencing and
Re-assembly

Benefits

Multilink PPP provides multivendor B-channel aggregation interoperability to the ISDN marketplace. This is especially helpful in the Internet service provider marketplace, where many different types of ISDN customer premises equipment (CPE) can be found. Multilink PPP also addresses some of the issues found with proprietary load-balancing aggregation techniques when using protocols such as IPX or AppleTalk. These protocols are less forgiving of out-of-order packets than IP. By providing sequencing and reordering, Multilink PPP removes such problems.

Considerations

At present MP is only implemented for dialup circuits. A later release of Cisco IOS software will be enhanced to provide aggregation for any link/interface supporting PPP encapsulation. MP is currently process switched. Due consideration should be given to performance in large hub implementations using multiple ISDN PRIs.

PPP interoperability can never be guaranteed with constantly changing MP software on different vendors' ISDN products. To reduce interoperability problems, Cisco regularly takes part in PPP interoperability testing. MP was last tested at the California ISDN User Group (CIUG) testing session at the Pacific Bell laboratories in mid-September 1995. At that time Cisco successfully interoperated with the 16 vendors outlined in Table F-29.

Table F-29 *Products with which Cisco IOS Multilink PPP Can Successfully Interoperate*

Company	Product	Software Release
3Com Corporation	Impact	
3Com Corporation	AccessBuilder 400	6.01 (unreleased)
3Com Corporation	NETBuilder Remote Office	Unreleased software
Ascend	Pipeline Max 4000	4.5
Gandalf	XpressWay	3.2
Eicon Diehl	PacketBlaster	SDK 20
Eicon Technology	SOHO/Connect DIVA	Unreleased software
ISDNtek	Cyberspace Freedom	CY123.2099
Shiva	Shiva PPP Client	4.0
ISC	SecureLink II	Unreleased software
Combinet (now Cisco)	2060	3.1
Microsoft	Windows '95	
Rockwell Network Systems	Dialup Router	4.1
Motorola	Bitsurfer Pro	
Xyplex	Network 3000	5.5
Network Express	Interhub	Unreleased software

IP Address Negotiation for ISDN

The sections that follow describe IP address negotiation for ISDN, including address assignments with local address pooling, Terminal Access Controller Access Control System Plus (TACACS+), and DHCP. The benefits of, and considerations for, IP address negotiation for ISDN are also covered.

Description

IP address negotiation for ISDN allows remote node PPP client software to request an IP address from a Cisco core router during call setup. This request occurs as part of the PPP IPCP setup negotiation.

This feature is specifically designed for remote node connectivity where the end user is operating a PC/Mac/workstation with a nonrouting device such as a Cisco LAN2LAN Personal Office ISDN PC card or an external ISDN terminal adapter such as a Motorola Bitsurfer.

IP addresses can be assigned either from a "local pool" that is held on the core router or from an external TACACS+ or DHCP server. Figure F-3 shows the solutions where IP address negotiation can be best utilized.

Figure F-3   *IP Address Negotiation*

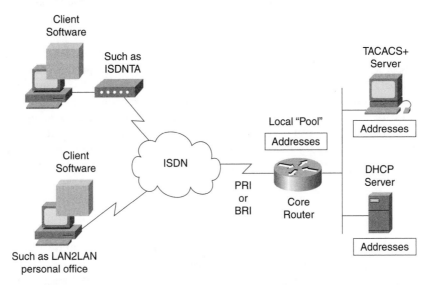

Note that multiple pooling types can be active simultaneously on the core router. It is possible for certain dialup users to be assigned an IP address from a local "pool" while others use a TACACS+ server.

Local Address Pooling

Several pools of IP addresses can be held on the core router. Each pool can hold up to 255 addresses. Each pool has a free queue containing available addresses and a "used" queue containing addresses currently in use. On receipt of the IPCP address negotiation request, the core router retrieves an address from the free queue. It is possible for the client to request the same address used in his or her last connection. If this address is in the free queue, it is assigned. If it is in use, another address from the free queue is assigned.

TACACS+ IP Address Assignment

You can configure TACACS+ to assign an IP address to a dialup user in one of two ways. An IP address can be assigned directly by the TACACS+ server while it is authorizing the remote node connection. As an alternative, the TACACS+ server can return a local address pool name, which allows the core router to assign the IP address from that local pool.

DHCP

When using DHCP, the core router acts as a DHCP proxy for the remote client. On receipt of the IPCP address negotiation request, the core router retrieves an IP address from the DHCP server. At the end of the session, the router returns that address to the server. For more information on DHCP, visit http://web.syr.edu/~jmwobus/comfaqs/dhcp.faq.html.

Benefits

Address negotiation allows an organization to manage its address space centrally. It also allows the use of IP addresses to be minimized. In most instances, dial-up services are oversubscribed. With address negotiation, it is only necessary to provide enough address space to cope with worst-case loading scenarios. Use of IP address negotiation also reduces configuration text in the core router. Because of the dynamic nature of IP address assignment, it is no longer necessary to maintain a specific dialer map statement for each remote node. IP address negotiation creates dynamic dialer maps for each connection and removes them at the end of the session.

Considerations

It is important to ensure that an address is being negotiated via the PPP IPCP. Some client software stacks support DHCP locally. If a DHCP request originates remotely, the core router cannot function as a DHCP proxy, and no return path will be available through this unit.

PPP Callback for ISDN

Refer to the "Cisco 750 Configuration" section for an example of PPP Callback for ISDN on Cisco IOS platforms. The sections that follow provide a general description for PPP callback for ISDN, as well as the benefits of and considerations for using PPP callback for ISDN.

Description

Callback for ISDN interfaces allows a Cisco router using a DDR interface and PPP encapsulation to initiate a circuit-switched WAN link to another device and request that it be called back. A Cisco ISDN router can also respond to a callback request from a remote device. The process uses PPP and the facilities specified in RFC 1570 (which you can find at http://info.internet.isi.edu/in-notes/rfc/files/rfc1570.txt). A typical negotiation would proceed as follows (see Figure F-4):

Step 1   Router A brings up a circuit-switched connection to Router B.

Step 2   Routers A and B negotiate PPP Link Control Protocol (LCP) with either Router A requesting callback or Router B initiating callback.

Step 3   Routers authenticate using PPP PAP or CHAP protocols. Router A is required to authenticate; Router B authentication is optional.

Step 4   Circuit-switched connection is dropped by both routers.

Step 5   Router B brings up circuit-switched connection to Router A.

Figure F-4   *PPP Callback Operation*

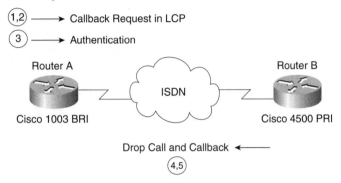

Benefits

Callback for ISDN/DDR provides centralized billing for sync dialup services. It also allows organizations to take advantage of tariff disparities on both a national and an international basis.

Considerations

Because callback for ISDN/DDR requires a circuit-switched connection to be established before the callback request can be passed, a small charge (dependent on local tariffing) will always be incurred by the router that initiated the call.

For more information on these features and the rest of the Cisco IOS ISDN feature set, refer to Cisco Connection Documentation CD-ROM and CCO.

AppleTalk DDR Update

Running AppleTalk over DDR links is problematic because of the number of broadcasts generated by AppleTalk devices. Name Binding Protocol (NBP) packets are at the top of the list of AppleTalk broadcast packets that bring DDR circuits up and down.

A variety of applications, including QuarkXpress, FileMaker Pro, and Datebook Pro, send out all-zone NBP broadcasts to check for licensing violations. For obvious reasons this is a bad strategy when usage-based DDR links are in use.

To alleviate the effects that NBP traffic imposes on DDR links, Cisco has introduced NBP Filtering with Release 11.0 of the Cisco IOS software.

In Release 11.0 and later, look for the addition to the **access-list** command for AppleTalk, as outlined in Table F-30.

Table F-30   *AppleTalk Filtering in a Cisco IOS Router*

Command and Parameters	Function
homer(config) #**access-list 601 deny ?**	
<1-65279>	AppleTalk network number
additional-zones	Default filter action for unspecified zones
cable-range	Filter on cable range
includes	Filter on cable range inclusively
nbp	Specify nbp filter
network	Filter an AppleTalk network
other-access	Default filter action
other-nbps	Default filter action for nbp
within	Filter on cable range exclusively
zone	Filter on AppleTalk zone

Under the NBP heading in the **access-list** command are the parameters outlined in Table F-31.

Table F-31   *AppleTalk NBP Filtering in a Cisco IOS Router*

Command and Parameters	Function
homer(config)#**access-list 601 deny nbp ?**	
<1-65536>	nbp sequence number
homer(config)#**access-list 601 deny nbp 1 ?**	
Object	Filter on nbp object
Type	Filter on nbp type
Zone	Filter on nbp zone
homer(config)#**access-list 601 deny nbp 1 object ?**	
LINE	NBP object filter
homer(config)#**access-list 601 deny nbp 1 type ?**	
LINE	NBP type filter
homer(config)#**access-list 601 deny nbp 1 zone ?**	
LINE	NBP zone filter

Example F-2 is a sample configuration used to filter all NBPs except AppleShare NBP traffic. All other traffic is permitted using the **other-access** command. Broadcast traffic is not permitted by using the **broadcast-deny** statement.

Example F-2   *An AppleTalk NBP Filter Configuration on a Cisco IOS Router*

```
!
 access-list 601 permit nbp 1 type AFPServer
 access-list 601 deny other-nbps
 access-list 601 permit other-access broadcast-deny
 !
 dialer-list 1 list 601
 !
```

To learn more about NBP packets in your LAN/WAN environment, use the NBP Test feature that is available on all Cisco IOS routers. To use this feature, use the commands outlined in Table F-32:

Table F-32   *Using the NBP Test Feature on a Cisco IOS Router*

Commands and Parameters	Function
cisco-router#	
cisco-router#**ping**	Invokes the extended ping function.
Protocol [ip]: **appletalk**	
Target AppleTalk address: **nbp**	This starts NBPtest facility.
nbptest> **?**	Type ? for help.
Tests are:	
lookup: lookup an NVE. prompt for name, type and zone	
parms: display/change lookup parms (ntimes, nsecs, interval)	
zones: display zones	
poll: for every zone, lookup all devices, using default parms	
help|?: print command list	
quit: exit nbptest	
nbptest> **parms**	Always start by adjusting the parms to these defaults.
maxrequests [5]: 1	These are TAC recommendations.
maxreplies [1]: 200	
interval [5]: 5	

The example in Table F-33 will look up all resources in the zone "Infosource".

Table F-33   *Using the NBP Test Feature on a Cisco IOS Router to Look Up Resources*

Commands and Parameters	Function
nbptest>	
nbptest> **lookup**	
Entity name [=]:	= is wild card, or type the exact name
Type of Service [=]:	that is, AFPServer
Zone [Twilight]: **Infosource**	Zone of interest
Output deleted due to length	

The example in Table F-34 will look up the types of services provided by "Sales Server".

Table F-34   *Using the NBP Test Feature on a Cisco IOS Router to Look Up Types of Services*

Commands and Parameters	Function
nbptest> **lookup**	
Entity name [=]: **Sales Server**	
Type of Service [=]:	
Zone [Infosource]:	
(7214n,35a,244s)[1]<-(7214.35.2)	
: `Sales Server:AFPServer@Infosource'	Syntax of output is as follows `Entity(object): Type@Zone'
(7214n,35a,8s)[1]<-(7214.35.2)	
: `Sales Server:SNMP Agent@Infosource'	Syntax of output is as follows `Entity(object): Type@Zone'
(7214n,35a,4s)[1]<-(7214.35.2)	
: `Sales Server:Workstation@Infosource'	Syntax of output is as follows `Entity(object): Type@Zone'
NBP lookup request timed out	
Processed 3 replies, 6 events	
nbptest>	
nbptest> **quit**	returns to the router prompt
cisco-router#	

This Windows NT Design and Implementation Guide was originally written by Cisco. It has been edited here for formatting.

Although this guide contains some information on older products and software, and refers to some "future" products, which are, in fact, now available, this guide does provide useful information regarding the design and implementation of Windows networks. Refer to the Cisco IOS™ and other product documentation for information on the latest products and features available.

Windows NT Design and Implementation Guide

The term "networking" covers a broad range of technologies that, when combined, allow computers to share information. Networking components can be segmented into end system applications, network operating systems, and networking equipment.

A network operating system is software run on all interconnected systems. Examples include Novell NetWare, Sun's Network File System (NFS), AppleShare, and Microsoft's implementation of a network operating system commonly called Windows Networking. Windows Networking is now extensively deployed, with over 100 million nodes.

This design guide explains the basic concepts of Windows Networking and provides insight on how to design networks (LANs and WANs) to best utilize Windows Networking. The guide also explains Windows protocols, naming, and scaling issues associated with Windows Networking.

What Is Windows Networking?

Windows Networking refers to the networking system shared by the software that comes with all the following Microsoft operating systems or servers:

- Microsoft LAN Manager
- MS-DOS with LAN Manager client
- Windows for Workgroups
- Windows 95
- Windows NT

Microsoft LAN Manager, the LAN Manager client for MS-DOS, and Windows NT 3.1 will not be discussed in this document except in an historical context.

Domains Versus Workgroups

Windows Networking has two concepts of a group of related computers—workgroups and domains. Workgroups can be any logical collection of computers; any computer on the network can join an existing workgroup or create a new one. More formal entities, domains are created and managed by a Primary Domain Controller (PDC) process that runs on a Windows NT server. A domain has security and administrative properties that a workgroup does not. Each domain must have at least one NT server. Windows Networking domains are not the same as Internet domain names as used by Domain Naming System (DNS).

What Protocol Does It Use?

Windows Networking uses the NetBIOS protocol for file sharing, printer sharing, messaging, authentication, and name resolution. NetBIOS is a session layer protocol that can run on any of these transport protocols:

- NetBEUI
- NWLink (NetBIOS over IPX)
- NetBIOS over TCP (NBT)

Although Microsoft recommends that clients use only one transport protocol at a time for maximum performance, this is not the default. You should pick a protocol to use for your entire network and then turn the other protocols off.

NetBEUI is the least scalable of the three protocols because it must be bridged. NetBEUI is only included to support very old services (for example, old versions of LAN manager). NetBEUI does not require any client address configuration.

NWLink is recommended for small- to medium-sized networks, especially if they are already running IPX. Like NetBEUI, NWLink requires no client address configuration. NWLink uses IPX type-20 packets to exchange registration and browsing information. To forward type-20 IPX packets across Cisco routers, you must configure **ipx type-20-propagation** on each interface on every router on your network.

Microsoft recommends NetBIOS over TCP (NBT) for medium-sized and large networks, or anytime the network includes a wide-area network (WAN). Because NBT uses TCP/IP, each computer must be configured to use a static IP address or to fetch an IP address dynamically with the Dynamic Host Configuration Protocol (DHCP).

Dynamic IP Addressing

Manually addressing TCP/IP clients is both time consuming and error-prone. To solve this problem, the Internet Engineering Task Force (IETF) developed DHCP, the Dynamic Host Configuration Protocol. DHCP is designed to automatically provide clients with a valid IP address and related configuration information (see DHCP Options). Each range of addresses that a DHCP server manages is called a Scope.

DHCP Scopes

You must configure a range of addresses for every IP subnet where clients will request a DHCP address. Each range of addresses is called a DHCP scope. You can configure a DHCP server to serve several scopes because the DHCP server or servers do not need to be physically connected to the same network as the client. If the DHCP server is on a different IP subnet from the client, then you need to use DHCP Relay to forward DHCP requests to your DHCP server.

DHCP Relay

DHCP Relay typically runs on a router. You can turn on DHCP Relay on a Cisco Internetwork Operating System (Cisco IOS™) router by configuring **ip helper-address** with the address of the DHCP server on each interface that will have DHCP clients. To prevent forwarding other broadcasts to the DHCP server, add the **ip forward-protocol udp bootpc** global command to the router configuration. DHCP Relay on the Cisco 700 series is planned for the last quarter of 1996.

DHCP Options

In addition to its IP address, a DHCP client can get other TCP/IP configuration information from a DHCP server, including the subnet mask, default gateway, and DNS information. These pieces of information, called DHCP Options, can be configured in the DHCP Manager on your Windows NT DHCP server (see Figure G-1).

Figure G-1   *Microsoft's DHCP Manager*

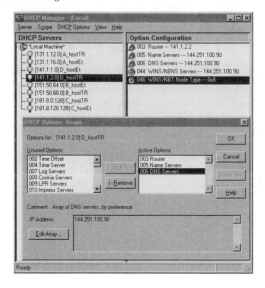

If your clients are using Windows Internet Name Service (WINS) for name resolution, as is discussed later, you should configure the address of the WINS server and the WINS node type. A brief list of node types is included in the Name Resolution section. p-node (0x2) is strongly recommended.

Cisco DHCP Server

Cisco shipped an integrated DHCP and DNS server for Windows NT, UNIX, and OpenVMS in the third quarter of 1996. This server has a graphical interface, support for secondary addressing, and many other enterprise features.

Microsoft LAN Services Browser

Windows Networking was originally designed to run on a single LAN segment or a bridged (flat) network. At that time, only the NetBEUI protocol was supported.

Microsoft developed the LAN Services Browser to enable the user to browse a list of all computers available on the network. Each Windows Networking client registered its NetBIOS Name periodically by sending broadcasts.

Every computer also had to send broadcasts to elect a browse master for the network. The browse master (and several backup browse masters) maintained the list of computers and their addresses. When a user browsed the network, the client would send a broadcast request, and one of the browse masters would respond.

Eventually Microsoft added support for NetBIOS over IPX and NetBIOS over TCP/IP, but Windows Networking still assumed that all clients and servers were on the same logical IPX network or IP subnet—they still sent broadcasts to register and find computers on the network.

This architecture, although simple to implement, generated an enormous burden on the network and on the CPU of each client on the network. Because of these scalability problems, Microsoft began to offer other methods of browsing and name resolution—ways for clients to map a name to the IP address of other computers on the network. Eventually Microsoft also provided a way to browse and resolve names without broadcasts.

Name Resolution

As of the release of Microsoft Windows NT 3.51, Windows Networking clients have a choice of four methods of name resolution:

- Broadcasts
- LMHOSTS
- WINS
- Internet DNS

Broadcasts

By sending broadcasts on a subnet, Windows Networking clients cause a browser election. The designated browse master maintains a list of all the resources available on that subnet. Because registrations, browser elections, and name queries all generate broadcasts, use of this method is not recommended.

Because this method is used by default on all Microsoft products, it is strongly recommended that you turn this feature off by setting the BrowseMaster setting to Disabled (the default is Automatic). For specific details, see Appendix A, "Turning Off Broadcast Name Resolution," in this document.

LMHOSTS

Windows Networking can consult a static table in a file called LMHOSTS. To use this method, the Primary Domain Controller (PDC) should maintain at the least a static list of all computers and their IP addresses in that domain and the names and addresses of the PDCs for all other domains in the network. All clients must then have an LMHOSTS file with the IP address of their PDC and the path to the master LMHOSTS file on the PDC.

Using this method alone, however, does not allow clients to browse the network. Because of the obvious administrative burden, this method of resolving NetBIOS names is recommended only if you are using a router running EveryWare (Cisco 700 series) and you need to control line charges. (See the Dial-on-Demand Routing section for more details.)

Windows Internet Name Service

WINS was created to allow clients on different IP subnets to dynamically register and browse the network without sending broadcasts. Clients send unicast packets to the WINS server at a well-known address. For compatibility with older MS Networking clients, however, broadcast name resolution is still turned on by default, even when WINS is also configured.

NOTE   *Important*: As shown in Figure G-2, browsing will not work on a subnet if any Windows 3.1 or Windows 95 computer on the subnet has broadcast name resolution turned on (that is, Browse Master setting to Automatic). Individual servers, however, are still reachable by name.

Figure G-2   *With WINS, Broadcast Name Resolution Must Be Turned Off*

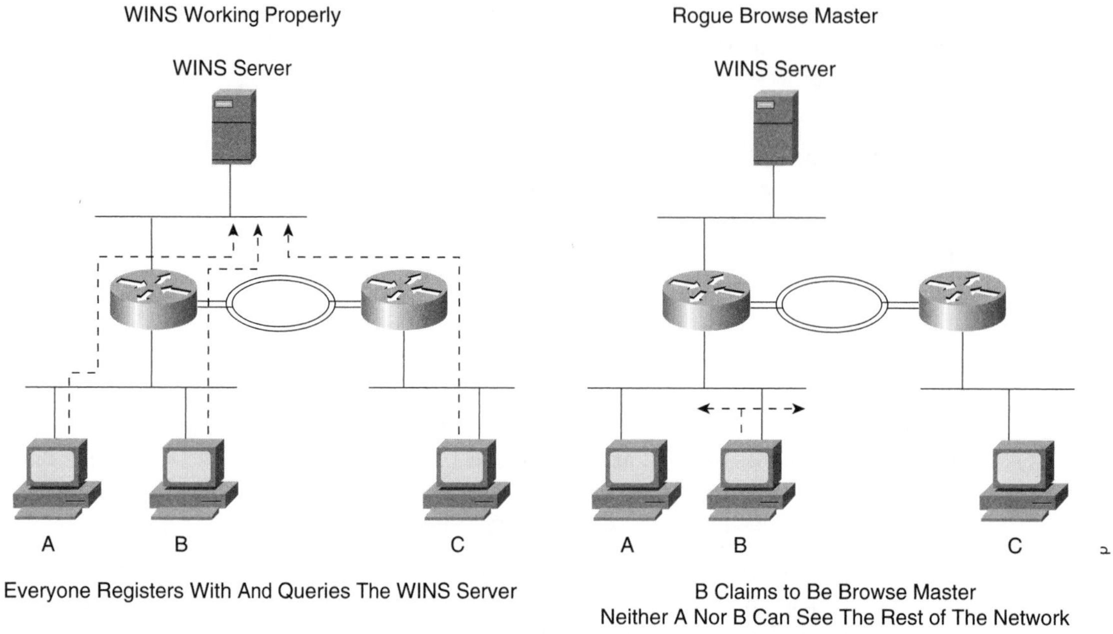

In Windows for Workgroups 3.11, broadcasts are turned off by adding a command to the system.ini file. (See Appendix A in this document for details.) In Windows 95 the Browse Master setting in Advanced File and Print Sharing Properties must be set to Disabled. Administrators can control broadcasts sent by DHCP clients by selecting the appropriate WINS node-type (p-node: 0x2). Table G-1 provides a complete list of WINS node types.

Table G-1   *WINS Node Types*

WINS Node Type	Name Search Order
b-node (0x1)	Broadcast only
p-node (0x2)	WINS only
m-node (0x4)	Broadcast, then WINS
h-node (0x8)	WINS, then broadcast

Internet DNS

Any DNS server can be configured statically to answer queries for computers with fixed IP addresses. This is useful if computers in your network have fixed IP addresses. When Windows systems use DHCP to get an IP address and WINS to register a NetBIOS name, you can set up a

Windows NT DNS server to query a WINS server for names or addresses that were not entered statically. In both cases, Windows and non-Windows systems can resolve IP addresses correctly.

If an administrator configures each Windows Networking server with a static IP address, it may be convenient to enter each server in the DNS system and use DNS for name resolution. Occasionally (for example, when using a dial-on-demand link), it is convenient to register clients with WINS and make queries with DNS. The Microsoft NT 3.51 Resource Kit and Windows NT 4.0 server both include a DNS server that can answer DNS queries by querying a WINS server in the background. For more information about how to configure this architecture, see Appendix B, "Configuring DNS Resolution of WINS Names," in this document.

Figure G-3 shows an example. Windows and non-Windows systems both send DNS lookups for a Windows NT server named Warthog. The DNS server does not have an entry for Warthog, so it queries the WINS server and returns the IP address.

Figure G-3   *WINS and DNS Servers Can Work Together to Answer Queries from Windows and Non-Windows Systems*

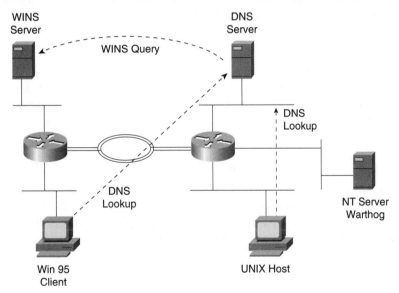

Scaling to Larger Networks—Trusted Domains

When planning a Windows network, consideration of what domain model to use is important. The following paragraphs discuss the benefits and drawbacks of several domain models. If you have several domains, you probably want to exchange data with other domains in your network. Trust relationships are a way to gain or grant access to a domain without having to manage each user individually. Each relationship permits trust in one direction only. For more information, see the *Windows NT Resource Kit, Volume 2, Chapter 4*.

Single Domain

This domain model is the simplest because the network has only one domain. This setup works for small or medium-sized installations without a WAN.

Global Trust

Designed for companies without a central administrative or IS organization, the global trust model is the easiest to understand and the most difficult to manage. Every domain trusts every other domain.

Master Domain

In this model, a master domain is trusted by all other domains, but the master domain trusts no one. This option is beneficial when departments or divisions want administrative control over their own services, but still want to authenticate centrally.

Multiple Master Domains

This model is designed to be a larger version of the master domain model. Several master domains all trust each other, and each of the master domains is, in turn, trusted by each departmental domain.

Replicating WINS

For redundancy or to optimize WAN traffic, sometimes having several WINS servers is desirable. Windows NT servers can replicate or resynchronize WINS databases in either or both directions. In Figure G-4, a large multinational company has several distributed WINS servers so that WINS queries do not have to travel across continents.

Figure G-4   *Example of an Enterprise-Wide Configuration for WINS Replication*

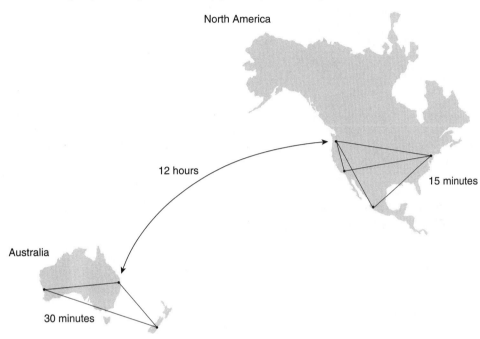

Modem Access

Windows NT comes with Microsoft's remote-access server (RAS), which uses the Point-to-Point Protocol (PPP). Customers often want to use Cisco access servers instead of NT RASs for their dial-in pools because of the better dial-in density and performance available on Cisco access servers.

NT supports TCP/IP, IPX, and NetBEUI (IPCP, IPXCP, and NBFCP control protocols for PPP). NetBEUI dial-in support was added to the Cisco IOS™ in Release 11.1. For NetBEUI dial-in, use the **netbios nbf** command (as shown in Example G-1) on each async interface or on a group-async interface on the access server.

Example G-1   *Enabling NetBEUI Dial-In*

```
interface group-async 0
  group-range 1 16
  netbios nbf
```

To configure IPX dial-in, use the **ipx ppp-client** command (as shown in Example G-2) on each async interface or on a group-async interface on the access server. This command requires you to configure an IPX network address on a loopback interface. Dial-in clients do not need to hear Service Advertisement Protocol (SAP) messages, so these messages should be turned off with the **ipx sap-interval 0** command.

Example G-2 *Enabling IPX Dial-In*

```
interface loopback 0
  ipx network <network number>
interface group-async 0
  group-range 1 16
  ipx ppp-client loopback 0
  ipx sap-interval 0
```

In order to assign IP addresses to dial-in clients, Cisco access servers can use a pool of local addresses or act as a proxy for a DHCP server. The access server requests an address from the DHCP server and uses that address during PPP negotiation. The client can also negotiate the address of its WINS server. Example G-3 illustrates this process.

Example G-3 *Assigning IP Addresses to Dial-In Clients*

```
ip dhcp-server n.n.n.n
async-bootp nbns-server m.m.m.m
async-bootp dns-server p.p.p.p
ip address-pool dhcp-proxy-client
!
interface group-async 0
  group-range 1 16
  peer default ip address dhcp
```

Dial-on-Demand Routing

Dial-on-demand routing (DDR) provides network connections across Public Switched Telephone Networks (PSTNs). Traditionally, WAN connections have been dedicated leased lines. DDR provides low-volume, periodic network connections, allowing on-demand services and decreasing network costs. ISDN is a circuit-switched technology. Like the analog telephone network, ISDN connections are made only when there is a need to communicate.

Cisco routers use dial-on-demand routing (DDR) to determine when a connection needs to be made to another site. Packets are classified as either interesting or uninteresting based on protocol-specific access lists and dialer lists. Uninteresting packets can travel across an active DDR link, but they do not bring up the link or keep it up.

As shown in Figure G-5, Windows for Workgroups and Windows 95 clients using WINS try to register themselves on the network every 10 minutes by sending a unicast packet to the WINS server (on User Datagram Protocol [UDP] port 137—the NetBIOS Name Service port).

Figure G-5   *Dial-on-Demand Link Up All the Time*

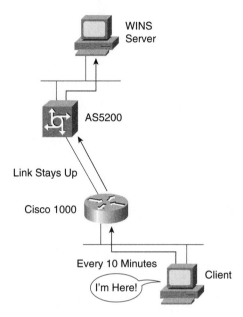

Sending a packet to the WINS server normally brings up the dial-on-demand link. If, however, this port is classified as uninteresting to the Cisco IOS™ software, as shown in the configuration in Example G-4 and in Figure G-6, then the router will neither bring up nor keep up the link. This feature is not currently available on the Cisco 700 series.

Example G-4   *Making Packets to the WINS Server Uninteresting, So They Do Not Bring Up the DDR Link*

```
interface bri 0
  dialer-group 1
!
dialer-list 1 protocol ip list 101
access-list 101 deny udp any any eq netbios-ns
access-list 101 permit ip any any
```

Figure G-6   *UDP Port 137 Is Uninteresting, Link Is Down*

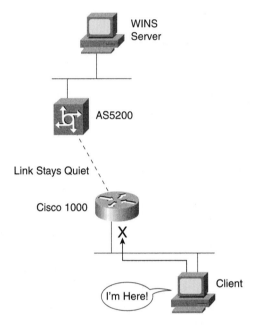

Unfortunately, making NetBIOS name service packets uninteresting can cause initial logins to time out or fail completely. The only reliable way to ensure that Windows for Workgroups and Windows 95 logins succeed while controlling line usage is to use the DNS method of NetBIOS name resolution.

Windows NT workstations and servers regularly send security messages to the domain controllers in their domain. This traffic is not spoofable. To prevent this traffic from keeping up your dial-on-demand connection, Cisco recommends that you create a separate trusted domain at the remote site. You might also want to use separate WINS servers on each side of the ISDN line and periodically replicate them.

ISDN Access

This section covers ISDN cards and terminal adapters (TAs). For information about using Windows networking with ISDN routers, see the previous section on dial-on-demand routing.

Cisco 200

The Cisco 201 and 202 are ISDN cards for Industry-Standard Architecture (ISA) bus computers. Open Data-Link Interface (ODI) drivers are available for Windows 3.1 and Windows 95, which support IP and IPX dial-on-demand routing. Network driver interface specification (NDIS) 3.1 drivers and drivers for the ISDN accelerator pack (both for Windows 95) were made available in September 1996. Windows NT drivers were released in the third quarter of 1996.

Adtran

Because Adtran and Cisco have worked closely during interoperability testing (PPP bakeoffs, for example), Adtran is a good candidate to consider for external terminal adapters. Adtran TAs support Multilink PPP (MP), Challenge Handshake Authentication Protocol (CHAP) and Password Authentication Protocol (PAP), synchronous or asychronous serial interfaces, and the Automatic Service Profile Identifier (AutoSPID) configuration.

Motorola BitSURFR

The simplest way to make a BitSURFR connected to a PC interoperate with a Cisco router is to turn on async/sync conversion with the command **AT%A2=95** (for more information, see page 7-1 of the BitSURFR manual). If you are using a BitSURFR Pro and want to use both B channels, you must use PAP authentication. The BitSURFR Pro cannot correctly answer the CHAP challenge sent when bringing up the second B channel. To place a call using two B channels you must enter the phone number twice. For example, if the phone number is 555-1212, you would enter **ATD555-1212&555-1212**. Table G-2 lists the commands to enter for several types of connections.

Table G-2   *Commands to Establish Connections on a Motorola BitSURFR*

Type of Connection	Command
Connect Using PPP	%A2=95
Use Both B channels (MP)	@B0=2
Use PAP Authentication	@M2=P
Data Termination Equipment (DTE) Speed (PC COM port)	&M
Place 64 kbps Calls	%A4=0
Place 56 kbps Calls	%A4=1
Place Voice Calls	%A98

Client Software

This section covers some Windows client software products available from Cisco.

CiscoRemote and CiscoRemote Lite

CiscoRemote™ Lite is a free TCP/IP stack and dialer application for Windows 3.1 and Windows for Workgroups.

CiscoRemote is a complete set of applications for "dial-up" remote computing in one package for the PC Windows and Apple Macintosh environments. All applications are optimized, tested, and supported by Cisco. This single product will link PCs with other computing resources within an enterprise network or across the worldwide Internet. CiscoRemote also includes the industry's first remote node accelerator to dramatically improve dial-up performance.

Cisco TCP/IP Suite 100

This TCP/IP stack for Windows 3.1 and Windows 95 directly replaces the Microsoft stack and adds features like router discovery and extensive configuration and management facilities. The full suite of TCP/IP applications include a Serial Line Internet Protocol (SLIP) and PPP dialer; a graphical File Transfer Protocol (FTP) client (with passive-mode support); a Telnet client with full VT420, tn3270, and tn5250 emulation and Kerberos support; a World Wide Web browser; Post-Office Protocol (POP) mail client; a Network File System (NFS) client; line printer daemon (LPD), Stream and PCNFSd printing; and best-in-class technical support.

IPeXchange Gateways

Customers using NWLink (NetBIOS over IPX) who want Internet access but do not want the complexity of configuring TCP/IP on each computer can use a Cisco IPeXchange gateway to run TCP/IP applications on a computer configured only with IPX. Only the IPeXchange Gateway requires a TCP/IP address.

Examples

This section shows four examples of Windows networks that include Cisco routers and access servers. Configurations are also provided for some of the devices.

Example 1

Example 1 (see Figure G-7) shows a small, single-domain network using NWLink (NetBIOS over IPX).

Figure G-7 *Small, Single-Domain Network Using NWLink*

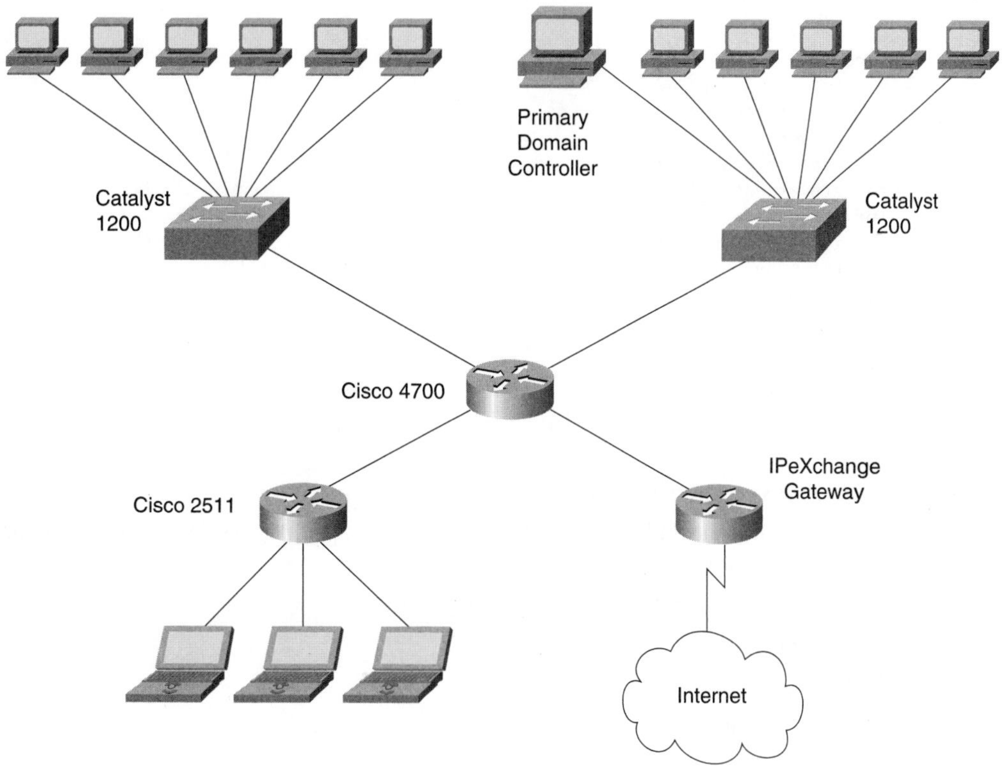

Configuration of Cisco 4700 Router

Example G-5 shows a sample configuration of the Cisco 4700 router in the network depicted in Figure G-7.

Example G-5   *Configuration of the Cisco 4700 Router in Figure G-7*

```
hostname 4700
ipx routing
!
interface ethernet 0
  ipx network 50
  ipx type-20-propagation
interface ethernet 1
  ipx network 60
  ipx type-20-propagation
interface ethernet 2
  ipx network 7B
  ipx type-20-propagation
interface ethernet 3
  ipx network 95
  ipx type-20-propagation
```

Configuration of Cisco 2511 Access Server

Example G-6 shows a sample configuration of the Cisco 2511 Access Server in the network depicted in Figure G-7.

Example G-6   *Configuration of the Cisco 2511 Access Server in Figure G-7*

```
hostname 2511
ipx routing
!
interface ethernet 0
 ipx network 98
interface loopback 0
 ipx network 163
interface group-async 0
 group-member 1 16
 ipx ppp-client loopback 0
 ipx sap-interval 0
 encapsulation ppp
 async mode dedicated
!
line 1 16
  modem inout
  speed 115200
  flowcontrol hardware
```

Example 2

Example 2 (see Figure G-8) shows a medium-sized network using NBT (NetBIOS over TCP) and static name resolution (LMHOSTS).

Figure G-8   *Medium-Sized Network Using NBT and LMHOSTS*

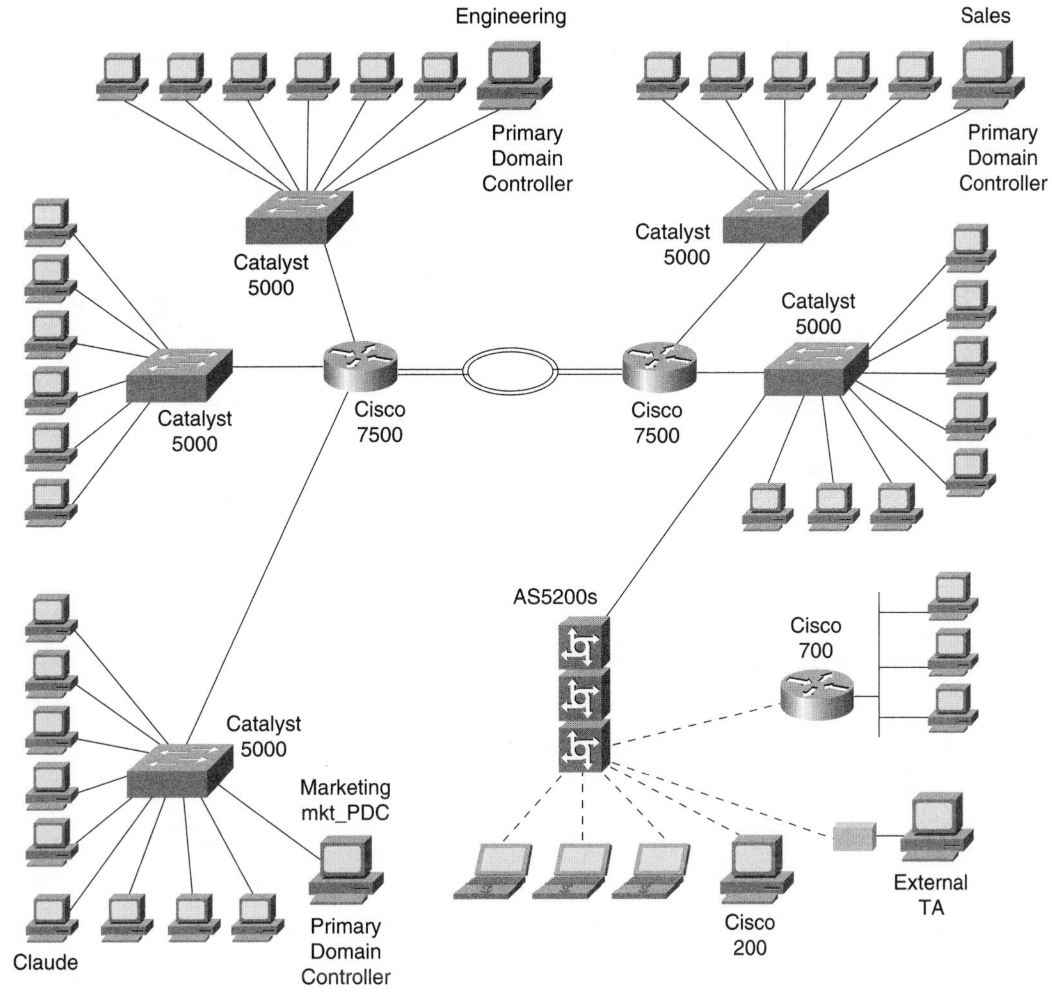

LMHOSTS Configuration on Claude (a Client in the Marketing Domain)

Example G-7 shows a sample LMHOSTS configuration for the client "Claude" in the network depicted in Figure G-8.

Example G-7   *LMHOSTS Configuration for Client "Claude" in Figure G-8*

```
1.2.1.8    mkt_PDC    #PRE
1.2.7.3    mkt_BDC    #PRE
#BEGIN ALTERNATE
  #INCLUDE \\mkt_pdc\public\lmhosts
  #INCLUDE \\mkt_bdc\public\lmhosts
#END ALTERNATE
```

LMHOSTS Configuration on mkt_PDC (Primary Domain Controller for the Marketing Domain)

Example G-8 shows a sample LMHOSTS configuration for the mkt_PDC in the network depicted in Figure G-8.

Example G-8   *LMHOSTS Configuration for the Marketing Domain PDC in Figure G-8*

```
1.1.1.3    eng_PDC    #PRE #DOM:eng
1.1.4.5    sales_PDC    #PRE #DOM:sales
1.2.1.4    sleepy
1.2.1.5    sneezy
1.2.6.2    martin
1.2.6.78   theresa
1.2.6.89   claude
```

Configuration of Cisco 7500 Router

Example G-9 shows a sample configuration for a 7500 router in the network depicted in Figure G-8.

Example G-9   *Configuration for a Cisco 7500 Router in Figure G-8*

```
hostname 7500
ip forward-protocol udp bootpc
!
interface ethernet 0
 ip address 1.5.6.1 255.255.255.0
 ip helper-address n.n.n.n
...
interface ethernet 23
 ip address 1.5.56.1 255.255.255.0
 ip helper-address n.n.n.n
```

Configuration of an AS5200 in a Stack Group

Example G-10 shows a sample configuration for an AS5200 in the stack group in the network depicted in Figure G-8.

Example G-10 *Configuration for an AS5200 in the Stack Group in Figure G-8*

```
hostname as5200-1
!
controller t1 0
 framing esf
 linecode b8zs
 pri-group
controller t1 1
 framing esf
 linecode b8zs
  pri-group
!
sgbp group as5200s
sgbp member as5200-2
sgbp member as5200-3
username as5200s password stackpassword
!
ip dhcp-server n.n.n.n
ip wins-server m.m.m.m
ip address-pool dhcp-proxy-client
!
interface ethernet 0
 ip address 192.168.2.1 255.255.255.0
!
interface group-async 0
 group-member 1 48
 peer default ip address dhcp
!
interface serial 0:23
 dialer rotary-group 1
 isdn incoming-voice modem
interface serial 1:23
 dialer rotary-group 1
 isdn incoming-voice modem
interface dialer 1
 ip unnumbered ethernet 0
 encapsulation ppp
 ppp multilink
 ppp authentication chap
 ppp use-tacacs
 dialer-group 1
!
dialer-list 1 protocol ip permit
!
line 1 48
 modem inout
 modem autoconfigure type microcom-hdms
 speed 115200
 flowcontrol hardware
```

Configuration of Cisco 700 Router

Example G-11 shows a sample configuration for the Cisco 700 router in the network depicted in Figure G-8.

Example G-11   *Configuration for the Cisco 700 Router in Figure G-8*

```
set system 700
cd LAN
 set ip address 1.4.3.1
 set ip netmask 255.255.255.248
 set ip routing on
 set ip rip update periodic
cd
set user as5200s
 set encapsulation ppp
 set ip framing none
 set ip routing on
set number 5551212
set ip route destination 0.0.0.0/0 gateway 0.0.0.0
cd
set active as5200s
set bridging off
```

Example 3

Example 3 shows a medium-sized network using NBT (NetBIOS over TCP) and a single WINS server (see Figure G-9).

Figure G-9   *Medium-Sized Network Using NBT and a Single WINS Server*

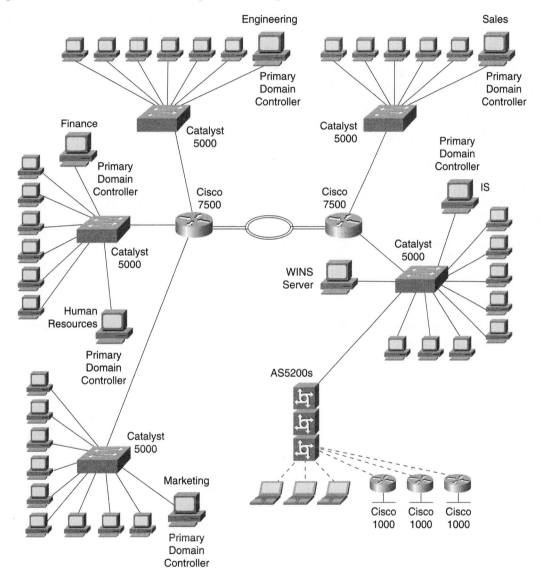

Configuration of a Cisco 1000 Router

Example G-12 shows a sample configuration for a Cisco 1000 router in the network depicted in Figure G-9.

Example G-12 *Configuration for a Cisco 1000 Router in Figure G-9*

```
hostname 1000
username as5200s password secret
!
interface ethernet 0
 ip address 1.4.3.1 255.255.255.248
interface bri 0
 ip unnumbered ethernet 0
 encapsulation ppp
 ppp multilink
 dialer string 5551212
 dialer-group 1
!
dialer-list 1 protocol ip list 101
access-list 101 deny udp any any eq netbios-ns
access-list 101 permit ip any any
```

Example 4

Figure G-10 shows a large network using NBT (NetBIOS over TCP) with multiple master domains and replicated WINS servers.

Figure G-10 *Large Network Using NBT with Multiple Master Domains and Replicated WINS Servers*

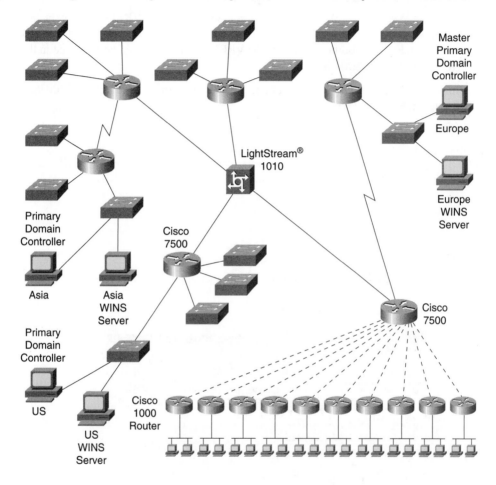

Appendix A: Turning Off Broadcast Name Resolution

This appendix covers how to turn off broadcast name resolution for the following systems:

- Windows for Workgroups 3.11
- Windows 95
- Windows NT 3.51

In addition, this appendix covers the proper Windows NT Registry settings to use to disable broadcast name resolution, as well as how to locate Windows 3.1 and Windows 95 workstations that are attempting to function as browse masters.

When Using Windows for Workgroups 3.11

When using Windows for Workgroups 3.11, a new browser file, VREDIR.386, which is included with Windows NT 3.5, must be used to allow browsing to work correctly. Windows 95 already includes this modified browser. The VREDIR.386 file is typically located in the C:\WINDOWS\SYSTEM directory.

Windows for Workgroups clients should make the change to the SYSTEM.INI file that is illustrated in Example G-13:

Example G-13 *SYSTEM.INI File Changes for Windows for Workgroups Clients*

```
; SYSTEM.INI
;
[Network]
MaintainServerList=No
```

Windows 95

Figure G-11 illustrates how to disable the Browse Master on Windows 95 client machines.

Figure G-11 *Turning Off Browse Master in Windows 95*

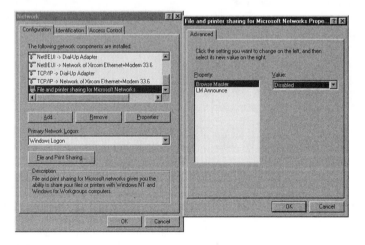

Windows NT 3.51

Windows NT 3.51 Workstations and Servers which are configured for WINS name resolution do not send broadcasts unless other computers on the network request a browser election. No action is required.

Windows NT Registry Entries

These entries in the hkey_local_machine\system\currentcontrolset\services\browser\parameters area of the Registry should be set as follows. MaintainServerList should be set to Yes, and IsDomainMaster should be set to False. These are the default settings.

The MasterPeriodicity setting (in seconds) specifies how often subnet browse servers query the domain master to obtain a browse list. When subnet browse servers and the domain master are separated by a low-speed or charge-per-packet link, you can set this to an hour or more.

Finding Rogue Browse Masters

Windows 3.1 and Windows 95 workstations cannot function as browse masters in a Windows NT network because they do not handle NT server and domain information. Unfortunately, by default, Windows 95 will attempt to become a browse master. A single workstation incorrectly claiming to be the browse master will hinder browsing for every computer on that entire subnet.

The Windows NT Server Resource Kit contains a utility called BROWSTAT. The easiest way to find a rogue broadcaster on a subnet is to run BROWSTAT on a Windows NT computer on the affected subnet.

Appendix B: Configuring DNS Resolution of WINS Names

The Microsoft NT 3.51 Resource Kit and Windows NT 4.0 server both include a DNS server that can answer DNS queries by querying a WINS server in the background. The WINS server and the DNS server must be on the same Windows NT machine. All DNS queries to a subdomain (in this example, wins.cisco.com) should be delegated to the DNS/WINS server.

For more information about DNS, see *DNS and Bind* by Paul Albitz and Cricket Liu (O'Reilly and Associates, 1992).

Example G-14 shows an example of a DNS boot file.

Example G-14 *The DNS Boot File*

```
;BOOT
cache    .       CACHE
primary  domain.com      domain.dom
primary  8.17.1.in-addr.arpa     1-17-8.rev
```

Example G-15 shows the DNS File for cisco.com.

Example G-15 *The DNS File for cisco.com*

```
;domain.dom
@   IN   SOA   ns.domain.com.   rohan.domain.com. (
        1  ; Serial Number
        10800  ; Refresh [3h]
        3600  ; Retry [1h]
        604800  ; Expire [7d]
        86400)  ; Minimum [1d]
@   IN   WINS   1.1.4.6 1.2.7.4
wins-server   IN   A 1.1.4.6
wins-server2   IN   A 1.2.7.4
```

This appendix contains information on Cisco's Network Address Translation obtained from Cisco's web site and from other Cisco courses.

Network Address Translation

IP address depletion is a key problem facing the Internet. To assist in maximizing the use of your registered IP addresses, Cisco IOS™ Release 11.2 software implements Network Address Translation (NAT). This feature, which is Cisco's implementation of RFC 1631, *The IP Network Address Translator,* is a solution that provides a way to use the same IP addresses in multiple internal stub networks, thereby reducing the need for registered IP addresses.

Why Use NAT?

Use NAT in the following situations:

- **When you want to connect to the Internet but not all the hosts have globally unique IP addresses**—NAT technology enables private IP internetworks that use nonregistered IP addresses to connect to the Internet. A NAT router is placed on the border of a stub domain (referred to as the *inside network*) and a public network such as the Internet (referred to as the *outside network*) and translates the internal local addresses into globally unique IP addresses before sending packets to the outside network.

  NAT takes advantage of the fact that relatively few hosts in a stub domain communicate outside of the domain at any given time. Because most of the hosts do not communicate outside of their stub domain, only a subset of the IP addresses in a stub domain must be translated into globally unique IP addresses when outside communication is necessary.

- **When you need to modify your internal addresses because of changing Internet service providers (ISPs)**—NAT can be used to translate the appropriate addresses. This enables you to change addresses incrementally, without changing hosts or routers other than those bordering stub domains.

- **When you want to do basic load sharing**—You can map outside IP addresses to inside IP addresses using the Transmission Control Protocol (TCP) Load Distribution feature.

NAT Terminology

When using NAT, the terms *inside* and *outside* networks are used, as shown in the example in Figure H-1. The terminology for NAT, as used in Figure H-1, is defined in Table H-1.

Figure H-1   *Network Address Translation Is Used to Translate Addresses between the* Inside *and* Outside *Networks*

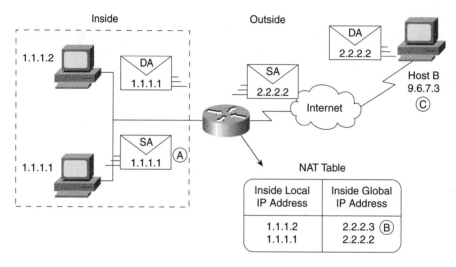

Table H-1   *NAT Terminology*

Term	Definition
Inside Local IP Address (A)	The IP address assigned to a host on the inside network. The address was globally unique but obsolete, allocated from RFC 1918, *Address Allocation for Private Internet Space*, or randomly picked.
Inside Global IP Address (B)	A legitimate IP address (assigned by the NIC or service provider) that represents one or more inside local IP addresses to the outside world. The address was allocated from a globally unique address space, typically provided by the ISP.
Outside Global IP Address (C)	The IP address that was assigned to a host on the outside network by its owner. The address was allocated from a globally routable address space.
Outside Local IP Address (not shown)	The IP address of an outside host as it appears to the inside network. The address was allocated from address space routable on the inside or possibly allocated from RFC 1918, for example.
Simple Translation Entry	A translation entry that maps one IP address to another. This is the type of entry shown in Figure H-1.
Extended Translation Entry (not shown)	A translation entry that maps one IP address and port pair to another.

Supported Features

Supported NAT features include the following:

- **Static address translation**—Establishes a one-to-one mapping between inside local and global addresses.

- **Dynamic source address translation**—Establishes a dynamic mapping between the inside local and global addresses. This is accomplished by describing the local addresses to be translated, the pool of addresses from which to allocate global addresses, and associating the two. The router will create translations as needed.

- **Address overloading**—Can conserve addresses in the inside global address pool by allowing source ports in TCP connections or User Datagram Protocol (UDP) conversations to be translated. When different inside local addresses map to the same inside global address, each inside host's TCP or UDP port numbers are used to distinguish between them.

- **TCP load distribution**—A dynamic form of destination translation that can be configured for some outside-to-inside traffic. Once a mapping is defined, destination addresses matching an access list are replaced with an address from a rotary pool. Allocation is done on a round-robin basis, and only when a new connection is opened from the outside to the inside. All non-TCP traffic will be passed untranslated (unless other translations are in effect).

NAT Operation

NAT can be used to perform several functions. This section discusses the operation of the following NAT functions:

- Translating Inside Local Addresses
- Overloading Inside Global Addresses
- Handling Overlapping Networks
- TCP Load Distribution

Translating Inside Local Addresses

Figure H-2 illustrates NAT operation when NAT is used to translate addresses from inside your network to destinations outside of your network.

Figure H-2 *Translating Inside Local Addresses*

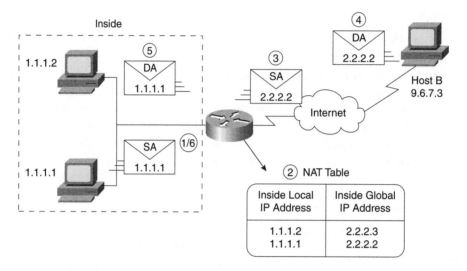

The process of translating inside local addresses, as depicted in Figure H-2, is described in the step-by-step list that follows.

Step 1 The user at Host 1.1.1.1 opens a connection to Host B.

Step 2 The first packet that the router receives from Host 1.1.1.1 causes the router to check its NAT table.

— If a translation is found because it has been statically configured, the router continues to step 3.

— If no translation is found, the router determines that address 1.1.1.1 must be translated. The router allocates a new address and sets up a translation of the inside local address 1.1.1.1 to a legal global address from the dynamic address pool. This type of translation entry is referred to as a simple entry.

Step 3 The router replaces Host 1.1.1.1's inside local IP address with the selected inside global address (2.2.2.2) and forwards the packet.

Step 4 Host B receives the packet and responds to Host 1.1.1.1 using the inside global IP address 2.2.2.2.

Step 5 When the router receives the packet with the inside global IP address, the router performs a NAT table lookup using the inside global address as the reference. The router then translates the address to Host 1.1.1.1's inside local address and forwards the packet to Host 1.1.1.1.

Step 6 Host 1.1.1.1 receives the packet and continues the conversation. For each packet, the router performs steps 2 through 5.

Overloading Inside Global Addresses

Figure H-3 illustrates NAT operation when a single inside global address can be used to represent multiple inside local addresses simultaneously.

Figure H-3   *Overloading Inside Global Addresses*

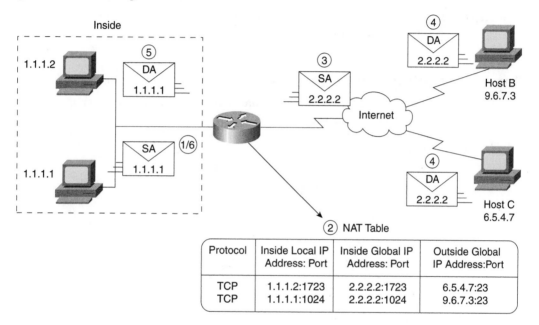

The process of overloading inside global addresses, as depicted in Figure H-3, is described in the step-by-step list that follows.

Step 1   The user at Host 1.1.1.1 opens a connection to Host B.

Step 2   The first packet the router receives from Host 1.1.1.1 causes the router to check its NAT table.

If no translation is found, the router determines that address 1.1.1.1 must be translated. The router allocates a new address and sets up a translation of the inside local address 1.1.1.1 to a legal global address (2.2.2.2). If overloading is enabled, and another translation is active, the router will reuse the global address from that translation and save enough information (the port number) to be able to distinguish it from the other translation entry. This type of entry is called an extended entry.

Step 3   The router replaces Host 1.1.1.1's inside local IP address with the selected inside global address (2.2.2.2) and forwards the packet.

Step 4   Host B receives the packet and responds to Host 1.1.1.1 using the inside global IP address 2.2.2.2.

Step 5 When the router receives the packet with the inside global IP address, the router performs a NAT table lookup using the inside global address and port number, and the outside address and port number as the references. The router then translates the address to Host 1.1.1.1's inside local address and forwards the packet to Host 1.1.1.1.

Step 6 Host 1.1.1.1 receives the packet and continues the conversation. For each packet, the router performs steps 2 through 5.

Handling Overlapping Networks

Figure H-4 illustrates NAT operation when addresses in the inside network overlap with addresses that are in the outside network.

Figure H-4 *Handling Overlapping Networks*

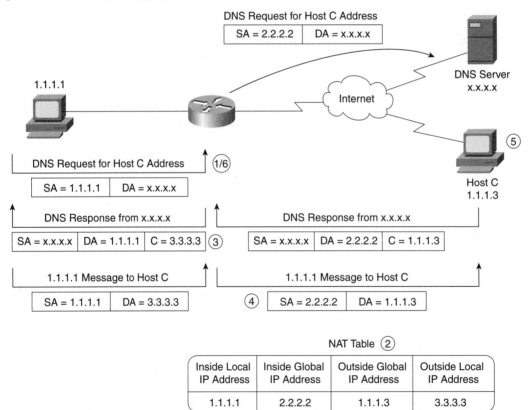

The process of handling overlapping addresses, as depicted in Figure H-4, is described in the step-by-step list that follows.

Step 1   The user at 1.1.1.1 opens a connection to Host C (1.1.1.3), causing 1.1.1.1 to do a name-to-address lookup to a DNS server.

Step 2   The router intercepts the DNS reply and translates the returned address if there is an overlap. In this case, 1.1.1.3 overlaps with an inside address. To translate the return address of Host C, the router creates a simple translation entry that maps the overlapping address 1.1.1.3 to an address from a separately configured outside local address pool. In this example, the address is 3.3.3.3.

Step 3   The router then forwards the DNS reply to Host 1.1.1.1. The reply has Host C's address as 3.3.3.3. At this point, 1.1.1.1 opens a connection to 3.3.3.3.

Step 4   When the router receives the packet for Host C (3.3.3.3), the router sets up a translation that maps the inside local and global addresses and outside global and local addresses. The router does this by replacing the source address of 1.1.1.1 with the inside global address 2.2.2.2, and by replacing the destination address of 3.3.3.3 with Host C's outside global address 1.1.1.3.

Step 5   Host C receives a packet and continues the conversation.

Step 6   For each packet sent between Host 1.1.1.1 and Host C, the router does a lookup, replaces the destination address with the inside local address, and replaces the source address with the outside local address.

TCP Load Distribution

Figure H-5 illustrates NAT operation when NAT is used to map one virtual host to several real hosts.

Figure H-5 *TCP Load Distribution*

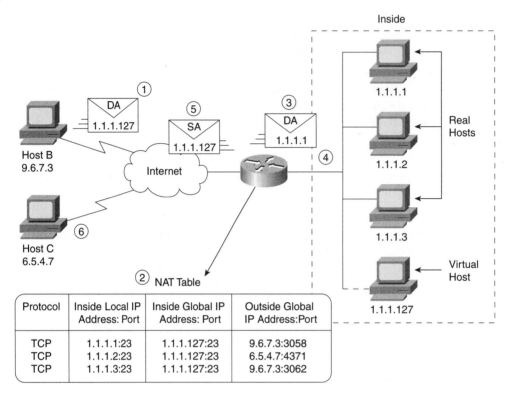

The process of TCP load distribution, as depicted in Figure H-5, is described in the step-by-step list that follows.

Step 1 The user on Host B (9.6.7.3) opens a TCP connection to the virtual host at 1.1.1.127.

Step 2 The router receives the connection request and creates a new translation allocating the next real host (1.1.1.1) for the inside local IP address.

Step 3 The router replaces the destination address with the selected real host address and forwards the packet.

Step 4 Host 1.1.1.1 receives the packet and responds.

Step 5 The router receives the packet and performs a NAT table lookup using the inside local address (1.1.1.1) and port number, and outside address (9.6.7.3) and port number as the key. The router then translates the source address to the address of the virtual host and forwards the packet.

Step 6 The next connection request will cause the router to allocate 1.1.1.2 for the inside local address.

Configuring NAT

This section includes details about how to configure various NAT capabilities.

Configuring NAT for Basic Local IP Address Translation

The procedure used to enable basic local IP address translation is as follows:

Step 1 At a minimum, IP routing and appropriate IP addresses must be configured on the router.

Step 2 If you are doing static address translations for inside local addresses, define the addresses using the following command:

```
Router(config)#ip nat inside source static local-ip global-ip
```

Step 3 If you are doing dynamic translations, define a standard IP access list for the inside network.

Step 4 If you are doing dynamic translations, define an IP NAT pool for the inside network using the following command:

```
Router(config)#ip nat pool name start-ip end-ip {netmask netmask ¦
prefix-length prefix-length}
```

This command defines a pool of contiguous addresses from the start address to the end address, using the netmask or prefix length. These addresses will be allocated as needed.

Step 5 If you are doing dynamic translations, define a map between the access list and the IP NAT pool using the following command:

```
Router(config)#ip nat inside source list access-list-number pool name
```

Step 6 Enable NAT on at least one inside and one outside interface using the following command:

```
Router(config-if)#ip nat {inside ¦ outside}
```

Step 7 Only packets moving between "inside" and "outside" interfaces can be translated. For example, if a packet is received on an "inside" interface but is not destined for an "outside" interface, it will not be translated.

An example configuration of basic inside local address translation is shown in Example H-1. This example uses a pool of addresses named *net-2* to translate inside local addresses 1.1.1.x to inside global addresses 2.2.2.x.

Example H-1   *An Example of Basic Inside Local Address Translation*

```
ip nat pool net-2 2.2.2.1 2.2.2.254 netmask 255.255.255.0
ip nat inside source list 1 pool net-2
!
interface Serial0
 ip address 171.69.232.182 255.255.255.240
 ip nat outside
!
interface Ethernet0
 ip address 1.1.1.254 255.255.255.0
 ip nat inside
!
access-list 1 permit 1.1.1.0 0.0.0.255
```

Configuring Inside Global Address Overloading

The procedure used to configure inside global address overloading is as follows:

Step 1   At a minimum, IP routing and appropriate IP addresses must be configured on the router.

Step 2   Configure dynamic address translation, as described in the "Configuring NAT for Basic Local IP Address Translation" section.

When you define the mapping between the access list and the IP NAT pool, add the **overload** keyword to the command, as follows:

```
Router(config)#ip nat inside source list access-list-number pool name
overload
```

Step 3   Enable NAT on the appropriate interfaces with the following command:

```
Router(config-if)#ip nat {inside ¦ outside}
```

Example H-2 shows an example configuration of inside global address overloading. This example uses a pool of addresses named *net-2* to translate inside local addresses 1.1.1.x to inside global addresses 2.2.2.x. Overloading of the inside global addresses will be done.

Example H-2   *An Example of Inside Global Address Overloading*

```
ip nat pool net-2 2.2.2.1 2.2.2.254 netmask 255.255.255.0
ip nat inside source list 1 pool net-2 overload
!
interface Serial0
 ip address 171.69.232.182 255.255.255.240
 ip nat outside
!
interface Ethernet0
 ip address 1.1.1.254 255.255.255.0
 ip nat inside
!
access-list 1 permit 1.1.1.0 0.0.0.255
```

Configuring NAT to Translate Overlapping Addresses

The procedure used to configure overlapping address translation is as follows:

Step 1   At a minimum, IP routing and appropriate IP addresses must be configured on the router.

Step 2   Define the standard IP access list for the inside network, as previously discussed.

Step 3   Define an IP NAT pool for the inside network, as previously discussed, using the following command:

```
Router(config)#ip nat pool name start-ip end-ip {netmask netmask ¦
prefix-length prefix-length}
```

Step 4   Define an IP NAT pool (with a different name) for the outside network using the following command.

```
Router(config)#ip nat pool name start-ip end-ip {netmask netmask ¦
prefix-length prefix-length}
```

Step 5   Define the mapping between the access list and the inside global pool, as previously discussed, using the following command:

```
Router(config)#ip nat inside source list access-list-number pool name
[overload]
```

Step 6   Define the mapping between the access list and the outside local pool using the following command:

```
Router(config)#ip nat outside source list access-list-number pool name
```

Step 7   Enable NAT on the appropriate interface, as previously discussed, using the following command:

```
Router(config-if)#ip nat {inside ¦ outside}
```

Example H-3 shows an example configuration of translating overlapping addresses. This example uses a pool of addresses named *net-2* to translate inside local addresses 1.1.1.x to inside global addresses 2.2.2.x. It also has a pool of addresses named *net-10* to translate outside global addresses 1.1.1.x to outside local addresses 10.0.1.x.

Example H-3   *An Example of Translating Overlapping Addresses*

```
ip nat pool net-2 2.2.2.1 2.2.2.254 prefix-length 24
ip nat pool net-10 10.0.1.1 10.0.1.254 prefix-length 24
ip nat inside source list 1 pool net-2
ip nat outside source list 1 pool net-10
!
interface Serial0
 ip address 171.69.232.182 255.255.255.240
 ip nat outside
!
interface Ethernet0
 ip address 1.1.1.254 255.255.255.0
 ip nat inside
!
access-list 1 permit 1.1.1.0 0.0.0.255
```

Configuring TCP Load Distribution

The procedure used to configure TCP load distribution is as follows:

Step 1   At a minimum, configure IP routing and appropriate IP addresses on the router.

Step 2   Define a standard IP access list with a permit statement for the virtual host.

Step 3   Define an IP NAT pool for the real hosts, making sure it is a rotary type pool, using the following command:

```
Router(config)#ip nat pool name start-ip end-ip {netmask netmask ¦
prefix-length prefix-length} type rotary
```

Step 4   Define a mapping between the access list and the real host pool using the following command:

```
Router(config)#ip nat inside destination list access-list-number pool name
```

Step 5   Enable NAT on the appropriate interface, as previously discussed, using the following command:

```
Router(config-if)#ip nat {inside ¦ outside}
```

Example H-4 shows an example configuration of TCP load distribution. This example uses an access list to translate the virtual server address 1.1.1.127 (the inside global address) to a pool of real hosts addresses from a pool named *real-hosts*.

Example H-4   *An Example of TCP Load Distribution*

```
ip nat pool real-hosts 1.1.1.1 1.1.1.126 prefix-length 24 type rotary
ip nat inside destination list 2 pool real-hosts
!
interface Serial0
 ip address 192.168.1.129 255.255.255.240
 ip nat outside
!
interface Ethernet0
 ip address 1.1.1.254 255.255.255.0
 ip nat inside
!
access-list 2 permit 1.1.1.127
```

Verifying NAT

This section lists **show** and **clear** commands that are used to verify NAT operation.

show **Commands**

Table H-2 presents the commands that can be used to verify NAT operation.

Table H-2   *show Commands to Verify NAT Operation*

Command	Description
show ip nat translations [verbose]	Shows active translations
show ip nat statistics	Shows translation statistics

Example H-5 shows a sample verification output for basic IP address translation.

Example H-5   *A Sample Verification Output for Basic IP Address Translation*

```
router#show ip nat trans
Pro  Inside global      Inside local      Outside local      Outside global
---  2.2.2.2            1.1.1.1           ---                ---
---  2.2.2.3            1.1.1.2           ---                ---
```

Example H-6 shows a sample verification output for IP address translation with overloading.

Example H-6   *A Sample Verification Output for IP Address Translation with Overloading*

```
router#show ip nat trans
Pro  Inside global      Inside local      Outside local      Outside global
udp  2.2.2.2:1220       1.1.1.1:1220      171.69.2.132:53    171.69.2.132:53
tcp  2.2.2.2:11012      1.1.1.2:11012     171.69.1.220:23    171.69.1.220:23
tcp  2.2.2.2:1067       1.1.1.1:1067      171.69.1.161:23    171.69.1.161:23
```

Clearing NAT Translation Entries

If you need to clear a dynamic translation entry, use the commands shown in Table H-3.

Table H-3   *Commands to Clear NAT Translation Entries*

Command	Description
clear ip nat translation *	Clears all translation entries.
clear ip nat translation inside *global-ip local-ip* [**outside** *local-ip global-ip*]	Clears a simple translation entry containing an inside translation, or both an inside and outside translation.
clear ip nat translation outside *local-ip global-ip*	Clears a simple translation entry containing an outside translation.
clear ip nat translation *protocol* **inside** *global-ip global-port local-ip local-port* [**outside** *local-ip local-portglobal-ip global-port*]	Clears an extended entry (in its various forms).

Example H-7 and Example H-8 provide two example outputs using the **clear** commands.

Example H-7 *Clearing NAT Translation Example 1*

```
router#show ip nat trans
Pro  Inside global      Inside local       Outside local       Outside global
udp  2.2.2.2:1220       1.1.1.1:1220       171.69.2.132:53      171.69.2.132:53
tcp  2.2.2.2:11012      1.1.1.2:11012      171.69.1.220:23      171.69.1.220:23
tcp  2.2.2.2:1067       1.1.1.1:1067       171.69.1.161:23      171.69.1.161:23
router#clear ip nat translation *
router#show ip nat trans
router#
```

Example H-8 *Clearing NAT Translation Example 2*

```
router#show ip nat trans
Pro  Inside global      Inside local       Outside local       Outside global
udp  2.2.2.2:1220       1.1.1.1:1220       171.69.2.132:53      171.69.2.132:53
tcp  2.2.2.2:11012      1.1.1.2:11012      171.69.1.220:23      171.69.1.220:23
tcp  2.2.2.2:1067       1.1.1.1:1067       171.69.1.161:23      171.69.1.161:23
router#clear ip nat translation udp inside 2.2.2.2 1220 1.1.1.1 1220 outside
  171.69.2.132 53 171.69.2.132 53
router#show ip nat trans
Pro  Inside global      Inside local       Outside local       Outside global
tcp  2.2.2.2:11012      1.1.1.2:11012      171.69.1.220:23      171.69.1.220:23
tcp  2.2.2.2:1067       1.1.1.1:1067       171.69.1.161:23      171.69.1.161:23
```

Troubleshooting NAT

If you need to use a trace on a NAT operation, use the **debug ip nat [list ¦ detailed]** command, which displays a line of output for each packet that gets translated .

Example H-9 shows example output using the **debug ip nat** command.

Example H-9 *Tracing NAT Operations with **debug ip nat***

```
router#debug ip nat
NAT:  s=1.1.1.1->2.2.2.2, d=171.69.2.132      [6825]
NAT:  s=171.69.2.132,     d=2.2.2.2->1.1.1.1  [21852]
NAT:  s=1.1.1.1->2.2.2.2, d=171.69.1.161      [6826]
NAT*: s=171.69.1.161,     d=2.2.2.2->1.1.1.1  [23311]
NAT*: s=1.1.1.1->2.2.2.2, d=171.69.1.161      [6827]
NAT*: s=1.1.1.1->2.2.2.2, d=171.69.1.161      [6828]
NAT*: s=171.69.1.161,     d=2.2.2.2->1.1.1.1  [23313]
NAT*: s=171.69.1.161,     d=2.2.2.2->1.1.1.1  [23325]
```

The debug output in Example H-9 can be decoded as follows (using the fourth line in the output as an example):

- The asterisk next to "NAT" indicates that the translation is occurring in the fast path. The first packet in a conversation will always go through the slow path (that is, it will be process-switched). The remaining packets will go through the fast path if a cache entry exists.
- **s=171.69.1.161** is the source address.
- **d=2.2.2.2** is the destination address.
- **2.2.2.2->1.1.1.1** indicates that the address was translated.
- The value in brackets is the IP identification number. This information might be useful for debugging because it enables you to correlate with other packet traces, from protocol analyzers for example.

Implementation Considerations

Some things to consider before implementing NAT are as follows:

- Translation introduces delays into the switching paths.
- NAT makes some applications that use IP addresses difficult or impossible to use. For example, public World Wide Web pages that have links expressed using local IP addresses rather than DNS names will not be usable by outside hosts. A list of traffic types supported and not supported by NAT is available on Cisco's web site, in the document at http://www.cisco.com/warp/public/cc/cisco/mkt/ios/nat/prodlit/792_pp.htm.
- NAT hides the *real* identity of hosts.
- All packets that need to be translated must go through the NAT router, which may place limitations on the network design.

Summary

This Appendix discussed how NAT operates and when it can be used. It also summarized how you configure, verify, and troubleshoot this feature.

This list of OSPF frequently asked questions was originally produced by Cisco. For further information on OSPF refer to Cisco's web site or to the Cisco Press title, "*OSPF Network Design Solutions*," by Thomas M. Thomas II. This list has been edited here only for formatting.

OSPF Frequently Asked Questions

Q — *What is OSPF?*

A — OSPF is a link state routing protocol developed for IP networks. Each router maintains an identical database describing its area's topology. Then each router calculates its routing table by constructing a shortest path tree.

Q — *What are the advantages of OSPF over other distance vector routing protocols like IGRP and RIP?*

A — OSPF, being a link state routing protocol, is designed to recalculate routes quickly in the face of topological changes. This is called Fast Network Convergence. It uses a minimum of routing protocol traffic, so it provides better convergence time. It also allows different subnets of the same IP network number to have different masks. This is called Variable Length Subnetting. It provides support for discontiguous networks.

Q — *It's said that OSPF routing protocol exchanges are authenticated. What does this mean?*

A — This means that only trusted routers can participate in the Autonomous System's routing. A single authentication scheme is used for each area. Each participating router can have a password.

Q — *What is an area?*

A — An area is a collection of networks, together with routers having interfaces to any of the included networks.

Q — *What is a stub area?*

A — A stub area is an area in which you don't allow advertisements of external routes.

Q — *When you define an area to be a stub area by the command **area xx stub** in every router in the stub area, do you need the **area xx default-cost yy** command in every router too?*

A — No, **area-default-cost yy** is only required in area border routers.

Q — *If your network has no externals, is there any benefit of using stub areas?*

A — No, you don't need the **stub area** command in the router if your network has no externals.

Q — *When OSPF is configured, does area 0 have to be there?*

A — There is no need to have area 0 if you have only one area in your network. You can use any number as the area id. You only need area 0 to connect multiple areas if you have more than one area. But, when the autonomous system is divided into areas, there has to be an area 0 which is the backbone area. The backbone must be contiguous. If the backbone is partitioned, then parts of the autonomous system will become unreachable. Virtual links can be configured to repair the partition.

Q — *Could you configure an autonomous system that contained one class B network and used multiple areas with backbone area 0?*

A — Yes.

Q — *Can you use an area ID based on IP addresses?*

A — Yes, Cisco's implementation takes area id both in IP address format and decimal number.

Q — *The 9.1 documentation states that if you set def=0, the router is ineligible to ever become the designated router. Then, two paragraphs later, it states that the default setting is 0. What does this mean?*

A — This is an error in the manual. If a router's priority is 0, then it is ineligible to become a designated or backup designated router. Cisco routers have a default priority of 1, as shown in the following example output of the **show ip ospf interface ethernet 0** command.

```
Ethernet 0 is up, line protocol is up
Internet Address 131.108.70.1, Mask 255.255.255.240, Area 0.0.0.0 AS
1099, Router ID 131.108.72.81, Network Type BROADCAST, Cost: 10
Transmit Delay is 1 sec, State DR, Priority 1
                                   ^^^^^^^^^^
Designated Router id 131.108.72.81, Interface address 131.108.70.1 No
backup designated router on this network Timer intervals configured,
Hello 10, Dead 40, Wait 40, Retransmit 5 Hello due in 0:00:09
Neighbor Count is 0, Adjacent neighbor count is 0
```

Q — *There is a command to set the Link-State Retransmit Interval. What is this?*

A — Each newly received link-state advertisement must be acknowledged. This is done by sending link-state acknowledgment packets. LSAs are retransmitted until they are acknowledged. Link-State Retransmit Interval defines the time between retransmissions.

Q — *IP-OPSF-Transmit-Delay: What is the purpose of this variable, which adds a specified time to the age field of the update?*

A — If the delay is not added before transmission over a link, the time in which the LSA propagates over the link is not considered. The default value is 1 second. This parameter has more significance on very low-speed links.

Q — *What is a virtual link? When and how is it used?*

A — The backbone area must be contiguous; otherwise, some areas of the Autonomous System will become unreachable. Virtual links establish connectivity to the backbone. The two end points of the virtual link are area border routers that both have virtual link configured. Whenever there is an area that does not have a connection to the backbone, the virtual link provides that connectivity. OSPF treats two routers joined by a virtual link as if they were connected by an unnumbered point-to-point network. Virtual links cannot be configured on unnumbered links or through stub areas.

Q — *A great deal of literature suggests that OSPF is a complete solution to the problems of discontiguous addressing in IP nets. However, many people were under the impression that only the static option of the virtual link in OSPF allowed discontiguous nets regardless of the mask propagation properties of OSPF. Is this an accurate statement?*

A — No. Virtual links in OSPF maintain connectivity to the backbone from nonbackbone areas, but they are unnecessary for discontiguous addressing. OSPF provides support for discontiguous networks because every area has a collection of networks and OSPF attaches a mask to each advertisement.

Q — *Is there a limitation on the number of routers in an area?*

A — No, but this all depends on your network, available memory, processing, and so forth. In general, in order for OSPF to scale well, you should have less than 40 routers in an area.

Q — *All advertisements are sent using multicast addressing. Are the multicast IP addresses mapped to MAC-level multicast addresses?*

A — Except for Token Ring, the multicast IP addresses are mapped to MAC-level multicast addresses. Cisco maps Token Ring to MAC-level broadcast addresses.

Q — *OSPF's default cost for an interface is inversely proportional to its bandwidth (10^8 / bandwidth). But whatever "bandwidth" is configured on a given interface, the cost calculated by OSPF is the same. Why?*

A — OSPF does not calculate interface costs automatically from bandwidth. The user has to set it manually using the following commands:

```
int e 0
  ip ospf cost xx.
```

(This depends on your level of Cisco IOS™.)

NOTE   Since version 11.0 of the IOS™, the router does calculate the OSPF costs automatically from the bandwidth configured on the interface if the **ip ospf cost** command is not used.

Q — *Does Cisco's OSPF implementation support IP TOS-based routing?*

A — Cisco only supports TOS 0, which means that routers route all packets on the TOS 0 path, eliminating the need to calculate nonzero TOS paths.

Q — *Does OSPF discover multiple routes to a destination?*

A — Yes, it discovers multiple equal-cost routes to a destination.

Q — *Will the **offset-list** subcommand work for OSPF or is it only implemented for IGRP, RIP, and Hello?*

A — It is only there for IGRP, RIP, and Hello. It does not work with OSPF.

Q — *Can an OSPF default be originated into the system based on external information (such as routes learned from some exterior protocol) on a router that does not itself have a default?*

A — OSPF will generate a default only if it is configured using the command **default-information originate** and if there is a default network in the box from a different process. The default route in OSPF is 0.0.0.0.

Q — *Can **distribute-list in/out** be used with OSPF to filter routes?*

A — The command **distribute-list in** does not work on OSPF routes. It is applied when OSPF routes are fed into the routing table. You cannot alter the database, and a link state will still be generated.

The command **distribute-list out** works only on the routes being redistributed from other processes into OSPF. It can be applied only to EXTERNAL_TYPE2 and EXTERNAL_TYPE1 routes and cannot be applied to INTRA and INTER routes.

Q — *Does Cisco support the OSPF MIB definitions defined in RFC 1253?*

A — Release 11.0 supports the OSPF MIB.

Q — *Does Cisco's software comply with RFC 1364, "BGP OSPF Interaction"?*

A — Yes.

Q — *Do you have to manually set up adjacencies for routers on the SMDS cloud with the **OSPF neighbor** subcommand?*

A — In Cisco IOS™ 9.1, you need the **OSPF neighbor** command to make OSPF work on SMDS. As of 10.0, you need the **ip ospf network broadcast** command on the designated router.

Q — *Why must the **neighbor** command be used when running OSPF over NBMA (Frame Relay, X.25, and so on)?*

A — You need the **neighbor** command to make OSPF to work on NBMA in Cisco IOS™ 9.1. As of 10.0, at the OSPF level, an NBMA network can be configured as a broadcast network, and OSPF would treat NBMA as a broadcast network only. You would need X.25 maps with the **broadcast** keyword to make it work.

Q — *Can I assume that when routes are redistributed between OSPF processes, all SPF metrics are preserved and the default metric value is not used?*

A — Metrics are not preserved. The redistribution between them is like redistribution between any two IP routing processes.

Q — *What do the states DR/OTHER, DR, and BDR mean in **show ip ospf int** output?*

A — DR means "Designated Router," BDR means "Backup Designated Router," and DR/OTHER means a router that is neither the DR nor the BDR. DR will generate a Network Link-State Advertisement representing that network, listing all the routers on that network.

Q — *I have the following setup:*

Figure I-1   *Routers Running OSPF over X.25*

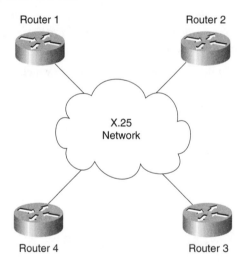

R1 through R4 are running OSPF, and each router is declared as neighbor in the other three. I want to connect R5, a fifth router, to that network. Can I declare R5 as neighbor of the Designated Router only and still get the whole routing table?

A — You need to list all the routers only in the routers eligible for DR/BDR. If you list R5 only in the present DR, you might have some problems when that DR goes down and routers are trying to become DR/BDR. If you think a router should not be allowed to become DR or BDR (its priority is set to 0), there is no need to list any routers in that router. As of Cisco IOS™ 10.0, Cisco routers allow these nonbroadcast networks to be configured as broadcast in order to avoid all this neighbor configuration.

Q — *How does Cisco accommodate OSPF routing on partial mesh Frame Relay Networks? What about other routing protocols, such as RIP and IGRP?*

A — You can configure OSPF to understand whether or not it should attempt to use multicast facilities on a multi-access interface. Also, if multicast is available, OSPF will use it for its normal multicasts.

Cisco IOS™ 10.0 includes a feature called "subinterfaces." This feature can be used with Frame Relay and similar interfaces to tie a set of VCs together to form a virtual interface, which acts as a single IP subnet. All systems within the subnet are expected to be fully meshed. This feature is routing protocol independent. As of 10.3 and 11.0, point-to-multipoint is also available.

RIP and IGRP have had other enhancements to deal with this same situation since Cisco IOS™ 8.3(3).

Q — *The area router subcommand associates router interfaces with OSPF areas, and it requires an address-wildmask pair. Which address-wildmask pair should be used for assigning an unnumbered interface to an area?*

A — Use the address-wildmask pair of the interface to which the unnumbered interface is pointing.

This OSPF Design Guide was originally written by Sam Halabi of Cisco Systems, Network Consulting Engineer—NSA group, and edited by Laura McCarty on April 9, 1996. This guide can also be found on Cisco's web site at http://www.cisco.com/warp/public/104/1.html. It has been edited here for formatting.

OSPF Design Guide

OSPF (Open Shortest Path First) protocol was developed due to a need in the internet community to introduce a high functionality nonproprietary Internal Gateway Protocol (IGP) for the TCP/IP protocol family. The discussion of creating a common interoperable IGP for the Internet started in 1988 and did not get formalized until 1991. At that time, the OSPF Working Group requested that OSPF be considered for advancement to Draft Internet Standard.

The OSPF protocol is based on link-state technology, which is a departure from the Bellman-Ford vector-based algorithms used in traditional Internet routing protocols, such as RIP. OSPF has introduced new concepts, such as authentication of routing updates, Variable Length Subnet Masks (VLSM), route summarization, and so forth.

This paper addresses the OSPF terminology, algorithm, and the pros and cons of the protocol in designing the large and complicated networks of today.

OSPF and RIP

The rapid growth and expansion of today's networks has pushed RIP to its limits. RIP has certain limitations that could cause problems in large networks:

- **RIP has a limit of 15 hops**—A RIP network that spans more than 15 hops (15 routers) is considered unreachable.

- **RIP cannot handle Variable Length Subnet Masks (VLSM)**—Given the shortage of IP addresses and the flexibility VLSM gives in the efficient assignment of IP addresses, this is considered a major flaw.

- **Periodic broadcasts of the full routing table will consume a large amount of bandwidth**—This is a major problem with large networks, especially on slow links and WAN clouds.

- **RIP converges more slowly than OSPF**—In large networks, convergence gets to be in the order of minutes. RIP routers will go through a period of a hold-down and garbage collection and will slowly time-out information that has not been received recently. This is inappropriate in large environments and could cause routing inconsistencies.

- **RIP has no concept of network delays and link costs**—Routing decisions are based on hop counts. The path with the lowest hop count to the destination is always preferred, even if the longer path has a better aggregate link bandwidth and slower delays.

- **RIP networks are flat networks**—There is no concept of areas or boundaries. With the introduction of classless routing and the intelligent use of aggregation and summarization, RIP networks seem to have fallen behind.

Some enhancements were introduced in a new version of RIP called RIP Version 2. RIP Version 2 addresses the issues of VLSM, authentication, and multicast routing updates. RIP Version 2 is not a big improvement over RIP (now called RIP Version 1) because it still has the limitations of hop counts and slow convergence, which are essential in todays large networks.

OSPF, on the other hand, addresses most of the issues presented in the preceding list on the limitations of RIP, including:

- With OSPF, there is no limitation on the hop count.

- The intelligent use of VLSM is useful in IP address allocation.

- OSPF uses IP multicast to send link-state updates. This ensures less processing on routers that are not listening to OSPF packets. With IP multicasting, OSPF sends updates only when routing changes occur, instead sending updates periodically. This ensures a better use of bandwidth.

- OSPF has better convergence than RIP because routing changes are propagated instantaneously and not periodically.

- OSPF allows for better load balancing based on the actual cost of the link. Link delays are a major factor in deciding where to send routing updates.

- OSPF allows for a logical definition of networks where routers can be divided into areas. This will limit the explosion of link state updates over the whole network. This also provides a mechanism for aggregating routes and cutting down on the unnecessary propagation of subnet information.

- OSPF allows for routing authentication by using different methods of password authentication.

- OSPF allows for the transfer and tagging of external routes injected into an Autonomous System. This keeps track of external routes injected by exterior protocols, such as BGP.

This of course would lead to more complexity in configuring and troubleshooting OSPF networks. Administrators that are used to the simplicity of RIP will be challenged with the amount of new information they have to learn in order to keep up with OSPF networks. Also, this will introduce more overhead in memory allocation and CPU utilization. Some of the routers running RIP might have to be upgraded in order to handle the overhead caused by OSPF.

What Do We Mean by Link States?

OSPF is a link-state protocol. We could think of a link as being an interface on the router. The state of the link is a description of that interface and of its relationship to its neighboring routers. A description of the interface would include, for example, the IP address of the interface, the mask, the type of network it is connected to, the routers connected to that network and so on. The collection of all these link-states would form a link-state database.

OSPF uses a link-state algorithm in order to build and calculate the shortest path to all known destinations. The algorithm by itself is quite complicated. The following is a very high level, simplified way of looking at the various steps of the algorithm:

Step 1   Upon initialization or due to any change in routing information, a router will generate a link-state advertisement. This advertisement will represent the collection of all link-states on that router.

Step 2   All routers will exchange link-states by means of flooding. Each router that receives a link-state update should store a copy in its link-state database and then propagate the update to other routers.

Step 3   After the database of each router is completed, the router will calculate a Shortest Path Tree to all destinations. The router uses the Dijkstra algorithm to calculate the Shortest Path Tree. The destinations, the associated cost, and the next hop to reach those destinations will form the IP routing table.

Step 4   In case no changes in the OSPF network occur, such as cost of a link or a network being added or deleted, OSPF should be very quiet. Any changes that occur are communicated via link-state packets, and the Dijkstra algorithm is recalculated to find the shortest path.

Shortest Path Algorithm

The shortest path is calculated using the Diskjtra algorithm. The algorithm places each router at the root of a tree and calculates the shortest path to each destination based on the cumulative cost required to reach that destination. Each router will have its own view of the topology, even though all the routers will build a shortest path tree using the same link-state database. The following sections indicate what is involved in building a shortest path tree.

OSPF Cost

The cost (also called metric) of an interface in OSPF is an indication of the overhead required to send packets across a certain interface. The cost of an interface is inversely proportional to the bandwidth of that interface. A higher bandwidth indicates a lower cost. There is more overhead (higher cost) and time delays involved in crossing a 56 kbps serial line than crossing a 10 MB ethernet line. The formula used to calculate the cost is:

Cost=100,000,000/bandwith in bps

For example, it will cost $10^8/10^7 = 10$ to cross a 10 Mbps Ethernet line and will cost $10^8/1544000 = 64$ to cross a T1 line.

By default, the cost of an interface is calculated based on the bandwidth; you can force the cost of an interface by using the **ip ospf cost** *cost* interface subcommand.

Shortest Path Tree

Assume we have the network diagram in Figure J-1 with the indicated interface costs. In order to build the shortest path tree for Router A, we would have to make Router A the root of the tree and calculate the smallest cost for each destination.

Figure J-1 *Building the Shortest Path Tree for Router A*

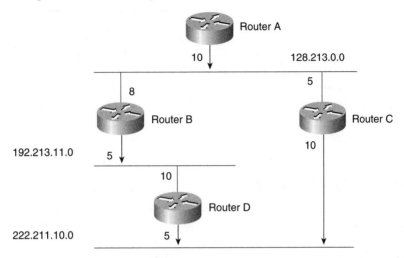

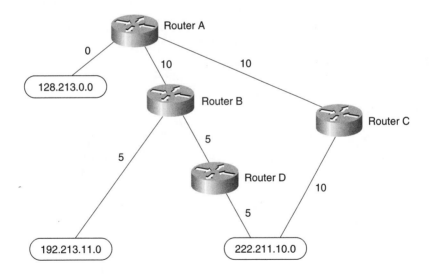

Figure J-1 is the view of the network as seen from Router A. Note the direction of the arrows in calculating the cost. For example, the cost of Router B's interface to network 128.213.0.0 is not relevant when calculating the cost to 192.213.11.0. Router A can reach 192.213.11.0 via Router B with a cost of 15 (10+5). Router A can also reach 222.211.10.0 via Router C with a cost of 20 (10+10) or via Router B with a cost of 20 (10+5+5). In case equal cost paths exist to the same destination, Cisco's implementation of OSPF will keep track of up to six next hops to the same destination.

After the router builds the shortest path tree, it will start building the routing table accordingly. Directly connected networks will be reached via a metric (cost) of 0, and other networks will be reached according to the cost calculated in the tree.

Areas and Border Routers

As previously mentioned, OSPF uses flooding to exchange link-state updates between routers. Any change in routing information is flooded to all routers in the network. Areas are introduced to put a boundary on the explosion of link-state updates. Flooding and calculation of the Dijkstra algorithm on a router is limited to changes within an area. All routers within an area have the exact link-state database. Routers that belong to multiple areas, called area border routers (ABR), have the duty of disseminating routing information or routing changes between areas. Figure J-2 shows two autonomous systems that have been divided into OSPF areas and the ABRs between the areas.

Figure J-2   *OSPF Uses Areas within an Autonomous System To Limit the Explosion of Link-State Updates*

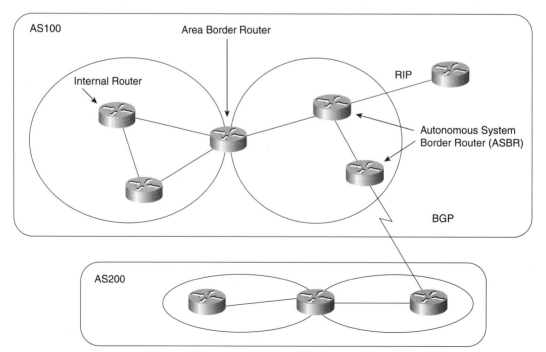

An area is interface specific. A router that has all of its interfaces within the same area is called an internal router (IR). A router that has interfaces in multiple areas is called an area border router (ABR). Routers that act as gateways (redistribution) between OSPF and other routing protocols (IGRP, EIGRP, IS-IS, RIP, BGP, Static) or other instances of the OSPF routing process are called autonomous system border routers (ASBR). Any router can be an ABR or an ASBR.

Link-State Packets

There are different types of link-state Packets; those are what you normally see in an OSPF database (see Appendix A, "Link-State Database Synchronization," in this document). Figure J-3 illustrates the different types of link-state packets.

Figure J-3   *Link-State Packet Types*

Router Links

Describe The State And Cost
of The Router's Links (Interfaces)
to The Area (Intra-Area).

Summary Links

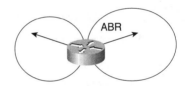

Originated by ABRs Only.
Describe Networks in The Autonomous
System But Outside of An Area (Interarea).
Also Describe The Location of The ASBR.

Network Links

Originated for Multiaccess Segments
with More Than One Attached Router.
Describe All Routers Attached to The
Specific Segment. Originated by A
Designed Router (discussed later on).

External Links

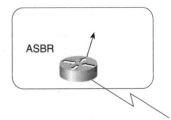

Originated by An ASBR.
Describe Destinations External to The
Autonomous System or A Default Route
to The Outside Autonomous System.

Router links are an indication of the state of the interfaces on a router belonging to a certain area. Each router will generate a router link for all of its interfaces.

Summary links are generated by ABRs; this is how network reachability information is disseminated between areas. Normally, all information is injected into the backbone (area 0), and, in turn, the backbone will pass it on to other areas. ABRs also have the task of propagating the reachability of the ASBR. This is how routers know how to get to external routes in other ASs.

Network Links are generated by a designated router (DR) on a segment (DRs will be discussed later). This information is an indication of all routers connected to a particular multi-access segment, such as Ethernet, Token Ring, and FDDI (NBMA also).

External Links are an indication of networks outside of the AS. These networks are injected into OSPF via redistribution. The ASBR has the task of injecting these routes into an autonomous system.

Enabling OSPF on the Router

Enabling OSPF on the router involves the following two steps in config mode:

Step 1   Enabling an OSPF process via the **router ospf** *process-id* command

Step 2   Assigning areas to the interfaces via the **network** {*network or IP address}*
mask **area** *area-id* command

The OSPF *process-id* is a numeric value local to the router. It does not have to match *process-id*s on other routers. It is possible to run multiple OSPF processes on the same router, but it is not recommended because it creates multiple database instances that add extra overhead to the router.

The **network** command is a way of assigning an interface to a certain area. The *mask* is used as a shortcut, and it helps when putting a list of interfaces in the same area with one line configuration line. The *mask* contains wildcard bits, where 0 is a match and 1 is a "do not care" bit. For example, 0.0.255.255 indicates a match in the first two bytes of the network number.

The *area-id* is the area number we want the interface to be in. The *area-id* can be an integer between 0 and 4294967295 or can take a form similar to an IP address A.B.C.D.

Figure J-4 shows an example of an ABR, Router A, between area 23 and area 0.0.0.0.

Figure J-4   *Example OSPF Area Configuration*

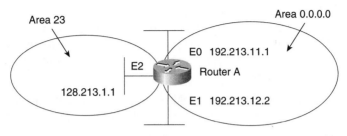

Example J-1 shows the configuration of OSPF on Router A in Figure J-4.

Example J-1   *Configuring OSPF on Router A in Figure J-4*

```
Router A#
interface Ethernet0
 ip address 192.213.11.1 255.255.255.0

interface Ethernet1
 ip address 192.213.12.2 255.255.255.0

interface Ethernet2
 ip address 128.213.1.1 255.255.255.0

router ospf 100
 network 192.213.0.0 0.0.255.255 area 0.0.0.0
 network 128.213.1.1 0.0.0.0 area 23
```

The first network statement will put both Ethernet0 and Ethernet1 in the same area (0.0.0.0), and the second network statement will put Ethernet2 in area 23. Note the mask of 0.0.0.0, which indicates a full match on the IP address. This is an easy way to put an interface in a certain area if you are having problems figuring out a mask.

OSPF Authentication

It is possible to authenticate the OSPF packets so that routers can participate in routing domains based on predefined passwords. By default, a router uses a Null authentication, which means that routing exchanges over a network are not authenticated. Two other authentication methods exist: Simple password authentication and Message Digest authentication (MD5).

Simple Password Authentication

Simple password authentication allows a password (key) to be configured per area. Routers in the same area that want to participate in the routing domain will have to be configured with the same key. The drawback of this method is that it is vulnerable to passive attacks. Anybody with a link analyzer could easily get the password off the wire. The following commands enable password authentication:

> **ip ospf authentication-key** *key* (this goes under the specific interface)
> **area** *area-id* **authentication** (this goes under **router ospf** *process-id*)

Example J-2 shows the configuration of simple OSPF password authentication on a router.

Example J-2 *Configuring Simple OSPF Authentication*

```
interface Ethernet0
 ip address 10.10.10.10 255.255.255.0
 ip ospf authentication-key mypassword

router ospf 10
 network 10.10.0.0 0.0.255.255 area 0 area 0 authentication
```

Message Digest Authentication

Message Digest Authentication is a cryptographic authentication. A key (password) and key-id are configured on each router. The router uses an algorithm based on the OSPF packet, the key, and the key-id to generate a "message digest," which gets appended to the packet. Unlike the simple authentication, the key is not exchanged over the wire. A nondecreasing sequence number is also included in each OSPF packet to protect against replay attacks.

This method also allows for uninterrupted transitions between keys. This is helpful for administrators who want to change the OSPF password without disrupting communication. If an interface is configured with a new key, the router will send multiple copies of the same packet, each authenticated by different keys. The router will stop sending duplicate packets after it detects that all its neighbors have adopted the new key. Following are the commands used for message digest authentication:

> **ip ospf message-digest-key** *keyid* **md5** *key* (used under the interface)
> **area** *area-id* **authentication message-digest** (used under **router ospf** *process-id*)

Example J-3 shows the configuration of Message Digest OSPF password authentication on a router.

Example J-3 *Configuring OSPF Message Digest Authentication*

```
interface Ethernet0
 ip address 10.10.10.10 255.255.255.0
 ip ospf message-digest-key 10 md5 mypassword

router ospf 10
 network 10.10.0.0 0.0.255.255 area 0
 area 0 authentication message-digest
```

The Backbone and Area 0

OSPF has special restrictions when multiple areas are involved. If more than one area is configured, one of these areas has be to be area 0. This is called the backbone. When designing networks, it is good practice to start with area 0 and then expand into other areas later on.

The backbone has to be at the center of all other areas that is, all areas have to be physically connected to the backbone. The reasoning behind this is that OSPF expects all areas to inject routing information into the backbone, and the backbone will, in turn, disseminate that information into other areas. Figure J-5 illustrates the flow of information in an OSPF network.

Figure J-5 *Information Flow in an OSPF Network*

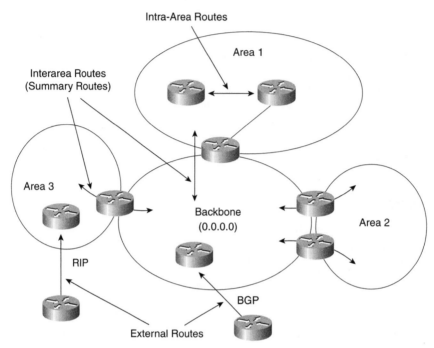

In Figure J-5, all areas are directly connected to the backbone. In the rare situations where a new area is introduced that cannot have a direct physical access to the backbone, a virtual link will have to be configured. Virtual links will be discussed in the next section. Note the different types of routing information. Routes that are generated from within an area (the destination belongs to the area) are called *intra-area routes*. These routes are normally represented by the letter **O** in the IP routing table. Routes that originate from other areas are called *interarea* or *Summary routes*. The notation for these routes is **O IA** in the IP routing table. Routes that originate from other routing protocols (or different OSPF processes) and that are injected into OSPF via redistribution are called *external routes*. These routes are represented by **O E2** or **O E1** in the IP routing table. Multiple routes to the same destination are preferred in the following order: intra-area, interarea, external E1, external E2. External types E1 and E2 will be explained later.

Virtual Links

Virtual links are used for two purposes:

- Linking an area that does not have a physical connection to the backbone
- Patching the backbone in case discontinuity of area 0 occurs

Areas Not Physically Connected to Area 0

As mentioned earlier, area 0 has to be at the center of all other areas. In some rare case where it is impossible to have an area physically connected to the backbone, a virtual link is used. The virtual link will provide the disconnected area a logical path to the backbone. The virtual link has to be established between two ABRs that have a common area, with one ABR connected to the backbone. Figure J-6 illustrates an example of establishing a virtual link between two ABRs.

Figure J-6   *Establishing a Virtual Link between Two ABRs.*

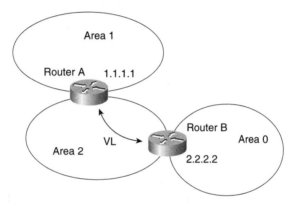

In this example, area 1 does not have a direct physical connection into area 0. A virtual link has to be configured between Router A and Router B. Area 2 is to be used as a transit area, and Router B is the entry point into area 0. In this way, Router A and area 1 will have a logical connection to the backbone. In order to configure a virtual link, use the **area** *area-id* **virtual-link** *router-id* subcommand on both Router A and Router B.

The *area-id* parameter represents the transit area. In Figure J-6, this is area 2. The OSPF *router-id* is usually the highest IP address on the box or the highest loopback address if one exists. The *router-id* is only calculated at boot time or anytime the OSPF process is restarted. In order to find the *router-id*, you can do a **show ip ospf interface**. Assuming that 1.1.1.1 and 2.2.2.2 are the respective *router-ids* of Router A and Router B, the OSPF configuration for both routers would look like Example J-4:

Example J-4   *Configuring Virtual Areas on the Routers in Figure J-6*

```
Router A#
router ospf 10
 area 2 virtual-link 2.2.2.2

Router B#
router ospf 10
 area 2 virtual-link 1.1.1.1
```

Partitioning the Backbone

OSPF allows for linking discontinuous parts of the backbone by using a virtual link. In some cases, different area 0s need to be linked together. This can occur if, for example, a company is trying to merge two separate OSPF networks into one network with a common area 0. In other instances, virtual links are added for redundancy in case some router failure causes the backbone to be split into two. Whatever the reason might be, a virtual link can be configured between separate ABRs that touch area 0 from each side and having a common area (see Figure J-7).

Figure J-7 *Configuring a Virtual Link to Link the Backbone*

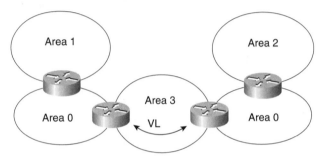

As depicted in Figure J-7, two area 0s are linked together via a virtual link. In case a common area does not exist, an additional area, such as area 3, could be created to become the transit area.

In case any area that is different than the backbone becomes partitioned, the backbone will take care of the partitioning without using any virtual links. One part of the partitioned area will be known to the other part via interarea routes rather than intra-area routes.

Neighbors

Routers that share a common segment become neighbors on that segment. Neighbors are elected via the Hello protocol. Hello packets are sent periodically out of each interface using IP multicast (see Appendix B, "OSPF and IP Multicast Addressing," in this document). Routers become neighbors as soon as they see themselves listed in the neighbor's Hello packet. This way, a two-way communication is guaranteed. Neighbor negotiation applies to the *primary address* only. Secondary addresses can be configured on an interface with a restriction that they have to belong to the same area as the primary address.

Two routers will not become neighbors unless they agree on the following criteria:

- **Area-id**—Two routers having a common segment; their interfaces have to belong to the same area on that segment. Of course, the interfaces should belong to the same subnet and have a similar mask.

- **Authentication**—OSPF allows for the configuration of a password for a specific area. Routers that want to become neighbors have to exchange the same password on a particular segment.

- **Hello and Dead Intervals**—OSPF exchanges hello packets on each segment. This is a form of keepalive used by routers in order to acknowledge their existence on a segment and to elect a designated router (DR) on multiaccess segments. The hello interval specifies the length of time, in seconds, between the hello packets that a router sends on an OSPF interface. The dead interval is the number of seconds that a router's hello packets have not been seen before its neighbors declare the OSPF router down.

  OSPF requires these intervals to be exactly the same between two neighbors. If any of these intervals are different, these routers will not become neighbors on a particular segment. The router interface commands used to set these timers are: **ip ospf hello-interval** *seconds* and **ip ospf dead-interval** *seconds*

- **Stub area flag**—Two routers also have to agree on the stub area flag in the hello packets in order to become neighbors. Stub areas will be discussed in a later section. Keep in mind for now that defining stub areas will affect the neighbor election process.

Adjacencies

An adjacency is the next step after the neighboring process. Adjacent routers are routers that go beyond the simple Hello exchange and proceed into the database exchange process. In order to minimize the amount of information exchange on a particular segment, OSPF elects one router to be a designated router (DR), and one router to be a backup designated router (BDR) on each multi-access segment. The BDR is elected as a backup mechanism in case the DR goes down. The idea behind this is that routers have a central point of contact for information exchange. Instead of each router exchanging updates with every other router on the segment, every router will exchange the information with the DR and BDR. The DR and BDR will relay the information to everybody else. In mathematical terms, this would cut the information exchange from O(n*n) to O(n), where n is the number of routers on a multi-access segment. The router model in Figure J-8 illustrates the DR and BDR.

Figure J-8   *A Router Model Shows the DR and BDR on a Multi-Access Segment, Used to Minimize the Required Information Exchange*

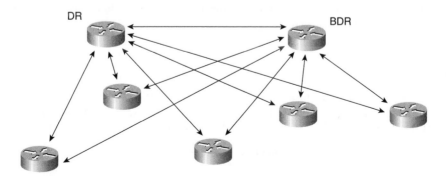

In Figure J-8, all routers share a common multi-access segment. Due to the exchange of hello packets, one router is elected DR, and another is elected BDR. Each router on the segment (which already became a neighbor) will try to establish an adjacency with the DR and BDR.

DR Election

DR and BDR election is done via the Hello protocol. Hello packets are exchanged via IP multicast packets (Appendix B) on each segment. The router with the highest OSPF priority on a segment will become the DR for that segment. The same process is repeated for the BDR. In case of a tie, the router with the highest RID will win. The default for the interface OSPF priority is one. Remember that the DR and BDR concepts are per multi-access segment. Setting the OSPF priority on an interface is done with the **ip ospf priority** *value* interface command:

A priority value of zero indicates an interface that is not to be elected as DR or BDR. The state of the interface with priority zero will be *DROTHER*. Figure J-9 illustrates the DR election.

Figure J-9 *Designated Router Election Process*

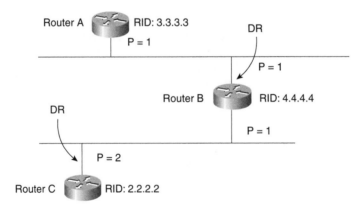

In Figure J-9, Router A and Router B have the same interface priority, but Router B has a higher RID. Router B would be DR on that segment. Router C has a higher priority than Router B. Router C is DR on that segment.

Building the Adjacency

The adjacency building process takes effect after multiple stages have been fulfilled. Routers that become adjacent will have the exact link-state database. The following is a brief summary of the states an interface passes through before becoming adjacent to another router:

Step 1 **Down**—No information has been received from anybody on the segment.

Step 1* **Attempt**—On nonbroadcast, multi-access clouds, such as Frame Relay and X.25, this state indicates that no recent information has been received from the neighbor. An effort should be made to contact the neighbor by sending hello packets at the reduced rate PollInterval.

Step 2 **Init**—The interface has detected a hello packet coming from a neighbor, but bidirectional communication has not yet been established.

Step 3 **Two-way**—There is bidirectional communication with a neighbor. The router has seen itself in the hello packets coming from a neighbor. The DR and BDR election would have been done at the end of this stage. At the end of the 2way stage, routers will decide whether to proceed in building an adjacency or not. The decision is based on whether one of the routers is a DR or BDR or the link is a point-to-point or a virtual link.

Step 4 **Exstart**—Routers are trying to establish the initial sequence number that is going to be used in the information exchange packets. The sequence number insures that routers always get the most recent information. One router will become the primary, and the other will become secondary. The primary router will poll the secondary for information.

Step 5 **Exchange**—Routers will describe their entire link-state database by sending database description packets. At this state, packets could be flooded to other interfaces on the router.

Step 6 **Loading**—At this state, routers are finalizing the information exchange. Routers have built a link-state request list and a link-state retransmission list. Any information that looks incomplete or outdated will be put on the request list. Any update that is sent will be put on the retransmission list until it gets acknowledged.

Step 7 **Full**—At this state, the adjacency is complete. The neighboring routers are fully adjacent. Adjacent routers will have a similar link-state database.

Figure J-10 shows an example of a multi-access network running OSPF.

Figure J-10   *OSPF on a Multi-Access Segment*

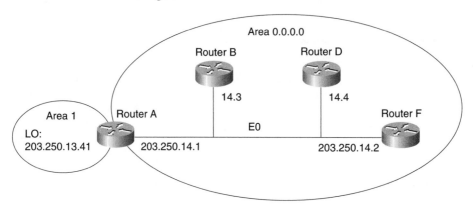

Router A, Router B, Router D, and Router F share a common segment (E0) in area 0.0.0.0. Example J-5 shows the configurations of Router A and Router F. Router B and Router D should have a similar configuration to Router F and will not be included.

Example J-5   *Configuring OSPF on Router A and Router F in Figure J-10*

```
Router A#
hostname Router A

interface Loopback0
 ip address 203.250.13.41 255.255.255.0

interface Ethernet0
 ip address 203.250.14.1 255.255.255.0

router ospf 10
 network 203.250.13.1 0.0.0.0 area 1
 network 203.250.0.0 0.0.255.255 area 0.0.0.0

Router F#
hostname Router F
interface Ethernet0
 ip address 203.250.14.2 255.255.255.0

router ospf 10
 network 203.250.0.0 0.0.255.255 area 0.0.0.0
```

The example shown in Figure J-10 and Example J-5 can be used to demonstrate a couple of commands that are useful when debugging OSPF networks: **show ip ospf interface** *interface* and **show ip ospf neighbor.**

The **show ip ospf interface** *interface* command is a quick check to see if all of the interfaces belong to the areas they are supposed to be in. The sequence in which the OSPF network commands are listed is very important. In Router A's configuration, if the "network 203.250.0.0 0.0.255.255 area 0.0.0.0" statement was put before the "network 203.250.13.41 0.0.0.0 area 1" statement, all of the interfaces would be in area 0, which is incorrect because the loopback is in area 1. Example J-6 shows the output for the **show ip ospf interface** command on Router A, Router F, Router B, and Router D.

Example J-6 *Output of the **show ip ospf interface** Command for the Routers in Figure J-10*

```
Router A#show ip ospf interface e 0
Ethernet0 is up, line protocol is up
  Internet Address 203.250.14.1 255.255.255.0, Area 0.0.0.0
  Process ID 10, Router ID 203.250.13.41, Network Type BROADCAST, Cost:
10
  Transmit Delay is 1 sec, State BDR, Priority 1
  Designated Router (ID) 203.250.15.1, Interface address 203.250.14.2
  Backup Designated router (ID) 203.250.13.41, Interface address
203.250.14.1
  Timer intervals configured, Hello 10, Dead 40, Wait 40, Retransmit 5
    Hello due in 0:00:02
  Neighbor Count is 3, Adjacent neighbor count is 3
    Adjacent with neighbor 203.250.15.1  (Designated Router)
Loopback0 is up, line protocol is up
  Internet Address 203.250.13.41 255.255.255.255, Area 1
  Process ID 10, Router ID 203.250.13.41, Network Type LOOPBACK, Cost: 1
  Loopback interface is treated as a stub Host

Router F#show ip ospf interface e 0
Ethernet0 is up, line protocol is up
  Internet Address 203.250.14.2 255.255.255.0, Area 0.0.0.0
  Process ID 10, Router ID 203.250.15.1, Network Type BROADCAST, Cost: 10
  Transmit Delay is 1 sec, State DR, Priority 1
  Designated Router (ID) 203.250.15.1, Interface address 203.250.14.2
  Backup Designated router (ID) 203.250.13.41, Interface address
203.250.14.1
  Timer intervals configured, Hello 10, Dead 40, Wait 40, Retransmit 5
    Hello due in 0:00:08
  Neighbor Count is 3, Adjacent neighbor count is 3
    Adjacent with neighbor 203.250.13.41  (Backup Designated Router)
```

continues

Example J-6 *Output of the **show ip ospf interface** Command for the Routers in Figure J-10 (Continued)*

```
Router D#show ip ospf interface e 0
Ethernet0 is up, line protocol is up
  Internet Address 203.250.14.4 255.255.255.0, Area 0.0.0.0
  Process ID 10, Router ID 192.208.10.174, Network Type BROADCAST, Cost:
10
  Transmit Delay is 1 sec, State DROTHER, Priority 1
  Designated Router (ID) 203.250.15.1, Interface address 203.250.14.2
  Backup Designated router (ID) 203.250.13.41, Interface address
203.250.14.1
  Timer intervals configured, Hello 10, Dead 40, Wait 40, Retransmit 5
    Hello due in 0:00:03
  Neighbor Count is 3, Adjacent neighbor count is 2
    Adjacent with neighbor 203.250.15.1  (Designated Router)
    Adjacent with neighbor 203.250.13.41  (Backup Designated Router)

Router B#show ip ospf interface e 0
Ethernet0 is up, line protocol is up
  Internet Address 203.250.14.3 255.255.255.0, Area 0.0.0.0
  Process ID 10, Router ID 203.250.12.1, Network Type BROADCAST, Cost: 10
  Transmit Delay is 1 sec, State DROTHER, Priority 1
  Designated Router (ID) 203.250.15.1, Interface address 203.250.14.2
  Backup Designated router (ID) 203.250.13.41, Interface address
203.250.14.1
  Timer intervals configured, Hello 10, Dead 40, Wait 40, Retransmit 5
    Hello due in 0:00:03
  Neighbor Count is 3, Adjacent neighbor count is 2
    Adjacent with neighbor 203.250.15.1  (Designated Router)
    Adjacent with neighbor 203.250.13.41  (Backup Designated Router)
```

The output in Example J-6 shows important information. Take a look at Router A's output. Ethernet0 is in area 0.0.0.0. The process ID is 10 (router ospf 10), and the router ID is 203.250.13.41. Remember that the RID is the highest IP address on the box or the loopback interface, calculated at boot time or whenever the OSPF process is restarted. The state of the interface is BDR. Because all routers have the same OSPF priority on Ethernet 0 (default is 1), Router F's interface was elected as DR because of the higher RID. In the same way, Router A was elected as BDR. Router D and Router B are neither a DR nor a BDR, and their state is DROTHER.

Also note the neighbor count and the adjacent count. Router D has three neighbors and is adjacent to two of them, the DR and the BDR. Router F has three neighbors and is adjacent to all of them because it is the DR.

The information about the network type is important and will determine the state of the interface. On broadcast networks such as Ethernet, the election of the DR and BDR should be irrelevant to the end user. It should not matter who the DR or BDR are. In other cases, such as NBMA media such as Frame Relay and X.25, this becomes important for OSPF to function correctly. Fortunately, with the introduction of point-to-point and point-to-multipoint subinterfaces, DR election is no longer an issue. OSPF over NBMA will be discussed in the next section.

show ip ospf neighbor is another command we need to look at. Example J-7 looks at Router D's output after executing the **show ip ospf neighbor command**.

Example J-7 *Output of the show ip ospf neighbor Command for Router D in Figure J-10*

```
Router D#show ip ospf neighbor

Neighbor ID    Pri State        Dead Time  Address      Interface

203.250.12.1    1  2WAY/DROTHER  0:00:37    203.250.14.3  Ethernet0
203.250.15.1    1  FULL/DR       0:00:36    203.250.14.2  Ethernet0
203.250.13.41   1  FULL/BDR      0:00:34    203.250.14.1  Ethernet0
```

The **show ip ospf neighbor** command shows the state of all the neighbors on a particular segment. Do not be alarmed if the *Neighbor ID* does not belong to the segment you are looking at. In our case, 203.250.12.1 and 103.250.15.1 are not on Ethernet0. This is "OK" because the *Neighbor ID* is actually the Router ID, which could be any IP address on the box. Router D and Router B are just neighbors, which is why the state is *2WAY/DROTHER*. Router D is adjacent to Router A and Router F, and the state is *FULL/DR* and *FULL/BDR*.

Adjacencies on Point-to-Point Interfaces

OSPF will always form an adjacency with the neighbor on the other side of a point-to-point interface, such as point-to-point serial lines. There is no concept of DR or BDR. The state of the serial interfaces is point-to-point.

Adjacencies on NBMA

Special care should be taken when configuring OSPF over multi-access, nonbroadcast medias, such as Frame Relay, X.25, and ATM. The protocol considers these media like any other broadcast media, such as Ethernet. NBMA clouds are usually built in a hub-and-spoke topology. PVCs or SVCs are laid out in a partial mesh, and the physical topology does not provide the multi-access that OSPF believes is out there. The selection of the DR becomes an issue because the DR and BDR need to have full physical connectivity with all routers that exist on the cloud. Also, because of the lack of broadcast capabilities, the DR and BDR need to have a static list of all other routers attached to the cloud. This is achieved using the **neighbor** *ip-address* [**priority** *number*] [**poll-interval** *seconds*] command, where the *ip-address* and **priority** are the IP address and the OSPF priority given to the neighbor. A neighbor with priority 0 is considered ineligible for DR election. The "poll-interval" is the amount of time an NBMA interface waits before polling (sending a hello) to a presumably dead neighbor. The neighbor command applies to routers with a potential of being DRs or BDRs (interface priority not equal to 0). Figure J-11 shows a network diagram where DR selection is very important.

Figure J-11 *OSPF DR Selection on an NBMA Network*

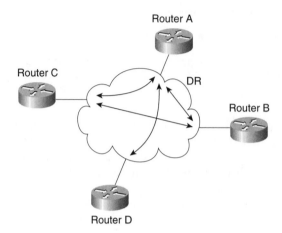

In Figure J-11, it is essential for Router A's interface to the cloud to be elected DR because Router A is the only router that has full connectivity to other routers. The election of the DR could be influenced by setting the OSPF priority on the interfaces. Routers that do not need to become DRs or BDRs will have a priority of 0; other routers could have a lower priority.

I will not dwell too much on the use of the **neighbor** command because it is becoming obsolete with the introduction of new means of setting the interface Network Type to whatever we want, irrespective of what the underlying physical media is. This is explained in the following section.

Avoiding DRs and the neighbor Command on NBMA

Different methods can be used to avoid the complications of configuring static neighbors and having specific routers becoming DRs or BDRs on the nonbroadcast cloud. Specifying which method to use is influenced by whether we are starting the network from scratch or rectifying an already existing design.

Point-to-Point Subinterfaces

A subinterface is a logical way of defining an interface. The same physical interface can be split into multiple logical interfaces, with each subinterface being defined as point-to-point. This was originally created in order to better handle issues caused by split horizon over NBMA and vector-based routing protocols.

A point-to-point subinterface has the properties of any physical point-to-point interface. As far as OSPF is concerned, an adjacency is always formed over a point-to-point subinterface with no DR or BDR election. Figure J-12 provides an illustration of point-to-point subinterfaces.

Figure J-12 *Point-to-Point Subinterfaces*

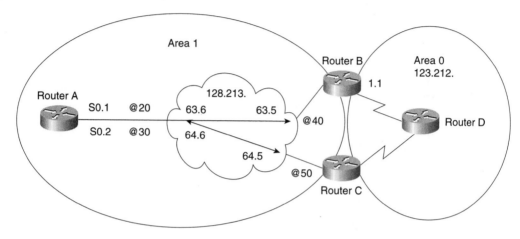

In Figure J-12, on Router A, we can split Serial 0 into two point-to-point subinterfaces, S0.1 and S0.2. This way, OSPF will consider the cloud as a set of point-to-point links rather than one multi-access network. The only drawback for the point-to-point is that each segment will belong to a different subnet. This might not be acceptable because some administrators have already assigned one IP subnet for the whole cloud.

Another workaround is to use IP unnumbered interfaces on the cloud. This also might be a problem for some administrators who manage the WAN based on IP addresses of the serial lines. Example J-8 shows a typical configuration for Router A and Router B.

Example J-8 *Configuring Subinterfaces on Router A and Router B in Figure J-12*

```
Router A#

interface Serial 0
 no ip address
 encapsulation frame-relay

interface Serial0.1 point-to-point
 ip address 128.213.63.6 255.255.252.0
 frame-relay interface-dlci 20

interface Serial0.2 point-to-point
 ip address 128.213.64.6 255.255.252.0
 frame-relay interface-dlci 30

router ospf 10
 network 128.213.0.0 0.0.255.255 area 1

Router B#

interface Serial 0
 no ip address
 encapsulation frame-relay

interface Serial0.1 point-to-point
 ip address 128.213.63.5 255.255.252.0
 frame-relay interface-dlci 40

interface Serial1
 ip address 123.212.1.1 255.255.255.0

router ospf 10
 network 128.213.0.0 0.0.255.255 area 1
 network 123.212.0.0 0.0.255.255 area 0
```

Selecting Interface Network Types

The **ip ospf network** {**broadcast** | **non-broadcast** | **point-to-multipoint**} command is used to set the network type of an OSPF interface.

Point-to-Multipoint Interfaces

An OSPF point-to-multipoint interface is defined as a numbered point-to-point interface having one or more neighbors. This concept takes the previously discussed point-to-point concept one step further. Administrators do not have to worry about having multiple subnets for each point-to-point link. The cloud is configured as one subnet. This should work well for people who are migrating into the point-to-point concept with no change in IP addressing on the cloud. Also, they would not have to worry about DRs and neighbor statements. OSPF point-to-multipoint works by exchanging additional link-state updates that contain a number of information elements that describe connectivity to the neighboring routers. Figure J-13 shows a point-to-multipoint interface.

Figure J-13 *Point-to-Multipoint Interfaces*

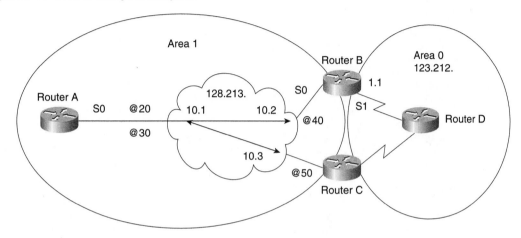

Example J-9 shows the configuration of Router A and Router B in Figure J-13.

Example J-9 *Configuring Point-to-Multipoint Interfaces on Router A and Router B in Figure J-13*

```
Router A#

interface Loopback0
 ip address 200.200.10.1 255.255.255.0

interface Serial0
 ip address 128.213.10.1 255.255.252.0
 encapsulation frame-relay
 ip ospf network point-to-multipoint

router ospf 10
 network 128.213.0.0 0.0.255.255 area 1

Router B#
interface Serial0
 ip address 128.213.10.2 255.255.255.0
 encapsulation frame-relay
 ip ospf network point-to-multipoint

interface Serial1
 ip address 123.212.1.1 255.255.255.0

router ospf 10
 network 128.213.0.0 0.0.255.255 area 1
 network 123.212.0.0 0.0.255.255 area 0
```

Note that no static **frame-relay map** statements were configured; this is because Inverse ARP takes care of the DLCI to IP address mapping. Example J-10 presents some **show ip ospf interface** and **show ip ospf route** outputs.

Example J-10 *Output of **show** Commands for Router A and Router B in Figure J-13*

```
Router A#show ip ospf interface s0
Serial0 is up, line protocol is up
  Internet Address 128.213.10.1 255.255.255.0, Area 0
  Process ID 10, Router ID 200.200.10.1, Network Type
POINT_TO_MULTIPOINT, Cost: 64
  Transmit Delay is 1 sec, State POINT_TO_MULTIPOINT,
  Timer intervals configured, Hello 30, Dead 120, Wait 120, Retransmit 5
    Hello due in 0:00:04
  Neighbor Count is 2, Adjacent neighbor count is 2
    Adjacent with neighbor 195.211.10.174
    Adjacent with neighbor 128.213.63.130Router A#show ip ospf neighbor


Router B#show ip ospf neighbor

Neighbor ID    Pri  State           Dead Time  Address        Interface
128.213.10.3    1   FULL/ -         0:01:35    128.213.10.3   Serial0
128.213.10.2    1   FULL/ -         0:01:44    128.213.10.2   Serial0

Router B#show ip ospf interface s0

Serial0 is up, line protocol is up
  Internet Address 128.213.10.2 255.255.255.0, Area 0
  Process ID 10, Router ID 128.213.10.2, Network Type
POINT_TO_MULTIPOINT, Cost: 64
  Transmit Delay is 1 sec, State POINT_TO_MULTIPOINT,
  Timer intervals configured, Hello 30, Dead 120, Wait 120, Retransmit 5
    Hello due in 0:00:14
  Neighbor Count is 1, Adjacent neighbor count is 1
    Adjacent with neighbor 200.200.10.1

Router B#show ip ospf neighbor

Neighbor ID    Pri  State           Dead Time  Address        Interface
200.200.10.1    1   FULL/ -         0:01:52    128.213.10.1   Serial0
```

The only drawback for point-to-multipoint is that it generates multiple Hosts routes (routes with mask 255.255.255.255) for all the neighbors. Note the Host routes in the IP routing table for Router B and Router C shown in Example J-11.

Example J-11 *Routing Tables for Router B and Router C in Figure J-13*

```
Router B#show ip route
  Codes: C - connected, S - static, I - IGRP, R - RIP, M - mobile, B - BGP
         D - EIGRP, EX - EIGRP external, O - OSPF, IA - OSPF inter area
         E1 - OSPF external type 1, E2 - OSPF external type 2, E - EGP
         i - IS-IS, L1 - IS-IS level-1, L2 - IS-IS level-2, * - candidate default

Gateway of last resort is not set

     200.200.10.0 255.255.255.255 is subnetted, 1 subnets
O       200.200.10.1 [110/65] via 128.213.10.1,  Serial0
        128.213.0.0 is variably subnetted, 3 subnets, 2 masks
O    128.213.10.3 255.255.255.255
            [110/128] via 128.213.10.1, 00:00:00, Serial0
O    128.213.10.1 255.255.255.255
            [110/64] via 128.213.10.1, 00:00:00, Serial0
C       128.213.10.0 255.255.255.0 is directly connected, Serial0
     123.0.0.0 255.255.255.0 is subnetted, 1 subnets
C       123.212.1.0 is directly connected, Serial1
Router C#show ip route
     200.200.10.0 255.255.255.255 is subnetted, 1 subnets
O       200.200.10.1 [110/65] via 128.213.10.1, Serial1
     128.213.0.0 is variably subnetted, 4 subnets, 2 masks
O       128.213.10.2 255.255.255.255 [110/128] via 128.213.10.1,Serial1
O       128.213.10.1 255.255.255.255 [110/64] via 128.213.10.1, Serial1
C       128.213.10.0 255.255.255.0 is directly connected, Serial1
     123.0.0.0 255.255.255.0 is subnetted, 1 subnets
O       123.212.1.0 [110/192] via 128.213.10.1, 00:14:29, Serial1
```

Note that in Router C's IP routing table, network 123.212.1.0 is reachable via next hop
128.213.10.1 and not via 128.213.10.2, as you normally see over Frame Relay clouds sharing
the same subnet. This is one advantage of the point-to-multipoint configuration because you do
not need to resort to static mapping on Router C to be able to reach next hop 128.213.10.2.

Broadcast Interfaces

This approach is a workaround for using the **neighbor** command, which statically lists all
existing neighbors. The interface will be logically set to broadcast and will behave as if the
router were connected to a LAN. DR and BDR election will still be performed, so special care
should be taken to assure either a full mesh topology or a static selection of the DR based on
the interface priority. The **ip ospf network broadcast** command sets the interface to broadcast.

OSPF and Route Summarization

Summarizing is the consolidation of multiple routes into one single advertisement. This is normally done at the boundaries of Area Border Routers. Although summarization could be configured between any two areas, it is better to summarize in the direction of the backbone. This way the backbone receives all the aggregate addresses and, in turn, will inject them, already summarized, into other areas. There are two types of summarization:

- Interarea route summarization
- External route summarization

Interarea Route Summarization

Interarea route summarization is done on ABRs, and it applies to routes from within the AS. It does not apply to external routes injected into OSPF via redistribution. In order to take advantage of summarization, network numbers in areas should be assigned in a contiguous way to be able to lump these addresses into one range. To specify an address range, execute the **area** *area-id* **range** *address mask* command in router configuration mode.

The *area-id* parameter is the area containing networks to be summarized. The *address* and *mask* parameters specify the range of addresses to be summarized in one range. Figure J-14 shows an example of summarization.

Figure J-14 *Interarea Route Summarization*

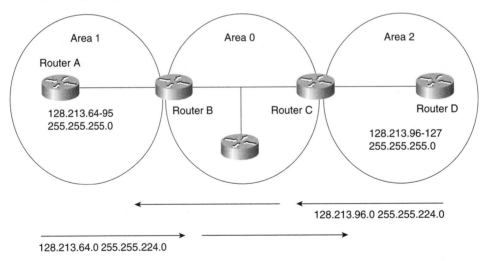

In Figure J-14, Router B is summarizing the range of subnets from 128.213.64.0 to 128.213.95.0 into one range: 128.213.64.0 255.255.224.0. This is achieved by masking the first three left bits of 64 using a mask of 255.255.224.0. In the same way, Router C is generating the summary address 128.213.96.0 255.255.224.0 into the backbone. Note that this summarization was successful because we have two distinct ranges of subnets, 64–95 and 96–127.

It would be hard to summarize if the subnets between area 1 and area 2 were overlapping. The backbone area would receive summary ranges that overlap, and routers in the middle would not know where to send the traffic based on the summary address.

Example J-12 presents the relative configuration of Router B.

Example J-12   *Configuring Router B in Figure J-14 for Interarea Route Summarization*

```
Router B#
router ospf 100
 area 1 range 128.213.64.0 255.255.224.0
```

External Route Summarization

External route summarization is specific to external routes that are injected into OSPF via redistribution. Also, make sure that external ranges that are being summarized are contiguous. Summarization overlapping ranges from two different routers could cause packets to be sent to the wrong destination. Summarization is done via the **summary-address** *ip-address mask* command.

This command is effective only on ASBRs doing redistribution into OSPF. Figure J-15 shows a network with two ASBRs, Router A and Router D.

Figure J-15   *External Route Summarization*

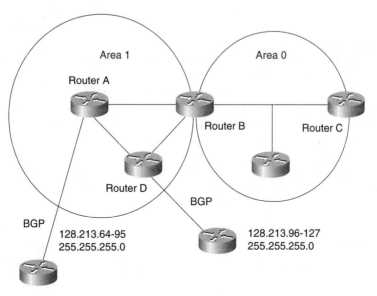

In Figure J-15, Router A and Router D are injecting external routes into OSPF by redistribution. Router A is injecting subnets in the range 128.213.64-95, and Router D is injecting subnets in the range 128.213.96-127. Example J-13 demonstrates what we can do in order to summarize the subnets into one range on each router.

Example J-13 *Summarizing Subnets into One Range on Router A and Router D in Figure J-15*

```
Router A#
router ospf 100
 summary-address 128.213.64.0 255.255.224.0
 redistribute bgp 50 metric 1000 subnets

Router D#
router ospf 100
 summary-address 128.213.96.0 255.255.224.0
 redistribute bgp 20 metric 1000 subnets
```

This will cause Router A to generate one external route 128.213.64.0 255.255.224.0 and will cause Router D to generate 128.213.96.0 255.255.224.0.

Note that the **summary-address** command has no effect if used on Router B because Router B is not doing the redistribution into OSPF.

Stub Areas

OSPF allows certain areas to be configured as stub areas. External networks, such as those redistributed from other protocols into OSPF, are not allowed to be flooded into a stub area. Routing from these areas to the outside world is based on a default route. Configuring a stub area reduces the topological database size inside an area and reduces the memory requirements of routers inside that area.

An area could be qualified a stub when there is a single exit point from that area or if routing to outside of the area does not have to take an optimal path. The latter description is just an indication that a stub area that has multiple exit points will have one or more area border routers injecting a default into that area. Routing to the outside world could take a suboptimal path in reaching the destination by going out of the area via an exit point that is farther to the destination than other exit points.

Other stub area restrictions are that a stub area cannot be used as a transit area for virtual links. Also, an ASBR cannot be internal to a stub area. These restrictions are made because a stub area is mainly configured not to carry external routes, and any of the previous situations cause external links to be injected in that area. The backbone, of course, cannot be configured as stub.

All OSPF routers inside a stub area have to be configured as stub routers because whenever an area is configured as stub, all interfaces that belong to that area will start exchanging hello packets with a flag that indicates that the interface is stub. Actually, this is just a bit in the hello packet (E bit) that gets set to 0. All routers that have a common segment have to agree on that flag. If they don't, they will not become neighbors, and routing will not take effect.

An extension to stub areas is what is called "totally stubby areas." Cisco indicates this by adding a "no-summary" keyword to the stub area configuration. A totally stubby area is one that blocks external routes and summary routes (interarea routes) from going into the area. This way, intra-area routes and the default of 0.0.0.0 are the only routes injected into that area.

The **area** *area-id* **stub [no-summary]** command configures an area as stub. The **area** *area-id* **default-cost** *cost* command configures a default-cost into an area. If the cost is not set using the **area** *area-id* **default-cost** *cost* command, a cost of 1 will be advertised by the ABR.

Figure J-16 shows an example of an OSPF network with a stub area.

Figure J-16 *A Network with a Stub Area*

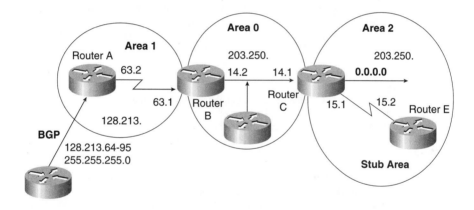

Assume that area 2 is to be configured as a stub area. Example J-14 shows the configuration of Router C and the routing table of Router E before configuring area 2 as a stub.

Example J-14   *Before Configuring a Stub Area in Figure J-16*

```
Router C#

interface Ethernet 0
 ip address 203.250.14.1 255.255.255.0

interface Serial1
 ip address 203.250.15.1 255.255.255.252

router ospf 10
 network 203.250.15.0 0.0.0.255 area 2
 network 203.250.14.0 0.0.0.255 area 0

Router E#show ip route
 Codes: C - connected, S - static, I - IGRP, R - RIP, M - mobile, B - BGP
        D - EIGRP, EX - EIGRP external, O - OSPF, IA - OSPF inter area
        E1 - OSPF external type 1, E2 - OSPF external type 2, E - EGP
        i - IS-IS, L1 - IS-IS level-1, L2 - IS-IS level-2, * - candidate default

 Gateway of last resort is not set

      203.250.15.0 255.255.255.252 is subnetted, 1 subnets
 C       203.250.15.0 is directly connected, Serial0
 O IA 203.250.14.0 [110/74] via 203.250.15.1, 00:06:31, Serial0
      128.213.0.0 is variably subnetted, 2 subnets, 2 masks
 O E2    128.213.64.0 255.255.192.0
             [110/10] via 203.250.15.1, 00:00:29, Serial0
 O IA    128.213.63.0 255.255.255.252
             [110/84] via 203.250.15.1, 00:03:57, Serial0
      131.108.0.0 255.255.255.240 is subnetted, 1 subnets
 O       131.108.79.208 [110/74] via 203.250.15.1, 00:00:10, Serial0
```

Router E has learned the interarea routes (O IA) 203.250.14.0 and 128.213.63.0 and it has learned the intra-area route (O) 131.108.79.208 and the external route (O E2) 128.213.64.0.

Example J-15 shows the necessary configuration to make area 2 a stub.

Example J-15   *Configuring a Stub Area on the Routers in Figure J-16*

```
Router C#

interface Ethernet 0
 ip address 203.250.14.1 255.255.255.0

interface Serial1
 ip address 203.250.15.1 255.255.255.252

router ospf 10
 network 203.250.15.0 0.0.0.255 area 2
 network 203.250.14.0 0.0.0.255 area 0
 area 2 stub

Router E#

interface Ethernet0
 ip address 203.250.14.2 255.255.255.0

interface Ethernet1
 ip address 131.108.79.209 255.255.255.240

interface Serial1
 ip address 203.250.15.1 255.255.255.252

router ospf 10
 network 203.250.15.0 0.0.0.255 area 2
 network 203.250.14.0 0.0.0.255 area 0
 network 131.108.0.0 0.0.255.255 area 2
 area 2 stub
```

Note that the **stub** command is also configured on Router E; otherwise, Router E would never become a neighbor to Router C. The default cost was not set, so Router C will advertise 0.0.0.0 to Router E with a metric of 1. Example J-16 shows the routing table for Router E now that area 2 is a stub area.

Example J-16   *Router E's Routing Table after Configuring a Stub Area*

```
Router E#show ip route
 Codes: C - connected, S - static, I - IGRP, R - RIP, M - mobile, B - BGP
        D - EIGRP, EX - EIGRP external, O - OSPF, IA - OSPF inter area
        E1 - OSPF external type 1, E2 - OSPF external type 2, E - EGP
        i - IS-IS, L1 - IS-IS level-1, L2 - IS-IS level-2, * - candidate default

Gateway of last resort is 203.250.15.1 to network 0.0.0.0

      203.250.15.0 255.255.255.252 is subnetted, 1 subnets
C       203.250.15.0 is directly connected, Serial0
O IA 203.250.14.0 [110/74] via 203.250.15.1, 00:26:58, Serial0
      128.213.0.0 255.255.255.252 is subnetted, 1 subnets
O IA    128.213.63.0 [110/84] via 203.250.15.1, 00:26:59, Serial0
      131.108.0.0 255.255.255.240 is subnetted, 1 subnets
O       131.108.79.208 [110/74] via 203.250.15.1, 00:26:59, Serial0
O*IA 0.0.0.0 0.0.0.0 [110/65] via 203.250.15.1, 00:26:59, Serial0
```

Note that all the routes show up except the external routes, which were replaced by a default route of 0.0.0.0. The cost of the route happened to be 65 (64 for a T1 line plus 1 advertised by Router C).

Example J-17 shows how to configure area 2 to be totally stubby and change the default cost of 0.0.0.0 to 10.

Example J-17   *Configuring a Totally Stubby Area on the Routers in Figure J-16*

```
Router C#

interface Ethernet 0
 ip address 203.250.14.1 255.255.255.0

interface Serial1
 ip address 203.250.15.1 255.255.255.252

router ospf 10
 network 203.250.15.0 0.0.0.255 area 2
 network 203.250.14.0 0.0.0.255 area 0
 area 2 stub no-summary

Router E#show ip route


 Codes: C - connected, S - static, I - IGRP, R - RIP, M - mobile, B - BGP
        D - EIGRP, EX - EIGRP external, O - OSPF, IA - OSPF inter area
        E1 - OSPF external type 1, E2 - OSPF external type 2, E - EGP
        i - IS-IS, L1 - IS-IS level-1, L2 - IS-IS level-2, * - candidate default

 Gateway of last resort is not set
```

continues

Example J-17   *Configuring a Totally Stubby Area on the Routers in Figure J-16 (Continued)*

```
        203.250.15.0 255.255.255.252 is subnetted, 1 subnets
C          203.250.15.0 is directly connected, Serial0
        131.108.0.0 255.255.255.240 is subnetted, 1 subnets
O          131.108.79.208 [110/74] via 203.250.15.1, 00:31:27, Serial0
O*IA 0.0.0.0 0.0.0.0 [110/74] via 203.250.15.1, 00:00:00, Serial0
```

Note that the only routes that show up are the intra-area routes (O) and the default-route 0.0.0.0. The external and interarea routes have been blocked. The cost of the default route is now 74 (64 for a T1 line + 10 advertised by Router C). No configuration is needed on Router E in this case. The area is already stubbed, and the **no-summary** command does not affect the hello packet at all, which the **stub** command does.

Redistributing Routes into OSPF

Redistributing routes into OSPF from other routing protocols or from static will cause these routes to become OSPF external routes. To redistribute routes into OSPF, use the **redistribute** *protocol* [*process-id*] [**metric** *value*] [**metric-type** *value*] [**route-map** *map-tag*] [**subnets**] command in router configuration mode.

The *protocol* and *process-id* parameters indicate the protocol that is injected into OSPF and its process-id if it exits. The **metric** is the cost we assign to the external route. If no metric is specified, OSPF puts a default value of 20 when redistributing routes from all protocols except BGP routes, which get a metric of 1. The **metric-type** is discussed in the next section.

The **route-map** is a method used to control the redistribution of routes between routing domains. The format of a route map follows:

```
route-map map-tag [[permit ¦ deny] ¦ [sequence-number]]
```

When redistributing routes into OSPF, only routes that are not subnetted are redistributed if the **subnets** keyword is not specified.

E1 Versus E2 External Routes

External routes fall under two categories, external type 1 and external type 2. The difference between the two is in the way the cost (metric) of the route is calculated. The cost of a type 2 route is always the external cost, irrespective of the interior cost to reach that route. A type 1 cost is the addition of the external cost and the internal cost used to reach that route. A type 1 route is always preferred over a type 2 route for the same destination (see Figure J-17).

Figure J-17 *Type E1 and E2 External OSPF Routes*

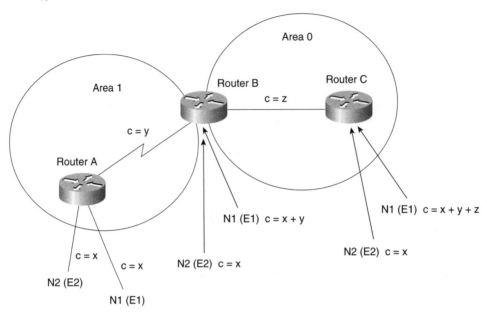

As Figure J-17 shows, Router A is redistributing two external routes into OSPF. N1 and N2 both have an external cost of **x**. The only difference is that N1 is redistributed into OSPF with a **metric-type** 1, and N2 is redistributed with a **metric-type** 2. If we follow the routes as they flow from Area 1 to Area 0, the cost to reach N2 as seen from Router B or Router C will always be **x**. The internal cost along the way is not considered. On the other hand, the cost to reach N1 is incremented by the internal cost. The cost is **x+y** as seen from Router B and **x+y+z** as seen from Router C. Type 2 routes are preferred over type 1 routes in case two same-cost routes exist to the destination. The default is type 2.

Figure J-18 shows another example of redistribution, with static routes.

Figure J-18 *Static Routes Configured on an OSPF Router*

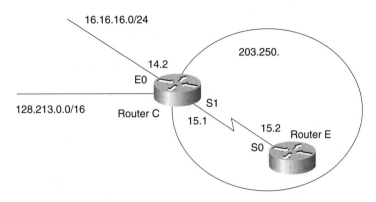

Suppose we added two static routes pointing to E0 on Router C: 16.16.16.0 255.255.255.0 (the /24 notation indicates a 24-bit mask starting from the far left) and 128.213.0.0 255.255.0.0. To show the different behaviors when different parameters are used in the **redistribute** command on Router C, start with the configurations in Example J-18.

Example J-18 *Configuring Router C and Router E in Figure J-18*

```
Router C#
interface Ethernet0
 ip address 203.250.14.2 255.255.255.0

interface Serial1
 ip address 203.250.15.1 255.255.255.252

router ospf 10
 redistribute static
 network 203.250.15.0 0.0.0.255 area 2
 network 203.250.14.0 0.0.0.255 area 0

ip route 16.16.16.0 255.255.255.0 Ethernet0
ip route 128.213.0.0 255.255.0.0 Ethernet0

Router E#

interface Serial0
 ip address 203.250.15.2 255.255.255.252

router ospf 10
 network 203.250.15.0 0.0.0.255 area 2
```

Example J-19 shows the output of the **show ip route** command on Router E.

Example J-19 *The Routing Table on Router E in Figure J-18*

```
Router E#show ip route
 Codes: C - connected, S - static, I - IGRP, R - RIP, M - mobile, B - BGP
        D - EIGRP, EX - EIGRP external, O - OSPF, IA - OSPF inter area
        E1 - OSPF external type 1, E2 - OSPF external type 2, E - EGP
        i - IS-IS, L1 - IS-IS level-1, L2 - IS-IS level-2, * - candidate default

Gateway of last resort is not set

     203.250.15.0 255.255.255.252 is subnetted, 1 subnets
C       203.250.15.0 is directly connected, Serial0
O IA 203.250.14.0 [110/74] via 203.250.15.1, 00:02:31, Serial0
O E2 128.213.0.0 [110/20] via 203.250.15.1, 00:02:32, Serial0
```

Note that the only external route that has appeared is 128.213.0.0 because we did not use the **subnet** keyword. Remember that if the **subnet** keyword is not used, only routes that are not subnetted will be redistributed. In our case, 16.16.16.0 is a class A route that is subnetted, and it did not get redistributed. Because the **metric** keyword was not used (or a **default-metric** statement under router OSPF), the cost allocated to the external route is 20 (the default is 1 for BGP). If we use the **redistribute static metric 50 subnets** command on Router C, Example J-20 shows the resulting change to the routing table on Router E.

Example J-20 *The Routing Table on Router E in Figure J-18 with Router C Redistributing Subnets*

```
Router E#show ip route
Codes: C - connected, S - static, I - IGRP, R - RIP, M
- mobile, B - BGP
        D - EIGRP, EX - EIGRP external, O - OSPF, IA - OSPF inter area
        E1 - OSPF external type 1, E2 - OSPF external type 2, E - EGP
        i - IS-IS, L1 - IS-IS level-1, L2 - IS-IS level-2, * - candidate default

Gateway of last resort is not set

     16.0.0.0 255.255.255.0 is subnetted, 1 subnets
O E2    16.16.16.0 [110/50] via 203.250.15.1, 00:00:02, Serial0
     203.250.15.0 255.255.255.252 is subnetted, 1 subnets
C       203.250.15.0 is directly connected, Serial0
O IA 203.250.14.0 [110/74] via 203.250.15.1, 00:00:02, Serial0
O E2 128.213.0.0 [110/50] via 203.250.15.1, 00:00:02, Serial0
```

Note that 16.16.16.0 has shown up now, and the cost to external routes is 50. Because the external routes are of type 2 (E2), the internal cost has not been added. Suppose we now change the type to E1 in the redistribute command on Router C, as follows: **redistribute static metric 50 metric-type 1 subnets.** Example J-21 shows the resulting change to the routing table on Router E.

Example J-21   *The Routing Table on Router E in Figure J-18 with Router C Redistributing Type 1 Routes*

```
Router E#show ip route
 Codes: C - connected, S - static, I - IGRP, R - RIP, M - mobile, B - BGP
        D - EIGRP, EX - EIGRP external, O - OSPF, IA - OSPF inter area
        E1 - OSPF external type 1, E2 - OSPF external type 2, E - EGP
        i - IS-IS, L1 - IS-IS level-1, L2 - IS-IS level-2, * - candidate default

Gateway of last resort is not set

     16.0.0.0 255.255.255.0 is subnetted, 1 subnets
O E1    16.16.16.0 [110/114] via 203.250.15.1, 00:04:20, Serial0
     203.250.15.0 255.255.255.252 is subnetted, 1 subnets
C       203.250.15.0 is directly connected, Serial0
O IA 203.250.14.0 [110/74] via 203.250.15.1, 00:09:41, Serial0
O E1 128.213.0.0 [110/114] via 203.250.15.1, 00:04:21, Serial0
```

Note that the type has changed to E1 and the cost has been incremented by the internal cost of Serial0 which is 64; the total cost is 64 + 50 = 114.

Assuming we added a route map to Router C's configuration, we would get the configuration shown in Example J-22.

Example J-22   *Configuring a Route Map on Router C in Figure J-18*

```
Router C#
interface Ethernet0
 ip address 203.250.14.2 255.255.255.0

interface Serial1
 ip address 203.250.15.1 255.255.255.252

router ospf 10

 redistribute static metric 50 metric-type 1 subnets route-map STOPUPDATE
 network 203.250.15.0 0.0.0.255 area 2
 network 203.250.14.0 0.0.0.255 area 0

ip route 16.16.16.0 255.255.255.0 Ethernet0
ip route 128.213.0.0 255.255.0.0 Ethernet0

access-list 1 permit 128.213.0.0 0.0.255.255

route-map STOPUPDATE permit 10
 match ip address 1
```

The route map in Example J-22 will only permit 128.213.0.0 to be redistributed into OSPF and will deny the rest. This is why 16.16.16.0 does not show up in Router E's routing table anymore, as shown in Example J-23.

Example J-23   *The Routing Table on Router E in Figure J-18 with Router C Configured with a Route Map*

```
Router E#show ip route
 Codes: C - connected, S - static, I - IGRP, R - RIP, M - mobile, B - BGP
        D - EIGRP, EX - EIGRP external, O - OSPF, IA - OSPF inter area
        E1 - OSPF external type 1, E2 - OSPF external type 2, E - EGP
        i - IS-IS, L1 - IS-IS level-1, L2 - IS-IS level-2, * - candidate default

Gateway of last resort is not set

     203.250.15.0 255.255.255.252 is subnetted, 1 subnets
C       203.250.15.0 is directly connected, Serial0
O IA 203.250.14.0 [110/74] via 203.250.15.1, 00:00:04, Serial0
O E1 128.213.0.0 [110/114] via 203.250.15.1, 00:00:05, Serial0
```

Redistributing OSPF into Other Protocols

When redistributing OSPF into other protocols, you should consider the following:

- The use of a valid metric
- The effect of using VLSM
- The effect of mutual redistribution

Use of a Valid Metric

Whenever you redistribute OSPF into other protocols, you have to respect the rules of those protocols. In particular, the metric applied should match the metric used by that protocol. For example, the RIP metric is a hop count ranging between 1 and 16, where 1 indicates that a network is one hop away and 16 indicates that the network is unreachable. On the other hand, IGRP and EIGRP require a metric in this form:

```
default-metric bandwidth delay reliability loading mtu
```

VLSM

Another issue to consider is VLSM (see the Variable Length Subnet Guide, covered in Appendix C, "Variable Length Subnet Masks [VLSM],"). OSPF can carry multiple subnet information for the same major net, but other protocols, such as RIP and IGRP (EIGRP is okay with VLSM), cannot. If the same major net crosses the boundaries of an OSPF and RIP domain, VLSM information redistributed into RIP or IGRP will be lost, and static routes will have to be configured in the RIP or IGRP domains. Figure J-19 illustrates this problem.

Figure J-19 *Example Using RIP and OSPF with VLSMs*

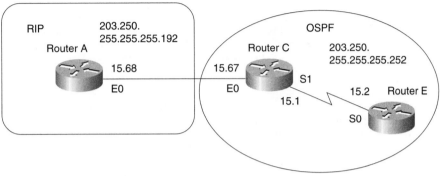

In Figure J-19, Router E is running OSPF, and Router A is running RIP. Router C is doing the redistribution between the two protocols. The problem is that the class C network 203.250.15.0 is variably subnetted; it has two different masks, 255.255.255.252 and 255.255.255.192. Example J-24 shows the configuration for Routers A, C, and E, and the routing tables of Router E and Router A.

Example J-24 *Configuration and Routing Tables for the Routers in Figure J-19*

```
Router A#
interface Ethernet0
 ip address 203.250.15.68 255.255.255.192

router rip
 network 203.250.15.0

Router C#
interface Ethernet0
 ip address 203.250.15.67 255.255.255.192

interface Serial1
 ip address 203.250.15.1 255.255.255.252

router ospf 10
 redistribute rip metric 10 subnets
 network 203.250.15.0 0.0.0.255 area 0

router rip
 redistribute ospf 10 metric 2
 network 203.250.15.0
```

continues

Example J-24   *Configuration and Routing Tables for the Routers in Figure J-19 (Continued)*

```
Router E#show ip route
 Codes: C - connected, S - static, I - IGRP, R - RIP, M - mobile, B - BGP
        D - EIGRP, EX - EIGRP external, O - OSPF, IA - OSPF inter area
        E1 - OSPF external type 1, E2 - OSPF external type 2, E - EGP
        i - IS-IS, L1 - IS-IS level-1, L2 - IS-IS level-2, * - candidate default

Gateway of last resort is not set

     203.250.15.0 is variably subnetted, 2 subnets, 2 masks
 C      203.250.15.0 255.255.255.252 is directly connected, Serial0
 O      203.250.15.64 255.255.255.192
           [110/74] via 203.250.15.1, 00:15:55, Serial0


Router A#show ip route
 Codes: C - connected, S - static, I - IGRP, R - RIP, M - mobile, B - BGP
        D - EIGRP, EX - EIGRP external, O - OSPF, IA - OSPF inter area
        E1 - OSPF external type 1, E2 - OSPF external type 2, E - EGP
        i - IS-IS, L1 - IS-IS level-1, L2 - IS-IS level-2, * - candidate default

Gateway of last resort is not set

     203.250.15.0 255.255.255.192 is subnetted, 1 subnets
 C      203.250.15.64 is directly connected, Ethernet0
```

Note that Router E has recognized that 203.250.15.0 has two subnets, whereas Router A thinks that it has only one subnet (the one configured on the interface). Information about subnet 203.250.15.0 255.255.255.252 is lost in the RIP domain. In order to reach that subnet, a static route needs to be configured on Router A, as in Example J-25.

Example J-25   *Configuring a Static Route on Router A in Figure J-19*

```
Router A#
interface Ethernet0
 ip address 203.250.15.68 255.255.255.192

router rip
 network 203.250.15.0

ip route 203.250.15.0 255.255.255.0 203.250.15.67
```

It is in this way that Router A will be able to reach the other subnets.

Mutual Redistribution

Mutual redistribution between protocols should be done carefully and in a controlled manner. Incorrect configuration could lead to potential looping of routing information. A rule of thumb for mutual redistribution is *not* to allow information learned from a protocol to be injected back into the same protocol. Passive interfaces and distribute lists should be applied on the redistributing routers. Filtering information with link-state protocols, such as OSPF, is a tricky business. The **distribute-list out** command works on the ASBR to filter redistributed routes into other protocols; **distribute-list in** works on any router to prevent routes from being put in the routing table, but it does not prevent link-state packets from being propagated—downstream routers would still have the routes. It is better to avoid OSPF filtering as much as possible if filters can be applied on the other protocols to prevent loops. Figure J-20 shows an example of a network with RIP and OSPF configured.

Figure J-20 *Example of Mutual Redistribution between OSPF and RIP*

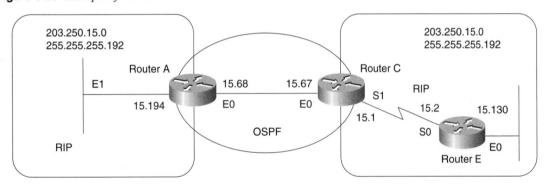

To illustrate, suppose Router A, Router C, and Router E are running RIP. Router A and Router C are also running OSPF. Both Router A and Router C are doing redistribution between RIP and OSPF. Let us assume that you do not want the RIP coming from Router E to be injected into the OSPF domain, so you put a passive interface for RIP on E0 of Router C. However, you have allowed the RIP coming from Router A to be injected into OSPF. Example J-26 shows the outcome. (DO NOT USE THIS CONFIGURATION!)

Example J-26 *Configurations and Routing Table for Routers in Figure J-20*

```
Router E#
interface Ethernet0
 ip address 203.250.15.130 255.255.255.192

interface Serial0
 ip address 203.250.15.2 255.255.255.192

router rip
 network 203.250.15.0

Router C#
interface Ethernet0
 ip address 203.250.15.67 255.255.255.192

interface Serial1
 ip address 203.250.15.1 255.255.255.192

router ospf 10
 redistribute rip metric 10 subnets
 network 203.250.15.0 0.0.0.255 area 0

router rip
 redistribute ospf 10 metric 2
 passive-interface Ethernet0
 network 203.250.15.0

Router A#
interface Ethernet0
 ip address 203.250.15.68 255.255.255.192

router ospf 10
 redistribute rip metric 10 subnets
 network 203.250.15.0 0.0.0.255 area 0

router rip
 redistribute ospf 10 metric 1
 network 203.250.15.0

Router C#show ip route
 Codes: C - connected, S - static, I - IGRP, R - RIP, M - mobile, B - BGP
        D - EIGRP, EX - EIGRP external, O - OSPF, IA - OSPF inter area
        E1 - OSPF external type 1, E2 - OSPF external type 2, E - EGP
        i - IS-IS, L1 - IS-IS level-1, L2 - IS-IS level-2, * - candidate default

Gateway of last resort is not set

     203.250.15.0 255.255.255.192 is subnetted, 4 subnets
C        203.250.15.0 is directly connected, Serial1
C        203.250.15.64 is directly connected, Ethernet0
R        203.250.15.128 [120/1] via 203.250.15.68, 00:01:08, Ethernet0
                        [120/1] via 203.250.15.2, 00:00:11, Serial1
O        203.250.15.192 [110/20] via 203.250.15.68, 00:21:41, Ethernet0
```

Note that Router C has two paths to reach the 203.250.15.128 subnet: Serial1 and Ethernet0 (Ethernet0 is obviously the wrong path). This happened because Router C gave that entry to Router A via OSPF, and Router A gave it back via RIP because Router A did not learn it via RIP. This example is a very small scale of loops that can occur because of an incorrect configuration. In large networks, this situation gets even more aggravated.

In order to fix the situation in our example, you could stop RIP from being sent on Router A's Ethernet0 via a passive interface. This might not be suitable in case some routers on the Ethernet are RIP-only routers. In this case, you could allow Router C to send RIP on the Ethernet; this way, Router A will not send it back on the wire because of split-horizon (this might not work on NBMA media if split horizon is off). Split-horizon does not allow updates to be sent back on the same interface they were learned from (via the same protocol). Another good method is to apply distribute-lists on Router A to deny subnets learned via OSPF from being put back into RIP on the Ethernet. The latter, illustrated in Example J-27, is the one we will be using.

Example J-27   *Configuring Distribute-List on Router A in Figure J-20*

```
Router A#
interface Ethernet0
 ip address 203.250.15.68 255.255.255.192

router ospf 10
 redistribute rip metric 10 subnets
 network 203.250.15.0 0.0.0.255 area 0

router rip
 redistribute ospf 10 metric 1
 network 203.250.15.0
 distribute-list 1 out ospf 10
```

Example J-28 shows the output of Router C's routing table.

Example J-28   *Router C's Routing Table with a Distribute-List on Router A*

```
Router C#show ip route
Codes: C - connected, S - static, I - IGRP, R - RIP, M - mobile, B - BGP
       D - EIGRP, EX - EIGRP external, O - OSPF, IA - OSPF inter area
       E1 - OSPF external type 1, E2 - OSPF external type 2, E - EGP
       i - IS-IS, L1 - IS-IS level-1, L2 - IS-IS level-2, * - candidate default

Gateway of last resort is not set

     203.250.15.0 255.255.255.192 is subnetted, 4 subnets
C       203.250.15.0 is directly connected, Serial1
C       203.250.15.64 is directly connected, Ethernet0
R       203.250.15.128 [120/1] via 203.250.15.2, 00:00:19, Serial1
O       203.250.15.192 [110/20] via 203.250.15.68, 00:21:41, Ethernet0
```

Injecting Defaults into OSPF

An autonomous system boundary router (ASBR) can be forced to generate a default route into the OSPF domain. As discussed earlier, a router becomes an ASBR whenever routes are redistributed into an OSPF domain. However, by default, an ASBR does not generate a default route into the OSPF routing domain.

To have OSPF generate a default route use the following command:

```
default-information originate [always] [metric metric-value] [metric-type type-
    value] [route-map map-name]
```

There are two ways to generate a default. The first is to advertise 0.0.0.0 inside the domain, but only if the ASBR itself already has a default route. The second is to advertise 0.0.0.0, regardless of whether the ASBR has a default route. The latter can be set by adding the keyword **always**—but be careful when using the **always** keyword. If your router advertises a default (0.0.0.0) inside the domain and does not have a default itself or a path to reach the destinations, routing will be broken.

The **metric** and **metric-type** are the cost and type (E1 or E2) assigned to the default route. The **route-map** specifies the set of conditions that need to be satisfied in order for the default to be generated.

Figure J-21 shows an example network using OSPF and RIP.

Figure J-21 *Example of Injecting a Default Route into OSPF*

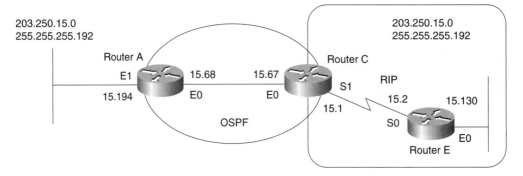

Assume that Router E is injecting a default-route 0.0.0.0 into RIP. Router C will have a gateway of last resort of 203.250.15.2. Router C will not propagate the default to Router A until we configure Router C with a **default-information originate** command as in Example J-29.

Example J-29 *Routing Tables and Configuration for Routers in Figure J-21 when Injecting a Default Route*

```
Router C#show ip route
 Codes: C - connected, S - static, I - IGRP, R - RIP, M - mobile, B - BGP
        D - EIGRP, EX - EIGRP external, O - OSPF, IA - OSPF inter area
        E1 - OSPF external type 1, E2 - OSPF external type 2, E - EGP
        i - IS-IS, L1 - IS-IS level-1, L2 - IS-IS level-2, * - candidate default

 Gateway of last resort is 203.250.15.2 to network 0.0.0.0

      203.250.15.0 255.255.255.192 is subnetted, 4 subnets
 C       203.250.15.0 is directly connected, Serial1
 C       203.250.15.64 is directly connected, Ethernet0
 R       203.250.15.128 [120/1] via 203.250.15.2, 00:00:17, Serial1
 O       203.250.15.192 [110/20] via 203.250.15.68, 2d23, Ethernet0
 R*    0.0.0.0 0.0.0.0 [120/1] via 203.250.15.2, 00:00:17, Serial1
               [120/1] via 203.250.15.68, 00:00:32, Ethernet0

Router C#interface Ethernet0
 ip address 203.250.15.67 255.255.255.192

interface Serial1
 ip address 203.250.15.1 255.255.255.192

router ospf 10
 redistribute rip metric 10 subnets
 network 203.250.15.0 0.0.0.255 area 0
 default-information originate metric 10

router rip
 redistribute ospf 10 metric 2
 passive-interface Ethernet0
 network 203.250.15.0

Router A#show ip route

 Codes: C - connected, S - static, I - IGRP, R - RIP, M - mobile, B - BGP
        D - EIGRP, EX - EIGRP external, O - OSPF, IA - OSPF inter area
        E1 - OSPF external type 1, E2 - OSPF external type 2, E - EGP
        i - IS-IS, L1 - IS-IS level-1, L2 - IS-IS level-2, * - candidate default

 Gateway of last resort is 203.250.15.67 to network 0.0.0.0

      203.250.15.0 255.255.255.192 is subnetted, 4 subnets
 O       203.250.15.0 [110/74] via 203.250.15.67, 2d23, Ethernet0
 C       203.250.15.64 is directly connected, Ethernet0
 O E2   203.250.15.128 [110/10] via 203.250.15.67, 2d23, Ethernet0
 C       203.250.15.192 is directly connected, Ethernet1
 O*E2 0.0.0.0 0.0.0.0 [110/10] via 203.250.15.67, 00:00:17, Ethernet0
```

Note that Router A has learned 0.0.0.0 as an external route with metric 10. The gateway of last resort is set to 203.250.15.67, as expected.

OSPF Design Tips

The OSPF RFC (1583) did not specify any guidelines for the number of routers in an area, the number of neighbors per segment, or what is the best way to architect a network. People have different approaches to designing OSPF networks. The important thing to remember is that any protocol can fail under pressure. The idea is not to challenge the protocol, but to work with it in order to get the best behavior. The following are a list of things to consider.

Number of Routers per Area

Experience has shown that 40 to 50 routers per area is the upper bound for OSPF. That does not mean that networks with 60 or 70 routers in an area won't function, but why experiment with stability if you don't need to. One of the main problems is that administrators let their backbone area grow too large. Try to outline the logical view of the network from the start, and remember that it doesn't hurt to start creating that other area.

Number of Neighbors

The number of routers connected to the same LAN is also important. Each LAN has a DR and BDR that build adjacencies with all other routers. The fewer neighbors that exist on the LAN, the smaller the number of adjacencies a DR or BDR have to build. That depends on how much power your router has. You could always change the OSPF priority to select your DR. Also, if possible, try to avoid having the same router be the DR on more than one segment. If DR selection is based on the highest RID, then one router could accidentally become a DR over all segments it is connected to. This router would be doing extra effort while other routers are idle. Figure J-22 shows two segments with four routers; a different router is chosen as the DR on each segment.

Figure J-22 *Try To Avoid Having the Same Router Be the DR on More than One Segment*

More neighbors = more work for DR/BDR

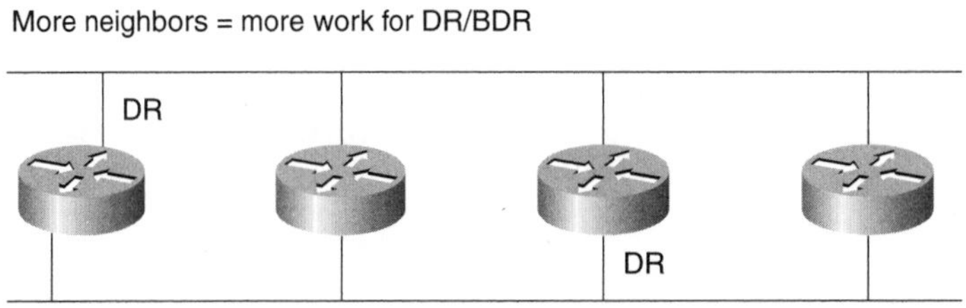

Number of Areas per ABR

ABRs will keep a copy of the database for all areas they service. If, for example, a router is connected to five areas, it will have to keep a list of five different databases. It is better not to overload an ABR. You could always spread the areas over other routers. The ideal design is to have each ABR connected to two areas only: the backbone and another area, with three areas being the upper limit. Figure J-23 shows the difference between one ABR holding five different databases (including area 0) and two ABRs holding three databases each. Again, these are just guidelines. The more areas you configure per ABR, the lower the performance you get. In some cases, the lower performance can be tolerated.

Figure J-23 *Try To Avoid Having One Router Be the ABR for More than Two Areas*

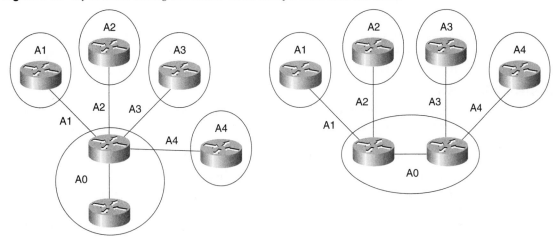

Full Mesh Versus Partial Mesh

Non broadcast Multiaccess (NBMA) clouds such as Frame Relay or X.25, are always a challenge. The combination of low bandwidth and too many link-states is a recipe for problems. A partial mesh topology has proven to behave much better than a full mesh. A carefully laid out point-to-point or point-to-multipoint network works much better than multipoint networks that have to deal with DR issues, as shown in Figure J-24.

Figure J-24   *Partial Mesh Has Proven To Behave Much Better than Full Mesh for OSPF*

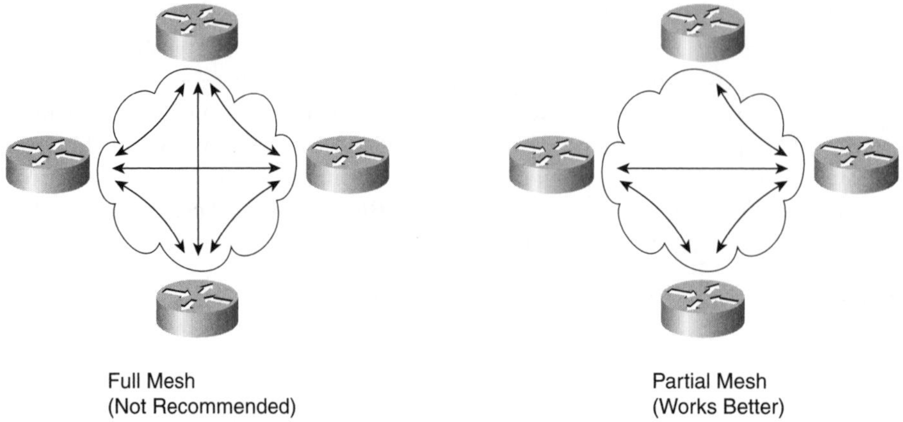

Full Mesh
(Not Recommended)

Partial Mesh
(Works Better)

Memory Issues

It is not easy to figure out the memory needed for a particular OSPF configuration. Memory issues usually come up when too many external routes are injected in the OSPF domain. A backbone area with 40 routers and a default route to the outside world would have less memory issues compared with a backbone area with four routers and 33,000 external routes injected into OSPF.

Memory could also be conserved by using a good OSPF design. Summarization at the area border routers and use of stub areas could further minimize the number of routes exchanged.

The total memory used by OSPF is the sum of the memory used in the routing table (**show ip route summary**) and the memory used in the link-state database. The following numbers are a rule-of-thumb estimate. Each entry in the routing table will consume between approximately 200 and 280 bytes, plus 44 bytes per extra path. Each LSA will consume a 100-byte overhead, plus the size of the actual link state advertisement, possibly another 60 to 100 bytes. (For router links, this depends on the number of interfaces on the router.) This should be added to memory used by other processes and by the IOS™ itself. If you really want to know the exact number, you can do a **show memory** with and without OSPF being turned on. The difference in the processor memory used would be the answer (keep a backup copy of the configurations).

Normally, a routing table with less than 500,000 bytes could be accommodated with 2 to 4 MB of RAM; large networks greater than 500,000 mighy need 8 to 16 MB (maybe 32 to 64 MB if full routes are injected from the Internet).

Summary

The OSPF protocol defined in RFC 1583 provides a high functionality open protocol that enables multiple-vendor networks to communicate using the TCP/IP protocol family. Some of the benefits of OSPF are fast convergence, VLSM, authentication, hierarchical segmentation, route summarization, and aggregation, which are needed to handle large and complicated networks.

Appendix A: Link-State Database Synchronization

As Figure J-25 shows, routers on the same segment go through a series of states before forming a successful adjacency. The neighbor and DR election are done via the Hello protocol. Whenever a router sees itself in his neighbor's hello packet, the state transitions to "2-Way." At that point, DR and BDR election is performed on multi-access segments. A router continues forming an adjacency with a neighbor if either of the two routers is a DR or BDR or they are connected via a point-to-point or virtual link.

Figure J-25 *Router OSPF State Transitions*

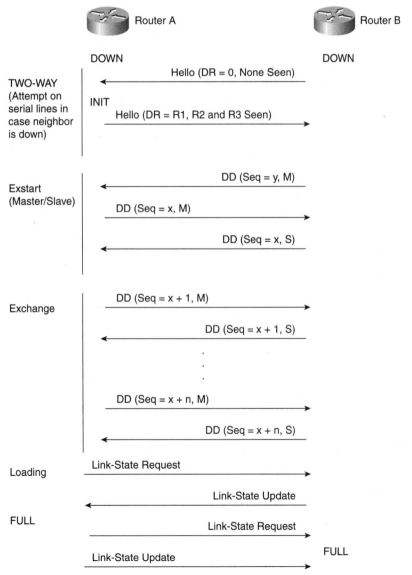

In the *Exstart* state, the two neighbors form a Master/Slave relationship, where they agree on a initial *sequence number*. The sequence number is used to detect old or duplicate Link-State Advertisements (LSA).

In the *Exchange* state, Database Description Packets (DD) will get exchanged. These are abbreviated link-state advertisements in the form of link-state headers. The header supplies enough information to identify a link. The master node sends DD packets, which are acknowledged with DD packets from the slave node. All adjacencies in exchange state or greater are used by the flooding procedure. These adjacencies are fully capable of transmitting and receiving all types of OSPF routing protocol packets.

In the *Loading* state, link-state request packets are sent to neighbors, asking for more recent advertisements that have been discovered but not yet received. Each router builds a list of required LSAs to bring its adjacency up to date. A *Retransmission* List is maintained to make sure that every LSA is acknowledged. To specify the number of seconds between link-state advertisement retransmissions for the adjacency, you can use the **ip ospf retransmit-interval seconds** command.

Link-state update packets are sent in response to request packets. The link-state update packets will be flooded over all adjacencies.

In the *Full* state, the neighbor routers are fully adjacent. The databases for a common area are an exact match between adjacent routers.

Each LSA has an *age* field that gets periodically incremented while it is contained in the database or as it gets flooded throughout the area. When an LSA reaches a *Maxage*, it gets flushed from the database if that LSA is not on any neighbors retransmission list.

Link-State Advertisements

Link-state advertisements are broken into five types:

- **Router Links** (RL) are generated by all routers. These links describe the state of the router interfaces inside a particular area. These links are only flooded inside the router's area.

- **Network Links** (NL) are generated by a DR of a particular segment; these are an indication of the routers connected to that segment.

- **Summary Links** (SL) are the interarea links (type 3); these links will list the networks inside other areas but still belonging to the autonomous system. Summary links are injected by the ABR from the backbone into other areas and from other areas into the backbone. These links are used for aggregation between areas.

- **ASBR-summary** are the other types of summary links. These are type 4 links that point to the ASBR. This is to make sure that all routers know the way to exit the autonomous system.

- **External Links** (EL) are the last type (type 5) of links. ELs are injected by the ASBR into the domain.

Figure J-26 illustrates these five different types of link-state advertisements.

Figure J-26 *The Five Types of Link-State Advertisements*

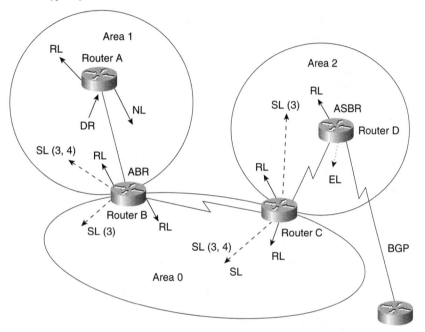

Router A generates a router link (RL) into area 1, and it also generates a network link (NL) because it happens to be the DR on that particular segment. Router B is an ABR, and it generates RL into area 1 and area 0. Router B also generates summary links into area 1 and area 0. These links are the list of networks that are interchanged between the two areas. An ASBR summary link is also injected by Router B into area 1. This is an indication of the existence of Router D, the autonomous system border router. Similarly, Router C, which is another ABR, generates RL for area 0 and area 2, and an SL (3) into area 2 (because it is not announcing any ASBR), and an SL (3,4) into area 0 announcing Router D. Router D generates an RL for area 2 and generates an EL for external routes learned via BGP. The external routers will be flooded all over the domain.

Table J-1 provides a summary of the link-state advertisements.

Table J-1 *Link-State Advertisements*

LS Type	Advertisement Description
1	Router Link advertisements. Generated by each router for each area it belongs to. They describe the states of the router's link to the area. These are only flooded within a particular area.
2	Network Link advertisements. Generated by Designated Routers. They describe the set of routers attached to a particular network. Flooded in the area that contains the network.
3 or 4	Summary Link advertisements. Generated by Area Border routers. They describe inter-area (between areas) routes. Type 3 describes routes to networks, also used for aggregating routes. Type 4 describes routes to ASBR.
5	AS external link advertisements. Originated by ASBR. They describe routes to destinations external to the AS. Flooded all over except stub areas.

If you look at the OSPF database in detail, using **show ip ospf d d**, you will see different keywords, such as *Link-Data*, *Link-ID*, and *Link-state ID*. These terms become confusing because the value of each depends on the link-state type and the link-type. We will go over this terminology and will provide a detailed example on the OSPF database as seen from the router.

The Link-State ID basically defines the identity of the link-state, depending on the LS type. *Router Links* are identified by the router ID (*RID*) of the router that originated the advertisement. *Network Links* are identified by the relative *IP address of the DR*. This makes sense because Network Links are originated by the Designated Router. *Summary Links* (type 3) are identified by the *IP network numbers of the destinations* they are pointing at. *ASBR Summary Links* (Summary Links type 4) are identified by the *RID of the ASBR*. Finally, *External Links* are identified by the *IP network numbers of the external destinations* they are pointing at. Table J-2 summarizes this information.

Table J-2 *Interpreting Link State ID in* **show ip ospf** *Commands, Based on Link-State Type*

LS Type	Link-State ID
1	The originating Router's Router ID (RID)
2	The IP interface address of the network's Designated Router
3	The destination network number
4	The router ID of the described AS boundary router
5	The external network number

In the high-level view of the database when referencing a router, the Link-State ID is referred to as the Link ID.

The following list describes the different links available:

- **Stub network links**—This term has nothing to do with stub areas. A stub segment is a segment that has one router only attached to it. An Ethernet or Token Ring segment that has one attached router is considered a link to a stub network. A loopback interface is also considered a link to stub network with a 255.255.255.255 mask (Host route).

- **Point-to-point links**—These could be physical or logical (subinterfaces) point-to-point serial link connections. These links could be numbered (an IP address is configured on the link) or unnumbered.

- **Transit links**—These are interfaces connected to networks that have more than one router attached, hence the name transit.

- **Virtual links**—These are logical links that connect areas that do not have physical connections to the backbone. Virtual links are treated as numbered point-to-point links.

The *link-ID* is an identification of the link itself. This is different for each link type. A *transit link* is identified by the *IP address of the DR* on that link. A *numbered point-to-point link* is identified by the *RID of the neighbor router* on the point-to-point link. *Virtual links are identical to point-to-point links*. Finally, links to *stub networks* are identified by the *IP address of the interface to the stub network*. Table J-3 summarizes this information:

Table J-3   *Interpreting Link ID in **show ip ospf** Commands, Based on Link Type*

Link Type	Link ID
Point-to-Point	Neighbor Router ID
Link to transit network	Interface address of DR
Link to stub network (In case of loopback mask is 255.255.255.255)	Network/subnet number
Virtual Link	Neighbor router ID

The Link ID applies to individual links in this case.

The *Link Data* is the *IP address of the link, except for stub network* where the link data is the *network mask*. Table J-4 summarizes this information.

Table J-4   *Interpreting Link Data in **show ip ospf** Commands, Based on Link Type*

Link Type	Link Data
Stub network	Network Mask
Other networks (applies to router links only)	Router's associated IP interface address

Finally, an *Advertising Router* is the RID of the router that has sent the LSA.

OSPF Database Example

Given the topology in Figure J-27 and the configurations and IP route tables in Example J-30, let us look at different ways of understanding the OSPF database.

Figure J-27 *Example OSPF Network*

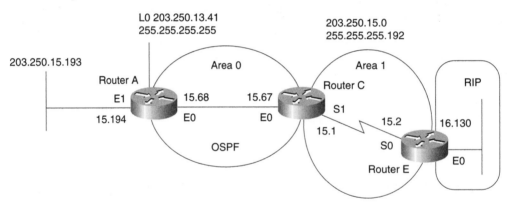

Example J-30 *Configurations and Routing Tables for Routers in Figure J-27*

```
Router A#
interface Loopback0
 ip address 203.250.13.41 255.255.255.255

interface Ethernet0
 ip address 203.250.15.68 255.255.255.192

interface Ethernet1
 ip address 203.250.15.193 255.255.255.192

router ospf 10
 network 203.250.0.0 0.0.255.255 area 0

Router A#show ip route
 Codes: C - connected, S - static, I - IGRP, R - RIP, M - mobile, B - BGP
        D - EIGRP, EX - EIGRP external, O - OSPF, IA - OSPF inter area
        E1 - OSPF external type 1, E2 - OSPF external type 2, E - EGP
        i - IS-IS, L1 - IS-IS level-1, L2 - IS-IS level-2, * - candidate default

Gateway of last resort is 203.250.15.67 to network 0.0.0.0

     203.250.16.0 255.255.255.192 is subnetted, 1 subnets
O E2    203.250.16.128 [110/10] via 203.250.15.67, 00:00:50, Ethernet0
     203.250.13.0 255.255.255.255 is subnetted, 1 subnets
C       203.250.13.41 is directly connected, Loopback0
     203.250.15.0 255.255.255.192 is subnetted, 3 subnets
O IA    203.250.15.0 [110/74] via 203.250.15.67, 00:00:50, Ethernet0
C       203.250.15.64 is directly connected, Ethernet0
C       203.250.15.192 is directly connected, Ethernet1
O*E2 0.0.0.0 0.0.0.0 [110/10] via 203.250.15.67, 00:00:50, Ethernet0

Router E#
ip subnet-zero

interface Ethernet0
 ip address 203.250.16.130 255.255.255.192
interface Serial0
 ip address 203.250.15.2 255.255.255.192

router ospf 10
 redistribute rip metric 10 subnets
 network 203.250.15.0 0.0.0.63 area 1
 default-information originate metric 10

router rip
 network 203.250.16.0

ip route 0.0.0.0 0.0.0.0 Ethernet0
```

continues

Example J-30 *Configurations and Routing Tables for Routers in Figure J-27 (Continued)*

```
Router E#show ip route
 Codes: C - connected, S - static, I - IGRP, R - RIP, M - mobile, B - BGP
        D - EIGRP, EX - EIGRP external, O - OSPF, IA - OSPF inter area
        E1 - OSPF external type 1, E2 - OSPF external type 2, E - EGP
        i - IS-IS, L1 - IS-IS level-1, L2 - IS-IS level-2, * - candidate default

 Gateway of last resort is 0.0.0.0 to network 0.0.0.0

      203.250.16.0 255.255.255.192 is subnetted, 1 subnets
 C       203.250.16.128 is directly connected, Ethernet0
      203.250.13.0 is variably subnetted, 2 subnets, 2 masks
 O IA    203.250.13.41 255.255.255.255
              [110/75] via 203.250.15.1, 00:16:31, Serial0
      203.250.15.0 255.255.255.192 is subnetted, 3 subnets
 C       203.250.15.0 is directly connected, Serial0
 O IA    203.250.15.64 [110/74] via 203.250.15.1, 00:16:31, Serial0
 O IA    203.250.15.192 [110/84] via 203.250.15.1, 00:16:31, Serial0
 S*   0.0.0.0 0.0.0.0 is directly connected, Ethernet0


Router C#
ip subnet-zero

interface Ethernet0
 ip address 203.250.15.67 255.255.255.192

interface Serial1
 ip address 203.250.15.1 255.255.255.192

router ospf 10
 network 203.250.15.64 0.0.0.63 area 0
 network 203.250.15.0 0.0.0.63 area 1

Router C#show ip route
 Codes: C - connected, S - static, I - IGRP, R - RIP, M - mobile, B - BGP
        D - EIGRP, EX - EIGRP external, O - OSPF, IA - OSPF inter area
        E1 - OSPF external type 1, E2 - OSPF external type 2, E - EGP
        i - IS-IS, L1 - IS-IS level-1, L2 - IS-IS level-2, * - candidate default

 Gateway of last resort is 203.250.15.2 to network 0.0.0.0

      203.250.16.0 255.255.255.192 is subnetted, 1 subnets
 O E2    203.250.16.128 [110/10] via 203.250.15.2, 04:49:05, Serial1
      203.250.13.0 255.255.255.255 is subnetted, 1 subnets
 O       203.250.13.41 [110/11] via 203.250.15.68, 04:49:06, Ethernet0
      203.250.15.0 255.255.255.192 is subnetted, 3 subnets
 C       203.250.15.0 is directly connected, Serial1
 C       203.250.15.64 is directly connected, Ethernet0
 O       203.250.15.192 [110/20] via 203.250.15.68, 04:49:06, Ethernet0
 O*E2 0.0.0.0 0.0.0.0 [110/10] via 203.250.15.2, 04:49:06, Serial1
```

General View of the Database

Example J-31 is a general look at the whole OSPF database. The database is listed according to the areas. In this case, we are looking at Router C's database, which is an ABR. Both area 1 and area 0's databases are listed. Area 1 is composed of router links and summary links. No network links exist because no DR exists on any of the segments in area 1. No Summary ASBR links exist in area 1 because the only ASBR happens to be in area 0. External links do not belong to any particular area because they are flooded all over. Note that all the links are the cumulative links collected from all routers in an area.

Example J-31 *OSPF Database on Router C in Figure J-27*

```
Router C#show ip ospf database

        OSPF Router with ID (203.250.15.67) (Process ID 10)

                Router Link States (Area 1)

    Link ID         ADV Router      Age     Seq#        Checksum Link count
    203.250.15.67   203.250.15.67   48      0x80000008 0xB112    2
    203.250.16.130  203.250.16.130  212     0x80000006 0x3F44    2

                Summary Net Link States (Area 1)

    Link ID         ADV Router      Age     Seq#        Checksum
    203.250.13.41   203.250.15.67   602     0x80000002 0x90AA
    203.250.15.64   203.250.15.67   620     0x800000E9 0x3E3C
    203.250.15.192  203.250.15.67   638     0x800000E5 0xA54E

                Router Link States (Area 0)

    Link ID         ADV Router      Age     Seq#        Checksum Link count
    203.250.13.41   203.250.13.41   179     0x80000029 0x9ADA    3
    203.250.15.67   203.250.15.67   675     0x800001E2 0xDD23    1

                Net Link States (Area 0)

    Link ID         ADV Router      Age     Seq#        Checksum
    203.250.15.68   203.250.13.41   334     0x80000001 0xB6B5

                Summary Net Link States (Area 0)

    Link ID         ADV Router      Age     Seq#        Checksum
    203.250.15.0    203.250.15.67   792     0x80000002 0xAEBD
```

continues

Example J-31 *OSPF Database on Router C in Figure J-27 (Continued)*

```
                   Summary ASB Link States (Area 0)

    Link ID          ADV Router       Age    Seq#        Checksum
    203.250.16.130   203.250.15.67    579    0x80000001  0xF9AF


                   AS External Link States

    Link ID          ADV Router       Age    Seq#        Checksum Tag
    0.0.0.0          203.250.16.130   1787   0x80000001  0x98CE   10
    203.250.16.128   203.250.16.130   5      0x80000002  0x93C4   0
```

We will mainly concentrate on the database in area 0. *The Link-ID indicated here is actually the Link-State ID. This is a representation of the whole router, not a particular link.* This is a bit confusing, but just remember that this high-level Link-ID (should be Link-State ID) represents the whole router and not just a link.

Router Links

In Example J-32, we start with the router links.

Example J-32 *Router Link States for Area 0 on Router C in Figure J-27*

```
                   Router Link States (Area 0)

    Link ID          ADV Router       Age    Seq#        Checksum Link count
    203.250.13.41    203.250.13.41    179    0x80000029  0x9ADA   3
    203.250.15.67    203.250.15.67    675    0x800001E2  0xDD23   1
```

There are two entries listed for 203.250.13.41 and 203.250.15.67 ; these are the RIDs of the two routers in area 0. The number of links in area 0 for each router is also indicated. Router A has three links to area 0, and Router C has one link. Example J-33 provides a detailed view of Router C's router links (in area 1).

Example J-33 *Detailed Router Link States for Router C Area 1 in Figure J-27*

```
Router C#show ip ospf database router 203.250.15.67

    OSPF Router with ID (203.250.15.67) (Process ID 10)

              Router Link States (Area 1)
    LS age: 1169
    Options: (No TOS-capability)
    LS Type: Router Links
    Link State ID: 203.250.15.67
    Advertising Router: 203.250.15.67
    LS Seq Number: 80000008
    Checksum: 0xB112
    Length: 48
    Area Border Router
     Number of Links: 2

      Link connected to: another Router (point-to-point)
       (Link ID) Neighboring Router ID: 203.250.16.130
       (Link Data) Router Interface address: 203.250.15.1
        Number of TOS metrics: 0
         TOS 0 Metrics: 64

      Link connected to: a Stub Network
       (Link ID) Network/subnet number: 203.250.15.0
       (Link Data) Network Mask: 255.255.255.192
        Number of TOS metrics: 0
         TOS 0 Metrics: 64
```

One thing to note here is that OSPF generates an extra stub link for each point-to-point interface. Do not get confused if you see the link count larger than the number of physical interfaces. Example J-34 is a continuation of the output in Example J-33 and provides a detailed view of Router C's router links (in area 0).

Example J-34   *Detailed Router Link States for Router C Area 0 in Figure J-27*

```
                    Router Link States (Area 0)

    LS age: 1227
    Options: (No TOS-capability)
    LS Type: Router Links
    Link State ID: 203.250.15.67
    Advertising Router: 203.250.15.67
    LS Seq Number: 80000003
    Checksum: 0xA041
    Length: 36
    Area Border Router
     Number of Links: 1

      Link connected to: a Transit Network
       (Link ID) Designated Router address: 203.250.15.68
       (Link Data) Router Interface address: 203.250.15.67
        Number of TOS metrics: 0
         TOS 0 Metrics: 10
```

Note that the Link ID is equal to the IP address (not the RID) of the attached DR; in this case, it is 203.250.15.68. The Link Data is Router C's own IP address.

Network Links

In Example J-35, we again see the network links part of the OSPF database for area 0 for Router C.

Example J-35   *Network Link States for Area 0 on Router C in Figure J-27*

```
                    Net Link States (Area 0)

    Link ID         ADV Router      Age    Seq#        Checksum
    203.250.15.68   203.250.13.41   334    0x80000001  0xB6B5
```

One network Link is listed, indicated by the interface IP address (not the RID) of the DR—in this case, 203.250.15.68. Example J-36 presents a detailed view of this entry.

Example J-36 *Detailed Network Link States for Area 0 for Router C in Figure J-27*

```
Router C#show ip ospf database network

        OSPF Router with ID (203.250.15.67) (Process ID 10)

                Net Link States (Area 0)

    Routing Bit Set on this LSA
    LS age: 1549
    Options: (No TOS-capability)
    LS Type: Network Links
    Link State ID: 203.250.15.68 (address of Designated Router)
    Advertising Router: 203.250.13.41
    LS Seq Number: 80000002
    Checksum: 0xB4B6
    Length: 32
    Network Mask: 255.255.255.192

        Attached Router: 203.250.13.41
        Attached Router: 203.250.15.67
```

Note that the network link lists the RIDs of the routers attached to the transit network; in this case, the RIDs of Router A and Router C are listed.

Summary Links

In Example J-37, we again see the summary network links part of the ospf database for area 0 for Router C.

Example J-37 *Summary Network Link States for Area 0 on Router C in Figure J-27*

```
                Summary Net Link States (Area 0)

    Link ID        ADV Router      Age    Seq#      Checksum
    203.250.15.0   203.250.15.67   792    0x80000002 0xAEBD
```

Area 0 has one summary link represented by the IP network address of the link 203.250.15.0. This link was injected by the ABR Router C from area 1 into area 0. Example J-38 shows a detailed view of this summary link (summary links for area 1 are not listed here).

Example J-38   *Detailed Summary Network Link States for Area 0 for Router C in Figure J-27*

```
Router C#show ip ospf database summary (area 1 is not listed)

                Summary Net Link States (Area 0)

    LS age: 615
    Options: (No TOS-capability)
    LS Type: Summary Links(Network)
    Link State ID: 203.250.15.0 (summary Network Number)
    Advertising Router: 203.250.15.67
    LS Seq Number: 80000003
    Checksum: 0xACBE
    Length: 28
    Network Mask: 255.255.255.192 TOS: 0  Metric: 64
```

Summary ASBR Links

In Example J-39, we again see the summary ASB links part of the OSPF database for area 0 for Router C.

Example J-39   *Summary ASB Link States for Area 0 on Router C in Figure J-27*

```
                Summary ASB Link States (Area 0)

    Link ID         ADV Router      Age    Seq#        Checksum
    203.250.16.130  203.250.15.67   579    0x80000001  0xF9AF
```

Example J-39 provides an indication of who the ASBR is. In this case, the ASBR is Router E represented by its RID 203.250.16.130. The advertising router for this entry into area 0 is Router C with RID 203.250.15.67. Example J-40 shows a detailed view of the summary ASBR entry.

Example J-40   *Detailed Summary ASB Link States for Area 0 for Router C in Figure J-27*

```
Router C#show ip ospf database asbr-summary

        OSPF Router with ID (203.250.15.67) (Process ID 10)

                Summary ASB Link States (Area 0)

    LS age: 802
    Options: (No TOS-capability)
    LS Type: Summary Links(AS Boundary Router)
    Link State ID: 203.250.16.130 (AS Boundary Router address)
    Advertising Router: 203.250.15.67
    LS Seq Number: 80000003
    Checksum: 0xF5B1
    Length: 28
    Network Mask: 0.0.0.0 TOS: 0  Metric: 64
```

External Links

In Example J-41, we again see the external link states part of the ospf database on Router C.

Example J-41 *External Link States on Router C in Figure J-27*

```
                     AS External Link States

Link ID          ADV Router       Age    Seq#        Checksum Tag
0.0.0.0          203.250.16.130   1787   0x80000001 0x98CE    10
203.250.16.128   203.250.16.130   5      0x80000002 0x93C4    0
```

We have two external Links: the first is the 0.0.0.0 injected into OSPF via the **default-information originate** command, and the other entry is network 203.250.16.128, which is injected into OSPF by redistribution. The router advertising these networks is 203.250.16.130, the RID of Router E. Example J-42 shows a detailed view of the external routes.

Example J-42 *Detailed External Link States on Router C in Figure J-27*

```
Router C#show ip ospf database external

        OSPF Router with ID (203.250.15.67) (Process ID 10)

                AS External Link States

Routing Bit Set on this LSA
LS age: 208
Options: (No TOS-capability)
LS Type: AS External Link
Link State ID: 0.0.0.0 (External Network Number )
Advertising Router: 203.250.16.130
LS Seq Number: 80000002
Checksum: 0x96CF
Length: 36
Network Mask: 0.0.0.0
      Metric Type: 2 (Larger than any link state path)
      TOS: 0
      Metric: 10
      Forward Address: 0.0.0.0
      External Route Tag: 10
Routing Bit Set on this LSA
LS age: 226
Options: (No TOS-capability)
LS Type: AS External Link
Link State ID: 203.250.16.128 (External Network Number)
Advertising Router: 203.250.16.130
LS Seq Number: 80000002
Checksum: 0x93C4
```

continues

Example J-42 *Detailed External Link States on Router C in Figure J-27 (Continued)*

```
Length: 36
Network Mask: 255.255.255.192
        Metric Type: 2 (Larger than any link state path)
        TOS: 0
        Metric: 10
        Forward Address: 0.0.0.0
        External Route Tag: 0
```

Please note the forward address. Whenever this address is 0.0.0.0, it indicates that the external routes are reachable via the advertising router—in this case, 203.250.16.130. This is why the identity of the ASBR is injected by ABRs into other areas using ASBR summary links.

This forward address is not always 0.0.0.0. In some cases, it could be the IP address of another router on the same segment. Figure J-28 illustrates this situation.

Figure J-28 *Example of when OSPF Forwarding Address Is Not 0.0.0.0*

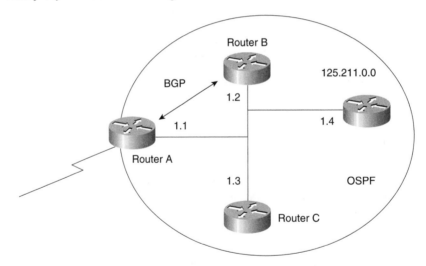

In the network in Figure J-28, Router B is running BGP with Router A and OSPF with the rest of the domain. Router A is not running OSPF. Router B is redistributing BGP routes into OSPF. According to OSPF, Router B is an ASBR advertising external routes. The forwarding address in this case is set to 125.211.1.1 and not to the advertising router (0.0.0.0) Router B. This makes sense because there is no need to make the extra hop.

NOTE   An important thing to remember is that routers inside the OSPF domain should be able to reach the forwarding address via OSPF in order for the external routes to be put in the IP routing table. If the forwarding address is reached via some other protocol or not accessible, the external entries would be in the database but not in the IP routing table.

Another situation would arise if both Router B and Router C are ASBRs (Router C is also running BGP with Router A). In this situation, in order to eliminate the duplication of the effort, one of the two routers will not advertise (will flush) the external routes. The router with the higher RID will win.

The Full Database

Finally, Example J-43 provides a listing of the whole database as an exercise. You should now be able to go over each entry and explain what is going on.

Example J-43 *Full OSPF Database on Router C in Figure J-27*

```
Router C#show ip ospf database router

         OSPF Router with ID (203.250.15.67) (Process ID 10)

              Router Link States (Area 1)

   LS age: 926
   Options: (No TOS-capability)
   LS Type: Router Links
   Link State ID: 203.250.15.67
   Advertising Router: 203.250.15.67
   LS Seq Number: 80000035
   Checksum: 0x573F
   Length: 48
   Area Border Router
    Number of Links: 2

    Link connected to: another Router (point-to-point)
      (Link ID) Neighboring Router ID: 203.250.16.130
      (Link Data) Router Interface address: 203.250.15.1
       Number of TOS metrics: 0
        TOS 0 Metrics: 64

    Link connected to: a Stub Network
      (Link ID) Network/subnet number: 203.250.15.0
      (Link Data) Network Mask: 255.255.255.192
       Number of TOS metrics: 0
        TOS 0 Metrics: 64
```

continues

Example J-43 *Full OSPF Database on Router C in Figure J-27 (Continued)*

```
Routing Bit Set on this LSA
LS age: 958
Options: (No TOS-capability)
LS Type: Router Links
Link State ID: 203.250.16.130
Advertising Router: 203.250.16.130
LS Seq Number: 80000038
Checksum: 0xDA76
Length: 48
AS Boundary Router
 Number of Links: 2

   Link connected to: another Router (point-to-point)
    (Link ID) Neighboring Router ID: 203.250.15.67
    (Link Data) Router Interface address: 203.250.15.2
     Number of TOS metrics: 0
      TOS 0 Metrics: 64

   Link connected to: a Stub Network
    (Link ID) Network/subnet number: 203.250.15.0
    (Link Data) Network Mask: 255.255.255.192
     Number of TOS metrics: 0
      TOS 0 Metrics: 64

                Router Link States (Area 0)

Routing Bit Set on this LSA
LS age: 1107
Options: (No TOS-capability)
LS Type: Router Links
Link State ID: 203.250.13.41
Advertising Router: 203.250.13.41
LS Seq Number: 8000002A
Checksum: 0xC0B0
Length: 60
AS Boundary Router
 Number of Links: 3

   Link connected to: a Stub Network
    (Link ID) Network/subnet number: 203.250.13.41
    (Link Data) Network Mask: 255.255.255.255
     Number of TOS metrics: 0
      TOS 0 Metrics: 1

   Link connected to: a Stub Network
    (Link ID) Network/subnet number: 203.250.15.192
    (Link Data) Network Mask: 255.255.255.192
     Number of TOS metrics: 0
      TOS 0 Metrics: 10
```

continues

Example J-43 *Full OSPF Database on Router C in Figure J-27 (Continued)*

```
        Link connected to: a Transit Network
         (Link ID) Designated Router address: 203.250.15.68
         (Link Data) Router Interface address: 203.250.15.68
          Number of TOS metrics: 0
           TOS 0 Metrics: 10


    LS age: 1575
    Options: (No TOS-capability)
    LS Type: Router Links
    Link State ID: 203.250.15.67
    Advertising Router: 203.250.15.67
    LS Seq Number: 80000028
    Checksum: 0x5666
    Length: 36
    Area Border Router
     Number of Links: 1

        Link connected to: a Transit Network
         (Link ID) Designated Router address: 203.250.15.68
         (Link Data) Router Interface address: 203.250.15.67
          Number of TOS metrics: 0
           TOS 0 Metrics: 10

Router C#show ip ospf database network

        OSPF Router with ID (203.250.15.67) (Process ID 10)

                Net Link States (Area 0)

    Routing Bit Set on this LSA
    LS age: 1725
    Options: (No TOS-capability)
    LS Type: Network Links
    Link State ID: 203.250.15.68 (address of Designated Router)
    Advertising Router: 203.250.13.41
    LS Seq Number: 80000026
    Checksum: 0x6CDA
    Length: 32
    Network Mask: 255.255.255.192
         Attached Router: 203.250.13.41
         Attached Router: 203.250.15.67

Router C#show ip ospf database summary

        OSPF Router with ID (203.250.15.67) (Process ID 10)
```

continues

Example J-43 *Full OSPF Database on Router C in Figure J-27 (Continued)*

```
                    Summary Net Link States (Area 1)
     LS age: 8
     Options: (No TOS-capability)
     LS Type: Summary Links(Network)
     Link State ID: 203.250.13.41 (summary Network Number)
     Advertising Router: 203.250.15.67
     LS Seq Number: 80000029
     Checksum: 0x42D1
     Length: 28
     Network Mask: 255.255.255.255 TOS: 0  Metric: 11

     LS age: 26
     Options: (No TOS-capability)
     LS Type: Summary Links(Network)
     Link State ID: 203.250.15.64 (summary Network Number)
     Advertising Router: 203.250.15.67
     LS Seq Number: 80000030
     Checksum: 0xB182
     Length: 28
     Network Mask: 255.255.255.192 TOS: 0  Metric: 10

     LS age: 47
     Options: (No TOS-capability)
     LS Type: Summary Links(Network)
     Link State ID: 203.250.15.192 (summary Network Number)
     Advertising Router: 203.250.15.67
     LS Seq Number: 80000029
     Checksum: 0x1F91
     Length: 28
     Network Mask: 255.255.255.192 TOS: 0  Metric: 20

                    Summary Net Link States (Area 0)

     LS age: 66
     Options: (No TOS-capability)
     LS Type: Summary Links(Network)
     Link State ID: 203.250.15.0 (summary Network Number)
     Advertising Router: 203.250.15.67
     LS Seq Number: 80000025
     Checksum: 0x68E0
     Length: 28
     Network Mask: 255.255.255.192 TOS: 0  Metric: 64

Router C#show ip ospf asbr-summary

        OSPF Router with ID (203.250.15.67) (Process ID 10)
```

continues

Example J-43 *Full OSPF Database on Router C in Figure J-27 (Continued)*

```
                        Summary ASB Link States (Area 0)

      LS age: 576
      Options: (No TOS-capability)
      LS Type: Summary Links(AS Boundary Router)
      Link State ID: 203.250.16.130 (AS Boundary Router address)
      Advertising Router: 203.250.15.67
      LS Seq Number: 80000024
      Checksum: 0xB3D2
      Length: 28
      Network Mask: 0.0.0.0 TOS: 0  Metric: 64

  Router C#show ip ospf database external

          OSPF Router with ID (203.250.15.67) (Process ID 10)

                  AS External Link States

      Routing Bit Set on this LSA
      LS age: 305
      Options: (No TOS-capability)
      LS Type: AS External Link
      Link State ID: 0.0.0.0 (External Network Number)
      Advertising Router: 203.250.16.130
      LS Seq Number: 80000001
      Checksum: 0x98CE
      Length: 36
      Network Mask: 0.0.0.0
            Metric Type: 2 (Larger than any link state path)
            TOS: 0
            Metric: 10
            Forward Address: 0.0.0.0
            External Route Tag: 10

      Routing Bit Set on this LSA
      LS age: 653
      Options: (No TOS-capability)
      LS Type: AS External Link
      Link State ID: 203.250.16.128 (External Network Number)
      Advertising Router: 203.250.16.130
      LS Seq Number: 80000024
      Checksum: 0x4FE6
      Length: 36
      Network Mask: 255.255.255.192
            Metric Type: 2 (Larger than any link state path)
            TOS: 0
            Metric: 10
            Forward Address: 0.0.0.0
            External Route Tag: 0
```

Appendix B: OSPF and IP Multicast Addressing

OSPF used IP multicast to exchange hello packets and Link State Updates. An IP multicast address is implemented using class D addresses. As shown in Figure J-29, the most significant four bits in a Class D address are set to binary 1110; thus a class D address ranges from 224.0.0.0 to 239.255.255.255.

Figure J-29   *The Most Significant Four Bits for a Class D IP Address*

Class D Addressing

Some special IP multicast addresses are reserved for OSPF:

- **224.0.0.5**—All OSPF routers should be able to transmit and listen to this address.
- **224.0.0.6**—All DR and BDR routers should be able to transmit and listen to this address.

The mapping between IP multicast addresses and MAC addresses has the following rule:

For multi-access networks that support multicast, the low order 23 bits of the IP address are used as the low order bits of the MAC multicast address 01-00-5E-00-00-00.

For example:

224.0.0.5 would be mapped to 01-00-5E-00-00-05 and
224.0.0.6 would be mapped to 01-00-5E-00-00-06

OSPF uses broadcast on Token Ring networks.

Appendix C: Variable Length Subnet Masks (VLSM)

Table J-5 provides a binary to decimal conversion chart, useful in IP addressing and VLSM calculations.

Table J-5   *Binary/Decimal Conversion Chart*

	0000		0001		0010		0011		0100		0101		0110		0111
0	0000	16	0000	32	0000	48	0000	64	0000	80	000 0	96	0000	112	0000
1	0001	17	0001	33	0001	49	0001	65	0001	81	000 1	97	0001	113	0001
2	0010	18	0010	34	0010	50	0010	66	0010	82	001 0	98	0010	114	0010

continues

Table J-5   *Binary/Decimal Conversion Chart (Continued)*

	0000		**0001**		**0010**		**0011**		**0100**		**0101**		**0110**		**0111**
3	0011	19	0011	35	0011	51	0011	67	0011	83	001 1	99	0011	115	0011
4	0100	20	0100	36	0100	52	0100	68	0100	84	010 0	100	0100	116	0100
5	0101	21	0101	37	0101	53	0101	69	0101	85	010 1	101	0101	117	0101
6	0110	22	0110	38	0110	54	0110	70	0110	86	011 0	102	0110	118	0110
7	0111	23	0111	39	0111	55	0111	71	0111	87	011 1	103	0111	119	0111
8	1000	24	1000	40	1000	56	1000	72	1000	88	100 0	104	1000	120	1000
9	1001	25	1001	41	1001	57	1001	73	1001	89	100 1	105	1001	121	1001
10	1010	26	1010	42	1010	58	1010	74	1010	90	10 10	106	1010	122	1010
11	1011	27	1011	43	1011	59	1011	75	1011	91	10 11	107	1011	123	1011
12	1100	28	1100	44	1100	60	1100	76	1100	92	11 00	108	1100	124	1100
13	1101	29	1101	45	1101	61	1101	77	1101	93	11 01	109	1101	125	1101
14	1110	30	1110	46	1110	62	1110	78	1110	94	11 10	110	1110	126	1110
15	1111	31	1111	47	1111	63	1111	79	1111	95	11 11	111	1111	127	1111
	1000		**1001**		**1010**		**1011**		**1100**		**1101**		**1110**		**1111**
128	0000	144	0000	160	0000	176	0000	192	0000	208	0000	224	0000	240	0000
129	0001	145	0001	161	0001	177	0001	193	0001	209	0001	225	0001	241	0001
130	0010	146	0010	162	0010	178	0010	194	0010	210	0010	226	0010	242	0010
131	0011	147	0011	163	0011	179	0011	195	0011	211	0011	227	0011	243	0011
132	0100	148	0100	164	0100	180	0100	196	0100	212	0100	228	0100	244	0100
133	0101	149	0101	165	0101	181	0101	197	0101	213	0101	229	0101	245	0101
134	0110	150	0110	166	0110	182	0110	198	0110	214	0110	230	0110	246	0110
135	0111	151	0111	167	0111	183	0111	199	0111	215	0111	231	0111	247	0111
136	1000	152	1000	168	1000	184	1000	200	1000	216	1000	232	1000	248	1000
137	1001	153	1001	169	1001	185	1001	201	1001	217	1001	233	1001	249	1001
138	1010	154	1010	170	1010	186	1010	202	1010	218	1010	234	1010	250	1010
139	1011	155	1011	171	1011	187	1011	203	1011	219	1011	235	1011	251	1011
140	1100	156	1100	172	1100	188	1100	204	1100	220	1100	236	1100	252	1100
141	1101	157	1101	173	1101	189	1101	205	1101	221	1101	237	1101	253	1101
142	1110	158	1110	174	1110	190	1110	206	1110	222	1110	238	1110	254	1110
143	1111	159	1111	175	1111	191	1111	207	1111	223	1111	239	1111	255	1111

The idea behind variable-length subnet masks is to offer more flexibility in dealing with dividing a major net into multiple subnets and still being able to maintain an adequate number of hosts in each subnet. Without VLSM, only one subnet mask can be applied to a major network. This would restrict the number of hosts given the number of subnets required. If we pick the mask so that we have enough subnets, we wouldn't be able to allocate enough hosts in each subnet. The same is true for the hosts; a mask that allows enough hosts might not provide enough subnet space.

For example, suppose you were assigned a class C network 192.213.11.0 and you need to divide that network into three subnets with 100 hosts in one subnet and 50 hosts for each of the remaining subnets. Ignoring the two end limits of 0 and 255, you theoretically have 256 addresses (192.213.11.0–192.213.11.255) available to you. This cannot be done without VLSM. Figure J-30 shows an example network, with the maximum number of host addresses on each network noted.

Figure J-30   *Example Network Requiring VLSM*

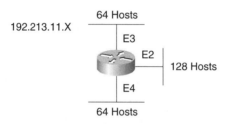

There are a handful of subnet masks that can be used; remember that a mask should have a contiguous number of ones starting from the left and the rest of the bits being all zeros. The last octet of the available subnet mask could be as follows:

-252 (1111 1100) The address space is divided into 64.
-248 (1111 1000) The address space is divided into 32.
-240 (1111 0000) The address space is divided into 16.
-224 (1110 0000) The address space is divided into 8.
-192 (1100 0000) The address space is divided into 4.
-128 (1000 0000) The address space is divided into 2.

Without VLSM, we have the choice of using mask 255.255.255.128 and dividing the addresses into two subnets with 128 hosts each or using 255.255.255.192 and dividing the space into four subnets with 64 hosts each. This would not meet the requirement. By using multiple masks, we can use mask 128 and further subnet the second chunk of addresses with mask 192. Figure J-31 shows how we have divided the address space accordingly.

Figure J-31 *Division of the Address Space for the Network in Figure J-30, Using VLSM*

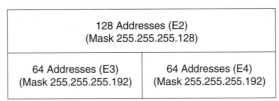

VLSM

128 Addresses (E2) (Mask 255.255.255.128)	
64 Addresses (E3) (Mask 255.255.255.192)	64 Addresses (E4) (Mask 255.255.255.192)

Now, be careful in allocating the IP addresses to each mask. After you assign an IP address to the router or to a host, you have used up the whole subnet for that segment. For example, if you assign 192.213.11.10 255.255.255.128 to E2, the whole range of addresses between 192.213.11.0 and 192.214.11.127 is consumed by E2. Likewise, if you assign 192.213.11.160 255.255.255.128 to E2, the whole range of addresses between 192.213.11.128 and 192.213.11.255 is consumed by the E2 segment.

Example J-44 is an illustration of how the router will interpret these addresses. Please remember that any time you are using a mask different than the natural mask—for instance, when you are subnetting—the router will complain if the combination IP address and mask will result in a subnet zero. To resolve this issue, use the command **ip subnet-zero** on the router.

Example J-44 *Configuration of the Router in Figure J-30, Using VLSM*

```
Router A#
ip subnet-zero
interface Ethernet2
 ip address 192.213.11.10 255.255.255.128
interface Ethernet3
 ip address 192.213.11.160 255.255.255.192
interface Ethernet4
 ip address 192.213.11.226 255.255.255.192

Router A#show ip route connected
      192.213.11.0 is variably subnetted, 3 subnets, 2 masks
C        192.213.11.0 255.255.255.128 is directly connected, Ethernet2
C        192.213.11.128 255.255.255.192 is directly connected, Ethernet3
C        192.213.11.192 255.255.255.192 is directly connected, Ethernet4
```

This Enhancements to EIGRP paper was originally written by Raja Sundaram of Cisco's Technical Assistance Center (TAC). It has been edited here for formatting.

Enhancements to EIGRP

This paper is an informational document describing Enhanced Interior Gateway Routing Protocol (EIGRP) and its continuing improvements as part of Cisco's ongoing effort to enhance its routing protocol technology. A project was undertaken to improve certain aspects of the EIGRP implementation. It was based on field experience gained from the initial implementation. The intent was not to add any features to EIGRP, but to improve the stability and scalability of the existing implementation. As such, the user-visible changes are very few. This document describes in general terms how EIGRP works, the changes and enhancements made, the implications for deployment, and the impact on the customer.

Introduction

There are two classifications of routing protocols: distance vector and link-state protocols. In a distance vector protocol, a router sends an update to its neighbor who in turn sends an update to its neighbor. These updates contain a vector of one or more entries, each of which specifies as a minimum, the distance to a given destination. Distance vector protocols are mainly based on variations of the Distributed Bellman-Ford (DBF) algorithm. The pitfalls of DBF during failures include persistent looping problems, large convergence times, and counting-to-infinity.

Link-state protocols, such as Open Shortest Path First (OSPF) and Intermediate System-to-Intermediate System (IS-IS), are being offered as an alternative. OSPF and IS-IS solve DBF's counting-to-infinity problem and convergence time by replicating topology information. However, replicating link states at every router becomes undesirable in large networks, and SPF is expensive.

This paper examines EIGRP, an advanced distance vector (ADV) protocol that uses the Diffusing Update Algorithm (DUAL) which is used to compute shortest paths in a distributed fashion without creating routing loops, incurring counting-to-infinity behavior, or exchanging link states.

How EIGRP Works

This section is a basic explanation of how EIGRP works including coverage of the neighbor table, topology table, feasible successor, and route states and how routes converge.

Neighbor Table

When a router is configured for EIGRP it dynamically discovers other routers directly connected to it. Each router maintains information that it has learned from its neighboring routers. This information is maintained in the Neighbor Table. The address and the interface through which the neighbor can be reached is recorded. The Neighbor Table also maintains an entry known as the HoldTime. HoldTime is the amount of time the router treats the neighbor as reachable and operational. HoldTime is calculated as 3 × hello time interval, but it can also be configured. The HoldTime is reported by a router as part of its hello message; this means that Hello interval and HoldTime values can be set independently on different routers without difficulty.

Topology Table

Once the router dynamically discovers a new neighbor, it sends an Update about the routes it knows to the new neighbor and receives the same from it. These Updates populate what is known as the Topology Table. This table does not contain all the information advertised by all the neighboring routers; much of the information is discarded, and only the current route and, possibly backup routes ("feasible successors") are kept (see the section that follows for an explanation of "feasible successor"). It is important to note that if a neighbor is advertising a destination, then it must be using that route to forward packets. This rule must be strictly followed by all distance vector protocols.

The Topology Table also maintains the metric that the neighbors advertise for each destination, and the metric that the router uses to reach the destination. This is the sum of the best advertised metric from all neighbors plus the link cost to the best neighbor. The topology table is also updated when a directly connected route or interface changes, or when a neighboring router reports a change to a route.

DUAL is the finite state machine that selects which information will be stored in the Topology Table, chooses the efficient loop free path to each destination from the Topology Table, and inserts it into the routing table. The routing table is essentially a subset of the Topology Table. The Topology Table contains more detailed information about each route, backup routes, and information used exclusively by DUAL.

Feasible Successor

The neighbor that is used to forward data packets to a destination (the "next hop") is known as a Successor. A Feasible Successor is a neighbor that is downstream with respect to the destination, but is not the least cost path and therefore is not used for forwarding data. Feasible Successors are kept in the Topology Table for use as backup routes. A Feasible Successor is a neighbor that meets the Feasibility Condition. The Feasibility Condition is met when a neighbor's advertised cost to a destination is less than or equal to the cost of a route used from the routing table through the current successor. The Feasibility Condition also guarantees that the Feasible Successor's route does not loop back through us.

Route States and How Routes Converge

The Topology Table entry for a destination can have one of two states: Active or Passive. A route is considered Passive when a router is not performing recomputation on that route. The route is in Active state when it is undergoing recomputation.

When the router loses a route, it will look at the Topology Table for a Feasible Successor. If one is available, the route will not go into an Active state; rather, the best Feasible Successor will be promoted to being the Successor and will be installed in the routing table. When there are no Feasible Successors, a route will go into Active state, and route recomputation occurs. Recomputation involves sending a Query packet to all neighbors on interfaces other than the one where the previous successor was located (the "split-horizon" rule), inquiring if they have a route to the given destination. Neighboring routers can Reply if they have a Feasible Successor for the destination (or if they have no route at all to the destination). However, if a router was using the querying router as its successor, it will in turn Query everyone else. This creates an expanding tree of Queries, effectively searching the network for a path. Once the router receives all the Replies to a given Query, the route state transitions to Passive and the route will reconverge. If the route was Active because it received a Query itself, it will return a Reply to the original Query at that point. Thus, the tree collapses back inward to the original point where the route was lost.

The Components of EIGRP

This section explains the four basic components of EIGRP, which are the following:

- Neighbor discovery/recovery
- A reliable transport mechanism
- The DUAL finite state machine
- Protocol dependent modules

Neighbor Discovery

When EIGRP is configured on an interface, the router will periodically multicast Hello packets on that interface. When a router running an EIGRP process with the same Autonomous System number receives another router's Hello packet, it establishes a neighbor relationship (Adjacency). Hello packets are sent at various time intervals depending on the media. They default to once every 5 seconds over a LAN and point-to-point links, and 60 seconds over NBMA.

This Hello mechanism is also used by the routers to discover the loss of their neighbors dynamically and quickly. If a Hello packet is not heard before the expiration of the HoldTime, then a topology change is detected. The neighbor adjacency is deleted, and all topology table entries learned from that neighbor are removed (as if the neighbor had sent an Update stating that all of the routes are unreachable; this may cause routes to enter Active state). This enables the route to quickly reconverge if an alternate feasible route is available.

Reliable Transport Mechanism

The next component of EIGRP is the reliable transport mechanism. This is responsible for the guaranteed, ordered delivery of packets to the neighbors. It supports intermixed transmission of multicast and unicast packets.

Packet Types

EIGRP supports five generic packet types. They are:

- **Hello**—Hello packets, as described earlier, are used for neighbor discovery. They are sent as multicasts and carry a zero acknowledgment number.

- **ACK**—The ACK is used for acknowledging other types of packets described below. ACKs are hello packets that are sent as unicasts, and contain a non-zero acknowledgment number.

- **Update**—An Update is sent to communicate the routes that a particular router has converged on. These are sent as multicasts when a new route is discovered, or when convergence has completed (and the route is Passive). They are also sent as unicasts when neighbors start up in order to synchronize the topology tables (since Updates are not sent periodically as in IGRP).

- **Queries**—When a router is performing route computation, and it does not have a feasible successor, it will send a Query packet to its neighbors asking if they have a feasible successor for the destination. Queries are always multicast.

- **Replies**—A Reply packet is sent in response to a Query packet. Replies are unicast to the originator of the Query.

All packets carrying routing information (Update/Query/Reply) must be sent reliably, since they are not sent periodically. Reliability is provided by assigning a sequence number to each reliable packet, and requiring an explicit acknowledgment for that sequence number. Acknowledgments and Hello packets, which help provide the reliability mechanism, by their nature are not sent reliably.

DUAL

The DUAL finite state machine embodies the decision process for all route computations. It tracks all routes advertised by all neighbors. The metric information is used by DUAL to select efficient loop free paths. DUAL selects routes to be inserted into a routing table based on feasible successors. DUAL is also responsible for the route recomputation process.

Protocol-Dependent Modules

EIGRP supports three protocol-dependent modules: IP, IPX, and Appletalk. These modules are responsible for network layer specific protocol requirements. The network layer protocol-dependent modules (PDM) are responsible for initializing, building, and decoding packets. They are also responsible for interfacing DUAL to the routing table, providing protocol-dependent support routines for DUAL, and configuration and runtime command support.

Changes to EIGRP in the Enhanced Code

The functionality of Diffusing Update Algorithm (DUAL) was not changed. The enhancements are in the transport mechanism and the way DUAL interfaces with it. The enhanced code does not change the EIGRP protocol itself in any significant way. The enhanced code will interoperate with the earlier code without difficulty, so phased upgrades may take place in whatever fashion the customer is comfortable with (though targeting problem areas may bring improvements in stability more quickly). It should be noted that the full benefits of the enhanced code may not be realized until it is fully deployed within the customer's network.

The enhanced version will significantly increase the various limits specified by the deployment guidelines. New guideline numbers cannot be determined until we have more field experience. The enhanced version is not expected to cause disruption of router functionality even under extreme circumstances, and adjacencies should not fail. Note that periods of 100% CPU utilization will still occur when a lot is happening; however, the enhanced code will regularly relinquish the CPU for other processes, and so the router should continue to function normally.

The only configuration issue to be aware of is that the EIGRP transport now uses the setting of the "bandwidth" interface parameter in order to control link utilization. The default bandwidth on serial lines is T1 (1544 Kbps). For the best results, the bandwidth parameter should be set so that it agrees with reality. The reasons for this are discussed on the following pages.

Bandwidth

The earlier code sends packets at full wire rate. This causes large spikes of traffic and most likely causes large amounts of packet loss on Frame Relay networks. In the enhanced code, the solution to this problem is throttling. There is an adjustable bandwidth limiter; by default EIGRP will not use more than 50% of the configured bandwidth (this percentage is configurable).

Bandwidth is also saved by suppressing ACKs. An ACK will not be sent if a unicast data packet is ready for transmission. The ACK field in any reliable unicast packet is sufficient to acknowledge the neighbor's packet, and so the ACK packet is suppressed to save bandwidth. This is a significant win on point-to-point links and NBMA networks, since on those media all data packets are sent as unicasts (and thus are able to carry an acknowledgment).

Configuring the "Bandwidth" Parameter

The enhanced code uses the **bandwidth** subcommand on interfaces and subinterfaces in order to determine the rate at which to generate EIGRP packets. This parameter is automatically set on fixed-bandwidth interfaces (such as LANs), but defaults to T1 (1544 Kbps) for all serial media. It is *strongly* recommended that this parameter be appropriately set. Failure to do so should not cause severe problems, but it may result in excessive retransmissions, packet loss, or degraded convergence if it is set too high, and degraded convergence if it is set too low.

For generic serial interfaces (PPP or HDLC framing), the bandwidth should be set to be equal to the line speed.

For Frame Relay, the safest setting would be equal to the committed information rate (CIR) (for point-to-point subinterfaces), or the sum of all CIRs (for multipoint configurations). However, a CIR of zero makes this difficult; in such cases, you'll have to pick a number that fits the following criteria:

- Low enough to be likely to work most of the time, and
- High enough so that EIGRP will converge in less than geologic time.

If for some reason the bandwidth parameter cannot be changed (most likely because it is set artificially in order to influence route selection), the **bandwidth-percent** command (explained later) can be used to adjust the transmission rate.

Building Packets

In the earlier code, when DUAL decided that a packet needed to be transmitted to a neighbor, that packet was created and placed on a queue in the transport. If the neighbor was slow in responding, or the link was slow, or there were many changes to transmit, this queue could grow without bound, and eventually consume all available memory. This was particularly problematic when an adjacency was first established, because essentially every route in the topology table was placed on the queue. Additionally, if a route was changing repeatedly, there could have been multiple packets containing the same route on the queue (with only the last packet being useful, and the earlier versions simply wasting link bandwidth).

In the enhanced code, packets are not actually generated until the moment of transmission. The transmit queues instead contain small, fixed-size structures that indicate which parts of the topology table to include in the packet when it is finally transmitted. This means that large queues will not consume large amounts of memory. It also means that only the latest information will be transmitted in each packet. If a route changes state several times, only the last state will be transmitted in the packet (reducing link utilization).

Adjacency Maintenance

In the earlier code, when congestion occurred, neighbor adjacencies often failed. The failing adjacencies in turn triggered more EIGRP traffic, which could cause even more congestion.

In the enhanced code, a new CPU process has been created called the Hello process. The Hello process is responsible for sending Hello packets, and for doing initial processing on all incoming EIGRP packets. The Hello process uses any incoming EIGRP packet from a peer as an indication that the neighbor is alive, and resets the Holdtime. Since the Hello process runs independently of the Router process, adjacencies should no longer be lost under periods of heavy CPU load or link utilization. This vastly improves stability.

Convergence on Intermediate State

Latency in networks allows routers to converge on a route which has old information. As the most current Updates arrive, the router will again converge. Multiple convergences cause CPU load and link utilization.

In the enhanced code, the packet is constructed based on the latest information in the Topology Table. Therefore, multiple convergence will occur less often, resulting in lower CPU and link utilization and more rapid convergence.

CPU Utilization

EIGRP can use very large amounts of CPU. In the enhanced code, the CPU cost of a route changing has been reduced to a constant, regardless of the database size. The enhanced code also relinquishes the CPU more often which results in a much lower impact on other processes, and ensures that the router will still be responsive even under periods of extreme load.

Memory Utilization

As mentioned earlier, the enhanced code does not generate packets until they are ready to be transmitted. This greatly reduces the amount of memory used during periods of network instability. In addition, the size of memory usage "spikes" that occur as the topology table takes on additional information during route convergence has also been reduced.

Stability for IPX EIGRP Networks

In the enhanced code, IPX/EIGRP SAP packets are interleaved with DUAL routing packets so that both receive sufficient bandwidth. This should improve convergence and stability in IPX/EIGRP networks with many services.

Immediate Response to Command Change

In the enhanced code, all configuration changes will take place without manual intervention. For instance, if an access list being used to filter routes is changed, then it will no longer be necessary to manually clear all neighbors for the changes to take effect. Configuration changes for interface bandwidth and delay are now reflected automatically in EIGRP (the topology table entry for the connected route is updated, and all neighbors on the interface are taken down in order to rebuild all the topology table entries received through that interface). Changes in the interface address or mask configuration and auto-summary setting are also reflected in EIGRP without any intervention; only the right set of neighbors are torn down.

New and Revised User-Visible Commands

There are a small number of new commands visible to users. In addition, some commands have additional parameters, and some displays have changed format slightly.

Controlling EIGRP Bandwidth

By default, EIGRP will use up to 50% of the bandwidth of an interface or subinterface, as set with the **bandwidth** parameter. This percentage can be changed on a per-interface basis by using one of the following interface subcommands:

```
ip bandwidth-percent eigrp as-number nnn
ipx bandwidth-percent eigrp as-number nnn
appletalk eigrp-bandwidth-percent nnn
```

In the preceding commands, *nnn* is the percentage of the configured bandwidth that EIGRP is allowed to use. Note that this can be set to greater than 100. This is useful if the bandwidth is configured artificially low for routing policy reasons. For example, the configuration in Example K-1 would allow EIGRP to use 40 kbps on the interface (it is essential to make sure that the line can handle the capacity).

Example K-1 *Allowing EIGRP to Use Up to 40 kbps on An Interface*

```
interface serial0
  bandwidth 20
  ip bandwidth-percent eigrp 1 200
```

Displaying the Topology Table

The **show** *<protocol>* **eigrp topology** command has two more options:

* **summary**—Displays a summary of the Topology Table contents
* **pending**—Displays Topology Table entries that need to be transmitted

Example K-2 shows what the **summary** output looks like.

Example K-2 *Displaying a Summary of the Topology Table Contents*

```
Router#show ip eigrp topology summary
IP-EIGRP Topology Table for process 1
Head serial 1, next serial 26
9 routes, 0 pending replies, 0 dummies
IP-EIGRP enabled on 5 interfaces, neighbors present on 4 interfaces
Quiescent interfaces: To0 To1 Et0 Et1
```

"Serial" numbers are an internal method of keeping track of which information needs to be transmitted. The third line of output in Example K-2 gives the count of entries in the topology table; **routes** refers to the number of entries in the topology table, **pending replies** gives the count of entries for which replies are in the process of being sent, and **dummies** refers to an internal data structure. The fourth line of output in Example K-2 shows how many interfaces EIGRP is enabled on, and how many of those interfaces have active neighbors. The last line in Example K-2 shows which interfaces are ready to transmit but have nothing to transmit.

The output of the **pending** option is a standard Topology Table entry.

The output of **show** *<protocol>* **eigrp** *as-number* **topology all"** includes a serial number on each route. This is for internal use.

Displaying Neighbor Information

The output of **show** *<protocol>* **eigrp** *as-number* **neighbors detail** now looks like Example K-3.

Example K-3 *Displaying Neighbor Information*

```
Router#show ip eigrp neighbors detail
  IP-EIGRP neighbors for process 1
  H   Address              Interface   Hold Uptime   SRTT   RTO  Q   Seq
                                       (sec)         (ms)        Cnt Num
  2   172.21.28.34         Et0            12 2d11h     38    342  0   77227
      Version 11.0/1.0, Retrans: 1757, Retries: 0
 12   172.16.21.152        To0            13 2d11h     46    276  0   77225
      Version 11.0/1.0, Retrans: 84, Retries: 0
 11   172.16.14.152        Et1            13 2d11h     47    282  0   77226
      Version 11.0/1.0, Retrans: 80, Retries: 0
 10   172.16.22.155        To1            11 2d11h     54    324  0   75900
      Version 11.0/1.0, Retrans: 86, Retries: 0
```

The first line is the same as in the earlier code. The **Version** field tells you the release running on the neighbor (11.0 in this case) and the EIGRP revision number (1.0 is the enhanced code, 0.0 is the earlier code). **Retrans** shows the count of retransmissions to this neighbor, and **Retries** shows the number of retransmissions of the current packet.

Displaying Interface Information

A new command to display EIGRP interface information has been added. The syntax is as follows:

```
show protocol eigrp interface [interface-name] [as-number]
```

If an interface name is specified, only that interface is displayed; otherwise, all interfaces configured for EIGRP are displayed. If an autonomous system number is specified, only information pertaining to that process is displayed; otherwise, information is displayed for all EIGRP processes. Example K-4 shows the output for the **show ip eigrp interface** command.

Example K-4 *Displaying Interface Information*

```
Router#show ip eigrp interface
  IP-EIGRP interfaces for process 1

                       Xmit Queue   Mean  Pacing Time   Multicast    Pending
  Interface    Peers   Un/Reliable  SRTT  Un/Reliable   Flow Timer   Routes
  Et0            1        0/0         21      0/10          84           0
  Et1            4        0/0        112      0/10          50           0
  To0            4        0/0         41      0/10          50           0
  To1            4        0/0         32      0/10          50           0
  Lo0            0        0/0          0      0/10           0           0
```

The first column contains the interface name. The second is the number of neighbors on the interface. The third is the number of unreliable and reliable packets in the interface transmit queue. The fourth is the average round-trip time for all neighbors on the interface. The fifth is the pacing time (interpacket gap) for unreliable and reliable packets on the interface. The sixth is the value of the multicast flow control timer (the amount of time the system will wait for all neighbors on a multicast interface to acknowledge the previous packet before going on to the next one). The last column shows the number of routes that still must be transmitted on the interface. Since the enhanced code does not build packets until they are ready to be transmitted, many routes pending transmission may not actually be in the transmit queue.

Displaying EIGRP Traffic Statistics

The commands **show ipx eigrp traffic** and **show appletalk eigrp traffic** were added to correspond to the existing **show ip eigrp traffic** command.

One line has been added to the end of the output of this command. Example K-5 shows the new output for the **show ip eigrp traffic** command.

Example K-5 *Displaying EIGRP Traffic Statistics*

```
Router#show ip eigrp traffic
IP-EIGRP Traffic Statistics for process 1
Hellos sent/received: 17598/49265
Updates sent/received: 45/59
Queries sent/received: 0/19
Replies sent/received: 10/0
Acks sent/received: 31/28
Input queue high water mark 15, 0 drops
```

The final line tells what the highest number of enqueued EIGRP packets were encountered, and how many packets have been dropped because the EIGRP process could not handle them in time.

Additional debug Commands

The **debug eigrp packets** command was enhanced with the following keywords:

- **ack**—Shows acknowledgments
- **hello**—Shows hello packets
- **ipxsap**—Shows IPX SAP packets
- **query**—Shows Query packets
- **reply**—Shows Reply packets
- **retry**—Shows retransmissions
- **update**—Shows Update packets

A new command, **debug eigrp transmit** was added. This command shows events at the interaction between DUAL and the transport. The possible keywords are as follows:

- **ack**—Shows acknowledgment events
- **build**—Shows packet building events
- **detail**—Shows more detail about the event
- **link**—Shows link-related events
- **packetize**—Shows packetization events
- **peerdown**—Shows peer down events
- **startup**—Shows peer startup events
- **strange**—Shows unusual events

A new command, **debug eigrp neighbors** was added. This command shows events related to the establishment of neighbor adjacencies.

Enhancement to the show memory free Command

The header displayed for **show memory** and **show memory free** has been changed. The old free list header address (which was not useful) has been removed, and a display of the "low-water mark" of free memory, the smallest value of free memory experienced since boot time, has been added as illustrated in Example K-6.

Example K-6 *Enhancement to the* **show memory free** *Command*

```
Router#show memory free
                Head    Total(b)   Used(b)    Free(b)    Lowest(b)  Largest(b)
 Processor      49C724  28719324   1510864    27208460   26511644   15513908
       I/O      6000000  4194304   1297088    2897216    2869248    2896812
      SRAM      1000      65536     63400      2136       2136       2136
```

Because EIGRP (and many other parts of the system) tends to have memory usage "spikes", in which large amounts of memory are used for a short time, this display can help diagnose potential low memory situations before they become critical. For example, one of the machines in the corporate network was showing free memory of almost 3 MB, but this display showed that at one point the machine had less than 200 KB left.

Logging Information

The enhanced implementation has the capability to log changes in neighbor adjacency state (up/down) and the reason for the change. This can be helpful for diagnosing stability problems (though most often it indicates some underlying problem, such as an unstable link).

Controlling the Logging of Neighbor State Changes

The log message is of the form illustrated in Example K-7.

Example K-7 *Neighbor State Change Log Messages*

```
%DUAL-5-NBRCHANGE: IP-EIGRP 1: Neighbor 172.21.28.33 (Ethernet0) is down:
 holding time expired
%DUAL-5-NBRCHANGE: IP-EIGRP 1: Neighbor 172.16.22.151 (TokenRing1) is up:
 new adjacency
```

By default this capability is disabled; it can be enabled by using the configuration shown in Example K-8:

Example K-8 *Enabling Logging of Neighbor State Changes*

```
appletalk eigrp log-neighbor-changes

router eigrp <as-number>
 eigrp log-neighbor-changes

ipx router eigrp <as-number>
 log-neighbor-changes
```

Logging Additional Information

The best way to gather information is to do it all through the log mechanism as demonstrated in Example K-9.

Example K-9 *Logging EIGRP Event Information*

```
router eigrp 1
 eigrp log-event-type [dual] [xmit] [transport]
 eigrp event-log-size <nn>
```

The default is to log only DUAL events, and to have an event log size of 500 events. The log is displayed in inverse order (the newest entry is first), and contains the time of day; this can be very useful for matching up events between multiple routers if they are time-synchronized using NTP.

The log can be viewed by typing in **show ip eigrp events**. The same is true for IPX and Appletalk.

This Workbook contains job aids such as procedures, tables, and checklists that you may use during the case studies and in your real designs later.

These items, referenced by chapter, are duplicated here from the chapters within the book so that you can easily find them at a later time. Most of the detailed instructions for completing the tables have not been duplicated in this Workbook; for those details refer to the appropriate chapter.

Workbook

The job aids reproduced in this Workbook from other chapters in the book will help you design scalable solutions that maximize your customer's satisfaction.

Chapter 2: Analyzing Small- to Medium-Sized Business Networks

The small- to medium-sized business solutions framework is represented as a triangle, as shown in Figure L-1.

Figure L-1 *Cisco's Framework for Identifying Small- to Medium-Sized Business Network Solutions*

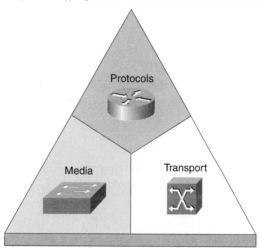

As illustrated in Figure L-1, use the following simple rules when designing solutions to customer problems:

- If the problems involve media contention, use LAN switching.
- If the problems are protocol related—for example, resulting in an excessive number of broadcasts—use routing.
- If the customer needs to transport payloads that require high bandwidth, use Fast Ethernet switching. In large networks where high bandwidth and predictable low latency are required, consider ATM switching.

Chapter 3: Characterizing the Existing Network

Complete the following steps to characterize a customer's network.

Step 1: Characterize the Customer's Applications

Use Table L-1 to characterize the customer's applications.

Table L-1 *Characterize the Customer's Applications*

Name of Application	Type of Application	Number of Users	Number of Hosts or Servers	Comments

Step 2: Characterize the Network Protocols

Use Table L-2 to characterize the customer's network protocols.

Table L-2 *Characterize the Network Protocols*

Name of Protocol	Type of Protocol	Number of Users	Number of Hosts or Servers	Comments

Step 3: Document the Customer's Current Network

Documenting the customer's current network is important before any changes are made. Items you should be most attentive to include the following:

- **Network topology**—On a separate piece of paper or in another application, draw a network topology map (or obtain a drawing from the customer). Include the type and speed of each major segment or link. Include the names and addresses of major internetworking devices and servers. See the Tip on drawing a network topology map, following this list.

- **Addressing schemes**—Document addressing schemes used in the current network design. Current addressing might impact your ability to modify the network structure. For example, current IP subnet masking might limit the number of nodes in a LAN or virtual LAN (VLAN).

- **Concerns about the network**—Document any concerns you have about the current topology and any additional information about the architecture of the internetwork that might not be obvious from the topology drawing. Characterize the overall network architecture to help you understand data flow patterns.

TIP   Draw the network topology map in the same, or a compatible, application with which you will be documenting your design. This will save you time later and will ensure that the existing topology is documented before any changes are made.

Step 4: Identify Potential Bottlenecks

Traffic that does not have a source or destination on the local network segment is considered nonlocal and may cause a bottleneck on the network.

Use a Protocol Analyzer to Determine Local Traffic

To identify potential network bottlenecks, obtain a protocol analyzer and determine how much of the network traffic on each major network segment is *not* local.

Specify how much of the traffic travels to different network segments, how much comes from different network segments, and how much just passes through this network segment.

Characterize Traffic That Is *Not* Local

Use Table L-3 to characterize how much of the traffic on each network segment is *not* local. Source and destination refer to source and destination network-layer addresses.

Table L-3   *Characterizing Traffic That Is Not Local*

Network Segment Identification	Both Source and Destination Are Local	Source Is Local, Destination Is Not Local	Source Is Not Local, Destination Is Local	Source Is Not Local, Destination Is Not Local
1				
2				
3				
4				

Step 5: Identify Business Constraints and Inputs to Your Network Design

After talking to your customer, check off as many of the following items as possible:

☐ I understand the corporate structure.

☐ I have analyzed the information flow in the corporation.

☐ The customer has identified any mission-critical data or operations.

☐ The customer has explained any policies regarding approved vendors, protocols, or platforms.

☐ The customer has explained any policies regarding open versus proprietary solutions.

☐ The customer has explained any policies regarding distributed authority for network design and implementation: for example, departments that control their own internetworking purchases.

☐ I have a good understanding of the technical expertise of my clients.

☐ I have researched the customer's industry and competition.

☐ I am aware of any politics that might affect the network design proposal.

☐ I am aware of any financial constraints that may influence the network design.

Document any concerns you have about the customer's business constraints.

Step 6: Characterize the Existing Network Availability

Gather statistics on network downtime and the mean time between failure (MTBF) for the internetwork. If some segments are known to be fragile, document the MTBF separately for those segments. Try to get the customer to express the cost of downtime by asking the following questions:

- What is the hourly cost by department for a network outage?
- What is the hourly cost to the company or organization for a network outage?

Use Table L-4 to help you determine the MTBF for each network segment and the internetwork as a whole.

Table L-4 *Characterize the Existing Network Availability*

Network/ Segment	MTBF	Date of Last Downtime	Duration of Last Downtime	Cause of Last Downtime
Internetwork				
Segment 1				
Segment 2				
Segment 3				

Step 7: Characterize the Network Performance

Use Table L-5 to document the results of any response time or performance measurements that you completed for each host on the network. This information will help you determine which areas of the network you should concentrate on for performance improvements and which are already satisfactory. This information will also provide you with benchmark measurements with which you can compare your new network.

Table L-5   *Characterize the Network Performance*

	Host A	Host B	Host C	Host D
Host A				
Host B				
Host C				
Host D				

Step 8: Characterize the Existing Network Reliability

Gather statistics about each major network segment using a monitoring tool, such as a protocol analyzer, network monitor, or network management tool. If possible, monitor each segment for at least a day. At the end of the day, record the following information seen on each segment:

- Total megabytes (MB)
- Total number of frames
- Total number of cyclic redundancy check (CRC) errors
- Total number of MAC layer errors (collisions, Token Ring soft errors, FDDI ring operations)
- Total number of broadcasts/multicast frames

Characterize the current network reliability by completing Table L-6. To calculate the *average network utilization*, add each hourly average and divide by the number of hourly averages. For the *peak network utilization*, record the highest hourly average. (If you have more granular data than hourly, record any short-term peaks.) For the *average frame size*, divide the total number of MB transferred on the network by the total number of frames.

The rate calculations are more complex. Your concern here is the number of errors or broadcasts compared to the amount of normal traffic. To calculate the *CRC error rate*, divide the total number of CRC errors by the total amount of MB. For the *MAC layer error rate*, divide the total number of MAC layer errors by the total number of frames. For the *broadcasts/multicasts rate*, divide the total number of broadcasts/multicasts by the total number of frames.

Table L-6   *Characterize the Existing Network Reliability*

Network Segment	Average Network Utilization	Peak Network Utilization	Average Frame Size	CRC Error Rate	MAC layer Error Rate	Broadcasts/ Multicasts Rate
Segment 1						
Segment 2						
Segment 3						
Segment 4						

Step 9: Characterize Network Utilization

Configure the monitoring tool to output an average network utilization statistic once each hour so you can determine when the peak usage hours are. If the network is saturated (that is, it is over-utilized), look at network utilization every minute. Especially on Ethernet, peak utilizations of over 40 percent that last for more than one minute cause noticeable performance degradation.

If time permits, characterize how much of the bandwidth on each segment is used by different protocols by completing Table L-7. Many network monitors let you specify the bandwidth used by protocols as relative or absolute bandwidth. Fill in the fields in Table L-7 as indicated:

- In the *Relative Network Utilization* field, enter the amount of bandwidth used by each protocol in comparison to the total bandwidth used on this segment.

- In the *Absolute Network Utilization* field, enter the amount of bandwidth used by each protocol in comparison to the total capacity of the segment (for example, in comparison to 10 Mbps on Ethernet).

- In the *Average Frame Size* field, enter the average frame size for each protocol.

- In the *Broadcasts/Multicasts Rate* field, enter the broadcast/multicasts rate for each protocol.

Table L-7   *Characterize Network Utilization*

Protocol	Relative Network Utilization	Absolute Network Utilization	Average Frame Size	Broadcasts/ Multicasts Rate
IP				
IPX				
AppleTalk				
NetBIOS				
SNA				
Other				

For major protocols, you might want to configure your network monitor to break down the data even further. For example, in an IP environment, it is useful to know how much bandwidth is used by each of the routing protocols, TCP-based applications, and UDP-based applications.

Step 10: Characterize the Status of the Major Routers

Characterize the status of the major routers in the network by completing Table L-8. Plan to spend about a day studying the routers. The following Cisco IOS™ commands will help you fill out Table L-8:

> **show interfaces**
> **show processes**
> **show buffers**

Complete Table L-8 every hour for each interface as follows:

- In the *Router Name* field, enter the name of each major router.

- To complete the remaining fields, add up the appropriate results from the **show interfaces**, **show processes**, and **show buffers** commands. Then divide the total by the number of samples to complete average values for the *5 Minute CPU Utilization, Output Queue Drops per Hour, Input Queue Drops per Hour, Missed Packets per Hour,* and *Ignored Packets per Hour* fields.

- In the *Comments* field, enter any comments that will help you characterize the status of each router.

Table L-8   *Characterize the Status of the Major Routers*

Router Name	5 Minute CPU Utilization	Output Queue Drops Per Hour	Input Queue Drops Per Hour	Missed Packets Per Hour	Ignored Packets Per Hour	Comments
Router 1						
Router 2						
Router 3						
Router 4						

Step 11: Characterize the Existing Network Management System and Tools

Document the type of platform and network management tools in use. If available, gather recent examples of daily, weekly, and monthly reports.

Step 12: Summarize the Health of the Existing Internetwork

Based on the data you have gathered from the customer's network, check off any of the items that are true in the following *Network Health Checklist*. On a healthy network, you should be able to check off all the items.

Note that these guidelines are just approximations. Exact thresholds depend on the type of traffic, applications, internetworking devices, topology, and criteria for accepting network performance. As every good engineer knows, the answer to most questions about network performance (and most questions in general) is "it depends."

☐ No shared Ethernet segments are saturated (no more than 40 percent network utilization).

☐ No shared Token Ring segments are saturated (no more than 70 percent network utilization).

☐ No WAN links are saturated (no more than 70 percent network utilization).

☐ The response time is generally less than 100 milliseconds (1 millisecond = 1/1000 of a second; 100 milliseconds = 1/10 of a second).

☐ No segments have more than 20 percent broadcasts/multicasts.

☐ No segments have more than one CRC error per million bytes of data.

☐   On the Ethernet segments, less than 0.1 percent of the packets result in collisions.

☐   On the Token Ring segments, less than 0.1 percent of the packets are soft errors not related to ring insertion.

☐   On the FDDI segments, there has been no more than one ring operation per hour not related to ring insertion.

☐   The Cisco routers are not over-utilized (5 minute CPU utilization no more than 75 percent).

☐   The number of output queue drops has not exceeded more than 100 in an hour on any Cisco router.

☐   The number of input queue drops has not exceeded more than 50 in an hour on any Cisco router.

☐   The number of buffer misses has not exceeded more than 25 in an hour on any Cisco router.

☐   The number of ignored packets has not exceeded more than 10 in an hour on any interface on a Cisco router.

Document any concerns you have about the health of the existing network and its capability to support growth.

Chapter 4: Determining New Customer Requirements

Steps for Determining a Customer's Network Requirements

Complete the following steps to determine the customer's network requirements:

Step 1   Identify business constraints

Step 2   Identify security requirements

Step 3   Identify manageability requirements

Step 4   Determine application requirements

Step 5   Characterize new network traffic

Step 6   Identify performance requirements

Step 7   Create a customer needs specification document (optional)

Characterizing Network Traffic

While reviewing the numbers, guidelines, and tables in this section, remember that the true engineering solution to most questions that characterize network traffic and performance is "it depends." The data provided in this section does not take the place of a thorough analysis of the network in question.

Broadcast Behavior

Table L-9 shows recommendations for limiting the number of stations on a single LAN based on the desktop protocol(s) in use. The table also applies to the number of stations in a virtual LAN (VLAN).

Table L-9   *Scalability Constraints for Flat (Switched and Bridged) Networks*

Protocol	Maximum Number of Workstations
IP	500
IPX	300
AppleTalk	200
NetBIOS	200
Mixed	200

Characterizing Traffic Loads and Behavior

Size of Objects Transferred Across Networks

Table L-10 identifies the approximate size of different objects transferred across networks.

Table L-10   *Approximate Size in MB of "Objects" Transferred Across Networks*

Type of Object	Size in MB
E-mail message	0.01
Spreadsheet	0.1
Computer screen	0.5
Document	1
Still image	10
Multimedia object	100
Database	1000

Source: McDysan and Spohn, "ATM: Theory and Applications," McGraw-Hill, 1995.

Note that the size of a computer screen image depends on the type of screen, the number of pixels, and the number of colors. A "dumb" terminal application transfers much less data than a windowed application. Telnet, for example, sends each character that the user types in one packet. Responses are also very small, depending on what the user is doing.

A 3270 terminal application transfers about 4000 bytes, including characters and "attribute" bytes that define color and style.

Traffic Overhead for Data Link Layer and Network Layer Protocols

Table L-11 illustrates the amount of traffic overhead associated with various protocols. Understanding the traffic overhead for protocols can be a factor when choosing the best protocol for your network design.

Table L-11 *Traffic Overhead for Various Protocols*

Protocol	Notes	Total Bytes
Ethernet	Preamble = 8 bytes, Header = 14 bytes, CRC = 4 bytes, Interframe gap (IFG) = 12 bytes	38
802.3 with 802.2	Preamble = 8 bytes, Header = 14 bytes, LLC = 3 or 4 bytes, SNAP (if present) = 5 bytes, CRC = 4 bytes, IFG = 12 bytes for 10 Mbps or 1.2 bytes for 100 Mbps	46
802.5 with 802.2	Starting delimiter = 1 byte, Header = 14 bytes, LLC = 3 or 4 bytes, SNAP (if present) = 5 bytes, CRC = 4 bytes, Ending delimiter = 1 byte, Frame status = 1 byte	29

continues

Table L-11   *Traffic Overhead for Various Protocols (Continued)*

Protocol	Notes	Total Bytes
FDDI with 802.2	Preamble = 8 bytes,	36
	Starting delimiter = 1 byte,	
	Header = 13 bytes,	
	LLC = 3 or 4 bytes,	
	SNAP (if present) = 5 bytes,	
	CRC = 4 bytes,	
	Ending delimiter and frame Status = about 2 bytes	
HDLC	Flags = 2 bytes,	10
	Addresses = 2 bytes,	
	Control = 1 or 2 bytes,	
	CRC = 4 bytes	
IP	With no options	20
TCP	With no options	20
IPX	Does not include NCP	30
DDP	Phase 2 (long "extended" header)	13

Traffic Caused by Workstation Initialization

The tables in this section identify the packets sent and received when different types of workstations initialize. Workstation initialization can cause a load on networks due to the number of packets and, in some cases, the number of broadcast packets.

Novell NetWare Workstation Initialization

Table L-12 shows the packets that a Novell NetWare client sends when it boots. The approximate packet size is also shown. On top of the packet size, add the data link layer overhead, such as 802.3 with 802.2, 802.5 with 802.2, or FDDI with 802.2, as shown in Table L-11. Network layer and transport layer overhead are already included in these examples. Depending on the version of NetWare being run, the packets generated might be slightly different than the ones shown here.

Table L-12 *Packets for NetWare Client Initialization*

Packet	Source	Destination	Packet Size in Bytes	Number of Packets	Total Bytes
GetNearestServer	Client	Broadcast	34	1	34
GetNearestServer response	Server or router	Client	66	Depends on number of servers	66 if 1 server
Find network number	Client	Broadcast	40	1	40
Find network number response	Router	Client	40	1	40
Create connection	Client	Server	37	1	37
Create connection response	Server	Client	38	1	38
Negotiate buffer size	Client	Server	39	1	39
Negotiate buffer size response	Server	Client	40	1	40
Log out old connections	Client	Server	37	1	37
Log out response	Server	Client	38	1	38
Get server's clock	Client	Server	37	1	37
Get server's clock response	Server	Client	38	1	38
Download login.exe requests	Client	Server	50	Hundreds, depending on buffer size	Depends
Download login.exe responses	Server	Client	Depends on buffer size	Hundreds, depending on buffer size	Depends
Login	Client	Server	37	1	37
Login response	Server	Client	38	1	38

AppleTalk Workstation Initialization

Table L-13 shows the packets that an AppleTalk station sends when it boots. The approximate packet size is also shown. On top of the packet size, add data link layer overhead, as shown in Table L-11. Depending on the version of Macintosh system software, the packets generated might be slightly different than the ones shown here.

Table L-13 *Packets for AppleTalk Client Initialization*

Packet	Source	Destination	Packet Size in Bytes	Number of Packets	Total Bytes
AARP for ID	Client	Multicast	28	10	280
ZIPGetNetInfo	Client	Multicast	15	1	15
GetNetInfo response	Router(s)	Client	About 44	All routers respond	44 if one router
NBP broadcast request to check uniqueness of name	Client	Router	About 65	3	195
NBP forward request	Router	Other routers	Same	Same	Same
NBP lookup	Router	Multicast	Same	Same	Same
If Chooser started:					
GetZoneList	Client	Router	12	1	12
GetZoneList reply	Router	Client	Depends on number and names of zones	1	Depends
NBP broadcast request for servers in zone	Client	Router	About 65	Once a second if Chooser still open; decays after 45 seconds	About 3000 if Chooser closed after 45 seconds
NBP forward request	Router	Other routers	About 65	Same	Same
NBP lookup	Router	Multicast	About 65	Same	Same
NBP reply	Server(s)	Client	About 65	Depends on number of servers	Depends
ASP open session and AFP login	Client	Server	Depends	4	About 130
ASP and AFP replies	Server	Client	Depends	2	About 90

An AppleTalk station that has already been on a network remembers its previous network number and node ID and tries 10 times to verify that the *network.node* combination is unique. If the AppleTalk station has never been on a network or has moved, it sends 20 multicasts: 10 multicasts with a provisional network number and 10 multicasts with a network number supplied by a router that responded to the *ZIPGetNetInfo* request.

NetBIOS Workstation Initialization

Table L-14 shows the packets that a NetBIOS station sends when it boots. The approximate packet size is also shown. On top of the packet size, add data link layer overhead, as shown in Table L-11. Depending on the version of NetBIOS, the packets might be slightly different than the ones shown here.

Table L-14   *Packets for NetBIOS Client Initialization*

Packet	Source	Destination	Packet Size in Bytes	Number of Packets	Total Bytes
Check name (make sure own name is unique)	Client	Broadcast	44	6	264
Find name for each server	Client	Broadcast	44	Depends on number of servers	44 if 1 server
Find name response	Server(s)	Client	44	Depends	44 if 1 server
Session initialize for each server	Client	Server	14	Depends	14 if 1 server
Session confirm	Server	Client	14	Depends	14 if 1 server

TCP/IP (without DHCP) Workstation Initialization

Table L-15 shows the packets that a TCP/IP station not running DHCP sends when it boots. The approximate packet size is also shown. On top of the packet size, add data link layer overhead, as shown in Table L-11. Depending on the implementation of TCP/IP, the packets might be slightly different than the ones shown here.

Table L-15 *Packets for Traditional TCP/IP Client Initialization*

Packet	Source	Destination	Packet Size in Bytes	Number of Packets	Total Bytes
ARP to make sure its own address is unique (optional)	Client	Broadcast	28	1	28
ARP for any servers	Client	Broadcast	28	Depends on number of servers	Depends
ARP for router	Client	Broadcast	28	1	28
ARP response	Server(s) or router	Client	28	1	28

TCP/IP (with DHCP) Workstation Initialization

Table L-16 shows the packets that a TCP/IP station running DHCP sends when it boots. Although a DHCP client sends more packets when initializing, DHCP is still recommended. The benefits of dynamic configuration far outweigh the disadvantages of the extra traffic and extra broadcast packets. (The client and server use broadcast packets until they know each other's IP addresses.)

The approximate packet size is also shown. On top of the packet size, add data link layer overhead, as shown in Table L-11. Depending on the implementation of DHCP, the packets might be slightly different than the ones shown here.

Table L-16 *Packets for DHCP Client Initialization*

Packet	Source	Destination	Packet Size in Bytes	Number of Packets	Total Bytes
DHCP discover	Client	Broadcast	576	Once every few seconds until client hears from a DHCP server	Depends
DHCP offer	Server	Broadcast	328	1	328
DHCP request	Client	Broadcast	576	1	576
DHCP ACK	Server	Broadcast	328	1	328
ARP to make sure its own address is unique	Client	Broadcast	28	3	84

continues

Table L-16   *Packets for DHCP Client Initialization (Continued)*

Packet	Source	Destination	Packet Size in Bytes	Number of Packets	Total Bytes
ARP for client	Server	Broadcast	28	1	1
ARP response	Client	Server	28	1	28
DHCP request	Client	Server	576	1	576
DHCP ACK	Server	Client	328	1	328

Chapter 6: Provisioning Hardware and Media for the LAN

Summary of Switching Versus Routing

Table L-17 summarizes the discussion of switching versus routing.

Table L-17   *Summary of Considerations for Switches Versus Routers*

	Routers	Switches
Problem solved	Protocol problems	Media (LAN switches), and Transport of large payload (Fast Ethernet and ATM switches) problems
Key Features	Many including filtering, addressing, connecting dissimilar LANs, security, load balancing, policy and QoS routing, multimedia	High bandwidth, low cost, ease of configuration
Broadcast and Bandwidth Domains	Reduces broadcast domain and bandwidth (collision) domain	Reduces bandwidth (collision) domain

Ethernet Design Rules

Table L-18 provides scalability information that you can use when provisioning IEEE 802.3 networks:

Table L-18 *Scalability Constraints for IEEE 802.3*

	10Base5	10Base2	10BaseT	100BaseT
Topology	Bus	Bus	Star	Star
Maximum Segment Length (meters)	500	185	100 from hub to station	100 from hub to station
Maximum Number of Attachments per Segment	100	30	2 (hub and station or hub-hub)	2 (hub and station or hub-hub)
Maximum Collision Domain	2500 meters of 5 segments and 4 repeaters; only 3 segments can be populated	2500 meters of 5 segments and 4 repeaters; only 3 segments can be populated	2500 meters of 5 segments and 4 repeaters; only 3 segments can be populated	See the Details on 100 Mbps Ethernet Design Rules Section that follows

The most significant design rule for Ethernet is that the round-trip propagation delay in one collision domain must not exceed 512 bit times, which is a requirement for collision detection to work correctly. This rule means that the maximum round-trip delay for a 10 Mbps Ethernet network is 51.2 microseconds. The maximum round-trip delay for a 100 Mbps Ethernet network is only 5.12 microseconds because the bit time on a 100 Mbps Ethernet network is 0.01 microseconds as opposed to 0.1 microseconds on 10 Mbps Ethernet network.

To make 100 Mbps Ethernet work, there are much more severe distance limitations than those required for 10 Mbps Ethernet. The general rule is that a 100 Mbps Ethernet has a maximum diameter of 205 meters when unshielded twisted-pair (UTP) cabling is used, whereas 10 Mbps Ethernet has a maximum diameter of 2500 meters.

10 Mbps Fiber Ethernet Design Rules

Table L-19 provides some guidelines to help you choose the right media for your network designs. 10BaseF is based on the fiber-optic interrepeater link (FOIRL) specification, which includes 10BaseFP, 10BaseFB, 10BaseFL, and a revised FOIRL standard. The new FOIRL allows data terminal equipment (DTE)—end-node—connections, rather than just repeaters, as allowed with the older FOIRL specification.

Table L-19 *Scalability Constraints for 10 Mbps Fiber Ethernet*

	10BaseFP	10BaseFB	10BaseFL	Old FOIRL	New FOIRL
Topology	Passive star	Backbone or repeater fiber system	Link	Link	Link or star
Allows DTE (end-node) Connections?	Yes	No	No	No	Yes
Maximum Segment Length (meters)	500	2000	1000 or 2000	1000	1000
Allows Cascaded Repeaters?	No	Yes	No	No	Yes
Maximum Collision Domains in Meters	2500	2500	2500	2500	2500

100-Mbps Ethernet (Fast Ethernet) Design Rules

100BaseT Repeaters

Table L-20 shows the maximum size of collision domains, depending on the type of repeater.

Table L-20 *Maximum Size of Collision Domains for 100BaseT*

	Copper	Mixed Copper and Multimode Fiber	Multimode Fiber
DTE-DTE (or Switch-Switch)	100 meters		412 meters (2000 if full duplex)
One Class I Repeater	200 meters	260 meters	272 meters
One Class II Repeater	200 meters	308 meters	320 meters
Two Class II Repeaters	205 meters	216 meters	228 meters

NOTE The Cisco FastHub 316 is a Class II repeater, as are all of the Cisco FastHub 300 series hubs. These hubs actually exceed the Class II specifications, which means that they have even lower latencies and therefore allow longer cable lengths. For example, with two FastHub 300 repeaters and copper cable the maximum collision domain is 223 meters.

Checking the Propagation Delay

To determine if configurations other than the standard ones will work, use the following information from the IEEE 802.3u specification.

To check a path to make sure the path delay value (PDV) does not exceed 512 bit times, add up the following delays:

- All link segment delays
- All repeater delays
- DTE delay
- A safety margin (0 to 5 bit times)
- Use the following steps to calculate the PDV:

Step 1 Determine the delay for each link segment; this is the link segment delay value (LSDV), including inter-repeater links, using the following formula. (Multiply by two so that it is a round-trip delay.)

LSDV=2 × segment length × cable delay for this segment.

For end-node segments, the segment length is the cable length between the physical interface at the repeater and the physical interface at the DTE. Use your two farthest DTEs for a worst-case calculation. For inter-repeater links, the segment length is the cable length between the repeater physical interfaces.

Cable delay is the delay specified by the manufacturer if available. When actual cable lengths or propagation delays are not known, use the delay in bit times as specified in Table L-21.

Cable delay must be specified in bit times per meter (BT/m).

Step 2 Add together the LSDVs for all segments in the path.

Step 3 Determine the delay for each repeater in the path. If model-specific data is not available from the manufacturer, determine the class of repeater (I or II).

Step 4 MII cables for 100BaseT should not exceed 0.5 meters each in length. When evaluating system topology, MII cable lengths need not be accounted for separately. Delays attributable to the MII are incorporated into DTE and repeater delays.

Step 5 Use the DTE delay value shown in Table L-21 unless your equipment manufacturer defines a different value.

Step 6 Decide on an appropriate safety margin from 0 to 5 bit times. Five bit times is a safe value.

Step 7 Insert the values obtained from the preceding calculations into the formula for calculating the PDV:

PDV=link delays + repeater delays + DTE delay + safety margin

Step 8 If the PDV is less than 512, the path is qualified in terms of worst-case delay.

Round-Trip Delay

Table L-21 shows round-trip delay in bit times for standard cables and maximum round-trip delay in bit times for DTEs, repeaters, and maximum-length cables.

NOTE Note that the values shown in Table L-21 have been multiplied by two to provide a round-trip delay. If you use these numbers, you need not multiply by two again in the LSDV formula (LSDV = 2 × segment length × cable delay for this segment).

Table L-21 *Network Component Delays*

Component	Round-Trip Delay in Bit Times per Meter	Maximum Round-Trip Delay in Bit Times
Two TX/FX DTEs	N/A	100
Two T4 DTEs	N/A	138
One T4 DTE and one TX/FX DTE	N/A	127
Category 3 cable segment	1.14	114 (100 meters)
Category 4 cable segment	1.14	114 (100 meters)
Category 5 cable segment	1.112	111.2 (100 meters)
STP cable segment	1.112	111.2 (100 meters)
Fiber-optic cable segment	1.0	412 (412 meters)
Class I repeater	N/A	140
Class II repeater with all ports TX or FX	N/A	92
Class II repeater with any port T4	N/A	67

Source: IEEE 802.3u—1995, "Media Access Control (MAC) Parameters, Physical Layer, Medium Attachment Units, and Repeater for 100 Mb/s Operation, Type 100BASE-T."

Calculating Cable Delays

Some cable manufacturers specify propagation delays relative to the speed of light (c) or in nanoseconds per meter (ns/m). To convert these values to bit times per meter (BT/m), use Table L-22.

Table L-22 *Conversion to Bit Times per Meter for Cable Delays*

Speed Relative to speed of light	Nanoseconds per meter (ns/m)	Bit Times per meter (BT/m)
0.4	8.34	0.834
0.5	6.67	0.667
0.51	6.54	0.654
0.52	6.41	0.641
0.53	6.29	0.629
0.54	6.18	0.618
0.55	6.06	0.606
0.56	5.96	0.596
0.57	5.85	0.585
0.58	5.75	0.575
0.5852	5.70	0.570
0.59	5.65	0.565
0.6	5.56	0.556
0.61	5.47	0.547
0.62	5.38	0.538
0.63	5.29	0.529
0.64	5.21	0.521
0.65	5.13	0.513
0.654	5.10	0.510
0.66	5.05	0.505
0.666	5.01	0.501
0.67	4.98	0.498
0.68	4.91	0.491
0.69	4.83	0.483
0.7	4.77	0.477
0.8	4.17	0.417
0.9	3.71	0.371

Source: IEEE 802.3u - 1995, "Media Access Control (MAC) Parameters, Physical Layer, Medium Attachment Units, and Repeater for 100 Mb/s Operation, Type 100BASE-T."

Token Ring Design Rules

Table L-23 lists some scalability concerns when designing Token Ring segments. Refer to IBM's Token Ring planning guides for more information on the maximum segment sizes and maximum diameter of a network.

Table L-23 *Scalability Constraints for Token Ring*

	IBM Token Ring	**IEEE 802.5**
Topology	Star	Not specified
Maximum Segment Length (meters)	Depends on type of cable, number of MAUs, and so on	Depends on type of cable, number of MAUs, and so on
Maximum Number of Attachments per Segment	260 for STP, 72 for UTP	250
Maximum Network Diameter	Depends on type of cable, number of MAUs, and so on	Depends on type of cable, number of MAUs, and so on

FDDI Design Rules

The FDDI specification does not actually specify the maximum segment length or network diameter. It specifies the amount of allowed power loss, which works out to the approximate distances shown in Table L-24.

Table L-24 *Scalability Constraints for FDDI*

	Multimode Fiber	**Single-Mode Fiber**	**UTP**
Topology	Dual ring, tree of concentrators, and others	Dual ring, tree of concentrators, and others	Star
Maximum Segment Length	2 km between stations	60 km between stations	100 meters from hub to station
Maximum Number of Attachments per Segment	1000 (500 dual-attached stations)	1000 (500 dual-attached stations)	2 (hub and station or hub-hub)
Maximum Network Diameter	200 km	200 km	200 km

Chapter 7: Provisioning Hardware and Media for the WAN

Provisioning Interface Description Blocks on Cisco Routers

On Cisco routers, Interface Description Blocks (IDBs) provide a central location in memory for storing information about network interface cards for use by interface driver code.

An IDB must be able to represent all kinds of interfaces, including subinterfaces. Therefore, IDB data structures use a lot of memory. To avoid problems with memory usage, the Cisco IOS™ software limits the number of IDBs. The current IDB limit is 300 per router.

Each physical interface on the router, whether it is configured or not and whether it is active or shut down, uses up one IDB.

Each configured channel on a channelized interface (such as the MultiChannel Interface Processor, MIP) uses one IDB. For example, if a MIP T1 port has 24 configured channels, the interface uses a total of 24 IDBs.

Each configured subinterface also uses one IDB. For example, if a Fast Serial Interface Processor (FSIP) port configured for Frame Relay has 10 configured subinterfaces, the interface uses a total of 11 IDBs (one for the physical interface and one each for the subinterfaces).

Subinterfaces use IDBs, but Frame Relay permanent virtual circuits (PVCs) do not. For example, if a Frame Relay interface has 10 PVCs but does not use any subinterfaces, it uses only a single IDB. If a Frame Relay interface has two subinterfaces, each terminating five PVCs (for a total of 10 PVCs at the interface), it uses three IDBs (one for the physical interface, and one for each of the subinterfaces).

Digital Hierarchy

WAN bandwidth is often provisioned in the United States using the North American Digital Hierarchy, depicted in Table L-25. Each format is called a digital stream (DS). The lower-numbered digital streams are multiplexed into the higher-numbered digital streams within a certain frequency tolerance. A DS0 is a 64 kbps stream. The term T1 is often used colloquially to refer to a DS1 signal. The term T3 is often used colloquially to refer to a DS3 signal. Similar hierarchies have also been developed in Europe and Japan. The term E1 refers to a 2.048 Mbps signal in Europe. The term J1 refers to a 2.048 Mbps signal in Japan.

Table L-25 *Signaling Standards*

Line Type	Signal Standard	Number of DS0s	Bit Rate
T1*	DS1	24	1.544 Mbps
T3*	DS3	672	44.736 Mbps
E1**	2M	30	2.048 Mbps
E3**	M3	480	34.064 Mbps
J1***	Y1	30	2.048 Mbps

*The T1/T3 format is used primarily in North America and parts of Asia.

**The E1/E3 format is used in most of the rest of the world.

***The J1 format is used primarily in Japan.

Provisioning Frame Relay Networks

Complete the following steps to provision Frame Relay links:

Step 1 Choose a committed information rate (CIR) based on realistic, anticipated traffic rates

Step 2 Aggregate all CIRs to determine core bandwidth required

Step 3 Determine the link speed and number of interfaces required on the core router

Step 4 Choose a router platform that can handle the job

Chapter 8: Designing a Network Layer Addressing and Naming Model

IP Addressing

IP addressing defines five address classes: A, B, C, D, and E. Only Classes A, B, and C are available for addressing devices; Class D is used for multicast groups, and Class E is reserved for experimental use.

The first octet of an address defines its class, as illustrated in Table L-26. The bits that represent network and subnet information in an IP address are known as the *prefix*; the number of such bits is known as the *prefix length*. The *Prefix Length* column in Table L-26 indicates the default prefix lengths for the three classes of addresses.

Table L-26   *IP Address Classes A, B and C Are Available for Addressing Devices*

Class	Format (N= network number, H= host number)	Prefix Length	Higher-Order Bit(s)	Address Range
Class A	N.H.H.H	8 bits	0	1.0.0.0 to 126.0.0.0
Class B	N.N.H.H	16 bits	10	128.0.0.0 to 191.255.0.0
Class C	N.N.N.H	24 bits	110	192.0.0.0 to 223.255.255.0

Reference: RFC 1700, available at http://info.internet.isi.edu/in-notes/rfc/files/rfc1700.txt

Private Addresses and Network Address Translation

Private addresses are reserved IP addresses to be used only internally within a company's network. These private addresses are not to be used on the Internet and therefore must be mapped to a company's external registered addresses when sending anything on the Internet.

RFC 1918, *Address Allocation for Private Internets*, available at http://info.internet.isi.edu/in-notes/rfc/files/rfc1918.txt, defines the private IP addresses.

The private IP addresses are as follows:

> 10.0.0.0 to 10.255.255.255
> 172.16.0.0 to 172.31.255.255
> 192.168.0.0 to 192.168.255.255

Network Address Translation (NAT) is a feature in the Cisco IOS™ Release 11.2 software that enables you to translate private addresses into registered IP addresses only when needed, thereby reducing the need for registered IP addresses.

IPX Addressing

A Novell Internetwork Packet Exchange (IPX) address has two parts, the network number and the node number. An IPX address is 80 bits long, with 32 bits (4 octets, or 8 hexadecimal digits) for the network number and 48 bits (6 octets, or 12 hexadecimal digits) for the node number. The node number is typically derived from the Media Access Control (MAC) address of an interface. IPX addresses are written in hexadecimal.

Steps for Designing Network Layer Addressing and Naming

The features of IP and IPX addressing are used when designing the network layer addressing and naming of your network. This section identifies eight steps to use in this aspect of your design.

Step 1: Design a Hierarchy for Addressing

Design a hierarchy for addressing as follows:

- Autonomous systems
- Areas
- Networks
- Subnetworks
- End stations

The hierarchy that you use will depend on the network layer protocol and routing protocol that you are using.

Step 2: Design Route Summarization

Summarization, also known as *aggregation,* allows one route to represent many routes, resulting in smaller routing tables. Route summarization is discussed in detail earlier in this chapter.

Step 3: Design a Plan for Distributing Administrative Authority for Addressing and Naming at the Lower Levels of the Hierarchy

Once the high-level plan is made for the network, lower-level addressing and naming may be delegated. For example, if the client has offices in Europe and Asia, as well as North America, the authority to name devices and assign addresses, within established guidelines, could be divided along these geographical lines.

Step 4: Design a Method for Mapping Geographical Locations to Network Numbers

Assigning network numbers by geographical location will also aid in the summarization task. For example, the client who has offices in Europe, Asia, and North America could assign a range of addresses to each continent (with the authority to distribute addresses within the range resting within the appropriate continent office). The summarized address for each continent would then encompass the entire range of addresses assigned to that continent.

Step 5: Develop a Plan for Identifying Special Stations Such as Routers and Servers with Specific Node IDs

To facilitate troubleshooting, devices such as routers and servers should have fixed addresses. For example, all routers could have an IP address with the node part in the range of 1 through 19, while all servers have the node part of their address in the range of 20 through 29. Then, if during troubleshooting there is a problem with an address that has a node part of 25, it is immediately obvious that this address belongs to a server.

Step 6: Develop a Plan for Configuring User Station Addresses

For scalability, user station addresses should be assigned dynamically, rather than statically, if possible. Dynamic address assignment allows the automatic assignment of addresses from a pool of addresses as user stations join the network; the addresses are released back into the pool if the device leaves the network. This simplifies the network administrator's task of changing IP addresses on user stations when users move to a new location, for example.

Use the Bootstrap Protocol (BOOTP) or the newer Dynamic Host Configuration Protocol (DHCP) for dynamic IP address assignment. Cisco's DNS/DHCP Manager product, described earlier in this chapter, can be used to aid in this task.

Step 7: If Necessary, Develop a Plan for Using Gateways to Map Private Addresses to External Addresses

As noted earlier, private addresses are reserved IP addresses to be used only within a company's network. These private addresses are not to be used on the Internet and therefore must be mapped to a company's external addresses when sending anything on the Internet. Use the Cisco IOS Network Address Translation (NAT) feature described earlier in this chapter to do this mapping.

Step 8: Design a Scheme for Naming Servers, Routers, and User Stations

Names should be meaningful to facilitate troubleshooting. For example, in the company with offices in Europe, Asia, and North America, the router and server names could all start with an abbreviation of the continent: EUR, ASIA, and NA. This could be suffixed with the last octet of the device's node address—for example, ERU03 for a router. The user's PCs could all have names that start with the abbreviation for the continent, followed by the letters PC, a hyphen, and the user's first initial and last name. An example is EURPC-JSMITH. To name devices in IP environments, install and configure DNS servers. Use Cisco's DNS/DHCP Manager, described in Chapter 8, to synchronize DNS names with dynamically assigned IP addresses.

Chapter 9: Selecting Routing and Bridging Protocols

Routed Protocols Supported

A specific routing protocol typically can only be used with one routed protocol. Table L-27 indicates the routing protocols available for use with the three most popular routed protocols, IP, IPX, and AppleTalk.

Table L-27   *Routing Protocols Available for Each Routed Protocol*

Routed Protocol	Routing Protocol
IP	IP RIP, IGRP, OSPF, IS-IS, EIGRP
IPX	IPX RIP, NLSP, EIGRP
AppleTalk	RTMP, AURP, EIGRP

Categories of Routing Protocols

There are two main categories of routing protocols: distance vector and link-state. A third category, hybrid, includes characteristics from both of the other two categories. Table L-28 summarizes how the various routing protocols fit in these categories.

Table L-28   *Categorizing Routing Protocols*

Category	Routing Protocol
Distance Vector	IP RIP, IGRP, IPX RIP, RTMP
Link-State	OSPF, NLSP, IS-IS
Hybrid	EIGRP

NOTE   The AppleTalk Update Routing Protocol (AURP) may also be used in AppleTalk networks. AURP, similar to a distance vector protocol, is discussed in Chapter 9.

Bandwidth Used By Distance Vector Routing Protocols

Distance vector routing protocols, being periodic in nature, use a defined amount of bandwidth for sending their routing updates. Table L-29 illustrates many characteristics of these routing protocols; you can use this information to determine the bandwidth used by the routing protocol in your network.

Table L-29 *Calculating Bandwidth Used by Routing Protocols*

Routing Protocol	Default Update Timer (Seconds)	Route Entry Size (Bytes)	Network and Update Overhead (Bytes)	Routes per Packet
IP RIP	30	20	32	25
IP IGRP	90	14	32	104
AppleTalk RTMP	10	6	17	97
IPX SAP	60	64	32	7
IPX RIP	60	8	32	50
DECnet IV	40	4	18	368
VINES VRTP	90	8	30	104
XNS	30	20	40	25

NOTE

For AppleTalk: DDP header = 13 bytes, RTMP header = 4 bytes, each route update = 6 bytes, maximum DDP data = 586. 586 – 4 = 582. 582/6 = 97 routes in a route update packet.

For NetWare: IPX RIP limits the number of routes in an update packet to 50. IPX SAP limits the number of SAPs in an update packet to 7. These limits apply regardless of the maximum transmission unit (MTU).

For IP: RIP is limited to 25 routes per update, regardless of the MTU.

Routing Protocol Administrative Distance

In some network designs, more than one IP routing protocol is configured. If a router learns about more than one route to a destination from different sources, the route with the *lowest administrative distance* is placed in the routing table. Table L-30 defines the default administrative distances for IP routes learned from different sources.

TIP

Think of the administrative distance as the *trustworthiness* of the source of the routing information. If a router has learned about the same network from more than one source (for example, from a static route and from RIP), it must decide which source is the most *trustworthy*. The lower the administrative distance, the more trustworthy the source.

Table L-30 *Default Administrative Distances for IP Routes*

IP Route	Administrative Distance
Connected interface	0
Static route using a connected interface	0
Static route using an IP address	1
EIGRP summary route	5
External BGP route	20
Internal EIGRP route	90
IGRP route	100
OSPF route	110
IS-IS route	115
RIP route	120
Exterior Gateway Protocol (EGP) route	140
External EIGRP route	170
Internal BGP route	200
Route of unknown origin	255

Time to Detect Link Failure

Table L-31 indicates the time required by an interface to detect a link failure, for common interface types.

Table L-31 *Time to Detect Link Failure*

Interface Type	Time to Detect Link Failure	Keepalive Timer
Serial lines	Immediate if Carrier Detect (CD) lead drops. Otherwise, between two and three keepalive times.	Keepalive timer is ten seconds by default.
Token Ring or FDDI	Almost immediate due to beacon protocol.	N/A
Ethernet	Immediate if caused by local or transceiver failure. Otherwise, between two and three keepalive times.	Keepalive timer is ten seconds by default.

Chapter 10: Provisioning Software Features

Access Lists Numbering

With the exception of named IP and IPX access lists, configuring an access list requires you to number the list. A range of numbers has been reserved for each type of access list, as identified in Table L-32.

Table L-32   *Access List Numbers*

Type of Access List	Range
IP standard	1–99
IP extended	100–199
Bridge type code	200–299
DECnet standard and extended	300–399
XNS standard	400–499
XNS extended	500–599
AppleTalk zone	600–699
Bridge MAC	700–799
IPX standard	800–899
IPX extended	900–999
IPX SAP	1000–1099
Bridge extended	1100–1199
NLSP route aggregation	1200–1299

Chapter 11: Selecting a Network Management Strategy

Summary of Cisco's Internetwork Management Applications

Table L-33 displays a brief summary of Cisco's internetwork management applications.

Table L-33   *Cisco's Network Management Applications*

Network Management Application	Devices Supported or Managed by the Application	Product Platform(s)
CiscoWorks	Various Cisco devices	SunNet Manager
		HP OpenView on SunOS/Solaris
		HP OpenView HP-UX
		IBM NetView for AIX
CiscoWorks Blue Maps	SNA-enabled Cisco routers	NetView for AIX on RS/6000
		HP OpenView on HP-UX on HP
		HP OpenView or SunNet Manager on Solaris on Sun
CiscoWorks Blue SNA View	SNA-enabled Cisco routers and SNA devices managed by mainframe	Requires CiscoWorks Blue Maps
CiscoWorks Blue Native Service Point	Cisco routers	IBM NetView
		Sterling NetMaster
Cisco Hub/Ring Manager for Windows	Cisco 2517, 2518, 2519 routers	PC with Microsoft Windows 3.1 or higher and HP OpenView Windows
CiscoWorks Windows	Cisco routers, switches, access servers, concentrators, adapters and ATM switches	PC with Microsoft Windows NT 3.51 or 4.0 or Windows 95 running CastleRock SNMPc (bundled with CiscoWorks Windows) or HP OpenView Windows (optional)
CiscoView	Cisco routers, switches, access servers, concentrators, adapters, and ATM switches (LightStream 100 and LightStream 2020)	Standalone on UNIX workstations
		Also bundled with CiscoWorks, CiscoWorks Windows, and CWSI
NETSYS Tools	Cisco routers	SunOS, Solaris, HP-UX, and AIX
NETSYS Baseliner for NT	Cisco routers	PC with Microsoft Windows NT 4.0

continues

Table L-33 *Cisco's Network Management Applications (Continued)*

Network Management Application	Devices Supported or Managed by the Application	Product Platform(s)
ControlStream StreamView VirtualStream	LightStream 2020	Sun SPARCstation with SunOS, and optionally, HP OpenView
TrafficDirector	RMON console management	SunNet Manager HP OpenView IBM NetView for AIX PC with Windows 95 or NT Standalone on UNIX workstations Version 5.2 is only available as part of CWSI (on Solaris and NT)
Total Control Manager/ SNMP	Modem and T1 cards in Cisco 5100 access server	PC with Microsoft Windows 3.1
CWSI (includes VlanDirector, TrafficDirector, CiscoView and others)	Comprehensive support for Cisco Catalyst switches	SunNet Manager on Solaris HP OpenView on Solaris PC with Windows NT
Resource Manager Essentials	Various Cisco devices	Solaris Microsoft Windows NT 4.0 AIX HP UNIX
CWSI Campus (includes VlanDirector, TrafficDirector, CiscoView, and others)	Comprehensive support for Cisco Catalyst switches	Solaris Microsoft Windows NT 4.0 AIX HP UNIX Resource Manager Essentials

Chapter 12: Writing a Design Document

Content of the Design Document

Your design document should include the following sections, at a minimum, although you may choose to include additional sections:

- Executive Summary
- Design Requirements
- Design Solution
- Summary
- Appendixes
- Cost

Chapter 13: Building a Prototype or Pilot

Steps to Build a Prototype

You can follow these steps to build a prototype network structure to prove to a customer that your design works:

Step 1 Review the customer requirements

Step 2 Determine how big the prototype needs to be

Step 3 Understand what your competition plans to propose

Step 4 Develop a test plan

Step 5 Purchase and configure the equipment

Step 6 Practice

Step 7 Conduct final tests and demonstrations

Steps to Build a Pilot

For small businesses, a pilot might be more practical. If applicable, the following are some minimum recommendations for a pilot of your design:

Step 1   Test the design

Step 2   Investigate the competition

Step 3   Script a demonstration of the test results

Step 4   Practice

Step 5   Schedule and present the demonstration

Chapter 14: Testing the Prototype or Pilot

Network Health Checklist

Use the *Network Health Checklist*, as given in Chapter 3, when checking a prototype or pilot for proper network functionality and scalability. This checklist provides guidelines, not rules. As mentioned in Chapter 3, the correct answer to questions regarding thresholds for network health usually is "it depends." Thresholds depend on topologies, router configurations, network applications, user requirements, how measurement tools calculate thresholds, and many other factors.

NUMERICS

10Base2. 10-Mbps baseband Ethernet specification using 50-ohm thin coaxial cable. 10Base2, which is part of the IEEE 802.3 specification, has a distance limit of 185 meters per segment. *See also* Ethernet, IEEE 802.3, and Thinnet.

10Base5. 10-Mbps baseband Ethernet specification using standard (thick) 50-ohm baseband coaxial cable. 10Base5, which is part of the IEEE 802.3 baseband physical layer specification, has a distance limit of 500 meters per segment. *See also* Ethernet and IEEE 802.3.

10BaseF. 10-Mbps baseband Ethernet specification that refers to the 10BaseFB, 10BaseFL, and 10BaseFP standards for Ethernet over fiber-optic cabling. *See also* 10BaseFB, 10BaseFL, 10BaseFP, and Ethernet.

10BaseFB. 10-Mbps baseband Ethernet specification using fiber-optic cabling. 10BaseFB is part of the IEEE 10BaseF specification. It is not used to connect user stations but instead provides a synchronous signaling backbone that allows additional segments and repeaters to be connected to the network. 10BaseFB segments can be up to 2,000 meters long. *See also* 10BaseF and Ethernet.

10BaseFL. 10-Mbps baseband Ethernet specification using fiber-optic cabling. 10BaseFL is part of the IEEE 10BaseF specification and, although able to interoperate with FOIRL, is designed to replace the FOIRL specification. 10BaseFL segments can be up to 1,000 meters long if used with FOIRL and up to 2,000 meters if 10BaseFL is used exclusively. *See also* 10BaseF, Ethernet, and FOIRL.

10BaseFP. 10-Mbps fiber-passive baseband Ethernet specification using fiber-optic cabling. 10BaseFP is part of the IEEE 10BaseF specification. It organizes a number of computers into a star topology without the use of repeaters. 10BaseFP segments can be up to 500 meters long. *See also* 10BaseF and Ethernet.

10BaseT. 10-Mbps baseband Ethernet specification using two pairs of twisted-pair cabling (Category 3, 4, or 5): one pair for transmitting data and the other for receiving data. 10BaseT, which is part of the IEEE 802.3 specification, has a distance limit of approximately 100 meters per segment. *See also* Ethernet and IEEE 802.3.

10Broad36. 10-Mbps broadband Ethernet specification using broadband coaxial cable. 10Broad36, which is part of IEEE 802.3 specification, has a distance limit of 3,600 meters per segment. *See also* Ethernet and IEEE 802.3.

100BaseFX. 100-Mbps baseband Fast Ethernet specification using two strands of multimode fiber-optic cable per link. To guarantee proper signal timing, a 100BaseFX link cannot exceed 400 meters. Based on the IEEE 802.3 standard. *See also* 100BaseX, Fast Ethernet, and IEEE 802.3.

100BaseT. 100-Mbps baseband Fast Ethernet specification using UTP wiring. Like the 10BaseT technology on which it is based, 100BaseT sends link pulses over the network segment when no traffic is present. However, these link pulses contain more information than do those used in 10BaseT. Based on the IEEE 802.3 standard. *See also* 10BaseT, Fast Ethernet, and IEEE 802.3.

100BaseT4. 100-Mbps baseband Fast Ethernet specification using four pairs of Category 3, 4, or 5 UTP wiring. To guarantee proper signal timing, a 100BaseT4 segment cannot exceed 100 meters. Based on the IEEE802.3 standard. *See also* Fast Ethernet and IEEE 802.3.

100BaseTX. 100-Mbps baseband Fast Ethernet specification using two pairs of either UTP or STP wiring. The first pair of wires is used to receive data; the second is used to transmit. To guarantee proper signal timing, a 100BaseTX segment cannot exceed 100 meters. Based on the IEEE 802.3 standard. *See also* 100BaseX, Fast Ethernet and IEEE 802.3.

100BaseX. 100-Mbps baseband Fast Ethernet specification that refers to the 100BaseFX and 100BaseTX standards for Fast Ethernet over fiber-optic cabling. Based on the IEEE 802.3 standard. *See also* 100BaseFX, 100BaseTX, Fast Ethernet, and IEEE 802.3.

100VG-AnyLAN. 100-Mbps Fast Ethernet and Token Ring media technology using four pairs of Category 3, 4, or 5 UTP cabling. This high-speed transport technology, developed by Hewlett-Packard, can be made to operate on existing 10BaseT Ethernet networks. Based on the IEEE 802.12 standard. *See also* IEEE 802.12.

A

AAL. ATM adaptation layer. Service-dependent sublayer of the data link layer. The AAL accepts data from different applications and presents it to the ATM layer in the form of 48-byte ATM payload segments. The AAL performs two main functions in service-specific sublayers of the AAL: a convergence function in the convergence sublayer (CS), and a cell segmentation and reassembly function in the segmentation and reassembly (SAR) sublayer. *See also* CS and SAR.

AAL5. ATM adaptation layer 5. One of four AALs recommended by the ITU-T. AAL5 supports connection-oriented variable bit rate services and is used predominantly for the transfer of classical IP over ATM and LANE traffic.

AARP. AppleTalk Address Resolution Protocol. Protocol in the AppleTalk protocol stack that maps a data-link address to a network address.

ABR. Area border router. Router located on the border of one or more OSPF areas that connects those areas to the backbone network. ABRs are considered members of both the OSPF backbone and the attached areas. They therefore maintain routing tables describing both the backbone topology and the topology of the other areas.

access layer. Layer in a hierarchical network that provides workgroup/user access to the network.

access list. List kept by routers to control access to or from the router for a number of services (for example, to prevent packets with a certain IP address from leaving a particular interface on the router).

access method. Generally, the way in which network devices access the network medium.

access server. Communications processor that connects asynchronous devices to a LAN or WAN through network and terminal emulation software. Performs both synchronous and asynchronous routing of supported protocols. Sometimes called a network access server.

accounting management. One of five categories of network management defined by ISO for management of OSI networks. Accounting management subsystems are responsible for collecting network data relating to resource usage. *See also* configuration management, fault management, performance management, and security management.

accuracy. The percentage of useful traffic that is correctly transmitted on the system, relative to total traffic, including transmission errors.

ACF. Advanced Communications Function. A group of SNA products that provides distributed processing and resource sharing.

ACK.

1. Acknowledgement bit in a TCP segment.

2. *See* acknowledgment.

acknowledgment. Notification sent from one network device to another to acknowledge that some event (for example, receipt of a message) has occurred. Sometimes abbreviated ACK. *Compare with* NAK.

address. A data structure or logical convention used to identify a unique entity, such as a particular process or network device.

address mapping. A technique that allows different protocols to interoperate by translating addresses from one format to another. For example, when routing IP over X.25, the IP addresses must be mapped to the X.25 addresses so that the IP packets can be transmitted by the X.25 network. *See also* address resolution.

address resolution. Generally, a method for resolving differences between computer addressing schemes. Address resolution usually specifies a method for mapping network layer (Layer 3) addresses to data link layer (Layer 2) addresses. *See also* address mapping.

adjacency. A relationship formed between selected neighboring routers and end nodes for the purpose of exchanging routing information. Adjacency is based on the use of a common media segment.

administrative distance. A rating of the trustworthiness of a routing information source. The higher the value, the lower the trustworthiness rating.

ADSP. AppleTalk Data-Stream Protocol. Protocol that establishes and maintains full-duplex communication between two AppleTalk sockets.

AEP. AppleTalk Echo Protocol. Used to test connectivity between two AppleTalk nodes. One node sends a packet to another node and receives a duplicate, or echo, of that packet.

AFP. AppleTalk Filing Protocol. Presentation and application layer protocol that permits AppleTalk workstations to share files across a network.

agent.

1. Generally, software that processes queries and returns replies on behalf of an application.

2. In NMSs, a process that resides in all managed devices and reports the values of specified variables to management stations.

aggregation. *See* route summarization.

alarm. A message notifying an operator or administrator of a network problem. *See also* event and trap.

algorithm. A well-defined rule or process for arriving at a solution to a problem. In networking, algorithms are commonly used to determine the best route for traffic from a particular source to a particular destination.

all-routes explorer packet. An explorer packet that traverses an entire SRB network, following all possible paths to a specific destination. Sometimes called a frame or an all-rings explorer packet or frame. *See also* explorer packet, local explorer packet, and spanning explorer packet.

analog transmission. Signal transmission over wires or through the air in which information is conveyed through a variation of some combination of signal amplitude, frequency, and phase.

ANSI. American National Standards Institute. A voluntary organization comprising corporate, government, and other members who coordinate standards-related activities, approve U.S. national standards, and develop positions for the United States in international standards organizations. ANSI helps develop international and U.S. standards relating to, among other things, communications and networking.

API. Application programming interface. A specification of function-call conventions that defines an interface to a service.

APPC. Advanced Program-to-Program Communication. IBM SNA system software that allows high-speed communication between programs on different computers in a distributed computing environment. APPC runs on LU 6.2 devices. *See also* LU 6.2.

AppleTalk. A series of communications protocols designed by Apple Computer. Two phases currently exist. Phase 1, the earlier version, supports a single physical network that can have only one network number and be in one zone. Phase 2, the more recent version, supports multiple logical networks on a single physical network and allows networks to be in more than one zone. *See also* zone.

application layer. Layer 7 of the OSI reference model. This layer provides services to application processes (such as electronic mail, file transfer, and terminal emulation) that are outside the OSI model. The application layer identifies and establishes the availability of intended communication partners (and the resources required to connect with them), synchronizes cooperating applications, and establishes agreement on procedures for error recovery and control of data integrity. Corresponds roughly with the transaction services layer in the SNA model.

APPN. Advanced Peer-to-Peer Networking. An enhancement to the original IBM SNA architecture. APPN handles session establishment between peer nodes, dynamic transparent route calculation, and traffic prioritization for APPC traffic. *See also* APPC.

area. A logical set of network segments and their attached devices. Areas are usually connected to other areas via routers, making up a single autonomous system. *See also* autonomous system.

ARP. Address Resolution Protocol. An Internet protocol used to map an IP address to a MAC address. Defined in RFC 826. *Compare with* RARP. *See also* proxy ARP.

ARPA. Advanced Research Projects Agency. A research and development organization that is part of the Department of Defense. ARPA is responsible for numerous technological advances in communications and networking. ARPA evolved into DARPA and then back into ARPA (in 1994). *See also* DARPA.

ARPANET. Advanced Research Projects Agency Network. A landmark packet-switching network established in 1969. ARPANET was developed in the 1970s by BBN and funded by ARPA (and later DARPA). It eventually evolved into the Internet. The term ARPANET was officially retired in 1990. *See also* ARPA, DARPA, and Internet.

AS. Autonomous system. A collection of networks under a common administration sharing a common routing strategy. Autonomous systems may be subdivided into areas.

ASA. Adaptive security algorithm used in Cisco's PIX Firewall.

ASBR. Autonomous system boundary router. An ABR located between an OSPF autonomous system and a non-OSPF network. ASBRs run both OSPF and another routing protocol, such as RIP. ASBRs must reside in a non-stub OSPF area. *See also* ABR, non-stub area, and OSPF.

ASP. AppleTalk Session Protocol. Protocol that establishes and maintains sessions between AppleTalk clients and servers.

asynchronous transmission. Digital signals that are transmitted without precise clocking. Such signals generally have different frequencies and phase relationships. Asynchronous transmissions usually encapsulate individual characters in control bits (called start and stop bits), which designate the beginning and end of each character. *Compare with* synchronous transmission.

ATM. Asynchronous Transfer Mode. An international standard for cell relay in which multiple service types (such as voice, video, or data) are conveyed in fixed-length (53-byte) cells. Fixed-length cells allow cell processing to occur in hardware, thereby reducing transit delays. ATM is designed to take advantage of high-speed transmission media, such as E3, SONET, and T3.

ATP. AppleTalk Transaction Protocol. A transport layer protocol that allows reliable request-response exchanges between two socket clients.

AURP. AppleTalk Update-Based Routing Protocol. A method of encapsulating AppleTalk traffic in the header of a foreign protocol, allowing the connection of two or more discontiguous AppleTalk internetworks through a foreign network (such as TCP/IP) to form an AppleTalk WAN. This connection is called an AURP tunnel. In addition to its encapsulation function, AURP maintains routing tables for the entire AppleTalk WAN by exchanging routing information between exterior routers. *See also* AURP tunnel.

AURP tunnel. A connection created in an AURP WAN that functions as a single, virtual data link between AppleTalk internetworks physically separated by a foreign network (a TCP/IP network, for example). *See also* AURP.

authentication. Verification of the identity of a person or process.

autonomous switching. With this type of switching, an incoming packet matches an entry in the autonomous-switching cache located on the interface processor. It is available only on Cisco 7000 series routers and in AGS+ systems with high-speed network controller cards.

AutoSPID. Automatic Service Profile Identifier. A feature of a terminal adapter that downloads SPID information from a compatible switch, eliminating the need for the user to enter the information.

availability. The amount of time that the network is operational, sometimes expressed as Mean Time Between Failure (MTBF).

B

backbone. The part of a network that acts as the primary path for traffic that is most often sourced from, and destined for, other networks.

bandwidth. The difference between the highest and lowest frequencies available for network signals. The term is also used to describe the rated throughput capacity of a given network medium or protocol.

bandwidth domain. Includes all devices that share the same bandwidth. Known as a collision domain for Ethernet LANs.

bandwidth reservation. A process of assigning bandwidth to users and applications served by a network. It involves assigning priority to different flows of traffic based on how critical and delay sensitive they are. This makes the best use of available bandwidth, and if the network becomes congested, lower-priority traffic can be dropped. Sometimes called bandwidth allocation.

baseband. A characteristic of a network technology in which only one carrier frequency is used. Ethernet is an example of a baseband network. Also called narrowband. *Compare with* broadband.

bastion host. A secure host that supports a limited number of applications for use by outsiders. It holds data that outsiders access, but is strongly protected from outsiders using it for anything other than its limited purposes.

Bc. Committed Burst. Negotiated tariff metric in Frame Relay internetworks. The maximum amount of data (in bits) that a Frame Relay internetwork is committed to accept and transmit at the CIR. *See also* Be and CIR.

B channel. Bearer channel. In ISDN, a full-duplex, 64-kbps channel used to send user data. *Compare with* D channel.

BDR. Backup designated router, in OSPF. The BDR is elected as a backup to the DR. If the DR goes down, the BDR will take over the DR's responsibilities. *See also* DR.

Be. Excess Burst. Negotiated tariff metric in Frame Relay internetworks. The number of bits that a Frame Relay internetwork attempts to transmit after Bc is accommodated. Be data is, in general, delivered with a lower probability than Bc data because Be data can be marked as DE by the network. *See also* Bc and DE.

bearer channel. *See* B channel.

BECN. Backward explicit congestion notification. A bit set by a Frame Relay network in frames traveling in the opposite direction of frames encountering a congested path. DTE receiving frames with the BECN bit set can request that higher-level protocols take flow control action when appropriate. *Compare with* FECN.

Bellman-Ford routing algorithm. *See* distance vector routing algorithm and DBF.

best-effort delivery. Delivery in a network system that does not use a sophisticated acknowledgment system to guarantee reliable delivery of information.

BGP. Border Gateway Protocol. An interdomain routing protocol that replaces EGP. BGP exchanges reachability information with other BGP systems. It is defined in RFC 1163. *See also* BGP4 and EGP.

BGP4. BGP Version 4. Version 4 of the predominant interdomain routing protocol used on the Internet. BGP4 supports CIDR and uses route aggregation mechanisms to reduce the size of routing tables. *See also* BGP and CIDR.

BIA. Burned-in address, another name for a MAC address.

binary. A numbering system that uses ones and zeros (1=on, 0=off).

bit. A binary digit used in the binary numbering system. Can be 0 or 1.

bit rate. The speed at which bits are transmitted, usually expressed in bits per second (bps).

BOD. Bandwidth-on-demand. A feature in Cisco routers that allows more links to the same destination to be brought up when the bandwidth of the current links is below a specified threshold.

BOOTP. Bootstrap Protocol. A protocol used by a network node to determine the IP address of its Ethernet interfaces in order to affect network booting.

BPDU. Bridge protocol data unit. A Spanning-Tree Protocol hello packet that is sent out at configurable intervals to exchange information among bridges in the network. *See also* PDU.

bps. Bits per second. Used in measurement of network throughput.

BRI. Basic Rate Interface. An ISDN interface composed of two B channels and one D channel for circuit-switched communication of voice, video, and data. *Compare with* PRI. *See also* ISDN.

bridge. A device that connects and passes packets between two network segments that use the same communications protocol. Bridges operate at the data link layer (Layer 2) of the OSI reference model. In general, a bridge filters, forwards, or floods an incoming frame based on the MAC address of that frame.

broadband. A transmission system that multiplexes multiple independent signals onto one cable. In telecommunications terminology, any channel having a bandwidth greater than a voice-grade channel (4 kHz). In LAN terminology, a coaxial cable on which analog signaling is used. Also called wideband. *Compare with* baseband.

broadcast. Data packet that is sent to all nodes on a network. Broadcasts are identified by a broadcast address. *Compare with* multicast and unicast. *See also* broadcast address.

broadcast address. A special address reserved for sending a message to all stations. Generally, a broadcast address is a MAC destination address of all ones. *Compare with* multicast address and unicast address. *See also* broadcast.

broadcast domain. The set of all devices that will receive broadcast frames originating from any device within the set. Broadcast domains are typically bounded by routers because routers do not forward broadcast frames.

broadcast radiation. The way that broadcasts and multicasts radiate from the source to all connected LANs in a flat network, causing all hosts on the LAN to do extra processing.

broadcast storm. An undesirable network event in which many broadcasts are sent simultaneously across all network segments. If there is redundancy in the network this could result in broadcasts continuously circling the network. A broadcast storm uses substantial network bandwidth and, typically, causes network time-outs.

BT/m. Bit times per meter. A measurement of round-trip delay per meter of a specific cable type. Used in the calculation of PDV for checking propagation delays in an ethernet network. *See also* PDV.

buffer. A storage area used for handling data in transit. Buffers are used in internetworking to compensate for differences in processing speed between network devices. Bursts of data can be stored in buffers until they can be handled by slower processing devices. Sometimes referred to as a packet buffer.

bus. A common physical signal path composed of wires or other media across which signals can be sent from one part of a computer to another. Sometimes called highway. *See* bus topology.

bus topology. A linear LAN architecture in which transmissions from network stations propagate the length of the medium and are received by all other stations. *Compare with* ring topology, star topology, and tree topology.

BVI. Bridged Virtual Interface. A software-based interface used in IRB.

byte. A series of consecutive binary digits that are operated on as a unit (for example, an 8-bit byte).

C

CA. Certification Authority. Used in IPSec, a CA is a third party that is explicitly trusted by the receiver to validate identities and to create digital certificates. Each device is enrolled with a CA. When two devices attempt to communicate, they exchange certificates and digitally sign data to authenticate each other. *See also* IPSec and IKE.

cable range. A range of network numbers that is valid for use by nodes on an extended AppleTalk network. The cable range value can be a single network number or a contiguous sequence of several network numbers. Node addresses are assigned based on the cable range value.

caching. A form of replication in which information learned during a previous transaction is used to process later transactions.

Category 1 cabling. One of five grades of UTP cabling described in the EIA/TIA-586 standard. Category 1 cabling is used for telephone communications and is not suitable for transmitting data. *See also* EIA/TIA-586 and UTP.

Category 2 cabling. One of five grades of UTP cabling described in the EIA/TIA-586 standard. Category 2 cabling is capable of transmitting data at speeds up to 4 Mbps. *See also* EIA/TIA-586 and UTP.

Category 3 cabling. One of five grades of UTP cabling described in the EIA/TIA-586 standard. Category 3 cabling is used in 10BaseT networks and can transmit data at speeds up to 10 Mbps. *See also* EIA/TIA-586 and UTP.

Category 4 cabling. One of five grades of UTP cabling described in the EIA/TIA-586 standard. Category 4 cabling is used in Token Ring networks and can transmit data at speeds up to 16 Mbps. *See also* EIA/TIA-586 and UTP.

Category 5 cabling. One of five grades of UTP cabling described in the EIA/TIA-586 standard. Category 5 cabling is used for running CDDI and can transmit data at speeds up to 100 Mbps. *See also* EIA/TIA-586 and UTP.

CCDA. Cisco Certified Design Associate. This certification is the first in the Network Design certifications path; it is a prerequisite to the CCDP certification. A CCDA can design simple routed LAN, routed WAN, and switched LAN networks.

CCDP. Cisco Certified Design Professional. This certification is a follow-on to the CCNA certification. A CCDP can design complex routed LAN, routed WAN, and switched LAN networks.

CCITT. Consultative Committee for International Telegraph and Telephone. An International organization responsible for the development of communications standards. Now called the ITU-T. *See* ITU-T.

CDDI. Copper Distributed Data Interface. An implementation of FDDI protocols over STP and UTP cabling. CDDI transmits over relatively short distances (about 100 meters), providing data rates of 100 Mbps using a dual-ring architecture to provide redundancy. *Compare with* FDDI.

CD-ROM. Compact Disk-Read Only Memory.

CET. Cisco Encryption Technology. Provides packet-level encryption that enables you to protect the confidentiality and integrity of network data traveling between cooperating (peer) encrypting routers.

CGMP. Cisco Group Management Protocol. A protocol that allows switches to participate in multicast groups by communicating to a router running IGMP. *See also* IGMP.

channel.

1. A communication path. Multiple channels can be multiplexed over a single cable in certain environments.

2. In IBM, the specific path between large computers (such as mainframes) and attached peripheral devices.

channel-attached. Pertaining to attachment of devices directly by data channels (input/output channels) to a computer.

channelized E1. An access link operating at 2.048 Mbps that is subdivided into 30 B-channels and 1 D-channel. Supports DDR, Frame Relay, and X.25. *Compare with* channelized T1.

channelized T1. An access link operating at 1.544 Mbps that is subdivided into 24 channels (23 B-channels and 1 D-channel) of 64 kbps each. The individual channels or groups of channels connect to different destinations. Supports DDR, Frame Relay, and X.25. Also referred to as fractional T1. *Compare with* channelized E1.

CHAP. Challenge Handshake Authentication Protocol. A security feature supported on lines using PPP encapsulation that prevents unauthorized access. CHAP does not itself prevent unauthorized access; it merely identifies the remote end. The router or access server then determines whether that user is allowed access. *Compare with* PAP.

CIDR. Classless interdomain routing. A mechanism developed to help alleviate the problem of exhaustion of IP addresses. The idea behind CIDR is that multiple Class C addresses can be combined, or aggregated, to create a larger (that it, more hosts allowed) classless set of IP addresses. Several IP networks appear to networks outside the group as a single, larger entity. *See also* BGP4.

CiscoFusion. An integrated network architecture developed by Cisco that includes multiple networking technologies operating at different networking layers to provide the right capabilities to handle different networking issues.

CIR. Committed information rate. The rate at which a Frame Relay network agrees to transfer information under normal conditions, averaged over a minimum increment of time. CIR, measured in bits per second, is one of the key negotiated tariff metrics. *See also* Bc.

circuit. A communications path between two or more points.

circuit switching. A switching system in which a dedicated physical circuit path must exist between sender and receiver for the duration of the call. Used heavily in the telephone company network.

classful routing protocols. Routing protocols that do not transmit any information about the prefix length. Examples are RIP and IGRP.

classless routing protocols. Routing protocols that do include the prefix length with routing updates; routers running classless routing protocols do not have to determine the prefix themselves. Classless routing protocols support VLSM. *See also* VLSM.

CLI. Command Line Interface. An interface that enables the user to interact with the operating system by entering commands and optional arguments. Co*mpare with* GUI.

client. A node or software program that requests services from a server. *See also* server.

client/server computing. Computing (processing) network systems in which transaction responsibilities are divided into two parts: client (front end) and server (back end). Both terms (client and server) can be applied to software programs or actual computing devices. Also called distributed computing (processing). *See also* RPC.

cluster controllers. *See* Establishment controllers.

CO. Central office. A local telephone company office to which all local loops in a given area connect and in which circuit switching of subscriber lines occurs.

CODEC. Coder-decoder. A device that typically uses PCM to transform analog signals into a digital bit stream and digital signals back into analog.

collapsed backbone. A nondistributed backbone in which all network segments are interconnected by way of an internetworking device. A collapsed backbone might be a virtual network segment existing in a device such as a hub, a router, or a switch.

collision. In Ethernet, the result of two nodes transmitting simultaneously. The frames from each device impact and are damaged when they meet on the physical media. *See also* collision domain.

collision domain. In Ethernet, the network area within which frames that have collided are propagated. Repeaters and hubs propagate collisions; LAN switches, bridges, and routers do not. *See also* collision.

common carrier. A licensed, private utility company that supplies communication services to the public at regulated prices.

communication controller. In SNA, the devices that manage the physical network and control communication links.

communications line. The physical link (such as wire or a telephone circuit) that connects one or more devices to one or more other devices.

community. In SNMP, a logical group of managed devices and NMSs in the same administrative domain.

community string. A text string that acts as a password and is used to authenticate messages sent between a management station and a router containing an SNMP agent. The community string is sent in every packet between the manager and the agent.

compression. The running of a data set through an algorithm that reduces the space required to store the data set or the bandwidth required to transmit the data set. *Compare with* expansion.

concentrator. *See* hub.

configuration management. One of five categories of network management defined by ISO for management of OSI networks. Configuration management subsystems are responsible for detecting and determining the state of a network. *See also* accounting management, fault management, performance management, and security management.

congestion. Traffic in excess of network capacity.

connectionless. Data transfer that occurs without the existence of a virtual circuit. *Compare with* connection-oriented. *See also* VC.

connection-oriented. Data transfer that requires the establishment of a virtual circuit. A Layer 4 protocol that creates with software a virtual circuit between devices to provide guaranteed transport of data. *See also* connectionless and VC.

convergence. The speed and capability of a group of internetworking devices running a specific routing protocol to arrive at a consistent understanding of the topology of an internetwork after a change in that topology.

core layer. Layer in a hierarchical network that provides optimal transport between sites.

cost. An arbitrary value, typically based on hop count, media bandwidth, or other measures, that is assigned by a network administrator and used to compare various paths through an internetwork environment. Cost values are used by routing protocols to determine the most favorable path to a particular destination: The lower the cost, the better the path. Sometimes called path cost. *See also* routing metric.

CPE. Customer premises equipment. Terminating equipment, such as terminals, telephones, and modems, supplied by the telephone company, installed at customer sites, and connected to the telephone company network.

CPU. Central Processing Unit. The main processor in a device such as a computer or router.

CRC. Cyclic redundancy check. An error-checking technique in which the frame recipient calculates a remainder by dividing frame contents by a prime binary divisor and compares the calculated remainder to a value stored in the frame by the sending node.

CS. Convergence sublayer. A sublayer of the AAL that performs a convergence function for ATM networks. Once a connection is established between communicating ATM devices, the CS accepts higher layer traffic for transmission through the network. Depending on the traffic type, certain header and/or trailer fields are added to the user data payload and formed into information packets called convergence sublayer protocol data units (CS-PDUs) and passed to the SAR sublayer for further processing. *See also* AAL and SAR.

CSA. Compression Service Adapter. Provides high-performance, hardware-based data compression capabilities by off-loading all compression- and decompression-related packet handling from the host processor. The CSA is available for Cisco 7500 series, Cisco 7000 series (equipped with the RSP7000), and Cisco 7200 series routers.

CSMA/CD. Carrier sense multiple access collision detect. Media-access mechanism wherein devices ready to transmit data first check the channel for a carrier. If no carrier is sensed for a specific period of time, a device can transmit. If two devices transmit at once, a collision occurs and is detected by all colliding devices. This collision subsequently delays retransmissions from those devices for some random length of time. CSMA/CD access is used by Ethernet and IEEE 802.3.

CSU. Channel service unit. A digital interface device that connects end-user equipment to the local digital telephone loop. Often referred to, together with DSU, as CSU/DSU. *See also* DSU.

custom queuing. A method of queuing that is used to guarantee bandwidth for traffic by assigning queue space based on protocol, port number, or other criteria. Custom queuing handles the queues in a round-robin fashion. *Compare with* priority queuing and WFQ.

cut-through packet switching. A packet-switching approach that streams data through a switch so that the leading edge of a packet exits the switch at the output port before the packet finishes entering the input port. A device using cut-through packet switching reads, processes, and forwards packets as soon as the destination address is looked up and the outgoing port is determined. Also known as on-the-fly packet switching. *Compare with* store and forward packet switching.

CWSI. CiscoWorks for Switched Internetworks. A suite of network management applications that enables you to configure, monitor, and manage a switched internetwork.

D

DARPA. Defense Advanced Research Projects Agency. A U.S. government agency that funded research for experimentation with the Internet. Evolved from ARPA, and then, in 1994, back to ARPA. *See also* ARPA.

data flow control layer. Layer 5 of the SNA architectural model. This layer determines and manages interactions between session partners, particularly data flow. Corresponds to the session layer of the OSI model.

datagram. A logical grouping of information sent as a network layer unit over a transmission medium without prior establishment of a virtual circuit. IP datagrams are the primary information units in the Internet.

data link control layer. Layer 2 in the SNA architectural model. This layer is responsible for the transmission of data over a particular physical link. Corresponds roughly to the data link layer of the OSI model.

data link layer. Layer 2 of the OSI reference model. This layer provides reliable transit of data across a physical link. The data link layer is concerned with physical addressing, network topology, line discipline, error notification, ordered delivery of frames, and flow control. The IEEE has divided this layer into two sublayers: the MAC sublayer and the LLC sublayer. Sometimes simply called link layer. Roughly corresponds to the data link control layer of the SNA model.

DBF. Distributed Bellman-Ford algorithm; distance-vector protocols are mainly based on variations of DBF.

DCE. Data communications equipment (EIA expansion) or data circuit-terminating equipment (ITU-T expansion). The devices and connections of a communications network that comprise the network end of the user-to-network interface. The DCE provides a physical connection to the network, forwards traffic, and provides a clocking signal used to synchronize data transmission between DCE and DTE devices. Modems and interface cards are examples of DCE. *Compare with* DTE.

D channel. Data channel. Full-duplex, 16-kbps (BRI) or 64-kbps (PRI) ISDN channel. *Compare with* B channel.

DDP. Datagram Delivery Protocol. An Apple Computer network layer protocol that is responsible for the socket-to-socket delivery of datagrams over an AppleTalk internetwork.

DDR. Dial-on-demand routing. A technique whereby a Cisco router can automatically initiate and close a circuit-switched session as transmitting stations demand.

DE. Discard eligible. A bit in a Frame Relay frame that, when set, indicates that the frame is eligible to be discarded because the frame contains data that is being transmitted in excess of the the CIR. *See also* Be and CIR.

decapsulation. The unwrapping of data from a particular protocol header. For example, when data is received on an Ethernet, the Ethernet header will be removed so that the data can be processed. *Compare with* encapsulation.

DECnet. Group of communications products (including a protocol suite) developed and supported by Digital Equipment Corporation.

decryption. The reverse application of an encryption algorithm to encrypted data, thereby restoring that data to its original, unencrypted state. *See also* encryption.

dedicated LAN. A network segment allocated to a single device. Used in LAN switched network topologies.

dedicated line. A communications line that is indefinitely reserved for transmissions, rather than switched as transmission is required. *See also* leased line.

default route. A routing table entry that is used to direct frames for which a next hop is not explicitly listed in the routing table.

default router. The router to which frames are directed when a next hop is not explicitly listed in the routing table. Also called a default gateway.

delay. The time between the initiation of a transaction by a sender and the first response received by the sender. Also, the time required to move a packet from source to destination over a given path.

Delay-sensitive traffic. Traffic that requires timeliness of delivery and varies its rate accordingly.

DES. Data Encryption Standard. A standard cryptographic algorithm developed by the U.S. National Bureau of Standards.

DES key. Data Encryption Standard key. A temporary session key, used in CET to encrypt data during the encrypted session. *See also* CET and DH.

designated router. *See* DR.

destination address. The address of a network device that is receiving data. *See also* source address.

DH. Diffie-Hellman. In CET, DH numbers are exchanged in the connection messages and are used to compute a common DES session key. *See also* CET and DES.

DHCP. Dynamic Host Configuration Protocol. Provides a mechanism for allocating IP addresses dynamically so that addresses can be reused when hosts no longer need them.

dial-up line. A communications circuit that is established by a switched-circuit connection using the telephone company network.

digital certificate. Used in IPSec. Contains information to identify a user or device, such as the name, serial number, company, or IP address. It also contains a copy of the device's public key. The certificate is itself signed by a Certification Authority (CA). *See also* CA, IKE, and IPSec.

distance vector routing algorithm. A class of routing algorithms that call for each router to send all or some portion of its routing table, but only to its neighbors. Also called Bellman-Ford routing algorithm and DBF. See also link state routing algorithm, DBF and SPF.

distributed switching. On Cisco 7500 series routers with an RSP and with VIP controllers, the VIP hardware can be configured to switch packets received by the VIP with no per-packet intervention on the part of the RSP.

distribution layer. Layer in a hierarchical network that provides policy-based connectivity.

DLCI. Data-link connection identifier. A value that identifies a PVC or SVC in a Frame Relay network. In the basic Frame Relay specification, DLCIs are locally significant (connected devices might use different values to specify the same connection). In the LMI extended specification, DLCIs are globally significant (DLCIs specify individual end devices). *See also* LMI.

DLSw. Data-link switching. An interoperability standard, described in RFC 1434, that provides a method for forwarding SNA and NetBIOS traffic over TCP/IP networks using data link layer switching and encapsulation. DLSw uses SSP instead of SRB, eliminating the major limitations of SRB, including hop-count limits, broadcast and unnecessary traffic, timeouts, lack of flow control, and lack of prioritization schemes. *See also* SRB and SSP.

DMZ. Demilitarized zone. A buffer between the corporate internetwork and the outside world. Also called an isolation LAN.

DNS. Domain Name Service, or Domain Name System. A protocol used in the Internet for translating names of network nodes into addresses.

domain.

1. In the Internet, a portion of the naming hierarchy tree that refers to general groupings of networks based on organization type or geography.

2. In Windows networking, a domain has security and administrative properties. Each domain must have at least one NT server.

DR. Designated Router. An OSPF router that generates LSAs for a multiaccess network and has other special responsibilities in running OSPF. OSPF routers elect one router to be a DR and one router to be a BDR on each multi-access segment so that the routers have a central point of contact for information exchange. Instead of each router exchanging updates with every other router on the segment, every router will exchange the information with the DR and BDR. The DR and BDR will relay the information to everybody else. *See also* BDR.

DS-0. Digital signal level 0. A framing specification used in transmitting digital signals over a single channel at 64-kbps on a T1 facility. *Compare with* DS-1 and DS-3.

DS-1. Digital signal level 1. A framing specification used in transmitting digital signals at 1.544 Mbps on a T1 facility (in the United States) or at 2.108 Mbps on an E1 facility (in Europe). *Compare with* DS-0 and DS-3.

DS-3. Digital signal level 3. A framing specification used for transmitting digital signals at 44.736 Mbps on a T3 facility. *Compare with* DS-0 and DS-1. *See also* E3 and T3.

DSS. Digital Signature Standard. A standard used in CET for generating public and private keys that are used to authenticate peer routers. *See also* CET.

DSU. Data service unit. A device used in digital transmission that adapts the physical interface on a DTE device to a transmission facility, such as T1 or E1. The DSU is also responsible for functions such as signal timing. Often referred to, together with CSU, as CSU/DSU. *See also* CSU.

DTE. Data terminal equipment. A device at the user end of a user-network interface that serves as a data source, destination, or both. DTE connects to a data network through a DCE device (for example, a modem) and typically uses clocking signals generated by the DCE. DTE includes devices such as computers, protocol translators, and multiplexers. *Compare with* DCE.

DUAL. Diffusing Update Algorithm. A convergence algorithm used in Enhanced IGRP that provides loop-free operation at every instant throughout a route computation. Allows routers involved in a topology change to synchronize at the same time, while not involving routers that are unaffected by the change. *See also* Enhanced IGRP.

duplexing. The same as mirroring disk drives on a file server, with the additional feature that the two mirrored hard drives are controlled by different disk controllers.

DVMRP. Distance Vector Multicast Routing Protocol. An internetwork gateway protocol, largely based on RIP, that implements a typical dense mode IP multicast scheme. DVMRP uses IGMP to exchange routing datagrams with its neighbors. *See also* IGMP.

dynamic routing. Routing that adjusts automatically to network topology or traffic changes. Also called adaptive routing.

E

E1. A wide-area digital transmission scheme used predominantly in Europe that carries data at a rate of 2.048 Mbps. E1 lines can be leased for private use from common carriers. *Compare with* T1. *See also* DS-1.

E3. A wide-area digital transmission scheme, used predominantly in Europe, that carries data at a rate of 34.368 Mbps. E3 lines can be leased for private use from common carriers. *Compare with* T3. *See also* DS-3.

efficiency. The measurement of how much effort is required to produce a certain amount of data throughput.

EGP. Exterior Gateway Protocol. An Internet protocol for exchanging routing information between autonomous systems. Documented in RFC 904. Not to be confused with the general term exterior gateway protocol. EGP is an obsolete protocol that has been replaced by BGP. *See also* BGP.

EIA. Electronic Industries Association. A group that specifies electrical transmission standards. The EIA and TIA have developed numerous well-known communications standards, including EIA/TIA-232 and EIA/TIA-449. *See also* TIA.

EIA-530. Refers to two electrical implementations of EIA/TIA-449: RS-422 (for balanced transmission) and RS-423 (for unbalanced transmission). *See also* RS-422, RS-423, and EIA/TIA-449.

EIA/TIA-232. A common physical layer interface standard, developed by EIA and TIA, that supports unbalanced circuits at signal speeds of up to 64 kbps. Closely resembles the V.24 specification. Formerly known as RS-232.

EIA/TIA-449. A popular physical layer interface developed by EIA and TIA. Essentially, a faster (up to 2 Mbps) version of EIA/TIA-232 capable of longer cable runs. Formerly called RS-449. *See also* EIA-530.

EIA/TIA-586. A standard that describes the characteristics and applications for various grades of UTP cabling. *See also* Category 1 cabling, Category 2 cabling, Category 3 cabling, Category 4 cabling, Category 5 cabling, and UTP.

EIGRP. *See* Enhanced IGRP.

EIR. Excess Information Rate. The maximum rate at which data can be transmitted in a Frame Relay network.

elastic. Traffic that is not sensitive to delay, such as file transfers. Traffic generated by these applications is called elastic because it can stretch to work under any delay conditions. *Compare with* inelastic.

electronic mail. A widely used network application in which mail messages are transmitted electronically between end users over various types of networks using various network protocols. Often called e-mail.

e-mail. *See* electronic mail.

encapsulation. The wrapping of data in a particular protocol header. For example, Ethernet data is wrapped in a specific Ethernet header before network transit. *Compare with* decapsulation. *See also* tunneling.

encapsulating bridging. Bridging that carries Ethernet frames from one router to another across disparate media, such as serial and FDDI lines. *Compare with* translational bridging.

encryption. The application of a specific algorithm to data so as to alter the appearance of the data, making it incomprehensible to those who are not authorized to see the information. *See also* decryption.

Enhanced IGRP. Enhanced Interior Gateway Routing Protocol. An advanced version of IGRP developed by Cisco. Provides superior convergence properties and operating efficiency, and combines the advantages of link state protocols with those of distance vector protocols. *Compare with* IGRP. *See also* IGP, OSPF, and RIP.

EPA. Encryption Port Adapter software for VIP2, available on the Cisco 7500 series platform.

Establishment controllers. In SNA, devices that control input and output operations of attached devices, such as terminals. Also known as cluster controllers.

Ethernet. A baseband LAN specification invented by Xerox Corporation and developed jointly by Xerox, Intel, and Digital Equipment Corporation. Ethernet networks use CSMA/CD and run over a variety of cable types at 10 Mbps. Ethernet is similar to the IEEE 802.3 series of standards. *See also* 10Base2, 10Base5, 10BaseF, 10BaseT, 10Broad36, and IEEE 802.3.

EtherTalk. A data link-layer implementation that allows proprietary AppleTalk protocols to communicate over Ethernet.

event. A network message indicating operational irregularities in physical elements of a network or a response to the occurrence of a significant task, typically the completion of a request for information. *See also* alarm and trap.

expansion. The process of running a compressed data set through an algorithm that restores the data set to its original size. *Compare with* compression.

explorer packet. A packet generated by an end station trying to find its way through a SRB network. Gathers a hop-by-hop description of a path through the network by being marked (updated) by each bridge that it traverses, thereby creating a complete topological map. Sometimes called an explorer frame. *See also* all-routes explorer packet, local explorer packet, and spanning explorer packet.

exterior routing protocols. See exterior gateway protocol.

exterior gateway protocol. Any internetwork protocol used to exchange routing information between autonomous systems. Not to be confused with Exterior Gateway Protocol (EGP), which is a particular instance of an exterior gateway protocol. *See also* BGP.

F

Fast Ethernet. Any of a number of 100-Mbps Ethernet specifications. Fast Ethernet offers a speed increase 10 times that of the 10BaseT Ethernet specification, while preserving qualities such as frame format, MAC mechanisms, and MTU. Such similarities allow the use of existing 10BaseT applications and network management tools on Fast Ethernet networks. Based on an extension to the IEEE 802.3 specification. *Compare with* Ethernet. *See also* 100BaseFX, 100BaseT, 100BaseT4, 100BaseTX, 100BaseX, and IEEE 802.3.

Fast EtherChannel. Grouping multiple Fast Ethernet interfaces into a single logical transmission path to deliver higher-speed connections.

fast switching. A Cisco feature whereby a route cache is used to expedite packet switching through a router. *Compare with* process switching.

fault management. One of five categories of network management defined by ISO for management of OSI networks. Fault management attempts to ensure that network faults are detected and controlled. *See also* accounting management, configuration management, performance management, and security management.

FCS. Frame check sequence. The extra characters added to a frame for error control purposes. Used in HDLC, Frame Relay, and other data link layer protocols.

FDDI. Fiber Distributed Data Interface. A LAN standard, defined by ANSI X3T9.5, specifying a 100-Mbps token-passing network using fiber-optic cable, with transmission distances of up to 2 km. FDDI uses a dual-ring architecture to provide redundancy. *Compare with* CDDI.

FDDI Ring Operations. When the FDDI ring becomes active from an inoperable state.

FDDITalk. A data link-layer implementation that allows proprietary AppleTalk protocols to communicate over FDDI.

FECN. Forward explicit congestion notification. A bit set by a Frame Relay network to inform DTE receiving the frame that congestion was experienced in the path from source to destination. DTE-receiving frames with the FECN bit set can request that higher-level protocols take flow-control action when appropriate. *Compare with* BECN.

FEP. Front-end processor. A device or board that provides network interface capabilities for a networked device. In SNA, typically an IBM 3745 device.

fiber-optic cable. A physical medium capable of conducting modulated light transmission. Compared with other transmission media, fiber-optic cable is more expensive but is not susceptible to electromagnetic interference, and is capable of higher data rates. Sometimes called optical fiber.

filter. Generally, a process or device that screens network traffic for certain characteristics, such as source address, destination address, or protocol, and determines whether to forward or discard that traffic based on the established criteria. *See also* access list.

firewall. A router or access server (or several routers or access servers) designated as a buffer between any connected public networks and a private network. A firewall router uses access lists and other methods to ensure the security of the private network. A firewall protects one network from another, untrusted network. This protection can be accomplished in many ways, but in principle, a firewall is a pair of mechanisms: one blocks traffic and the other permits traffic.

Flash memory. A technology developed by Intel and licensed to other semiconductor companies. Flash memory is nonvolatile storage that can be electrically erased and reprogrammed. Allows software images to be stored, booted, and rewritten as necessary.

flash update. A routing update sent asynchronously in response to a change in the network topology. *Compare with* routing update.

floating static route. A static route that has a higher administrative distance than a dynamically learned route so that it can be overridden by dynamically learned routing information.

flooding. A traffic-passing technique used by switches and bridges in which traffic received on an interface is sent out of all the interfaces of that device, except the interface on which the information was originally received.

flow control. A technique for ensuring that a transmitting entity, such as a modem, does not overwhelm a receiving entity with data. When the buffers on the receiving device are full, a message is sent to the sending device to suspend the transmission until the data in the buffers has been processed.

FOIRL. Fiber-optic interrepeater link. A fiber-optic signaling methodology based on the IEEE 802.3 fiber-optic specification. FOIRL is a precursor of the 10BaseFL specification, which is designed to replace it. *See also* 10BaseFL.

fractional T1. *See* channelized T1.

fragmentation. The process of breaking a packet into smaller units when transmitting over a network medium that cannot support a packet of the original size. *See also* reassembly.

frame. A logical grouping of information sent as a data link layer unit over a transmission medium. Often refers to the header and trailer, used for synchronization and error control, that surround the user data contained in the unit.

Frame Relay. An industry-standard, switched data link layer protocol that handles multiple virtual circuits using HDLC encapsulation between connected devices. Frame Relay is more efficient than X.25, the protocol for which it is generally considered a replacement. *See also* X.25.

Frame Relay traffic shaping. Rate enforcement, generalized BECN support, and priority/custom queuing support on a per-VC basis. *See also* traffic shaping.

FSIP. Fast Serial Interface Processor. The default serial interface processor for Cisco 7000 series routers, providing four or eight high-speed serial ports.

FTP. File Transfer Protocol. An application protocol, part of the TCP/IP protocol stack, used for transferring files between network nodes. FTP is defined in RFC 959.

full duplex. The capability for simultaneous data transmission between a sending station and a receiving station. *Compare with* half duplex and simplex.

full mesh. A network in which devices are organized in a mesh topology, with each network node having either a physical circuit or a virtual circuit connecting it to every other network node. *See also* mesh and partial mesh.

G

gateway. In the IP community, an older term referring to a routing device. Today, the term router is used to describe nodes that perform this function, and gateway refers to a special-purpose device that performs an application layer conversion of information from one protocol stack to another. *Compare with* router.

GNS. Get Nearest Server. A request packet sent by a client on an IPX network to locate the nearest active server of a particular type. An IPX network client issues a GNS request to solicit either a direct response from a connected server or a response from a router that tells it where on the internetwork the service can be located. GNS is part of the IPX SAP. *See also* IPX and SAP (Service Advertisement Protocol).

GUI. Graphical user interface. A user environment that uses pictorial as well as textual representations of the input and output of applications and the hierarchical or other data structure in which information is stored. Use of conventions, such as buttons, icons, and windows are typical, and many actions are performed using a pointing device (such as a mouse). Microsoft Windows and the Apple Macintosh are prominent examples of platforms utilizing a GUI. *Compare with* CLI.

H

half duplex. The capability for data transmission in only one direction at a time between a sending station and a receiving station. *Compare with* full duplex and simplex.

handshake. A sequence of messages exchanged between two or more network devices to ensure transmission synchronization.

HDLC. High-Level Data Link Control. A bit-oriented synchronous data link layer protocol developed by ISO. Derived from SDLC, HDLC specifies a data encapsulation method on synchronous serial links using frame characters and checksums. *See also* SDLC.

header. Control information placed before data when encapsulating that data for network transmission.

hello packet. A multicast packet that is used by routers for neighbor discovery and recovery. Hello packets also indicate that a client is still operating and network ready.

Hello protocol. A protocol used by OSPF systems for establishing and maintaining neighbor relationships.

helper address. An address configured on an interface to which broadcasts received on that interface will be sent.

holddown. A state into which a route is placed so that routers will neither advertise the route nor accept advertisements about the route for a specific length of time (the holddown period), so that the entire network has a chance to learn about the change. Holddown is used to flush bad information about a route from all routers in the network. A route is typically placed in holddown when a link in that route fails.

hop. The passage of a data packet between two network nodes (for example, between two routers). *See also* hop count.

hop count. A routing metric used to measure the distance between a source and a destination. IP RIP uses hop count as its sole metric. *See also* hop and RIP.

host. A computer system on a network. Similar to the term node except that host usually implies a computer system, whereas node generally applies to any networked system, including access servers and routers. *See also* node.

host number. Part of an IP address that designates which node on the subnetwork is being addressed. Also called a host address.

HSRP. Hot Standby Router Protocol. Provides a way for IP workstations to keep communicating on the internetwork even if their default router becomes unavailable, thereby providing high network availability and transparent network topology changes.

HTML. Hypertext markup language. A simple hypertext document formatting language that uses tags to indicate how a given part of a document should be interpreted by a viewing application, such as a WWW browser. *See also* hypertext and WWW browser.

HTTP. Hypertext Transfer Protocol. The TCP/IP protocol used to send hypertext documents.

hub.

1. Generally, a device that serves as the center of a star-topology network.

2. A hardware or software device that contains multiple independent but connected modules of network and internetwork equipment. Hubs can be active (where they repeat signals sent through them) or passive (where they do not repeat, but merely split, signals sent through them).

3. In Ethernet and IEEE 802.3, an Ethernet multiport repeater, sometimes referred to as a concentrator.

hypertext. Electronically stored text that allows direct access to other texts by way of encoded links. Hypertext documents can be created using HTML and often integrate images, sound, and other media that are commonly viewed using a World Wide Web browser. *See also* HTML, HTTP and WWW browser.

I

IAB. Internet Architecture Board. A board of internetwork researchers who discuss issues pertinent to Internet architecture. Responsible for appointing a variety of Internet-related groups such as IANA. *See also* IANA.

IANA. Internet Assigned Numbers Authority. An organization operated under the auspices of ISOC as a part of IAB. IANA delegates authority for IP address-space allocation and domain-name assignment to the NIC and other organizations. IANA also maintains a database of assigned protocol identifiers used in the TCP/IP stack, including autonomous system numbers. *See also* IAB and NIC.

ICMP. Internet Control Message Protocol. A network layer Internet protocol that reports errors and provides other information relevant to IP packet processing. Documented in RFC 792.

IDB. Interface Description Blocks. Provides a central location in memory for storing information about network interface cards for use by interface driver code.

IEEE. Institute of Electrical and Electronics Engineers. A professional organization whose activities include the development of communications and network standards. IEEE LAN standards are the predominant LAN standards today.

IEEE 802.1d. An IEEE specification which describes an algorithm that prevents bridging loops by creating a spanning tree. The algorithm was invented by Digital Equipment Corporation. The Digital algorithm and the IEEE 802.1 algorithm are not exactly the same, nor are they compatible. *See also* spanning tree, spanning-tree algorithm, and Spanning-Tree Protocol.

IEEE 802.2. An IEEE LAN protocol that specifies an implementation of the LLC sublayer of the data link layer. IEEE 802.2 handles errors, framing, flow control, and the network layer (Layer 3) service interface. Used in IEEE 802.3, IEEE 802.5, and FDDI LANs. *See also* IEEE 802.3 and IEEE 802.5.

IEEE 802.3. An IEEE LAN protocol that specifies an implementation of the physical layer and the MAC sublayer of the data link layer. IEEE 802.3 uses CSMA/CD access at a variety of speeds over a variety of physical media. Extensions to the IEEE 802.3 standard specify implementations for Fast Ethernet. Physical variations of the original IEEE 802.3 specification include 10Base2, 10Base5, 10BaseF, 10BaseT, and 10Broad36. Physical variations for Fast Ethernet include 100BaseT, 100BaseT4, and 100BaseX.

IEEE 802.5. An IEEE LAN protocol that specifies an implementation of the physical layer and MAC sublayer of the data link layer. IEEE 802.5 uses token passing access at 4 or 16 Mbps over STP cabling and is similar to IBM Token Ring. *See also* Token Ring.

IETF. Internet Engineering Task Force. A task force consisting of more than 80 working groups responsible for developing Internet standards.

IGMP. Internet Group Management Protocol. A protocol used by IP hosts to report their multicast group memberships to an adjacent multicast router. *See also* multicast router.

IGP. Interior Gateway Protocol. An Internet protocol used to exchange routing information within an autonomous system. Examples of common Internet IGPs include IGRP, OSPF, and RIP. *See also* IGRP, OSPF, and RIP.

IGRP. Interior Gateway Routing Protocol. An IGP developed by Cisco to address the problems associated with routing in large, heterogeneous networks. *Compare with* Enhanced IGRP. *See also* IGP, OSPF, and RIP.

IKE. Internet Key Exchange protocol. Used in IPSec to exchange digital certificates with the CA. *See also* CA, digital certificate and IPSEc.

inelastic. Traffic that is sensitive to delay, such as multimedia network applications. Traffic generated by these applications is called inelastic because it requires that certain minimum numbers of bits be transferred within a specific time frame. *Compare with* elastic.

interface.

1. A connection between two systems or devices.

2. In routing terminology, a network connection.

3. In telephony, a shared boundary defined by common physical interconnection characteristics, signal characteristics, and meanings of interchanged signals.

4. The boundary between adjacent layers of the OSI model.

Interior routing protocols. Routing protocols used by routers within the same autonomous system, such as RIP, IGRP, and Enhanced IGRP.

Internet. A term that refers to the largest global internetwork, connecting tens of thousands of networks worldwide and having a "culture" that focuses on research and standardization based on real-life use. Many leading-edge network technologies come from the Internet community. The Internet evolved in part from ARPANET. At one time, called the DARPA Internet. Not to be confused with the general term internet. *See also* ARPANET.

internet. Short for internetwork. Not to be confused with the Internet. *See also* internetwork.

internetwork. A collection of networks interconnected by routers and other devices that functions (generally) as a single network. Sometimes called an internet, which is not to be confused with the Internet.

internetworking. The industry that has arisen around the problem of connecting networks together. The term can refer to products, procedures, and technologies.

intranet. A network, internal to an organization, based on Internet and World Wide Web technology, that delivers immediate, up-to-date information and services to networked employees.

I/O. input/output. Typically used when discussing ports on a device where data comes in or goes out.

IOS™. Cisco's Internetworking Operating System.

IP. Internet Protocol. A network layer protocol in the TCP/IP stack offering a connectionless internetwork service. IP provides features for addressing, type-of-service specification, fragmentation and reassembly, and security. Documented in RFC 791.

IP address. A 32-bit address assigned to hosts using TCP/IP. An IP address belongs to one of five classes (A, B, C, D, or E) and is written as four octets separated with periods (dotted decimal format). Each address consists of a network number, an optional subnetwork number, and a host number. The network and subnetwork numbers together are used for routing, and the host number is used to address an individual host within the network or subnetwork. A subnet mask is used to extract network and subnetwork information from the IP address. Also called an Internet address. *See also* IP and subnet mask.

IP multicast. A routing technique that allows IP traffic to be propagated from one source to a number of destinations or from many sources to many destinations. Rather than send one packet to each destination, one packet is sent to a multicast group identified by a single IP destination group address.

IPCP. Internet Control Protocol. The part of the PPP protocol that negotiates an IP connection over PPP.

IPSec. A framework of open standards developed by the IETF. IPSec provides security for transmission of sensitive information over unprotected networks such as the Internet. IPSec acts at the network layer.

IPv6. IP version 6. Replacement for the current version of IP (version 4). IPv6 includes support for flow ID in the packet header, which can be used to identify flows. Formerly called Ipng (IP next generation).

IPX. Internetwork Packet Exchange. A NetWare network layer (Layer 3) protocol used for transferring data from servers to workstations.

IPX address. An IPX address is 80 bits long, with 32 bits for the network number and 48 bits for the node number.

IRB. Integrated Routing and Bridging. A Cisco IOS™ feature that interconnects VLANs and bridged domains to routed domains within the same router. IRB provides the capability to route between bridged and routed interfaces using a software-based interface called the BVI.

IS. Information Systems. A broad term used to describe the use of information technology in organizations. This includes the movement, storage, and use of information.

IS. Intermediate System. Routing node in an OSI network. *See also* IS-IS.

ISDN. Integrated Services Digital Network. A communication protocol, offered by telephone companies, that permits telephone networks to carry data, voice, and other source traffic. *See also* BRI, and PRI.

IS-IS. Intermediate System-to-Intermediate System. An OSI link-state hierarchical routing protocol based on DECnet Phase V routing whereby ISs (routers) exchange routing information based on a single metric to determine network topology.

ISL. Inter-Switch Link. A Cisco-proprietary protocol that maintains VLAN information as traffic flows between switches and routers.

ISO. International Organization for Standardization. An international organization that is responsible for a wide range of standards, including those relevant to networking. ISO developed the OSI reference model, a popular networking reference model.

ISOC. Internet Society. An international nonprofit organization, founded in 1992, that coordinates the evolution and use of the Internet.

isolation LAN. A buffer between the corporate internetwork and the outside world. The isolation LAN is called the demilitarized zone (DMZ) in some literature.

ISP. Internet service provider. A company that provides Internet access to other companies and individuals.

IT. Information Technology. Computers, networking devices, and networks used to transport, store, and manage information.

ITU-T. International Telecommunication Union Telecommunication Standardization Sector. An international body that develops worldwide standards for telecommunications technologies. The ITU-T carries out the functions of the former CCITT. *See also* CCITT.

J–K

kbps. Kilobits per second.

keepalive interval. The period of time between each keepalive message sent by a network device.

keepalive message. A message sent by one network device to inform another network device that the circuit between the two is still active.

L

LAN. Local area network. A high-speed, low-error data network covering a relatively small geographic area (up to a few thousand meters). LANs connect workstations, peripherals, terminals, and other devices in a single building or other geographically limited area. LAN standards specify cabling and signaling at the physical and data link layers of the OSI model. Ethernet, FDDI, and Token Ring are widely used LAN technologies. *Compare with* MAN and WAN.

LANE. LAN Emulation. Technology that allows an ATM network to function as a LAN backbone. The ATM network must provide multicast and broadcast support, address mapping (MAC-to-ATM), SVC management, and a usable packet format.

LAN Manager. Distributed NOS, developed by Microsoft, that supports a variety of protocols and platforms.

LAN switch. A high-speed switch that forwards packets between data-link segments. Most LAN switches forward traffic based on MAC addresses. This variety of LAN switch is sometimes called a frame switch. LAN switches are often categorized according to the method they use to forward traffic: cut-through packet switching or store-and-forward packet switching. Multilayer switches are an intelligent subset of LAN switches. *See also* cut-through packet switching and store and forward packet switching.

LAPB. Link Access Procedure, Balanced. A data link layer protocol in the X.25 protocol stack. LAPB is a bit-oriented protocol derived from HDLC. *See also* HDLC and X.25.

latency.

1. The delay between the time a device requests access to a network and the time it is granted permission to transmit.

2. The delay between the time a device receives a frame and the time the frame is forwarded out of the destination port.

leased line. A transmission line reserved by a communications carrier for the private use of a customer. A leased line is a type of dedicated line. *See also* dedicated line.

link. A network communications channel consisting of a circuit or transmission path and all related equipment between a sender and a receiver. Most often used to refer to a WAN connection. Sometimes referred to as a line or a transmission link.

link flapping. Links going up and down, which means a link is intermittently nonoperational. Link flapping can be caused by noise, misconfigurations or reconfigurations, or hardware failures.

link-state routing algorithm. A routing algorithm in which each router broadcasts or multicasts information regarding the cost of reaching each of its neighbors to all nodes in the internetwork. *Compare with* distance vector routing algorithm.

LLC. Logical Link Control. The higher of the two data link layer sublayers defined by the IEEE. The LLC sublayer handles error control, flow control, framing, and MAC-sublayer addressing. The most prevalent LLC protocol is IEEE 802.2, which includes both connectionless and connection-oriented variants. *See also* data link layer and MAC.

LLC2. Logical Link Control, type 2. A connection-oriented OSI LLC-sublayer protocol. *See also* LLC.

LMI. Local Management Interface. A set of enhancements to the basic Frame Relay specification. LMI includes support for a keepalive mechanism, which verifies that data is flowing; a multicast mechanism, which provides the network server with its local DLCI and the multicast DLCI; global addressing, which gives DLCIs global rather than local significance in Frame Relay networks; and a status mechanism, which provides an ongoing status report on the DLCIs known to the switch. Known as LMT in ANSI terminology.

load balancing. In routing, the ability of a router to distribute traffic over all of its network ports that are the same distance from the destination address. Good load-balancing algorithms use both line speed and reliability information. Load balancing increases the utilization of network segments, thus increasing effective network bandwidth.

local explorer packet. A packet generated by an end system in an SRB network to find a host connected to the local ring. If the local explorer packet fails to find a local host, the end system produces either a spanning explorer packet or an all-routes explorer packet. Sometimes called a local explorer frame. *See also* all-routes explorer packet, explorer packet, and spanning explorer packet.

LocalTalk. An Apple proprietary baseband protocol that operates at the data link and physical layers of the OSI reference model. LocalTalk uses CSMA/CD media access scheme and supports transmissions at speeds of 230 kbps.

LSA. Link-state advertisement. A broadcast packet used by link-state protocols that contains information about neighbors and path costs. LSAs are used by the receiving routers to maintain their routing tables. Sometimes called a link-state packet (LSP).

LSDV. Link segment delay value. The delay, in bit times, caused by a link segment. Used in the calculation of PDV for checking propagation delays in an ethernet network. *See also* PDV.

LSP. Link-state packet. *See* LSA.

LU. Logical unit. A primary component of SNA, an LU is an NAU that enables end users to communicate with each other and gain access to SNA network resources.

LU 6.2. Logical Unit 6.2. In SNA, an LU that provides peer-to-peer communication between programs in a distributed computing environment. APPC runs on LU 6.2 devices. *See also* APPC.

M

MAC. Media Access Control. The lower of the two sublayers of the data link layer defined by the IEEE. The MAC sublayer handles access to shared media, such as whether token passing or contention will be used. *See also* data link layer and LLC.

MAC address. A standardized data link layer address that is required for every port or device that connects to a LAN. Other devices in the network use these addresses to locate specific ports in the network and to create and update routing tables and data structures. MAC addresses are 6 bytes long and are controlled by the IEEE. Also known as a hardware address, a MAC-layer address, or a physical address. *Compare with* network address.

MacIP. A network layer protocol that encapsulates IP packets in AppleTalk packets for transmission over AppleTalk network.

MAN. Metropolitan-area network. A network that spans a metropolitan area. Generally, a MAN spans a larger geographic area than a LAN, but a smaller geographic area than a WAN. *Compare with* LAN and WAN.

managed device. In network management, a network device that can be managed by a network management protocol.

management database. A database containing information about managed devices.

management entity. An entity within an NMS that manages the network, using a network management protocol.

management proxy. An entity that provide management information on behalf of other entities.

MAU. Multistation access unit. A wiring concentrator to which all end stations in a Token Ring network connect. Also known as MSAU.

MB. Megabyte.

Mbps. Megabits per second.

MD5. Message Digest 5. An algorithm used for message authentication in SNMPv2. MD5 verifies the integrity of the communication, authenticates the origin, and checks for timeliness.

media. Plural of medium. The various physical environments through which transmission signals pass. Common network media include twisted-pair, coaxial and fiber-optic cable, and the atmosphere (through which microwave, laser, and infrared transmission occurs). Sometimes called physical media.

mesh. A network topology in which devices are organized in a manageable, segmented manner with many, often redundant, interconnections strategically placed between network nodes. *See also* full mesh and partial mesh.

message. An application layer (Layer 7) logical grouping of information, often composed of a number of lower-layer logical groupings such as packets.

metric. A standard of measurement, such as performance, that is used for measuring whether network management goals have been met. *See also* routing metric.

MHS. Message Handling Service. Netware message-delivery system that provides electronic mail transport.

MIB. Management Information Base. A management database that is used and maintained by a network management protocol such as SNMP. The value of a MIB object can be changed or retrieved using SNMP commands. MIB objects are organized in a tree structure that includes public (standard) and private (proprietary) branches.

millisecond. 1/1000 of a second.

Microsoft Access. A relational database application.

Microsoft Exchange. A messaging and collaboration application.

MIP. MultiChannel Interface Processor. An interface processor on the Cisco 7000 series routers that provides up to two channelized T1 or E1 connections via serial cables to a CSU. The two controllers on the MIP can each provide up to 24 T1 or 30 E1 channel-groups, with each channel-group presented to the system as a serial interface that can be configured individually.

mirroring. Synchronizing two disks on a file server, for redundancy.

MIS. Management of Information Systems. The design, implementation, management, and use of information technology in organizations.

modem. Modulator-demodulator. A device that converts digital signals to and from analog signals. Modems allow data to be transmitted over voice-grade telephone lines.

MPPP. Multilink Point-to-Point Protocol. A standard for aggregating multiple PPP links, defined in RFC 1717, that allows for multivendor interoperability. MPPP defines a way of sequencing and transmitting packets over multiple physical interfaces and defines a method of fragmenting and reassembling large packets.

MTBF. Mean time between failure. The average time between failures of a device. Used as a standard for comparing the availability of devices.

MTU. Maximum transmission unit. The maximum packet size, in bytes, that a particular interface can handle.

MTU Discovery. A function that allows software to dynamically discover and use the largest frame size that will traverse the network without requiring fragmentation.

multicast. Single packets copied by the network and sent to a specific subset of network addresses. These addresses are specified in the destination address field. *Compare with* broadcast and unicast.

multicast address. A single address that refers to multiple network devices. Synonymous with group address. *Compare with* broadcast address and unicast address. *See also* multicast.

multicast group. A dynamically determined group of IP hosts identified by a single IP multicast address.

multicast router. A router used to send IGMP query messages on their attached local networks. Host members of a multicast group respond to a query by sending IGMP reports, noting the multicast groups to which they belong. The multicast router takes responsibility for forwarding multicast datagrams from one multicast group to all other networks that have members in the group. *See also* IGMP.

multilayer switch. A switch that filters and forwards packets based on MAC addresses and network addresses. A subset of LAN switch.

N

NAK. Negative acknowledgement. A response sent from a receiving device to a sending device indicating that the information received contained errors. *Compare with* acknowledgement.

NAT. Network Address Translation. A feature in the Cisco routers that enables you to translate private addresses into registered IP addresses only when needed, thereby reducing the need for registered IP addresses.

NAU. Network addressable unit. An SNA term for an addressable entity. Examples include LUs. NAUs generally provide upper-level network services. *Compare with* path control network.

NBMA. Nonbroadcast multiaccess. A multiaccess network that either does not support broadcasting (such as X.25) or in which broadcasting is not feasible (for example, an SMDS broadcast group or an extended Ethernet that is too large).

NBP. Name Binding Protocol. An AppleTalk transport layer protocol that translates a character string name into an internetwork address.

NBT. NetBIOS over TCP. A transport layer protocol for transporting the NetBIOS session layer protocol over TCP/IP.

NC. Network computer. A computer with limited local functionality, used to access server-based applications and data.

NCP. NetWare Core Protocol. A series of server routines designed to satisfy application requests.

NDIS. Network driver interface specification. The specification for a generic, hardware- and protocol-independent device driver for NICs. Produced by Microsoft.

neigboring router. In OSPF, two routers that have interfaces to a common network.

NetBIOS. Network Basic Input/Output System. NetBIOS is a session layer protocol. It is used by applications on a LAN to request services from lower-level network processes.

NetFlow switching. Cisco's NetFlow switching identifies traffic flows between internetwork hosts and then, on a connection-oriented basis, switches packets in these flows at the same time that it applies relevant services, such as security, QoS, and traffic accounting.

NetWare. A popular distributed NOS developed by Novell. Provides transparent remote file access and numerous other distributed network services.

network. A collection of computers, printers, routers, switches, and other devices that are able to communicate with each other over some transmission medium.

network address. A network layer address referring to a logical, rather than a physical, network device. Also called a protocol address. *Compare with* MAC address.

network layer. Layer 3 of the OSI reference model. This layer provides connectivity and path selection between two end systems. The network layer is the layer at which routing occurs. Corresponds roughly with the path control layer of the SNA model.

network management. Systems or actions that help maintain, characterize, or troubleshoot a network. *See also* NMS.

network management protocol. The protocol that management entities within NMSs use to communicate with agents in managed devices. The Simple Network Management Protocol (SNMP) is a well-known network management protocol.

NFS. Network File System. As commonly used, a distributed file system protocol suite developed by Sun Microsystems that allows remote file access across a network.

NIC.

1. Network interface card. A board that provides network communication capabilities to and from a computer system. Also called an adapter.

2. Network Information Center. An organization that serves the Internet community by supplying user assistance, documentation, training, and other services.

NIS. Network Information Services. A protocol developed by Sun Microsystems for the administration of network-wide databases. The service essentially uses two programs: one for finding a NIS server and one for accessing the NIS databases.

NLM. NetWare Loadable Module. An individual program that can be loaded into memory and function as part of the NetWare NOS.

NLSP. NetWare Link Services Protocol. A link-state routing protocol for IPX, based on IS-IS. *See also* IS-IS.

NMS. Network management system. A system responsible for managing at least part of a network. An NMS is generally a reasonably powerful and well-equipped computer such as an engineering workstation. NMSs communicate with agents to help keep track of network statistics and resources.

node. An endpoint of a network connection or a junction common to two or more lines in a network. Nodes can be processors, controllers, or workstations. Nodes, which vary in routing and other functional capabilities, can be interconnected by links and serve as control points in the network. Node is sometimes used generically to refer to any entity that can access a network and is frequently used interchangeably with device. *See also* host.

Non-local traffic. Traffic that needs to travel to different network segments. This is a potential bottleneck in the network.

Non-stub area. A resource-intensive OSPF area that carries a default route, static routes, intra-area routes, interarea routes, and external routes. *Compare with* stub area. *See also* ASBR and OSPF.

NOC. Network Operation Center. The organization responsible for maintaining a network.

NOS. Network operating system. A generic term used to refer to what are really distributed file systems. Examples of NOSs include NetWare, NFS, and VINES.

NSM. Cisco's Netsys Service-Level Management Suite, an integrated end-to-end network management solution combined with service-level management.

NT1. Network Termination 1. In ISDN, a device that provides the interface between customer premises equipment and central office switching equipment.

NTP. Network Time Protocol. Protocol built on top of TCP that assures accurate local time-keeping with reference to radio and atomic clocks located on the Internet.

NVRAM. Nonvolatile RAM. RAM that retains its contents when a unit is powered off.

NWLink. NetBIOS over IPX. A transport layer protocol for transporting the NetBIOS session layer protocol over IPX. NWLink uses IPX type-20 packets to exchange registration and browsing information.

O

ODBC. Open Database Connectivity. An API for database access. It uses SQL as its database access language.

ODI. Open Data-Link Interface. A Novell specification providing a standardized interface for NICs (network interface cards) that allows multiple protocols to use a single NIC. *See also* NIC (network interface card).

optimum switching. Optimum switching is available on the Route/Switch Processor (RSP) only, on Cisco 7500 series routers. Optimum switching is similar to fast switching but is faster.

OSI. Open System Interconnection. An international standardization program created by ISO and ITU-T to develop standards for data networking that facilitate multivendor equipment interoperability.

OSI reference model. Open System Interconnection reference model. A network architectural model developed by ISO and ITU-T. The model consists of seven layers, each of which specifies particular network functions such as addressing, flow control, error control, encapsulation, and reliable message transfer. The highest layer (the application layer) is closest to the user; the lowest layer (the physical layer) is closest to the media technology. *See* application layer, data link layer, network layer, physical layer, presentation layer, session layer, and transport layer.

OSPF. Open Shortest Path First. A link-state, hierarchical IGP routing algorithm proposed as a successor to RIP in the Internet community. OSPF features include least-cost routing, multipath routing, and load balancing. OSPF was derived from an early version of the IS-IS protocol. *See also* Enhanced IGRP, IGP, IGRP, IS-IS, and RIP.

OUI. Organizational Unique Identifier. Three octets assigned by the IEEE, used in the 48-bit MAC addresses.

P

packet. A logical grouping of information that includes a header containing control information and (usually) user data. Packets are most often used to refer to network layer units of data. *See also* PDU.

packet switching. A networking method in which nodes share bandwidth with each other when sending packets.

PAP.

1. Password Authentication Protocol. An authentication protocol that allows PPP peers to authenticate one another. The remote router attempting to connect to the local router is required to send an authentication request. Unlike CHAP, PAP passes the password and host name or username in the clear (unencrypted). PAP does not itself prevent unauthorized access, but merely identifies the remote end. The router or access server then determines whether that user is allowed access. PAP is supported only on PPP lines. *Compare with* CHAP.

2. Printer-Access Protocol. AppleTalk protocol that allows client workstations to establish connections with servers, particularly printers.

partial mesh. A network in which devices are organized in a mesh topology, with some network nodes organized in a full mesh, but with others that are connected to only one or two other nodes in the network. *See also* full mesh and mesh.

PAT. Port Address Translation. A feature in the Cisco routers that allows you to translate private addresses into registered IP addresses, in a many-to-one relationship, by using port numbers. This translation is done only when needed, thereby reducing the need for registered IP addresses.

path control layer. Layer 3 in the SNA architectural model. This layer performs sequencing services related to proper data reassembly. The path control layer is also responsible for routing. Corresponds roughly with the network layer of the OSI model.

path control network. An SNA concept that consists of lower-level components that control the routing and data flow through an SNA network and handle physical data transmission between SNA nodes. *Compare with* NAU.

payload. The portion of a frame that contains upper-layer information (data).

PC. Personal Computer.

PCMCIA card. Personal Computer Memory Card International Association card, for a PC.

PDC. Primary Domain Controller. A process that runs on a Windows NT server to create and manage domains.

PDM. Protocol-dependent modules, at the network layer in EIGRP.

PDU. Protocol data unit. An OSI term for packet. A packet of data consisting of control information and user information that is to be exchanged between communicating peers in a network. In general, a PDU is a segment of data generated by a specific layer of a protocol stack, usually containing information from the next higher layer, encapsulated together with header and trailer information generated by the layer in question. *See also* BPDU and packet.

PDV. Path delay value. The total round-trip propagation delay in an ethernet network.

performance management. One of five categories of network management defined by ISO for management of OSI networks. Performance management subsystems are responsible for analyzing and controlling network performance including network throughput and error rates. *See also* accounting management, configuration management, fault management, and security management.

physical control layer. Layer 1 in the SNA architectural model. This layer is responsible for the physical specifications for the physical links between end systems. Corresponds to the physical layer of the OSI model.

physical layer. Layer 1 of the OSI reference model. The physical layer defines the electrical, mechanical, procedural, and functional specifications for activating, maintaining, and deactivating the physical link between end systems.

pilot. A pilot of a network is a scaled-down prototype used to demonstrate basic functionality, typically used for smaller networks. *See also* prototype.

PIM. Protocol Independent Multicast. A multicast routing architecture that allows the addition of IP multicast routing on existing IP networks.

ping. Packet internet groper. An ICMP echo message and its reply. Often used to test the reachability of a network device.

PIX. Cisco's Private Internet Exchange Firewall. *See also* firewall.

PLP. Packet level protocol. A network layer protocol in the X.25 protocol stack. Sometimes called X.25 Level 3 or X.25 Protocol. *See also* X.25.

policy routing. A routing scheme that forwards packets to specific interfaces based on user-configured policies. Such policies might specify that traffic sent from a particular network should be forwarded out one interface, while all other traffic should be forwarded out another interface.

port.

1. An interface on an internetworking device (such as a router).

2. In IP terminology, an upper-layer process that receives information from lower layers.

3. To rewrite software or microcode so that it will run on a different hardware platform or in a different software environment than that for which it was originally designed.

POS. Packet-over-SONET. A technology that maps IP packets into SONET frames in hardware and transports them over the optical SONET network.

PPP. Point-to-Point Protocol. A successor to SLIP that provides router-to-router and host-to-network connections over synchronous and asynchronous circuits. *See also* SLIP.

pps. Packets-per-second. Used as a measurement of throughput and performance of networks and networking devices.

presentation layer. Layer 6 of the OSI reference model. This layer ensures that information sent by the application layer of one system will be readable by the application layer of another. The presentation layer is also concerned with the data structures used by programs and therefore negotiates data transfer syntax for the application layer. Corresponds roughly with the presentation services layer of the SNA model.

presentation services layer. Layer 6 of the SNA architectural model. This layer provides network resource management, session presentation services, and some application management. Corresponds roughly with the presentation layer of the OSI model.

PRI. Primary Rate Interface. ISDN interface to primary rate access. Primary rate access consists of a single 64-kbps D channel plus 23 (T1) or 30 (E1) B channels for voice or data. *Compare with* BRI. *See also* ISDN.

priority queuing. A method of queuing that is used to guarantee bandwidth for traffic by assigning queue space based on protocol, port number, or other criteria. Priority queuing has four queues: high, medium, normal, and low; the high queue is always emptied first. *Compare with* custom queuing and WFQ.

private addresses. Reserved IP addresses, defined by RFC 1918, to be used only internally to a company's network. The addresses are: 10.0.0.0 to 10.255.255.255, 172.16.0.0 to 172.31.255.255, and 192.168.0.0 to 192.168.255.255.

proactive network management. Monitoring the network even when it is not having problems.

process switching. An operation that provides full route evaluation and per-packet load balancing across parallel WAN links. Involves the transmission of entire frames to the router CPU, where they are repackaged for delivery to or from a WAN interface, with the router making a route selection for each packet. Process switching is the most resource-intensive switching operation that the CPU can perform.

protocol. The formal description of a set of rules and conventions that govern how devices on a network exchange information.

protocol stack. A set of related communications protocols that operate together and, as a group, address communication at some or all of the seven layers of the OSI reference model. Not every protocol stack covers each layer of the model, and often a single protocol in the stack addresses a number of layers at once. TCP/IP is a typical protocol stack.

protocol suite. See protocol stack.

prototype. A prototype of a network is an implementation of a portion of the network to prove that the design meets the requirements typically used for larger networks. *See also* pilot.

provisioning. Defining the type of WAN, including the specifications and options, desired.

proxy. An entity that, in the interest of efficiency, essentially stands in for another entity.

proxy ARP. Proxy Address Resolution Protocol. A variation of the ARP protocol in which an intermediate device (for example, a router) sends an ARP response on behalf of an end node to the requesting host. Proxy ARP can lessen bandwidth use on slow-speed WAN links. *See also* ARP.

proxy explorer. A technique that minimizes exploding explorer packet traffic propagating through an SRB network by creating an explorer packet reply cache, the entries of which are reused when subsequent explorer packets need to find the same host.

PSDN. Packet-switched data network. A network that utilizes packet-switching technology for data transfer.

PSTN. Public Switched Telephone Network. The variety of telephone networks and services in place worldwide.

PVC. Permanent virtual circuit. A virtual circuit that is permanently established. PVCs save bandwidth associated with circuit establishment and tear down in situations where certain virtual circuits must exist all the time. Called a permanent virtual connection in ATM terminology. *Compare with* SVC.

Q

QoS. Quality of service. A measure of performance for a transmission system that reflects its transmission quality and service availability.

query. A message used to inquire about the value of some variable or set of variables.

queue.

1. Generally, an ordered list of elements waiting to be processed.

2. In routing, a backlog of packets waiting to be forwarded over a router interface.

R

RAM. Random-access memory. Volatile memory that can be read and written by a microprocessor.

RARP. Reverse Address Resolution Protocol. A protocol in the TCP/IP stack that provides a method for finding IP addresses based on MAC addresses. *Compare with* ARP.

Rate-sensitive traffic. Traffic that is willing to give up timeliness for guaranteed rate.

RDP. Router Discovery Protocol. Protocol that allows a workstation to learn the address of a router.

reassembly. The putting back together of an IP datagram at the destination after it has been fragmented either at the source or at an intermediate node. *See also* fragmentation.

redistribution. Allowing routing information discovered through one routing protocol to be distributed in the update messages of another routing protocol. Sometimes called route redistribution.

redundancy. The duplication of devices, services, or connections so that, in the event of a failure, the redundant devices, services, or connections can perform the work of those that failed.

reliability. The ratio of expected to received keepalives from a link. If the ratio is high, the line is reliable. Used as a routing metric.

repeater. A device that regenerates and propagates electrical signals between two network segments. *See also* segment.

Response time. The amount of time to receive a response to a request for a service from the network system.

RFC. Request For Comments. A document series used as the primary means for communicating information about the Internet. RFCs are available online from numerous sources.

RFP. Request for proposal. A formal document inviting proposals to be submitted for a project (for example, to perform a specific task or to sell a product). The RFP may specify the contents and format of the proposal as well as details of what is expected for the final project.

ring. A connection of two or more stations in a logically circular topology. Information is passed sequentially between active stations. Token Ring, FDDI, and CDDI are based on this topology.

ring topology. A network topology that consists of a series of repeaters connected to one another by unidirectional transmission links to form a single closed loop. Each station on the network connects to the network at a repeater. Although logically a ring, ring topologies are most often organized in a closed-loop star. *Compare with* bus topology, star topology, and tree topology.

RIP.

1. Routing Information Protocol. A distance vector IGP, RIP uses hop count as a routing metric. *See also* Enhanced IGRP, hop count, IGP, IGRP, and OSPF.

2. IPX Routing Information Protocol. A distance vector routing protocol for IPX.

RJ connector. Registered jack connector. Standard connectors originally used to connect telephone lines. RJ connectors are now used for telephone connections and for 10BaseT and other types of network connections. RJ-11, RJ-12, and RJ-45 are popular types of RJ connectors.

rlogin. Remote login. A terminal emulation program, similar to Telnet, offered in most UNIX implementations.

RMON. Remote Monitoring. An MIB agent specification that defines functions for the remote monitoring of networked devices. The RMON specification provides numerous monitoring, problem detection, and reporting capabilities.

ROM. Read-only memory. Nonvolatile memory that can be read, but not written, by the microprocessor.

route. A path through an internetwork.

routed protocol. A protocol that can be routed by a router. A routed protocol contains enough network-layer addressing information for user traffic to be directed from one network to another network. Routed protocols define the format and use of the fields within a packet. Packets that use a routed protocol are conveyed from end system to end system through an internetwork. Examples of routed protocols include AppleTalk, DECnet, and IP.

route summarization. The consolidation of advertised addresses in a routing table. Summarizing routes reduces the number of routes in the routing table, the routing update traffic, and overall router overhead. Also called route aggregation.

router. A network layer device that uses one or more metrics to determine the optimal path along which network traffic should be forwarded. Routers forward packets from one network to another based on network layer information. Occasionally called a gateway (although this definition of gateway is becoming increasingly outdated). *Compare with* gateway.

routing. The process of finding a path to a destination host. Routing is complex in large networks because of the many potential intermediate destinations a packet might traverse before reaching its destination host. Routing occurs at Layer 3, the network layer.

routing domain. A group of end systems and intermediate systems operating under the same set of administrative rules.

routing metric. A standard of measurement, such as path length, that is used by routing algorithms to determine the optimal path to a destination. This information is stored in routing tables. Metrics include bandwidth, communication cost, delay, hop count, load, MTU, path cost, and reliability. Sometimes referred to simply as a metric. *See also* cost.

routing protocol. A routing protocol supports a routed protocol by providing mechanisms for sharing routing information. Routing protocol messages move between the routers. A routing protocol allows the routers to communicate with other routers to update and maintain routing tables. Routing protocol messages do not carry end-user traffic from network to network. A routing protocol uses the routed protocol to pass information between routers. Examples of routing protocols are IGRP, OSPF, and RIP.

routing table. A table stored in a router or some other internetworking device that keeps track of routes to particular network destinations and metrics associated with those routes.

routing update. A message sent from a router to indicate network reachability and associated cost information. Routing updates are typically sent at regular intervals and after a change in network topology. *Compare with* flash update.

RPC. Remote-procedure call. The technological foundation of client/server computing. RPCs are procedure calls that are built or specified by clients and executed on servers, with the results returned over the network to the clients. *See also* client/server computing.

RS-232. A popular physical layer interface. Now known as EIA/TIA-232. *See* EIA/TIA-232.

RS-422. A balanced electrical implementation of EIA/TIA-449 for high-speed data transmission. Now referred to collectively with RS-423 as EIA-530. *See also* EIA-530 and RS-423.

RS-423. An unbalanced electrical implementation of EIA/TIA-449 for EIA/TIA-232 compatibility. Now referred to collectively with RS-422 as EIA-530. *See also* EIA-530 and RS-422.

RS-449. A popular physical layer interface. Now known as EIA/TIA-449. *See* EIA/TIA-449.

RSP. Route/Switch Processor (RSP), on Cisco 7500 series routers.

RSRB. Remote source-route bridging. An SRB over WAN links.

RSVP. Resource Reservation Protocol. A protocol that supports the reservation of resources across an IP network. Also known as Resource Reservation Setup Protocol.

RST. Reset bit in a TCP segment.

RTMP. Routing Table Maintenance Protocol. An AppleTalk distance vector routing protocol.

RTP. Real-time Transport Protocol. A protocol used for carrying packetized audio and video traffic over an IP network.

S

SAP.

1. Service access point. A field defined by the IEEE 802.2 specification that is part of an address specification.

2. Service Advertisement Protocol. An IPX protocol that provides a means of informing network clients, via routers and servers, of available network resources and services. *See also* IPX.

SAR. Segmentation and Reassembly. A sublayer of the AAL that segments each CS-PDU received from the CS into smaller units and adds a header and/or trailer field, depending on the traffic type, to form 48-byte payloads called segmentation and reassembly sublayer protocol data units (SAR-PDUs).

SDLC. Synchronous Data Link Control. An SNA data link layer communications protocol. SDLC is a bit-oriented, full-duplex serial protocol that has spawned numerous similar protocols, including HDLC and LAPB. *See also* HDLC and LAPB.

security management. One of five categories of network management defined by ISO for management of OSI networks. Security management subsystems are responsible for controlling access to network resources. *See also* accounting management, configuration management, fault management, and performance management.

segment.

1. A section of a network that is bounded by bridges, routers, or switches.

2. In a LAN using a bus topology, a continuous electrical circuit that is often connected to other such segments with repeaters.

3. In the TCP specification, a single transport layer unit of information.

server. A node or software program that provides services to clients. *See also* client.

session. A related set of communications transactions between two or more network devices.

session layer. Layer 5 of the OSI reference model. This layer establishes, manages, and terminates sessions between applications and manages data exchange between presentation layer entities. Corresponds to the data flow control layer of the SNA model.

shielded cable. A cable that has a layer of shielded insulation to reduce electromagnetic interference.

silicon switching. With this type of switching, an incoming packet matches an entry in the silicon-switching cache located in the SSE of the SSP module. This module is available only on Cisco 7000 series routers.

simplex. The capability for data transmission in only one direction between a sending station and a receiving station. *Compare with* full duplex and half duplex

SIN. Ships-in-the-night model of routing used in EIGRP. Each network layer client protocol has its own separate hellos, timers, and metrics.

single-route packet. A packet in an SRB network that follows only one specific path to its destination. Also known as a single-route frame. *See also* SRB.

sliding window flow control. A method of flow control in which a receiver gives a transmitter permission to transmit data until a window is full. When the window is full, the transmitter must stop transmitting until the receiver advertises a larger window. TCP, other transport protocols, and several data link layer protocols use this method of flow control.

SLIP. Serial Line Internet Protocol. A standard protocol for point-to-point serial connections using a variation of TCP/IP. A predecessor of PPP. *See also* PPP.

SMDS. Switched Multimegabit Data Service. A high-speed, packet-switched, datagram-based WAN networking technology offered by the telephone companies.

SMI. Structure of Management Information. A document (RFC 1155) specifying rules used to define managed objects in the MIB. *See also* MIB.

SMTP. Simple Mail Transfer Protocol. An Internet protocol that provides electronic mail services.

SNA. Systems Network Architecture. A large, complex, feature-rich network architecture developed in the 1970s by IBM. Similar in some respects to the OSI reference model, but with a number of differences. SNA is essentially composed of seven layers. *See* data flow control layer, data link control layer, path control layer, physical control layer, presentation services layer, transaction services layer, and transmission control layer.

SNMP. Simple Network Management Protocol. A network management protocol used almost exclusively in TCP/IP networks. SNMP provides a means to monitor and control network devices, and to manage configurations, statistics collection, performance, and security. *See also* SNMP communities and SNMPv2.

SNMP communities. Authentication scheme that enables an intelligent network device to validate SNMP requests from sources such as the NMS. *See also* SNMP.

SNMPv2. SNMP Version 2. Version 2 of the popular network management protocol. SNMPv2 supports centralized as well as distributed network management strategies, and includes improvements in the SMI, protocol operations, management architecture, and security. *See also* SNMP.

socket. A software structure operating as a communications endpoint within a network device. In an AppleTalk node, a unique, addressable location.

SOHO. Small office/home office.

SONET. Synchronous Optical Network. A high-speed (up to 2.5 Gbps) synchronous network specification developed by Bellcore and designed to run on optical fiber. Approved as an international standard in 1988.

source address. The address of a network device that is sending data. *See also* destination address.

spanning explorer packet. A packet that follows a statically configured spanning tree when looking for paths in an SRB network. Also known as a limited-route explorer, or a single-route explorer packet or frame. *See also* all-routes explorer packet, explorer packet, and local explorer packet.

spanning tree. A loop-free subset of a network topology. *See also* Spanning-Tree Algorithm and Spanning-Tree Protocol.

Spanning-Tree Algorithm. An algorithm used by the Spanning-Tree Protocol to create a spanning tree. Sometimes abbreviated STA. *See also* spanning tree and Spanning-Tree Protocol.

Spanning-Tree Protocol. A bridge protocol that utilizes the Spanning-Tree algorithm, enabling a learning bridge to dynamically work around loops in a network topology by creating a spanning tree. Bridges exchange BPDU messages with other bridges to detect loops, and then remove the loops by shutting down selected bridge interfaces. Refers to both the IEEE 802.1 Spanning-Tree Protocol standard and the earlier Digital Equipment Corporation Spanning-Tree Protocol on which it is based. The IEEE version supports bridge domains and allows the bridge to construct a loop-free topology across an extended LAN. The IEEE version is generally preferred over the Digital version. Sometimes abbreviated STP. *See also* BPDU, spanning tree, and Spanning-Tree algorithm.

SPF. Shortest path first. A routing algorithm that iterates on length of path to determine a shortest-path spanning tree. Commonly used in link-state routing algorithms. Also called Dijkstra's algorithm. *See also* link state routing algorithm.

SPID. Service profile identifier. A number that some service providers use to define the services to which an ISDN device subscribes. The ISDN device uses the SPID when accessing the switch that initializes the connection to a service provider.

split horizon. A routing rule that states that a router cannot send routing information about a network out the same interface from which it learned that information. A router knows the interface that it learned information from by looking in its routing table. Split-horizon updates are useful in preventing routing loops.

SPP. Sequenced Packet Protocol. Xerox Networking Systems (XNS) transport mechanism.

SPX. Sequenced Packet Exchange. A reliable, connection-oriented protocol that supplements the datagram service provided by the IPX protocol. Novell derived this commonly used NetWare transport protocol from the SPP of the XNS protocol suite.

SQL. Structured Query Language. Used for accessing databases.

SQL server. A server running the Structured Query Language. A relational database and relational database management system for the Microsoft Windows platform.

SRB. Source-route bridging. A method of bridging originated by IBM and popular in Token Ring networks. In an SRB network, the entire route to a destination is predetermined, in real time, prior to the sending of data to the destination. *Compare with* transparent bridging.

SRT. Source-route transparent bridging. An IBM bridging scheme that merges the two most prevalent bridging strategies, SRB and transparent bridging. SRT employs both technologies in one device to satisfy the needs of all nodes. No translation between bridging protocols is necessary. *Compare with* SR/TLB.

SR/TLB. Source-route translational bridging. A method of bridging in which source-route stations can communicate with transparent bridge stations with the help of an intermediate bridge that translates between the two bridge protocols. *Compare with* SRT.

SSE. Silicon Switching Engine. A routing and switching mechanism that compares the data link or network layer header of an incoming packet to a silicon-switching cache, determines the appropriate action (routing or bridging), and forwards the packet to the proper interface. The SSE is directly encoded in the hardware of the SSP of a Cisco 7000 series router. It can therefore perform switching independently of the system processor, making the execution of routing decisions much quicker than if they were encoded in software. *See also* silicon switching and SSP.

SSP.

1. Silicon Switch Processor. A high-performance silicon switch for Cisco 7000 series routers that provides distributed processing and control for interface processors. *See also* silicon switching and SSE.

2. Switch-to-switch protocol. A protocol specified in the DLSw standard that routers use to establish DLSw connections, locate resources, forward data, and handle flow control and error recovery. *See also* DLSw.

S/T interface. In ISDN, the connection between a BRI interface and an NT1 device.

star topology. A LAN topology in which endpoints on a network are connected to a common central switch by point-to-point links. A ring topology that is organized as a star implements a unidirectional closed-loop star, instead of point-to-point links. *Compare with* bus topology, ring topology, and tree topology.

static route. A route that is explicitly configured and entered into the routing table.

store and forward packet switching. A packet-switching technique in which frames are completely processed before being forwarded out the appropriate port. This processing includes calculating the CRC and checking the destination address. In addition, frames must be temporarily stored until network resources (such as an unused link) are available to forward the message. *Compare with* cut-through packet switching.

STP.

1. Shielded twisted-pair. A two-pair wiring medium used in a variety of network implementations. STP cabling has a layer of shielded insulation to reduce EMI. *Compare with* UTP. *See also* twisted pair.

2. *See* Spanning-Tree Protocol.

stub area. An OSPF area that carries a default route, intra-area routes, and interarea routes, but does not carry external routes. *Compare with* non-stub area. *See also* ASBR and OSPF.

stub network. A stub network is a part of an internetwork that can only be reached by one path; a network that has only a single connection to a router.

subinterface. One of a number of virtual interfaces on a single physical interface.

subnet. *See* subnetwork.

subnet address. A portion of an IP address that is specified as the subnetwork by the subnet mask. *See also* IP address, subnet mask, and subnetwork.

subnet mask. A 32-bit number that is associated with an IP address; each bit in the subnet mask indicates how to interpret the corresponding bit in the IP address. In binary, a subnet mask bit of one indicates that the corresponding bit in the IP address is a network or subnet bit; a subnet mask bit of zero indicates that the corresponding bit in the IP address is a host bit. The subnet mask then indicates how many bits have been borrowed from the host field for the subnet field. Sometimes referred to simply as mask. *See also* IP address.

subnetwork. In IP networks, a network sharing a particular subnet address. Subnetworks are networks arbitrarily segmented by a network administrator in order to provide a multilevel, hierarchical routing structure while shielding the subnetwork from the addressing complexity of attached networks. Sometimes called a subnet. *See also* IP address, subnet address, and subnet mask.

SVC. Switched virtual circuit. A virtual circuit that is dynamically established on demand and is torn down when transmission is complete. SVCs are used in situations where data transmission is sporadic. Called a switched virtual connection in ATM terminology. *Compare with* PVC.

switch.

1. A network device that filters, forwards, and floods frames based on the destination address of each frame. The switch operates at the data link layer of the OSI model.

2. An electronic or mechanical device that allows a connection to be established as necessary and terminated when there is no longer a session to support.

SYN.

1. The synchronize bit in a TCP segment, used to indicate that the segment is a SYN segment (see definition 2).

2. The first segment sent by the TCP protocol, used to synchronize the two ends of a connection in preparation for opening a connection.

synchronous transmission. Digital signals that are transmitted with precise clocking. Such signals have the same frequency, with individual characters encapsulated in control bits (called start bits and stop bits) that designate the beginning and end of each character. *Compare with* asynchronous transmission.

Syslog. A service that receives messages from applications on the local host or from remote hosts (for example, a router or a printer) that have been configured to forward messages. Syslog directs messages to a log file.

T

T1. A digital WAN carrier facility. T1 transmits DS-1-formatted data at 1.544 Mbps through the telephone-switching network. *Compare with* E1. *See also* DS-1.

T3. A digital WAN carrier facility. T3 transmits DS-3-formatted data at 44.736 Mbps through the telephone switching network. *Compare with* E3. *See also* DS-3.

TA. Terminal adapter. A device used to connect ISDN BRI connections to existing interfaces such as EIA/TIA-232.

TAC. Cisco's Technical Assistance Center. The TAC provides around-the-clock support to Cisco customers worldwide.

TACACS. Terminal Access Controller Access Control System. An authentication protocol that provides remote access authentication and related services, such as event logging. User passwords are administered in a central database rather than in individual routers, providing an easily scalable network security solution.

tag edge routers. Routers at the boundaries of a network that perform network layer services and apply tags to packets. *See also* tag switching.

tag switches. The ATM switches or routers within the network that can switch tagged packets based on the tags.

tag switching. A high-performance, packet-forwarding technology that integrates network layer (Layer 3) routing and data link layer (Layer 2) switching and provides scalable, high-speed switching in the network core. Tag switching is based on the concept of label swapping, in which packets or cells are assigned short, fixed-length labels that tell switching nodes how data should be forwarded. *See also* tag edge routers, tag switches, and TDP.

TCP. Transmission Control Protocol. A connection-oriented transport layer protocol that provides reliable full-duplex data transmission. TCP is part of the TCP/IP protocol stack. *See also* TCP/IP.

TCP/IP. Transmission Control Protocol/Internet Protocol. A common name for the suite of protocols developed by the U.S. DoD in the 1970s to support the construction of worldwide internetworks. TCP and IP are the two best-known protocols in the suite. *See also* IP and TCP.

TDP. Tag Distribution Protocol. Protocol used to distribute tag information between devices in a Tag Switching network.

Telnet. A standard terminal emulation protocol in the TCP/IP protocol stack. Telnet is used for remote terminal connection, enabling users to log in to remote systems and use resources as if they were connected to a local system. Telnet is defined in RFC 854.

terminal. A simple device at which data can be entered or retrieved from a network. Generally, a terminal has a monitor and a keyboard, but no processor or local disk drive.

TFTP. Trivial File Transfer Protocol. A simplified version of FTP that allows files to be transferred from one computer to another over a network.

Thinnet. A thinner, less expensive version of the cable specified in the IEEE 802.3 10Base2 standard. *See also* 10Base2, Ethernet, and IEEE 802.3.

throughput. The quantity of data successfully transferred between nodes per unit of time, usually seconds.

TIA. Telecommunications Industry Association. *See also* EIA.

TN3270. Terminal emulation software that allows a terminal to appear to an IBM host as a 3278 Model 2 terminal.

TokenTalk. A data link-layer implementation that allows proprietary AppleTalk protocols to communicate over Token Ring.

Token Ring. A token-passing LAN developed and supported by IBM. Token Ring runs at 4 or 16 Mbps over a ring topology. Similar to IEEE 802.5. *See also* IEEE 802.5 and ring topology.

topology. The physical arrangement of network nodes and media within an enterprise networking structure.

TOS. Type of service. A field in an IP datagram that indicates how the datagram should be handled. It specifies reliability, precedence, delay, and throughput parameters.

traffic shaping. The use of queues to limit surges that can congest a network. Data is buffered and then sent into the network in regulated amounts to ensure that the traffic will fit within the promised traffic envelope for the particular connection. Traffic shaping is used in ATM, Frame Relay, and other types of networks. Also known as metering, shaping, and smoothing. *See also* Frame Relay traffic shaping.

transaction services layer. Layer 7 in the SNA architectural model. Represents user application functions, such as spreadsheets, word processing, or electronic mail, by which users interact with the network. Corresponds roughly with the application layer of the OSI reference model.

translational bridging. Bridging between networks with dissimilar MAC sublayer protocols. MAC information is translated into the format of the destination network at the bridge. *Compare with* encapsulating bridging.

transmission control layer. Layer 4 in the SNA architectural model. This layer is responsible for establishing, maintaining, and terminating SNA sessions, sequencing data messages, and controlling session level flow. Corresponds to the transport layer of the OSI model.

transparent bridging. A bridging scheme often used in Ethernet and IEEE 802.3 networks in which bridges pass frames one hop at a time based on tables associating end nodes with bridge ports. Transparent bridging is so named because the presence of bridges is transparent to network end nodes. *Compare with* SRB.

transport layer. Layer 4 of the OSI reference model. This layer is responsible for reliable network communication between end nodes. The transport layer provides mechanisms for the establishment, maintenance, and termination of virtual circuits, transport fault detection and recovery, and information flow control. Corresponds to the transmission control layer of the SNA model.

trap. A message sent by an SNMP agent to an NMS, console, or terminal to indicate the occurrence of a significant event, such as a specifically defined condition or a threshold that has been reached. *See also* alarm and event.

tree topology. A LAN topology similar to a bus topology, except that tree networks can contain branches with multiple nodes. Transmissions from a station propagate the length of the medium and are received by all other stations. *Compare with* bus topology, ring topology, and star topology.

TTL. Time To Live. A field in an IP header that indicates how long a packet is considered valid.

tunneling. An architecture that provides a virtual data link connection between two like networks through a foreign network. The virtual data link is created by encapsulating the network data inside the packets of the foreign network. *See also* encapsulation.

twisted pair. A relatively low-speed transmission medium consisting of two insulated wires arranged in a regular spiral pattern. The wires can be shielded or unshielded. Twisted pair is common in telephony applications and is increasingly common in data networks. *See also* STP and UTP.

U

UDP. User Datagram Protocol. A connectionless transport layer protocol in the TCP/IP protocol stack. UDP is a simple protocol that exchanges datagrams without acknowledgments or guaranteed delivery, requiring that error processing and retransmission be handled by other protocols. UDP is defined in RFC 768.

U interface. The connection between an NT1 device and the ISDN network.

UNI. User-to-Network Interface. An ATM Forum specification that defines an interoperability standard for the interface between ATM-based products (a router or an ATM switch) located in a private network and the ATM switches located within the public carrier networks. Also used to describe similar connections in Frame Relay networks.

unicast. A message sent to a single network destination. *Compare with* broadcast and multicast.

unicast address. An address that specifies a single network device. *Compare with* broadcast address and multicast address. *See also* unicast.

Utilization. Percentage of the total capacity (bandwidth) of a network segment.

UTP. Unshielded twisted-pair. A four-pair wire medium used in a variety of networks. UTP does not require the fixed spacing between connections that is necessary with coaxial-type connections. Five types of UTP cabling are commonly used: Category 1 cabling, Category 2 cabling, Category 3 cabling, Category 4 cabling, and Category 5 cabling. *Compare with* STP. *See also* EIA/TIA-586 and twisted pair.

V

V.24. An ITU-T standard for a physical layer interface between DTE and DCE. V.24 is essentially the same as the EIA/TIA-232 standard. *See also* EIA/TIA-232.

V.25bis. An ITU-T specification describing procedures for call setup and teardown over the DTE-DCE interface in a PSDN.

V.32. An ITU-T standard serial line protocol for bidirectional data transmission at speeds of 4.8 or 9.6 kbps.

V.32bis. An ITU-T standard that extends V.32 to speeds up to 14.4 kbps.

V.34. An ITU-T standard that specifies a serial line protocol. V.34 offers improvements to the V.32 standard, including higher transmission rates (28.8 kbps) and enhanced data compression.

V.35. An ITU-T standard describing a synchronous, physical layer protocol used for communications between a network access device and a packet network. V.35 is most commonly used in the United States and Europe and is recommended for speeds up to 48 kbps.

VC. Virtual circuit. A logical circuit created to ensure reliable communication between two network devices. A virtual circuit is defined by a VPI/VCI pair and can be either permanent (a PVC) or switched (an SVC). Virtual circuits are used in Frame Relay and X.25. In ATM, a virtual circuit is called a virtual channel. Sometimes abbreviated VC. *See also* PVC and SVC

VINES. Virtual Integrated Network Service. A NOS developed and marketed by Banyan Systems.

VIP. Versatile Interface Processor. Interface card used in Cisco 7000 and Cisco 7500 series routers. The VIP provides multilayer switching and runs Cisco IOS™.

VIP2. The most recent version of VIP.

VLAN. Virtual LAN. A logical, rather than physical, grouping of devices. The devices are grouped using switch management software so that they can communicate as if they were attached to the same wire, when in fact they might be located on a number of different physical LAN segments. Because VLANs are based on logical instead of physical connections, they are extremely flexible.

VLSM. Variable length subnet mask. The capability to specify a different subnet mask for the same network number on different subnets. VLSM can help optimize available address space. Some protocols do not allow the use of VLSM. *See also* classless routing protocols.

VPN. Virtual Private Network. Enables IP traffic to travel securely over a public TCP/IP network by encrypting all traffic from one network to another. A VPN uses tunneling to encrypt all information at the IP level. *See also* tunneling.

VTAM. Virtual telecommunications access method. A set of programs that control communication between LUs. VTAM controls data transmission between channel-attached devices, is responsible for establishing all sessions and for activating and deactivating resources, and performs routing functions.

W

WAN. Wide-area network. A data communications network that serves users across a broad geographic area and often uses transmission devices provided by common carriers. Frame Relay, SMDS, and X.25 are examples of WANs. *Compare with* LAN and MAN.

weighted fair queuing. See WFQ.

WFQ. Weighted Fair Queuing. A method of queuing that prioritizes low-volume traffic over high-volume traffic in order to ensure satisfactory response time for common user applications. *Compare with* custom queuing and priority queuing.

wildcard mask. A 32-bit quantity used in conjunction with an IP address to determine which bits in an IP address should be ignored when comparing that address with another IP address. A wildcard mask is specified when setting up access lists.

window. The number of data segments the sender is allowed to have outstanding without yet receiving an acknowledgement.

windowing. A method to control the amount of information transferred end-to-end, using different window sizes.

WINS. Windows Internet Name Service. Allows clients on different IP subnets to dynamically register and browse the network without sending broadcasts.

workgroup. A collection of workstations and servers on a LAN that are designed to communicate and exchange data with one another.

WWW. World Wide Web. A large network of Internet servers providing hypertext and other services to terminals running client applications such as a WWW browser. *See also* WWW browser.

WWW browser. A GUI-based hypertext client application, such as Mosaic, used to access hypertext documents and other services located on innumerable remote servers throughout the WWW and Internet. *See also* hypertext, Internet, and WWW.

X–Y

X.25. An ITU-T standard that defines how connections between DTE and DCE are maintained for remote terminal access and computer communications in PDNs. X.25 specifies LAPB, a data link layer protocol, and PLP, a network layer protocol. Frame Relay has to some degree superseded X.25. *See also* Frame Relay, LAPB, and PLP.

XNS. Xerox Network Systems. A protocol suite originally designed by the Palo Alto Research Center. Many PC networking companies, such as 3Com, Banyan, Novell, and UB Networks, used or currently use a variation of XNS as their primary transport protocol.

X terminal. A terminal that provides a user simultaneous access to several different applications and resources in a multivendor environment through implementation of X Window. *See also* X Window.

X Window. A distributed, network-transparent, device-independent, multitasking windowing and graphics system originally developed by MIT for communication between X terminals and UNIX workstations. *See also* X terminal.

Z

ZIP. Zone Information Protocol. An AppleTalk session layer protocol that maps network numbers to zone names.

zone. In AppleTalk, a logical group of network devices. *See also* ZIP.

INDEX

Numerics

10 Mbps Ethernet, calculating maximum packets-per-second 461–462

100 Mbps (Fast Ethernet), design rules 124, 126–130

16, Mbps Token Ring, calculating maximum packets-per-second 462–463

80/20 rule 120

A

AARP (AppleTalk Address-Resolution Protocol) 27

abbreviated commands, Cisco 750 series 480–481

ABRs (area border routers) 576–577
    areas, density 621
    summary links 580
    virtual links 582–583

access layer, hierarchical network topology models 91, 93

access lists 214
    applying to interfaces 215
    alphanumeric names, assigning 216
    example configuration 217
    NetFlow switching 219–220
    numbering 215–216
    router performance, affect on 218
    statements, ordering 215
    wildcard masks 216–217

access servers 9

access-group command 215

accessing Internet 394–395
    NAT (Network Address Translation) 106
    See also connectivity

ACF/VTAM (Advanced Communication Facility/Virtual Telecommunication Access Method) 28

ACK (acknowledgements) 650

acquisition (corporate), Combinet, Inc. 473

Active state (EIGRP routes) 649

adaptive retransmission algorithms 75

addressing
    AppleTalk 28
        AARP (AppleTalk Address-Resolution Protocol) 27
        cable ranges 26
    consolidation, distance vector routing protocols 180
    discovery
        AppleTalk 96
        ARP (Address Resolution Protocol) 95
        explicit configuration 95–96
        HSRP (Hot Standby Router Protocol), 96–97
        IPX (Internetwork Packet Exchange) 96
        RDP (Router Discovery Protocol) 96
        routing protocols 96
    encapsulation 6
    hierarchical designs 170–172
    IP 18–20 159
        ANDing 20–21
        binary to decimal conversion chart, 642–643
        Cisco DNS/DHCP Manager 164–165
        classes 18, 160
        default gateway 95
        inside global IP addresses 167
        inside local IP addresses 167
        ISDN address negotiation 510–512
        most significant bits 160
        octets 18, 159
        outside global IP addresses 167
        outside local IP addresses 167
        prefixes 160
        private addresses 166–167
        route summarization 161–163
        subnets 19–20
        VLSM (variable-length subnet masking) 161

B

F

G

H

I

N

P

Q

R

S

W

X-Z

CCIE Professional Development

Cisco LAN Switching

Kennedy Clark, CCIE; Kevin Hamilton, CCIE

1-57870-094-9 • AVAILABLE AUGUST 1999

This volume provides an in-depth analysis of Cisco LAN switching technologies, architectures, and deployments, including unique coverage of Catalyst network design essentials. Network designs and configuration examples are incorporated throughout to demonstrate the principles and enable easy translation of the material into practice in production networks.

Routing TCP/IP, Volume I

Jeff Doyle, CCIE

1-57870-041-8 • AVAILABLE NOW

This book takes the reader from a basic understanding of routers and routing protocols through a detailed examination of each of the IP interior routing protocols. Learn techniques for designing networks that maximize the efficiency of the protocol being used. Exercises and review questions provide core study for the CCIE Routing and Switching exam.

Advanced IP Network Design

Alvaro Retana, CCIE; Don Slice, CCIE; and Russ White, CCIE

1-57870-097-3 • AVAILABLE NOW

Network engineers and managers can use these case studies, which highlight various network design goals, to explore issues including protocol choice, network stability, and growth. This book also includes theoretical discussion on advanced design topics.

Large-Scale IP Network Solutions

Khalid Raza, CCIE; Salman Asad, CCIE; and Mark Turner

1-57870-084-1 • AVAILABLE NOW

Network engineers can find solutions as their IP networks grow in size and complexity. Examine all the major IP protocols in-depth and learn about scalability, migration planning, network management, and security for large-scale networks.

CISCO SYSTEMS

CISCO PRESS

www.ciscopress.com

Cisco Career Certifications

CCNA Exam Certification Guide

Wendell Odom, CCIE

0-7357-0073-7 • AVAILABLE NOW

This book is a comprehensive study tool for CCNA Exam #640-407 and part of a recommended study program from Cisco Systems. *CCNA Exam Certification Guide* helps you understand and master the exam objectives. Instructor-developed elements and techniques maximize your retention and recall of exam topics, and scenario-based exercises help validate your mastery of the exam objectives.

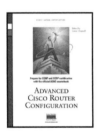

Advanced Cisco Router Configuration

Cisco Systems, Inc., edited by Laura Chappell

1-57870-074-4 • AVAILABLE NOW

Based on the actual Cisco ACRC course, this book provides a thorough treatment of advanced network deployment issues. Learn to apply effective configuration techniques for solid network implementation and management as you prepare for CCNP and CCDP certifications. This book also includes chapter-ending tests for self-assessment.

Introduction to Cisco Router Configuration

Cisco Systems, Inc., edited by Laura Chappell

1-57870-076-0 • AVAILABLE NOW

Based on the actual Cisco ICRC course, this book presents the foundation knowledge necessary to define Cisco router configurations in multiprotocol environments. Examples and chapter-ending tests build a solid framework for understanding internetworking concepts. Prepare for the ICRC course and CCNA certification while mastering the protocols and technologies for router configuration.

Cisco CCNA Preparation Library

Cisco Systems, Inc., Laura Chappell, and Kevin Downes, CCIE

1-57870-125-2 • AVAILABLE NOW • CD-ROM

This boxed set contains two Cisco Press books—*Introduction to Cisco Router Configuration* and *Internetworking Technologies Handbook,* Second Edition— and the *High-Performance Solutions for Desktop Connectivity* CD.

CISCO SYSTEMS

CISCO PRESS

www.ciscopress.com

Cisco Press Solutions

Designing Network Security
Merike Kaeo
1-57870-043-4 • AVAILABLE NOW

Designing Network Security is a practical guide designed to help you understand the fundamentals of securing you corporate infrastructure. This book takes a comprehensive look at underlying security technologies, the process of creating a security policy, and the practical requirements necessary to implement a corporate security policy.

Top-Down Network Design
Priscilla Oppenheimer
1-57870-069-8 • AVAILABLE NOW

Building reliable, secure, and manageable networks is every network professional's goal. This practical guide teaches you a systematic method for network design that can be applied to campus LANs, remote-access networks, WAN links, and large-scale internetworks. Learn how to analyze business and technical requirements, examine traffic flow and Quality of Service requirements, and select protocols and technologies based on performance goals.

Internetworking Technologies Handbook, Second Edition
Kevin Downes, CCIE, Merilee Ford, H. Kim Lew, Steve Spanier, Tim Stevenson
1-57870-102-3 • AVAILABLE NOW

This comprehensive reference provides a foundation for understanding and implementing contemporary internetworking technologies, providing you with the necessary information needed to make rational networking decisions. Master terms, concepts, technologies, and devices that are used in the internetworking industry today. You also learn how to incorporate networking technologies into a LAN/WAN environment, as well as how to apply the OSI reference model to categorize protocols, technologies, and devices.

OSPF Network Design Solutions
Thomas M. Thomas II
1-57870-046-9 • AVAILABLE NOW

This comprehensive guide presents a detailed, applied look into the workings of the popular Open Shortest Path First protocol, demonstrating how to dramatically increase network performance and security, and how to most easily maintain large-scale networks. OSPF is thoroughly explained through exhaustive coverage of network design, deployment, management, and troubleshooting.

CISCO SYSTEMS

CISCO PRESS

www.ciscopress.com

Cisco Press Solutions

Internetworking Troubleshooting Handbook
Kevin Downes, CCIE, H. Kim Lew, Spank McCoy,
Tim Stevenson, Kathleen Wallace

1-57870-024-8 • AVAILABLE NOW

Diagnose and resolve specific and potentially problematic issues common to
every network type with this valuable reference. Each section of the book is
devoted to problems common to a specific protocol. Sections are subdivided
into symptoms, descriptions of environments, diagnosing and isolating problem
causes, and problem-solution summaries. This book aims to help you reduce
downtime, improve network performance, and enhance network reliability
using proven troubleshooting solutions.

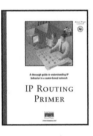

IP Routing Primer
Robert Wright, CCIE

1-57870-108-2 • AVAILABLE NOW

Learn how IP routing behaves in a Cisco router environment. In addition to
teaching the core fundamentals, this book enhances your ability to troubleshoot
IP routing problems yourself, often eliminating the need to call for additional
technical support. The information is presented in an approachable,
workbook-type format with dozens of detailed illustrations and real-life
scenarios integrated throughout.

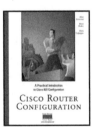

Cisco Router Configuration
Allan Leinwand, Bruce Pinsky, Mark Culpepper

1-57870-022-1 • AVAILABLE NOW

An example-oriented and chronological approach helps you implement and
administer your internetworking devices. Starting with the configuration
devices "out of the box," this book moves to configuring Cisco IOS for the
three most popular networking protocols used today: TCP/IP, AppleTalk, and
Novell Interwork Packet Exchange (IPX). You also learn basic administrative
and management configuration, including access control with TACACS+ and
RADIUS, network management with SNMP, logging of messages, and time
control with NTP.

For the latest on Cisco Press resources and Certification and

Training guides, or for information on publishing opportunities, visit

www.ciscopress.com.

CISCO SYSTEMS

CISCO PRESS

**Cisco Press books are available at your local bookstore,
computer store, and online booksellers.**

Cisco Press

Staying Connected to Networkers

We want to hear from **you**! Help Cisco Press **stay connected** to the issues and challenges you face on a daily basis by registering your book and filling out our brief survey.

Complete and mail this form, or better yet, jump to **www.ciscopress.com** and do it online. Each complete entry will be eligible for our monthly drawing to **win a FREE book** from the Cisco Press Library.

Thank you for choosing Cisco Press to help you work the network.

Name _____

Address _____

City _____ State/Province _____

Country _____ Zip/Post code _____

E-mail address _____

May we contact you via e-mail for product updates and customer benefits?
❏ Yes   ❏ No

Where did you buy this product?

❏ Bookstore	❏ Computer store	❏ Electronics store
❏ Online retailer	❏ Office supply store	❏ Discount store
❏ Mail order	❏ Class/Seminar	

❏ Other _____

When did you buy this product? _____ Month _____ Year

What price did you pay for this product?

❏ Full retail price	❏ Discounted price	❏ Gift

How did you learn about this product?

❏ Friend	❏ Store personnel	❏ In-store ad
❏ Catalog	❏ Postcard in the mail	❏ Saw it on the shelf
❏ Magazine ad	❏ Article or review	❏ Used other products
❏ School	❏ Professional Organization	

❏ Other _____

What will this product be used for?

❏ Business use	❏ Personal use	❏ School/Education

❏ Other _____

How many years have you been employed in a computer-related industry?

❏ 2 years or less	❏ 3-5 years	❏ 5+ years

CISCO SYSTEMS
CISCO PRESS®

www.ciscopress.com

CISCO SYSTEMS

CISCO PRESS

www.ciscopress.com

Which best describes your job function?

❐ Corporate Management ❐ Systems Engineering ❐ IS Management
❐ Network Design ❐ Network Support ❐ Webmaster
❐ Marketing/Sales ❐ Consultant ❐ Student
❐ Professor/Teacher

❐ Other _____

What is your formal education background?

❐ High school ❐ Vocational/Technical degree ❐ Some college
❐ College degree ❐ Masters degree ❐ Professional or Doctoral degree

Have you purchased a Cisco Press product before?

❐ Yes ❐ No

On what topics would you like to see more coverage?

_____
_____

Do you have any additional comments or suggestions?

_____
_____

Designing Cisco Networks (1-57870-105-8)

Cisco Press

201 West 103rd Street
Indianapolis, IN 46290
www.ciscopress.com

Place
Stamp
Here

Cisco Press
Customer Registration
P.O. Box 189014
Battle Creek, MI 49018-9947